URGENCY

URGENCY

ONE MINISTER'S QUEST TO SAVE THE WORLD

FRANK SHELTON, JR.

Designed by: Vince Pannullo
Printed in the United States of America by
One Communications LLC 800-621-2556

ISBN: 978-0-578-92471-7

CONTENTS

"For we wrestle not against flesh and blood, but against principalities, against powers, against the rulers of the darkness of this world, against spiritual wickedness in high places. Wherefore take unto you the whole armor of God that ye may be able to withstand in the evil day, and having done all, to STAND.

Stand therefore, having your loins girt about with truth, and having on the breastplate of righteousness; And your feet shod with preparation of the gospel of peace; above all, taking the shield of faith, wherewith ye shall be able to quench all the fiery darts of the wicked. And take the helmet of salvation, and the sword of the Spirit, which is the word of God.

Praying always with all prayer and supplication in the Spirit and watching thereunto with all perseverance and supplication for all saints; and for me, that I may open my mouth boldly, to make known the mystery of the Gospel, for which I am an ambassador in bonds that therein I may speak boldly, as I ought to speak. (Ephesians 6:12-20)."

DEDICATION

This is <u>dedicated</u> to Jesus my Savior. Christ saved my soul. God told me to write the book
My parents, Frank & Sharon Shelton
My wife, Ruth and two children, Hannah & Andrew
My siblings, Matt & Jaime
I love you more than Websters could define.

I also dedicate this book to the men and women of our law enforcement community and your respective families. As talk screams louder to "defund the police" it is my honor to defend and stand with the law enforcement rank and file. Elvis Presley once said, "If God didn't give me a voice to sing, I would have liked to be a policeman." I thank the Lord for that long line of blue and each of you are my heroes.

To the lawmakers that I have the high honor to speak life into and help lead a weekly Bible study I salute you and cherish our friendship. Your valiant and selfless service is an inspiration to me and many others. Thank you for honoring God daily and for realizing that public service when done right is not only noble and necessary but in these last days is needed more than ever. Our state and nation are better because you answered the call and your ministry to God and your respective constituents is appreciated and welcomed. You are a light in the dark and Ambassador of Hope.

To Sylvester Stallone. I met you as a child (age 13), but your movies inspired me to take risks, be bold when needed and fight for what is right as an adult while often going against incredible odds, larger than life opponents and dangerous terrain. In the movies you went to Russia, Afghanistan and Burma and I figured I could to a small degree try to follow those footsteps. My godmother, Judy Henderson and I shared the Gospel with you in Hollywood, CA in 1985. I was touched that on Easter 2021, you used your social media platform to encourage millions to watch the story of Christ. It thrills my heart that you know that the Gospel is the greatest message of Hope and Charlton Heston was correct when he said, "The Good News of Jesus is the greatest story ever told." Blessings on your beautiful wife and gorgeous daughters. Sir, never stop punching or praying because with God in your corner you forever a winner! Jesus is still the biggest star of them all and much love champ! #Yo

To our ministry partners, board members, prayer warriors and friends, we are grateful to march forward "By Faith" with each of you in these unique days. More than ever, we live to love even those different than us and be encouraged fellow Christian as time ticks, take heart that the Lord not Satan holds the game clock in His hand and the King always has one more move. I have read the end of the best-selling Book of all time and the born-again Christians WIN!

Finally, to the person concerned with the signs of the times but is not yet a born-again

Christian. Jesus told Nicodemus, "You must be born again!" May you come to a saving relationship with Christ. Apart from Him, nothing else matters. You are loved and God bless you richly.

ENDORSEMENTS

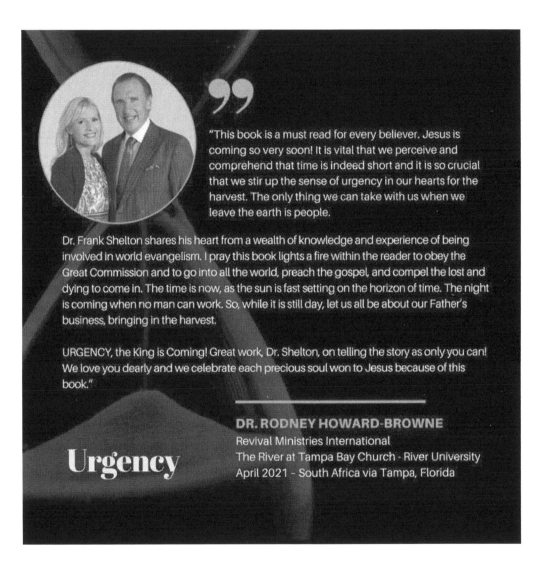

"This book is a must read for every believer. Jesus is coming so very soon! It is vital that we perceive and comprehend that time is indeed short and it is so crucial that we stir up the sense of urgency in our hearts for the harvest. The only thing we can take with us when we leave the earth is people.

Dr. Frank Shelton shares his heart from a wealth of knowledge and experience of being involved in world evangelism. I pray this book lights a fire within the reader to obey the Great Commission and to go into all the world, preach the gospel, and compel the lost and dying to come in. The time is now, as the sun is fast setting on the horizon of time. The night is coming when no man can work. So, while it is still day, let us all be about our Father's business, bringing in the harvest.

URGENCY, the King is Coming! Great work, Dr. Shelton, on telling the story as only you can! We love you dearly and we celebrate each precious soul won to Jesus because of this book."

DR. RODNEY HOWARD-BROWNE
Revival Ministries International
The River at Tampa Bay Church - River University
April 2021 - South Africa via Tampa, Florida

Dr. Rodney Howard-Browne
Revival Ministries International
The River at Tampa Bay Church - River University
April 2021 – **South Africa via Tampa, Florida**

"I have known Dr. Frank Shelton and his family for several years. He is a real man who loves Jesus. He is one of the few men I know, who not only have a passion for preaching the gospel, but also has a passion for winning souls for Christ!

With his unique insight in this book on "Urgency," Dr. Frank gently reminds us all, that God is in full control of all things and He is still on the throne! We are therefore asked to redeem our time and occupy ourselves to doing His will on earth. "IF you have faith and do not doubt" (Matt. 21:21).

Doubt is a doorway through which Satan enters into our lives. It causes the "Fight of faith' to become the "Flight of faith." When we fear, confusion, discouragement, and despair take up residence within us. They rob us of our confidence, joy, and peace. I pray that this book strengthens your faith in Christ and your walk with Him. Remain strong and keep the Faith!"

Urgency

DR. SAMUEL A. THOMAS
President & CEO
Hopegivers International - Kota, India

Dr. Samuel A. Thomas
President & CEO
Hopegivers International - Kota, India

"I've known Frank for over two decades. He is the real deal! He is willing to take a bullet for cause of Christ. His love for America, our freedoms, our children, and the TRUTH is CONTAGIOUS! The urgency in his heart, like mine, for the time we have left to save this country, is what has kept our friendship strong and focus on Christ, even stronger. I HIGHLY recommend this book and urge you to pray for this man and support his ministry. Frank's message MUST get out to the masses!"

——— COUNTER CULTURE MOM,
TINA MARIE GRIFFIN
www.CounterCultureMom.com – Nashville, Tennessee

Urgency

~ **Counter Culture Mom, Tina Marie Griffin**
www.CounterCultureMom.com – **Nashville, Tennessee**

"Dr. Frank Shelton's book accurately and literally exemplifies its title "Urgency." There has never been a greater need, nor opportunity for The Church of Jesus Christ to arise and shine and take its place as the light in the darkness around us. A shaken world is seeking solace, the broken are seeking restoration, a divided humanity seeking solidarity and a weary world seeking authenticity. Exposure of global corruption, the fragility and volatility of secular structures and world systems has given way to prepare the hearts of the world for the greatest global revival this planet has ever seen!

This compelling read breathes new life and fresh insight into the timeless message and assignment of followers and ambassadors of Jesus Christ. Time is short... but the mission is vast! Fear is not an option, silence is intolerable and simply spectating, inadequate. This final stretch of the race requires us all to make a stand, step out into the supernatural power of God and live out the very words we read in the Scriptures."

DR. BRAD NORMAN

Founder SFTN Churches UK
Director, FaithUK TV Channel
President RBI – London, England

Dr. Brad Norman
Founder SFTN Churches UK
Director, FaithUK TV Channel
President RBI - London, England

"As the conclusion of the Age of Grace draws near, the truth of the Gospel must be heralded throughout the world. Frank is a longtime friend who is passionate to see a great end-time harvest and expresses the "urgency" of the hour in his new book. "Urgency" will ignite a fire within you and is a must read for all."

Evangelist Sharon Bolan
Dallas, Texas

Urgency

Evangelist Sharon Bolan
Dallas, Texas

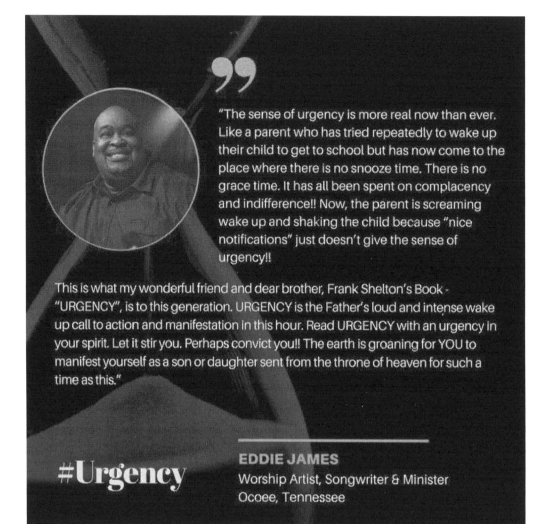

"The sense of urgency is more real now than ever. Like a parent who has tried repeatedly to wake up their child to get to school but has now come to the place where there is no snooze time. There is no grace time. It has all been spent on complacency and indifference!! Now, the parent is screaming wake up and shaking the child because "nice notifications" just doesn't give the sense of urgency!!

This is what my wonderful friend and dear brother, Frank Shelton's Book - "URGENCY", is to this generation. URGENCY is the Father's loud and intense wake up call to action and manifestation in this hour. Read URGENCY with an urgency in your spirit. Let it stir you. Perhaps convict you!! The earth is groaning for YOU to manifest yourself as a son or daughter sent from the throne of heaven for such a time as this."

#Urgency

EDDIE JAMES
Worship Artist, Songwriter & Minister
Ocoee, Tennessee

Eddie James
Worship Artist, Songwriter & Minister - Ocoee, Tennessee

"If you are a sincere pursuer of truth, you and renowned author/evangelist Frank Shelton have a lot in common. His newest book entitled URGENCY will attest to that. Like Frank, the Lord has likely been giving you growing levels of awareness about the urgent signs of the times. This new book will help inspire you and sharpen your focus about these last of the last days. If are not a believer in the soon-coming-Messiah, but you sense things are going awry in the world, Frank's scripture-filled book "URGENCY" will be more important for you! His crisp and distinctive storytelling will captivate your mind and help you make sense of the senseless events unfolding before you. Read it and become activated into Christ's role for you today. This is your time, and this should be your next read!"

— CAZ TAYLOR
*Prophetic Teacher & Author – Salem Media Group & broadcaster
San Diego, CA*

#Urgency

Caz Taylor
**Prophetic Teacher & Author – Salem Media Group & broadcaster
San Diego, CA**

"We all know Jesus is coming back really soon and it's imperative that we prepare ourselves for His return. I recommend this reading. We are in an urgent hour to wake up!"

——— ANNA KHAIT
Lover of Jesus, Patriot & contestant on CBS "Survivor"
– Brooklyn, New York

Anna Khait
Lover of Jesus, Patriot & contestant on CBS "Survivor" – Brooklyn, New York

"For students of Scripture, specifically Bible prophecy, it is more than apparent that we are living in the times the Apostle Paul called "perilous" in 2 Timothy 3:1. The "Pandemic Year" of 2020 rocketed us forward toward the end-time scenario perhaps more than any event in our lifetime. My friend, Evangelist Frank Shelton, has had his finger on the pulse of our nation and world for years. But his insight into where we are currently is particularly powerful and pertinent! I have known Frank for several years, and it has been an absolute delight to co-labor with him in a variety of ministry ventures, including on Capitol Hill and at the United Nations. He is a man of conviction, courage, and contagious passion – attributes that uniquely qualify him to speak on the topic of "URGENCY."

I cannot recommend strongly enough to you his new book. Filled with Frank's stellar wit and wisdom, "URGENCY" will challenge you to place your confidence in the One Who still controls a world that appears to be completely out of control. As you will learn in "URGENCY," now is the time to run TO in faith, not FROM in fear, placing our unwavering hope, not is science, but the Savior!"

DR. DAVE KISTLER

President, HOPE Ministries International
President, HOPE To The Hill
Host, Stand In The Gap Radio – Washington, DC

Dr. Dave Kistler
President, HOPE Ministries International
President, HOPE To The Hill
Host, Stand In The Gap Radio – Washington, DC

"Frank Shelton, Jr. is a master communicator and educator. He has a anointing to make the most complex issue simple and understandable in a powerful and impactful way. There is no doubt in my mind that Urgency will be life changing for anyone who embraces this message. You will be forever changed, and God will be glorified."

KrisAnne Hall
Constitutional Attorney
President of Liberty First University
Sunshine State - Florida

#Urgency

KrisAnne Hall
Constitutional Attorney
President of Liberty First University
Sunshine State - Florida

"This timely book is a MUST read!!! The is no better book title in 2021 than "Urgency!" Our world is on the tail end of a pandemic that brought with it paralyzing fear, difficulty and much uncertainty about the future

Many times, in our history God has moved in power during times like these. For example: the First Great Awakening (1730-1740's), Second Great Awakening (1820's-1850's), Chicago Revival (1875-1885) and the Revival in America/Jesus Movement (1910-1970's). All of these powerful movements of God happened during seasons of fear and uncertainty. We are ripe for another major movement! However, the church MUST mobilize and get back to the mandate Jesus gave us before He ascended, the GREAT COMMISSION! The time is short. Jesus is coming soon! Please read this book and then share your faith with someone who's lost. Jesus is the only ANSWER!!

#Urgency

PASTOR/EVANGELIST RONNIE COLEMAN
SoulQuest Ministries
Jackson, Tennessee

Pastor/Evangelist Ronnie Coleman
SoulQuest Ministries
Jackson, Tennessee

"Frank Shelton has been a friend and fellow laborer for nearly a decade. I have watched God use him to reach people all over the globe. In the more recent months, I have witnessed a divine calling on Frank to discover and disseminate the information that others are either unaware of or too afraid to speak of. Frank has been faithful to shine the light of truth into the dark places of our society

As you read the pages of this book, my prayer is that you will discover a revelation from the Spirit of God that will allow you to see beyond the surface of what is going in in the world today; to understand that we are not at war against flesh and blood but against principalities and powers; to see that Satan has been playing the long game with our health, with our education, and with our church leadership.

Frank has responded to Holy Spirit's leading to call for a generation of pastors, lay leaders, and believers who will not only recognize the Satanic influence in Hollywood, government, "health industry," and education, but to also remember that the eternal God of creation cannot be overcome, outmaneuvered, or derailed. His plan will stand, His will shall come to pass, His people are victorious. Right now, we stand in the moment before our Lords return, and our orders are clear... Do not grow weary... Do not grow cold... Do not grow fearful... But with divine wisdom, grace, and love GO! To the highways and byways, GO! To those who are your political rivals, GO! To the ends of the earth GO!" And Lo I Am With You," Jesus' promises to all who will GO! For years I have not only heard Frank preach this message, but I have watched him model this with every fiber of his being. Here in lies the message that transcends the current events, troubles conventional wisdom, and transforms hardened hearts. May the Peace of God dwell in you richly as you discover, or rediscover, His mission through the pages of this book."

PASTOR RANDALL SNIPES
Oak Grove Baptist Church
Colonial Beach, Virginia

#Urgency

Pastor Randall Snipes
Oak Grove Baptist Church - Colonial Beach, Virginia

"Frank Shelton is shaking nations! In this book, as you immerse yourself in every chapter, you will feel Frank's heart and love for people. This book "Urgency" will certainly challenge you to do what God has called you to do and to be bold not cold. God is using ordinary people to do extraordinary things, whether in the supermarkets, gas stations, parks, parking lots, etc. it is time for Christians to not be afraid. They also need to be filled with the Holy Spirit, walking in power, and the miraculous. This will cause a "Greater is He that is in me, than those who oppose the Gospel" in you, every day of your life."

Alma Rivera
Singer, Evangelist & Ordained Minister - Nesconset, New York

#Urgency

Alma Rivera
Singer, Evangelist & Ordained Minister - Nesconset, New York

"What we need now more than ever are voices like these - generals of God - who will be heaven's bulldozers to plough through the lies and fear created by a very evident anti-Christ agenda sweeping across the earth! Evangelist Frank Shelton does exactly that in his latest book "Urgency". He does not just create the much-needed urgency and wake up call, but also hits the nail on the head sharing informed intelligence that many are too afraid to share for fear of being labelled. He is unintimidated in his approach and message! A man of God with astounding generational favour in the political arena and even the White House! He sounds a trumpet of truth, with no apology. A must read for this hour! Touché friend - excellent work!

—— EVANGELIST LINDY-ANN HOPLEY
founder of Beautiful Witness Ministries - Cape Town, South Africa

#Urgency

Evangelist Lindy-Ann Hopley
founder of **Beautiful Witness Ministries – Cape Town, South Africa**

"Urgency is the resounding impression from the Spirit of God in these last days. There is an undeniable pulling and call from God to redeem the times and stand strong. There are seconds left in the timeline of this world. May we make them count for eternity. The hour is eminent for Christ to return, but He plans to come back to a vibrant, living, and growing church.

There has never been a time where the gospel must be preached, and the love of God seen more than now. While many may be feeling uneasy or worried, let hope swell in your heart. This is not the end of good things; it is the beginning of something greater. This is the church's finest hour.

Frank Shelton has captured the truth of the moment we are living in. Frank is a man that lives and preaches the Word. He has a love for people and has been used to reach so many with the gospel in the wildest of ways. His long span career for the Lord has had him write a story unlike any others. May this book inspire you to action and to live a life packed full of adventuring with God. Your best is still in front of you and if you truly know Christ, then there is nothing left for you to fear. The future is grand. Read this book and let it leave a desire in your heart to see this generation encounter God."

#Urgency

PASTOR CALEB RING
The River - Clermont, Florida

Pastor Caleb Ring
The River – Clermont, Florida

"My friend, Frank, has produced a timely and poignant book for such a time as this where voices of truth are desperately needed in a world consumed by confusion, doubt, and unbelief. As an evangelist, Frank has dedicated his life to reaching a lost and hurting world with the love of the Lord accompanied with the power of the Spirit. He is a man of uncompromising character which uniquely qualifies him to speak to the nations, calling them to a higher level of Kingdom living. This book is not only a powerful resource but a blessing to everyone who reads the wisdom contained within, challenging readers to think through today's realities from a biblical perspective. It's time to level up!"

—— TAMAR KLAYMAN SAMS
Israel & Cleveland, Ohio

#Urgency

Tamar Klayman Sams
Israel & Cleveland, Ohio

"The BAD NEWS is, one of the greatest deceptions in human history is happening before our eyes. In a few short months, we have gone from freedom and prosperity to massive fear, lockdowns, masks, and seeing churches and businesses closed. But the GOOD NEWS is, during this chaos, the truth is shining forth! Frank Shelton's book, "Urgency" unmasks the deception! It is a ray of HOPE and a wakeup call to follow the TRUTH in this dark hour!"

BRUCE CREVIER
Husband, Father of 12 children, Author, Speaker/Performer
Finalist on "America's Got Talent"
5x World Record Holder Basketball Handler
Elkton, South Dakota

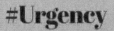

#Urgency

Bruce Crevier
Husband, Father of 12 children, Author, Speaker/Performer
Finalist on "America's Got Talent"
5x World Record Holder Basketball Handler
Elkton, South Dakota

"Urgency", by my good friend, Frank Shelton is a very timely book. Why? Because time is running out! It is no longer time, to be the "silent majority." It is high time to be bold! It's time to speak up, it's time to rise up, it's time to stand up, and be heard. One hundred years ago it was known as the "Roaring 20's" but this is not the time to roar, it's the time to SOAR. So wise up, mount up, armor up and get ready because we are in a war. A spiritual battle like never in the history of mankind. This is not the time to bury your head in the sand, this is the time to stand tall, stick your chest out, pick up your shield of faith and the sword of the spirit. We are privileged to help usher in the return of the Messiah, Jesus. Let's do this!

Nikita Koloff #Urgency
Koloff for Christ Ministries
5x World Wrestling Champion – Concord, North Carolina

Nikita Koloff
Koloff for Christ Ministries
5x World Wrestling Champion – Concord, North Carolina

"Just hearing that my wonderful friend, Dr. Frank Shelton, has released a book entitled, "URGENCY" is all the motivation that I need to pick up a copy. I know this man's life and I know his message. He is constantly and consistently finding opportunities to share the Good News with anyone that he can and to intentionally encourage someone else in their walk with Jesus! He is a walking Bible, ready to be opened and shared at a moment's notice.

I have never seen Dr. Frank without a smile on his face, radiating the love of God and sharing a word in-season to someone (even a stranger) that causes them to open their heart and receive a Word that can transform their life. He knows that the hour is late, and that time is winding down to rescue lives from the trap that the devil has laid for them. He is instant in-season and out. At a time when chaos and confusion seem to be clouding people's minds, Dr. Shelton knows how to deliver a word from God that cuts through the lies of the enemy and impacts their hearts for eternity! He has a bold word, but it is delivered in such love and packaged with such kindness that people do not realize what they received until it explodes inside of them, changing their life forever, from darkness to light! You do not want to miss the message that God has given him in the pages of this book. Expect a transformation! Expect for the Holy Spirit to blow through your life in a powerful way! Expect the Fire of God to be freshly lit inside your heart, never to grow dim again. Expect the unexpected because there is an URGENCY for this message to be delivered!"

— DR. TODD HOLMES

The River of Tri-Cities
Johnson City, TN

Dr. Todd Holmes
The River of Tri-Cities
Johnson City, TN

"URGENCY should be read by every Christian! Frank Shelton has a way with words. This book is so readable, so accessible, and written in an amazingly simple style, yet absolutely forceful in creating the sense of urgency we need for such a time as this. The Lord is using Frank to impress upon us the importance of faith, trust & holiness. Throughout the book, Frank reminds us that, no matter what is going on in the world around us, Jesus is our only answer. He will never let us down. God has not given us a spirit of fear and this is one of those books that makes you feel convicted and inspired at the same time."

Michelle Moore Winder
UNREDACTED TRUTH – San Diego, California

#Urgency

Michelle Moore Winder
UNREDACTED TRUTH – San Diego, California

"Urgency" is one of the timeliest books of all-times. We are certainly living in the latest of what the Bible speaks of when it uses the term "the Last Days". The hourglass Is speeding up and very few grains of time remain on this earth. This is our moment in history! You and I were born as Queen Esther of the old testament, for such a time as this. It is not the time to despair or allow fear or compromise to direct our decisions. I am elated to be part of a generation that God has hand-picked for this hour. In a relay race, the best runners are saved for last. That is, you and me.

We must stand for Christ, The Bible, freedom, and the constitution. However, we have watched countless pastors cave, churches close, and people scatter like sheep having no shepherd. Where are the over-comers, the water-walkers, and fire-starters? I am so happy to be part of a group of people who will not bow or grow weary in well-doing, Evangelist and author Frank Shelton is one of those God has raised up in this hour to help show us the way. He has taken a stand and paid a price. I am honored to call him my friend and to have him as a guest speaker at our Washington State Stand. He has been involved in many levels of the political scene but is first and foremost an ambassador for Christ. I pray and believe that "Urgency" will unveil truth to you. Your eyes will be opened as never before, and you will be given the practical steps to live victoriously in this hour."

DR. DEBBIE RICH-RESTER

Debbie Rich Ministries – Olympia, WA

Dr. Debbie Rich-Rester
Debbie Rich Ministries – Olympia, Washington

"My friend Author / Evangelist Frank Shelton has written one of the timeliest books ever written! "Urgency" is a holy call to arise and be Ambassadors for Christ! In a day and age of cancel culture, radical agendas, and the perversion of identity we must have a Revelation 3:20 awakening! This book will not only stir your heart for more of Jesus, but it will mandate your spirit to join the Romans 11:5 Remnant! Lord willing, generations from now this powerful book may be one of the compass's that Jesus used to help usher in the last day awakening! Get this book! Send this book to friends and family!! Together, we can lead a spirit revolution! God is not done with America or the nations!"

PAT SCHATZLINE
Author, Evangelist & CEO
Remnant Ministries International – Argyle, Texas
www.RaiseTheRemnant.com

Pat Schatzline
Author, Evangelist and CEO of Remnant Ministries International – Argyle, Texas
www.RaiseTheRemnant.com
Https://coach.optavia.com/teamschatzline

"If ever there was a time that "We," as God Fearing American, Patriotic Kingdom Driven Men and Women of the "Most High God" need to be Awakened to the Moment of "Urgency" – The "TIME IS NOW!" Never in my 30 years of business, public speaking, and ministry around the U.S.A. and Internationally, have I seen such a lethargic spiritual attitude in people who have been lulled to sleep with the media's voices, blinding all the Truth. There is an "Awakening" that must take place, so the masses will not just believe anything they hear or see any longer - Accepting it as truth!

The voices opposing our democracy today simply portray the opposite of the current state of reality. It is past time for our stance towards those things we hold dear to our hearts in America, become that of an advancement of "Urgency" to keep this nation from sinking into a state of socialism and Marxism. We have been called to act, not just sit on the sidelines. From the "Church House to the White House," we must come together and unite against the evil of an elitist agenda and arise again to defend our "Nation's History" now for our children and the future generations. Our Heavenly Father breathed "Inspirational Wisdom" – To our "Founding Fathers," as they wrote the "Framework of our Freedom" in our Great American Constitution! These are our "Foundational Principles" that we hold dear to us, that allows us to be a "Free Republic for which it Stands - One Nation under God, Indivisible, with liberty and justice for all!" I applaud my dear friend, Frank Shelton Jr. for his research and candid truth in this book "Urgency!" My prayer is all reading would be "Awakened to Truth" and then Arise with such an urgency to advance with the same Spirit of those Patriots who bled and died for the "Freedom" we now see being taken from us."

DR. BRETT WATSON
CEO, Pastor, International Speaker
Brett Watson Ministries, Inc - Viera, Florida

Dr. Brett Watson
CEO, Pastor, International Speaker
Brett Watson Ministries, Inc. – Viera, Florida

"Frank Shelton is one of the most passionate, interesting and transformational individuals I have ever met. His passion to lift the name of Jesus and exhaust all means necessary to see that "ONE" come to Jesus is consistent and contagious. His heart burns to dream big with those that have large platforms while equally dreaming big with those that have smaller platforms, even if they live in the middle of nowhere. This book entitled; "URGENCY" is sure to be an explosive call to redeem the time as we are rushing into eternity. You have one shot at doing exploits for Jesus and this book reminds us that the hourglass of time in this life on earth is running out. Frank Shelton will take you on a journey in this book that will charge you to take your eyes off the storm of what is happening globally and fix them on Jesus, who is the Author and Pioneer of our faith. As you read this book you are sure to be infused with fresh faith to occupy and advance the kingdom of God until Jesus Christ cracks the clouds and time has ran out."

DR. CALEB COOPER

Pastor – New Hope Revival Church. Author of "Jesus Focused Awakening End-time Prophetic Strategy, The Convergence of Revival and the King's Arrival, The Call For Strong Godly Leadership." CalebCooperMinistries.com - Truth or Consequences, New Mexico

#Urgency

Dr. Caleb Cooper, Pastor – New Hope Revival Church. Author of "Jesus Focused Awakening End-time Prophetic Strategy, The Convergence of Revival and the King's Arrival, The Call For Strong Godly Leadership." CalebCooperMinistries.com - **Truth or Consequences, New Mexico**

"The Urgency is NOW! Global Evangelist Frank Shelton, Jr. is a Front Runner for the Glory of God! Frank has been given Holy Spirit insight and revelation on the frontal attacks from the demonic forces as well as God's Power to pierce through ALL darkness in Jesus Name!

This on time relevant exposure of the plots of the enemy from the occult societies, deep state, the antichrist, and Marxist agendas will open the eyes of all! The earth is quaking for the awakening of the Sons of God to manifest with signs, wonders, and miracles unto Salvation. The bold truth and hope of the Gospel of Jesus Christ must be proclaimed Now!

Frank and I met in 2014 as State Coordinators for the Billy Graham Evangelistic Association and God has woven an unbreakable Kingdom Friendship! I've personally witnessed Frank's unashamed and undeniable Holy Spirit boldness to proclaim Jesus and all truth throughout the Nations. May The Holy Spirit inspire you through this book with the urgency to get back into the Fight of Faith with hunger to bring transformation to the nations for the end time harvest of souls unto salvation and mobilization in Jesus' name!"

#Urgency

STAN LOVINS II
Evangelist/President
Stan Lovins II Ministries
Victory Fire with Stan Lovins II
Sandlot Ministries

Evangelist Stan Lovins II
Revivals For Jesus
RevivalsForJesus.com – Indianapolis, Indiana

"It is with great honor that I recommend this wonderful work of my good friend Frank Shelton. I know this book will be a blessing to all who will read it. I have known Frank for many years as we both labored together with the Olympic team as chaplains. We have traveled together to the last two summer Olympics: London, UK and Rio de Janeiro, Brazil. Recently, Frank came to California to preach at the 115th anniversary celebration of the Azusa Street Revival.

#Urgency

We both agree that we are in the latter days and expect prophetic fulfillment of scriptures leading us to the coming of the Lord. It is imperative that we make ourselves ready for His coming! Frank is a sold-out warrior for Jesus Christ. I call him my battle buddy. Frank carries his cross of Christ like a true soldier and will never let go of the good news of Jesus. He is a true evangelist after the order of Billy Graham. You can trust Frank's zeal for Christ and his discipline to walk worthy of the calling. Frank is a balanced preacher of the gospel of the Kingdom of God. He is a demonstrator of the Lordship of Jesus Christ over sin, sickness, demons, nations, and people. Frank carries an anointing for the last days and will release that same grace into your life as you read!

APOSTLE FRED BERRY

AzusaStreetMission.org
Los Angeles, California

Apostle Fred Berry
AzusaStreetMission.org
Los Angeles, California

PRELUDE

THE book that you hold in your hands was the easiest and hardest I ever wrote. Since childhood, speaking and writing came easy. It is a fact, that nine out of ten people would rather die than speak to a crowd, but I never felt more alive than when addressing an audience. As a former speechwriter to a Member of Congress some would say I have a way with words. Truthfully, I have been writing my own speeches since elementary school when I was the keynote at both my elementary and junior high graduation.

Since that time, I have now been invited to speak face to face to over one million people in person. In 2020, I was booked to address crowds in TEN countries in twelve months and was excited about what the future had in store. However, I knew intimately that the sands of time were sliding rapidly through the proverbial hourglass. In my heart I sensed by faith that the walls were caving in and life as we know it was about up. In full disclosure, I knew with eyes of faith the "lockdown" would eventually happen before we all saw it. Since a youth, I had an innate sense that either God was coming back to rapture His Church, or I was on my way out! Billy Joel sang, "Only the good die young" and I would not voluntarily suggest I was *good,* but I loved God and I knew if we were not in the bottom of the ninth, we were certainly in the top of the ninth literally and figuratively.

When the Covid-19 hit, like you, all of our plans were tossed out the window, but my mission was crystal clear: To love God, love others and lead the lost to our Lord. God led me to write this book and I started in April 2020. Within two months, I had written 235 pages and it was as if I was reading it as I was writing. The Lord had downloaded in me this text and we went to work, and many nights burned the midnight oil and for several consecutive weeks I was up at four in the morning starting or completing another chapter.

I knew the book needed to be released and similar to a woman late in pregnancy I was certain this baby needed to be birthed. Then another curve ball was thrown and the book you now hold in your hand almost never happened. I wrote it twice and lived it once but in July 2020, with just three chapters remaining to be written, things got bumpy. Real bumpy! In twenty-one days, all Hell broke loose. The Saturday before the Fourth of July (2020) my father and I were in my car on the Harry Nice Memorial Bridge connecting Maryland to King George, Virginia. We were driving across the Potomac River on a three-mile two lane bridge, nearly 150 feet up in the air. As we were nearing the crest of the bridge, my car died on one of the busiest Saturdays of the summer, tying up traffic on both sides of the bridge with no place to go.

After God providentially bringing "an angel" in a tractor trailer just two cars stuck behind me and three of Maryland's finest stationed just on the other side of the bridge, we were back and running in half an hour. The fact is it felt like an eternity on top of a bridge with wall-to-wall weekend traffic. God works in mysterious ways because one of the assisting police officers recognized my father and his aunt served with my Dad at the United States Capitol Police in Washington, D.C. It was a comfort to have help even in a jam and it was a pleasant reminder that God was on the scene even in a storm. Police are some of my heroes and the Lord has used many of them to be His extended hands and feet. The Bible says, "Blessed are the peacemakers for they shall be called the children of God." Thank God for those wear the blue! That long, line of blue goes a long way!

By God's grace and some divine help, we finally got the car started again and what was interesting was the two cables to my battery had both been detached. I am still uncertain a year later how that could be but regardless, if intentional or just rattled loose, either way Satan was trying to stop my progress or as the teens today would say, "Stop my roll!"

I can prove it because after finally getting the cables securely fastened and crossing the bridge so hundreds of cars and occupants, we tied up on the bridge could now enjoy their pre "Fourth of July" festivities, we finally made it to the other side. We crossed onto land and saw firsthand the sign, "Welcome to Virginia" and did not go another six miles when the car died again! That is now twice in one day on a car that was immaculate, and one could eat off the engine. While waiting for the tow truck that never came in Maryland, we had apparently overwhelmed the alternator and drained the battery. When we finally were rolling once more, we were on borrowed time and now coasting to the side of the road hoping not to get hit. The perfect Saturday with my father on the road was now everything but and once again we are stuck and going nowhere fast. Two hours later, we finally got a tow and every shop in Colonial Beach, Virginia was closed and thankfully my friends, Frank and Frank, Jr. at F&A Corvettes were able to help us get the car to their shop that had just closed at three on a scorching summer Saturday afternoon. To their credit they worked overtime not for another sale but because they were willing to help old friends. Lately, with all the stress I had been under I was aging by the second and my father at seventy-three was looking better than ever. However, the heat does not help!

No matter how bad things get, I can always trace God's Hand in the sunshine, snow, sleet, or storm. He is indeed faithful. My wife, mother and son came to collect us an hour from home across the state line and when we all the reunited the five of us got some bottled water at a Wawa convenient store in Virginia while heading home to Maryland. It was already a humid 95 degrees and it felt like 110 after sitting twice counting the bridge between two states and stuck again on the side of the road in Virginia. For a Baptist preacher, that was as close to purgatory as one could be. Sweating profusely after buying a 12-ounce water bottle for each of us, I looked at the receipt and did not have to read it twice. The bill was $6.66! I knew because Satan had been kicking me all day long on this trip. That was strike one.

Three days later, my eleven-year-old son, Andrew and I drove 900 miles to Tampa, Florida in another car to attend a revival meeting with my dear friend, Pastor Rodney Howard - Browne. On the Fourth of July (the following Saturday) he allowed me to preach on that festive day to a packed outdoor celebration. My remarks aired LIVE to over 65 million homes nation-wide on DirecTV and other television outlets around the world.

We were already in a lockdown and nearly all holidays were on hiatus. The irony is across America most were forced to wear a mask but when Halloween rolled around no one could wear one. Cue the Twilight music!

All the fireworks had fizzled, but Pastor does everything big and we were told his church was the only one still shooting them off and they were incredible! I preached that night as we celebrated God, Country and grateful for the Constitution and the next day we headed back for the long trip home. We drove nearly two thousand miles in just four days, and my son was with me but when I said "we" it was just God and me because Andrew was still too young to drive. Exhausted, I finally got home and slept soundly in my own bed and could rest knowing I was not going to crash while doing all the driving.

The next day I went into our home office and apparently the electricity had gone out the day before while we were gone. My computer had been turned off and when logging back in I noticed a Microsoft application that I had not signed up for and I knew in my spirit this was not good. Some things had been changed and re-arranged and I could see some files had been moved around. After closer inspection I had that innate sinking feeling that my book that I had been writing feverishly had disappeared or worse, been deleted. My fears were proven true almost immediately. Instantly, I had four friends who are computer professionals from three states each try to resurrect or resuscitate that document to no avail. We had folks prophesy that it would be restored and yet it was a mute point, dead on arrival and we were up the creek.

The application had corrupted the file and deleted the rest and my two hundred and thirty-five page nearly completed manuscript which had been almost ready for editing and printing, now did not exist. I remember back in college that I had an entire semester to write a seventeen-page term paper and I thought that took some work but when you write over two hundred plus pages only to have it vanish will "bless you" and almost break you. At first, I was in shock, secondly, beyond sad and I did not know whether to cry, die, or try vomiting! God had downloaded this book in me and one week my car died on a bridge and now my book that you now hold in your hand died in my computer. That was strike two!

As God is my witness, you cannot make this stuff up and the Lord impressed on me to go exercise the following Saturday morning and to quote Schwarzenegger in "Commando," – "Let off some steam!" I got out of bed at seven because those four in the morning wake up calls while producing this book did not pan out to well so I "slept in" a bit. I finally got my focus back and made a mental declaration that I was going to walk it off, let off some steam and then get back and start writing. Perseverance has always been a constant theme of mine, but this test had pushed the limit and everything in me was screaming "quit" but I knew I had an assignment from God and a word that needed to be released. At 7:04AM I walked into my garage in a t-shirt and shorts while barefoot and still half asleep. I was going to put on my tennis shoes in the garage next to the door only to get my steps in and exercise on.

While wiping the sleep out of my eyes and still "sleep walking" as I descended from the house steps to the garage, I felt a scratch on my left foot. Initially, I thought our son Andrew had left a sharp toy or metal object out of place only to scratch my bare foot. The sleep was now completely out of my eyes when I saw what was now staring at me. The scratch I hoped was from a misplaced toy was a coiled snake that was sitting on the top step of our garage and struck with two fresh fang marks on my left foot! Three weeks before a dead car, the previous week a dead book and now either a dead snake or author. No joke, I made a point right then and there it wasn't going to be me!

Very few could describe that time was ticking more accurately than me but I knew my time was not up yet. Had this happened a couple years before the snake incident would have really thrown me in a tailspin but I think the snake was more shocked than me to see in the words of Sir Elton John, "I'm Still Standing." I recalled instantly Paul in the New Testament when he was bit by a viper and he threw it in the fire and I could almost hear former Minnesota Governor Jesse "The Body" Ventura say from his iconic quote in the movie "Predator" also starring Arnold Schwarzenegger, "I ain't got time to bleed!" Like Paul, the Lord had given me a message and mandate to finish this book and I did not have time to allow a snake or anything or anyone sideline me.

Anytime you are moving forward in your calling you can expect pushback and opposition. Interesting enough, the day after I was stuck on the bridge with my Dad, I learned that my sermon I had taped weeks before was airing to millions in Pakistan. The Good News was going to reach countless Muslims in Pakistan for Christ! Where Satan tried to sideline me in a car on the ground that Saturday, the Lord used me the next day on Sunday halfway around the world to take the airwaves back for His glory against the Devil. The next week, when Pastor Rodney graciously invited me to preach to his packed church crowd on the Fourth of July to additional millions more across America, I would get home only to find my book was either deleted or stolen. I was delivering God's mail only for my manuscript to be removed immediately afterwards. Coincidence? Not a chance. The following week I would be bitten by a snake and the term "snake bitten" did indeed cross my mind but I knew I could not let the Devil get the last say or bite, so I pressed in and pressed on.

A month later, my car had an accident and then spent three weeks in the shop with $7,500 damage but fortunately my car insurance covered it. The interesting thing was the more I was in His will the Devil tried to take my wheels. The very hour of the accident we were eighteen minutes from airing our first inaugural television show "BY FAITH with Frank Shelton" to over 180 million on another Christian Television network airing across America and in dozens of countries in Africa. Every single time we were on assignment moving forward for God, the Devil did all he could to stop us, derail us or take us out. Our son, who is not even a teen told me, "Dad, Satan is going to not only throw the kitchen sink at you but he's getting ready to throw the kitchen, too!" You know it is spiritual warfare when your child can not only see it but prophesy before it happens.

Since then, we have had some highs and lows. Lost several friends in death and life throws curveballs but praise God, the Lord got the last word. May this book bless you, convict you, stretch you, minister to you and encourage you that He that began a good work in you shall complete until the day of Jesus Christ's return. Buckle up because this is a wild ride and I pray it is less painful on you than me. Praise the Lord and glory to God and I am just the messenger delivering His mail.

On April 5, 2020, I did a FB Live video and over a thousand watched it immediately with some glowing comments and thanking me for staying true and speaking out in love. True proponents of society stand up when it would be easier to sit out. True prophets are willing to lose their neck or be sent to prison. Many in ministry dreamed to be known with their names on seminaries but the best and most used of God are known in penitentiaries. In those remarks I said with no notes but from the heart, "Friends, no matter what happens God is in control. I spoke a few years ago in India as a keynote graduation speaker of Bible college students and that venue has produced more martyrs for the cause of Christ than any other on earth. I got up in the same pulpit as Dr. John Maxwell and others had stood before me in years past and I finally could relate to what Dr. Charles Spurgeon when he said, "He preached as a dying man to dying men."

In closing, I am not here to make you feel scared but rather to help you stand strong. Our Constitution is under attack, folks have sold their soul to the New World Order and we are emptying out prisons to make room for others. We are now in a culture that celebrates evil at the expense of good, decency and purity. Concentration camps have been known to exist around the world but when folks stand up and speak truth sometimes heads roll. When Presidents Lincoln and Kennedy spoke truth to power, they were assassinated. You will learn in these pages my family throughout the years met them both. When Dr. Martin Luther King and President Reagan respectively stood up both men were gunned down. One lived and the other died but better to be die prematurely standing for truth than live long cowardly existing and adapting to a lie.

I want to do whatever it takes. God did not call me to preach to become popular. He did not call me to preach to be famous. He did not call me to preach to make money, but God did call me to preach the Word and stand for Truth. I come from a long line of detectives and for a century and half my family were police officers in our Capital City. At one time my dream was to follow suit, but the Lord had other plans. At one of my interviews with United States Secret Service, the Special Agent in charge of Baltimore Field Office told me a decade and half ago, "*Shelton, you would make one Hell of an agent.*" What a compliment from one of the best but today as preacher of the Gospel around the world and my past years on Capitol Hill; I did not stop thinking. If you think I have turned off my mind as I have climbed into the pulpit and stuck my head in the sand like a defeated ostrich you are out of your mind!

If one day, they make it mandatory to take this or another version of a vaccine or as Revelation talks of the "Mark of the Beast" I am already cleansed and clean because I have been washed in the blood of the Lamb. If that means losing my life to warn you then I did my job. I have read the Bible cover to cover, and we WIN when we trust Christ as Savior. The line has been drawn in the sand and you are either standing with God and what is good or the Devil and his downward agenda. We better get right, or you will be left, and I am not talking politically but literally and spiritually."

The same crowd today that demands "tolerance" is the least tolerant in the world. In

1985, Michael Jordan's game changing "Air Jordans" shook the shoe world, and they were banned. At first what was devastating for MJ was brilliant strategy for Nike. The "higher ups' in the NBA tried to ground the inaugural pair of "Air Jordan's" because they were colored and not the typical white shoes. Today, social media executives are banning folks today left and right for speaking truth and not following their false agenda. The same fact checkers are being played and at times paid by people who are part of the problem.

I warned pastors in the middle of the pandemic not to be satisfied or filled with false pride over your online views. It is possible that one day big tech will pull the plug on you and then you will realize you should have adhered to the Bible and not stop assembling in church because then that window would have passed. A few thought I was wrong but when the President of the United States was banned and deplatformed do not think that you are immune. However, if you do not follow their agenda, you may be next. Shoes being banned are bad enough, but the soul of a nation and global society are in play and unlike some players, I will not sit this one out.

The Bible reminds us that "nothing new is under the Sun." The three Hebrew boys stood up to the fake news of their day. Daniel did not dishonor his God to appease their false gods and they would all attest better to be persecuted for the Lord than promoted with the world's new order. Make no mistake, come Hell or high water that the Savior stands with us in the storm and if God be for you – who can be against you? For the last four years, I lead and co-lead a Bible study to lawmakers that is open to all (bipartisan). Very few appreciate the Book of Romans when it talks about obeying those in authority. We are at a crisis now because some failed to remember that true Authority is in Christ not Congress. What is Truth? I shared once on Fox News in New York that is it not a program, product, or policy but a Person, Jesus the Christ. Grace has a Face, and His Name is the Son of the Living God. Truth is in Lord not law of the land that at times can be against the Bible but make no mistake, our Constitution beats communism all day long. Lately, some prefer to subtract both Christ and the Constitution and wonder why we are in a decline morally and corporately in our nation.

Join with me and praying for all your leaders at the national, state, and local levels and an assault is not only against America but our public officials. There is nothing better than when pastors, police and politicians honor God and work together. However, there is nothing worse than when they turn their back on God and promote death and destruction more than liberty and life. I sense in my Spirit some were already on the wrong side either intentionally or accidentally, but the Gospel of Jesus extends grace and forgiveness, and repentance is still a prayer away. You can be forgiven today, and we do not need a global reset pushed by man, but we do need a revival by the blood of the Lamb! Jesus Christ is the Lamb of God that taketh away the sin of the world!

Months before the lockdown, I was invited to speak on the floor of Congress in Nicaragua. I shared with their president and vice president who were seated over my shoulder and to the packed crowd of their elected leaders seated in front of me, "Nations have succeeded when they honored the Bible. History has shown that nations have fallen when they disobey God." Pastor Jentezen Franklin was correct when he said, *"Christianity can survive without America, but America cannot survive without Christianity."* More than ever time is short, and Australia is affectionately known as the "Land down under." It was brilliant marketing for the Aussies, but America was to be that city set on a Hill and when her lamp goes dim our days are numbered.

Rolex makes an incredible watch, and it is a beautiful piece of art. The authentic watch has a second hand that never skips. The counterfeit watch despite their logo is easy to spot because the second hand hesitates like almost every other watch manufacture in the world. Despite its value and fame, I have always been intrigued by the "Days of our Lives" hourglass. Why? It reminds us all, rich or poor, black or white, Democrat or Republican, citizen of America or some remote village around the globe, that one day time will run out. My prayer is that your ears will hear not only the end time clock ticking but the sand silently racing towards the end is perhaps your last warning to get your heart and home right with God. Hell is too long to be wrong.

My former boss, Dr. Billy Graham was the beloved international evangelist who helped share the Gospel with more people face to face than anyone since the Apostle Paul. It was an honor to serve nearly five years on his staff and I was preaching in India when I got the news in February 2018, that he departed this world and was ushered into the presence of God. Years ago, at the height of his prominence and popularity he was listening to a young minister preach. Three quarters through his sermon a local pastor leaned towards the revered reverend and inquired in his ear, *"What do you think of this young minister?"* Dr. Graham known for rarely criticizing another publicly whispered in private, "He will never make it as an evangelist!" Shocked by his rare rebuke his colleague inquired, "Why?"

Rev. Graham replied, "There is no <u>URGENCY</u> in his message." Our prayer is that he that hath hears let them hear and may we get right with God before it is too late because time is not only ticking but running out. Jesus said, "Behold, I come quickly (Revelation 22:12)."

PAKISTAN

IT was a chilly night in the Nation's Capital, and I was having dinner for the first time with three new friends. Another year on the calendar had turned and we just entered a new decade and for just a few weeks into 2020 on the outside looking in many would think the sky was the limit.

Leadership gurus had been boasting for the last few remaining months of 2019 that in 2020 we are going to have 20/20 vision! Little did most know that in a few short months the world as we knew it would be turned upside down. For many it would come to a screeching halt! If they believed they would see clearly, we were heading into airspace with zero visibility. Truth be told, Ray Charles and Steve Wonder could SEE better what was ahead because unless you are naturally blind you are not used to seeing in the supernatural. It is an art to see in the dark. However, I could sense the train coming down the tracks for several years and it was already moving too fast, and, in my Spirit, it was getting ready to come off the rails. It was as if I was hearing the beat of a different drummer. Perhaps that is one reason the classic, "Little Drummer Boy" touched me so much. For most of my life it felt like it was just God and me.

Ministry had become more and more lonely to me because too many Christians, clergy and churches were not concerned about winning souls anymore and fewer were preaching the second coming of Christ. Everyone wants to have it all now and regardless, if callous or indifferent to the reality of the Lord's imminent return. David in the Old Testament had to encourage himself daily in the Lord and I loved the Lone Ranger as a kid; but it was getting old as an adult. It was not that I was advocating an all alone walk with God, but the fact is leadership is both lovely and at times lonely. Some in ministry want to grow a big church to build their ego. What happened to seeing people saved and when did it become about being the best or biggest church in town? My only competition is Satan; and we are running out of time (hence the cover of this book). While some were counting seats, I was counting souls and while others were excited about dollars I was still impressed with the Divine.

Two of my dinner companions that night in the capital city were originally from the United States but now serving with the great ministry of a very a respected pastor, Dr. Anwar Fazal known as the "Billy Graham of Pakistan." His ministry is beloved by many, and his church has over 30,000 attend each week in Lahore on Sunday mornings and Wednesday night services and he is the face of Isaac TV reaching scores for Christ. He has organized events and preached to multiplied millions all over Pakistan and I had been familiar with him from afar but my good friend, Stan Lovins II connected us together and now finding myself face to face with them at the table, thanks to his introduction.

Stan and I served in the past as State Coordinators when on staff with the Billy Graham Evangelistic Association. Stan represented Indiana and I served in Maryland, Delaware and Washington, D.C. respectively. He was a former minor league baseball player but in the Majors in my book when it came to ministry. As a pitcher he was clocked at throwing a baseball nearly ninety-three miles an hour but had led countless thousands to Christ. Both were impressive but in the game of life the eternal was more important that the temporal. We had much in common, but both knew time was ticking and we are almost out of time. Cher sang, "If I could turn back time" and Marty McFly's DeLorean in Back to the Future tags read "OUTATIME" and the proverbial sands of time were slipping fast through the hourglass.

The night before Stan was on a television show with Anwar during his visit to the United States and he said, "You absolutely need to meet Frank Shelton!" To Anwar and his team's credit they rearranged their plans and drove from Indianapolis to Capitol Hill all night to meet me from Maryland! I felt extra special and the next day after our meeting in Washington they flew to California to meet with leaders at the largest Christian television ministry in the world. The week before, they were with the leadership at Daystar TV and with one of the President of the United States' spiritual counsellors. To detour, pivot and make a pitstop for me was both humbling and a confirmation. Jesus said, "a prophet is respected everywhere but their hometown."

When I refer to eating dinner, for full disclosure I was at the table but did not eat since I was fasting, and gladly picked up the tab for their meal. I can share it now because the Bible warns of bragging when we do things unto the Lord for by doing so, we would have already received our reward. Lord willing, I still want a few surprises in Heaven and the Bible tells us to not let our right hand know what our left hand is doing. I am at a point in my life and ministry if God knows and the one, I minister to know, not everyone else needs to know.

Now that the fast is past, I am free to share to encourage you reading today, testify of God's goodness and report the URGENCY of the hour that had been alarmed in my spirit. Like a fireman awakened out of his sleep to hear that siren scream and out of a slumber by repetitive training put on his gear to fight another fire and hopefully save a soul. The Bible tells us daily to also put on "the full armor of God." Millions love to hit the snooze button in the morning for a few more winks but in this late hour in life I needed less sleep and more pep in my step. Elvis sang a song that I wish more professors and students in seminaries would sing, "Little less conversation and a lot more action!" I knew intimately that the clock was going to strike soon for the last time and the Lord would appear and life on this Earth as we know it would be over. REM sang a song, "It's the end of the world as we know it and I feel fine." Truth was I am 'ok' but millions are clueless to what was to come. Frank Sinatra sang, "My Way" but in these unprecedented seasons with time still on the clock if I would be any good for God and humanity, I needed to do it "His Way" in these last days.

A country song has been popular for over a decade now and one of the lyrics says, "We all want to go to Heaven but just not today!" To an extent I think we all feel like we have some unfinished business they would like to take care of before heading Home. Rocky Balboa told Adrian's brother Paulie about having "some stuff left in the basement." Perhaps you have a bucket list of things you want to accomplish but one thing I have learned that we may make plans, but the Lord orders our steps and tomorrow is not guaranteed. Over the years, I have crisscrossed our great country too many times to count. The international travel was starting to take a toll on my body and a flight from DC to LA seemed like a small trip around the corner after racking up air miles to London, Israel, Paris, Romania, Brazil, India, Africa, and the Philippines. There was an upcoming trip to Tokyo next on my schedule to name a few.

I read where Reinhard Bonnke the famous African evangelist who God used to shake the entire continent had flown so much during his ministry that the circulation in his legs began to have serious problems. He had to take precautions and wear therapeutic socks while travelling and despite preaching on the solid rock his legs at times would feel like they would collapse. He was indeed a man's man, but Satan has a way to weaken any minister or ministry. Through it all we must totally lean on God.

Many armchair quarterbacks today and throughout history want to throw rocks at folks who are sitting in First Class both dining and reclining while they are whining in coach class wishing they were up front. After countless flights up and down, north, and south, east to west I know all too well about being smashed in a middle seat or stuck next to the lavatory where folk's congregate waiting their turn to use the flying toilet. I am not one to complain but when the environment stinks and that is before the door of the lavatory is opened to really get a whiff, I have come to relate flying on a plane and trying to get rest is like sleeping in a hospital for me both are nonexistent. When you finally get a reprieve to feel like you are sleeping you either get hit by the metal beverage cart racing down the aisle on the plane by the stewardess or poked with a needle by a nurse drawing more blood.

In a conversation with my friend and former basketball Hall of Famer Meadowlark Lemon, who was arguably the greatest Harlem Globetrotter of all time, I asked, "Why do you always fly first class?" With his million dollars smile he said, "Brother Frank, rich people need Jesus too!" I am starting to agree with the late, living legend more than ever. He is now with the Lord and I think of him often and he was also a powerful preacher of the Gospel. It is indeed a privilege to preach and see life change, families restored, captives set free, souls saved, and eternal destinies altered but the privilege and the platform come with a price. At times I have flown so much the joke was I traveled as much as some of my Air Marshal friends.

The reason I was fasting on this night in Washington with my new friend from Pakistan is because God made it crystal clear that if was going to be used in these last days, I needed to be all in. Like a boxer who did not waste his punches yet ran many miles to get in shape before climbing in that ring. I also knew that I could not be satisfied with business as usual in the ministry. I needed more of God and God wanted more of me.

I knew two things and one of them was if I were to go to the next level with the Lord, I had to be intentional in many areas of my life. I needed discipline in my diet because you cannot fight off the Devil and his demons if I could not put down my fork from an awaiting plate at dinner. Secondly, by dying to my flesh I would *activate my faith*. Another reason was I felt compelled and called for this last hour. Just as Uncle Sam drafted many out of the blue to go to war, the Lord was telling me that my number was picked, and I was off to war. I had seen how the church had grown overweight and sluggish. Sometimes when we eat too much, we get sleepy. Sadly, before my very eyes the church was asleep at the wheel and did not even realize it or worse some could care less.

Perhaps you recall in the first "Vacation" movie with Chevy Chase when they show the entire family asleep on a road trip in that pea green station wagon with the wood paneled side. As the camera showed the kids in the back knocked out and then the wife with a smile snoring in the passenger side and then we find our trusted and beloved father Chevy Chase asleep at the wheel! It was hilarious in the movies, but it is a crying shame in ministry. Last year in America (2019) over 9,000 churches didn't baptize a single soul. We boast about donating to missions and brag about building bigger buildings, but the truth is seeing souls saved is declining in many denominations. God is not coming back for beautiful, brick buildings but for blood bought believers!

Over 2,000 pastors throw in the towel every single month and hundreds of churches close their doors for sale annually. Satan has had a field day in getting us to let off the gas, fighting among the saints and callous to things of God. One of the things God has pricked my heart to is awaken a sleeping church. I preached in India where they dream to die for the cause of Christ and yet some in church circles in America are content to not even live for Him. The Apostle Paul said, "For me to die is gain!"

As I had my third glass of water while everyone was enjoying dinner the conversation quickly turned to evangelism, crusade events and winning souls. This is my crowd when they are excited about seeing souls snatched out of a Devil's Hell and won to the Family of God with a home reserved in Heaven! The three men at the table were seasoned saints and powerful preachers. Pastor Anwar is considered by some as a general of the faith and they all knew intimately a lifestyle of prayer and fasting. I was learning more each day that it had to become more of a staple in my journey because time is of the essence. Pastor Anwar had preached to as many as 1.5 million people at once in person. Another time he had preached to 1.3 million. Billy Graham's largest crowd was in Korea in 1971 where over 1.1 million came to hear him preach and for as far as the eye could see folks were packed like sardines to hear the Gospel message.

As a child I heard Dr. Graham preach in person and early on I daydreamed of preaching to massive crowds. It was not egotistical, but a calling embedded deep into my heart to proclaim God's love to a lost and dying world. After hearing Dr. Graham preach in 1982 at RFK stadium where some 55,000 came to hear him preach in the home of the Super Bowl Champions Washington Redskins as we exited that famous arena while holding my mother's hand I said, "That is one of the most amazing things I have ever seen! If God could do just a little of that in my life just once that would be amazing."

When the disciples tried to get Jesus to eat, at times He would reply, "I have food that you not of." Sometimes when we are so busy doing a work, we don't take time to eat. Snickers would have you believe in their commercials that only their candy bar can satisfy but I tasted in 1979 and found firsthand that "the Lord is good" and Christ, not chocolate, is the only thing that satisfies. Desperate times call for desperate and drastic measures and the conversation at dinner came up about two of their upcoming crusades. Both were going to be in Pakistan, but one was going to be with over a million souls in the Fall of 2020 and the other was to be to nearly 150,000 the second week of March 2020.

The million plus crowd intrigued me because I had seen it "by faith" since childhood but the 150,000 caught my focus. Let me ask you a question, if someone offered you a million dollars later or $150,000 now what would you choose? A lot of variables go into play but let me show you, my rationale. Both were an answer to prayer, an assignment of God and a signal for me to go as an evangelist. The first two letters of God's name spell "Go." The first two letters of Gospel spell "Go" and the first two letters of Good News spell "Go." God has already given me the green light to get going but too many saints on Sunday were satisfied sitting on the sidelines.

Another aspect that touched and intrigued me was that both crowds were to minster to Muslims. Mainstream media in selling their "fake news" are oblivious of the Good News of the Gospel. Jesus commanded us to "Go into all of the world and preach the Gospel, baptizing them and making disciples." Twenty-two years ago in 1999, I was among the youngest to receive a scholarship and attend a weeklong conference at the Billy Graham School of Evangelism in Monterey, California. The closing guest speaker was one of my all-time favorite preachers, Dr. E.V. Hill and he preached with power on the Great Commission. His text that night was from Matthew 28:18 and in his iconic voice that resonated like a black freight train he screamed behind the pulpit to a capacity crowd of clergy with authority from on High and love below, *"All power is given unto me in Heaven and in Earth."* He then read a few more verses and closed with verse 20, "Teaching them to observe all things whatsoever I have commanded you: and, lo, I am with you always, even unto the end of the world."

 He then paused and said, "In verse 18 circle ALL POWER." He then told us to look at your neighbor and repeat after me, "I got the power!" The place went crazy, and I had just been deputized to evangelize! For a guy who recently graduated college and had never done drugs I was as high as a man on cocaine that night because crack has nothing on Christ and the greatest "high" is in service to the Most High God. Following his remarks, I waited in line to have a brief encounter with one of my heroes of the faith. I had watched him preach on television frequently but now waiting for my turn to shake his hand, look him in the eye and thank him for his ministry. When we finally connected, he was tired, sitting on a stool provided by the host and I could tell he was well spent in service to his Lord.

I do not normally do this practice, but I asked him that night to sign my Bible and he autographed his name on the inside cover and wrote Psalms 71. He told me that entire chapter had comforted him many days and nights throughout his ministry. He had been harassed by the KKK and threatened by the Black Panthers. He said, "When you got the whites and blacks after you without the Lord you are in trouble!" He received countless death threats, crosses were set on fire in his front yard at night to terrorize him, rocks thrown through the windows of his home scaring his family, car bombs installed around his vehicle to take him or his wife out and the relentless attacks of the enemy seemed endless.

I never dreamed that those same verses that comforted him would begin to minister to me decades later as a traveling preacher. He often tagged teamed with another one of my heroes, Dr. Adrian Rogers and their "ebony and ivory" combo preached massive crusades together at home and abroad. He preached frequently on Trinity Broadcast Network and a time when their channel was a tad over the top his message was always on point. Their dream together was to lead one million souls to Jesus. I have a feeling when the number is revealed at the Great White Throne Judgement, they indeed hit that mark. The great Wayne Gretsky who dominated hockey said, "I missed every single shot I didn't take." One of the problems of having nothing to aim for is that you miss the target every single time.

Hands down, one of the greatest sermons I ever heard was from Dr. Hill when he preached the funeral of his first wife. You can find it online and to this day pound for pound among the most powerful sermons ever. He preached with clarity and great power to a capacity crowd next to his beloved wife's casket about God's faithfulness and his love for her. He wove the Gospel message into that eulogy and revival broke out at the funeral. He reminded me so much of Christ because only the Lord can put funeral home directors out of business. Dr. Hill went on to be with the Lord not long after we met but I still preach almost every sermon, revival, radio broadcast and television appearance with that same battered Bible he signed for me that night on the West Coast. It is scarred and battle-tested and still gives hope to the hurting today! I like to believe some of that same power is on me today. My friends have said since day one that I may be white on the outside but got a lot of "soul" on the inside.

The lame stream media have misrepresented and maligned many Christians as if we hated Muslims. One of the primary reasons I had the desire to go to Pakistan was to preach with love that God loves them! I pictured myself sharing God has a plan for your life, your days can be filled with hope, joy, and peace. You can have confidence today and enthusiasm for tomorrow. I wanted to tell them God wants to communicate with you daily and draw you to His heart and become best friends. I pictured preaching to that crowd that Christ is the only way to Heaven. Millions of Muslims have bought the lie that Mohammed leads to Heaven; but it is through Jesus' death, burial, and resurrection alone that we have access to Almighty God and find forgiveness of sin.

Yes, the idea of speaking to either event with Pastor Anwar was a huge honor and not everyone is wired or gifted to speak to that many souls at once. Before I could even share at the table what door I should go is when Pastor and his team shared, "Frank, we want you to come but honestly the first one is too dangerous." What I did not share and now you will see my mindset and heart was the million plus crusade for the Fall was in a safer part of Pakistan but the one scheduled in less than a month was considered the most dangerous region in their nation. The man who is beloved across Pakistan and spent his adult life preaching there had never ministered on a large scale in that dangerous vicinity. When a Pakistani is saying Pakistan is dangerous one should take note. In fact, it was mere miles from where Team Six of the Navy Seals killed Osama bin Laden. Pastor Anwar then looked at me and with complete sincerity said, *"Frank you can come but you may not come home alive."*

The crowd of well over 150,000 Muslims that I was invited to preach to while on that platform was not only in bin Laden's backyard, but Pastor Anwar paused and said you will be surrounded by the Taliban when you preach. No one was eating at this juncture and some of you may have lost your meal at this point but when you are fasting you tap into a focus that few will know only once you have been in the "secret place" with God.

I recall at a press conference in Rocky IV when Balboa agreed to fight the Russian after he killed his best friend Apollo, a reporter asked Rocky, "Has the fight date been set yet?" In his unmistakable Italian, deep voice, "December 25th." Instantly another reporter barked, "Why Christmas?" Rocky calmly replied, "That's what I was told." Another correspondent chimed, "Where will it be?" He replied, "It's in Russia." His brother-in-law Paulie who was seated near him with the cameras rolling said emphatically, "Are you nuts?" A loud reporter in the back yelled, "Rocky, how much are you making for this fight?" Rocky said, "No money. It's not about money." It has been said that right before you die your life flashes before your eyes. I cannot verify that, but I do know that within milliseconds, this movie scene from exactly thirty-five years ago danced through my head. I could recall the entire script from the scene from 1985 as my new friends at the dinner table were inviting me to preach in Pakistan the next month, March 2020.

My former United States Marine friend once said, "Better to go fight the enemy overseas than wait till they come home here." Personally, I could not think of a single pastor off the top of my head that would buy their own flight to Pakistan, fly all alone halfway around the world with no spouse, special assistants, or security detail in one of the most dangerous venues in the world. This is not game six of the 1998 NBA finals where Jordan and the Chicago Bulls flew west to Utah to play the Jazz inside the Delta Center, now known as Vivint Smart Home Arena in Salt Lake. This was not Rocky fighting a Russian in Moscow in a Hollywood film on a safe studio set. This was me from Maryland preaching perhaps for the last time in Pakistan not far from one of the world's most dangerous terrorist's former compound surrounded by one of the most lethal military snipers on the face of the Earth.

This was no ego trip, but mission trip and I saw "Death Wish" as a kid, but I am no Charles Bronson as an adult. Call me crazy but I have travelled enough for so long on my own that I honestly did not expect any other option to be on the table. I did ask if my dear friend, Mike Neifert from Delaware could accompany me; but they said seeing two Americans on that Pakistani platform would be too risky and draw additional attention. Just as a running back looks for a hole to break through to gain yards as an evangelist; I was taught to look for a way in when everyone else is looking for a way out.

Leaving that night from dinner in DC, I was grateful for the invite but also concerned. Even Jesus in the Garden of Gethsemane sweated drops of blood on the eve of the crucifixion and prayed to His Father if possible that He would not have to face the cross and die. However, Christ was born to die yet rise again! As I drove home that evening one of the reasons for going to preach in Pakistan was to share the Good News that Christ can forgive from sin, save the soul, and extend eternal life by faith and grace. Secondly, it was to befriend the Muslims who were still enslaved to a lie and false religion. Third, I have seen more than once that love is greater than hate, faith is greater than fear and the Gospel is more powerful than the Pentagon. What could be a dead end could be result in a u-turn to get on the right road with God.

The week before my dinner date in DC I had just preached in Birmingham to pastors and leaders at the Alabama Baptist Convention that the ingredient missing in their ministry was a lack of *urgency*. Too often we have a resume, but most didn't have the burning fire to turn the tide. Too many are fighting over War Eagle or Roll Tide that we are were distracted by the bigger battle. The biggest game in town is not over sports but it is the fighting for the souls of men. I just preached to a room full of pastors in Alabama that if I can preach in Pakistan than you better be on post in Birmingham. It was basically a "drop the mic" moment.

I had served as a Chaplain and Evangelism Chairman at the Summer Olympics in London in 2012, in Rio de Janeiro in 2016, and was scheduled to do the same that July at the 2020 Olympics in Tokyo. I was asked to come to Alabama to speak to, encourage and help mobilize leaders to prepare for the upcoming World Games. I was asked to cast vision and help shed light on how to effectively evangelize to athletes and fans with over 100,000 coming to Alabama the following summer. One of the biggest surprises for me in ministry was how low a priority it often is on a pastor's radar to reach people who have yet to have a personal relationship with God. We are so busy feeding sheep on a day-to-day basis that we often don't look out of the four walls of our church office.

Before reaching my driveway from our dinner with Pastor Anwar on Capitol Hill with my three new friends it was clear to me that either scores of souls would respond to Christ, or I would be gunned down from a kill shot by a member of the Taliban. I am part preacher but also part promoter and I knew that the sermon may go viral on YouTube and whatever it took for the Gospel to go forth I made a point that live or die I was going to die trying. I knew most of the Church was asleep and that makes ministry lonelier for me, but the blessing is it forces one to talk to God more. For a good part of my life, I have dedicated my time to preach the Gospel, invite folks to respond to Christ and see revival in our land. The same crowd that does not desire revival or hold services anymore for renewal and refreshing were not going to be the one to preach to the masses and warn the end is near. I was doing it then and still doing it now with greater accuracy and urgency.

With the help of their staff and that of Sarah from North Carolina (who is a genius in administration) I was able to secure a visa to Pakistan in record time. What could take weeks was done in days. That was another confirmation from the Lord that the trip was good to go. We bought my airline ticket that would have me depart Dulles International near Washington and change planes in Dakar and arrive in Lahore, Pakistan. It would be an entire day and half traveling and then fly like Han in Star Wars "solo" and then pray to navigate through customs only to be monitored probably by their government the entire time. Spiritual warfare is intense on any mission trip, but most folks are oblivious to the sheer emotional duress that comes from this type of ministry. You are dealing with a hostile ideology in a foreign setting with the Taliban looming.

I have joked that the reason I shop at Walmart is because *Target* is on my back! I penned this in my notes prior to flying overseas while preaching revival in Orange Country, California. When I tell you I already saw it I truly did. Below were my remarks and then I was going to share as I approached the pulpit on social media the night of the big event in Pakistan. I was not advertising on my website itinerary I was going to the Middle East until already there. Mentors gave me wisdom years ago to not let the enemy know you were there until "wheels up" coming home but since I was not guaranteed to come home alive; I felt it was good to get the word out for saints to pray.

My heroes as a kid were Mister Rogers, Superman, Evel Knievel and the Six Million Dollar Man. The irony was I was voted the nicest kid in my class like Mr. Rogers and because I did not have Superman's cape, I had to rely on Qatar Airlines, but I recall thinking even Evel may have hesitated to try this feat in Pakistan. Jumping over a fountain at Caesars Palace in Vegas was one thing but dodging potential Taliban bullets as target practice in Pakistan was probably riskier. Unlike Lee Majors, I did not have a six-million-dollar life insurance policy for my wife and kids had I came home in a box. I think that both Evel and Elvis must have had the same tailor because they each had the white jumpsuit, Napoleon collar, matching cape, and same love for America.

I had seen literally thousands, perhaps tens of thousands, get born again at the stadium events in Africa. I know the power of the Gospel to redeem even the worse sinner and I still believed God could do it again in Muslim dominated Pakistan. In one vision I could see those beautiful people hanging on to every word of the sermon with a hunger I had seen in other places of the world and in record numbers would come to saving faith in Christ. Keep in mind, many of the Muslims in this region have NEVER heard the Gospel. So, when I asked you earlier in this chapter would you go after a million in a safe region who had heard the Gospel or 150,000 most of whom have never heard The Good News of Christ, now you can see my logic to choose the latter group.

Plus, I knew time was short and something was coming against our nation. I couldn't prove it but I could sense that the event in the Fall may not happen. In 2015, I preached at a Romanian Pentecostal Church in Phoenix, Arizona and said in my sermon, "A tidal wave never seen before was coming to the United States and most were not prepared for it." That wave proved true with an invisible virus that crossed nations and crashed on our shores and we are still passing out life preservers today and yet many died while on ventilators. What is suspicious is that the same tool that prolonged life lately almost seemed programmed to produce premature death. A friend of the family in April 2020 got COVID-19 and he said the moment they hooked him up the ventilator it had a reverse effect on him where he felt it was hindering his breathing and he was begging to be removed. Fortunately, he lived but others died and when you hear some were getting a kick back of $40,000 USD for every death while on a ventilator you start wondering if it was more financially lucrative to allow others die than to live? More than ever, we are up against pure evil and our only Hope is Christ.

Since childhood, I had this unique feeling either the Lord was coming back very soon, or I was going to Heaven. This sense of <u>urgency</u> had been in my biological clock for some time. God had impressed on me for several years that the chance to see a harvest for souls was growing slimmer by the day. The walls were closing in and repeated dreams and nightmares in my sleep reminded me far too frequently that time was almost up. Another scenario I had was while preaching to those hungry hearts, perhaps right before giving the invitation to repent of sin, turn from the Muslim false belief system and trust Christ as Savior, a flurry of gunfire could easily take me out. Perhaps bleeding profusely with a bullet riddled body, while gasping for air and still holding to the Holy Bible not Qaran remind that capacity crowd with love in my eyes and parting words on my dying lips would be that Jesus Saves! This is what I penned and was **going to share** that day on social media in the biggest pulpit of my life getting ready to possibly deliver my last sermon.

"Today, I'm in Pakistan. This was an undercover mission and very few know I am here but in such a short time I have fallen in love with their beautiful people and this country. In a few

minutes I will be speaking to the largest crowd of our ministry to date. They tell me over 150,000 souls are present, and locals have confirmed I'm in the most dangerous part of this nation.

The Taliban is on roof tops overlooking the massive outreach with their weapons and I am scheduled to preach in ten minutes. I am the only American on stage. As I see this vast crowd before me, I can relate to Christ when He wept over Jerusalem because they resembled sheep with no Shepherd. The entire crowd as far as the eye can see are Muslims and this area has been unreached to date with the Gospel. I am certain that there are militant Muslims in the mix but I'm also hearing promising reports that many Muslims recently are forsaking the dead prophet for the Living Lord. Praise JESUS! Heaven and Hell are in play today and Eternity is no joke!

On the entire flight over here I have been praying that multiplied thousands will give their life to Jesus today. Perhaps tens of thousands! I didn't come here to play games. Truthfully, I saw this crowd a long time ago as a younger man in my mind and under the circumstances this is hands down the most volatile place I have ever preached.

Over the years, I have ministered to Hells Angels in the USA, Muslim Priests in London, armed drug lords in Rio de Janeiro, African tribes in Uganda, preached in the very pulpit that produced more martyrs for Christ than any other in the world only for me to be removed repeatedly in the midnight hour from multiple hotels in India with extremists threatening to kill the message, messenger, movement or all three. I preached with love to police in communist Nicaragua, the Coronavirus is threatening what would be my next stop as evangelism chairman of 2020 Olympics outreach in Tokyo and traveled by bus on the Gaza Trip from Israel to Egypt with possibility of armed to teeth guerillas hijacking us anytime and ministered to a few other people and places in between and around the globe but this venue today is indeed different.

Some think it's bold as a football fan to represent wearing a Redskins jersey at Cowboys stadium in Dallas but it's another level representing Christ here in Pakistan. I knew coming in that I was not guaranteed to come home alive after this sermon, but I still believe that one man can make a difference because 2,000 years ago, I met "by faith" that Man who made all the difference. Life begins and ends with Christ.

I still believe LOVE is greater than hate, GOOD triumphs evil every time and JESUS not Mohammed is the only way to Heaven. I still believe the song I sang as a boy in Sunday School is true, "red, yellow, black and white are ALL precious in God's sight" and at this moment I have the peace and power of God on me as I am ready to approach the pulpit. I am prayed up and ready to be poured out and it could be the last time I preach but I'm willing to risk it to enable for this multitude to hear the Gospel for the first time and others for the last time.

Sadly, our culture and corrupt media has misled millions to believe the Bible is hate speech when it is a letter of love not from a celebrity but the Creator of the Universe. Jay Z did not die for you, but JC did! Charlton Heston was correct when he said, "the Gospel is the greatest story ever told" and for forty years I have loved to tell the Story. I believe we make history every time we share His Story.

I have said for years that prayer is more powerful than the Pentagon and one preacher from the past said, "God's man is virtually indestructible until the Lord is done with him." The Lord led me on this assignment, and I do not know many people or pastors that would have flown all alone from America to Pakistan to preach today to this crowd but since childhood; I found a confidence in Christ, a boldness with the Bible and an internal fire because of my faith.

One friend once called me, "Rambo without a gun" and looking back the friendliest guy in the county was also one of the boldest in the <u>country</u>. Niceness is never weakness, and it takes a real man to honor the Lord. When you kneel before God in private you can STAND before any man in public. On the law enforcement memorial in Washington, DC etched in marble is a Bible verse, "The righteous are as bold as a lion but the wicked flee when no man pursues." When you are right with God you can run forward not backward and like any rescue mission, I was taught to look for a way IN not out.

I'm in, I'm here, I'm on post and I'm once again going to soon lovingly but powerfully point the lost to the Lord. I am just the mailman delivering His mail and it's still all about Jesus and scores of souls are hungry to meet the Hope of Heaven. The answer in life is not a product, program or policy but a Person and His Name is JESUS, The Christ.

Presently, I may be surrounded by the Taliban, but God is my rock, shield, and mighty fortress. I love the new Michael W. Smith song "Surrounded" and have listened to it repeatedly lately and the lyrics comfort me now. Bill Gaither once said, "If you live long enough the lyrics will catch up to you." Today the lyrics caught up to me and I found tremendous peace with the Prince of Peace. One famous evangelist from a century ago said, "I want to chase Hell with a water gun telling them about God's love" and today I am following his footsteps. Twenty-five years ago, I worked on the floor of the United States Senate and heard some of the greatest orators speak daily but over the years I found my own voice and today I have something to say.

At this moment, I am no longer looking at the enemy around me but the Divine within me who called me today to bring "Good News" and I have a front row seat to watch Him once again set the captives free. Christianity was never a spectator sport and those that call Christ, or the Bible boring do not know either. Indeed, I have tasted and found the Lord is good. I have not only tasted but tested Jesus again and again and found Him true because He's "The Way, The Truth & The Life" (John 14:6).
Please do not pray for me because I'm fine either way. Pray for my family at home and that these precious misguided Muslims before me that Christ bled and died for will repent of sin and live for Jesus. I am believing many Muslims will join the family of God in the next few minutes. You come to a point in your life when you either believe it or you don't, and I STILL DO. More than ever!

Personally, I am praying even members of the Taliban adorning weapons will come to saving faith in Jesus. God is greater than guns and sometimes the worst sinners become the best saints. I learned that Saul became the Apostle Paul, and it can happen again today. While some theologians "play it safe" and sit on the couch and play armchair quarterback and debate behind a computer in the comfort of their living room the Lord called me as an evangelist to share, "JESUS SAVES!"

Spurgeon preached as a dying man to dying men and today in this moment I am halfway there. I am fully reminded of the prayer of the prophet from the Old Testament, "Here I am Lord, send me."

Thank you to all my family and friends at home who encouraged, prayed, and financially supported us. We could not do it without you and our sole mission is still souls and it's an honor to be on the winning team with you. I never felt smart, but the Bible says, "He that wins souls is wise." I am praying the churches in America will wake up from their slumber and be wise because wisdom goes after souls. We are called to "do the work of an evangelist" not a Calvinist and I answered the call and over the years preached to millions and saw multiplied tens of thousands saved. All glory to Him and we sow seeds, but Christ alone saves the soul.

My time is now and all glory to His Name. God loves Pakistan, God loves America, God loves the world, God loves you and because I know He loves me I can stand and share today whatever the outcome with boldness, "I know that my Redeemer Lives!" Mine eyes have seen the coming of the Lord."

#LetsRoll #TeamJesus #TCB #LoveYouRuthHannahAndrew #InTheLineOfFire #ElvisHasLeftTheBuilding #BillyGraham2 #DesmondDoss #Rambo #TheLoneRanger #Lincoln #EvilKneivel #John316 #Souls #FrankShelton.com

2 Timothy 4:5-8

5 "But watch thou in all things, endure afflictions, do the work of an evangelist, make full proof of thy ministry.

6 For I am now ready to be offered, and the time of my departure is at hand.

7 I have fought a good fight, I have finished my course, I have kept the faith:

8 Henceforth there is laid up for me a crown of righteousness, which the Lord, the righteous Judge; shall give me at that day: and not to me only, but unto all of them also that love His appearing." THE HOLY BIBLE

Days before I was scheduled to depart for Pakistan, I learned from Pastor Anwar's team that the government had pulled the permits before the big crusade because of the violence that may have ensued. To say, I was disappointed would be an understatement. I wanted so badly to lovingly preach the Gospel to those precious people and hopefully point many to salvation found only in Christ. Anwar was disappointed, I was disappointed, everyone was disappointed (except for my wife).

The original plan was for me to fly late on a Monday night and then arrive at four in the morning in Pakistan on Wednesday local time. Hopefully find a bed to crash and then preach that evening at Pastor Anwar's church to approximately 30,000 Muslims and encourage them in their faith. I don't know of another church in America running 30,000 in attendance for a midweek service, but Anwar and his team are doing incredible things! Then we would together travel on Thursday several hours "under the radar" to the darkest place in Pakistan near the bin laden compound and preach Friday with him to over 150,000 Muslims and hopefully get back to Lahore for a Sunday flight and live to tell it. Talk about the belly of the beast! I loved movies as a child and you throw in Indiana Jones, Mission Impossible, RAMBO and cast a younger Billy Graham as lead and this would be the movie of my life.

Unfortunately, the outdoor event was now cancelled despite all the prayers, promotion and preparation leading up to it and all I could think about was the souls that might have been saved and snatched out of the Devil's grasp and by grace now heading for Heaven. The Lord gave me a vision in advance to preach to that crowd and now it was on hold. The door was still open for me to fly halfway around the world and back alone and preach to his church on Wednesday night which is no small invite. The average church runs about 150 across America and to preach to 30,000 Muslims plus millions on television was an honor but something still was off, and I could not put my finger on it.

The week leading up to the departure my spirit was torn and restless. It was not that I was afraid; well to an extent I was because as a human the thought of fear and "what if" did cross my mind. Like Desmond Doss from "Hacksaw Ridge" I was trying to ask the Lord to give me one more soul to rescue during the war, but it was if God was blocking the door. My wife Ruth had NO peace, and she has called me since our marriage her library book who selflessly loans me out to the world knowing I am coming back. However, this trip was different. She cried for days, and she knew I may not come home.

The Scriptures teach that in the multitude of counsellors we find safety and wisdom. I called a few pastors that I trust, and one was Stan who I mentioned earlier who served with me at the Billy Graham Evangelistic Association. He is a great soul winner, powerful preacher and prophet and he said, "Frank it sounds like the Lord is telling you to wait this one out."

My friend Dave Kistler who ministers to Members of Congress told me to sit out too and will elaborate later but for the trifecta I called my dear friend, Dr. Rodney Howard - Browne during the day. To his credit he caught up with me later at midnight via text. This dear preacher friend just two weeks later would be falsely arrested and made international news for having church and honoring the Constitution and his text to me that night was, "I wouldn't go to Pakistan at this time. We need help in America." He has preached in 85 countries and one of the greatest evangelists of our time and for a brother who only knows forward by faith does not reverse or retreat I was confused because he was also telling me to stay.

The Lord had used my Godly wife and THREE wise, committed soul winners, without knowing previous conversations, all gave me the same counsel: Not this time! God is not the author of confusion, and it became clear that had I boarded that plane that evening alone by the time I would have been halfway to Dakar the Coronavirus had already began to halt travel and it was rippling around the globe. Pastor Anwar, who was already back in Pakistan said, "Frank it was wisdom that you didn't come."

That same week, President Trump shut down most travel coming back from the East, and I would have been a man without a country. For a Baptist who does not believe in Purgatory I may have died in an airport with no money, no bed, and no chance to return. Death by Taliban was looking more attractive by the minute.

It is all starting to make sense. My heart was pure, my motives sincere and I knew as much as anyone that scores of souls could be saved in Pakistan. Lives changed, families encouraged only try to navigate as the lone American through that tough terrain trying to leave undetected, get through Customs and trust the Lord to get back home safe and sound to the United States to live another day. Nothing was guaranteed this side of Heaven and no monies were to be given. Like Paulie said to Rocky about Russia, "Are you nuts?" Maybe I was nuts, but for all the right reasons. Some folks would not do it for a million bucks, and I am willing to risk all of this for nothing. You ask why? One word.

#URGENCY

CONSTITUTION HALL

(Ruth Mizell & Dr. Rodney Howard-Browne.
Ruth was beloved on Capitol Hill and married to a former Member of Congress)

ALLOW me to go back in time a few years and share my story leading up to the current day. No, I am not borrowing a DeLorean, nor will we hit 88 mph, but the stories are real and all glory to God.

I was on a conference call with Pat Schatzline in the spring of 2014. He is a well-known and very respected evangelist from Alabama and God is using he and his wife, Karen mightily. He invited me to be on a call with him and halfway through he introduced me to his friends and shared some of my Capitol Hill background and current work as an evangelist residing just outside of Washington, D.C. in Southern Maryland. After finishing my remarks, immediately, a man on the line with a thick South African accent chimed in and said, "Who is this young man? I need to meet him!" I learned it was Dr. Rodney Howard - Browne and he texted me his private cell. Following the call, we were on the phone, and he shared with me he was coming to Washington and God gave him an assignment to preach the Gospel in our Nation's Capital. He informed me he was going to rent out the iconic DAR Constitution Hall and would also be ministering to Members of Congress while in town.

Only God could have orchestrated that phone conference and for Pat to selflessly have me share briefly on that national call and then for Dr. Rodney Howard - Browne to connect with me was a Kingdom connection. I could sense instantly that Rodney was a soul winner and had an incredible vision and determination to see our nation turn back to God. My wife Ruth is a program manager of a Christian-Spanish radio station in the DC region and over-sees two other stations in Philadelphia and Richmond. We were able to invite Pastor Rodney and some of his team to be a guest in the studio to promote his upcoming event. Over the years I have learned that many preachers learned in Bible college how to promote God but somehow failed to learn how to promote others without feeling threatened or inferior. I was taught when we promote others the Lord smiles.

When Ruth and I finally met Pastor Rodney in person, we found him gracious and generous out of the gate and as his big event approached, I had several ministry friends encourage me privately not to attend his event. Some said, "We don't like his style of preaching." Another said something about a scandal of making folks laugh in the service. I recall thinking if that was the biggest flaw, they could find then they, too, should attend and get a fresh dose of the Holy Ghost and the joy that comes from knowing Jesus. I had been in ministry long enough to realize that most criticism is rooted in jealousy. When you stare at the last five letters of jealousy it spells LOUSY! One went so far as to say, "You come from a Baptist background, and he is Pentecostal" and you should stay in your own lane.

God showed me long ago that He was bigger than my Baptist box. Jesus is more wonderful than the Wesleyans, more powerful than the Pentecostals and mightier than the Methodists. You cannot label the Lord or put Him in a box. You cannot even keep Him dead in a tomb because Truth always rises to the top. A few even hinted to me that attending this evangelistic event could hurt my ministry. The fact is I am just a spoke on God's wheel but in His will and the Lord is the one with the ministry. Plus, as one of the only fulltime evangelists in the DC region I would look exceedingly small and insecure if I could not help another to reach our region for Christ. Too often and far too many in ministry only assist or attend if they are on a poster beforehand or scheduled to be preaching on the platform the night of the event, but I wanted to be around a genuine move of God. The Lord gave me a great gift to speak but He also gave me two ears for a reason, and I need to listen and learn, too.

On opening night at Constitution Hall, I was getting additional and heated pushback by some clergy and was told to stay home. The Lord told me to go, and I was en route alone to Constitution Hall. This is a fact that those who are trying to build their own kingdom are territorial but those who labor for God's Kingdom know no boundaries. Satan was teasing me on the entire trip to turn around. The Devil and his demons whispered in my ear that I would not find parking, etc. Faith moves forward but fear is stuck in reverse, and I was moving ahead!

Any doubts I had soon disappeared upon arriving at the iconic venue. Their staff had me sit right down front on the floor and treated me like some VIP. Read that again! Faith will get in the door while fear while keep you on the outside. I was two or three rows from the front to the right of the stage and their praise team is second to none. God was in that place and without question there was a sweet Spirit in the house! Right before Pastor Rodney preached, he did something that I was not expecting and was totally selfless. Pastor Rodney invited any or all clergy to come up on to the platform to be recognized at that historic venue. I honestly did not want to move but someone sitting next to me knew I was a preacher and tapped me and implored me to go up on stage.

The thought danced through my mind that this is crazy! I drove all alone and less than half an hour after already being positioned on the floor in a place of honor this minister took time to take the spotlight off himself and over one hundred and fifty pastors from the region are now being recognized a block from The White House. We are standing on one of the world's most recognized and respected stages and God honors those who honor Him. That was extremely selfless of Dr. Rodney to honor others that evening, but I learned then and countless times since that he is both powerful in the pulpit but generous off the platform. He did not get to his level by burning bridges but by blessing others and preaching Jesus.

From the corner of my eye, I could see from stage left one of his team members carrying a large frame about four feet tall and placed it gingerly next to the podium front and center. They do everything over the top with their ministry and this next gesture solidified my appreciation and respect for Pastor Rodney forever. This international evangelist in his own right in front of a great crowd took time out to present a lifetime achievement award for my hero of the faith, Dr. Billy Graham. This Pentecostal evangelist was pausing to honor the world-famous statesman and at the time in his late nineties he was unable to make the trip but flew Dr. Jim Wilson (Billy Graham's son-in-law) from Montreat, North Carolina to attend the service. Jim had married GiGi Graham and was on hand to receive the prestigious award. At this juncture the crickets of criticism that my Baptist colleagues had said in the past were long gone because he was showing more honor to Graham than many of them in recent years. Our convention was now leaning more towards Calvinism than evangelism.

Dr. Wilson received the award on behalf of his father-in-law, and he was visibly both impressed and touched by Pastor Rodney's generosity and respect. The gift was so large that one of Pastor's assistants carried the gift off the stage and as all the clergy began to find their seats, I just happened to walk off in the same direction towards the back with Billy Graham's son-in-law. In that moment ordained by God, I was able to introduce myself and shared that his stepson recently wrote the foreword to my last book. He stopped dead in his tracks and said, "Is that right?"

I replied, "Yes sir." I shared faster than a Ferrari with no brakes that I was a huge fan of Dr. Billy Graham and attended over a dozen of his crusades. I told him that I just received a free scholarship to attend an evangelism conference at The Cove in Asheville, N.C. It is owned and operated by the Billy Graham Evangelistic Association and his eyes lit up. Pastor Rodney was getting ready to preach, everyone else is sitting in the auditorium and the world's most famous evangelist's son-in-law and I are standing on the stage in the back corner getting ready to disappear so Dr. Howard Browne can finally preach.

Over the years, I have learned that the greats are gracious. Dr. Wilson said, "Frank, here is my business card and let me know the exact dates you will be in town and if I am home and my schedule permits than I would like to meet you for a coffee or meal." For a guy who had never done drugs at that moment I was as high as a kite, and I do not recall if my feet hit the floor as I headed back to my seat to take in the rest of the service. Pastor Rodney was already preaching and all I could think of was three things; if I left now, it was incredible! Pastor Rodney is a general in God's Army and I almost missed it if I listened to the voices of those back home deterring me from coming.

As the service concluded, I left looking for my car and on the way home thought about the powerful evening of praise, preaching and the privilege to grow as friends better with Pastor Rodney and to meet Dr. Wilson. The next morning, I received a text from Dr. Rodney Howard - Browne at seven A.M. I thought I was seeing things and he was inviting me to meet him for breakfast. He told me, "Frank, I know what Billy Graham means to you and why don't you join me and Dr. Wilson for a meal before I take him back to the airport?" I was floored and most folks try to cut people out of the equation, but Pastor Rodney wanted to include me with his time with Billy Graham's son-in-law. That was big of him to do that, and I thanked him for the kind invite but had to politely decline since I already promised to take my son to summer camp for the week and could not do both simultaneously.

I was afraid that I would hurt his feelings by declining but if there is anything that Pastor understands is that family comes first especially after traveling so far and so fast preaching the Gospel. We do not have forever to raise our children and he understood but I forever will cherish that one of the generals of the faith was trying to bless me. Two weeks later, I reached out to Dr. Wilson and shared I was indeed coming to Asheville and was inquiring if he would have an hour or two to spend time together. He responded almost immediately and said "absolutely!" I was so happy because I have been around enough people that some will say something to you publicly but when you follow up in private, they have amnesia and almost forget the conversation.

The Graham family did not get to their level by compromise or cutting corners. I felt like a kid in the candy store and was excited to learn that in a few days I would be having fellowship with one of Billy Graham's family members in Montreat, North Carolina.

GOING TO CAROLINA

WHEN you live "by faith" you do not take anyone or anything for granted. The moment the Lord opened the door for me to head south to North Carolina I was excited! Packing for this trip was not a problem and the Tar Heel state is special to me for a couple of reasons. My Dad's mother was from Wadesboro, North Carolina and we had distant cousins in Raleigh, Greensboro, and Charlotte.

Unfortunately, we only saw them on rare occasions, and it was either a wedding, funeral, or family reunion but I found them to be among the nicest people in the world. I learned quickly that they may talk slow, but they sure drive fast! Perhaps to make up time for talking to friends but either way they made up for any lost time. I had a cousin that was a cheerleader at UNC Chapel Hill and my cousin from Maryland married Michael Butler who was a baseball pitcher for NC State. He was an ACC All Star and was even drafted by the Angels. I was also a proud graduate of Gardner Webb University in Boiling Springs, North Carolina and had made a few trips since returning to see faculty and friends and preach revivals both on and off campus.

Before kissing my wife to leave that morning, I had our SUV packed and I was once again heading out all alone. The conference would start on Monday, and I was scheduled to preach the next day in Asheville, North Carolina. My good buddy, Brent Ramsey opened the door for me to preach at a Presbyterian Church near his home and we had done some ministry events before. He is a great guy and I still smile when he texted me a picture of himself under a tree in Kenya reading my last book under the African sun. For quite some time I had a vision to take the Gospel around the world and we were already halfway there.

With time ticking, I said "goodbye" and like Elvis, I had left the building (house). I said a quick prayer, threw on my seatbelt and was excited about the 425-mile trip before me. With my pit stop at a Cracker Barrel and stops for gas, I calculated the trip to be about eight hours. I had made this trip many times over the years, and it was always therapeutic heading south. James Taylor penned a classic, "In My Mind I'm Going to Carolina" hence the title of this chapter. After pulling out of my driveway I had not driven seven miles when suddenly my 2004 Lincoln Aviator began to shudder and came to a complete stop. After throwing on the hazard lights, I found myself stuck on the side of the road. The good news is I was still in my hometown, but the bad news was I had eight hours before me, and it was already almost noon on Saturday.

Strike number two was I called my wife and there was no answer. I called one of my best friends and he did not pick up. I called another friend but in baseball three strikes and someone is out! The late, great Regis Philbin had a popular show at the time called "Who Wants to Be a Millionaire?" I was rich in faith and broke according to my bank and I was out of lifelines.

Satan was teasing me. Mocking me! Frank, you should just give up now. You will never make it! Your free scholarship at the Billy Graham Training Center is not going to work out. Plus, you should forget the breakfast with his son in law on Monday morning. Where is your God in all of this? If it were meant to be, it would be much easier than this! The mental verbal assaults were overwhelming, but I had taken some shots in life before to the head and heart and I will not say you get used to it but I had learned through those trials to keep moving forward.

I was able to call a tow truck and he was on his way. The Bible talks about "count the cost" and my mind was already calculating time lost, the repair and towing expenses, and Satan relentlessly telling me that this working vacation was over before it started. My wife Ruth will tell you that perseverance probably could have been my middle name and just because I am sidelined does not mean we are not in the game.

The good news was the tow truck was on his way but an hour and half later I am still sitting stuck in my hometown on the side of the road with time ticking. The Bible says, "Be still and know that I am God" and I was certainly still and aware that God was going to have to do it because I was going nowhere fast! Two hours later, my help came, and he got my black SUV truck on the back, and I climbed in with my carry-on luggage and sat up front in his big cab. Satan was saying "STOP" but God said, "Go!" Just remember when Satan tries to give you a red card that the Lord already gave you the green. Faith moves forward but fear keeps you in reverse or stuck on the couch (or on the side of the road).

It was comical as we pulled into the rental car place. I rolled in a big, black tow truck about half the size of an eighteen-wheeler and climbed out with a suitcase and signed some papers and rented a car. I was sweaty, fatigued and starting to run low on faith. After dropping me off, the tow truck driver was now headed to take my car to my mechanic. Satan was running his mouth in my ears about what the cost that would be. At this point, I could not control anything other than I knew I had to get to North Carolina. Some of the folks were staring at me as I rolled into the rental place. Not sure if it was because of my predicament or because most folks do not come in with their luggage or an Uber that is a tow truck, but I was a man on a mission and with a message and time was ticking and I had to get out of Maryland.

The rental place was getting ready to close. It was already three in the afternoon on Saturday and apparently, they close early on weekends. Five minutes later and they would have already closed for the day. That was one thing I could be thankful for, and I am still trying to look for the good and not dwell on the bad. I got a small car and was just thankful for something that looked clean and had a full tank of gas, so I grabbed the keys, and I was off to the races.

I have now been in three vehicles since leaving my house and three hours later still had not gotten out of town. My SUV was now heading to a shop, and I am in a rented car and could not stop any longer. I said another prayer for protection and provision and grateful to God to be moving forward. As I finally graduated from park to drive, I was all too familiar with the time, and I had lost nearly four hours and this eight-hour trip was going to put me in Asheville close to midnight.

One thing I have learned in life, leadership and living for the Lord is that whenever Satan hits you it is probably because you are heading towards the Promised Land. No one said living for God would be easy! In fact, it is downright hard at times but if God be for you who can be against you? The Devil has knocked many out of commission because rather than pressing into the Lord and persevering, too many complained, quit or both. Take this to the bank and make a note that when Satan starts messing with you then God is getting ready to bless you to the next level.

I am a little different and some suggest a tad slow. One friend said, "I was so slow it took me two hours to watch '60 Minutes!" I may be slow, but I do tend to see the big picture through the eyes of faith. Where others may have quit, I would get more determined. At times, Satan may have done better to leave one alone because where others quit, I would be ramping up. Dr. Johnny Hunt is the former pastor of the great First Baptist Church of Woodstock, Georgia. He served previously as the President of the Southern Baptist Convention. He is a Cherokee Indian and one of my favorite preachers on the planet. We both graduated from Gardner-Webb University, and he spoke my junior year at chapel, and it was still one of the greatest sermons I had ever heard. Very few preached with his passion and that made such a profound impact on me. He said, "When an African American is happy, he preaches extra good! When a white pastor gets mad, he tends to preach really good" after pausing with a smile and said, "but when you are Indian you preach good all the time!" Everyone laughed but the fact is I was a tad mad from Satan sidelining me, but I was going to make him pay more than ever.

The first song that came to my mind was the theme from "Smokey & The Bandit" and I love the line, "*Eastbound and down, loaded up and trucking! We're gonna do what they say can't be done! We got a long way to go and a short time to get there. I'm eastbound and watch that Bandit run!*" Someone once said that the reason your rear-view mirror is smaller than your windshield is because where you are going with God is more important than where you have been with the Devil. At this juncture, I had to leave a few loose ends behind but had to keep the pedal to the medal and roll on and that is what we did.

I use the word "we" because God was with me each mile of the way. When you have problems, I learned to turn up the praise. After crossing the Governor Harry Nice Bridge leaving my beloved Maryland and officially in King George, Virginia I was heading south. After a time of prayer and praise my problems seemed to dissipate but God was in that car! Satan threw the sink at me before and he tried again that day, but I have learned when all Hell is coming at you take heart that all of Heaven is for you!

Before I was thinking of the Bandit's song but more than ever, I could hear James Taylor in the soundtrack of my life, "In My Mind I'm Going to Carolina." With the praise music on and Satan no longer taking rent free space in my head I flew through Virginia like a Lambo in Los Angeles but ironically in a Hyundai about two hundred and fifty thousand dollars less. It was refreshing to finally see "Welcome to North Carolina" and it was now dinner time and I still made time for Cracker Barrel. I love that place and the tea and hospitality is "sweeter" the farther south one travels. I did not sit in the rocking chairs this time, but it was still good to eat that southern cooking.

The Lord was stretching my faith and the joy had come back. When Satan tried to halt me, I could see Christ was getting ready to <u>catapult</u> me! It was about eleven that evening when I rolled into town, and I stayed at my friend Brent's place. I never like showing up that late at a friend's house but sometimes life throws a curve, and it was out of my control.

It was like old times reuniting with him and we stayed up a couple hours and it was long past midnight, and I went to bed to get a few hours of rest before preaching in the morning at the country church nestled in beautiful Western North Carolina. The next day I was ready to go and survived the delay from the day before and was fired up and ready to roll! I got up to preach that morning and it was surreal because I knew God was on me and that message out the gate. While I was preaching, I almost felt like I was watching from the side opposed to front and center and it very well could be because I was in the passenger seat and the Lord was preaching in the pulpit. God had kicked me into overdrive, and it was no flesh and all faith and that is a wonderful place to be!

God shook the place in that Presbyterian church and when I gave the invitation, we had EIGHTEEN souls call on Jesus for salvation. I am not going to get into an elect argument or debate here but all I know is that souls were saved that day and the Lord was in our midst in a tangible way. They graciously took an offering for me which was a blessing but what they did next floored me. I do not recall this ever happening before or since in my ministry but someone in the church brought up the fact that I arrived in a rental car. I did not broadcast that my car died on the way down nor had revealed that I was in a rental and what they did next ministered to this minister.

They took a second offering to help with the expenses and would you believe it not only paid for the rental car and the repair to my Lincoln back home, but I also had some spending money while in North Carolina for the evangelism conference starting the next day! I was told when "God guides He provides" and when we are in His Will it will be on His bill. God made a way when it seemed to be no way. He works in ways we cannot see, and He made a way for me and won't fail you either!

Dr. Billy Graham's wife, Ruth had a Presbyterian background, and he was ordained Southern Baptist and that wonderful church ministered profoundly to this traveling evangelist. I still smile every time I think of them, and God bless each of those saints who assisted near Asheville. Brent and his family took me out to lunch after the service and folks were really encouraged by the sermon and a sweet Spirit was lingering all day. We had a great time the rest of the afternoon and even played a little golf on a gorgeous course near the house I was staying. The mountains of North Carolina in that region are spectacular.

The following morning, I had to leave a tad early to meet Dr. Jim Wilson for breakfast. Just a couple weeks before I was invited by Dr. Rodney Howard - Browne to have breakfast with the two of them but having to politely cancel had set the table for this meal in Montreat, North Carolina. I recall being so excited to reconnect and a few moments with Jim and recall thinking this was about as close to the Graham Family as I would get. For starters, the Denny's we were going to meet for breakfast was nestled in Montreat just down from where Dr. Billy Graham resides in Black Mountain, NC. As a youth I had visited the respected Southern Baptist retreat center called Ridgecrest just miles away, but proximity wise I had never been this close to the world-famous preacher's home.

Over the years, I had the honor to have met Will Graham (Billy Graham's grandson) at a couple events and we became friends. He was a guest on my radio show in the past and it was my privilege to have met Franklin Graham a couple years before at Grandfather Mountain in Boone, North Carolina. My college friend, Brad Huss went on to become Dr. Graham's number two photographer and invited me to attend the Billy Graham staff picnic. I was not on staff at the time, but Brad brought me as his personal guest, and he hoped to introduce me to Billy, but we learned later that Dr. Graham was not feeling well that day and had to decline coming to the lunch after all. I always smile when I think of Brad because some friends act more like enemies when they hear you have a dream and opposed to helping, they often intentionally hinder the process. Brad forever will get extra credit in my book just for trying to make the connection, but it was not meant to be this side of Glory.

As I pulled up in the rental car, I was seven minutes early. Less than 36 hours earlier I was on the side of the road in Maryland with a dead car. However, I was not going to allow Satan to hold me back. For most of my life I had prayed to grow as friends with the Billy Graham Evangelistic Association and just over five hundred miles in another car and preaching my heart out the day before I was now getting ready to have breakfast with Billy's son-in-law.

The Lord is never in a hurry but always on time and despite the Devil's thwart to hold me back I was seven minutes early! The number seven is symbolic of "perfection" and completeness. Some would say "restoration." God always has the last word. I whispered a quick prayer in the parking lot, thanking the Lord for the privilege to be present and asked Him to have his way with this meeting.

With a smile and happy heart, I walked inside and shortly after reunited with Dr. Wilson and with his congenial southern hospitality he pointed towards a booth, and we sat down. What a treat to be with him and Jim is a broad-shouldered man and tall in person and the only thing bigger than his frame is his heart and booming voice. Many have commented over the years that he has Dr. Graham's unmistakable accent, and it sounds as if God were speaking directly through him. The only two other voices that are as distinct to me were both Dr. Adrian Rogers and my friend, Dr. Lloyd Ogilvie. They both had the "voice of God."

Jim was so gracious and made it easy to talk to and that was the trademark of Dr. Billy Graham. He made everyone feel at ease and was more concerned about hearing you than hearing himself speak. After we looked at the menu and the waitress took our order he said, "Frank, I know you are one of my father-in-law's biggest fans and we are literally about two miles from his home. As you may know, he has his good days and bad days and I already asked if I could take you up to meet him today, but Franklin said "unless family" it would be best not for him to see any visitors today.

My heart dropped because although I had heard him speak thirteen times before in several states, I had never met him. However, I was thankful that Jim would even try, and it goes to show you that the greats are gracious. He was not trying to block but bless and just trying goes a long way. Evangelism since a child had been one of my passions and I shared the story when my parents took me to hear Billy Graham at RFK Stadium in Washington, DC. It was home to the Super Bowl Champion Washington Redskins and hearing Dr. Graham preach to that massive crowd I was mesmerized.

My mother reminded me as we exited that sports stadium of a statement that I said to her, "Mom that was one of the greatest things I have ever seen. No one could be Billy Graham but if God could use me one day even in the slightest way would be one of the most incredible privileges ever." Brother Jim smiled, and I began to share with him the various cities I had seen Dr. Graham and I could name the stadium and the date. He was floored and knew I was telling the truth. I joked if some folks followed the Grateful Dead, I could follow the Grahams who promoted eternal life! We both laughed and began to eat our meal.

We talked for about an hour and my time was up. Like the title of this book eventually time will run out. Right before we adjourned to get up and leave, he said, "Frank, my wife, GiGi works at The Cove where you are heading, and she looks forward to meeting you." I had to look over my shoulder to see if another man named Frank was sitting directly behind me. As we exited to our cars, I gave him a hug and it felt like I was hugged by a bear and left smiling wider than ever as I headed towards the Billy Graham training center.

Rolling into the majestic campus was something I still recall vividly. In my mind I had been there before, and it is more beautiful in person. I grabbed my bags and raced into the lobby to check in to the conference. When I arrived, I dropped off my bags in my room and it was clean and spacious. It smelled brand new, and I laid on the bed for just a moment, but I was so excited to be there I did not want to waste a minute resting. I was so excited to be there that although the first session was not until a few more hours I felt compelled to go back upstairs in the main lobby and connect with old friends, fellow evangelists and meet new brothers and sisters in Christ.

While running into some dear friends I heard my name and turn around and Billy Graham's daughter was calling me. All my friends stopped and thought who in the world is this guy that Gi Gi Graham called me by name. She said, "*Frank, my husband Jim told me all about you and he had the absolute best time with you for breakfast and he wanted me to ask you if you had time to meet him again for lunch tomorrow?* Without missing a beat, I said "Yes!" Truth be told, I was still trying to figure out why he wanted to spend more time with me? I had a couple youth pastors in my hometown who would not even take the time to return my call, but I have the heavyweights in ministry, pro sports, Hollywood, and politicians wanting to connect. I have always said, "the winners are wonderful, but it is the wannabes you have to watch out for."

She was so kind, and you do not get to the top constantly stepping on others, but leaders elevate those around them. I was honored, humbled and happy to be with him again the next day and what was Hell two days before trying to get out of town in Maryland was turning into Heaven on Earth now in North Carolina. God gave me a pep to my step as I headed into the conference, and I could see clearly that Satan was trying to prevent me from experiencing in person this moment and training.

It was a treat to soak in all the material and it was like drinking water from a fresh mountain stream and to be in the room with some of your heroes and likeminded colleagues was both rare and refreshing. I was a kid in the candy store, and this was my crowd, and I was having the time of my life. Although the accommodations at The Cove are second to none I do not recall sleeping too much because I was so wired and happy to be there. In baseball terms, I was in my "sweet spot" and the next day while in the morning session we paused for lunch and this time as I had round two with my dear friend, Dr. Jim Wilson and he brought his colleague with him, Mr. Greg Matthews.

Greg was his supervisor for the MY HOPE with Billy Graham project for that entire northeast team for the USA. After the introduction and enjoying another lunch, Jim said, "Frank I need your resume." I recall thinking for what? He said, "We don't have anyone to represent my father-in-law in that part of the country and I believe you are our man!" This Baptist preacher turned Pentecostal and I almost fell out on the floor. Only God could orchestrate this and had I not gone to Constitution Hall, I would have missed out on the connection that Pastor Rodney orchestrated for me with Dr. Jim Wilson.

Indeed, I was thankful for the three-day scholarship that my good friend, Dennis Nunn gave me to come to the evangelism retreat and despite Hell trying to hinder, hamstring and hold me back we made it "by faith." What I was thinking was for a three-day reprieve, retreat and refresher was a game changer and huge open door to come on staff with the Billy Graham Evangelistic Association. This not only enabled me to learn from the best but mature as an evangelist. Opportunity may only knock once! Ministry minus URGENCY equals Catastrophe. What was to be a 72-hour conference became over a four-year contract and I am so thankful to God for that incredible experience. Remember, when Satan is holding you back, the Lord may be setting you up!

DECISION AMERICA

(Rev. Franklin Graham & Frank's Family) - Dover, DE

FOR several years since quitting my Capitol Hill career in 2007, I was praying that the Lord would allow me to be a treat to clergy not a threat. I was hoping to be a colleague and cheerleader to them not some cocky competition. My private prayer was, "Lord, when I call a pastor to add value to them personally and their church corporately, I don't want them to roll their eyes trying to get me off the phone thinking I am begging for a booking to preach even though we sure could use the money."

God answered that request a thousand times when the door opened to serve contractually on staff with the Billy Graham Evangelistic Association. For the first year we were gearing up for Dr. Graham's 95th birthday and one of his caretakers in his humble log cabin home in Black Mountain, NC asked the revered reverend was there anything you need? The nurse was thinking a glass of milk or cookies to nibble on but arguably the most powerful evangelist since the Apostle Paul said, "Give me one more sermon!" Her eyes grew wide, and his request immediately trickled back down the mountain to Franklin Graham and the BGEA team.

When I first heard that quote my mind raced to ROCKY II when Balboa was sidelined from training handcuffed by love in a hospital to his wife, Adrian's bedside as she suffered complications prior to giving birth. Rocky's manager Mickey was growing restless by the second because the biggest rematch since Ali vs Frazier was only a couple weeks away and Apollo had not wasted a minute in the gym training, but the great contender had not been in a ring to train since their last bout. Right when it appeared that all hope was gone, the fight would be over before it started, and the proverbial parade of redemption passed by, his wife awoke out of a coma and strung together the greatest sentence of affirmation to dance on the silver screen in Hollywood history. Adrian whispered to her haggard husband with the manager in tow listening to every word, "Rocky, there is one thing I want you to do for me – WIN!"

Immediately, the trumpets began to blast; and the brass horns began to belt out the now iconic theme "Gonna Fly Now" and that was music to both Rocky and Mickey's ears and the rest is history! Rocky went on to beat Apollo Creed to win the Heavyweight Championship of the world and when Dr. Graham on the mountain of his Montreat, NC home said to his nurse, "Just give me one more sermon," I cannot prove it, but every great lion has one more fight in him and I wouldn't be surprised if trumpets started blowing in my former boss' ears. If not his, certainly Franklin and most of the crusade team and immediately thought creatively how they could help honor his request to preach one last sermon to the whole wide world.

They moved quickly and time was ticking; and Dr. Graham did not get to the pinnacle of his profession by accident. He knew God called him, but he also had a unique pulse on what time it was, and urgency was on the table and his internal clock. All great evangelists know what time it is both literally and spiritually. I would also add they see the signs of the times in advance long before others read it in the newspaper. Dr. Graham knew his days were limited, he knew the Lord could return any time and the country was in desperate need of direction.

The staff initially tried to have the senior statesman stand behind his famous pulpit, but he was too weak. Later in his ministry just before retirement he could sit down in a chair, and it would raise up behind the podium but from the outside of the pulpit it appeared that he was standing when in fact he was sitting. The near century year old Gospel preacher had a hard time with that, too. Strike number two!

Someone brilliantly suggested that they film his last sermon from his living room chair. Talk about home court advantage it worked! Dr. Don Wilton of the great, First Baptist Church of Spartanburg, S.C. for the last several years became a close friend to Dr. Graham and became the world-famous evangelist's pastor. He would make the trek weekly from South Carolina to North Carolina to lead Dr. Graham in a sermonette and devotion.

For continuity, the staff shot on several different days but had Dr. Graham dressed the same for each take. At times for those in attendance while filming said it was touch and go with his health and failing memory but when it came to the simple, Gospel message that he had preached thousands of times in 180 countries his mind was alert and as sharp as a tack. Dr. Graham got his wish and leading up to his birthday the first week in November, churches across America were encouraged to not only watch it but have house parties inviting family and friends who were unchurched or not born-again Christians to hear the Gospel. For some it would be the first time and others the last time and the Gospel is good news only if it arrives on time.

When it aired on his birthday multiplied millions tuned in one last time to hear the timeless Truth from God's Ambassador. Fox News, TBN and other news outlets world-wide ran with it and some speculate that almost as many people tuned into that one sermon as several decades of filling stadiums in person. What look like was the end was God's way of saying, "I'm just warming up!" Dr. Graham had been faithful to God throughout his career and the Lord was indeed faithful to him at the end granting him one more wish. He said something decades before that resonated with me as a young man still in high school, "I am just a Western Union messenger boy delivering a telegram of God's love to the door of humanity." One more time the mailman was delivering God's Mail (Gospel) for what would be his last sermon.

The next couple of years, it was my job and high honor to serve as the Washington, DC Coordinator for the MY HOPE with Billy Graham project and my terrain also included Northern Virginia, half of Maryland and all of Delaware. That was a lot of bandwidth for one person. since almost every other state coordinator in the country was assigned to only one state. I recall joking with the VP of BGEA, "I don't know if you see potential or you are trying to kill me" because no other state coordinator was tasked to cover that much ground, but I ran to the challenge and I could also hear the clock ticking. I knew time was short, the sands of time had almost slipped through the hourglass and most of society including too many Christians were oblivious to how late in the game we really are. The Lord allowed me to see it through the eyes of faith and we crisscrossed the states at a feverish pace. It was almost inhumane. Where Rocky and Billy Graham heard "Gonna Fly Now" I could hear the soundtrack to "Smokey and the Bandit" that we have a long way to go and a short time to get there!"

Truthfully, I heard both. Meeting Stallone as a child inspired me in a profound way. The unknown Billy Graham met his baseball hero, Babe Ruth at a game when his dad took him to an exhibition game in Carolina. Meeting his hero as a teen enabled him to stand toe to toe with ease meeting world leaders later. Regardless, if "ROCKY" or "RAMBO" both taught me directly and indirectly the value of prayer, patriotism, and perseverance. Rambo danced through my head more than once preparing for the top-secret mission to Pakistan and if

Rocky could fight alone in Russia perhaps God and I could do it together in the Middle East. #Yo

Life indeed imitates art sometimes and more than ever this late in the game we all must emulate and imitate Christ. He does not call us to play it safe but preached JESUS SAVES! The next several months I logged countless miles throughout the Northeast. When I prayed that pastors would not see me as a threat it was so much easier to say for those who did not know me, "Hi, I am Frank Shelton with the Billy Graham Evangelistic Association." I was promoting God, the Gospel, and the Grahams in that order but many doors did open, and we give God all the glory. We contacted thousands of Christians and untold hundreds of clergies and churches of multiple dozen denominations. We taught personal evangelism, how to share your faith, promote church growth and mobilize countless Christians. It was an honor to even on occasion teach some of my peers and colleagues with the Graham Team on effective ways to share the Gospel, promote an outreach and grow the church.

It was the best of times and trying at times too! The presidential election was a year out and many had already believed that Hillary Clinton had it all wrapped up. I got the impression that Franklin may have been watching the news at home one night and where Elvis shot the television with a gun perhaps like me you may have been prone to throw the remote once or twice at the flat screen on the wall and basically say, "Not on my watch!" God gave Franklin an assignment to go to each of the fifty states and hold a prayer rally. It would not be political nor tell anyone who to vote for but encourage all to be involved in the political process, exercise your God given right to vote and choose candidates that aligned with the Bible. It is important that we vote our faith!

When his colleagues and Daddy's former crusade team heard of his request some thought he missed the boat. One allegedly said, "Franklin, your Daddy preached in all 50 states but not all in one calendar year." Franklin probably hinted I am not my Daddy and God told me to do it. The team began to "urgently" seek permits, construct a ground game, and map out a course to best pull it off. However, nothing happens without prayer and pray we did! From an outsider it would be easy to think that everything the Graham organization did turned to gold. That was not the case but almost everything was given to God and that makes it better than gold. Satan relentlessly hit us all and anytime you are on the front end of advancing the Gospel you can expect pushback. Sometimes violently! For years, I joke the reason I shop at Walmart is because TARGET is already on my back!! When you preach that Christ is coming soon and the only way to Heaven, the bullseye gets even bigger on your head, chest and back.

We continued to press into God and after receiving our marching orders we moved forward by faith. America was truly at a crossroads and Franklin Graham aptly noted that the only hope for our country was Almighty God. The Republicans nor Democrats could not fix it and we needed heart surgery and Christ is the Great Physician. The road of the cross will help make all the difference when at a crossroads. Several years later, I would preach on the floor of Congress in communist Nicaragua and in my remarks to a packed crowd of their national leaders with the President over my shoulder on television I shared, "Nations have fallen when they have turned their back on God. However, He blesses those that honor Him."

To say in that moment; I was inspired by Dr. Billy Graham (now with the Lord) and Rambo would be an understatement. However, I was just one of God's ambassadors still delivering the Mail and the Gospel Truth. It is humbling but by my 47th birthday I had ministered with both a U.S. President and Communist President over my shoulder. One of the reasons I believe God used me is because I would give an invitation wherever I go, I would not be deterred by a crowd's size (big or small) and I had been around power and prominence my entire life. Since a child, I would wear my Sunday best and walk the corridors of Congress with my Dad at work. In fact, I believe I may have been the youngest in history when the United States Senate took a photo i.d. card for me when I was 12 years old!

The BGEA team worked tirelessly to mobilize churches, encourage clergy, and invite folks to come to one of the fifty state prayer rallies. We had intense opposition not only from the unchurched but also from some clergy within the Christian camp, but neither we nor Franklin were running a popularity contest but humbly trying to honor God and do what He told us to do. Many were on board, but some argued that it was automatically 'political' because we were congregating outside on the lawns of state capitols. Let me park the car and take a few critics to school regarding Christians not being engaged in the public square. For starters, one of the reasons our world is in the shape we are presently in is because too many spineless pastors have told their congregants that politics is evil, not a worthy profession and we should not be engaged in public debate or policy. Secondly, we are to be salt and light, and one cannot bring change if you exclude yourself from all conversation. Martin Luther King, Jr. said, "God called us to be THERMOSTATS not thermometers." Read that again!

You cannot change the tone or temperature if you boycott the process. I volunteered serving in four different White House administrations of both political parties. I made a point years ago that I wanted more than one party represented at my funeral. The Apostle Paul was "all things to all people to win some" and I learned in elementary school math class what you do to one side you need to do to the other. When Billy Graham, after ministering to thirteen U.S. Presidents, was asked by a reporter, "Reverend, are you after the right wing or left wing?" Without hesitation, he replied brilliantly, "I am after the whole bird!"

Everyone needs Jesus and it was also attributed to Dr. King, "If you don't show up if invited to the dinner table you will eventually be on the menu, and they will eat you alive." I heard it for decades of various political leaders that some would scream, "That's not my president! I am boycotting a visit to The White House!" For every failed visit that was one less chance to be an Ambassador of Hope. Personally, for every college and professional sports team that turns down a visit with a sitting President they may have just flunked a course in dealing with someone regardless of if you agree with them or not.

Too many in our culture today are winning professionally but failing personally because of a lack of respect for authority and will not dialogue or do business with someone opposite of them. Unless we want to graduate students with a broken mindset of having an attorney on speed dial and sue your way to the top when your feelings are hurt or melt like a snow-flake, we are going to strike out in the game of life. Eventually we will all have to work with a boss, organization or colleagues who think differently than us and unless you want to live in a false bubble and cannot cross the street much less shake hands with different people you are doomed for disappointment.

If my Dad would be willing to have died for seven different United States Presidents before retiring as Acting Assistant Chief of America's Police Department (United States Capitol Police) and another ten years with the Department of Justice as a contractor in security, why is it so hard for others to be courteous and kind? If Dad and my ancestors would have DIED for them why can't others at least say HI to someone? #Hello

Speaking of the Apostle Paul, this may be the greatest eye opener for many ministers who boycott anything politically. Paul was previously named Saul before his Damascus Road encounter with Jesus. I never dreamed in few short years when the world would enter a lockdown over a virus with a 99 percent survival rate and forced to wear a mask, I too would preach on the road to De MASK us! That is good preaching!

Previously, Paul was rebellious but now after becoming righteous he went from perse-cuting Christians to arguably the greatest evangelist apart from Christ. The first eight out of nine converts that Paul led to salvation in Christ were PUBLIC SERVANTS! Are you ready for this? Put on your seatbelt and take out a pen because class has started on Evangelism 101. Three of those were governors!! Read that again and if Paul thought it wise and Biblical to also share the love of God and Gospel with leaders why are too many today in ministry failing to lead them to Christ?

The Church has been great over the centuries ministering to the poor but somehow failed to minister in love to the prominent and powerful. I asked Basketball Hall of Fame inductee and legendary Harlem Globetrotter Meadowlark Lemon one time at lunch why he flew First Class? I will never forget his response. With a twinkle in his eye and million dollars smile the Clown Prince of Basketball said to me, *Brother Frank, rich people need Jesus too!* That statement really put my ministry into overdrive and for the rest of my days I would be intentional and relational to those in the political arena as well.

With the national election less than a year away, the campaigns were in full swing for candidates on both sides of the aisle trying to win their party nomination for the highest office in the land. I was invited to the second Decision America rally to get a firsthand look of what to expect. I will never forget it was a bitter, cold day with a foot of snow on the ground and dismal four degrees! The wind made it worse and when I got a cup of hot choco-late it was cold within thirty seconds! The night before we had a nice dinner with our team and stayed in a warm, clean hotel and several of the candidates and their staff stayed in the same hotel and as they were jockeying for votes with hopes to win the Presidency, we were trying to get Jesus elected to the hearts across America.

It was almost surreal seeing tour buses wrapped with candidates of both sides in the snow while we were also in town. Then again, we were knee deep in marketplace ministry and knee deep literally because we had been praying for God to turn things around. This tour was neither an indictment against the Democrats nor a pass for Republicans but collectively calling all to seek God and repent personally and corporately as a nation. We are bankrupt without the grace and mercy of God. Leading up to one of the first Decision America tour stops in the frigid Northeast corridor we were elated to see two thousand souls stand in the snow praying for the Lord to heal our land. I was encouraged then and there that if they can stand in the snow our region had no excuses standing in the sun a few months away to repeat the process. We were freezing on the outside but their support for God warmed our hearts for the rest of the tour.

It was the late, great Dr. Adrian Rogers who was President of the Southern Baptist Convention and beloved pastor at Bellevue Baptist in Memphis said, "Our job is to fill the pulpit and it is God's job to fill His Church." We are responsible for OBEDIENCE, but God oversees the outcome. To borrow a line from "Field of Dreams", "If you build it; they will come!" And come they did -- in droves! They came in rain, sleet, and snow and when it was all over, we had a quarter of a million souls come out and pray for America! Over ten thousand repented of sin and trusted Christ as Lord and Savior and multiplied millions were energized and encouraged to vote and be part of the process.

Before the bus rolled into Delaware; I had made so many trips there and racked up tens of thousands of miles crisscrossing the First State that it was home away from home. I have since been verbally offered a key to a city but was starting to think Delaware may follow suit and do the same. During that season I almost spent more time there than home in Maryland. The crusade team at the Billy Graham Evangelistic Association told me a few months prior, "Frank if you can help us get a thousand people on the lawn of the Dover Capitol we will be pleased." I really believe most folks fail today not because the bar is set too high, but we have repeatedly put it too low. One of my first trips to Delaware representing the Graham Team, I left at five in the morning and drove three hours to meet four pastors representing four churches in Dover. The Bible reminds in Deuteronomy, "don't despise the day of small beginnings." We had a time of prayer and one of the pastors led a brief Bible study, but it was a blessing because getting pastors to carve out time and fellowship with one another is not only a lost art but happening less and less.

It was a treat to be with that band of brothers and they not only represented different churches, but the best part was that three of them were of different denominations. The Greek word for denomination is division. Sadly, we have been so divided by the name on the church door that we have failed to mobilize and multiply on the ground floor. Two big blessings came out of that small eight o'clock in the morning meeting. First, they graciously prayed for me as I had the task to represent both God and the Graham ministry while ministering to pastors and mobilizing their church to come to a future prayer rally. Second, one of the pastors said, "You need to meet Nicole Theis." I had heard of her name before; but we never met. She is the President of the Delaware Family Policy Council, and the same pastor gave me her cell number.

Before getting out of the parking lot as I set my GPS to my next appointment with the female voice talking in my ear leading me the way I had already called Nicole on my cell and miraculously she answered on the third ring! I now had two women talking in my ear!! One from GPS and the other sent by God!!! Truth be told, Nicole is one of the most respected leaders in her state and that first conversation cemented our friendship. We eventually met and began to work closely together on a variety of projects, and I asked her and another friend, John Radell to both collaborate and be co-city captains of Franklin Graham's visit to Delaware. Both are conscientious, dedicated and well-respected leaders and together we worked unceasingly to promote the prayer rally.

I reached out to my friends, Pastor Ennio & Maribel Zaragosa. They co-pastor the wonderful Maranatha Life Changing Church, a diverse, multi-lingual church nestled just blocks from Legislative Hall at the State Capitol. With time ticking and no time to waste we invited clergy to show up for a free lunch at the other end of the state and figured if we wanted them to come to Dover, we needed to go to them first. John Radell is a strong Catholic and has strong contacts and Pastor Ennio is Spanish speaking and Nicole and I did our best networking, working the phones and knocking on scores of doors. Nicole literally sent out one mass text to her key leaders and what was just four pastors at a prayer meeting the day of our luncheon we had 107 pastors and their spouses attend our FREE vision casting. The Vice President of the Billy Graham Evangelistic Association flew up from Charlotte and after a time of prayer, praise music and enjoying a nice meal catered at an upscale hotel I had the honor to get up and share a brief message and then introduce our VP and he gave the challenge and the urgency of the hour to have "all hands-on deck" leading up to Franklin Graham's future arrival.

Excitement was in the air, but it was still an uphill battle, and I was told I may have been one of the only state coordinators tasked to lead an entire state that they did not even live in. God has constantly given me incredible role models in my life and if I have the honor to pen one more book it will probably be called, "I Had Some Help." It has been said, 'if you see a turtle on a fence post it didn't get there by accident it had some help." Frankly, I had a LOT of help and I learned from the best. My father would never tell you this but although we try to stay humble, I am proud to say my father was named the Chairman of the Inaugural Committee planning and providing protection for the first inauguration of President William Jefferson Clinton on January 20, 1993. Dad was a top cop in our nation's Capital and retired as Acting Assistant Chief of the U.S. Capitol Police in Washington, DC. At the time, it was the largest attended inaugural in history on the West Front and my great, great, great grandfather hand carried President Abraham Lincoln across the street from Ford's Theater on Good Friday, April 1865 the evening of the assassination.

One Shelton (at no mistake of his own) lost one President while on duty to God and Country and Dad did not want to be the second. He worked relentlessly for six months, seven days per week and often 16-hour days preparing for the inaugural. My Mother, Sister, Aunt Barbara and Uncle Joe and I sat in the fourth row of that capacity crowd. Barbara Streisand was a dozen rows behind us! However, it was because of Dad and his team's nonstop work ethic, and they knew about integrity, loyalty, and urgency. True leadership and ministry are often "caught" more than taught and I was blessed to glean from giants.

I recall thinking vividly if Dad could help with over a half million coming to the United States Capitol at the biggest venue for a political transfer of power than with the Lord's help and a few friends we could get a couple thousand in Dover. The Lord opened some wonderful doors, and I was so blessed to meet countless pastors as for the next few fleeting months I travelled all over Delaware to every corner of the state. If an aspiring county commissioner could go door to door to get out the vote, I needed to do it for God as well.

Yes, one will always have push back doing the Lord's will but at this juncture I will not elaborate on what went wrong but what God did to make a way. Pastors began to open their pulpits for me to preach on Sunday and then invite their congregation to the future prayer rally with Franklin Graham.

John the Baptist was the forerunner to Jesus, but I was speaking at so many venues and churches that the joke on the ground was when introducing me that people were calling me the forerunner to Franklin Graham. I will go to my grave recalling the privilege it was to represent the Billy Graham Evangelistic Association. I spoke in dozens of churches and preached weeklong revivals, spoke in schools, and even visited a radio station or two along the way. One night I was invited to speak at a Republican event promoting Franklin's visit and when getting up to address the crowd and many thought I was a younger version of his father.

I preached the Gospel at a Republican event, and I gave an invitation right then and there to repent of sin and come to faith in Christ. Nearly a dozen souls that night became born again and I shared in my remarks, "Your politics can be right and still LEFT out! It is not about being a Republican but are you redeemed by the blood of the Lamb. True peace is not in being a conservative but coming to Christ." When it was over one gentleman said, "I wasn't sure if I came to a political event or accidentally showed up to church but either way, we had revival."

Leading into the rally, I met for lunch with African American clergy who often leaned to the left politically but loved on them and encouraged them with their ministry and invited them to come. Over the years I was employed by both political parties and appointed a bi-partisan figure with the United States Senate serving all one hundred at one time and more than ever I knew God trumped politics and people need the Lord. Several of my new African American friends to their credit came and stood with us in prayer the day of the big event. The week before the rally I recall going to the lawn at the State Capitol and it was a beautiful fall day and no one else was on the grounds. It was empty and I had two friends, David Moorman, and his wife film me with the State Capitol over my shoulder.

Someone said, "If you don't see it before you see it than you will never see it." I looked towards the camera on my phone and after saying a silent prayer before filming invited them to come. God gave me the idea and I shared, "Today, I am standing on the beautiful lawn of the Dover State Capitol. As you can see it is empty but one week from today I, with the eyes of faith, believe this place will be jam packed. I am encouraging you on behalf of the Billy Graham Evangelistic Association to make plans to bring your family, friends, church members and co-workers to a time of prayer for our beloved nation."

We uploaded it to Facebook and multiplied thousands watched it, commented on, and shared it. One of the leaders with the crusade team said, "Frank that was invaluable what you did and you're thinking out of the box made a huge difference." Other state coordinators began to do similar things for their state and the night of the DECISION AMERICA rally I was still a tad nervous. I had been sharing in my message across Delaware that when Franklin rolls into town, "Don't miss the bus!" His father, Dr. Billy Graham often said in his sermons when giving an altar call, "The buses will wait" but the fact is Franklin was rolling in and out. Plus, I did not want him to hear crickets when he stood up to speak.

While starring at my ceiling trying to go to sleep early in the morning of the big day, I was reflecting on all the miles covered, churches visited, posters placed in storefronts, endless emails and personally mailing hundreds of letters to pastors reminding them of the event. I had been in politics long enough and could relate to the public servant wondering did we knock on enough doors and erect enough signs to win the election? I had done my part and now it was totally in God's Hands.

One last thing that I am proud of that the Lord told me a long time ago, "If you minister to the unknown then you will have something to say when you meet the well-known." God burned in my heart to follow up with a homeless shelter in Wilmington, Delaware and I got permission by the executive director to transport 50 of their homeless men on a free trip to attend our rally. My wife and I forked out nearly a thousand dollars of our own money, knowing we would not get reimbursed by BGEA and I don't know any other state coordinator that thought of that or did it but God gave me the assignment and we are not swimming in money, but we were obedient.

I knew most of those precious men had not caught a break in years and had little to look forward to. Under the radar, Ruth and I chartered a bus equipped with a television and they came as our invited guests to Dover the day Franklin Graham came to town. The director told me afterwards that the men not only loved the trip and prayer rally, but several made personal commitments to Christ that day on the way home! You cannot put a price tag on that.

The morning started and I prayed we had enough votes. God knows we got out the vote, so to speak, but even greater than the soul of a nation, the souls of mankind were at stake. We had heard chatter for weeks that folks were coming and not everyone that says, "yes" to your face publicly is really on board privately. Several months before in the snow I saw buses around town promoting presidential races but, on this day, we saw scores of buses around town promoting prayer. I rode that morning on a chartered bus with my parents and our bus was filled and praying silently and simultaneously that the lawn around the corner would be as well. We were invited to a private event that morning with Franklin Graham and his team before the big event later that morning. It was great getting to reunite with Will Graham IV (Billy's grandson) and reintroduced him to my parents and Nicole and a few pastors who were crucial in the success of this day.

As we re-boarded the bus for the final few miles towards the Capitol for the prayer rally in Dover, I just remember what little fear or apprehension that was there had now dissipated and I saw buses everywhere. It was packed with people and when we turned the corner the lawn was filling fast with over an hour still before the start time. This was great! God was indeed moving, and the Lord had blessed all our efforts for His glory. What a glorious day and it was so good to reunite with so many friends we had met in the last year on the ground. Pastors from multiple denominations, Christians coming up to say hello and take a picture it was incredible!

The event started precisely on time and Franklin was in good spirits. It is exhausting crisscrossing the country and one truly must be called of God to have that stamina. Rock stars and politicians have been known to be hospitalized for exhaustion and Franklin was the evangelism energizer bunny and he kept going and going! The Billy Graham Evangelistic Association is incredibly careful to give God all the credit and intentionally not exaggerate any numbers pertaining to crowds or conversions. When it was all over that day, I was told it was perhaps the biggest surprise in the East Coast on that tour. What started with four pastors just half a year before at a Bible study, but thanks to God, Nicole, John, Pastor Ennio and countless, concerned Christians and citizens we had FOUR THOUSAND that day on the lawn in Dover. The crusade team said, "Frank we will be thrilled if you get a thousand" and God can still do above and beyond all you ask or think.

We had nearly one hundred receive Christ that day as well and Heaven knows exactly what truly transpired on that tour stop! I had even made a previous chapel visit to a respected Christian school in Dover two months before and encouraged their principal to make it a field trip for the students. It is not every day that a Graham comes to town and being at the Capitol it was both historical and a time to be prayerful. They agreed and over 300 students, teachers and parents attended. To Franklin's credit when he heard that they were in attendance he took a picture with their entire school in front of his tour bus. It not only made front page news but was on the school homepage on their website for the rest of the year. We had students to senior citizens, legislators came with local pastors and fifty of Delaware's finest from the Wilmington homeless center. At the foot of the cross, the ground is level. A special shout out to the law enforcement that day that worked the event but even they would agree despite a large crowd we were a delight to work with and prayer rallies are greater than rioting, looting and violent protest any day of the week.

One of the highlights birthed out of that revival is another dozen clergy began to meet regularly for Bible study, fellowship and many friendships were forged out of that prayer rally. When we see each other as colleagues and not competition we can really cover ground quickly. As the bus pulled out of town, I had to race in two weeks, and I was co-hosting the Annapolis DECISION AMERICA rally coming to Maryland. My dear friend, Lori

Boutieller and I both shared Maryland as co-state coordinators and God used her skills in incredible ways. Where almost every other state coordinator could crash and decompress after their rally I was still racing.

We had over 4,000 crammed onto the lawn in Annapolis and then the VP of BGEA dispatched me to Richmond, Virginia. We were a tad behind heading into that rally and I worked nonstop two weeks out helping my dear friend, Tom Holland who did an exceptional job leading up to his event that he was in charge. We called, emailed, contacted several thousand churches, pastors, and Christians to attend and we trusted God to fill in the blanks. That day we saw over 8,400 attend the Virginia rally and I treated Tom to a steak dinner that day celebrating a job well done. The only thing was I had no time to spare because after throwing down the t-bone I was racing to the Richmond Airport for a flight to Charlotte to attend the final stop in Raleigh, North Carolina. When I say I almost missed the flight I sure did! For the first time in my life I was almost on two wheels rolling into the Richmond airport and since I still had to park I dropped off my car at a valet parking that I had never used on a departing flight, threw my keys to a parking attendant and told him to leave the receipt under the floor mat and had to trust God and him that "Honest Abe" my black Lincoln SUV would still be there when I returned. Yes, it was much more expensive to pay for valet but more costly to miss that flight.

Once more I was not walking, jogging but resembling O.J. running through an airport minus his infamous murder court case. Why was I running? I was not only a man on a mission with a message, but Billy Graham would agree at "urgency" both in and out of the pulpit. Talk about planes, trains, and automobiles I hit them all and we had nearly ten thousand show up the next day in Billy Graham's backyard! Yes, when I returned to Richmond the fare was higher than normal; but praise God "Abe" was still there, and you cannot put a price on souls saved.

I had the honor to attend TEN of Franklin's DECISION AMERICA rallies and helped host two of them (Dover and Annapolis) and assisted on others coast to coast from the Rose Bowl in Pasadena and Washington State to Vermont, New Hampshire, and half a dozen more on the East Coast. That prayer rally was a massive turning point in that election and over eighty two percent of Christians went out to vote and the world was shocked. Probably no one more than Hillary Clinton but once again we were just encouraging all to seek the Lord and His will be done. We prayed intentionally for the Clintons and all those in public office. I heard stories of several folks who attended one of our state prayer rallies and then felt called of God to run for office. Many won! Christians should be engaged in the public arena, and they need more of our prayers not less.

Speaking of decision, our nation and world both collectively and individually must decide where we will spend eternity. Millions make plans for a vacation during the summer, but many have not given much thought as to where their reservation will be forever in the next life. Regardless of if you believe it or not, your soul will spend somewhere, and it is either Heaven or Hell, but you cannot pick both. The beauty about the Gospel of Jesus is that He is in the soul saving business and if you have breath, you still have a chance. The Bible, says, "Choose ye this day who you will serve." Heaven is only a prayer away and Hell is too long to be wrong. The reason we relentlessly traveled the nation on this tour was not to win the presidency but encourage souls to vote Christ as their personal Savior. Thank God for grace and as for me and my house, we will serve the Lord.

THE FIRST STATE

LET'S take first things first and get back to basics. Dover, Delaware was becoming my second home in that season, and I had racked up thousands of miles making frequent trips to mobilize churches and minister to clergy privately. Most Uber drivers could not keep up with me and I was a "Road Scholar" with some street smarts, but God told me to go, and I was long gone!

The Holy Spirit had been preparing my heart for a few years before about investing in The First State. Yes, I had prayed as a child for influence in Washington, DC, and New York City along with Los Angeles and He had answered that prayer repeatedly, but He was also adding another assignment to my preaching portfolio. It is hard to explain, but to those who know the Lord and the power of the Holy Spirit, you know when God is prompting you.

Delaware was indeed "The First State" but also a small state but like Iowa it has pull politically and many controversial bills are promoted here first. It is a very blue state and other than when General George Washington sailed those icy waters across the Delaware River on Christmas Eve 1776 during the Revolutionary War the state had not had much national prominence since. During my countless trips there I quickly fell in love with the fine people of that great state and some of my best friends are from there.

During my tenure with BGEA and my own ministry, I had the honor to preach in dozens of churches, met hundreds of pastors and ministered to thousands of people along the way since being dispatched to bless their state adjacent to my home state of Maryland. Maryland was not for the Terrapins, but I had come out of my shell a long time ago and Delaware was like a walk in the park compared to traveling to Tokyo. However, it was not right around the corner because it was at least three hours every time I left my house to visit, and I did my best to meet them where they were. Plus, you do not get far being lazy, playing it safe or sitting on the couch. When God says, "Go" we must get going!

In those couple of years, I met wonderful business owners, caring educators, compassionate hospital workers, selfless public servants and loving clergy ministering to those under their care. When one pastor friend lost his wife of nearly thirty years I jumped in the car and drove the six-hour round trip commute and stood in line to pay my respects. As a minister, when others are hurting, we often do, too, and God prompted me to minister to the grieving minister.

The line was wrapped clear out of the sanctuary, down the hallway and almost out the church door and that was before the dreaded "social distancing." The line was so long that day out of respect and love for the pastor and his late wife that had it been in the current time as I write this, we all would still be waiting today! As Pastor Bill was hugging church members who were broken as well over the news of their First Lady's passing when he saw me four people next in line his reaction was worth the drive. Through his blurry vision with tear filled eyes it was almost when he saw me, he saw Dr. Billy Graham. I was on staff and serving the Grahams as the Delaware State Coordinator but there was only one Billy Graham. However, when he hugged me it was therapeutic for both of us, and that precious preacher clung to me and it was as if he did not want to let go. That brother is one of my heroes and for several years he has valiantly led that church widowed and still single. Ladies, if you love the Lord and in the market for a Godly man, I know his number and he is first class!

While leaving that day I knew God used me and Dr. Graham would have been pleased. In Bible college many daydreamed to preach to crowds, but you cannot discount the power of ministering to one, particularly when they are broken. I have always said anyone can show up in the sunshine, but they do not forget you when you show up in the storm. A step further I believe unless you can sit with someone in their valley you are unfit to stand with them in victory. True friends show up when others walk out.

While building many friendships and relations with the fine folks of Delaware it was truly a Divine Appointment. It was not long before that I only knew of one person in that state, and we just met briefly when I was appointed two decades before to work as a bi-partisan figure on the floor of the United States Senate as one of their three Doorkeepers. Senator Joe Biden (D-DE) was a powerful Member of Congress and well dressed. Fast forward he was now the Vice President of the United States of America. Since General George Washington's boat ride the Vice President had put Delaware back in the spotlight. From that humble prayer meeting with the four pastors in Dover and then connecting me to Nicole Theis and a few other key leaders we were off to the races. God used that first meeting in the First State to help catapult our efforts in expanding the Gospel.

At home in Maryland, I got the news that Vice President Biden's son, Beau had passed of cancer. He was the Attorney General and many already speculating that the sky was the limit for him politically as well with talks of him running for Governor one day. He was handsome, smart, served his country, well-spoken and sharp dresser. It seemed he had a deep desire to serve his Country and a deeper desire to his honor his father. I had never met him but admired him for that and you must tip your hat to those that want to serve.

Once again, the Lord prompted me to pay my respects and drive all the way to Dover for the viewing of the Vice President's son. For this occasion, I found myself driving all alone, but I knew like the Blues Brothers I was on a mission from God. The entire trip leaving Maryland you can guess who was once again whispering doubt in my ear? You guessed it! The lying Devil and he was relentless shouting in my head, "What are you doing? You don't have to drive three hours each way for this!" I kept moving forward and now while on the Bay Bridge heading closer towards Delaware the snake was talking more trash, "What if you get there and you are not allowed in?" Then the Devil hinted, "You may not find a place to park. It is not worth it just turn around and go back home now!"

There comes a time when you just must leave the Devil in the dust. Two hours into my drive towards Dover, the Devil was still running his mouth but mark this down when he tempts you to quit is often when you are at the door of the Promised Land. I arrived at Dover and miraculously in record time and as I got closer, I could see the Capitol around the bend. Legislative Hall is a stately brick edifice and houses both the House and Senate chambers. It does not have the columns or dome like many other state house capitols but it still impressive. The Devil is a liar because I found a place to park in almost an empty lot less than a block away. Satan scolded me a couple hours before that the line would be wrapped around the building and down two or three street blocks. It was as the morning wore on but because I drove early, I was the tenth person in line outside the door. That day I probably drove the furthest in that morning crowd but was right up front.

Satan had also been teasing me that the Vice President may not be present and why drive that far if he was not there? It is not healthy to have a conversation with the Devil because he will twist your words and God's word regardless. The moment I walked towards that temporary outdoor tent and saw the x-ray machines and the uniformed United States Secret Service officers on post, it was evident that the Vice President was inside. As I passed through both the magnetometer outside with the Secret Service outside and then again with the police indoors, the first thing, I saw to my right was the American Flag draped casket in the Senate Chamber. Standing next of the coffin on the left was the Vice President of the United States. As we inched closer to the line that stretched from the main lobby to the right and around the chamber to the coffin, I prayed silently with my eyes opened that God would use me somehow to speak life and offer comfort during their time of great grief.

Recently I drove to Delaware to pay my respects to a preacher's wife and now I am doing the same with the Vice President of the United States of America's son. I am now a person away next in line to say hello and when it was my turn, I looked Vice President Biden in the eye, shook his hand firmly and told him I was deeply sorry for his son's passing and told him we would continually be praying for he and his family. I reminded him that I used to work on the floor of the United States Senate, and he was a powerful senator, and I was a staffer, but some joked we were two of the best dressed on the Senate side. He asked what I was doing lately, and I told him I stepped out by faith from my Capitol Hill career and became a preacher and now serving as the DC, Maryland and Delaware State Coordinator for the Billy Graham Evangelistic Association.

I will never forget that he was truly broken that day but while still shaking my hand the Vice President looked me in the eye and said, "Please, please, please keep me and my family in your prayers." I vowed I would and standing next to him was Dr. Jill Biden and I had the honor to say hello to her and extend our condolences to her and Beau's wife and now widow next to her. Looking back, I believe Hunter and the whole gang was there that day, but I was impressed that despite broken the Vice President was doing his best to love on everyone as they came through the line. Earlier while standing in line they had local news reporters interviewing people and asking them different questions.

Reporters and news crews were interviewing various folks and when asked where I was from, I replied, "Maryland." They said, "You came from a good distance." I said, "Yes" and when asked was I a Republican or Democrat I remember thinking, "I am a caring American and born-again Christian." Twenty years ago, I worked on the floor of the United States Senate and part of my job was serving all 100 U.S. Senators. I spent half the day serving the Republicans and the other half serving the Democratic side of the aisle. I was not on friendship terms with Biden but had the privilege to serve him and his colleagues when I was appointed as a bi-partisan figure on the Senate floor during his time as Senator from Delaware. I didn't have the privilege to meet Beau either, but I wanted him to know that he wasn't all alone in the dark night of despair and when the bottom fell out."

Once again, what you do to one side we should be intentional to do to the other. I remember when President Ronald Reagan was shot by a would-be assassin and my Dad's friend was within feet of the 40th Commander in Chief the day. A bullet almost took the president's life, and he was rushed to the nearby George Washington University Hospital. The "Gipper" was going in and out of consciousness and was surrounded by a team of doctors and he saw a bright light. Later, he thought he was indeed dying and going to Heaven. Arguably the greatest president since Lincoln when it came to telling a joke, President Reagan then said to the doctors hovering above him, "I hope you are all Republicans!" The head cardiologist on duty who happened to be a staunch Democrat, responded with the perfect answer: "Mr. President, today we are all Republicans!" That gracious word uttered in a crucial moment helped save the day by God's grace and the skillful hands of the physicians.

That reference from Reagan way back in 1981 when I was only nine years old helped me decades later to respond to the reporter's question about my visit today in Delaware. The Vice President was now the second most powerful man in the world but in tough times the Lord can use others to be a blessing when the bottom falls out. As I drove home, the Devil was no longer laughing or taunting me because God gave the breakthrough and obedience always proceeds ministry. The Bible says, "Without faith it is impossible to please God."

The trip felt even shorter heading home and once again I found the "sweet spot" by being willing to be used as one of God's ambassadors. Looking back, if I did not drive to bless the preacher when his wife died, I may not have been ready to show up when the Vice President's son died.

The doors you open for others God may open for you. Only God could orchestrate this but shortly after that time trying to show respect and minister to the Vice President, I was asked out of the blue to begin leading a weekly Bible study to lawmakers in that same building. For almost the last four years, I have continued a weekly basis to make the six-hour round trip commute to Dover when Legislative Hall was in session to minister to the lawmakers. I was blessed to help facilitate, teach Bible and minister to some of Delaware's most powerful public servants and as I have said before, "The Church has been great ministering to the poor but failed at times to minister to the powerful."

My supervisor at the time was leading the White House Cabinet Bible study and gave us access and permission to use his teaching materials to the state senators and legislators. Sometimes God has us start from the bottom and work our way up but in Delaware the Lord had me minister with the Vice President at a funeral and then lead those under him. Once you stand toe to toe with Goliath everything else falls into place. Others may want to only show up with the heavyweights but if we neglect everyone else, we are unfit to speak life even if the opportunity presented itself. Everyone is important to God and only He could write that script.

Many know that had I not answered the call to preach I would have loved to either be a special agent or enter politics. Public service is a noble calling when done with integrity. A politician is thinking of the next election, but a statesman thinks of the next generation and more than ever we need some statesmen and stateswomen! God used those years in the halls of Congress on both sides of the aisle and Capitol at the national level to minister to those in the state and local level. Just as when Billy Graham met Babe Ruth, he was ready to converse with heads of state and my resume, service and training in the past equipped me to be a blessing now. God works all things together for our good and He does all things well in His time.

IN THE LINE OF FIRE

WHILE serving on staff with BGEA, I was still traveling more than ever before as an evangelist. The last year while I was working fulltime on Capitol Hill in 2007, I had preached 105 times in 52 weeks in 14 states while holding down a fulltime government job. Read that again. The Apostle Paul made tents by day but was preaching along the way! I was a walking billboard for Jesus in the halls of Congress but praying and preparing for my next sermon and often caught a flight on weekends to preach. A decade before, in 2006, I was preaching a weeklong revival all over Alabama at multiple churches, school assemblies and even did some radio and television messages while in town.

If memory serves me correct, I preached sixteen times in five days and while most in the state are debating and dissecting Roll Tide or War Eagle I was rolling with JESUS! I remember closing the revival at a Baptist church and was completely exhausted and the next day was on a Southwest Airlines flight from Birmingham back to Baltimore. It was the premise of my first book "Career vs. Calling?" and I was 33,000 feet in the air but never felt further away from God. I had a dilemma and was not sure if I should keep my secure, government job on Capitol Hill or step away BY FAITH to preach the Gospel. Without question, the Lord had used me in DC but the calling to preach the Gospel was burning deeper in my heart and it was obvious God was calling me out.

The next day I was back in Maryland, and I was training as a recruit officer with the United States Capitol Police, and we were on a one-year probationary period. At one time I had the "In the Line of Fire" Clint Eastwood movie poster in my college dorm room back in the day and wanted to join the U.S. Secret Service as a Special Agent but God had other plans. While training with the U.S. Capitol Police, I was injured and tore my right thigh muscle so badly that my kidneys crashed. I was running an obstacle course and was sprinting up and down a fire escape and it had rained previously but that summer morning it was already a very humid 90 degrees. The desire to enter law enforcement was fading with each passing day and although some of my heroes are in the long line of blue and our family heritage not only goes back to policing to presidents for a century and half but before that our ancestors were police in England with ties to the Queen.

My Dad never once pressured me to follow his footsteps. He encouraged me to follow the footsteps of God and be happy in whatever I chose. For months, I was wrestling with do I become the sixth generation Washington DC police officer in my family, and I had my eye on either one time perhaps being the Spokesperson for the Department (PIO) or Special Agent with the Dignitary Protection Detail. Women may like a man dressed in uniform, but a nice suit and cufflinks were more my style perhaps with my political and pastoral background. I prayed that morning that if the Lord did not want me to continue in law enforcement to shut the door. That morning while training with the USCP I was still fatigued from preaching nonstop in Alabama the day before. Burning both ends of the candle was my middle name and eventually something had to give or tear.

I just landed the night before and in my first book "Career vs Calling?" I confessed in writing because I was uncertain what to do if God wanted to go ahead and crash the plane it would be all right by me. However, I also learned that indecision is still a decision, and I was told to honor God above and my parents below.

For years, Washington DC was the murder capital of the world in the mid 1990's and my mother often prayed with tears and fear wondering if my father would make it home alive. The blessing is that although he was an official with his own unmarked car to take to and from work, he was also a visible target sitting at red lights coming home. Our culture since the fall of Adam and Eve has slowly deteriorated to a society of death. We do not respect life and know little about honoring authority. For some, shooting a cop was extra credit in their warped playbook.

By God's grace, on his shift and throughout his career he never lost a President nor died on duty but when he finally could relax Mom was encouraging me more than ever to continue the family tradition that dated over a century and half on Capitol Hill. I wondered periodically half-jokingly in my mind if she may want me to dead if she was demanding that I join the force. Without question and all joking aside, she genuinely wanted the best for me, and all her children and women think security and safety and we all knew it was a noble calling as a police officer and good pay with great benefits. Plus, having a good and clean last name did not hurt but that morning while running the obstacle course I was injured at the top of the staircase. Firemen also trained on the same steps, and it was a challenging obstacle course that had weeded many recruits out over the years.

I did not know then but know now that when your body is dehydrated your muscles are weak and easily tear. I heard a violent rip across my right thigh muscle and keep in mind at this time I was nearly 36 years old and the cut off to become a federal law enforcement officer is 37. Time was ticking and urgency seems to have followed me like a shadow since birth.

My mind was doing one thing while my body another, but my heart was screaming something else. The Bible says, "A double minded man is unstable in all his ways" and the only thing now louder than my head torn between a secular or spiritual job was the fresh tear clear across my thigh muscle. I am in the middle of a race and my right leg is literally dangling like Jell-o. With the clock ticking in the obstacle course, I now find myself with no leg to plant on top of a four-story fire staircase. It was one hundred steps and I had to run up and down four times and after completing that run full sprint only to the final stretch to pick up a 110-pound mannequin and drag it fifty yards. With the tear and excruciating pain, I was now running up and down the final two hundred steps almost completely by my two hands on the rail with one left leg as the right dangled helplessly like a spaghetti noodle in the morning sun.

The word quit was never in my vocabulary and no one had to remind me my last name.

I was not looking for favors or hand outs and now trying to hide the pain and terror in my eyes that something was seriously wrong a female Sergeant raced around the corner and screamed, "Shelton you need to run-run-run!" At that juncture, many may have quit, and it was the wise thing to do but quit did not come easy to me. With her now "cheering me on" despite not knowing the injury I hobbled to the final leg of the race. It was literally the last leg of the course, and I am also on my last leg and with each step it became painfully obvious to every else that indeed something was sincerely wrong.

With no embellishment, the only thing I can share is with next to zero gas in my tank, sweating profusely, dehydrated and half dead, I now have the task to pick up a mannequin half my weight and drag him half a football field. The key was with time ticking, I am dying but still trying to finish albeit with NO right leg. It is hard to pick up much less move when you have nothing to plant down with and too often, we do not know what we have until its gone.

At this point, I am on sheer adrenaline, and I picked up that one-hundred-and-ten-pound dummy and dragged him twenty feet and then crashed. At this juncture, I do not know who the bigger dummy was; the mannequin or me for still going! The mannequin and I are both down and now not only are the clocking ticking, but the proverbial referee was starting to count me out. I remember thinking just days before in Alabama I was preaching on ROCKY, and it is not wrong to be knocked down but dead wrong to stay down! I remember thinking, "Lord, I got to practice what I preach" and once again got up and carried that mannequin another twenty-five yards and despite mustering every ounce of strength I toppled and fell again. Strike two!

This time the mannequin fell on top of me and had pinned across my body. If we were wrestling, he would have probably had me pinned but because the Bible says to "fight the good fight" I was reminded I was a boxer down but not out! What made this fall different was that while hitting the pavement both my elbows slammed on the street and were now bleeding with the full weight of the dummy strewn across my body. Two minutes before I am participating in a track and field race with two strong legs and now in a wrestling match, I did not sign up for minus one right leg and nearly pinned. I am not sure what you are made from or what you would have done at that time, but I knew that I had to get up once more. Like a battered boxer beaten to a pulp but trying one last time to climb the ropes before getting counted out I staggered to my feet and with my right thigh on fire and all my peers watching in disbelief I hobbled backwards once again pulling this lifeless mannequin to the finish life. Looking back, I wondered did most of those watching think was I more lifeless on my feet or the dummy I was carrying but either way I was going to die trying.

After all, I had a lot to live up to and I shared in an interview one time that, "Living up to history can be heavy, but missing your Divine Destiny can be deadly." Dad was a Chief with the nationally respected police department, my Uncle Charlie was a Lieutenant and in charge of their entire K-9 division and I could not quit even though my leg gave out. This same female official that was screaming, "run-run-run" now had eyes the size of a frisbee, and she was no longer scolding me but scared for me and I saw in her face that she pushed way too hard and did not realize how injured I was. To her credit, she was the first screaming and waiving for the ambulance parked off to the side in case emergency occurs in training.

It is amazing what runs through your mind when your body is in shock, and she resembled Lawrence Taylor (#56) of the New York Giants on 'Monday Night Football' when he broke Washington Redskin's quarterback Joe Theismann's leg on national television but to his credit he was the first frantically calling for all paramedics to assist. I began to lose consciousness at that juncture and learned later that my kidneys crashed. As medics put me on a stretcher some of my fellow recruit officers and senior staff gingerly and promptly were getting ready to lift me up into the ambulance. I recall dozing in and out of consciousness and they were telling me to, "hold on" and "stay with me." Holding on was all I have ever known and the next thing I recall was finally being hoisted into the back of the ambulance. I had four technicians crammed inside the parked hospital on wheels and I was lying completely on my back and I recall begging for ice, water, or something cold to put in my mouth but they would not give me anything. It is embarrassing to write this, but I violently vomited while lying completely on my back and hit all four of them with projectile vomit. It was almost demonic out of some horror film, but those Emergency Medical Technicians are true champions.

My body was spent, kidneys collapsed, right leg thigh muscle torn from side to side, and I resembled Denzel Washington "Man on Fire." Just then someone closed the doors of the ambulance and after banging on the back door to tell the driver up front, we were clear to roll. With the sirens blaring and during the uncomfortable ride to the hospital I got the sign that the Lord answered the prayer I had prayed a few hours earlier on the way to the training facility. My prayer was, "God, if you don't want me to stay here and become a police officer, please close the door" and He did just that.

While arriving at the hospital I was hooked up to IV and had more wires in me than a 70-inch flat screen television display at Best Buy. Still no water on the horizon for this thirsty soul and maybe that is why Jesus said, "I am the Living Water." If you are in a dry, dusty desert you do not crave Coca-Cola but iced cold WATER! After a few hours, my parents made it safely from the Eastern Shore in Maryland and Mom's first words were, "Frankie, I got good news we spoke to the Captain and they will allow you after a couple months of light duty to retake the test all over again and you will be as good as new." I had already heard from the Lord and my mother was encouraging me to stay with the department.

After a couple days, one of the doctors advised my parents that I may be on dialysis the rest of my life because of the trauma done to my kidneys and we were not out of the woods yet. After six days I was sent home to spend another week in bed on my back with next to no movement and now 13 days later I was slowly moving. The bill was nearly $40,000 for the first few days in the hospital and physical therapy and several visits later but the good news is the police department paid for everything because it was an on-the-job injury.

Indeed, it was an honor to be on light duty and for the next year! I had several posts, but the two best assignments were working briefly in the Internal Affairs Office and in the Office of the Assistant Chief. The irony of ironies I was on the top floor of the United States Capitol Police Headquarters Building that my Dad had worked so hard in planning and seeing it come to fruition. I recall vividly when visiting him as a child in the much older, dilapidated brick building just a few feet from the new one. It reminded me of a "Hill Street Blues" vibe, but Dad was tasked to help with making the move into the new building.

The United States Capitol Police was formed in 1828 and Dad began reviewing blueprints so much I believe he was seeing them in his sleep. His colleagues named the new USCP Headquarters the unofficial, "Shelton Sheraton." Dad was also responsible for placing the x- ray machines in the Hart Senate Office Building in the late 1980's and early 90's. Dad even proposed that a checkpoint for security would be at least one hundred feet from outside the U.S. Capitol. Dad foresaw the problem of allowing everyone in the building first before checking and clearing them. Yes, it was called "The People's House," but you cannot trust every single person that wants to walk through your front door.

Dad testified in a hearing before the Speaker of the House Tom Foley (D-WA) that security measures should be in place outside the majestic building. The Speaker basically said, "Thanks for your input Chief but we have our way of doing things and will take it from here." Just a year or so later two of the US Capitol Police finest were gunned down and murdered INSIDE the United States Capitol in Washington, DC. The first officer was Jacob Chestnut a respected police officer who had been on the force for three decades and was less than a calendar year away from retirement. He was a beloved member of the department and African American. He was placed by an x-ray machine and tourists from around the globe would ask questions and the police are not professional tour guides but because of their love of country and respect for the building and kindness to visitors they often take on more than their job description.

The magnetometer went off, but they do all day long and as Officer Chestnut was searching for any weapon or contraband while answering a tourist's question when he was attempting to stand back up a gunman had placed a 9mm to the officer's temple and shot him execution style. As Chestnut fell to the ground in a pool of blood in those marble halls of the corridors of Congress and pinnacle of political power, the assailant made a left turn to an adjacent door. The Special Agent to the House Leader (Tom DeLay R-TX) came around the corner. Detective John Gibson had been on the Dignitary Protection Detail (DPD) for years and when he heard the first gunshot, without hesitation ran towards the blast that was not echoing and bouncing off those same walls. It was reported that his gun jammed, and he was shot multiple times in the chest.

John was a family friend and he and I had been friends for nearly ten years. In one of my early summer internships on Capitol Hill I worked for the United States Senate Postmaster and often sorted the mail for senators and staff and even on occasion personally hand delivered their checks. That was long before direct deposit and Senator Orrin Hatch's son Jess worked with me one year and he was a great, down to earth guy. Vice President Dan Quayle's son had worked in the same mailroom a couple summers before. In Washington, it seemed everyone knew someone, but Dad taught me long ago, "I may be able to help open a door, but it is up to you to be kind, work hard and move up and down the floors." It has been said, "Credentials may get you in a door, but Character will keep you there."

In the early 1990's I drove a government van and delivered some of the White House mail and often took it to the New Executive Building for screening twice weekly. One day I was summoned to the Senate Postmaster's Office, and she personally instructed me to purchase $15,000 worth of postage stamps at the Brentwood facility in downtown DC. The catch was it would be in cash stuffed in a suitcase and I was entrusted to carry the satchel with all the money! I had never held that much money at once and I was assigned with two Special Agents and one of them who drove me and accompanied me that day was John Gibson. He was a true professional, he was from Boston, and he loved his job at the Capitol.

We often saw each other in the halls and then a couple of summers later I was promoted to work as a Doorkeeper in the Senate Gallery. Daily, I would interact with lawmakers and tourists from around the world. On any given day we could meet people from homeless to Hollywood and for a "people person" it was a dream come true to work in such a distinguished place. Truthfully, I had walked those halls since a child and between my Dad staring at blueprints for both the USCP Headquarters and the Capitol Complex and all my decades working and walking in those halls very few know the layout as well as us. My mother was also on staff years before working at the United States Capitol Historical Society. At times, tour guides with the U.S. Capitol would often politely pause and let me take over when sharing facts in the building and several confessed, they did not know some of the details I was sharing.

Agent Gibson and I, while working in the Senate Gallery, often had a little competition as to who may have the best joke of the day. Sometimes I won and other times he did even though the Shelton's are known for their quick wit. I knew John was the best of the best but I had this inner thought in my heart that John may one day die in the line of fire. When the tragedy happened a couple years later, long after our jokes subsided in the Senate side of the Capitol; John was trained by the best and he became one of America's best. He ran straight towards the battle and died valiantly helping save untold lives that day. It was no joking matter and he also helped save his boss, a Member of Congress in the leadership and countless other lawmakers and tourists. A true American hero! While the world watched on CNN, Fox, NBC, ABC, CBS, or C-Span these were not just strangers but family friends. We were not only professional but personal and the police had always done right by Congress and now the Members honored these two brave souls. One black and the other white, both were courageous guardians of America. Their coffins were side by side with the ultra-rare privilege of being laid in honor in the Rotunda of the United States Capitol. With the US Capitol Police honor guard keeping watch and American flags draping the matching coffins these patriotic policemen were honored by the whole world.

When the smoke settled it was obvious that my father, Deputy Chief Franklin C.

Shelton's assessment to the Speaker of the House was correct. Had the proposed security measures been adopted and implemented, the gunman would not have been in the building before the fatal shootings. Dad, who was now retired and who was never one the kind to say, "I told you so" watched as Congress threw nearly one billion dollars towards the Capitol Visitor Center which is about a hundred feet out on the East Front Plaza. It is filled with priceless heirlooms, a gift shop, state of the art technology and a gorgeous auditorium but make no mistake its main purpose is enhanced security. My Dad's legacy is far-reaching. Whether working to enhance measures to provide an added layer of protection for visitors, Members of Congress and police officers, or planning the new multi-million-dollar police headquarters building or planning and implementing the security for the inauguration of the most powerful person on the planet. Looking back, you can see Dad's fingerprints all over the place. The beautiful thing was he did not like the spotlight nor seek it out and was hands down considered one of the most respected people in the Capitol community. Everyone from janitors to the Joint Chiefs would say, "Hi" and Dad befriended everyone from custodian to Commander-in-Chief and to everyone in between. He had met Bob Hope and Billy Graham and when tourists saw his uniform with the brass glistening on his shoulders while walking through the Capitol folks seemed to stand taller out of respect.

This was in the mid 1990's but it was now 2006 when I got insured and it was obvious God was re-positioning me. While on light duty, I was assigned to not only the top floor in the Office of the Chief suite, but I was in the same office my father was in when he was serving as Acting Assistant Chief of America's Police Department. We have over 3,200 counties in the United States and where a Sheriff has enormous power in his region and a "top cop" in the county; Dad was one of the top cops in the country. The difference was it never went to his head. I had the honor to work for my boss and longtime family friend, Deputy Chief Larry Thompson. He and Dad had the same position and Chief was a Lieutenant serving with my Dad when he was towards the top. On occasion I would drive the Assistant Chief in a Capitol Police car (both marked and unmarked) and years before I was a full-time driver to a Member of Congress, and it was an easy adjustment driving the Chief in our new police cars.

One of the officials said, "Frank, it took me over two decades to get to park near Headquarters and you are right out front." A couple of the officials would joke when they saw me on light duty behind perhaps my Dad's old desk, "Hello Chief Shelton! Good to see you!!" The fact is I could never replace Dad and even with that injury I think the Lord allowed me to be around his old stomping grounds and when it was my time to leave I did. The fact that Dad climbed so high I did not think I had any other assignment left or unfinished business left in law enforcement. As a child, when I would wear my Sunday best and occasionally accompany my Dad, I recall a few times that his colleagues would often surround me walking through the halls of Congress. As I was employed years later as an adult sometimes when tourists saw a bubble of police walking with me some inquired who was the young man in the dark navy suit, white shirt, red tie with cuff links? One Special Agent joked, "the junior senator from the northeast."

Our entire family has been providing protection to world leaders for a century and half but maybe God had another task and on occasion others may protect me? I wrote this prelude about Alabama and now will tie it all together. On that flight from Birmingham to Baltimore-Washington International (BWI) I was so torn about whether to take the government job and stay and serve the Lord in DC or step out "by faith" to preach the Gospel coast to coast and around the world? Although I would have been fine with the plane crashing and society never knowing what I was going to do with my life sometimes it is easier to die than live, but God did not call me to quit.

After much prayer and agonizing what to do, the Lord made it plain and clear that He wanted me to step out by faith and preach the Gospel. It was one of the hardest but most liberating days of my life and on July 27, 2007, after being in the line of fire, I did not get fired but resigned and officially left the department that we admired and loved so much. I had to stop by several stations on multiple floors in the human resource department and sign several documents stating I was leaving. Everyone was so nice, but several were also trying to talk me in to staying. It was tempting but I just knew I had to leave. That day I got in my car and as I headed home, I looked into the rear-view mirror and could see the United States Capitol and it will always be a special place to me.

SWEET HOME ALABAMA

ALABAMA played a role after I preached that revival in 2006 and now a decade later in 2016, I was flying into Mobile, Alabama to preach a city-wide revival. Repeatedly in my life I could see that God often brought me back to a place I had been before or had unfinished business.

Over twenty-five churches were coming together and my friend, John Bush from "Across Festivals" had a relationship with a Godly man in Florida who had access to a 2,000-seat tent. I had preached all over Alabama before and was even a call-in guest for a couple years with my friends "Wendy & Ken" who were disc jockeys on the largest Christian radio station near Tuscaloosa. Every Friday, I would call WDJC 93.7FM and do different celebrity impressions over the air LIVE and share a brief morning devotional reaching many across their great state. Those were good times and now I am invited to speak at a large, outdoor tent revival in the middle of Monroeville, Alabama. Previously I was in the air but now was back on the ground in a tent.

Much prayer and preparation had been done in advance leading up to the tent revival and members of the community even held a prayer rally and bonfire the week before, invoking God to meet with us. The key to any revival is **prayer**, **promote** the event, and **invite** folks to participate and then during the revival, **pray some more**, have **praise music honoring the Lord** and then **preach the Word**. A couple days before the big event, an eighteen-wheeler showed up and local high school athletes assisted in setting up the big tent. It was like "Ringling Bros. & Barnum Bailey" Circus coming to town and a couple of the pastors hinted, "Do we set up three hundred or four hundred chairs?" I recall thinking, "In a 2,000-seat tent?" One of them confessed, "We have never done anything like this before" and at least they were honest, but I recall thinking, "You either need to shrink that tent or grow your faith real fast." Why? Because we don't have time to play games and must trust God that souls will come and attend, they did!

That first Sunday morning, I preached three times in three different churches to not only preach the Word but promote the revival starting that night. As I preached my heart out; I would go from a joke to Jesus almost faster than a Gulfstream jet and then quietly and respectfully slip out to the awaiting car and race to the next church and repeat it two more times in less than three hours. Anyone that has seen me preach knows I usually only preach one speed – full throttle. Previously I was nonstop promoting Franklin Graham's rallies in the Northeast. Now we hoped and prayed we did all we could to encourage folks to attend the revival services. On the morning of the big tent revival, we were still swinging for the fence.

One of the most beautiful sites in our ministry was the night of the event I was driven over to the property and it was on a prime piece of real estate right on a busy road in the middle of town. Everyone, and I mean everyone, could see the massive white tent with a big blue cross in the center. It represented a Canvas Cathedral and thirty minutes before the start the place was electric! Cars were everywhere, people were coming from all over the region and church vans with different denominational names on the side were dropping their members off by the bus load. I love when churches UNITE! Kids were playing with their friends and adult couples were walking hand in hand into the tent. The praise team had an incredible ensemble of local choirs together and our worship leader, Gerald Simmons took us to the Throne of God. The music was off the charts! For a white dude that brother had some soul, and everyone loved the worship.

Over 1,800 showed up on opening night and for a town of six thousand we had almost one third of the entire community under that tent! The pastors were no longer doubting about the seating situation and fear keeps you shackled but FAITH helps us move forward. Exhausted but excited, I was now preaching my fourth full sermon in the fourth different venue of the day and God was in that place. The crowd loved it! Why with such passion? The call and time were of the essence. The Gospel is good news only if it arrives on time.

The following day was off to the races and if preaching four times was not enough on Sunday; I was now being whisked throughout the county to three public schools to do assemblies to jammed packed auditoriums. When I was on staff with my congressman that man was never lazy and if he went nonstop, I could and should as well. Adults will politely listen to you, but kids will throw tomatoes at you if you are not on their level, bring your "A" game or if they feel you are insincere. Truthfully, I need the public-school assemblies as much as students may need the message because it keeps me on my toes, and it is a win-win!

My years as serving as Student Government President in junior high at John Hanson

Middle School in Waldorf, Maryland was incredible training to respect teachers, connect with students and lead my peers. I was writing my own speeches since seventh grade and addressing nearly 1,000 students and staff by twelve years old. It was an honor to give the morning announcements to the entire student body from the principal's office daily and most pastors with a degree speak to about 250 on Sunday in their forties but I was doing it before a teenager to much larger crowds. Looking back, I gave my fifth-grade graduation address to 500 parents, peers, and principal at Malcolm Elementary. Over 1,200 to my eighth-grade graduation with parents, peers and family members packed in that gym in 1986 and for my senior year I was crowned "Prom King" and received a standing ovation with 2,000 in attendance in 1990.

Leadership had always come easy and now I am speaking to crowds of all sizes in both public and private school settings. From churches, colleges to corporate America and another previous visit I was asked to speak to the Fellowship of Christian Athletes (FCA) at the University of Alabama! One high school assembly I spoke to 3,500 students in Alabama and not everyone can be placed in the middle of a gym floor, given a microphone and hold a crowd of teenagers in the palm of their hand. It is a gift and I had been doing it for as long as I can remember and that Monday after hitting three consecutive public schools I was taken to a Christian school. It was my fourth talk of the day and I tend to talk on Character messages in the public school and can preach Christ in the private school. My friend, Ken Freeman shares something that I incorporated in some of my talks that "people make choices and choices make people." Show me your friends and I will show your future. Who you hang out with today often will dictate what happens tomorrow and you can pick your friends; but you cannot pick your consequences.

Part of my story growing up as proud product of the public schools I share, "*If you promote Character* then character will promote you!" I often tell them you do not have to buy the lie that you are a loser if you are kind, considerate or respectful. You do not have to drink, do drugs, or sleep around to be accepted. We are not called to "fit in" but STAND OUT and my testimony in school was to be kind to everyone because winners build others up; but wannabes tear down. The Christian school assembly was great and even though I was growing tired the Lord was moving in a powerful way. After a quick bite to eat on the road I was able to return briefly to the hotel. Shower and close my eyes for less than an hour power nap and then my ride would be driving me back to the tent revival that was scheduled nightly from Sunday-Thursday.

Now with four school assemblies done I was gearing up for my fifth talk in one day. If you are counting with the four speeches in four different venues the day before I was now entering my ninth message in just over a day! I recall a precious senior pastor friend in Virginia who invited me to preach at his church last year and bless his heart he was a little nervous, "Frank, I know you evangelists don't usually preach more than one or two times per day and I speak three back-to-back services on Sunday. Not sure if you can keep up!" The comical thing is most clergy could not keep up with my schedule.

Some were preparing for a slight dip in attendance on Monday night because after all it is a school and weeknight with parents working and busy schedules. However, three things really paid off. One with us being in the public schools all day we invited them to come out at night to hear as Paul Harvey would say, "The Rest of the Story." I shared before leaving the schools if you would like to hear more or learn the "secret to my success" come out tonight. The students did! Another brilliant idea was to have advertised the night before that we would have food trucks on the property and after work and school do not worry about cooking dinner but come to the tent and eat prior to the event! It worked!!

We had another 1,700 on a Monday night which is almost unheard of. My dear friends Johnny and Rosalyn Sales with a Christian pilot ministry was filming LIVE nightly and airing it on Facebook and literally thousands of people were watching online! It is hard to go to sleep after such a high and sadly I could see how Elvis and other rock stars could be tempted to take "uppers" and "downers" to go to sleep at night. Plus, sleeping in hotels may look glamorous but living out of a suitcase gets old quick. After finally getting to sleep we often had a seven in the morning departure to drive another half hour to speak at another school. No rest for the weary! Without question, the third element regarding the crowds is attributed to prayer. When God is in it that is a sacred moment in time. However, I have also learned firsthand when God is moving so is the Devil (and religious spirits).

After another two forty-minute public school assemblies on Tuesday, I was invited to appear on a radio show. We met and recorded in a car dealership, and they were broadcasting live next to new automobiles on the dealership floor. I love cars so I was right at home and my years driving the Congressman played a pivotal role. I not only drove him but watched him how he handled the press both radio and television and lately it had been me in the driver's seat although often transported on this trip in the passenger seat. I never once forgot that this is the Lord's show; and I am just a small spoke on the wheel but glad to be in His will.

That radio show went so well with folks calling in and crowding up the phone lines that they came that night under the tent in droves. One interview led to another, and I was even asked to cut lunch short and do another live interview with a country station called the "Flying Pig." You can't make this stuff up, but I was with God's anointing bringing home the bacon! Most would agree I can go from a joke to Jesus but now I was going from George Strait and Garth Brooks to God, Himself. I even quoted Garth's hit "Unanswered Prayers" and a decade before I met Garth in the U.S. Capitol. It never ceases to amaze me how God can order our steps and look back and see how God did that in the past and now make sense in the present. Plus, their listeners loved the fact that I could speak about George, Garth, and God (not to mention on staff with the Graham's). What up G? #SlapYourNeighbor

The Lord is faithful and that Tuesday we hit one more public-school assembly and although I was dead tired, something would happen en route to each school assembly. Almost supernaturally, God would give me strength the moment I was introduced. A second before I was on the ropes and Satan tempting me to "throw in the towel" but the next second the Devil was on the ropes and another victory ensured. The crowd could not notice how tired I was but the team traveling with me were floored that when I looked like I was dead and done, suddenly found a second wind the moment my speech began. That is both the anointing and power of God and His grace to continue. Despite being tired, I had fallen before carrying a one-hundred-pound mannequin with crashed kidneys and couldn't quit now. The finish line was still a way off and we had come too far to throw in the towel now.

As much as I love speaking; I enjoy connecting with the students and teachers more. We were intentional with treating everyone with respect and trying to speak life into people. We instantly connected with the jocks and star athletes but also intentional of conversing with those who were obviously shy or socially aloof. We signed a few autographs, took several "selfies," and even filmed a few testimonials from principals and teachers grateful for our presentation and then like Elvis, "left the building."

Once back in the car we had another temporary high and it is a privilege to be well spent in a noble cause and then I would slowly start to decompress again in the car. Another quick pitstop to the hotel for a shower and it was already close to the time to begin heading back to the tent for third night of the revival. For the fine pastor worried about me preaching three services in a row I was now up to my sixteenth sermon (each about 40 min) including the three radio interviews on both a country and a Christian station. The Lord was blessing in a powerful way, but I noticed and sensed the tension from the Devil in a most unique setting.

We now had seen over 150 souls repent of sin and publicly accept Christ as Lord that week of the tent revival and we were only at day three. Did you know when the U.S. Coast Guard is aware of someone stranded in the water, they do not communicate that a person is stuck but they report a SOUL is struggling at sea? It is amazing that they military has the terminology correct but many in ministry no longer focus on lost souls heading for Hell. Souls are no longer their focus and those stranded in society's sin, sick sea are not on the radar because too many got enamored with building bigger buildings at the expense of building the Kingdom. God is not coming back for big budgets or bigger buildings but souls who were lost and now redeemed by the blood of the Lamb. Just as the Coast Guard must move intentionally and swiftly to rescue the perishing, we must have that same sense of URGENCY!

As more souls had been saved out the gate and concern over whether the crowd would come made some folks thrilled and others angry! It is interesting that sometimes the ones most jealous over the years have been in leadership positions of a church, denomination, or ministry. At times, it wasn't the ACLU, or the town drunk but a pastor, Director of Missions or a Treasurer who were in a public role allegedly representing Christ and yet they would sulk, be sour and sometimes try to stop a move of God. While in Alabama, it became obvious that a couple pastors were very much against the altar call and all the great preachers will tell you that invitation is even more important than an introduction. Some of the same clergy that had little skin in the game and who did not expect God to move were now murmuring behind the scenes with what God was doing. I learned long ago that the last five letters of jealousy spell LOUSY!

Something surreal happened that night when I stood up to preach. From the pulpit, I could literally feel a demonic tension in the crowd. However, it was not everywhere just in one section of the tent. That night I preached my heart out once again and Jesus said, "If I be lifted up; I will draw all men unto Himself." Right as I lifted my hands towards Heaven and invited sinners to respond, repent, accept Christ as Lord and to come forward publicly, I could finally see in the natural what I sensed in the supernatural. The one section where the tension was extra thick was a row of about five or six local pastors. They were reformed in theology and when folks began to come forward to get saved, they stood up and walked out. While sinners were coming to get right with God, we had a few ministers who stormed out. The Bible says, "The angels rejoice over one sinner that repents." If all of Heaven throws a party each time someone is born again; and you cannot celebrate, one starts to wonder are you on the wrong team? #Hello

As an evangelist and as Christians, we are all called to be fishers of men. Sadly, some I have heard over the years and met firsthand; their least favorite card game is "Go Fish!" Church growth or evangelism is not stealing fish from another aquarium but rescuing the lost and getting them into the boat.

Part of me was shocked and ultimately sad. From my vantage point standing on the platform, not everyone could see what I saw but for those that did see, it was embarrassing. Not against God or me, but it just exposed them. Despite the few who walked out, we had another ONE HUNDRED and EIGHTEEN souls who walk up the aisle that night under the tent and get born again into the family of God. We now had seen 268 souls saved and snatched from a Devil's Hell in just three days! Let me park the car here. Sadly, last year over 9,000 churches in America did not baptize one person and to see just shy of three hundred souls graduate from Hell to Heaven in an old-fashioned tent revival proved that God was not only still moving but He was also still in the soul-saving business. The same camp that said for far too long that "revivals don't work" were the same missing in action believers who were not willing to be part of the Kingdom building process.

For several decades I not only sensed my internal clock ticking but could picture the proverbial "Days of our Lives" hourglass with the sands of time slipping rapidly through the glass. One of my dear ministry friends is Brenda Epperson-Moore who for seven seasons she played "Ashley" on the "Young & Restless." We have done several ministry events, television and radio appearances and wrote a book together. She still lives in California, but I was restless when I remembered the hourglass was both ticking and fading fast. Just as a woman knows when her biological clock is ticking towards a potential pregnancy, I could sense with great urgency that the game clock was evaporating at a rapid rate, the walls were closing sooner than ever, and the Lord could appear at any time. Some of the harshest critics are often jealous and dogs do not chase parked cars but only bark after something moving! God was certainly on the move in Alabama and more than ever so were the critics; but I am also mindful that in a canoe if two folks are in the boat it is always the one complaining most that is rowing the least. Thank God I was a rower and not a groaner nor complainer. We had a job to do, and time was of the essence.

I recall a story of a young lad who entered a summer race; and they had an obstacle course that went uphill with ropes wrapped around the thick oak trees every twenty feet. For nearly two decades when the gun went off and the kids ran, they always started out strong but eventually one by one would quit. Interesting enough, instead of pushing, pulling, and praying for the kids to succeed, some of the folks on the sidelines found it easier to criticize, complain and critique them; some even demanding that they stop. Some screamed from the sidelines, "Quit! You are going too fast!! You are making us look bad" or my personal favorite, "We used to do that!" Sadly, one by one the runners quit.

However, one year when the cowardly crowd screamed louder, this one young boy ran faster. For the first time in years this one lad finally finished what he started and completed the race. What made the difference? Unbeknownst to the campers, contestants or those criticizing in the crowd the one that WON was born deaf. In these turbulent times, more than ever we need to learn the art of turning a deaf ear to our critics!

Despite the few misguided ministers that played armchair quarterback rather than be in the game, the Lord was all over that town and tent. Men just released from prison walked the aisle to repent of sin and receive Christ as Savior. We also saw families coming together at the altar, relationships that were on the rocks were now reconciling and those addicted to drugs were being set FREE. You cannot put a price on that and as my driver quietly drove me in the dark through the maze of parked cars to our hotel it was always special being on that sacred ground.

Over the years, I have gotten sick because of being soaked to the skin from preaching under the hot lights, and I have learned that it is wise to go back to the hotel and get clean and dry. However, the intensity from Satan was not only teasing me but taunting me at an almost inhuman pace. For half that trip I was staying at a hotel and the other half I had generously been given access to a beautiful lakefront home. It was therapeutic on the water, but it gets dark at night and when the owls and other branches start snapping in the midnight hour and you are all alone your mind starts playing tricks on you. When God starts blessing you can count that the Devil will start messing!

I served on an advisory board for a large ministry in Tuscaloosa, Alabama and two of those on the board with me were both running backs for two University of Alabama National Championship football teams. I recalled stories of grown African American men built bigger than Stallone and almost as strong as Arnold tell me in confidence with trepidation that there were still pockets in the deep south that even they feared for their life. This brother from another mother was white on the outside but had some soul on the inside and I could relate to their concerns.

That night I do not think I slept at all and Satan hounded me all evening. I tossed and turned and the last time I glanced at my clock it was after four in the morning. Somehow, I finally got a few hours of sleep only to hit the ground running again to another school assembly. What was interesting was we had more and more adults who wanted to accompany us to the schools just to see how God was blessing and using me in the assemblies. No doubt part of the excitement generated was all the students and staff we met, and they shared with all their friends and parents about me being in town and the revival services being held nightly in the tent down the road.

The irony was I had a couple pastors who could not compliment me to save their life, but we were seeing lives changed everywhere we went. A reporter from a local paper out to capture what was happening in the school, interviewed a local pastor who became a good friend on that weeklong trip. He interviewed Rev. James Henry who was quoted, "I don't know anyone that has a gift like Frank Shelton to speak night after night to so many diverse people of different races and denominations and then to hold hundreds upon hundreds of students from a public school in the palm of his hand. They love his humor, celebrity impressions and powerful story of living a life of character and they love his message! Plus, many come back out at night to hear more!!"

Pastor James became a breath of fresh air and water to my thirsty soul, and it takes a big man to promote others. Some leaders run a big crowd but act small in respecting others. Now we were at day four of the county revival and near my twentieth talk and the clock indeed was ticking. The greats know what time it is and where some communicate as if they have thirty years to make a point the evangelist was usually allotted thirty minutes. However, there was always an URGENCY on the message that was often omitted accidentally, subliminally, or intentionally in many other minister's messages. My body had hit a wall and the fact is I started to grow fatigued. Who would not! Most would probably be dead or would have given up, but I knew we had to press on. I could see the finish line for this revival, but it was still far off. I have been told that every runner catches his second wind, and I am starting to wonder was that second wind elusive to me? Either way, I was praying it would kick in soon because I was running on empty.

After another radio interview and a quick bite for lunch we raced clear across town to speak at another Christian school assembly. If I were running for office, we not only intentionally touched all the bases, but we probably would have won! It was a nice school with an older gymnasium out back and the students were already filling into the assembly quickly. I met the principal and was shaking hands with some of the teachers with a few fleeting minutes prior to talk number twenty-one. The gym was a tad musty and dusty, and the bleachers were blue, but you could sense optimism in the air. One of the student government leaders was giving a few housekeeping instructions to their peers nestled on the bleachers and I saw some of them in me during my younger days. While they were addressing the students to kick off the assembly, I do not recall ever being that tired right before a talk in my life.

With my eyes open I whispered a prayer that God would show up. That He would do what only He could and fill in the holes. That I would disappear, and His presence would be so thick and almost tangible in that room. After saying, "amen" under my breath right before I would receive the microphone to speak and a polite applause from the audience; I could sense something off to the left of the room. The more I matured in the ministry the Lord was allowing me to sense things that were unseen to the eye. Dr. Johnny Hunt once chimed, "If you don't see it before you see it you will never see it." The Holy Spirit was showing me more than ever who was sincere and who was a counterfeit. Who was real and who was not and who resembled Jesus and those that resembled Judas? Not everyone in your crowd is in your corner. Read that again! #Boom

After accepting the microphone, the Lord made it crystal clear with no notice I was to preach on Hell to that Christian school. You may say, "*Frank why in the world would you preach on* Hell?" I had been around long enough to know that they are some demons that run around the Christian community including private schools. Where I was utterly exhausted minutes before the Lord was quickening me and it was as if I was no longer speaking but watching myself from a few feet away as God took over. In baseball terms, that is known as the "sweet spot" and balls tend to jump off the bat and sail over the fence with more frequency and this chapel to this Christian school was going to be no different. In fact, it was not a homerun, but Grand Slam! God had me preached with such pinpoint precision and the power of the Gospel thundered off the rafters of that aged gym and the students and staff were spellbound.

When I talked about the fumes and flames of Hell a teacher told me afterwards, "You could almost feel the fire when you spoke!" The message was hot, and my heart and eyes were filled with love and I shared again, "Hell was too long to be wrong." When I finished; we had over ONE HUNDRED students pray publicly to receive Christ as Lord. God shook the place and teachers were weeping and students crying and folks consoling each other and one official from the school came up and said with tears, "Thank you! We have prayed for years for God to touch the hardened hearts of our students. They have heard speaker after speaker preach and nothing happened; but you show up and God truly met with us today!" Truly, when we are weak God is strong! It was all the Lord and once again we were swamped with students wanting to say thank you, take pictures, sign books and despite being weary I wanted to bless them before I left.

My Spirit was strong, but my body and emotions were spent. Just as I was about to head to the car for the long trip across the county and to prepare to preach under the tent again that night to a capacity crowd, the enemy attacked. The discernment before my sermon that something was off to the left in the corner was now standing toe to toe with me. A young, novice preacher pastoring his first church down the street running less than fifty on Sunday was berating me in front of the remaining students and staff about how he thought I was wrong to preach the Gospel and mention Hell in my sermon to a Christian school. He was a Calvinist; and I am an evangelist and he stood about five foot five. He was hardly twenty-five years old, and he was not only wrong in his approach or attitude but had the audacity to give me a piece of his mind when the love of Christ was nowhere on his lips or evident in this juncture in his life.

At 6'1 and twice his age I towered over him in not only height and years but had been around the block longer than he had been alive. It was grace that I was in the fruit of the Spirit because anyone else in the flesh may have starting laying on the hands. Two wrongs do not make a right and I am a lifelong student and he had never preached to millions on television or thousands in person and I had just preached my twenty second sermon in half a week. Including the hundred new born-again converts we just witnessed with a front row seat as God had saved over three hundred souls now in three and a half days. My guess was that he probably had not led three to Christ since graduating from seminary. We just saw more saved in a service than he ministers to in two weeks! It never fails to surprise me that the person with four friends on Facebook is throwing rocks at the one running ten thousand on Sundays. Bigger is not always better but modeling Christ in and out of the pulpit is the standard and the goal.

I was extra gracious; and I was always told to debate ideas but never destroy individuals and just because he was wrong, I was looking for a way to make it right. The fact is I was voted the nicest person in my school in elementary, middle, and senior high. That may be a record to win "Friendliest" in twelve years of school. However, as the ministry expanded; I was still kind and outgoing off the platform but bold as a lion on the platform. The young man continued to lecture me how dare I give an altar call for the students to respond to Christ. He said, "How can you be sure that all those people are now going to Heaven?" I told him that the Bible says, "Whosoever calls upon the Lord shall be saved." Plus, if he preached and never INVITED them to come to faith in Christ then they most assuredly would not be ready in that moment to stand before a Holy God.

I love what one friend said years ago, "I'd rather be a used car salesman for God than a spineless preacher." When pressing for the answer he replied, "at least the car salesman will have the guts to ask for the sale before you leave the lot." That made a powerful impression on me and Billy Graham would give an invitation after every single sermon. Jesus said, "Today is the day of salvation." It was almost comical that this young preacher would make a beeline to insult a minister not only twice his age but one who was also completely exhausted after nonstop ministry in his community. Rather than thanking me, he was yelling at me, but jealousy and poor theology make the religious mad. Satan does not play fair, and the Devil was using that minister fresh out of seminary more than he realized. In that moment, he was an ambassador of Heaven resembling an agent of Hell. I learned later that he was part of the little fraternity with those clergy across town boycotting the altar call at the tent revival. Bless his heart, but he probably got orders to try to hit me to appease them. When you have a pastor attacking another pastor someone may not be saved or may perhaps be living a double life.

In leaving, I looked him in the eye and told him I would be praying that he too would know the power of preaching the Gospel and see souls saved. I was kind but when I left his mouth was wide open and his eyes popped out of his head. The conversation was over and after a few final fist bumps, high fives with students and thanking a janitor on the way out the door we were back in a three-car motorcade heading back for the Wednesday night service. The young pastor who just tried to call me outside of class was just outclassed by someone twice his age and God took him to school. I am still praying for him today and just because you preach Heaven publicly doesn't mean you have the right to live like the Devil privately.

Drained and dripping wet and now back at the lake house I had to look in the bathroom mirror to see if I had Everlast embroidered on my face because at times I did feel like I was a punching bag. The irony is some of the cheap shots were thrown by jealous and clueless clergy. Over the years, I have said more than once the reason I shop at Walmart is because I have Target on my back! Folks would always roar with laughter but only I could pen that comedic statement because I had endured it.

It has been said the only thing different from enemy and friendly fire is one is noble, but the fact is NOTHING is different. It is admirable to say you died fighting ISIS while being buried with honors at Arlington National Cemetery but when Mike from Missouri mishandled the machine gun and shot you in the back accidentally or intentionally, the death is not only senseless but seems less honorable. The Christian Army is the only battalion that tends to wound its own and more than ever I was a cheerleader not a combative, callous competitor.

The inner turmoil and stress were escalating at a level that would knock out many others in the fight. My legs were weary and my body tired; but I recalled Elton John's classic, "I'm Still Standing." I asked to intentionally be picked up a tad later than night for the drive to the tent. Partially because I needed to catch my breath, collect my bearings, and pray on my knees that God would do His thing. The attacks were greater than ever; but the blessings were as well. As we made our way into town, the traffic was packed and the tent already full. Seeing car lights and buses heading to the revival is something I will never forget.

The local police, first responders and EMTs were a big help, and they had a green room assembled for me just off the canvas cathedral. We would drive slowly under the radar and the police knew the car driving me each night and would park us around back. I love our first responders! The security would usher me into a private tent with just two adults providing hospitality and food for me to nibble alone. I love people but after pouring out into thousands day after day, a few fleeting minutes by myself helped me catch a breather and time needed to talk to God. Plus, you can say something stupid when you are that tired and running your mouth nonstop.

Personally, I do not like to eat much before preaching but could throw down a good steak afterwards. It is hard to preach on a full stomach and Pastor James Henry and Shannon Moses another pastor from the community would walk with me while the revival had already begun. We circled the exterior of the tent under cover and prayed for God to move and at the same time ask God to fill me and sustain me because I was running on empty.

Approximately another 1,800 or so were present at that Wednesday night service and most people had absolutely no clue what I was privately facing with demonic warfare and intense ridicule from a handful of pastors. It was the best of times and the worst of times like the classic book said and walking with Pastor James and Shannon was not only good for my soul but something I will cherish to my dying days. While everyone was inside worshipping it allowed me to privately walk the perimeter in prayer. A decade and half before I recall going to see Michael W. Smith in concert in Fairfax, Virginia and the music had already started for the opening act and I had to use the restroom but when I came back over 8,000 folks were in their seat. While walking back towards mine, I saw Michael himself standing there with an assistant. It was surreal but it was like he was also prayer walking, and I am no "Smitty" but now I found myself doing the same thing.

While the revival was going on and with the praise worship going up, it was my honor to go and shake hands one by one with as many officers as possible, thanking them for their presence and service. They were surprised to see me; and I was elated to have them there and Mom always told me to "dance with the one that took you to the prom." I was raised to honor those who were honorable; and the Bible reminds us to respect authority.

I was pleading with God to move in the hearts of men and to equip me with His power to speak to that crowd. Unless you have been there, most have no clue how much stress is on a person before addressing an audience and then when you are dealing with demons and spiritual warfare it is almost through the roof. Fear tormented me more than ever and the grumblings were coming from a small sect about the revival. Ninety five percent absolutely loved it and I met the "five guys" that loathed it, but the Bible says, "The fear of man brings a snare." You could almost feel the tension in the air and good verse evil was battling for the souls of men. This was STAR WARS for real on the ground and I may have been a Jedi for Jesus but my light sabre on the outside was well worn but it had been time tested and it had not lost a duel yet. The Word of God is sharper than any two-edged sword.

Just as the last praise song was finished; we had made it back to the rear of the tent. Together, the three of us said one more prayer and then I was introduced, the curtain opened, and I appeared on the platform standing behind the pulpit. One consolation was an eighty-five-year-old preacher had just testified that in his sixty years of ministry it was the greatest move of God he had ever seen! That sure blessed me, and it was like a shot of spiritual steroids in my veins. I must tip my hat to my dear friend, John Bush. He is not only a great evangelist in his own right but the consummate companion and the best counselor I have ever met. He was trained by both the Billy Graham Evangelistic Association and Luis Palau organization. We had done several events and the last two years in a row on New Year's Eve he opened the door for me to preach at a large youth event with 2,000 teenagers in Myrtle Beach, South Carolina. Well known Christian bands "For King & Country," "Big Daddy Weave," and "Hawk Nelson" led in music and Evangelist Ken Freeman and I both preached nightly and saw hundreds of souls saved.

John had trained 81 counsellors for this tent revival in Alabama and seeing his face in the crowd was comforting to this worn out but fired up Gospel preacher. Another consolation was seeing a group of the high school students we had met while crisscrossing the county and they were coming to hear more of the message of Hope not hype, and several gave their life to Christ. I could also see my "friends" who were there to both critique and boycott and I was hearing through the grapevine that they felt one of them should be preaching on the platform. The Devil is a liar! Interesting!! The same folks who had no faith before the revival wanted to be front and center and God showed up and the crowds came. That is not only hypocrisy but void of Heaven.

The Lord was lifted up again that night and dozens flooded the altar and just a few pastors left in disgust as the rest came forward to make decisions and become disciples for Christ. It was a sweet spirit in that place, and no one wanted to leave. As I exited the back of the tent every night, the awaiting car was always in place and ready to take me back. We would quickly but quietly disappear out the rear of the tent while everyone else lingered under the presence of God in that canvas tent. When the announcer said in the 1970's, "Elvis has left the building" he was in fact gone!

It was always a little rocky leaving the property; but it was nice departing "under the radar" and more than anything I just wanted the focus to be on God not man. Only the Lord could write this script because what were the odds but my boss, Franklin Graham was coming to Montgomery, Alabama in the morning for his DECISION AMERICA tour. It was about a three-hour trip the next day to attend and his big rally was on the steps of the State Capitol. One of the blessings was having absolutely no responsibility for this stop and it was nice stopping briefly by Dr. Martin Luther King, Jr's church next door while walking to the Capitol. Dr. King and Dr. E.V. Hill had their share of obstacles while heading to the "Promised Land" and I had a few obstacles myself.

Once again, I could sense a disturbance in the Force and knew Satan was close at hand and playing games. Franklin Graham did a great job preaching the Gospel like he had done across America and to his credit he gave a bold, clear, and strong invitation on the State Capitol steps for folks to come to Christ. It was nice running into a few friendly faces and team members and as we turned to walk back towards our awaiting van for the three-hour trip for the final scheduled tent service, the main organizer from the county tent revival cornered me and began to share some concerns. He was a respected minister and had been a big help and looked me in the eye and said, "Frank we have a small problem with some of the clergy and I think you know who I am talking about" I said, "Yes sir." He said, "The main concern is this revival is going very well and there is talk of it being extended." For years, I had heard of times past when God was moving so much that a revival continued and who would think this would be a bad thing? Particularly with folks in fulltime ministry but keep in mind when God is blessing, the Devil starts messing, and religious spirits get angry when the Lord is on the move.

He then said, "One or two of them are hinting, actually suggesting and almost demanding, that if the revival continues that one of them, not you, should be one of the main speakers." I remember thinking "how convenient." The same crowd that did not help much at the start was demanding to be front and center when it took off towards the end. A friend told me years ago that the same folks who did not invite you to a preseason game demand that you take them to the Super Bowl. How true!

I knew why they were mostly angry. It was due to jealousy and their theology. Calvinist do not give an altar call and the evangelist almost never fails to give one. They were upset that one of their own was not preaching and secondly were frustrated that I invited others to respond to Christ every night. The Latin phrase on protocol is spelled in four capital letters,

RSVP. It was an honor that someone took time to invite you to a party, birthday, retirement, wedding, etc. but it is customary and appropriate to reply in advance whether you are either coming or not. Two thousand years ago due to the fall of man, Almighty God sent His only Son to die in our place for our sins. By his death, burial, and resurrection we could be forgiven and made right with God. Christmas brought God to man, but Easter brought man to God.

My friend bearing the bad news said, "Frank, they are insisting if you do stay another two nights after the final night of the scheduled revival this evening, they are imploring that you DO NOT give an invitation." He then proceeded, "This is my first rodeo helping with a large, outdoor revival and just wanted you to know what I am hearing." As folks were leaving Franklin Graham's DECISION AMERICA stop in Montgomery, we were both dead in our tracks just steps from the State Capitol.

God gave me this on the fly and I said in love to my friend who at least had the guts to share what I already knew we were up against, and I pointed over my shoulder to a now empty podium as Franklin and his team had exited the platform and said, "Thank you for your update and we both just heard today from one of the world's most respected evangelists. Standing on the steps of this very state capitol, Billy Graham's son not only preached the Gospel but unapologetically gave a public invitation inviting folks to respond to Christ."

Faster than a Ferrari I shifted gears and said, "I realize today is still the final scheduled night and I came to this town as an invited guest not a celebrity. You have two options: I will preach my heart out again tonight and implore folks once again, unapologetically, to repent of sin and trust God by faith. My flight is still scheduled out of Mobile at 9AM tomorrow morning and no one will know that you all caved to allow one of these misguided ministers to preach and I will not say a word. Or you allow me to continue for the next two nights as it is extended to Saturday and ride the wave and watch the Lord draw more souls to Himself. Sir, if you think I am going to miss two more days away from my house and from my family who loves and misses me and speak for forty minutes and then at the end of my sermon assume that everyone under the sound of my voice in that tent is ready to stand before a Holy God and not give an invitation, then you have me mixed up with someone else. The Lord called me to be a minister not a motivational speaker and if I am here then the Gospel will be clear, and I will draw the net."

We headed back to the awaiting van, and he really is a great man of God. He was stuck in between two freight trains and was sincerely weighing both sides; but I also learned long ago that the fear of man brings a snare and when I am on my knees before God in private, I can stand before any man in public. To say the spiritual warfare was through the roof would be an understatement and Billy, Franklin and Will Graham came with an entourage and nine times out of ten it was just Jesus and me. The Bible says, "If God be for you than WHO can be against you?"

Three hours later we were back in town and less than two hours before the starting time of the revival. I do not even remember eating that afternoon and Jesus said, "I have food that you know not of" and over the years I found a feasting in fasting. It seems slow but becomes spiritual steroids when pressing into God. Once again, I had my friend assigned to pick me up drive me intentionally later that night and held back for what was the last scheduled night of the revival. Rumors were already hopeful that it could go another night or two. What very few knew was that it was stretching me to a place I do not recall being in ministry. Billy Graham said at times when he gave an invitation it felt like the Devil was tearing him in two.

Quite honestly, to a small extent I understood now what Jesus must have felt in the Garden of Gethsemane when He prayed that the bitter cup would be removed from Him, But He still was facing an arrest, unfair trial, and crucifixion. That night may have been the largest attended or if not, very close to the size of our opening night crowd and it was packed! The music was Heavenly and once again we slowly arrived unannounced behind the tent. After a brief wave to the couple manning the "green room" I told them about no food for me tonight but grateful it was prepared, and I was hungry for God like never before! I needed a fresh touch more than French fries! Pastor James and I, along with Pastor Shannon once again made our rounds praying over the perimeter asking and begging for the Lord to do it again! We complimented the police as we circled by and they were surprised to see me but started to realize I was sincere and the power and comfort I garnered in those last-minute prayer walks. It is hard to explain it was bittersweet and at times felt like I was being led to a coliseum with a couple lions licking their chops.

After walking about half mile around the packed parking lot it was humbling to know that with faith the size of the mustard seed the Lord can still do miraculous things. This was His show, live or die, succeed or fail, we were back behind the tent as the praise team was concluding the last song. It was said Elvis Presley in his jewel crusted jumpsuit would be known to bow his head in prayer asking the Lord for strength with thousands of awaiting fans on the other side of the curtain. He knew he needed God to help him almost minister to them. He came out after the iconic "2001" theme song and now the summer of 2016 my time was next. Lord knows, I am not Elvis but was friends with his stepbrother and have met a few friends over the years that either sang with him or protected him while in his inner circle.

At this juncture resembling Dr. Graham and a play from Elvis playbook we asked God once more to do what only He could do, and this was His show and Christ alone the Star. The music was over, and the kind introduction came, and the crowd was too gracious, and I find myself behind the pulpit once more before a packed house in Alabama and getting ready to preach for my twenty fourth time in just five days. After opening in prayer, we came out blazing and the Lord rocked the House. It was an on-time Word and God shook the place and once again dozens of souls responded and forsook sin and came to faith in Christ. It comes with a price but never gets old!

The last few nights with the eighty-one trained counselors on hand they were often in the adjacent tent another forty minutes to an hour with the brand new born again converts. My awaiting car was running, and my temporary driver was just off the right side of the stage, and I am the consummate people person but despite the lack of sleep, weary schedule, soaking wet clothes and warfare that tangible the rear curtain was opened and once again we swiftly disappeared into the night getting a jump on all the cars crammed on both sides of the highway and wrapped clearly around the canvas cathedral. We never failed to wave to the police who were gracious to wave as we pulled out on the highway to live another day.

God was moving and all glory to His Name and after getting another hot shower it was pushing ten thirty in the evening. After half dead on the couch wearing sweatpants and a t-shirt, I propped my feet on the coffee table and was thrilled to hear of all those who just trusted Christ as their Lord and Savior. We rejoiced together with all God was doing but John Bush was one of the true friends I could bounce things off and many people would love to have a platform, but they are not prepared to pay the price in any profession. I was notified about eleven that evening that indeed the revival had been extended and the community was asking me to continue to preach. On one hand my initial reaction was "Praise the Lord" but the other was it may get rough the next forty-eight hours.

The next morning was Friday and other than one more radio interview we had no more school assemblies. I had now done over twenty-five full messages and was feeling more like a muffler with each passing hour. Why? Because I was "exhausted!" No, I am not blowing smoke either and preaching to the masses was not a "pipe dream" for me but I had come too far to quit. No matter what city I go into there is always at least one suggesting or thinking all of us in ministry are in it for the money. I find that interesting because when a professional sports player signs a multi-million-dollar contract I do not once recall a broadcaster on ESPN share that he or she is "in it for the money."

God is indeed faithful, but I had preached in some towns where I almost had to borrow money to leave, and the joke was where was the "love" in the love offering? Lately, preaching abroad and at home the stress that comes with a growing ministry and accusations and temptations not counting the cheap shots from clueless clowns in the crowd, one should almost be entitled to hazardous pay. I had flown into cities and countries on my own dime with no compensation while there and with no guarantee to make it home alive or in one piece. It is a privilege to serve the Lord, but it does come with a price.

We had a nice brunch that Friday morning with some of the team and the word on the street was buzzing around town about the newly announced extended revival. You know it is a genuine move of God when no one is praising the singer or speaker but the Savior alone. Because my trip was longer than I signed up for I had to go to Walmart for some extra items and I met this older woman running the register and regardless, if at barber shops, in the halls of high schools, city hall, nail salon, local restaurants or this scenario at the cash register at Walmart, this sweet lady brings up the revival. She said to me, "Have you heard about the revival in town?" At first trying to figure out if she is joking and she was happy as a clam and I said, "Yes I have." She says, "That is the talk around town and the people are loving it!"

She then smiled and said, "I am hearing great reports about it and considering going myself." I looked at her and said, "That is fantastic! Maybe I should attend one night too." She then says, "I hear it just got extended tonight and tomorrow." I replied, "Super!" She then said, "Honey, you need to go tonight too because the Lord is there and the reports, I am hearing is it is awesome!" With a smile and my dimples coming out of retirement, I said, "I just may show up tonight too!" After grabbing my purchased items in a bag, I thanked her and wished her a good day but left smiling because it was God's Show and for His glory alone.

That afternoon was my first day without nonstop meetings, school assemblies or racing rapidly through the county. Some folks do not like to work but I do not see anywhere in the Bible where God blesses being lazy. If the early bird gets the worm, then maybe God honors hard work while we "wait on Him." We were now in extra innings revival speaking and I had heard about all the crusades and tent meetings that were prolonged in years past and all that praying paid off because we were now seeing it firsthand in our ministry. The good news it is real but the truth is one is stretched beyond your comfort zone but that is not a bad thing but often a God thing.

That Friday night was electric, and the weekend added additional attendance and momentum. Folks had travelled from out of the county earlier in the week but now reports of them coming hours away and across state lines. I was told years before, "If it is ALIVE, it is worth the drive" and travel they did! Thousands more were reached online and what was amazing that after five nights of revival some were still coming for the first time. The expectations get higher with each passing night and prayer helps take some of the pressure away. Billy Graham said, "If you don't take all the credit you don't have to take all the criticism." More than ever, we were trying to be empty of self and be full of His Gospel and kindness.

As the Friday service kicked off, once again the strain and stress were almost suffocating. Ninety five percent of the folks were elated that we were continuing but the Devil was using a few of the clergy to cause havoc. It is interesting to me that those who promote Heaven can act like Hell at times and truth be told, we can all drop the ball and get misdirected. I was not only preaching grace but still had to give it, but it does take being intentional to be Christ like because as the crowds get bigger, the stage wider and the lights brighter there is not much room or margin for error.

Once again, we did our customary prayer walk around the tent while everyone else was inside and the blessing was as I looked out towards the highway car lights were as far as the eye could see and almost every one of them were being directed to park. For several nights, buses were set up because the main lots were full, and cars were being parked a mile away at local school and church parking lots.

Fear had overwhelmed me the last couple nights and I had not had a full night of sleep since being back in town. The Bible reminds us to put on the full armor of God and you cannot go to war without your equipment and the Devil loves to blind side you with or without the helmet. My head had been rattled too many times to count and I did not know if I had PTSD, ESP or both but God was allowing me to pick up things in the supernatural. It is at times a blessing and curse, but it is also a protective measure to see who is legit and who is not. Even Jesus had His haters, and some folks are not only downright mean but dangerous.

For five nights in a row when I came out on stage to my right would be my main contact and driver. It seems as if almost everyone packs heat down south, and the police had done an exceptional job with their presence to provide security. I was told specifically that night to just get in the car immediately after the invitation and do not stick around to shake hands or work the crowd. Keep in mind being around Capitol Hill all my life and friends with musical artists "working the crowd" to them and me was like air to my lungs. I believe ministry is more off a platform than on it and to start eliminating that was not only a learning curve but something I did not like. A true Shepherd walks slowly among the crowd and more than ever I am instructed to be both a minister and magician and know the art and act of "disappearing."

As the crowds get bigger it is tempting to get a bigger ego, but I gave up on that long ago because with a bigger head becomes a bigger bullseye for others to aim. I heard a preacher tell me a few years before even boasting, "We can strut like a peacock and be arrogant at times" and I remember thinking where was that in the Bible or Fruit of the Spirit? Unfortunately, he is in prison today and a mentor shared with me two things long ago, "never put someone on a pedestal because they can fall off" and we are all capable of being a step away from stupid. I never forgot that 'step away from stupid" because I love alliteration and probably snore in my sleep stringing like sounding sentences together, but it is true.

Ministry like any other vocation can be like golf. Once you hit a good shot if you are not careful and focused you can hit the next two shots in the woods, and I am not talking "Tiger." But even Tiger Woods could relate but God loves Tiger and comeback performances. Even Christ came back from death, and you cannot keep a good man down. We prayed just behind the curtain, and I came out with just my Bible, and I had met Garth Brooks at the U.S. Capitol a few years before but took my wife to also see George Strait in concert at Cowboys Stadium in Texas. I was impressed that he came out just wearing a denim shirt, Wrangler jeans, boots and a nice hat and his guitar that produced fifty number one hits. "Pure Country" is one of my favorite movies and sometimes the fame, lights and smoke machines can get you sidetracked and in a bad place. Strait came out with his guitar, and it was just God, me and my battered Bible that had been halfway around the world.

It is amazing what goes through one's head and just as I was getting to the podium, Satan was whispering that this is where you will get shot tonight. Not in Afghanistan but "Sweet Home Alabama." Do not get me wrong, I adore that state and their football is tops, sweet tea incredible, BBQ among the best and the fine people who reside there second to none and some of my best friends live there but lately it had been wild to say the least and enemy fire and friendly fire is no different.

When I opened my Bible and scanned the crowd the first thing, I noticed was that the man who had been positioned night after night was missing in action. I looked and a man who had never been there before is now standing with a vest and knew in my Spirit that he was packing extra heat and higher up the food chain in law enforcement but then my mind was playing tricks and Satan taunting me in overdrive, "Was there a threat and no one told me to scare me?" Elvis had received multiple death threats in Vegas and the FBI encouraged him to cancel a couple shows and he had some of his own bodyguards sitting behind him in plain clothes as part of the orchestra." In the middle of a show, a guy in the balcony screamed, "Elvis!" and his team already on high alert saw Elvis pivot in his white jumpsuit and turned to his side because as a black belt in karate he knew how to become a smaller target and even "The Big E" thought this is where it may end on stage.

After an awkward pause the man finished, "Can you play Hound Dog." They said with laughs backstage that Elvis obliged and played it like he never sang it before." I am no Elvis but that night we were "taking care of business." The second group I saw was my "friendly clergy" in the non-cheering section and I often pray for them hoping they are serving the Lord today. Sadly, those who cause problems along the way usually fizzle or fall later down the road.

The Bible reminds us, "Perfect peace whose mind is stayed on thee" and at this juncture it is all I can do to concentrate on Christ, my text for the sermon and preach to those in the crowd and not dwell on a few. The Lord has given me a great gift with humor and celebrity impressions to break the ice but on this night, it was no jokes and all JESUS. I remember gazing to the back left of the tent under the lights and saw the sweet lady that ran the register at Walmart who had asked me if I were coming to the revival and her eyes were bigger than the offering buckets when she realized I was the guest preacher. We had a good laugh and ministry is not about me being seen but the Gospel proclaimed.

About two minutes into my message the fear was replaced by faith and Holy confidence. Arrogance and confidence have a small line between them, and one can easily step out of bounds. Arrogance is depending on self, but confidence is depending on God and more than ever I was leaning into the Lord. God was in that tent and the place was packed and folks were enjoying every word. I heard that the news had sent one of their helicopters clear from the next big city and was filming LIVE aerial views while hovering over the tent and grounds while I preached. That night at eleven o'clock that small town made big news while I preached the Good News. At this point, I want to thank every single pastor, deacon, church leader, caring Christian and concerned citizen and even the gentleman that graciously donated his farmland rent free for a move of God. Folks had prayed for years for this week, and some wondered if it would ever happen, but the Lord is never in a hurry but always on time.

I preached on the Cross and Jesus said, "If I be lifted up, I will draw all men unto Me." We lifted Christ higher than ever and one thing good about persecution is it makes you simplify your message and just as George Strait stuck to basics with his guitar, I was coming straight with the Gospel out of my time tested and battered Bible. The same one Dr. E.V. Hill signed in California was with me in Alabama. Over the years, I had folks try to steal that Bible including a pastor. Another woman in North Carolina after the sermon told me, "God told her that I was supposed to give her my Bible." I believe in being generous and at times to a fault, but the Lord did not tell me to and that Book is filled with blood, sweat and tears.

I am nobody but sometimes I wondered if folks thought it would be in the Smithsonian or Museum of the Bible because it was so well read and worn. God knows I am far from perfect but was doing my best to seek the Lord.

The power is in the Gospel not me; but God honors His Word. That night like a boxer not wasting his punches, no clichés or cool quotes, just straight Scripture and Jesus. That night God gave me great liberty preaching and uncanny confidence when extending the altar call that night. Praise God despite the private Hell we had another sixty-five walked the sawdust aisle turning their back on sin and the Devil and now citizens heading to Heaven and born again into the family of God.

When it was over, I noticed my one-man security guy and I have never been one to run away from anything but even Jesus had to slip away at times and now my mind is playing tricks on me as I follow him out the tent and now jump in an awaiting SUV with a man I never met. Plus, I am in a totally different vehicle and was privately hoping we are on the same team.

It had been the same driver and car for five nights but now without warning, I was assigned to another vehicle and I know this brother is packing heat. Even the president usually meets his special agents at least once before while in the line of fire and I am being whisked away by an unknown person and hoping we are going back to a safe place. That evening a few friends eventually came up to my room to check in, share the praise reports of all the life change and some on one hand knew how taxing the entire tent revival had been on me. We had a core team pray for me around the globe and it meant more to me that Webster's Dictionary could define. I had poured myself out ministering to their hometown and they were grateful and now pouring into this minister.

As the Gospel was moving greatly, the nightmares were increasing rapidly, and my parents were not only watching from afar online but even contemplated flying in to be part of this great move of God. They were also concerned because they could hear from my voice the stress that comes from being out front for God. I did not pick the ministry, but the ministry picked me, and I could relate to Dr. Graham at times when I felt like Satan was tearing me apart piece by piece. After tossing and turning that night in Alabama and sleep escaped me completely; I was ready for the final night of the revival. It was now Saturday morning and that evening I would have preached (counting radio and school assemblies both public and private) TWENTY-SEVEN times. If you see my preacher friend from Virginia wondering if I can handle three morning sermons on a Sunday, tell him he is a tad rattled but will be simply fine.

God was truly blessing, and the night before came with a great cost to me emotionally, but the Kingdom of Heaven expanded with the six dozen souls now registered in the Lamb's Book of Life. They made the right call by extending the revival and allowing me to preach and give the invitation. Indeed, God can use anyone, but He often uses a man and sometimes when you have ten speakers it is usually eight or nine too many. Plus, folks get familiar with the voice that God is using and if the crowds keep coming that could also be a sign the Lord has His hand on that man and mission.

I was weary from the week but not weary because of the work. Serving God and being spent in His service is a noble effort but I would be lying to you if I were not longing for home. Ruth has called me her library book joking she loans me to the world knowing I am coming back but days, weeks, and months away from home make one's heart homesick. I often temporarily kissed my family "goodbye" so sinners could say HELLO and one day welcome home to Heaven for eternity. I left my family that the Family of God could grow. Someone asked Billy Graham how many people he had saved. His answer is the same is mine, "None." He added, "I do the preaching and Jesus does the saving." It is our job to sow the seed but God's job to save the soul.

The last night resembled once again the county fair with folks laughing, playing, and having fun. Folks who think Christianity is boring do not know Christ and the tent could be seen half a mile away from the road and the only difference between Ringling Brothers and Barnum Bailey Circus was our tent had a big blue cross lit up at night for all to see but hands down the revival was the biggest show in town. My familiar car and driver picked me up the last night and I was happy to see him and live another day to thank him for his friendship and help all week. Many folks saw me, but it was the scores of clergy and others who made it possible. The Bible says, "Many who are first will be last and many last will be first." Today, I am not only trying to finish strong but love on everyone along the way. Even those critics that can be cruel and rather than giving them a piece of my mind I am praying to give them more of His heart. Two wrongs do not make a right but two, three lefts can make a right and at this juncture with a right turn we are back in our private spot conveniently located behind the tent.

I stood a tad longer in the green room that night and thanked the hospitality team for all their help that week. Part of me elected to stay back in the private reserved hospitality tent because they voluntarily agreed to serve me all week. They made me feel most comfortable and they did but I needed more of God above than any man below and that is why I walked in prayer night after night. We took a few pictures and shared hugs and I recall grabbing a bottled water and granola bar and we went walking one last time praying around the tent for God to do His thing. After a few handshakes and fist bumps with the county's finest and parking lot attendants who selflessly served behind the scenes so God and I could be on the scene I found myself once more behind the canvas flap leading me into the massive tent.

Just prior to entering I was told once again to come off the platform and head straight to the car. Without telling those around me I was not going to race to an awaiting car but intentionally come off the platform and love on the people regardless of the cost. I was preaching faith, I have a radio and television show about faith, I wrote books about faith and have experienced saving faith through God's grace, but Satan was having a field day with me on fear. Perhaps you can relate?

Sylvester Stallone was in a movie called "Lock Up" and he was a prisoner who was arrested for a small offense and serving time when the warden harassed him unceasingly and tempted to trip him up to make him serve more on his sentence. The warden's ego was bigger than the prisoner's infraction, and he was taken in the middle of the night from a low-grade prison to maximum security and made his life a living Hell. On paper it was called a "routine transfer", but it was really because a man's pride outgrew his profession. Sometimes we can become worse than the people under our care or supervision.

When the warden and his guards had threatened to rape the love of his life and told them they were en route to carry out their evil plot, he planned the escape to rescue her. When he was set up from the inside, he was accused of what the warden wanted and that was to add more time behind bars. When Stallone finally could have run free, he said a line that resonates with me today and the last night of the revival in Alabama. He looked the warden square in the eyes and said with his trademark bass voice coming out of his slightly deformed lips caused by a doctor at birth said, "*I am not going to spend the rest of my life running from you!*"

That moment when his running stopped, he found fear flew out the window and faith won the day! Plus, the warden was now incarcerated for his unethical behavior on the job and the prisoner went free. Sometimes you must face your fears head on and forgive those who will never say, "I'm Sorry." Over the years, I have found that more than not that those accusing others leave enough rope to hang themselves. Billy Graham was asked how he responded to his critics and the world's most respected reverend said, "I out loved them and out lived them!" Wow!! That will preach!!!

The time was now and for the last time I came in stage left and entered that canvas cathedral and the lights were bright, the music was out of sight, and we were at sermon twenty-eight on the very last night. A couple chapters before I was quoting James Taylor's classic, "In My Mind I'm Going to Carolina" but on this night I am in Alabama already daydreaming at night about Maryland. If I can quote the old rock and roll lyric, "Honey, I'm coming home!" God gave me great grace and freedom that night and even opened with an oldie but goody joke from the past and the crowd roared with laughter. When they laughed I did too, and I knew we were going to be alright.

Another forty souls walked the aisle on the last night for salvation and hundreds more came forward for the final altar call making various decisions. Some decided to recommit their commitment to Christ with greater focus and intensity. Addicts were getting clean, families restored, friends making amends and others weeping on their knees that God would use them like He did me that week in Alabama. It was no longer Roll Tide but Roll Jesus and no one was thinking War Eagle, but Satan is a liar, and we have an all-out attack against the Devil. For too long, we are fighting the wrong battles, placing too much premium stock on temporal things and must return to what matters most: **Loving God, loving others** and **rescuing lost souls**. If we stay focused on those three things, we are less likely to do stupid stuff. In some of our largest denominations today and mark this down -- When the baptisms and soul winning are down, lawsuits go up. We begin to fight within then we cannot be soldiers against the enemy; and we are fighting the wrong camp.

My driver and car that I started with was back on post but to his surprise I came off the platform with boldness and freedom. Opposed to leaving backwards I walked forward. President Lincoln said, "I walk slowly, but I never walk backwards." One of my favorite Bible verses is etched in marble in Washington, DC at the national law enforcement memorial with all the heroic guardians who died in the line of duty. It is from the Old Testament and says, "The righteous are as BOLD as a lion but the wicked flee when no man pursueth." Guilt flees but grace runs into harm's way and when religion and sin left the Lord's people walk right in. Van Halen sings a rock classic, "When Love Walks In."

While the revival was going on and the praise worship going up, the little security bubble that I had tried to catch up with me but honestly, I knew I did not need them because if God be for you WHO can be against you? I think I shook every single hand that night, took countless pictures, signed a dozen Bibles and despite dripping with sweat, I like to think I had the aroma of Christ smelling like Heaven. Someone said to me a statement that made a profound impact on me, "You are not much of a Shepherd if you cannot smell sheep on your clothes." Folks came to me crying thanking me for the breakthrough in their lives that week and it is humbling to hear the affirmation, but I had to keep reminding them and myself that it was the Lord's doing. It was His Son that came, died, and rose again and I am just a messenger delivering His mail.

My back was on fire but no longer from the proverbial bullseye that I knew all too well but the sleepless nights and grueling week schedule of preaching Heaven while going through a bit of Hell on Earth. Sometimes being out front comes with a price. Moses in the Bible was growing weary and when his hands were upright, he and his companions were winning but when they were lowered by fatigue and loss they began to lose. Forever, I will be indebted to all those who lifted my hands that week and it has been said all is well that ends well. The next morning after one last sleepless night in a hotel I knew I would be flying back to Maryland and despite the ups and downs, the Lord forever touched that town. Even devoid of sleep, I still look back and can say "Sweet Home Alabama."

The plan initially was for me to be assigned to another couple and they would drive me the long two- and half-hour trek to the airport for my early departure but I do not demand much and try not to be a prima donna on the road, but it was the one time I insisted that my dear friend, John Bush drive me. He had worked as hard as anyone in that "Fire in the Field" and he is a general in God's Army but my mother taught me "to dance with the one you went with." This may surprise you but in middle and high school I saw folks dance with everyone except for the one they walked in the door with.

Plus, John was the rare one with which I could let my guard down, decompress and like George shoot it "Straight" without fear of judgement or attack because John was in the battle with me. During that drive to the airport John ministered to me, a minister who was content but completely depleted and I forever will be grateful to him. I recall hearing a story a decade before that I have closed with on rare occasion when preaching to pastors or a room full of leaders and it applies here.

The modern-day story was of a man who was successful personally but struggling personally. He was in a different hotel almost every week and one night after a light night at work he came to his hotel only to find his rented room phone with a red glowing informing him he had a voice message. He pressed the button only to hear his wife emphatically say, "When you get back home the two kids, and I are gone. The marriage is over, and we are done!" The man's world took a tailspin and one minute where things were great and then the bottom fell out.

His now deceased grandmother's counsel echoed in his ears alone in a hotel in the middle of nowhere in the midnight hour. She said from years before when he was just a boy, "Honey, if you ever get in trouble read the Bible or call a preacher." He had been in enough hotels in his career on the road to know both a Gideon's Bible and Yellow Pages were in almost every room in America. He frantically picked up the Holy Bible and began to read but because he did not know the author personally it was hard to comprehend the meaning. Thoughts of suicide danced in his head, and it is now just after one in the morning. With one last effort, he picked up the Yellow Pages and skimmed for C section and found churches locally listed. Not sure what church or denomination to call and with Satan taunting him that you will wake someone up and why bother just go ahead and throw in the towel here alone on the road in a hotel room.

He called and fortunately a pastor answered the phone from a dead sleep. The man on the road was speaking so fast that the clergy while clearing the cobwebs out of his mind was kindly asking the man to slow down. The man's personal plane was coming in hot, and the train was coming off track. The pastor of a country church said to the man talking a hundred miles a second, "Sir what hotel are you at?" The man told him, and God alerted the minister that time was of the essence and like the title of the book it would be safe to say it was "URGENT." The pastor got dressed, found his shoes, and grabbed his keys and was out the door to try to help one more soul.

The man from out of town was in the lobby and it just past two in the morning and even the person usually manning the front desk was nowhere to be found. After a handshake, the two sat down in the cheap couch in a mid-level hotel and once again the man was off to the races pouring out his heart. The pastor tapped him on the knee interrupting him midsentence and said, "Sir I am honored to pray for you, but I have something for you. In my hand are two complimentary tickets to see the visiting circus and I have been told the world's greatest clown is with them and this guy has a gift that folks come far and wide to see him do his thing." The clergy continued saying, "I have two free tickets that I am giving you and tomorrow when the sun comes up invite a friend and this guy has been known to help folks forget all their problems."

With tears now streaming down the out of towner's face, the pastor confused and only trying to help said, "Did I say something wrong?" With tears cascading like Niagara Falls the man said, "Preacher, when I called you over an hour ago, I told you I am in a different city and hotel almost weekly." The minister with his eyes wide open and speechless left room for the out, of town stranger to finish saying, "Sir, I am that clown that folk come from miles around to help forget their problems."

The clown without the makeup dropped his head as tears danced off the cold floor of a motel early in the morning and that preacher's heart stopped momentarily. The moral of the story is who do we go to as leaders, executives, coaches, elected officials, artists, pro sports star and yes, ministers when the bottom of our barrel is dry? Robin Williams, the world-famous comedian shortly before my preaching in Alabama took his own life and was quoted as saying, "I had a gift to make millions laugh but couldn't make myself smile." Robin was the best and had a net worth upwards $100 Million but felt bankrupt in the midnight hour. I pray to God someone tried to point him to Jesus.

By God's grace, my parents' unceasing prayers, well wishes of friends sprinkled across America and in a few pockets around the world, I knew I was never alone, and I constantly went to Jesus for my strength and support. However, I could relate to the clown and I was now heading home leaving the tent behind fortunately to a wife and family still in love and waiting for me. God has been too good. John Bush is a cherished and treasured friend and one I trust whole heartedly. We have served side by side and been in foxholes together in the heat of battle and I knew it was extra work for John, but I needed him to carry me to the airport.

After a hug and closing prayer, he dropped me off at Mobile's small little airport and I love big crowds and large stadiums but find the smaller airports refreshing. Bigger is not better but smaller is better and flying home was even greater. As I boarded the Southwest flight and picked a chair because like life you can pick your friends and your own seat when flying on this airline. I sat down, buckled my seat belt, and finally breathed a sigh of relief. It was now exactly one week on the ground in Alabama because I flew in Saturday afternoon the week prior only to hit the ground running and preach four times in four venues the next day kicking off the revival. Approximately from what we knew for certain that FOUR HUNDRED and FIVE souls repented of sin and trusted Christ by faith as their Lord and Savior in a town of about six thousand. On any given night nearly a third of the town was under the tent and as the plane raced down the runway leaving Alabama heading back towards the city of my birth; I just now processed what God was doing.

At the beginning of this chapter, I shared that a decade before I was content if the Lord wanted to kill me on the flight from Birmingham back towards the DC region the city of my birth. However, despite the pain, getting injured at work with the United States Capitol Police, kidneys crashed while recovering in the hospital only to hear God say "step out" I would have missed not only the last ten years of this life God has blessed me with but even more important, multiplied thousands of souls that have now found freedom in Christ and on their way to Heaven. Sometimes when it looks like it is all over is when God steps in and says, "I am just warming up!" Praise the Lord!

SUNSHINE STATE

River Church – Tampa, FL

THE day before leaving Alabama I was contacted by the producers of Christian Television Network in Clearwater, Florida. They are one of the largest Christian television networks in the world and reached out inquiring if I could come back and be a guest on their network and share for a full hour what God had been doing with the ministry. It is always an honor to sit on their Oprah-like couch and share with a large audience about the goodness of God.

I shared previously that when God starts **blessing** it never fails that the Devil starts **messing** with you but more than ever, we do not stop **CONFESSING** how good the Lord is! You can set a timer to this, and it has become a welcomed reminder in my own life that when I am being harassed in one area, the Lord would send a helper for me to go to the next level. If getting the run around by someone in Little League I would get a call from one who plays in the Major Leagues! Literally!! One day, I had a youth pastor try to undermine me and within the hour I get a shout out from Billy Graham's grandson sending affirmation and appreciation out of the blue! My friend, Dr. Junior Hill said, "Little thinkers make big stinkers" and he was correct, and it still holds true now.

I had gotten pressure from just a few ministers *locally* in Alabama and yet during that same week got invited to come on national television in Florida and preach about Jesus globally. Sometimes you must be rejected at home before God can use you abroad. That will preach! Plus, when you have ministered in London and Los Angeles sometimes those in La Plata can get overwhelmed, intimidated, or jealous. Jesus said, "*A prophet is with honor everywhere but His hometown.*" Some lose sleep hoping to catch you in a scandal opposed to being preoccupied in Jesus' sandals! #WalkThisWay

The key is to stay humble and keep honoring Christ and happiness is moving forward while honoring Him. God always has the last laugh, last word and last move and He always settles the score and makes the crooked straight. Keep in mind that resistance is what helps an airplane lift off the runway. Lately, I had enough push back, but you cannot keep God's man down and praise the Lord after only one day back at home I was on another flight back to the Sunshine State.

After a week of next to no sleep on the road and completely exhausted after speaking nearly thirty times in six days I was able to throw my clothes in the laundry, kiss my wife, hug the little one and sleep a solitarily night in my own bed in Maryland only to be touching down in Tampa. Satan was teasing me and even imploring me to stay home but if you keep your eyes open and heart clean you can see the tactics of the enemy. The Devil tried to side-line me multiple times before and just because you are down does not mean you are out. Most recently, Satan tried to discourage me when my SUV died before going to the Billy Graham School of Evangelism a couple years before. Where most would have quit, we not only progressed but got promoted with a job. Go God!

I had been on their television network before and their founder, Bob D'Andrea is a legend in Christian circles and has become a dear friend. The Lord has used him and his team at their station to reach multiplied millions daily with the Gospel. After landing alone in Florida, I rented a small rental car and once again flying "Solo" like Han from STAR WARS but where he was still trying to determine if "The Force" was real I knew that Faith in God certainly is and all powerful. Despite being weary from the week of nonstop ministry and travel I had a sweet peace that only comes from being in that "sweet spot" with the Lord.

It was one of the absolute rare times that I was already dressed in my suit on the flight departing Washington. Typically, I like to travel casual and then shower and get dressed in the hotel before speaking at an appearance but once again time was of the essence and urgency was the clarion call of the hour. No time to waste and the clock was ticking. Racing in my rental in the warm weather wearing French cuffs and cufflinks is not the ideal attire when near the beach but the television taping was in less than an hour and I had a thirty-five-mile drive! With God in my heart and GPS directing me I pulled into the parking lot and for a guy that was on fumes physically and financially I had a pep to my step. I walked into the reception area of the studio and after signing in was intentional about greeting all those in the area from receptionist to janitor. Everyone is important and just because we are preaching the Gospel on television does not mean we can arrogantly bypass everyone heading to the next sermon.

They always make everyone feel special at CTN and the producer who sent me the invite to be a guest on the show appeared and was now leading me to the Green Room. It is always interesting after sitting down staring at a vanity mirror with lights and someone starts putting make up on you moments before going live. Fortunately, I had not gotten too sweaty in that race to the studio and after freshening up and makeup on I was invited to another room where I sat down on a nice couch to reconnect with the founder of the television network and his beautiful bride. We laughed and had the best time and after a time of prayer it was our time to go inside the studio.

It is always a good ten to fifteen degrees cooler in the studio which is fine by me because the heat in Florida coupled with me wearing a suit, it was a welcomed bonus. As another stage assistant began to place a microphone on my lapel while simultaneously hiding the wire inside my jacket one stagehand began to count down from t-minus thirty seconds before filming. I fixed my tie and handkerchief at the twenty second mark and said one last silent prayer asking God would use me, give me clarity, stamina, and His strength to now preach one more message but this time to a few more million people. One of my very pictures in the past that touches me was one of Billy Graham praying on set in CNN studios right before going "Live" with Larry King. I was not BG but if he would pause to pray at CNN in Atlanta, I needed to as well at CTN in Clearwater. It is hard to resemble Heaven if you do not call in periodically and I knew more than ever I need more not less prayer. The two thousand seat tent was incredible, but this was a moment ordained by God and I was so glad I did not stay home.

After whispering, "Amen" silently to my private prayer the producer's voice said, "three – two – one" and you could hear the music intro theme song playing in the monitor. The founder and host opened with a brief introduction and then pitched it to me, and JESUS smashed a grand slam from there! Over the years, the Lord gave me great ease because it is seemed the bigger the platform the more at ease I became. That hour flew by faster than the hour I had spent in the rental from Tampa International to get to the television station and everyone was thrilled with the segment. After taking a picture to capture the moment back on their network and thanking Bob and his team for the privilege to be back, I started heading outside. I learned it was better to say, "thanks" twice than not at all. While leaving, I made sure to try to make eye contact and shake hands with everyone on the way out the door. Their work and ministry is every bit as important as anyone else if not more! In fact, if they were not faithful doing their thing, I could not do what God called me to do.

After a pit stop in the bathroom to wash the makeup off, loosen my collar and take off my jacket, I was almost out. After splashing some water on my face and wiping the sweat from my brow I began to head to my car. While folding my suit coat on my arm and waving goodbye to one last employee out the door I was now in the car and getting ready to throw the car in reverse to head to the hotel. I had yet to check in. Sometimes we can be so busy we can fail to pause and give thanks and with the car still in park and I was finally able to breathe I said one more prayer of thanksgiving to God. Despite a non-stop week and having preached in a dozen public and private schools to thousands of teens plus six nights to capacity crowds under that canvas cathedral, gave multiple interviews on local radio shows and endured intense spiritual warfare, still by God's grace I was able to preach one more time to a global audience and was not a minute late.

Gratitude does your heart good and now after leaving the studio I was heading back to the hotel. I was like a muffler on a car because I was "exhausted" and could finally go find my rented bed and crash. It was still late in the afternoon but after thirty sermons I was about done. Ask any preacher, one sermon will wear you out. It has been said, "One hour in the pulpit is equivalent to an eight-hour day of manual labor." When you are fighting Satan and criticism from a few Fruit Loops it is more taxing than the IRS. When you preach thirty times in a week it is almost inhuman but there are countless people that swear that ministers only work an hour a week. Nice try!

Yes, I had every right to go to bed and probably could have slept nonstop from seven that night until nine the next morning because I did not have a flight until after lunch. Finally, the first time in a week I could get some rest even if in a hotel. The Lord reminded me while heading to the hotel that Pastor Rodney Howard - Browne had a church in the Tampa region. Satan was whispering once again in my ear, "Frank, take a break. You don't need to call him." Despite being tired I felt the Lord leading me to call Pastor Rodney. I also knew I had just preached my heart out probably more than any single person that week in America (no exaggeration) and as a minister of the Gospel and more importantly a born-again Christian I needed to hear a word from the Lord myself.

It is a dangerous day when as ministers or musicians we only "show up" at church if we are on a poster or platform. A mentor told me long ago, "If you are too small to serve off the stage then you don't deserve to be on one." My first paid church job was as a part time janitor in 1989-1991 at First Baptist Church of Waldorf, Maryland. For two years in high school and early at the community college I cleaned weekly both floors of the church for extra money and to keep the house of God clean. More than once I recall vacuuming the floors not only to His glory but to the best of my ability. We need to do everything with excellence. I also recall praying more than once in that empty sanctuary, "Lord if you could ever use me to preach once or on occasion to lift up your Name, share my testimony of what you've done for me or to help another, please use me. However, if you would rather me to push this vacuum, take out the trash and clean the bathrooms that will be fine, too."

Satan was still running his mouth to tell me to take a break. It is wise to do the exact opposite of what the Devil is saying, particularly when it comes to life and ministry. I should not confess this but with the GPS and the Devil directing me to the airport while driving from Clearwater back towards Tampa I grabbed my cell and scrolled to find Pastor Rodney's number. Keep in mind, other than a couple visits in Washington and rare texts or calls we had not reunited since the last event at Constitution Hall. Once again, the Devil was saying while I was looking at his contact in my cell doing sixty miles an hour, "Don't embarrass yourself! He will not answer the phone!! Even if you leave a message do you really think someone of his stature would call you?"

It is amazing what lies the enemy can race through your head while you're in a rental car visiting out of state, but I have been around the block in my journey with Jesus and I know that Satan is at ease lying anywhere and anytime. He did not get named "The Father of Lies" by telling the truth! I had to learn to be like the boy who won the obstacle course race and turn a "deaf ear" to not only my critics but to the Devil, himself. With one hand on the wheel and the other now calling Pastor Rodney the phone began to ring. Satan tried to say another outlandish lie and I just had to press into FAITH more than fear and on the second ring the great preacher with that familiar South African accent answered my call!

Excitedly I shared, "Pastor! Hello my friend. Don't you have a church in Tampa somewhere?" He said, "Yes! The River Church." I said, "Great! Are you having Wednesday night service this evening?" He said, "Yes we are at 7PM!" I replied, "Great! I would like to come and worship with you all this evening." He said, "You're in town?" I said, "Yes sir!" What he said next floored me and almost wrecked me." The great evangelist said to me while flying down the Florida highway, "I don't want you to come worship with us tonight." I thought, "Yikes! The man of God doesn't even want me on his property!" Just as Satan the slimy snake almost wiggled his way back into casting doubt and negativity in my mind, the renowned preacher replied in his matter-of-fact tone, "Frank, if you are in town, I don't want you to sit in the crowd; I want you to stand on the platform and preach to my people tonight!"

As some of my friends the inner city would say, "Slap Your Neighbor!" That is an expression when one is not only happy but elated! Can I get a witness? This is not proper grammar but pure Gospel when I type, "Ain't God good!" Indeed, He is!! Holy smokes, I am now higher than a kite for a man who has never touched cocaine. I was now three times higher than that dreaded drug. A minute before I was on fumes but now it was like a dozen firecrackers had just exploded in my veins and I was almost back on all cylinders. Opposed to crashing at the hotel to rest I was honored to preach in the pulpit of one of America's most powerful preachers. With no time to spare I headed straight for the church and was blown away with the beauty of their church campus. Plus, the palm trees are a beautiful bonus!

The buildings were first class, the grounds second to none and the atmosphere and worship off the charts. The best part was the Presence of the Living God was in that place. Nobody shows honor and kindness like the staff at The River Church in Tampa, and they made this out-of-town preacher feel like a V.I.P. They ushered me to the front and after the congregation sat after the incredible worship and a very gracious introduction, I am now standing behind the pulpit before a great crowd in a mega church in Florida. The Lord reminded me of that private prayer in Maryland decades before in my hometown Baptist church and now I am on stage of one of the greatest ministries in America. Truthfully, they have been used by God to lead multiplied millions to Christ locally, regionally, nationally, international and to their global television audience.

I had just preached on LIVE television two hours before at the third largest Christian television network in the world and wrapped thirty sermons in Alabama the same week under a 2,000-seat tent but now once again getting ready to preach the Gospel to a televised audience watching on DirecTV. It has been said, "Who you respect is who you attract" and one reason some will not go and grow to the next level in their profession because they do not know how to honor others. No joke, I said a prayer for my "friend" back in Alabama who was trying to lecture me after seeing one hundred souls saved at the Christian school. He was either strategizing with the wrong crowd or probably stuck in reverse. It is free to be nice but costly to be rude and when you honor God and respect others you can go a long way. Jealousy is a terrible theology and more than reformed that young minister needed revival.

Secondly, I had wanted to humbly sit in the crowd to receive a Word but now for the thirty second time this week I was tasked by God to "Preach the Word!" If you are unwilling to serve God when no one is looking you are unfit to be used by God if almost everyone is watching. The Gospel for me was never about being seen but that His message may be heard and since leaving Capitol Hill and after collapsing in training with the police academy I was still willing to die trying. Many want the platform but are not willing to pay the price. I still smile when my senior pastor friend in Virginia is curious if I could preach three times in one Sunday. If you see him, tell him "hi" and we are still in the game having fun!"

As I stood behind that beautiful state-of-the-art clear pulpit and scanned the crowd in that massive sanctuary, I whispered once again that God above would use me again below. It was a far cry from pushing the vacuum back home, but I am thankful for every ministry opportunity. My dear friend, Dr. Todd Holmes gave me the kindest greeting that night and after a friendly joke, like a boxer or bull coming out of his corner, the Lord and I came out swinging truth bombs and the place came unglued!

Pastor Rodney is a selfless saint and not only a General in God's Army but hands down perhaps the most generous man in ministry you will ever meet. Secondly, he is like a major league baseball coach and has this innate gift to know when to pinch hit someone or send a reliever to close out the game. Plus, he is so secure in who he is in the Lord he can afford to let others shine. One of the greatest sins in the church today is not adultery or lack of integrity but false theology and personal jealousy. It takes a big man to promote others and Pastor Rodney Howard - Browne promotes others with the best of them. Even greater, he smiles when they are in their element. We all win when we cheer each other on.

The Lord allowed me to preach with great liberty and power that night and I had great confidence when giving the altar call that night. On a Wednesday evening service, we had several souls saved and the entire altar was full of folks coming forward, weeping, getting right with God and with a fresh burden for souls who needed the Lord. They are a soul winning church, and they also have a School of Government training future leaders to run for elected office. It is not uncommon to have elected officials, Members of Congress, Ambassador or even a "presidential arrival" a time or two. They also have a Constitutional Scholar and attorney on staff and teach students to win their generation for Christ at The River Bible University. Students from almost every state in America come each year to learn from the absolute best and one of my high honors is growing as friends with this great ministry.

As I exited that Wednesday night service in Florida the sun had faded but the Son of God was glowing ever brighter in my heart. Spent in His service but genuinely satisfied, I finally started heading towards my hotel at ten that evening. It has been a long day from the flight from Washington, DC and taping an hour television appearance in Clearwater and just finished preaching again in Tampa, the Lord really blessed. I could not help but think of the five-foot seven pastor who was barely out of Bible college who just days before had the audacity to attack me in that Christian gymnasium after seeing over one hundred souls born again in Alabama. Bless his heart, the Devil was using him in Alabama but after back-to-back sermons on live television the Lord was using me in Florida and a couple millions more around the globe. I prayed once more for all the opposition and right or wrong, it can force us to draw closer to God. After asking God to bless them and gave thanks for one of the greatest weeks of our ministry I had to remind myself of where I had fallen in the past. Right then and there before moving forward I asked for forgiveness where I dropped the ball and would from now on wish them all well and leave it behind. Satan wants us looking backwards but faith in the present propels us forward and sometimes you just must move on.

Yes, the "greats are gracious" and both Bob D'Andrea and Dr. Rodney Howard - Browne are tops. Finally arriving at the hotel, I grabbed my only carry on luggage and now completely drenched from the heat of those hot lights while preaching I checked in. After a quick shower and call home to Ruth I finally climbed into bed and called it a night. While staring at the ceiling I closed my eyes once more not to sleep but say thanks in prayer to God for once again ordering my steps and opening doors. I was reminded of Moses and God did not part the Red Sea a year in advance, a month in advance nor the day before. The water did not part a minute prior, but it was when his sandals slapped the sea when God did it. He had to be in before God showed up and too often, we want easy street when God promotes obedience. After whispering, "Amen" I was finally out like a light for the night.

After a restful sleep I showered and grabbed breakfast and then received a text from Pastor Rodney inviting me to lunch at the Capital Grille in Tampa. It is a high-end restaurant, and it was a treat for me to dine at his table at a lunch for two. I am usually at Chick-Fil A, Cracker Barrel or for a nice dinner Carrabba's. Just like my report card, it was all "C's!" LOL. Pastor Rodney is next level and one of the greatest visionaries I have ever met. Honestly, I think Walt Disney would have had his hands full keeping up with this man of God. He is on the cutting edge of everything from technology, trends and perhaps most important these turbulent times. He had his finger on the pulse and like a true prophet he could see things happen before they did. One thing I noticed was my Baptist friends were faithful and consistent but had extraordinarily little urgency when reaching others for Christ. I am so thankful for my background, but we all have different strengths but one blind spot for sure was lacking in generosity, prophecy and chasing souls for eternity. One element also missing is how to deal with spiritual warfare. It could also be at some folks cannot teach from a place they have never been. When you start speaking in stadiums and studios it does not make you superior but lonely trying to navigate from a place without counsel. One consistent voice over the last thirty years is my home pastor, Rev. Marvin Harris. He is affectionately called "Starvin' Marvin" and we all love him! That brother is a soul winning machine, and the world is better because of friends like his wife Dona and their family.

We ordered a nice steak which was a treat for me, and Pastor Rodney is first class in everything he does. We talked about family, ministry, politics, and current events. He shared about some of his past crusades both at home and overseas and his passion for souls, generosity towards others, devotion to family and work ethic are almost unrivaled. True ministry is caught more than taught and I was trying to catch this Gospel gladiator was throwing at me. After giving the Lord thanks for the meal before us we dined on that delicious steak and the television playing adjacent to us brought breaking news that "Prince" had died. The artist who helped make purple popular had died and it was surreal hearing that Prince was gone but with the commentary in back I was still hearing from one of the world's most gifted evangelist remind me in conversation that The King is alive and well. No, we were not talking Elvis but all Jesus.

True leadership is spending time with others and subsequent meetings with him both corporately and privately accelerated my ministry in more ways than I could count and still processing today. It is like drinking out of a fire hydrant when he speaks, and you are doing your best just to keep up with him. After our meal he graciously picked up the check and said, "Let's go for a walk." The restaurant was connected to a beautiful shopping mall and many fancy stores were inside and I had a blast just shadowing him. We have much in common and his faith is an encouragement to all. Both he and his beautiful bride, Adonica came to the United States of America as missionaries from South Africa with three small children and three hundred dollars! Everyone can see their platform now but not the price along the way!

Pastor's wife, Dr. Adonica is a phenomenal teacher and thousands of women come to her annual Women's conference from all over the world. I love Rodney's and her accent, and I had the biggest crush on the actress starring next to Mel Gibson in "Lethal Weapon 2!" I was still at the junior college when the movie was released and saw it many times. It was an honor to meet Mel years later in New York on a red-carpet premiere of "Hacksaw Ridge." The actress was drop dead gorgeous blonde from South Africa and when she spoke in the movie she said, "I'm from South Af-ree-Ka." My heart skipped in that theater. I was single but I would have married her just for that accent alone! Reminiscing, I do not know if I was more in love with her looks or her voice, but Pastor Rodney and Adonica not only have her similar voice, but the difference is the power of God when they talk. My wife, Ruth and I agree that Pastor Rodney and Adonica have become our favorite couple in ministry. They are a powerful force together and complement each other so well and blessed with a beautiful family all serving the Lord in every area of ministry.

Over the years I have learned that "Those who come the furthest tend to go the farthest." Plus, when you display your faith, the Lord will show you His favor. Faith is the currency of Heaven, and I told a mega church pastor one time in passing after he kept quizzing me on my ministry. He was trying to learn my model or method as if it were a three-step program one could buy online and duplicate. He could not comprehend that it was the simple fact of His amazing grace and my obedience in faith. Still frustrated with my reply I shared with him, "Some church leaders may out finance me, but most will never out faith me." Some boast and rely on their savings in the bank but I am still depending totally on my Savior in my heart. That makes all the difference and Pastor Rodney and I both have faith and at times that is all we had but that is what makes one rich in the eyes of God.

Strolling through the mall on that day shadowing Pastor Rodney was one I will remember until I die, or the Lord soon splits the sky. I recall thinking as we walked that this would be a great reality show with cameras following us both on a Thursday afternoon in the middle of a mall. We went into a store, and he said, "Frank, I want to give you a gift." I vividly recall thinking to myself, "No! You have done so much for me and I cannot accept anything else." He then replied, "I want to bless you." This brother had already blessed me in such a short time that I could never repay him. Pastor proceeded and said, "I want to buy you something that you don't forget me." I was thinking how in the world could I forget you after all this? You just let me preach on a moment's notice in your church, aired on television halfway around the world and then treat me to a steak lunch. This is more than I deserve!

Truth be told, it is amazing how many get amnesia over the years and fail to remember what God and others have graciously done for us. Pause right now and the first person that comes to mind who helped you in the past, pray a blessing over them. Second, send a text or handwritten note by morning thanking them for their investment on you. At Pastor's level I knew he knew firsthand and all too well the pain of others taking you for granted. Plus, I have now learned that one of his love languages is giving. Personally, I believe we are never more like God when we are giving and for<u>giving</u>. Once again, *giving* is in both of those words and Jesus and Pastor Rodney are givers!

I was always generous since childhood and my Mother can attest to giving my lunch to homeless and buying gifts and clothes for friends and complete strangers. I was never swimming in money but what I had I freely gave away. After spending more time with Pastor in subsequent conversations and time in his presence I have become intentional more than ever with my giving. He told me more than once, *"Generosity towards others eliminates pride in us."* Read that again! Dr. Johnny Hunt once said with pinpoint accuracy, "Money is like manure because it stinks if you don't spread it around." At this juncture I find myself next to him as he is examining beautiful handmade silk ties. He said, "Do you like this?" I said, "Yes sir but I am fine." He said, "Seriously, I want you to have this."

It was a gorgeous blue tie, and I am not one to peek at a price in public especially when someone is gifting it to me, but the tag revealed $200! In near disbelief I chimed, "Pastor

Rodney, I have suits that I bought over the years that didn't cost me two hundred bucks!" With a smile but stern look interrupted and said, "It will look good on you." I quickly realized that you do not argue with this brother, and I started thinking he didn't like my tie from the night before and wanted to help me out to elevate my wardrobe. Maybe Adonica saw the sermon too and told her husband, "Help a brother out!" Either way, I humbly but thankfully followed him to the counter, and he graciously blessed me with the nicest tie I have ever owned. One of the clerks recognized him from his church and another said "hello" to him as we were leaving the store perhaps because of his television ministry. Two preachers in a casual setting having fun together while out and about and I found myself walking straighter and stood taller when next to him.

Those that make fun of folks are often jealous that they are on the outside looking in. I have found more than not that those that throw rocks are envious that they are not at the level of the one they privately and publicly pick apart. I recall our first breakfast together in Washington, DC and conversation about lost souls and he instantly began to weep. He shared what the opening page in this book revealed that most in ministry no longer have a genuine passion for rescuing lost souls. Watching his tears fall down his cheeks at that breakfast for two in the corner was something I will forever recall. You cannot fake that and without an audience or camera why try? It came out of a genuine brokenness for souls.

Secondly, he made a vow to God that the Devil would pay when his child died in his arms on Christmas day. Already one of the most respected soul winners in Christendom losing his girl emboldened him to go after the lost more after losing his most precious gift but had the fortitude and faith to lay her on the altar in service to our Lord. Most men and ministers may have crumbled, cursed God, and threw in the towel but this General pressed in and pressed on. While those in little league throw rocks this Major League minister built not a monument or memorial but a movement to equip thousands to see souls saved for the end time harvest.

Pastor Rodney had been discredited at times for laughter, but it is a miracle he was still able to smile after burying his daughter. Meadowlark Lemon was named "The Clown Prince of Basketball" and brought JOY to millions of fans over every race and creed world-wide but told me privately he was unable in those early years to eat in restaurants because of segregation and racial discrimination. If anyone had a reason to frown, sulk, curse, fight, quit or die it would be these two men respectfully; but God healed their heart and helped heal ours in the process with both a basketball and Bible. To have become friends with both Meadowlark and Pastor Rodney are two welcomed honors in my life. I have been with presidents but being with those two preachers was icing to my cake.

My watch on my wrist reminded me once again that time was ticking and in my whirlwind 24 hour visit to the Sunshine State was up. Pastor gave me a hug and we went our separate ways, and I was back in the rental racing to Tampa International Airport to return the car and me to return to my family. After returning the car and checking in my bags I reached in my pocket and finally looked at the love offering that was in an envelope from the night before and my heart skipped. While waiting at the gate to board the plane I peeked at the check and in front of a crowd almost cried. Pastor Rodney and his incredible church family blessed me with a gift that took my breath away. Once again, the General of generosity was blessing others and again it happened to be me.

Their church gave me more for preaching that one Wednesday night service than many churches over the years had given me for preaching a four-day revival (Sunday-Wednesday). It was never about the money but many times I had next to no money and salvation is FREE, but discipleship and ministry comes with a cost. Plus, Pastor Rodney did not get to his level by being stingy, backstabbing, or undermining others. What only God and my wife, Ruth in Maryland knew was she was privately praying for a year to one day go to Israel and walk where Jesus walked in the Holy Land.

Ruth had been invited two times before but both times declined one due to finances and two because her beloved Dad and my father-in-law has been a preacher of the Gospel for sixty years and never had the honor to visit the Holy Land. He preached about it, sang praises about it, and prayed for it to happen but was not a reality yet. The year before Ruth's brother, Noe sacrificially saved some money for my father-in-law and my mother-in-law to finally go to Israel. My in-laws had the time of their lives, and they are the salt of the Earth and humble people residing in El Salvador.

Since God finally allowed Ruth's parents to go, she felt it was now appropriate for her to try to go. She did not want to go before her parents. Read that again boys and girls because that is called "honor" and respect both characteristics that are lost today. No wonder America and civilization are in a tailspin. We were just shy of three thousand dollars that we were saving in the cupboard for Ruth to go to Israel with friends. God does all things well in His time, Dr. Antonio Bolainez is a cherished friend and powerful evangelist, and he was leading a trip and although Ruth had been invited before we were hoping to afford sending her on this trip. We had prayed, fasted, and saved and when I looked at the check it was exactly the remaining balance that Ruth needed to go to Israel. Go God!

What Pastor Rodney did not know that his church generosity enabled my wife to go with her friends to the Holy Land and it happened to be during Mother's Day. Ruth cried when she arrived in Tel Aviv and cried when she was boarding the plane to come home. I stood home to watch Andrew because it was all we had to send her but so glad it worked out and dreams come true. Once again, Pastor Rodney made me look good by blessing Ruth to go on that trip. We forever will be thankful. After placing the check safely in my left pocket, I found myself now boarding the plane departing Tampa and flying back to our Nation's Capital. As we hit thirty thousand feet it dawned on me flying over the state with arguably the best sunsets that I would have missed so much if I did not honor another in ministry and willing to call him by faith.

Opposed to crash in a hotel I was preaching with one of my heroes and got a new tie in the process! More importantly, he gave me his time and the honor to grow as friends. Plus, that connection helped Ruth walk where Jesus walked and who you respect is who you attract? What a week of ministry and it is amazing what God will do when we step out in faith and obey His commands. Florida did live up to its name and the sky was shining brighter after the intense thunder the week before in Alabama. I love both states, but it is a blessing when the sun is shining! Thank you, Jesus.

CHRIST, THE REDEEMER – BRAZIL

AFTER the nonstop sprint of ministry in both Alabama and Florida I was home for a brief break. I was still trying to be a good husband, father while still juggling my role connecting with dozens of pastors weekly and my own ministry preaching but stress was overwhelming. Weekly reports were mandatory with the Billy Graham Evangelistic Association, and I had been working around the clock preparing for Franklin Graham's upcoming Decision America Tour coming to my region.

The 2016 Olympics was on my doorstep, and this was the second Olympiad I would have the honor to be a chaplain. Dr. Sam Mings is the founder of the respected Lay Witnesses For Christ International and he had ministered at every Olympics since the 1984 games in Los Angeles. Dr. David Allbritton had ministered for years as the International Evangelism Chairman of the Olympic outreach as they minister to world class athletes and fans from around the world.

We became friends online and began to talk on the phone and he extended me the invite to go to the 2012 Olympics in London, England. His connection made it possible for me to grow as friends with Dr. Mings who has led thousands of athletes to Christ. Two months before the trip to London I got a call from Dr. Mings that Pastor David Allbritton who was an international evangelist and beloved pastor in Texas was diagnosed with a brain tumor. I had to sit down when I got the news, and it knocked the wind out of my sails. Dr. Mings shared that it was aggressive and not only would he not be going to the Olympics but most likely not live to watch it on television.

Dr. Mings then said, "Frank, I am tapping you to be our International Evangelism Chairman." My heart dropped and it was surreal. Within weeks one of God's generals and a mentor from afar was gone. The irony we had yet to meet in person but with phone calls and his constant encouragement online was a welcomed blessing. The greats are indeed gracious, and he was both. The man who opened the door for me to go was now gone and I was able to connect with his amazing wife, Linda and their awesome son, Matt who I have incredible respect for, and I know David is smiling down on them and his beautiful daughter with great pride and admiration.

He ministered at multiple Olympics and now I am asked to go without him. He was the epitome of a selfless servant but was also a powerful preacher. Someone suggested that we take a pair of Dr. Abritton's shoes to London and when they found out we wore the same shoe size I was asked if I would wear them. Rocky may have worn Apollo's colors in "ROCKY III" but I did not feel comfortable wearing his shoes. What God had done through him was incredible over the years and I figured I could best honor him by preaching the Gospel, staying humble because of this door and follow Jesus and His footsteps not so much wearing his shoes.

We did take them and felt like he was with us each step of the way. Now four years later I am a day away from flying alone once again to Rio de Janeiro, Brazil. The Olympics certainly picks some beautiful places, and I was doing last minute errands around the house because it is always three times harder on Ruth when I am on the road. Billy Graham often said three things, "His wife, Ruth was the greatest Christian he had ever known." We both had a Ruth, and that statement could be true in my life too. God has been too good to me! He went on to say, "In Heaven, she will receive probably more rewards than him." I believe that as well. If she was clingy and forbid me to go than scores of souls may not be in the Kingdom. We joke that I am her library book, and she loans me out to the world knowing I am coming right back." Thirdly, Dr. Graham believed it was a TEAM effort and the audience often sees

Billy, but it was the army of donors, volunteers, staff, and prayer warriors behind the scenes who helped make it happen.

We had a restful sleep that night and like the Lone Ranger I am finding myself flying halfway around the Lord with just a Bible and bag but knew intimately time was ticking and people need the Lord. It was a decent flight, and the longer trips were wearing me down. Plus, it was an uncomfortable feeling to sense that you may be on someone's radar. With my background in politics and family lineage of a century and half of law enforcement I could pick up plain clothes agents and air marshals a mile away and even at 30,000 feet.

What was interesting was I could tell there was a shift in our society, and it was one thing to be monitored by another nation but distressing to feel you were being under surveillance with your government. At times I would get up to use the restroom once on a ten-hour flight and the same Marshal would be watching me as if I were going to blow up the plane. The nights were already dark, but I could see with spiritual eyes and Biblical binoculars that the days were growing darker too.

After landing in Rio, it was as beautiful as a postcard, and they have some of the most gorgeous beaches in the world. We hit the ground running and that was another thing about being on mission that it was no rest for the weary. We were running on both anointing and adrenaline and putting in sixteen-hour days ministering to over twenty different nations. It was a treat to catch a few of the matches and games and usually we are so busy ministering outside that we do not get to enjoy too much on the inside.

Another fellow chaplain, Randy Shepherd had the honor to connect with some of the USA Men's Basketball team and had ministered to Kobe and Lebron, among others. A few of us were able to watch the USA Women's Basketball team win gold and that was a special moment. During the sunup to sundown ministry, we also would speak at night at multiple outreaches hosted by local churches. We would bring former gold medal winners and past Olympians from our team, and they would share their testimony that God means more than gold to them. We would have gifted musicians and soloists sing and then we would be ready at a moment's notice to share a sermonette to a crowd or one on one.

(Preaching @ 2016 Olympics - RIO)

We led two Uber drivers to Christ, and I have learned that sometimes we are so "professional" that we can lose the personal touch. We were able to take in a few tourists stops along the way and the famed beaches and restaurants were wonderful. Now as I write this in a middle of a lockdown too many took our liberties for granted. Halfway into our time at the 2016 Olympics we went to the iconic Christ, The Redeemer statue. It is one of the seven wonders of the world and President Obama called it "magical" when he and his family toured it.

Just as the Eiffel Tower and Paris are synonymous the Christ statue and Rio go hand in hand. I learned quickly that folks do not hesitate to pay $30 dollars to stand in line to see firsthand the famed sculpture. It is breathtaking and The Redeemer stands tall above all else with open arms overlooking beautiful Brazil below. Today it reminds us of while time is left that no sinner is too far from saving if we just come "by faith" in repentance.

The statue was built in 1931 by Portuguese artist, Cristo Redentor. It stands 98 feet tall and his horizontally stretched hands spanning 92 feet. Truly, Christ also represents the cross and regardless up close or far away you can see it. The statue stands on a base of 26 feet making it nearly 130 feet from top to bottom and it is officially the largest Art Deco style sculpture in the world.

It is certainly a tourist attraction, and it generates millions of dollars annually. What was interesting is that folks do not mind paying thirty bucks to see a statue but bypass His salvation for FREE. Many want the religion without relationship, but truth be told the thirty dollars is less costly than to genuinely follow Christ.

As we patiently waited in line and it slowly snaked up the mountain before finally being lifted towards the top of the mountain, we had tourists all around us. It was a hot, humid day in Rio, but everyone was excited that the Olympics were in town. Bruce Cavier and his family have performed across America and used their basketball dribbling and acrobatic skills to dazzle over half of the NBA arenas. They were even invited to do game six of an NBA Finals and when everyone comes to see Steph Curry or King James during the game the fans do not leave their seats at halftime when they come out.

Bruce and Randy were with us on the trip, and both handle a basketball as well as almost anyone. Randy had been friends with Michael Jordan since he was sixteen and played on the same team with him at a camp in North Carolina the year before MJ went to play for Dean Smith at UNC.

One of them pulled out a ball from their bag and started spinning it and since we already had a captive crowd, they did their thing. After weaving the Gospel message while the ball was spinning on his finger when he finished, he gave an invitation to receive Christ. The family of four right there gave their hearts to Christ. About an hour later after taking pictures on top of the majestic mountain with the multi-million-dollar view below we ran into the same family. Before we met them, they looked a tad sad but after receiving Christ below and seeing them above near the Redeemer they were all smiles.

I will never forget this memory etched in my mind because when we caught up with them, they were getting in position to take a family picture. All four of them with the widest smiles imaginable were at the base of the Christ statue and were under His outstretched saving arms. They heard of the statue below but officially knew the Savior now above. That is why we leave family, endure hostility, travel around the globe to help see souls saved one at a time. Despite being tired we were all thrilled, and our team slowly descended the mountain.

That trip in Rio was rough on my back. Our hotel accommodations fell through, and I slept on the floor of a dorm room with a small mattress. It was nice and clean inside but on the floor was tough for ten nights and adding the long days it was exhausting. We had already seen just shy of five hundred people accept Christ on this trip and with one full day off we did something different. To be frank, it was downright dangerous. It has been said do stupid things and you get stupid prizes but when you are flowing in the power of God and march to His orders you can have confidence in the assignment.

Some of our chaplain team was invited to tour the most dangerous place in all of Rio de Janeiro. It was called the "City of God" but even the locals referred to it as the place of death. We were told the police department just outside that town did not even like to go in because it seemed like a gun fight ensued each time.

I was trying to call home to Ruth almost every day but between the time difference halfway around the world and our nonstop schedule it was not conducive or realistic. We probably briefly spoke every other day while I was in Brazil but when she inquired what I was doing on my day off I did not feel I should worry her. Trying to pacify her, I told her some of the team was going sightseeing and hoped to put on an evangelistic event going to the other side of town. I casually said while trying to sound upbeat, "keep us in your prayers" and after saying "I love you" we hung up.

Technically, we were going to do some "sightseeing." Our prayer was to find favor with God and those inside that dangerous villa to see us a treat and not threat and allow us to share the Gospel. I will never forget the bus ride and I recall twenty years before I was on a bus driving on the Gaza Strip and that was a hairy experience. Those rivaled that but perhaps worse was we had armed guards on our bus in Israel and Egypt but now in Rio it was God and us.

A local pastor from Rio accompanied us but he also had faced death threats in his ministry. It is interesting that the ones spreading love are hated so much. On that borrowed yellow school bus were about a dozen of our chaplains and it really was a unique group. We had a former Dallas Cowboys cheerleader on board. A former Harlem Globetrotter and two Olympians from the past. We had a family that was featured in the Guinness Book of world records and Randy Shepherd who was a basketball standout in college and friends with MJ. This was his fifth Olympics as a chaplain and although I was invited to three counting the Winter Games in Russia that I politely declined this was my second.

The closer we got to this "mission trip" it was eerily quiet on the bus. In my old school days playing Varsity basketball at times the trip was wild, fun, and filled with my teammates either teasing each other or talking smack about what they were going to do to the opponents. However, if was an away game with a team that was red hot and known to be good it seemed like it was silent.

We were instructed to stay on the bus, and I read people's eyes and even the local pastor onboard with us looked nervous. That is not usually a good sign! I was seated three quarters of the way back on the driver's side near the rear when we pulled up to this gate and we stopped. The dust seemed to be a mushroom cloud that made our situation even more intense. In the Old Testament sometimes God followed His people by a cloud by day and maybe this was another miracle to hide us now. We heard some chatter in their native language and I am starting to reflect on what I last ate because that may have been my "last supper."

After being waived in we turned a corner and the first thing I noticed it looked like a war zone and the beautiful beaches just half hour away seemed like in another hemisphere. It was dusty, dirty, and resembled death. It looked like part military and full poverty and resembled little life. We were slowly winding down as we all silently looked at the window trying to process what we were seeing, and I could hear others praying that God would use us regardless the cost.

The bus finally came to a stop and when it did some were relieved, and others were more nervous. It is harder to hit a moving target and they implored once more stay on the bus until we were instructed otherwise. About five minutes later I saw something on my side of the bus that wrecked me to my core. I saw a boy about eight years old run around the corner with no shoes and he was dirty from head to toe. After watching him what appeared to be his younger sister was now in the picture right behind him.

They were the only sign of life on that entire dismal backdrop and what transpired next was a game-changer. The two siblings were now standing in front of a garbage commercial size dumpster and the little boy was now hoisting his sister on his shoulders as she was trying to find scraps of food. I had seen enough, and it was as if the Lord was prompting me to graduate from the bus and get in the game.

I stood up and walked to the front of the bus and exited. Love is greater than hate and compassion is better than indifference and with each step I got bolder, and my mission now was to head straight towards those kids. Immediately, a military helicopter with guns affixed on the side flew over my head and I heard it before but seeing it was another poignant reminder that we were over our heads.

Once again, Rambo without a gun and I did not even have a water pistol at this juncture, but Christianity isn't a spectator sport. Billy Graham said when you take a stand it strengthens the spines of others behind you, and I now had two more come with me to assist. I had two pockets full of Brazilian dollars and I wish to God I had more, but I gave those kids everything I had. Their eyes lit up like the Fourth of July and with a female Portuguese translator now assisting it was obvious to learn they were so thankful. The kids after jumping up and down and seeing their excitement as if they just won a mini lottery, they took off to finally get some real food.

Now with most of our team all on the bus peeking outside the one side breathing a sigh of relief I could hear trouble coming straight for us. A man in his late twenties was racing towards us on a dirt motorcycle. He was wearing a grey tank top, but everything had to be grey in that neighborhood with the dirt and little optimism. Thirty feet away I could also tell he had bulging biceps with bullets strewn over his shirt resembling an X over both shoulders. From ten feet before coming to a halt I noticed a gun on his hip and a larger gun strapped to his back and darn if he did not look like John J. Rambo from 'First Blood' after he escaped that small town Sheriff's Office and just stole a motor bike.

As his dirt bike came to a halt and the dust cleared, he is now three feet from us. He had done this entrance before and now face to face it was obvious he had a 9mm on his hip, an AK-47 on his back and that x shaped row of bullets all over his chest. I met Sly as a kid, and I am now meeting his misguided stunt double half a world of way. They have insurance on Hollywood sets, but we are not in California anymore or Kansas! He was angry, agitated and spouting off some obscenities in his language but ignorance is bliss, and I could not understand a word.

The local pastor that was on the bus now whispered to me that the man we are toe to toe with is the drug lord of this corrupt community intentionally hidden from society.

Meadowlark told me that First Lady Nancy Reagan and he helped kids, "Say No to Drugs" but Lark was not with me on this leg and I don't think this man on the motorcycle with matching guns would have listened anyways.

They play by their rules and the Lord or law is not in their language. He was the gate-keeper and I had received red carpet treatment before but was not expecting it here. Randy and I were standing before him as he calmed down and with our interpreter began to have a dialogue. Randy is bold and when you are on the Lord's side you can have confidence and then he said, "Hello. We are from America." He did not look impressed, but it was clear to him we were not undercover police sent by the locals, but we were in fact on a mission from God. We were not quite the "Blue Brothers" but this white brothers from another mother did have a nice farmer's tan while being in Brazil.

I wanted to talk but I deferred because Randy was already moving forward. He looked him square in the eye and told him, "We come in peace." The translator continued and then he hit him with a compliment which was brilliant, "You are a warrior." The man with two guns and bullets wrapped around him acknowledged with hardly saying a word but with a cocky "yes." Randy said what I was thinking but he went straight for the jugular and said, "you are a warrior – but a warrior for the wrong team."

Here is the moment of truth. It was a pregnant pause, and this could really incite him, and he had the biceps, bullets, and home court advantage to prove it. We were on his turf, but we were on God's timetable and just like that the in the live or die moment the drug lord who was the unofficial mayor of that town dropped is head and shame. Randy without hesitation and precision from the Lord said, "God wants you to be a warrior for Him." The man's head snapped back, and it was as if the lightbulb that had been dark in his world finally turned on. With the translator in disbelief tried to keep up with Randy plus momentum is everything and it had swung now to the Lord. Not to lose territory he said, "God has a great plan for your life. He wants to use you in a big way." The man with a machine gun and banana clip on his back shook his head in agreement. Randy continued, "Jesus loves you and He is the only way to Heaven."

Now faster than the motorcycle he rode up on us with he went to close the deal and said, "Your sin separates you from a Holy God. For you to go to Heaven you must repent of your sin and confess Jesus as Lord." It was wild because as I looked over my shoulder it seemed like every other window of that side of the school bus had a head peeking outside watching what was going down at high noon at the OK Corral. God was in the middle of us, and truth be told all the guns and helicopters at that point had eliminated all fear and He was calling the shots now.

Randy reached for his hand and asked would you like to be forgiven of your sins, find freedom in Christ and go to Heaven when you die? With no pushback he said, "yes!" To say that we were not relived would be an understatement and I grabbed our soon to be new brother in Christ's other hand and together we bowed our heads and right there in Rio de Janeiro he trusted Jesus as his personal Savior. Everyone is going "nuts" now and one by one everyone was off the bus! Indeed, when you take a stand, it strengthens the spines of everyone behind you. That moment would become a catalyst for me and many others four years later when the world would be locked down.

Saul in the New Testament was a murderer, thief and caused harm to society but one day on the road to Damascus he met Jesus and it changed his whole life. In four short years, Pastor Rodney and I would also be encouraging others after the pandemic on the road to De MASK us. He went from Saul to the Apostle Paul and became one of the greatest evangelists in history of the world. The drug lord minutes before blocking us while we stared death in the eye was now our tour guide. With no embellishment he slowly drove his motorbike leading us door to door and gave us permission to invite folks to a soccer clinic we would be hosting in an hour.

While we were going door to door with their leader the rest of our team was unloading games, food and sound system equipped with speakers, microphone, and long extension cord. As a kid, I loved "The A-Team" and every character had a role to play and I could hear Hannibal's saying in my ears, "I love it when a plan comes together!" Indeed, it was and within minutes they had set up a makeshift place for us to bring some fun and faith in a place that looked foolish just half hour before. Randy and I were not only talking to the people as they came out of their little dirt filled rooms, but they were happy to hear of the event going to transpire in minutes.

We canvased that entire community and the guy that was against us was now leading the way and I am part preacher but full promoter. My friends at times called me "the white Don King" and it is a gift to get a crowd. To expedite the process, I will forever recall what occurred next and Hollywood could not draft this script. The man who had just received Christ was now summoning for Randy to jump on the back of his motorcycle. Randy is on the back of the motorcycle and holding on to his hips with an AK-47 between them. They took off and Randy was spinning his ball on his right finger as they went off around the corner. By God's grace we lived another day to tell the story and later than night we posted a video on Facebook and nearly 10,000 views watched it immediately. As the rest of us caught up with our team the circus had come to town and the music was playing and kids were coming from all four corners of that town. What was grey with optimism was now blue skies when they heard the rich, red blood of Royalty died for them too!

Now they are no longer looking in dumpsters but clapping and smiling as we passed out what food and treats, we had remaining. One of our chaplains began to do a demonstration with the ball and then God showed up. A couple gave a testimony what Jesus means to them, and one female sang. The Dallas Cowboys cheerleader was so pretty some of that community, were in awe just by looking. Sometimes the best sermons do not say a word, but we were already friends, I was married, and she did not sound South African, so I just kept on moving. LOL Plus, I am from Washington. #HailToTheRedskins

After about half an hour the crowd had surrounded us and parents, grandparents and kids had swarmed us. We each got a chance to speak and after the Gospel was given an invitation was extended and over one hundred souls gave their life to Christ!

An hour and half before we appeared to be entering a dead end and no man's land and it resembled the "city of death." However, by the time we left it resembled their name and it was indeed under new ownership the city of God. A soccer game broke out and everyone was having fun and many of the kids were wearing no shoes. I wish I had a connection with Foot Locker because I would have loved to buy every child a brand-new pair.

No, we could not save the world, but we could reach some one at a time. After the music faded and the equipment packed it was time to say "goodbye." The drug lord from the past had this glow that radiated from him, and we both gave him a hug, high five and handshake. We took a picture from a keepsake but the pastor on the bus implored us never to post it on social media. Should his superiors learn that he gave his life to Christ they could execute him because he would be perceived as "soft." In fact, it takes a man to serve the Lord. I look forward to seeing him in Heaven. God has really used Randy over the years and a big shout out to him and Jamie Johnson at Crossfire Ministries. They are the real deal!

The bus was quiet coming in but ecstatic going out! It was like going against Goliath and watching God topple him and coming home with the victory. I smiled on the back of the bus and reflected on my days on the high school basketball team and when you win on the road against a big rival it was celebration all the way home. God gave us the victory; souls were saved and that man on the motorbike was now on the winning team. Looking back, the drug lord despite armed to the teeth with bullets and an automatic rifle on his back and pistol on his side was "out gunned" by God and two soul winners. Where some thought he might one day end up dead this new brother in the Lord found eternal life.

Some may say, "Frank you put your colleagues in danger when you disobeyed the orders to remain on the bus" but when I saw those kids, I knew I had to put feet to my prayers and God said, "go" and I was going to help. The Lord used everyone that day and once again Randy was on point and he is a cherished friend, phenomenal basketball player and one of America's greatest evangelists. His annual ACC All Star Basketball Classic has touched tens of thousands of youths over the last three decades. He is a winner on and off the court. We eventually made it back to our compound and I retreated to my small bed on the floor but slept a tad better knowing God saved the day and another hundred souls in the most dangerous region of that city. Indeed, the statue we just saw of Christ the day before still has outstretched arms today. No matter what you have done or where you have been the Bible is still true, "Whosoever shall call upon the Name of the Lord shall be saved (Romans 10:13)."

The next day when I caught up with Ruth on the phone, she asked how my day off in Rio go? I just smiled and said something to the effect, "Brazil is a beautiful place" and left it at that. God had allowed me to survive the drug lord the day before, but my wife would have killed me if I told her what we did. However, when returning I told her what God did and all was well, and I look forward to help welcoming them all Home in Heaven. That night was a great renewed bounce for the entire team and by the end of our final ministry event we saw 1,054 souls won to Christ during the 2016 Olympic games in Brazil.

With the final night upon us and closing ceremonies started I elected to try to race out of town early. I had been in town for the opening ceremonies for London in 2012 but on this closing night of 2016 I was trying to resemble Elvis and leave both the building and Brazil. I was racing to the airport and there were threats that the electricity could shut down. Time was ticking but lately that had been the story of my life and as I got to the airport I ran through the terminal and got the last seat on the plane.

It was wild and I realized that several others had the same idea and I noticed I was surrounded by over forty-five Olympians that were on that flight to Sao Pao with me departing Rio. It was one of those "pinch yourself" moments and some were still wearing their medals around their neck and others had it safely hidden deep in their carry on bags. Either way, it resembled the bus ride home a couple days before with a common share of elation and joy permeating throughout the cabin. The only difference was this bus was now racing down the runway and we were now airborne in the sky and as we looked to the right, we could see the stadium aglow in the distance.

It was a short flight before a five-hour layover in Sao Pau and that was brutal. I was so exhausted, and I had been nonstop for a week and half. I was wearing a beautiful aqua blue jacket with the Olympic rings on it, and we all know that airports have the worse chairs in the world in a terminal. With the chrome arm rest between each seat, it is impossible to stretch out and sleep and being six feet, one is a tad more difficult. After nonstop ministry I did something, I had not done since a child, but I took of my Olympic jacket and balled it up to make a pillow and slept on the floor of the airport. Where is Mike Lindell when you need a pillow? In that moment, and on the cold floor of that airport I was a man without a country and half a world away from home but purely spent in service to the Lord. Better cold and alive on the floor than dead in a cold morgue with a toe ring. God won and souls were won but I was down for the count physically and drained spiritually and went to sleep 4,739 miles from home.

After a two-hour nap, I was able to throw water on my face and was on the first flight in the morning heading back to Washington. Indeed, God is greater than gold.

HOLDING PATTERN

FOR full disclosure, I have talked about airplanes taking off and landing in previous chapters but now we come to the proverbial holding pattern. Perhaps you too have been in the air only to circle the runway half a dozen times. It is a frustrating feeling when you can see the goal but are prevented from landing.

God was still blessing in life and ministry, but it was in fact one step forward and two steps back. I mentioned flights coming and going but now will like to unpack to you the "holding pattern." The Catholic Church promotes a false theory of purgatory, but the Bible is clear you are either in or out. Jesus even said in Revelation if you are lukewarm, I would spit you out of my mouth.

Ruth and I married on July 7, 2007 (07/07/07) and I joke I hit the jackpot with her and for a guy that has rarely gambled I won! However, when we married, I learned after returning from the honeymoon and moving into her house she had purchased while single, that one of her "friends" had sold her a bogus loan for her mortgage. She thought it was a thirty-year fixed loan, but we learned with horror that for several years she had been unknowingly paying interest only and it was negative amortizing. That is a big word meaning that the money she was not paying towards principle was now being added on the back of the loan every single month.

I had known enough in that business could hurt someone gravely if they did not know what they were doing. The pitfall was when the stock market crashed and housing market tanked, many folks could be left holding the bag and possibly homeless. Where she paid $257,000 for a house in the past with the additional money being added monthly to her note on the back end we were in a serious bind and downward spiral. We were fortunate to quickly see that despite her never missing a monthly payment towards the house now owed approximately $305,000! Nearly ten years of her paying what she thought was a debt down, it ballooned up. What made matters worse that when the market crashed the house was now valued at half that price! We lived in Maryland but all I could think of was the iconic phrase from Apollo 13, "Houston, we have a problem." It was nothing short of a miracle, but we were able to hold on to the house it resembled the Titanic because we were on a sinking ship. The only difference was the RMS was brand new and we were in a thirty-year-old house that needed repairs.

I often wonder what happened to that friend of my wife who misguided her just to get a commission and preyed on her while she was single. The good news was we still had a roof over our heads, but it was indeed an uphill climb. Fast forward a few years in the house while still traveling the country living on love offerings, it was stressful. Before leaving my Capitol Hill career and secure government job with great benefits it was easy to swing a house payment. The joke is as a traveling minister that sometimes you wonder where the "love" in the love offering is. The second real scenario was after leaving my job "by faith" was when I tried to get health insurance since leaving my federal job I was denied because of a "precondition health issue." I could not believe but all the health carriers were holding an on-the-job injury to my thigh and kidneys against me.

While remaining on the job I had the best insurance in a group plan, and they did pay for all the expenses of my hospital and therapy. I even got a green light to return but when God called me out, I had no idea that trying to pick up health insurance would be so hard. I was quoted over $1,300 per month to cover me and that was in 2007! I could not afford the coverage nor afford to get sick! We kept moving by faith and then a couple years later picked up some medical share plan that gave some coverage and in case of an accident you would still be admitted to a hospital. The bill would be shared with a pool of other clients and hope you did not lose the house. Ruth was always a hard worker and God had blessed her managing three Christian radio stations on the East Coast, but it was disappointing for us to realize that fact that we were upside down twice what the house was worth. It was not that we were ungrateful or keeping up with the Joneses, but we were honestly just trying to stay lock step with Jesus.

Thousands of souls had been won to Christ while I traveled the country preaching but a colleague shared years ago that just because you have a full calendar speaking, it does not mean you will have a full checking account. The irony is there is always one clueless person who wants to scream we are all in it for the money. Quite frankly, we were getting used to not having much money, but we were being obedient to the call. All my friends were easily making six figures annually with the government and some of my retired police officer friends were double dipping and one family friend was now making nearly a quarter of a million a year providing security.

It is not wrong to make money, but it is wrong to not be able to pay your house note. We wrote countless letters to the mortgage lender and told them our dire situation and with a perfect track record paying the bills on time would they be lenient and grant us a reduced mortgage? Some of my friends had just stopped paying the mortgage altogether but it was like playing "Russian Roulette' because you never knew if it would go well in your favor or cost you everything. I was raised if you signed a contract, it was your responsibility to pay it and after two years of no assistance it really got discouraging. We were trying to be faithful and fruitful, but finances were hit or miss and living just fifteen miles from the Nation's Capital is not cheap.

We both were working nonstop and blessing multiplied lives, but it was still tight financially, but I had start laying up my treasures above long ago. We may have a simple house here but by God's grace would probably give the Biltmore House a run for its money in Heaven. You cannot out give God and Heaven was looking sweeter each day. After a while it seemed that the banks and mortgage companies got a thrill seeing so many hard working and on-time paying customers like us struggle and it was apparent that they just did not care. We had submitted papers, documents, and hardship letters so many times that I felt like Staples was my second home because we kept running out of toner and ink to print their demands. Only for them to tell us they misplaced it or never received it.

Finally, after much prayer and perseverance some consolation came but their plan was not to reduce the loan to benefit us, but we would be forced to have a short sale and benefit someone else. The house that we still owed over three hundred thousand on now went to an investor for just over $110,000. The bank gave it to someone at a third of what we owed. The irony is he had no skin in the game and had not paid a red cent, but he was being blessed. Indeed, the rich get richer and the poor….

The one silver lining was the bank would forgive the income taxes on the loss and the debt where we were upside down on but honestly between an economy that tanked and the friend who set her up to fail with a horrible loan, the Lord honored us on the way out the door. The good news we were free but with the temporary stigma on Ruth's credit because the house was in her name, and she was making most of our income we could not run out and qualify for another house. Looking back, you can see God's provision and protection and I can honestly attest now that the "holding pattern" was the Lord setting us up for a big blessing.

However, when circling the runway of life, you do not always view it as positive. The new owner did not have anyone lined up to rent the house to and we were able to live another nine months in our old house. The blessing was because he bought it for pennies on the dollar our new rent payment was peanuts compared to what we had been paying on our mortgage. This allowed us to stay in the house even when we thought we were gone, and also able to both save some money and bounce back a bit.

While both working harder than ever and crisscrossing the country in ministry, we began to look for another home. The first one we found was a two-story brick colonial in LaPlata, Maryland. It was a beautiful home with neighbors with nice, manicured lawns and was listed right at what we could afford. We visited it, liked it, and put a deposit on it and then turbulence hit. The owner was demanding to see all our private financial records when our bank was approving us a loan to purchase the house. He began to play games and we did not feel comfortable disclosing our finances only for him to keep the keys and deed to his house while holding on to our pertinent information. As much as we liked the house, we had more to lose than play games with a guy that did not come across as sincere. God just liberated us from one place and did not want any problems at a new address. We had encountered strike number one on the new house hunt.

We did not have peace although we could see us living there but God shut the door. I almost felt like I was back lying in an ambulance and could almost hear comedian Jeff Foxworthy say in his voice, "Here's Your Sign!" It was discouraging but we kept pressing forward and praying daily. I would browse the home listings almost nightly on my phone as we were still in our old house now paying rent to another, but God was blessing even in the holding pattern. The year was late 2016 and we kept looking and I bet we looked at dozens of homes, but the market was hot. Either the house we loved was out of our range or it needed work or looked good online but show up and it is next to a septic field.

Ruth remained hopeful and we both worked harder than ever. We were still blessed with each other and where we lacked in finances, we were wealthy in faith, family, and friends. One night I came across a home that instantly looked familiar while scrolling through my phone and I recall thinking this is it! I told Ruth I swear I have seen this house before. The next day we made an appointment to see it and it was in my childhood hometown of Waldorf, MD. We had moved there when I was three and it was nestled in Charles County. It was a beautiful brick two story home, and it was on Trumpeter Court. For all my friends who love the 45th President this was a sign. Literally, it was the name of the street and when we arrived my heart was beating. The curb appeal was spectacular and as we walked up the driveway and rang the doorbell, I realized that indeed I had been to this house before.

My parents came to look at this same house twenty-five years before when it was the stunning model in the middle of the cul-de-sac and considered buying it. The door flew opened and we were greeted by a friendly realtor who was "sitting" on the house. It had beautiful floors with the massive two-story foyer and spiraling staircase, and I immediately remembered the step-down dining room to the right that featured a custom fireplace which was a nice added touch. What I also remembered and loved was the colonial columns separating the foyer and the dining room. Anything with columns not only inspired me and impressed me. Perhaps because both at The White House and Graceland had them and I loved since childhood southern colonial antebellum homes. We could not afford those, but this was just within our price range, and I told my wife and realtor what was around the corner. The Realtor was really impressed when I told her I knew the name of the home "Saratoga." She had to review her notes and she was floored! Literally, her mouth hit the entry floor in the foyer because even she did not know it, but I recalled it from a quarter of century before.

The special agent in charge with the US Secret Service was right when he said, "You would make one Hell of an agent." Friends said for years that my memory recalled things that everyone else forgot but when it came to people, patterns, and things notable or out of place we could hold our own. My father once saw a polaroid picture of a man that he had not seen in forty years and not only remembered his name but knew where the picture was after running into him again. Regardless, if national or my detective friends with the Charles County Sheriff's Office I could help teach their up-and-coming class. Ministry and politics help to have a great memory but most important genuine care for people. Honor and respect not only go a long way, but our nation was failing rapidly because those two traits were becoming less. I may not be able to tell you what I just ate for lunch, but I often recall the craziest details with names, dates, and faces. Math was not always my thing, but my memorization skills were off the charts.

The back of the house had a beautiful flowing floor plan and the windows to the back-yard were icing on the cake. We went upstairs and I was also retracing the steps I climbed years before and I am always looking for symbolism or where God may be leading. The fact that my parents loved the house and considered buying it intrigued me more to see perhaps this would be right for us now. The master bedroom was big and had a fireplace and hot tub and massive walk-in closet. I did not need to see anymore, and I was just praying that if it were God's will that the house on Trumpeter would be ours. While leaving we put in a sales offer and headed back home to our humble house. Looking for houses is a draining process filled with ups and downs and sometimes it is like catching lightening when in the market to buy. Just because you like it and qualify does not mean it was yours.

The last couple of years had been both incredible and devastating. We gave it to the Lord and about half hour later the realtor called and said, "Good news! It looks like they are going to accept your offer." You may recall in the movie "Christmas Vacation" after unsuccessful attempts to turn the lights on, Chevy Chase struck out again and again. It is one thing to fail privately but it is much more embarrassing to lose in front of your spouse, kids, parents, and in-laws. Right when it looked bleak and he already began to kick Rudolph and Santa, he tried with one more desperate attempt and the lights kicked on and the Heavenly choir sang in the background, "HALLELEJUAH!" It was one of the most epic scenes of the movie and the crowd went wild. They rejoiced with him because they knew how hard he tried.

We were ecstatic and could already picture moving into that beautiful home. The Lord was too good, and it was finally making sense. So many years of moving backwards and now blessed beyond our dreams! God is never in a hurry but always on time and just as I was fantasizing about moving in, we received another call from our agent. I was expecting her to give additional good news and details, but my heart dropped when she said, "We have bad news! Another couple just showed up and gave a full cash offer." What appeared to be our future home just minutes before was now no more. To say we were disappointed would be an understatement. We had a history with that house, and we were first but some in society still believed that "cash was king" even though we had The King of kings on our side but struck out again.

In baseball three strikes and you are out but we were now on our second and the air to our proverbial sails had dwindled. Ruth was really crushed, and our time was running out on the rental as well. The owner was ready to allow another renter to move in even though we paid in advance and I could not only see the handwriting on the wall but the sand swiftly falling through the hourglass. Time was of the essence and the clock was ticking in more ways than one.

Anyone can sing God's praises in the sunshine, but it takes discipline to praise Him in the storm. Ruth continued to shine a light at the radio station touching thousands of lives weekly both on and off the air. She was like a celebrity in the DMV (DC, MD & VA) region and I was still ministering locally and regionally representing the Billy Graham Evangelistic Association as well as my own ministry nationally. About two weeks later, I was scheduled to be in New York City to meet with an Ambassador at the United Nations for a couple meetings and the night before I came across another house online. When I saw it was as if time stood still and I had seen that house before over the years in my travels.

I recall over the years flying down that road and I would see that house and remember thinking, "that is a beautiful home." It was also a two-story brick colonial with a two-car garage nestled on one full acre and was the first home on the corner as you pull into the nice neighborhood. The other two homes were great, but this was at another level. The others had brick front and the standard vinyl on the back to save money, but this was one of the rare homes that was solid brick all the way around.

The home had just been listed that night and it was about ten in the evening when I saw it on my phone on the realtor listing. I had a five in the morning departure on an Amtrak train leaving from Union Station in Washington, DC to Penn Station in NYC next door to Madison Square Garden. I showed Ruth the online listing and bless her heart she was still so depressed from the last two strike outs that she did not even want to bother looking. It hurts when you have been hurt and it is human nature to guard your heart, so your hopes do not get dashed again.

I said, "Honey, this is the house! I can't go with you tomorrow morning because I am on that train to New York but promise me that you and Gloria our competent realtor will both be at this house at nine in the morning!" She said, "Frank why so early?" I said, "Ruth, I guarantee you that everyone and their brother will want to tour this house over the weekend, and they will be lined up in the morning." I then shared, "If this house looks half as good as it does in the pictures, I don't want you to call me but go ahead and put an offer before you leave the property." She said, "Why the rush?" I knew that urgency also sounds like emergency and time was ticking and we were almost on the street. To some we may have been out of luck, but we had all the Lord and just because you are down does not mean you are out! I said, "Because I am certain folks will also be immediately putting in a contract and a bidding war could go into the weekend, and we have to strike first." She rolled her eyes, but I could hardly sleep that night. I finally fell to sleep close to midnight only to hear my alarm clock wake me three and half hours later. I was out the door by quarter to four in the morning and once again I was flying solo but this time up the highway with no traffic heading into the city of my birth.

I arrived at the train station at 4:25 in the morning and after parking I was inside the iconic Union Station that is dead across the street from the United States Capitol. I greeted the friendly Amtrak clerk, and she gave me my ticket and then grabbed a fresh cup from Starbucks at 4:44 am and was now boarding the train to the Big Apple. After putting my leather briefcase in the seat next to me and my winter coat above me, I finally got seated in my coach class seat. For a man who was constantly on the move I loved the nostalgia of the train. Yes, planes were much faster and could fly higher but there is nothing like watching houses pass you by on the old school train. Over the years, I was fortunate to be a guest multiple times on Fox News and appeared in their NYC studio as well as Dallas, TX and twice on Capitol Hill.

Lauren Green is the Chief Religion contributor for Fox News, and I was blessed to be on her program a half dozen times and was once interviewed by Kim Guilfoyle formerly of "The Five" who was now dating Donald Trump, Jr. It was an honor to also speak on Sean Hannity's show one night and that was also taped in New York. You may recall I prayed since childhood that God would give me favor and a platform in New York and God put that plate on the table. This time I was racing back to the largest city in America for meetings and a private lunch with the Ambassador and friend.

While sipping my coffee and still seeing the homes aglow before the sun arose, I prayed that God would bless us as Ruth and Gloria went to this house in a few hours. Urgency is key and in baseball three strikes and you are out, but I had a friend once tell me that God liked bowling! When I inquired why they said with a smile, "because in bowling when you get three strikes it means you are on a roll!" Perspective is everything and after reading a book, listening to some music on my iPod and going over notes for the meeting at the UN I realized by my watch that it was after nine.

I was praying that God would guide Ruth's steps and give us favor with the realtor and owner and that His will be done that morning. A quick fix could be a big problem and time was ticking and this would be a grand slam if God gave us this home. About forty minutes later my wife called and she was so excited, and she said, "Frank it is gorgeous and even prettier in person." She told me as she was leaving and walking towards the driveway that the owner of the home pulled up in her new Mercedes. It can be awkward in a situation like this, but she was very cordial, and they briefly talked and said, "She was praying that a good Christian family would buy it and enjoy it as much as they had." They were the original owners and took pristine care of the home and property.

To their credit, Ruth and Gloria told their realtor they wanted to put in a contract for it and as she was leaving another couple was pulling in. I knew it was going to get wild with folks looking at the home. I loved both the interior and exterior and the lawn resembled a golf course with thick green grass and mulch around the trees with gorgeous rose bushes. The front door also led to the two-story foyer, but this home had brand new marble floors and custom drapes. The staircase towards the second floor had a beautiful brass chandelier suspended from that twenty-foot ceiling and the catwalk above allowed one bedroom to connect to the master bedroom. We had always wanted a hot tub and contemplated buying one at the other house we lived for ten years but the deck was do dilapidated that we were afraid it could not hold the weight of that tub so declined and kept dreaming.

As you step outside on the back deck you can see the nice green lot and a hot tub was bubbling in the corner. Ruth fell in love with the kitchen and the house was exceptionally clean and their children were grown, and it was evident that they took great pride in the home. It was exciting hearing Ruth's voice, but she was also hesitant to get too worked up because we had been let down one too many times. My train was now rolling into the station, and we prayed again and gave it to the Lord asking that His perfect will be done.

After hanging up I collected my coat and briefcase and was now with a spring to my step looking for a cab to take me to the United Nations. My friend picked me up a couple block from the iconic venue overlooking the water and it is situated on sovereign soil. I could not dwell too much on the house because I am now entering an important meeting, but I would lie if I did not daydream a couple times about that house. That day was a treat being at the UN and we made some great strides and my friend who works for the Ambassador and her girlfriend said, "The Lord told me that house is yours. It will get a little bumpy right before closing but the house is yours and it is done."

It is not every day that you get a word from the Lord like that with such certainty through another, but I was believing God with them and now after a full day in New York I was being dropped off for my return trip back on the train to Washington. Just like before, Satan began to run his mouth in my ear saying it was not going to happen, but I was trusting God that it was. My friend, Michael English is a Grammy Winner and has one of the greatest voices in the world. He won dozens of awards in both secular and Christian circles and very few could sing like this brother. He had a new song that was recently released called "He's Able." I had listened to that song repeatedly and his lyric of each verse was speaking life into my weary soul and we were trusting that God would make a way.

With every doubt from the Devil, I would counter and claim a promise of God from the Bible and kept playing that song over and over on the train trip home. The words touched my heart profoundly and the lyrics elevated my soul. The song says,

"Exceedingly, abundantly all you could ask or think according to the power that worketh in you; God is able to do just what He said He would do. He's going to fulfill every promise to you don't give up God because He won't give up on you. He's able!"

That song resonated deep within me and knowing that the days we could remain in our old house were drawing to a close. When the problems come is when our prayers and praises must go up and we pressed into God more than ever. When Lazarus died, the Lord did not race to the funeral. In fact, it appeared that the Master was MIA (missing in action). Mary and Martha were weeping and one of them scolded the Lord for being late insinuating with her hands on her hips I picture waving her finger in the God of the Universe's face, "If you would have been here my brother wouldn't have died!"

NEWS FLASH! Unless on the first train out of here on the rapture we ALL are going to die. The Bible says, "It is appointed for everyone to die and then face the judgement." The Lord to those on the outside looking in was not one day late or two days late and not even three but FOUR dates late. Some scholars have suggested that medical physicians say that the body not only stinks but begins to decay after three days. When the Lord showed up his friend was not only dead but decaying and almost decomposing. But when the Light of the world, Lover of my Soul and the Lord of Lords showed up, Lazarus had no option but to GET UP! The Lord is never in a hurry but always on time. God delights in resurrecting the dead, restoring the broken and offering rehab to the addicted. When the world says, "All hope is gone" the Lord shows up and shows off.

As my Amtrak car was bumping back and forth on the track at about 75mph that silver bullet heading back to Washington was moving! While listening to Michael's song for about the tenth time straight on repeat singing over and over, "He's able" the music stopped in my ears to notify my eyes that I was receiving a call on my cell. I will forever remember when Gloria's cell popped up and I answered it on the first ring and she said, "Frank we got good news! The owners of the house that Ruth and I just looked at this morning agreed to accept your offer. The other couple did in fact put in a contract but opposed to letting a long, drawn-out bidding war start through the weekend or longer, they are going to sell the house to you and Ruth!"

GOD DID IT! The setbacks, tears, frustration, delay and striking out with two other offers not counting losing our last house was God graciously setting us up for a big blessing. The word my friends in New York just shared was true and "the house is yours, but it will get a little bumpy around closing, but God will work it out." What a blessing and that last part was correct, and things got a tad dark two days before and bumpy before closing but God ironed everything out. We are grateful to Gloria and her husband, Ricardo for all they did, and the transaction would not have been possible without the guidance and generosity of my parents as well. As my train arrived in DC, I had the biggest smile on my face and in my heart and the Lord is faithful and He does not neglect His own. To God be the glory! Great things He hath done!

WELCOME TO THE NEIGHBORHOOD

THE Lord is faithful and indeed God is good. You may recall a country song that had a phrase, "God is good, but people are crazy!" There is a lot of truth to that statement at times and we are called to try to model Christ and love people even when they are not acting loveable.

We were so thankful to finally be released from our old home in Accokeek, Maryland in Prince George's County and had moved just six miles away, but back across the county line into Charles County in April 2017. It was my hometown where I had grown up, but I knew in advance that coming back across that county line would be both a blessing and burden. The Lord told me in advance that we would experience some turbulence and growing up through grade school and a proud product of public schools we were blessed.

I was the President of Student Government in middle school and played three years of basketball and crowned Prom King my senior year of high school of 1,200. Our colors for all three schools were blue and gold and that was a nice touch of continuity and consistency in my childhood years. Now that we started our own ministry very few are as patriotic red, white and blue as me and my family, but we elected the blue and gold for our ministry logo. It was a tip of the hat to remember my formative years and it is imperative to never forget where you come from.

After being a staffer at the national level of politics for decades and connections with folks around the world it can be inspiring to some yet intimidating to others. Maryland is known for our blue crabs which are loved across America as a seafood delicacy. What is interesting about crabs is if you throw them in a bushel basket the moment when one is climbing towards the top you get the rest at the bottom trying to hold you back with their claws. Personally, I think we all win when cheering each other on but the mindset of the Devil is selfish but the Christian desires to be selfless. God had blessed regardless over the years, and you do not get to the top by compromising, cheating, cut corners or clawing your friends to advance your agenda or profile.

All I have wanted to do was love God and love people but when you have a few folks that are trying to do what we did years ago some still do not know how to honor or celebrate another because they see you as a threat. Growing up I was among the most respected but lately at times I felt the most rejected but that is a sign of growth and of God stretching my influence. The Bible says, "Be careful when all men speak well of you."

To save money we did not have a moving company to assist us but we rented a truck and did it ourselves. You wouldn't think a twelve-mile commute back and forth from our old house to the new home could rack up so many miles, but we did. Partly, because we rented a smaller box truck, and my back was in excruciating pain after those endless trips getting our new home in order and moving out from the old. However, we were so thankful and thrilled and each time we pulled up into our new driveway I had to pinch myself to see if it was not just a dream.

God had been too good to us, and we were looking forward to growing as friends with our neighbors around us. The neighbors across the street were a wonderful couple and very gracious and she was retired from the Department of State. We had several friends in common and it was always a treat to connect with them. On our second Saturday in our new home, we were watching a movie as a family, and we were all sitting on the couch. It was about ten at night and the doorbell rang and I thought it was a tad late for someone to be on our front step. We were not expecting any company and none of us ordered a pizza, so I sprung up to go to the door and no one was there. I was at the door in less than fifteen seconds after it rang but nothing or no one was present. In the dark I looked to the right and left and nothing. Came back inside and then looked around back and nada.

After coming back in the house, I went to the garage and opened the door and a red car with its high beams was just sitting there at the bottom of my driveway. The irony is when I approached the car just to say 'hello' and see who it was, they threw the car in reverse and sped off. That was a little odd, but I went back inside and resumed watching the film. That night we went to bed in our new happy home and for the next week or so I could sense something off in our home and neighborhood.

We continued to be grateful of the blessing God bestowed to us and usually when someone moves to town you tend to get a few waves of welcome or someone to drop off a small gift but that was minimal. One sign was when I was outside by our mailbox and a neighbor at the end of the street walked by and I said "Hi" hoping to break the ice and exchange greetings. If looks could kill, she murdered me. It was as if she burned holes through my head and with an iced cold stare, she kept on going.

For a guy who was voted "friendliest" in elementary, middle, and senior high in his class for next to twelve years growing up, for some reason we were having a hard time connecting with those on our street. Two nights later exactly at three in the morning someone was banging on our living room window just below our master bedroom. Faster than a Ferrari I raced down to look out despite my eyes trying to get adjusted from being awakened out of a dead sleep and I could hear two people laughing in the dark as they ran out of the bushes. Last time I checked; "W" was no longer near DC but I have some "friends" in the dark at night who came to get out the vote with the bushes! That was interesting and when folks are playing games that early in the morning you know something is off and someone is not right.

It was the Lord's Day and after coming home from church with the family I was thinking hopefully some of the odd behavior would cease tonight. For starters it was a Sunday and second the next morning was a work and school day. Part of the reason our country is in the state she is in is folks do not honor others nor respect authority. Ruth and I were still finishing with some final touches to make our house feel like home and went to bed about eleven that evening and what are the odds but exactly at three in the morning once again they were back. This time they were banging louder and began to play on your emotions.

The next day I came home and about five feet from the side of my driveway in the grass I saw my Billy Graham business card with my name and contact on it. What was interesting, it was torn in half and for gangs and folks who like to harass that is an age-old technique of intimidation. It was their minor league way to let me know that someone was on our property and did not appreciate us back in town.

My family had protected Presidents and world leaders and stood toe to toe with folks with less than stellar intentions and I was not going to let some local losers push me. Jesus was not a weakling but warrior but still trying to extend grace and kindness to all we meet. In the next week on two different occasions; we had either run errands or one night went to have dinner in a restaurant but both times upon returning you could tell and feel that someone had been in the house.

We had locked the doors, turned off all the lights and shut down the televisions but both times when we returned, the lights would be on and something intentionally seemed out of place. While staring at each other in disbelief and searched the rest of the house only to hear noise upstairs we found our fifty-inch flat screen television in our master bedroom was not only on, but the volume turned up loud! This is all right after moving into our home!! I saw part of the movie "Poltergeist" briefly as a kid but walked out of the theater in the middle and I did not like it then and did not care for it now.

The very next day we did what should have done on day one and change the door locks. A week later I was having breakfast with my former boss at a Cracker Barrel in my hometown. Deputy Chief Thompson has recently retired from the United States Capitol Police and was at the time working as a security consultant in the powerful office of House Sergeant at Arms. He knew the Capitol as well as anyone and it was super having breakfast with him. We met frequently both on and off The Hill and often talked about life, family, ministry and sports and our time in DC. We were both blessed to make some special friendships and we both enjoyed keeping in touch. Chief worked with my Dad when my father had his position, and he was also a respected friend of the family and distinguished leader in his own right with an incredible career with the one of the best police departments in the world. It was my honor to officiate his beautiful daughter's wedding and both he and his wife are first class.

Over breakfast I shared with him about the new house, and he was so happy for us. It takes maturity and self-confidence to compliment others and Chief was always a blessing to me. While eating bacon, eggs and their famous hash brown casserole I shared briefly about some of the odd behavior around the house. Our time was almost up, and he had to head back to the U.S. Capitol for work but to his credit he wanted to come by the house to see our place. He knew how blessed were but also knew the heartache of securing a home the last couple years. Just as I picked up the tab to pay for our meal and leaving a tip while turning to push in my chair, I noticed our newly elected Sheriff sitting right behind me and said hello. He was wearing a nice red polo shirt with a badge on his chest, and I do not miss much. The irony is Chief affiliated with the national police department did not see him, but I pick up on almost everyone and everything. Plus, he had a lot going on at Capitol Hill and it is another world dealing with billion-dollar budgets and every other person in the hallway is a national leader. However, Sheriff's in their space have great power locally but soon we will see who is for Christ and the Constitution or will cave and cower to communism.

After proceeding to pay for the bill, retired acting Assistant Chief Thompson followed me to my home. I just said hello to our top cop in the county and now one of the best in the country was following me home. At times, I drove Chief while in DC in one of our US Capitol Police cars but now, we are together again. Upon arriving he complimented us on the house, and we are most grateful.

It was an honor to have him inside and when we walked up the driveway towards the front door, he was gracious and impressed with the home and landscaping. When I entered the door with Chief in tow to my surprise, we found Ruth who was disoriented had just got up with help from our son and she had fallen completely down the steps.

With her back sore and ribs in pain she said that she had been on the floor for several minutes before Andrew found her at the base of the steps. We both were worried about her, but she was embarrassed that was not the welcome or greeting she would have desired to give my former boss and friend. Ruth is outgoing and the queen of hospitality but on this day, we were doing our best to welcome her and make her comfortable. It was comforting that one of America's top cops was in our foyer and when we finally needed a good policeman he was already in the house! Ruth still trying to hold back the tears and catch her breath said, "I was at the top of the staircase, but it felt like a man came behind me and shoved my back and pushed me down the steps."

Ruth has never been one to see things or misinterpret what was reality, but the fact is only she and Andrew were in the house, and she experienced a force from behind push her down our two-story foyer and she landed below on the marble floor. She said it was not like I was carrying laundry and missed a step, "I genuinely felt a push from behind!" Chief and I looked at each other and relieved she was ok, but we had never seen anything like that but after welcoming him inside the house we gave him the quick tour. We had worked our way upstairs in my office and he was enjoying seeing some of our mementos I collected from Washington and around the world and Ruth had called me on the phone. I paused to take her call and she despite being in pain was already outside getting ready to leave in the car to go to work and said some guy outside was asking unique questions. One of them was, "is anyone else home?" "Can I speak to your husband?"

Chief and I headed down the stairs and curious to see who was outside. The first thing I noticed was an older green Chevy Suburban. It was a large SUV but had seen better days and the second thing I noticed fifty feet away was the out of state tags. With the number two DC police official over my shoulder, we both picked up immediately the Colorado license plates. It was a younger African American male behind the wheel and the first thing I said to him was "you are a long way from home."

I noticed a computer like keyboard all over his dashboard and it was not the DeLorean from Back to the Future nor an unmarked police car. He looked nervous and said he was doing some "research", but I also knew in my spirit was that he was canvasing and monitoring our home and was looking for intel that would benefit him more than me. I was born in the morning but not yesterday morning and was not going to allow this misguided brother to take the lead, so I had him take out a pencil and proverbial piece of paper and was getting ready to take him to school. After politely but firmly letting him know, we were not interested we wished him well and he left and Chief looked at me and said, "that was really strange." Our tour was cut short, and he had to leave our house to go to the House of Representatives and had to bolt. Later that same evening the same Suburban came back but when he saw me, he was too afraid to make eye contact. Plus, he was doing fifty miles an hour in a twenty mile per hour in a residential zone. The guilty are often in a hurry and do not like to look you in the eye. A few hours before he is camped out waiting for me but now that he is back and driving like a bat out of Hell, he pretends he was Ray Charles.

In subsequent days we did not see him but an avalanche of students about college age were going door to door trying to sell us home security. I could tell by their pressing questions they were trying to see what we did and did not have and with our recent visitors banging on the windows at three in the morning they very well could be coming back when we were out of town. The Bible says, "Let your words be few" and I could just tell something was off about them and the entire sales pitch. The same folks that push fear are trying to sell you a remedy and I was old enough to see through the insincere. That is why when the "pandemic" would come three years later I had seen Satan's schemes too many times. Repeat after me, "The Devil is a liar!"

For the next couple days, I noticed that cars would be sitting on the side of our property sometimes at great lengths of time. We noticed utility trucks and cars that were not from our neighborhood, but they just seemed to park on the edge of our property. I realize that a plumber or electrician could have been just wrapping up at a neighbor's home and park in the shade on the side of our house to stall time before their next appointment, but it seemed like we were being monitored and a magnet for some reason.

At that time, Ruth was starting to feel uncomfortable, and I was as well but as the man of the house I didn't want to show my cards. That evening as were ready for bed I recall thinking of all the bizarre behavior around the house. We still absolutely loved the house and knew it was a gift from God but the turbulence that He forewarned me was a tad tougher than I was expecting. Truthfully, it was much more than I was desiring. It has been said new levels bring new Devils and that is true. Anytime God promotes you one can expect pushback almost instantly. This was more than pushback if Satan had his way, he would have bulldozed our house.

I had recently met Pastor Jentezen Franklin at a worship service, and he is an authority on both fasting and spiritual warfare. He wrote bestselling books on both, and I had devoured one and was wrapping up an incredible read, "The Spirit of Python." He talks about all the ways that Satan schemes and slides his way in people's heads, hearts, and homes.

That night while sleeping I had a dream and the Lord showed that a long black snake was on the far-right side at the end of my driveway near the street. In all my years, I had not had that one before but in the words of Indiana Jones, "I hate snakes!" Some dreams you forget and others you wish you could, but I took note and perhaps God was giving me a heads up. The very next day, Andrew and I were playing catch on the side of the yard when a black truck pulled up in front of our house. It was four that afternoon and I tend to pick up on people and patterns and when new folks arrive unannounced, or something is out of place I take notice. It could have been the century and half of law enforcement and detectives in my blood line that flows through my veins, but I have an antenna that picks up on frequencies that most could not detect. Plus, the Holy Spirit is the greatest Special Agent of all time and when we are in tune with God the Trinity reveals what is pure and what may be a problem.

The second thing I detected was the black pickup truck did not park in my driveway but in the middle of the road with his hazards flashing. The only one causing a hazard was him and at first, I thought it was someone coming to talk to me about my lawn. I had inquired about a respected local lawn care company to come out to help our yard stay dark green and healthy and figured he showed up in his personal vehicle. My game with Andrew temporarily ceased as I walked towards the driveway to say "hello" and when I asked him if he were with the lawn company, he rebuffed it as if that was beneath him.

He then told me he was a neighbor that lived at the end of the street and wanted to say hello. I figured we were now entering the three-month mark but better late than never. Often, I am the one out front being kind and accommodating but we always prayed to be a ray of hope wherever we go and maybe he was taking the initiative. However, with his car in the middle of the street and condescending towards the occupation I mistook him I had a quick feeling that he was less than sincere. The fact that he was standing exactly where the black snake was in my dream the night before was another sign and after the third flag I really was listening.

We shook hands and I looked him in the eye and then he ripped into me and said, "So you are on staff with the Billy Graham?" I said, "Yes sir." He had white hair and appeared in his mid-sixties and then with machine gun fire, "Did you vote for Trump?" I told him I served on staff with both national parties and enjoyed serving them over the years, but I could tell he was fishing and then I switched gears. Jesus had a unique way of answering a question with a question and after he paused, he defiantly said, "I did forty years with the Treasury Department." Without missing a beat, I said, "Great! We have some dear friends with Treasury" hoping to find some common ground. Without saying it my dear family friend and former boss was Assistant Secretary of Treasury under President Clinton. For decades, the United States Secret Service was under the umbrella of Treasury and now Homeland Security.

He already showed me that the local lawn car guy was beneath him but now he was insinuating that both the Secret Service and Homeland Security was not at his level. He pompously said with his hands on his hips "I was with the IRS!" He then scolded, "and my wife did 40 years with the IRS!!" With a smile and not to let him rattle me I said, "Great! My godmother was a GS-15 with the Internal Revenue Service and how high did you climb?" He paused for a second and back to Treasury I told him, "I worked for four years for Congressman Steny H. Hoyer in both his Waldorf and Washington Office." His eyes grew big and almost with a sinister sneer said, "I can't stand Steny Hoyer!" I replied, "I love him, and he went to the junior prom with my Aunt Barbara Shelton at Suitland High School in 1957." It was almost as if the blood went out of his face and his eyes grew wide.

Without question, I was voted the nicest in my class but even Jesus had to flip a table or two. Kill them with kindness is mostly the approach we take because a gentle answer turns away wrath but sometimes you must beat them at their game. He then walked past me and now standing uninvited inside my garage. The word of the day is #Trespassing. He was scanning for anything or everything and with or without the IRS some folks are trained to lie about their political or religious affiliation. I am not sure if he were looking for political banners, but he was just "off" and out of tune and he continued to rant and he is now hovering over my car. The Lord blessed me with a 1992 Corvette that I have driven only six hundred miles in four years. Most do not even know I have it and Tiger Woods had a multi-million-dollar yacht called "Privacy" and I have a thirty-year-old Vette that on rare occasion drive to get fresh air.

His eyes were now completely fixated on the car and then proceeded to show me a picture of his car not to be outdone on his cell phone. He said with pride, "Do you see this car?" I am a lover of cars and said, "Yes that is nice!" The truth is the car was nice but had seen much nicer, but I was trying to appease him and still be friendly particularly on our first conversation and I said, "looks like a 1968 Firebird." He then said with a Cheshire cat grin, "Do you know how I got it?" I said, "No, tell me." He replied, *From a guy who wasn't paying his taxes and I confiscated it.*" I remember thinking in my mind, "This brother needs Jesus!" Plus, not only is it inappropriate for agents to seize property for their personal gain but to boast about it would be both unethical and no class. He then showed me another car and I interjected that is a 1980's era Corvette." If he were looking to beat me on a pop quiz on cars, I would run circles around him. He said with his chest out, "Yep! Got that one the same way too." He then took another long look at mine and I could tell what he was thinking, and I said, "God is good. It's already paid for and I am giving it to my son as a present when he gets older."

I had met his kind before, and they would hurt others to get ahead. The fact is you do not get ahead living in reverse. I finally got him heading out the garage and we are standing back out on my driveway. I asked him if he went to church and he mentioned two different local churches and I mentioned both their pastors' names and he immediately switched the subject and said, "Lately I just sit at home and watch televangelists." I remember thinking,

"Good! Keep watching me preach and you just might get "born again." He then said looking up at me, "My wife has a unique gift to listen to people and while they talk, she takes mental notes." He then placed his finger in his mouth like a lure to a fish and said if she hears anything "fishy" she makes a report. If either one of us hears something out of the ordinary than we just make a call back to our friends at the IRS and we send a little audit in the mail. He then closed, "I would like to drop her off at your house so the two of you can get acquainted." At that moment I remember thinking two things, "what man would drop off his wife at another man's house so they can talk alone?"

I am six foot one and he was about five seven and with me standing toe to toe I was that much taller than him standing at the top of the driveway, and I replied, "I'd love to meet her one day but unless your wife now works for FedEx or UPS, we won't be accepting anymore packages." As he was heading back towards his truck, he told me he bought another brand-new truck, and she had an Infinity SUV. At this juncture, I did not ask nor care but it was obvious he was insecure, materialistic or both.

He then walked up to Andrew who was eight at the time and heard the entire conversation and stooped down towards his eye level and said sarcastically, "Don't play in the street. People get hurt in the street." He was trying to seem sincere, but it was like fingers running down on a chalk board. The irony is he was the clown parked in the middle of the street blocking traffic with his hazards on flashing in the afternoon sun. What we accuse others is often where we are guilty, and I began to add him to my prayer list because he was a few fries short of a happy meal plus I do not think he smiled once in our conversation. Perhaps God was revealing to us that he was the one to watch out for. The fact that he was standing in the exact spot as the snake the night before left little room for doubt.

It was at that moment after several crazy encounters that I finally felt as if Satan was saying, "Welcome to the neighborhood!" I took the high road and said, "Good to meet you" but it is a fact that oil and water don't mix and when he left about two minutes later, I looked at Andrew and said, "Come on buddy we are going for a little walk."

Andrew grabbed his plastic Nerf gun and we started walking down the street to visit some of the "neighbors." You guessed it we headed straight towards his house at the end of the block and when you met Jesus and "Rambo" as a youth you acquire some of their boldness as an adult. If you listen to someone long enough, they tell on themselves and sometimes you give someone enough rope they will hang themselves. It probably looked comical that Andrew with a water gun and I were heading south towards the end of our street, but we just wanted to check things out. Plus, while he was boasting to me minutes before in my driveway, he had just told me all his cars and cards that would be parked in his driveway. Indeed, some folks are not playing with a full deck. It was easy to find his house at the end of the caldesec and sure enough some of his toys were out front.

I will never forget his next-door neighbor who was watering his lawn out front saw Andrew and me walking, and it was as if he did a double take and could not believe we came down the street. His mouth dropped, his eyes grew wide, and his garden hose went limp. If they thought I was just a spineless preacher at the top of the street than he failed that exam. However, my daughter's middle name is "Grace," and I am looking to extend an olive branch as often as possible and whispered a prayer for him whatever his intentions. I knew in my heart that was a confirmation from the night before. Plus, sometimes when someone lashes out at a Christian is because they are upset with God but taking it out on you. Regardless, of one's age they are too small to honor others. I have also seen instances when someone told a lie about another, and others were gullible enough to believe it. It could also be out of jealousy and some folks have a hard time complimenting. Others are like a junk yard dog and just trying to mark their territory. He and his wife probably lived on the street longer than anyone now that the couple we bought the house from recently moved. He may have heard about my resume and wanted to let me know that he was somebody too. Thanks to God we are all somebody but as we walked back, I knew were not finished yet.

Two days later, I was boarding a flight to Silicon Valley in sunny California and was invited to spend a couple days with Ron Kardashian. He picked me up in a beautiful black six figure Mercedes and once again it never fails. Talk about "keeping up with the Kardashians" I had one personally pick me up in his luxury car curbside at the airport giving me the VIP treatment, yet I have a neighbor who cannot even make us feel at home in our new house. The greats are gracious, but the rest need some work. It has been said, "winners are wonderful but the wannabes you have to watch out for."

I was reminded one time a couple years before, I preached a funeral in my hometown at a country church in Maryland and a woman yelled at me but the very next day I was on a flight to Santa Ana, California to preach at Trinity Broadcast Network to their world-wide audience. The funny thing was I was picked up in Jan Crouch's personal chauffeured black SUV and they were thrilled to see me. Sometimes you must be rejected locally before God can use you globally and it hurts at first but helps in the long road. Jesus was correct, "A prophet is with honor everywhere but his hometown." God must really be using me and expanding me because now I was having a hard time being accepted on my own street. It gets dangerous quick when we start to believe our own press clippings and the only person God cannot use is the person full of himself. It was still a blessing for me while preparing me, but they still will have to repent and give an account to the Lord.

Over the years, I have met some clergy who are so competitive and carnal that they would ask members of their circle or congregation to try to spread lies and undermine others. You cannot represent God and use the Devil's playbook and expect the Lord to be pleased. You cannot act like Hell to accomplish Heaven and God gave me a word if you are a pastor but cannot say "hi" to another pastor than you may be an imposter. #DropTheMic

Ron Kardashian rolled out the red carpet and he has friends everywhere and I forever will appreciate the kindness he lavished on me while in town. He took me to the nicest hotel in San Francisco and with his connections they gave me a tour of the Presidential Suite and I had never seen a hotel room like that. In fact, as we walked out on the balcony of that top floor suite looking over that high rent region, I learned that was the same balcony that Sean

Connery filmed a scene from "The Rock." I can still hear his trademark voice, "*Welcome to the Rock*!" What was interesting I had guy down the street that could not even be polite and welcome me to the <u>block</u>.

In my spirit, I knew something was brewing back home and sure enough when I returned would you believe I had a friendly letter from the Internal Revenue Service. In all my 45 years at the time I had never once got a letter or been audited. I have had professionals for years do my taxes and you do not get ahead cutting corners. Plus, when your parents exude the highest integrity, I feared God and them more than doing something wrong with the law. When I opened it, they said we owed $2,000 from a past return! I called my accountant, and she was confused. The fact is we were in the right and as an ordained minister we are entitled also to housing benefits and the truth is we have probably paid too much over the years.

I called my godmother the next day who worked for the IRS, and she was livid. She said, "Frank, no IRS agent has the right to show up at your house or business unless you get a letter in the mail first. Secondly, they do not get to acquire any assets that are seized. Third, regardless of if he were still on staff, retired or impersonating one that is a serious problem, and we all know the wheels move slow with government. I was trying to give the benefit of the doubt and most form letters from any agency can take weeks to generate. However, it is extremely suspicious that having been paying taxes for nearly thirty years at the time and never in just shy of 11,000 days ever received a letter from the Internal Revenue Service hinting of any audit and a week after my friendly neighbor's "welcome to the neighborhood" visit I get a letter.

If they were trying to see if we were square, we passed with flying colors and they would be embarrassed to learn we were not two million, two hundred thousand or even twenty thousand in question but two thousand dollars that technically we were not in arrears. Opposed to bringing in the forces I went ahead and paid a payment plan to resolve the alleged amount they said owed. For a year, he began to resemble the young man with Colorado tags and was afraid to look my way. However, I was told to take the high road and always be willing to forgive when wronged. It could have been a huge misunderstanding but either way Satan used a guy down the street to try to play with us. Regardless, if it was our windows being banged on late after the midnight hour or televisions turned on after off while away or a torn business card on my property, I was not going to give the Devil any victory.

A mentor told me long ago, "Frank you will go far in life as long as you don't let others make you bitter." For each car that drove by or jogger run near the house I just waved and smiled. Billy Graham when asked how he handled his critics he laughed and replied, "I out loved them and then out lived them." Good advice and I was going to do the same.

EUROPEAN VACATION

FOR years I had been a huge Chevy Chase fan and his debut on "Saturday Night Live" and films like "Fletch" were classics but National Lampoon's "Vacation," and "Christmas Vacation" were EPIC! Initially I was not a huge fan of the "European Vacation" edition, but it certainly had its comedic moments, and I was now getting ready to live it.

The past couple weeks had been a whirlwind and I had felt like a I was thrown in a washing machine and was starting to wonder what side was up or down. Between nonstop ministry and the subliminal surveillance around the house it was growing emotionally exhausting. My next trip to preach was not one but back-to-back trips to Europe in less than a week! Flying across the pond is one thing but add another trip plus the spiritual warfare at home and abroad it can drain your battery quick. Over the years, I was starting to think I should get "hazardous pay" for the stuff we put up with and once again and worth repeating there is always someone in the crowd that swears, we are in the ministry for money.

Less than seventy-two hours before my departure from Dulles Airport to Bucharest, Romania my wife was talking in her sleep. So much that it woke me up and she began to scream "They are breaking down the back door!" It was obvious she was having a nightmare and I was trying to gingerly wake her without her frantically hitting me next to her thinking I am one of the intruders. She said while almost out of breath, "Frank, they were trying to come in the house!!" I inquired who and she said two men and God had already revealed the snake in the driveway on a recent night before and after that came to pass, I now have a confirmation from my wife that we need to ramp up security.

The catch is I am scheduled to fly once again alone to Europe, but I cannot leave my family vulnerable while on the road or at home. I had seen "Rambo II" three times in the theater as a kid and I am now I am applying some of it as an adult. One of my favorite scenes was earlier in the movie when he received the orders from Colonel Trautman to fly solo to Vietnam and look for American prisoners of war. The catch was he was not to engage the enemy and only take pictures! With the clock ticking, the plot thickening and his biceps bulging he began to scramble and his assemble his arsenal. Just as Billy Graham may have or not have heard the ROCKY trumpets when he told his nurse, "I just need one more sermon" the irony is I was hearing the RAMBO soundtrack as I now began to secure our home with the clock ticking. Urgency had been a theme and song on my personal playlist for some time and now you may be start putting the pieces together.

I feverishly studied, shopped and with a friend's help installed several security cameras around our property. Truthfully, it was part anointing and adrenaline, and my wife will verify I do not ever recall working that quickly as I did in that three-day window before my flight. Despite some of the recent distractions, unwelcome visits and folks trespassing on the property I not only had to pray up but man up and layer up. Now with Ruth more concerned than ever I was a Ferrari with no brakes to help safeguard the family.

My friend is a master electrician, and he was helping install our security cameras and I know God is ultimately our alarm system and my friends in Delaware said, "ADT security stands for Almighty, Divinity and the Trinity" protecting us." So true! While installing another camera above the front door overlooking our lawn I picked up on another neighbor. I had recognized his car but not had the pleasure to meet him officially. He must have gone to the same failed summer course with the other guy because he also parked out front with the hazards on. That was the first flag! Since I had already taken a walk and inventory with Andrew after the first incident, I knew he was neighbors with my other new "friend." You know something is wrong with them when they cannot get along with the nicest around.

The second red flag was we have these things in America called *sidewalks* and they are a nice addition and been around for centuries. What piqued my focus now was not just his vehicle in the road with the hazards, but he is now running across my manicured front lawn as he too parked in the middle of the road. Most folks would have "keep off the grass" but because I value friendship more than vanity, I let it slide. Where the first neighbor parked blocking the driveway the other was on the street out front of my house.

By scanning the neighborhood on occasional walks to exercise and make sure folks were on the up and up I knew he lived three doors down from the other guy. What really picked up my internal antenna was with the similar Cheshire cat grin as the neighbor before and both their smile looked insincere. What confirmed it as he too was trying to welcome me to the neighborhood, he was more focused on the brand of security we were installing. He was intent at staring at the empty box on the ground than looking me in the eye and giving me the right hand of fellowship. Perhaps he had friends who had supported the "Bushes" lately and I do not mean 41 & 43.

What was odd after seeing the brand of our security camera immediately ran back across our lawn once again bypassing the sidewalk and left promptly in his vehicle. I knew long before his vehicle had tags with the DC police logo but when your family has been in the major leagues you can pick up on those also in the game. We had two retired DC detectives on our street, but my grandfather was a captain and chief of detectives with Metropolitan Police. He would have been their superior in both cases not because of race but resume and rank. Sadly, we live in a culture today that does not respect authority nor always plays by the rules. You can cancel all you want but you should add class while you are subtracting. Plus, you can cancel culture, and continue to try to handcuff the Church but you cannot cancel Christ.

Now with just a few hours before my flight and knew more than ever time was of the essence. Perhaps you are finally getting an idea of the title of this book because it seemed as of late everything was urgent! It was touch and go and for the first time in my entire ministry I was tempted to miss intentionally a flight. In my Spirit I was really concerned that something could happen while I was gone and as an evangelist being used mightily of the Lord to help save the world, I am not sure how I could handle if I lost one of my family while gone. You have heard of whistle while you work well; we prayed around the clock with not a second to spare and reluctantly packed for my flight later that night.

We had even checked for tracking mechanisms under the wheel wells of my car because more than ever it was obvious, I was being monitored. The guy who drove daily a Member of Congress to and from his work and on occasion one of the top cops in America and been invited to some cool places was under someone's watch list. It is ok because God told me years ago that when it got late in the Game of Life this would be par for the course.

I recall racing to Dulles airport after kissing and hugging my wife and son "goodbye" that with each mile like never before was tempted to return. Just like going to Vice President Biden's son funeral when Satan was imploring me to go back the Lord was telling me to keep moving forward by faith. I remember being on a phone call with my friend who works at Andrews Air Force Base and does the President of the United States of America flight schedule for "Air Force One." He is a strong Christian brother and dear friend and he prayed for me as I pulled my car into the airport parking garage and jumped out of my Lincoln

SUV. Our family was friends with the former President and with a tip of the hat to our sixteenth commander in chief my daily driver was a Lincoln.

I was already soaked before my long flight overseas and looking back it was a miracle how we were able to accomplish what we did in just over two and half days. I was hoping to have more peace of mind with the cameras installed and security implemented but we all know that nothing can completely safeguard you apart from God's protection. The late, Dr. Jerry Falwell said frequently, "God's man is virtually indestructible until He is done with him." I was starting to wonder how much time we had as a world collectively and me personally. I grabbed my carry on luggage and I had learned long ago to travel pretty light and started racing across the busy Dulles parking lot like the 80's arcade game Frogger only to safely check in for my flight. Plus, being an international trip requires extra time and after getting my boarding pass, went through security and took a tram towards my gate.

My heart was pounding, my mind was racing, and I could not help being concerned with my family back home. I recall being on a call with a friend from Nashville and we both had our pulse on where our society was racing. She is also a nationally known communicator and we have been friends for twenty years. Several times over the years we had shared the pressure of not only being censored but could sense we were being monitored individually while on the road ministering.

I recall vividly one time while on the phone our call dropped off three times in a row. We could not help but think "big brother" was listening in and that is why it is imperative to live clean nonstop. The Bible is clear, "be sure your sin will find you out" and my dear friend is a former NFL chaplain, and he preaches repeatedly, "make sure your backstage aligns with the front stage." What he is implying is that we cannot live a double life and folks are looking to silence any voice that speaks or represents Truth.

Now at my gate despite the Devil whispering "go back" I felt the Lord was saying, "Frank you be about my business, and I will be about yours." It was as if God was saying you keep preaching and I will keep providing and protecting your family. After boarding the flight, I worked my way back to my seat and my friends joked so much at times I have traveled so much that my U.S. Air Marshal friends almost thought I traveled as much as them. With my background in politics and law enforcement I could also pick up out of a lineup plain clothes officers or agents. However, over the years it felt like I was being monitored more than ever. You know you are from Washington when you not only know the names of Presidents and Members of Congress but pick out of a crowd special agent with the United States Secret Service and you not only know their name, but they know you! It has happened many times!!

After finding my seat and throwing my lone luggage above me I sat back, turned off my phone, fastened my seatbelt and whispered a silent prayer with my eyes open asking God to take it from here and protect Ruth and the family back there. I was going to have to trust Him more than ever and nine minutes later we were wheels up heading to Romania. After an uneventful flight my dear friend, Cornel Ilioi from Arizona met me at the Bucharest airport and his smile was a welcomed sight. We became dear friends on Facebook, and he is a native of Romania but had me preach for him four different times in Phoenix, Arizona. I had the honor to even preach at his nephew's funeral and he told me multiple times he wanted me to preach for him in his homeland. Some folks promise the moon, but this brother delivered, and I was invited to preach at multiple events in their country.

Dr. Billy Graham had an entourage when he came to town, and it was almost like a presidential arrival when arrived. He had an advanced team, security team, accountability partners and friends accompanying but for most of my ministry it was me and my three friends – God, The Father. Jesus, The Son and the Holy Spirit." I probably resembled Rambo more than the revered reverend because like the U.S. Marines you do not need a lot of them to get the job done! However, once we got in the pulpit the Gospel machine gun opened and more often than I could count friends would tell me they could hear Dr. Graham's heart and at times his voice on my message. The fact is it was God's Heart because we both preached the simple Gospel but there is only ONE Billy Graham.

After a long flight with next to no sleep I was able to finally crash in a comfortable hotel. Cornel had become a cherished friend to me, and he is one brother that I can be real, relax and even share some concerns. Very few know the enormous pain and stress that comes from being out front in the Lord's Army. Some in the crowd think you are on an ego trip; others think you are in it for the money and some throw rocks at you from the sidelines. What no one knew was I had just left one of the most stressful weeks of my life and I am flying clear to Romania in a communist country thousands of miles from home and I was going to preach my heart out night after night only to receive ZERO compensation the entire time on the ground. However, I knew the Lord called me to this ministry and all my years on Capitol Hill, interacting with Congressional leaders, vast lineage in law enforcement almost unparalleled going back to President Lincoln and linked with the Billy Graham Evangelistic Association enabled me to have a unique perspective on current events. Plus, I could preach the Gospel with clarity and tie the two together.

Many folks see the hour on a platform publicly but do not see the pain and price privately off the stage. Joyce Meyers is a well-known minister and she said she received many letters over the years saying, "I want to be like you" and she laughed, "No you don't! Others see the hour of Heaven while ministering but not the twenty-three hours of Hell." God has blessed tremendously, and we had seen scores come to faith over the years and we give Him all the glory, but the call comes with a price. More than ever, I am just a mailman delivering His mail and intentionally trying to stay close and clean to the Lord.

Looking back the hotel I stayed in Bucharest was a beautiful place with its own unique charm. It can be a little daunting at times traveling overseas alone but despite the turbulence as of late at home it was a brief respite on the road. Make no mistake my mind constantly was tormenting me, and Cornel was as always, a calming comfort. His counsel over the last ten years have been a welcomed gift and his heart is bigger than his five- and half-foot frame. His beautiful bride and their family are the salt of the Earth.

Time was ticking and after a nice meal overlooking the hotel balcony and a great conversation, we prayed there in Romania that God would indeed have His will be done. That He would use me as He saw fit on this trip and that souls would be saved and encouraged. One common denominator I have noticed that at times when we are empty personally is the time, we are most full of God spiritually. Better to be full of Christ than full of self. Plus, we resemble Jesus when ministering from broken place. Cracked pots leak water and broken Christians tend to ooze out Jesus when the storms of life hit.

We raced off to preach at my first church while in their country and it certainly has its beauty but there is still in the air despair from years of oppression. When I arrived at the church I went off to a small room and shut the door and asked God to use me. The service had started, and the crowd was nearly packed, and I preached, and the Lord was in that place. Several years before while preaching at Romanian-Pentecostal Church at the invite of Cornel in Phoenix, Arizona I will never forget ministering on a Sunday night. The crowd was packed, and I was preaching with a translator and when I finished it was a slight pause and then people started coming to the altar. I noticed both Cornel and another pastor was crying, and I thought they were upset with the service, but he told me, "Frank, you don't understand in our Romanian culture they rarely respond to alter calls! Your sermon tonight touched them, and we are most happy."

God gave me great liberty while preaching and the Lord over the years gave me a unique love for folks wherever I may be. President Ronald Reagan said, "the camera doesn't lie" and I knew that to be true. Regardless, if preaching in Israel, Africa, Egypt, Jamaica, El Salvador, Canada, England to name a few it was like I could adopt on a dime. Not because I was a chameleon or charlatan but as an Ambassador of Heaven my desire was to be a conduit for Heaven's love to flow through me while connecting with them. If it would just start working at home again like in high school that would be great. I can still hear Elvis Presley's stepbrother, Rick Stanley who told me in my car once as I dropped him off at Ronald Reagan National Airport, The King of Rock n Roll's little brother by Vernon's second marriage said, "Frank, folks want you to do good -- just not really good!" He was right but I was like his brother with the Lord's help, keep "Taking Care of Business!"

We had a phenomenal service and folks were invited to attend another church service where I would be preaching and many of them came! The food was always nice, and the folks made me feel at home and many of the leaders wanted to talk about living in the United States and my experience on Capitol Hill. Later that evening, I was taken to preach at one of the larger churches in Bucharest and it was an honor. It was a large indoor facility adjacent to their massive sports coliseum next door.

Prior to my message that night they were baptizing two dozen people and it is always exciting to see folks in their journey with Jesus. Once again, Cornel was by my side, and I would not want anyone else to translate for me as we shared the platform. He had repeatedly and selflessly opened doors for me and despite his smaller stature he was a giant to me in the ministry. It was God that brought us together. A couple years before I posted I was open to preach that Sunday and if anyone were interested, please respond. Immediately, I got a reply from a man he said, "Yes! We want you to come to my church."

It was a Wednesday and because the date was on Sunday, I was thinking someone in a 100-mile radius would reach out but when I checked this man lived in Arizona! After politely reminding him, I was 2,500 miles away he said, "We want you! I have been following your ministry for some time and we would be honored to have you." A man in his church worked at an airport and they flew me that weekend and our friendship has been great ever since. That church that had to cancel me back home was a Divine Appointment and those various trips to Phoenix since now have me preaching on this large stage in Eastern Europe.

At times, Mark Zuckerberg at Facebook has taken enormous heat, but I do want to thank he and his staff for helping multiplied millions at one time connect with friends and complete strangers. It can be a blessing and burden but on this connection with Cornel it was a grand slam. As I was en route to the Sunday evening service the Lord impressed on me to preach a message on Hell. That is not the most popular topic among preachers today but the Lord made it clear to bring the heat now so others could miss it later.

God was all over the sermon out the gate and with Cornel side by side with me and his rapid translation keeping up with me the Lord used us both. A translator can make or break you and Cornel always came through and when I gave the invitation, we had a great response to the altar. One woman came up to me with tears and pointed to a man and said, "The first man to respond to your message tonight is my brother." As she stammered with tears streaking down her face she said, "I have prayed for years that he would give his life to Christ. He was no doubt on his way to Hell but your message revealing God's love made the difference! Thank you!!" At this juncture we both were crying, and I found out later that the man who was saved was a multi-millionaire and folks were rejoicing to hear he was no longer bankrupt with God. Poor is the person whose only wealth is in their wallet.

After back-to-back preaching in multiple churches that day I was invited afterwards to participate in a wedding ceremony. I have now had the honor to preach a funeral, help officiate a wedding and preach revival for my Romanian friends and so thankful for Cornel who opened the door. Truly, it takes a big man to promote others. It had been a whirlwind and after a brief tour of the city and one more speaking event the following day my time in Romania was already up. Sometimes less is more but I had to hit the States but no rest yet.

In three days, I was scheduled to preach in Paris, France and looking on the map they are relatively close and both in Europe. However, I promised my dear friend, Dale Dukes in Delaware who hosts the annual Sussex County Prayer Breakfast that I would be his keynote speaker. The year before, I was present when my buddy, Bill Alexson the dean of NBA chaplains was the main speaker. For over twenty-six years he was the chaplain to the Boston Celtics and we both served at the 2012 Olympics together in London. With a promise that was made, and my parents taught me your word is your bond I was summons back to the First State in the United States and was heading back to the airport.

One last meal with Cornel and a hug goodbye I was heading back to America. The long flight back was tiring and no, I did not sleep much but the moment I landed I raced straight from Dulles Airport in Virginia just outside of Washington to Delaware. I did not get into my hotel until midnight that night and my body clock was off because of jet lag. After a dozen hours flying and nearly three more to Delaware, I finally got to bed about two that morning only to be up four hours later to speak at seven to seven hundred people. Nearly two dozen politicians were present along with pastors and civic leaders from that great state.

It was an honor to address that capacity crowd and with next to no sleep and no time to waste I preached the simple Gospel message, and we had a dozen souls trust Christ! Dale is a great leader, and his family is incredibly special to me. He graciously surprised me and took another love offering for me and truth be told I needed it because after preaching for free in Europe every bit helps. He told the crowd that I just landed from Europe last night and flying back tomorrow to France. Where was the Concorde when you needed it? All joking aside, I could not afford it but it sure would have made travelling a tad easier, but Christ did not call me to Easy Street. Promises made and promise kept and sometimes my heart is bigger than my head, but I would not have done it differently.

After working the crowd and connecting with some dear friends I was out the door for my three-hour trip home, and I resembled a muffler. Why? I was EXHAUSTED and three times during the morning drive back I had the window down with air in my face trying to keep me awake. With little rest and no chauffeur once again, it was God and me and Carrie Underwood sang, "Jesus take the wheel" but I was doing most of the driving! Upon my arrival, I was able to finally sleep in my own bed and the next day was washing clothes from that trip and packing my suitcase for this one. The blessing was Ruth was accompanying me on this trip and they say you cannot go to Paris without taking your wife. Our church graciously helped provide for Ruth to go with me and it was a treat that I was not traveling alone back to Europe.

This time with time ticking we were not flying out of Washington, Baltimore, or Virginia but Philadelphia, Pennsylvania. Our dear friends, Mike, and Lisa Neifert with the invite of their pastor, Bill Breon from Delaware opened the door for us to minister on this trip. If I recall on this trip, I let Ruth do most of the driving while I tried to get a few winks in, and we caught up with our friends after going through security. We grabbed dinner in the airport, and we would be flying with British Airways on a jumbo 747 jet. It was a beautiful plane, and we would stop for a two-hour layover in London.

Mike and Lisa are incredible, and they are wise beyond their youthful years. They also had a huge heart for evangelism and missions but also knew the sting of folks hurting them in church. They are among some of the most anointed people I know but sadly even in ministry folks can be jealous and they along with Cornel and myself could relate to being overlooked at times, bypassed, or misunderstood. Indeed, God often uses the foolish to confound the wise and those were rejected locally are used by God nationally and globally. I said it before but reminding myself and you as well. If you think Satan is going to give you a free pass you are crazy, but God is faithful and crazy about you!

We took a picture of the four of us in front of the big plane moments before boarding and we were now departing the US heading to the UK. Since childhood, I loved to fly. It was always a thrill for me, and I am still amazed that those massive planes filled with people can get off the ground. It was a double treat for me to get on the iconic 747 and I have been blessed a few times to board the current "Air Force One" and that Boeing 747 is second to none, but it was a treat to be on this one. The 747 are not in service as much as they were in the past and it was getting rarer to fly on them, but I still think they are perhaps the most beautiful.

We found our seats and the four of us were all in one row towards the back. Matter fact we were about three quarters of the way back of the plane but literally our chairs were leaning up against a wall partition. It was no way to lean our chair back and another flight across the pond in less than a week I knew while still on the runway before takeoff that this may be a long trip. Over the years, the thrill as a child of flying was now like the sand in an hourglass slipping quickly and had taken a toll on me. It was therapeutic on this trip flying with my wife and friends and not one to complain it was a boost for me personally to have their company.

In 2012, I mentioned I had the honor to spend almost ten days in England. Many of my African American friends told me that when they went to Africa for the first time it was like they had been there before. To an extent, I could see what they were saying my first trip to England. Some are familiar with our heritage linked in Washington and interacting with U.S. Presidents, but our family originally was from England. In fact, The Shelton family is a family that was once prominent in the English gentry and based in Norfolk. Their family seat was Shelton Hall. John De Shelton, the first Lord of the Manor, was born c. 1140. It is said that Nicholas De Shelton was among those barons presenting Magna Carta to King John, while Sir Ralph Shelton was knighted for his services to Edward III at the Battle of Crecy (1346). In the Tudor period Sir John Shelton, the twenty-first Lord of the Manor, and his wife Anne Boleyn Shelton were entrusted with the custody of Princess Mary and Princess Elizabeth as children, partly because Anne was the aunt of Queen Anne Boleyn and the mother of Mary Shelton, the mistress of Henry VIII during his marriage to Anne. They reached the peak of their influence during the Tudor period, when Mary Shelton became the mistress of Henry VIII.

For those tracking my thirteenth great grandfather, 21st Earl Sir John William Shelton (born 12/12/1472) married Lady Anne Boleyn (born 11/28/1475). John William Shelton was the Uncle of Queen Anne Boleyn Shelton (second wife of King Henry VIII). A special thank you to my Mom, Sharon Shelton who not only worked at the U.S. Capitol Historical Society in the 1960-1970's but our official historian at home and most grateful for this information from my Dad's cousin, Danny Mitchell's daughter Pamela for all her research to connect the dots.

We were not only linked to President Lincoln in the United States but the Queen in the United Kingdom. Not linked politically but biblically and spiritually as kids of The King (JESUS). Henry VIII married Anne Boleyn (Shelton) not once but twice. He married her, divorced her, and then beheaded her and lately on the road both home and abroad I had a few who wanted to knock my block off at times too.

Had I stayed with the United States Capitol Police I would have been the sixth consecutive generation Washington, DC police officer in our family all the way back to 1850's. The Shelton Family that came from England have been also traced to various parts but mostly near Nottingham, region where Robin Hood was from, and they are recorded to have been some type of law enforcement too.

It was a treat to see Buckingham Palace while in London during the Olympic summer games and I had just met a friend in Africa who was friends with the current Queen. I was not invited to have tea, but I did have several cups of coffee to keep me going on this flight now with Ruth, Mike and Lisa.

We had not hit 33,000 feet and the captain just removed the seatbelt sign when the passenger in front of me slammed his seat back and pinned my knees. Mike, the forever champion of compassion eyes grew big and was willing to let the guy in front of me know that I was in a tough spot for a long flight. The fact that we could not recline due to our seats up against the wall made me look like an accordion. It was almost comical if not so uncomfortable, but I had to remind myself that I am a servant not a celebrity and just because my lineage goes back to presidents and queens, I must represent The King.

I politely waived Mike off and did not bother the man in front of me and the next couple hours politely endured it until our plane touched down at Heathrow. After deplaning I probably resembled the Hunchback of Notre Dame, but I was slowly starting to stand taller with each step off the plane and for a guy who resembled a question mark I was back in England to help share The Answer.

Ruth and I ducked into a cute airport store, and they tend to all look alike around the world but what caught my eye was a beautiful replica tea set from Buckingham Palace but after seeing the price I figured it looked better on the display table than our home. We were able to grab breakfast and after finally back to vertical we boarded our flight to Paris. Once again, we were air born and this time our seats in commercial were fine but with all my travel and more and more internationally it really is hard on the body. Those who make fun of those flying "First Class" are either frustrated they do not have the funds or most likely do not travel for a living. You start racking up flights coast to coast and halfway around the world it really is hard and comes with a price literally and physically. I have never demanded first class but if someone wanted to bless our family or ministry with an upgrade, I would NOT want to rob them of a blessing! #HelpABrotherOut

Over the years, I had flown 20 hours to a destination only to immediately preach after my feet hitting the ground and going through Customs. At times, I was half dead before climbing up to the pulpit. Satan is already attacking relentlessly, and rest goes a long way. When you are fatigued, tired and running on empty the Devil can really play games with you. We can all do things we regret when going too fast, too long.

We had a great time the first day and I was still borderline sleep walking, and it is hard to be "on" with nonstop travel and not one to intentionally be rude the bigger the platform the more people can expect. I have had to adopt Jesus' model more than ever and disappear and get alone with God. We are not good for anyone if we are never alone with Him plus,

He allows us to rest and find renewal. We stayed in a guest room in Paris of friends that we just met through Mike and Lisa and we did our best to try to rest but at times I struggle on the road sleeping.

The next day we went to the church and met some local leaders, and we had a meeting with the pastor and local preachers. It was an honor to talk to them about evangelism and encourage them to consider hosting a revival, but it was like pulling teeth. Lately, I noticed that not only were some of our churches asleep, but the clergy were as well. They had no sense of urgency and yet I could feel the walls closing for some time and I knew we did not have forever to reach the world for Christ. Time was ticking and most pastors were not genuinely looking for revival.

I was doing my best to hang on during the meeting but the back-to-back flights to Europe and preaching in Delaware in less than a week was almost more than I could take. I could tell I was beginning to get sick, and I went upstairs and found a hidden room with a couch above the church and layed down. When my wife and friends checked on me, I had already developed a fever and was quickly getting ill. My body started to shut down and I had push myself hard over and over and probably could have got up and preached but sometimes a leader needs to know when to step aside and let others step up.

After prayer, I think I surprised them but said, "You three take this service" and they did a super job. Ruth and Lisa shared their testimony and what God meant to them and Mike gave an encouraging message, and they just naturally flow in ministry. Everyone told me afterward they loved it and I was able to finally show up at the end and gave a brief word and extended an invitation and a Muslim had come forward to repent of sin and trust Christ as his Savior. Mike, Lisa, and Ruth were ministering to all those who came forward and laying hands on all of them and it was so rewarding to see them in their element. Plus, when you are part of a great team, we all have interchangeable parts. Everyone was happy and I was still struggling, and I finally found another bed back at the home we were staying in France and slept for 23 hours straight! I was down for the count and felt much better after sleeping through an entire day of my life.

They have some delicious bagels in France, but I will forever recall eating French onion soup at a cute restaurant in Paris. The soup was splendid, and the fellowship was sweet but what was surreal was staring at the iconic Eiffel Tower two blocks away. It is a magnificent trophy in architecture and the back story was it was despised by the locals when it was built. Mr. Gustave Eiffel along with Stephen Sauvestre, Maurice Koechlin and Emile Nouguier, respectively built the famed tower standing 1,063 feet at its tip. The massive steel structure was completed in 1889 and was built for the World's Fair. The citizens of France initially perceived it as an eyesore and demanded that it would be dissembled the moment the fair was over.

Ironically, what was considered worthless became the symbol of Paris and what was once looked upon as a disgrace helped put them on the map. The morale of the story is if you are going to stand tall in coming days you need a track record of being overlooked a time or two.

Jesus said, "be careful when all men speak well of you" and I have been in ministry, politics, and life long enough to realize that the very ones that were falsely promoted to the top or considered the chosen one often is not only lacking in leadership but missing in action when the game is on the line. Truth be told, many are now not even serving or in the picture.

As we dined eating our French onion soup in France the four of us in our lives had been blessed but bypassed and could relate to the lone Eiffel Tower and Christ's statement, "a prophet is with honor everywhere but their hometown." Again, sometimes you must be rejected locally before God can use you globally and looking back, we would not change a thing. We were not trying to be famous but faithful and keep sharing the message while time was still on the clock.

Before wrapping up with our table for four with the Tower to our left aglow in the almost midnight hour, Lisa shared something that made the hair on my forearm stand up. The night was late, and it was still June 26, 2017, but this put me on the fast track instantly. She shared about a friend of her who the year before was at a Bible study in Delaware with her pastor and his wife. A woman shared in that inner circle that she had information that trains were already being implemented with handcuffs. The information that she heard resembled passenger cars from the outside but when you viewed inside almost all the chairs had been removed. No food car, no dining area and no business or first-class seats.

She said what made it eerie was that it was a sole solidary steel pole the length of the cars from the ceiling and folks would be jammed like sardines holding to the rail above. I had traveled enough at home and abroad to picture that immediately. Regardless, if a tram on the runway to or from an airport or on a crowded bus or METRO train in DC or the MARTA in Atlanta I was familiar what it was liked to be packed with passengers holding on for dear life to a steel pole above while the vehicle moved.

What got my attention was when she turned the conversation from just being inside with a bunch of strangers holding a steel pole to her mentioning handcuffs had shackled everyone to that above. Interesting! Lisa quickly went on to elaborate that after hearing that detailed conversation from her friend began to have reoccurring daydreams and occasional nightmares about that possibility. Several months later one of her son's friends came over their home and the conversation somehow got on the end times, persecution towards Christians and a host of other topics. Lisa shared to her son and his friend about the conversation the previous calendar year about what she heard about trains being equipped with handcuffs.

Immediately, all the blood went out of her son's friends face and he said, "How did you know?" Lisa expecting some outlandish pushback or the roll of eyes like you have lost it now was opposite and said a second time but with more passion, "How did you know??" Lisa replied, "My friend told me from a Bible study." He countered, "You know what I do for a living right?" Lisa curious said, "No!" He said, "I am a welder and we had received a shipment of thousands of steel handcuffs and we already started installing those cuffs to the pole in trains that you referenced." Both of their eyes popped out of their heads and mouths dropped and he elaborated, "When I asked what we were installing his supervisor shot back that they were for future prisoners."

The Bible says, "In the last days that evil will be called good and good would be called evil." I too have been having occasional nightmares for the past six or seven years. As our ministry expanded and the platform was getting bigger, I could sense the proverbial walls caving it. At times I would see a UN or military like police force coming door to door and taking key Christians and leaders from their home and detaining them.

I recall watching a movie that came out in 1998 called, "Enemy of the State" starring Gene Hackman, Will Smith and Jon Voight and it was about an upstanding American that was deemed his own government's enemy and they began to falsely accuse, harass, and chase him. While in the theater that day my hair on my forearm stood up then like it did when Lisa and her husband, Mike told Ruth and I in Paris about trains equipped with handcuffs. That day at the theater nearly twenty years before (1998-2017) I felt as if the Holy Spirit whispered to me while the film was playing, "Frank that could be you and some of your Christian and patriotic friends one day who would be deemed an "Enemy of the State!"

Ray Boltz, a Christian singer who I always admired his music and saw in concert with my mother sang a song four years before that movie (1994) that became a huge hit, "I Pledge Allegiance to the Lamb." The video has millions of views on YouTube and that seven-minute miniature movie showed that in the last days about choosing to honor God or the government. They would have to choose to follow the Master or be marked for not taking The Mark of the Beast. The faithful were willing to die for Christ than live a lie on Earth.

Eventually, he and the other saved saints were confiscated and handcuffed by a government police and the rest would be history. Then and now it was a confirmation that our days were numbered, time was short, and the sand indeed was sliding out of the hourglass. #Urgency

The French Onion soup that night was still the best I ever had but starting to think it resembled more of the "last supper" than a luxury dinner dining next to one of the world's most iconic edifices. Just as Eiffel was rejected locally and loved globally in a short irony of symbolism, we all knew our assignment. With time ticking, as we wrapped up and begin to leave without a saying a word as we walked towards the car with our respective spouses, I knew that we too would have to stand tall like the tower and glow like a nightlight in the last days as a beacon of hope and truth remining folks to get right with God because the King was coming. Plus, live or die we would do our best to research and preach the Gospel to all who would listen.

After a wonderful evening we headed back to our host home we stayed for our final night in France before departing in the morning back home. Back-to-back trips to Europe for me in just over a week and my spirit was strong but my body was growing fatigued. With little sleep but happy to be on a plane with friends we waived goodbye to Paris and now racing down the runway to return to the United States. Sadly, most had no clue what was coming, and leadership indeed is lovely but lonely and the future was going to get bumpy.

I joked naming this chapter "European Vacation" because despite the privilege to travel and see beautiful people, cities, and architecture it was not always a vacation for me personally. Professionally, it was exhausting and when God starts elevating a man or ministry others get nervous including not only foreign governments but my own as well.

OUT OF AFRICA

AFTER adjusting upon returning and still being alert to subliminal harassment locally I still pressed into God more than ever to complete the assignment before me. Without question, I knew probably more than most ministers how urgent our times were. Over the years, I had some well-respected Christian leaders of large churches even hint or flat out tell me I was wrong or worse, wasting my time desiring to reach lost souls as an evangelist. They were not only clueless but callous, but I prayed for them regardless.

The calling of the evangelist was lonelier than ever and the same churches that said revivals do not work are often the same ones that saw little Kingdom growth. Just shy of ten thousand churches in America the year before did not baptize one person in one calendar year. They would run a full-page press release when a church saw nine saved at a Vacation Bible School but could not comprehend when a guest evangelist saw over a hundred walk the aisle after a single sermon. Dr. Billy Graham was right that many sitting week after week in church were never born again.

Knowing full well the clock was ticking, and the proverbial sand is racing through the hourglass I knew I could not change the thinking of clergy and convert lost souls simultaneously. Like Nehemiah in the Old Testament when he was up building a brick wall, he did not have time to come down and hold a press conference or debate those who were asleep at the wheel. The Lord told me in love to wish them well, keep building and remember Lot's wife and "don't look back!"

With every opposition on Earth comes Kingdom promotion and those who have been blinded by their own ambition or jealousy and unable to see your worth in the present will eventually need and realize your value later. Please do not think I am being dismissive but transparent. I have been tasked to also mentor and disciple other ministry leaders and upcoming evangelists and it is a lie to think that you will encounter no pushback, opposition or hate mail when you are delivering God's love letter. Read that again and marinate on that.

Just because you get blindsided, chewed out or falsely accused does not mean to stop and certainly is not proof you are wrong. In fact, you must be moving forward in the right direction when the religious camp and jealous crowd get rowdy! In the wise words of Rocky Balboa, *It ain't about how hard you hit, it's about how hard you can get hit and keep moving forward.* That's how winning is done !"

At this juncture from the Fall of 2017 to the New Year 2018 the door was opening to bigger and bigger speaking venues. In a previous chapter I wrote, "When God starts blessing the Devil starts messing with you" and it is true. I have also seen the opposite true that when Satan is messing the Lord is fixing to really bless you, but either way we cannot be ignorant of the Devil's devices. Mark this down: deception, division and disinformation are the Devil's calling cards and it is a playbook that he has executed since the beginning of time.

Several months before we moved into our new home, I want to show you a blessing. The past five out of six New Year's Eve I had preached at various celebrations. It was always coupled with great worship or praise music, and I would be one of the closing guest speakers. As an evangelist from the moment, I was starting with my opening joke I was already thinking of Jesus and when beginning my introduction in my mind I was already heading to the invitation. Dr. Billy Graham believed that the invitation was the most important part of the service and if you listen to some of his past sermons, he was pointing people the entire time throughout his message about Christ, His Cross, His Coming Again and you have a CHOICE today to accept Jesus or reject Him. He often proclaimed that "Today is the day of salvation."

The first two years I am referring I had the honor to preach back-to-back New Year's Eve in Poplar Bluff, MO. My dear friend and former World Wrestling Champ Nikita Koloff, "The Russian Nightmare" had connected me to his dear friend and mentor in ministry, The Rev. Ronnie Dean "The Preaching Machine." It was instantly a match made in Heaven and we are all three close friends. It is worth the price of admission to see us together doing life and ministry. The best part is just cutting up and having clean fun.

Both years in Missouri bringing in the New Year was super, and we had packed crowds both times and while most of the world is watching the ball drop in New York I was someone lifting the Gospel and drawing the net to see souls saved. The next two years my dear friend, John Bush (mentioned previously in the "sweet home Alabama" chapter) opened the door for me to preach at the Big God Conference in Myrtle Beach, South Carolina. For twenty years, Evangelist Dean & Gayna Forrest and their awesome son, Jeffrey hosted arguably the largest two-day New Year's conference in the old Ronnie Milsap Theater just miles from the beach.

It was a speaker's dream venue, and it was state of the art with nearly 2,000 seats including balcony seating and I had the honor to preach back-to-back years. Each year they would bring in the most respected bands in Christian music and always have one or two guest evangelists and Jeff Smith a well-known comedian in youth circles. Ken Freeman is a legend in evangelism and public-school assemblies, and he was booked almost every year and was loved by all.

My first year flying to speak at that conference was exciting and Big Daddy Weave, Hawk Nelson and For King & Country were the three bands during that two-year tenure. One of the toughest days of my ministry was my beautiful daughter, Hannah was scheduled to be with me while in Myrtle Beach but at the last second, she was invited to Disney and as she and her friends went to see Mickey I felt like Goofy.

What no one knew as I stood to preach to that massive crowd was there was one front row seat empty out of the entirely sold-out venue and it was reserved for her. As I prayed backstage for strength backstage with a hole in my heart the size of Houston, I preached to two thousand teens and the one that mattered most could not make it that night. Ken preached first and I followed and between the two of our sermons when I gave the invitation, we had 166 souls born again that night. What may have been even more interesting is we had nearly nine hundred respond to the altar car to grow closer to Christ in the New Year. While I was giving away Heaven publicly, I was going through Hell privately, but God does use broken people.

After returning home that was now four New Year's Eve services in a row while preaching on the road between Missouri and South Carolina. The Lord deliberately had me stay home and rest and spend time with the family the next year. On New Year's Eve I was lying in bed and saw an almost viral video of a friend of mine on Facebook. Pastor Chuck Balsamo is a giant and lives in Virginia and pastors a thriving church and in a world of cubic zirconia he is the real deal. I saw this man preaching at a massive stadium and he resembled a young Billy Graham. As I watched it was a sea of people as far as the eye could see and I learned quickly it was the iconic Nelson Mandela Soccer Stadium. It had to be over 100,000 people crammed in that massive venue and the President of Uganda was also on the platform with him. He was one of the only white brothers in that service and he was representing a small delegation from America.

My heart jumped with excitement when I saw him, and I was glued to my tablet on my chest while I was home for the first time in five years on New Year's Eve. The crowd was electric, and the atmosphere was jubilant and there is my buddy bringing the Good Word. I wrote on his Facebook page under the video and thousands had already watched with hundreds of comments below. As quickly as I could I wrote, "Pastor Chuck, I am so proud of you! God is using you in AMAZING ways and I couldn't be prouder of you."

About twenty years before, I was ordained at Cresthill Baptist Church in Bowie,

Maryland and I shared with some friends and deacons in the congregation that the Lord showed me I would speak to a sea of people as far as the eye could see. It was not arrogant but accurately sharing what the Lord showed me and the crowd was African American. One or two may have rolled their eyes but the others did not doubt.

As a child, little Johnny's teacher asked him what he wanted to be when he grew up and he replied with a grin, "a professional baseball player" and everyone laughed. In middle school his teacher asked him again what he wanted to be and after starting and staring for his Little League team he replied, "a professional baseball player" and a few laughed. His senior year when asked the same question by another teacher and after just winning the State Championship he said, "A professional baseball player" and no one laughed! Johnny Bench went on to play for the Cincinnati Reds and became one of the greats to play the game and today is in the Hall of Fame.

A month after I had commented on his video, Pastor Chuck called me out of the blue and I was happy to hear from him and quickly answered. I complimented and was so happy for him and he told me the whole story how God gave him favor and opened that massive door for him and he said something that I will take to my grave and anyone with a heart-beat and head screwed on who desires to be in leadership needs to take notes of this next conversation.

Chuck said, "Frank, you know that video basically went viral." I replied, "I know I was one of them watching." He then said, "You know it got scores of views and hundreds of comments." I said, "I know! I was one of them." He then said, "I am calling to thank you." I was thinking, thank me? What did I do? He said, "Frank I went back and read the comments twice and you were one of the only other ministers who took time to celebrate what God was doing and complimenting me on the biggest stage of my ministry." I was floored but my mind reminded me of a conversation I had with Elvis Presley's stepbrother, Rick Stanley. While dropping the King of Rock n Roll's stepbrother off at Reagan National Airport to fly back to Tennessee one time, he looked at me while sitting in my passenger seat and said, "Frank do you know the one thing many ministers won't forgive you for?" That was a unique question and I started running down a laundry list of sin and character flaws and said, "Drugs, Adultery, Cheating" and he interrupted and said an emphatic "No." I went on quickly, knowing time was ticking and he had a plane to catch and threw out, "Lying, stealing, boasting" and he said another firm, "No." He looked me square in the eye and basi-cally said, "If you are ever more anointed or successful in the ministry than they are, many will hold it against you."

My mouth dropped and I realized shortly afterwards that he was right. Too many see other clergy as competition and not colleagues and I would rather die a cheerleader prema-turely than live long and be a critic. #ThatWillPreach

Pastor Chuck said, "Frank, out of all those comments on my Facebook page with my recent visit to Uganda you, to my knowledge, were the only other preacher friend that complimented me on that stage at the biggest door of my ministry." My heart dropped!

Could some clergy truly be insecure and clueless failing to compliment but also thankful that I passed that pop quiz. I reminded him again how proud I was of him and told him I was cheering him on.

Fast forward eight months and Pastor Chuck called me at seven in the morning. It was the week of Thanksgiving, and I was still in bed, but something told me to not let it go to voicemail. I answered trying to pretend that I had already been on a treadmill, had breakfast, took a shower and on my second cup of coffee but he could detect that I was still at Bedside Baptist! He said, "Frank, I know it is early, and you are not going to believe this, but I honestly thought my sermon last year in Africa was just a onetime event. I went to my mailbox yesterday and I open a letter with a flyer in it with my picture on it with the stadium in the background! I guess this is their way of inviting me, but it is less than a month away and I can't back out now!!" He then elaborated, "The reason I am calling you now is because when you selflessly complimented last year I am thinking of you this year! I am going to call the host of the stadium event in Africa and ask Dr. Joseph Serwadda if you can come preach with me to over 120,000 people this New Year's Eve!"

At this juncture, my eyes were out of my head; my feet were now on the floor and my heart rate was up as if I had been on the treadmill an hour and on my FIFTH cup of coffee. In the last chapter, "European Vacation" I tipped my hat to Chevy Chase but in the Christmas Vacation you may recall when he finally got the lights to turn on and lit up the entire block and drain all the electricity in the Windy City the chorus "Hallelujah" came on and it was magic to his ears? That happened in my home too!

Within weeks, we scrambled and trusted God and He took care of everything from a sweet couple in Alabama who paid for my flight to Uganda. Robbie and Tracy Whigham from Choctaw County blessed me, and God used that couple to help me get to Africa. We met at another tent revival in Alabama and where I had a few misguided ministers try to block me, this couple resembled Christ and blessed me. We went from Roll Tide to Roll Jesus!

The Lord enabled me to get my passports and vaccines in record time and even had some spending money placed in my hand as I went to preach "by faith" on December 27, 2016, to fly to Uganda. I had seen it a million times in my head, but the Lord showed me back in the summer of 1998 after being ordained that I would speak to a sea of people at a stadium event. At the time, I was not sure if it were the Bahamas or Jamaica, but the crowd was dark skinned, and you could see their huge smiles and dark faces, but I wasn't sure where they were at the time.

After kissing my family goodbye, I met Chuck at Dulles Airport with his awesome son, Coree who is a world traveler and missionary with incredible insight and a huge heart for others. While going through security I met Eric Newberry from Ohio who sold real estate by day but had a heart for missions as well. The four of us were "high as a kite" and like kids opening our presents on Christmas morning. Mark this down: there is no high like the Highest.

As we boarded the massive jet and found our seats, it was a dream to be on the plane heading to Africa to preach to the largest crowd of our ministry. It was all grace, Chuck's generosity and to think if I were "too small" to compliment him months before I would not be on the runway now racing towards liftoff to preach in Uganda. It is worth repeating but "Who you respect is who you attract" and "If you don't see it before you see it then you will most likely never see it."

Africa is half a world away but despite the long flight, the hope in our heart made it more bearable. The flights had been taking a toll on my body for some time, but it is an honor to be spent in God's service. If one is to be exhausted in any work, may it be in doing the Lord's assignment and it is never time wasted. While we were nearly 40,000 feet flying east about halfway into our flight, the Lord impressed on me, "Frank do you trust Me?" I knew it was the prompting of the Holy Spirit and I said, "Yes Lord." He then said, "Change your sermon."

Immediately, I knew what that meant. I had been in ministry long enough that the Lord was stretching me, and He got me this far and He opened this massive door and now I had to be totally vulnerable and get out of the way. Even preachers can wrestle with the flesh, and I had to lean into FAITH more than ever. Satan was reminding me, "It is going to be in a stadium with over 120,000 people. You don't want to bomb in front of everyone preaching a new message you have never delivered, do you?"

Satan has been lying since the Garden of Eden and I had to kick that slimy snake out of my thoughts once again, and I proceeded to pull out a pen and paper and whispered to God, "Go ahead and write it from here." Right there on the plane, the Lord downloaded to me a sermon that I had never preached before and in less than 20 minutes I had the message that I would speak to that crowd in the coming days." God gave me great peace with that sermon, and it is satisfying to know you are in the center of His will.

After watching a few movies in the air and listening to some music we finally landed in Uganda. It was nearly a full day of travel and when we arrived, media swarmed Chuck and our small delegation as we landed. Pastor Chuck is a national celebrity because of his past ministry in their country and they wrapped around us like a drive-in line at Chick-Fil-A. Chuck is a man's man and has a full beard and one of the most creative geniuses you could ever connect with. In his past life, he was a mogul in real estate, selling hundreds of millions of dollars of property over a decade ago. Today, even after accepting the call into ministry, he still coaches business and real estate leaders nationwide on how to grow their business. Too often, we wrongfully think a preacher is just some poor person when in fact some could have become CEOs to an airline, held national office or made ten figures a year in business.

At four in the morning the parking lot of the Uganda airport was lit up because of all the cameras that were in our faces welcoming us to Africa and interviewing Chuck on what his New Year's Eve message would be at Mandela Stadium. I was glad to carry both his and my luggage because it was by God's grace and Chuck's generosity we were there, and I was trying to free him to talk to the reporters. It really was surreal to be in that moment and as we found our awaiting driver and van, they relieved us all of our luggage and we jumped in the back as we gingerly navigated through the crowd for the half hour drive to our hotel.

Despite being dead tired they treated us as if we were "The Beatles" arriving not in America but on Ugandan soil. My family back home was a tad worried about the conditions of where we stayed but it was a five-star hotel and top of the line in their nation. We all felt better with armed security both outside and x-ray machines to enter the lobby. It had marble floors and we almost felt guilty staying at such a nice place.

I had just climbed into bed with about half hour of sleep with hopes of sleeping for at least eight hours to play catch up, only to find out I was summoned to preach to a thousand pastors and parishioners at a Bible conference. I was thinking it was an April Fool's joke but after clearing the cobwebs from my mind, it was still very much December, and the joke was on me! Overseas it is rude to turn down an invitation and plus it was an honor to speak into some precious ministers' lives to encourage them.

As we caught a cab to speak at the event our taxi driver's eyes grew wide and said, "You are Frank Shelton!" He reached back to shake my hand and I was thinking I am halfway around the world and how does he know who I am? Before I could open my mouth to ask him, he had a flyer on his passenger seat with all our pictures on it promoting the massive upcoming New Year's Eve service and he treated us like royalty. Just as Chuck had woke me up a month before out of a dead sleep with the invite to preach, I was now fully awake and happy I did not miss meeting this taxi driver who was thrilled about the celebration in just a couple days! His excitement was just what I needed and when travelling on mission there is usually no rest for the weary.

After arriving to the pastor's conference in Kampala the people were ecstatic. Their praise was over the top and they genuinely were seeking the Lord. They ushered us in the front row, and I was invited to preach, and God gave me great liberty when ministering. For someone who literally just got off a plane with no sleep the Lord blessed, and I did not want to miss this moment. After all, we flew over not as rock stars but as servants of the Highest and with time ticking, we came to be a blessing. They were with me out of the gate, and I was taught years ago to walk slowly among the people. Those that act as if they are too good or would rather be somewhere else are often the ones that fall into trouble down the road.

A wise mentor told me years ago, "You are not much of a shepherd if you cannot smell sheep on your clothes." I never forgot that, and I had the aroma of Christ and Uganda all over me as I slowly loved on each African in that crowd. It was one hundred degrees outside and probably ten degrees hotter inside and my suit jacket was soaking wet with sweat, but it was a privilege spent in service to my Lord.

After four hours we slowly started to head out of the church. Some Americans are restless after an hour-long service, but they were just warming up at the three-hour mark. To say we were hugging babies, taking countless pictures, and working the crowd like a visiting head of state would not be an exaggeration. They were loving on us and we were loving on them! Drenched and dead tired, we finally got in our awaiting vehicle and our driver took us back to finally crash and catch up on some rest. To be honest, I had one eye on the clock and other on the door just waiting for someone to tell me "No time to rest" and we got another speaking event but after half an hour my body figured maybe it was indeed safe to sleep and despite broad daylight I was finally out like a light and down for the count. I slept nine hours straight and jet lag is a powerful thing, and it can take several days to get back into a rhythm.

Almost my entire ministry, I have flown coach class, but I no longer allow folks to make fun of those that fly First Class. Often, they speak out of either jealousy or ignorance. To fly halfway around the world in a seat built for someone half your size next to the lavatory you are already about dead when you land. More than ever, we are trying to build margin to be in a better position of rest when we arrive so we can hit the ground running to minister while in town.

While in Africa we were able to do some sightseeing and minister at a couple preliminary services leading up to the large New Year's Celebration. For many it was their highlight of the year to come from all over the country to be in that stadium celebrating and worshipping while bringing in the New Year! We were thrilled to be part of it and with each passing hour the excitement was building.

With time ticking and no time to spare as New Year approached, my buddy Pastor Chuck Balsamo had an idea. It was a God idea, and it would be a miracle to pull it off. He is from Virginia and I am from Maryland and he told us over a meal that he wanted to add a visual to his sermon to that capacity crowd to lift their spirits. When Elvis Presley sang in Hawaii in 1973 to the first ever global audience via satellite, he told his jumpsuit designer he wanted something that screamed "America" with the whole world watching. In record time, Bill Belew designed a dazzling white jumpsuit with red, blue, and gold crusted jewels with a big American bald eagle on the front, back and down the sleeves and pants. The matching Eagle belt and cape honored the request perfectly and when "The King" sang "American Trilogy" at the end of the concert and threw the matching cape and belt in the crowd Elvis' father Vernon almost died of a heart attack on national television. The jumpsuit was reported to have cost nearly $50,000 and that was in 1973!

Elvis wanted something "Americana" but my fellow American, Chuck needed something to elevate a nation and God gave him an idea. He had used a four-foot-tall stuffed dog named "Maguja" that weighed nearly forty pounds in the previous sermon from the last year. The crowd loved it and it endeared them to Chuck more and a movie sequel is a blessing and burden. It is a blessing because folks already know the storyline and players but a burden because the expectations are higher than ever. Only a few sequels in Hollywood History come close to the first success of the original and I can think of two out of the gate, "Empire Strikes Back" and "ROCKY II."

With less than a day before our big stadium sermon, God gave Chuck the download to make that stuffed animal fly! Where in the world is David Copperfield when you need him? Just as God had me re-write my sermon on the plane it was obvious that Chuck was pressing into God and aligning his new message to coincide with this miracle message. Many people and even pastors "preach faith" but most do not operate in it and add the biggest platform of one's ministry I would dare to say most would chicken out and do something safe. God spoke and it was clear we had to adjust our sails to His wind and do it without looking back. A few around us tried to say it could not be done and when Chuck called back home a few ministry friends said, "Don't do it!" Others said, "You will bomb in front of that capacity crowd" but God said, "Go" and we were running on the ground to try to make it work.

Pastor Chuck has a diverse group of faithful members back in Virginia at his awesome church and among them are a couple of engineers. My Uncle Frank was an electrical engineer who graduated from the University of Maryland and he is a very bright guy. They see things in their sleep that most miss wide awake and Chuck and I are both visionaries and we can tell you we are going to the Moon, but we need a few helping hands to help us build the rocket but make no mistake we are going up!

Chuck and a few of our team members went to two local shops in Uganda trying to get air. We did not need helium to blow up a couple birthday party balloons but big tanks to help a four-foot-tall stuffed animal not only get off the ground but disappear out of the stadium two hundred feet off the ground! We had crazy faith but on a shoestring budget and the cards stacked against us in the natural but if God be for us who can be against us?

Keep in mind when you are halfway around the globe in a third world country the selection gets smaller to put the pieces together. The hour was getting late, and time was indeed urgent, and the first strike was the first two shops did not have the correct helium we needed. The other strike came when we found it but they wanted to gouge us on the price. I always thought it was interesting when you have outsiders who have already paid their way to bless their nation only to find a couple locals trying to make big bucks on another's generosity and goodwill.

Chuck and another shop owner finally agreed on a price and despite being still too high we knew that this bear better fly even higher tomorrow night. The Super Bowl has millions of dollars to spend to make the halftime show "through the roof" and we had peanuts and a prayer to make the dog fly out of the roof! Who would you have bet on to succeed? The endless funds of the Super Bowl or a couple white brothers from the United States working feverishly by faith (around the clock) to see this sermon come to life and FLY!

Two hours before the start of the New Year's Eve sermon we still had a few folks on the ground and back home on phone imploring us not to try it. They thought it was too risky but there is a reason that Pastor Chuck and I were on that platform that night and not them. Yes, it was grace we were there, but God gave us an assignment and our faith got us to this point and we were not giving up now!

A pastor on staff at a larger church in my region one time asked to meet for lunch and during our conversation he was inquiring how we got to the level we have in ministry? I told him it was all the Lord. He then proceeded, "What is your method?" I told him with a smile, "The Holy Spirit" and then he pushed, "What is your model?" I knew where he was going and I said, "Jesus." He said, "I know that! Seriously, how are you doing it?" In love, I told him the difference between me and most in ministry especially those in a mega church where all too often pride can creep in and I said, "The difference between me and you are you all may out finance me but most likely will never out faith me." Some rely on their savings, but I am still depending on my Savior and some churches arrogantly act unless they can write a check for it and take the credit for it, they will not have the faith to trust God to pull it off. The conversation kind of ended after that drop the mic moment but I now found myself in the bowels of the iconic Nelson Mandela National Soccer Stadium and folks since childhood said, "You remind me of Billy Graham" and now we are getting ready to preach in a stadium like my childhood hero.

Talk about a small world, my college roommate George Odembo was from Nairobi, and he played on the Kenya National Soccer Team. We were together so much on campus that they called us "Ebony & Ivory." Of course, black lives matter, and I had been living that my entire life, because everyone is important to Christ. When George was on their Olympic Team, he had told me in the past that he played in the same stadium when they played Uganda. Now I am ninety minutes away from preaching in the same arena. Only God could write the script to put two college roommates in North Carolina and then twenty years later allow me to stand on the same field that he played. I love that verse, "Whatever your hand finds to do – do it for God's glory." George dominated in soccer and in just over an hour I was preaching to a nation but in the same stadium all for the glory of our Lord.

With the clock ticking, crowd electric and the music thumping, Pastor Chuck, his son, Coree, Eric from Ohio and yours truly were under the bleachers of the main stage in that iconic stadium named after the late President from South Africa and the four of us white brothers from all different mothers were trying to bring HOPE and healing to their nation and great continent. Picture this, we are all in our Sunday best attire each wearing suit, tie, handkerchiefs, and I am wearing my Capitol Hill cufflinks and French cuffs. All the while trying to put the finishing touches on to the bear! You heard of whistle while you work but the four of us were putting feet to our prayers and praying nonstop while we worked!

It was now less than an hour before Chuck preached but I am up to speak to the largest crowd of my life and in fifteen minutes I am preaching. With sweat on my forehead and no longer time to go over my notes nor had time to worry about me but we were laboring together to make sure Chuck's illustrative sermon would not only touch hearts but take flight! With the massive helium tanks, we were tying the final balloons according to the engineer's calculations and trusting God and the scientists back home that it would work. With time ticking, we had to throw out doubt and have faith the Lord would pull it off and that stuffed animal would fly up in front of that packed crowd.

Teamwork makes the dream work, and I forever will smile when reflecting when the four of us with no time to spare were pulling together to help Chuck's vision become a reality. With two minutes to spare someone signaled for me to come back up on stage and I grabbed a towel and wiped my brow and sat down just moments before being introduced. A staff member assigned to help us just notified me that the President of Uganda just ordered those 35 million homes would watch our sermon LIVE across Uganda! No pressure here and the irony is I got a "D" in public speaking in high school, but I was born for this moment. God uses the foolish to confound the wise and I am up next.

Someone handed me my tattered Bible that I have preached from in two dozen countries and with no time to get nervous I said a silent prayer that God would use both me now and Chuck after me to present the Living Jesus to this crowd. The Lord said in His Word, "If I be LIFTED up, I will draw all men unto me" and between my sermon and Chuck's illustrative message we were indeed going to lift Christ. The moment I closed my prayer, "In Jesus Name, amen" the announcer introduced me and with a thousand flickering lights and the roar of a soccer crowd I found myself taking nine steps to the center of that global stage half a world away from home and placed my Bible on the pulpit and with a smile while scanning the crowd, I bragged on Jesus. I had seen it in my mind two decades before and where I thought it may have been Bahamas or Jamaica it was Uganda when the Lord showed me in 1998 that I would speak to a sea of people.

After bringing greetings from America and my wife, Ruth, and kids back home I shared with both peace and passion this statement that resonated throughout the soccer stadium. I wrote it days before on the plane and saw it firsthand three days before with no sleep before preaching at the pastor's conference. I shared, "In America we have WEALTH but in Africa you have WORSHIP and truth be told, you are richer because of it." The crowd roared as if one of their country's best soccer players just scored a goal and the applause went on for over a minute. It was thundering not in lightening but with love for our Lord and God shook the place! Literally.

(118,000 souls @ Mandela Stadium)

Switching gears into overdrive I shared, "When Winston Churchill visited Uganda years ago, he called your country "The Pearl of Africa." The crowd erupted like a volcano once again through my interpreter. Ironically, I just met the man who would translate for me when I stood up to preach but when God is in the middle, He can do AMAZING things. I shared about the pearl of great price in Scripture, and I said that capacity crowd of over one hundred and twenty thousand strong with thirty million plus watching on television that, "Uganda – you are the pearl of great price that God is looking for! Tonight, I have good news – God loves Uganda!!" The stadium went bonkers, and you would have thought they just won the World Cup after that statement.

I recall as a kid when Elvis hit a note in the Aloha from Hawaii special with half the world watching, he looked to his left and with a wink to his fellow band member signaling between the two that he nailed it. I remember in real time looking over my shoulder and to my left was Pastor Chuck now on the platform and with a wink we both had that look that God just nailed it and his sermon up next was going to be both EPIC and through the roof! There was no doubt that the Lord was in the House and we both were pulling for each other.

Faster than a Ferrari, I switched gears again and took them from my American hands to His nail scarred hands and with the power of God on me as I preached. Next to no notes, no nervousness but all business while preaching Jesus and they hung on every word. When using a translator, it is a unique situation, but I had watched Evangelist Billy Graham do it a million times on television and in person and leadership is caught more than taught. Anyone who has ever heard me preach at times would say I resemble a machine gun but with an interpreter the words are much more concise. Plus, it is mandatory to pause for the other to translate. This not only allowed me to catch my breath and focus on the next sentence but more importantly prayer briefly that God would fill in the gaps. The best part of preaching overseas is that all the unnecessary "fluff" and jokes are out the window. It forces one to preach the pure Gospel and that is what we need more of now more than ever before -- the matchless message of Christ, His Cross and He's coming again!

It was over one hundred degrees that night and it was even hotter on the platform. The lights are so bright it is almost impossible to see past the first few rows, but I kept delivering the mail "by faith" because that is all I have ever known and would not change now if I could try. Faith is the currency of Heaven and when we display faith the Lord will reveal His favor. No surprise that faith comes before favor even in the dictionary and without faith it is impossible to please God.

As I was winding down third and heading home, I knew that it was time to land the plane. Dr. Billy Graham believed the invitation was even more important than the introduction and with the message resembling an airplane on "Final Approach" it was high time to draw the net. I closed my Bible and lifted my hands towards Heaven and like I had done thousands of times before was inviting souls to repent of sin and trust Christ by faith as their personal Lord and Savior.

Something happened in that sacred moment but as my hands went towards Heaven both of my legs buckled at the knees simultaneously and I almost fell on the ground. I am not sure if it was evident to anyone in the crowd or to those behind me, but I forever will recall that moment. It happened so fast, but both my hands grabbed the podium to stop my fall and without missing a beat I continued, and I have thought about that a hundred times, and I can only come up with two scenarios.

Dr. Graham said often in interviews that he felt as if the Devil himself was tearing the evangelist apart as we stand in the gap for the souls of men. I have shared more than once in this book the phrase, "new levels bring new devils." Bible College did not teach or prepare me for this stage in this stadium on this moment in time. Very few in ministry will ever know intimately what it is like to speak to that many people at one time. The stakes are much higher, and the temptations are greater when you arrive to a place of this magnitude. One renowned Bible teacher said, "Be very careful not to cheat or compromise your way to the next level in ministry because if you get there prematurely you will find a dozen devils laughing and licking their chops getting ready to devour you because you are not ready."

Fortunately, I knew the Lord had put me there but either the sheer weight of that moment standing in the gap with Heaven and Hell at play for all eternity it was as if Satan was either trying to knock me down or God politely reminding me that this was His show, and He alone gets all the glory! Another unique element of co-laboring with a translator is the pregnant pause in between sentences. As I gave the invitation for folks to pray to receive Christ as Dr. Graham, Reinhard Bonnke, Rodney Howard-Browne, Charles Spurgeon, John Wesley, E.V. Hill, and countless evangelists have in the past it seemed a tad awkward at first. I gave the first sentence but after the translator repeated, other than my two kids' first cries when they were born, it was the most special sound I have or possibly will ever hear. With no exaggeration or embellishment, it sounded like one third of that soccer stadium repeated back the sinner's prayer with us to confess Christ as their Savior!

The Lord took us all home that night at the end of the sermon and when it was all said and done, tens of thousands may have quite literally trusted Christ and were now born again with reservations made in Heaven. I prayed since I was a teenager that if Paul could see three thousand saved at Pentecost at one time after one sermon, perhaps God could do it again with me? After speaking to forty times that crowd (120,000) not counting the multiplied millions watching via television God only knows how many did receive Christ.

God is the same yesterday, today and forever and if He did it then we believed He could do it again! The Lord did it and right before concluding I told them my best friend was in the house. I borrowed an idea I got from comedian Steve Harvey and ran with it but told that crowd tonight I introduce to you not a President, Prime Minister, Professional Athlete or Pope but the Prince of Peace, King of Kings, Lord of Lords, Great I Am, Almighty God, Wonderful Counsellor and the Savior of the Universe, Jesus The Christ" and by the time I said his name all one hundred thousand plus didn't need a translator to tell them where we were going and love and our Lord is the universal language and they gave God a standing ovation and I walked back to my seat and disappeared as the Lord appeared.

It was one of the most amazing moments of my life and indeed God was high and lifted and sometimes we as ministers and musicians must learn from a magician and know when it is time to disappear. That stadium was rocking, and video footage does not do it justice the night all of Uganda ushered in the New Year on their feet in adoration of our risen Lord. To God be the glory!

I humbly sat down and got a fist bump of affirmation from my three fellow Musketeers (Chuck, Coree and Eric) and it takes maturity to compliment others and that was a sweet moment. Once again, I was half a world away and soaked to the skin from sweat and completely spent in service to my Savior, but it was worth it. After a song selection, Pastor Chuck was up next as we were drawing to the hour before the New Year's celebration. Chuck had been tasked to close out the service and with our calculations we had three prayer requests. First, that his sermon would wrap up right before the clock ticking into the New Year. Second, that dog would indeed get off the ground, take flight and soar out of the stadium and inspire an entire nation in person and those watching at home on television. Third, anyone that did not trust Christ after my message would be touched and repent of sin after being inspired by his message.

Pastor Chuck was introduced, and they gave him an enthusiastic round of applause and it was like a hero's welcome. He was white but considered an honorary Ugandan and may have yet to get a key to the city, but he already had the key to their hearts. You cannot fake love and there is nothing inauthentic about Dr. Chuck Balsamo. That brother got up and flat out preached the stars down and the paint off the walls.

It took all three of us to bring the official mascot out who was beloved the year before and when we did the crowd roared again. Not because of us but because of the dog that Chuck made special in the stadium the previous year. We quickly got out of the way and it was Jesus, Chuck and the stuffed dog front and center.

His first point was talking about as a nation you (Uganda) may have been knocked down before, but you must get on your knees! He said, "Regardless of if you are doing good or bad it is imperative to seek God and there is power when on your knees in prayer!"

We had put balloons on the arms of the stuffed animal and prayed we had the correct amount. Too little or too much could kill the sermon and we were totally depending on God and the wisdom of his saints back home at Chuck's church who had excelled in science class. We also had a few weights on the animal to tie him down until it was time to fly. After removing a few weights immediately that bear slowly was elevated to its knees and the place went NUTS!

Then Chuck eloquently told them once you have found strength and wisdom on your knees from the Lord it is important to stand up. He removed a few more weights and Maguja slowly started to stand up on his own two feet. We were behind Chuck the entire time during the sermon (literally) and praying unceasingly but when that dog was standing erect that stadium went BONKERS!! The crowd was louder than it had been since I introduced Jesus and then Chuck passionately said, "As a nation you may have been down. You find strength on your knees in prayer but then once you stand up God will take you to heights you have only dreamed!" And with that, a few more cords were cut, the weights were off and darn if that forty-pound dog didn't take off!"

Maguja was ten feet off the ground, twenty feet, thirty feet, forty feet and at fifty feet the roar of that stadium crowd dwarfed a World Cup and World Series victory combined. God used Chuck's sermon to not only elevate a team but a Nation and with each foot that stuffed animal climbed it represented what God could do in the life of everyone who believed. If someone sold ear plugs before that sermon, they would have been a multi-millionaire and the noise was deafening but nobody cared. Maguja was now over a hundred feet and climbing and everyone who had been looking down was now looking up with kids pointing towards the night sky and tears of joy in adults' eyes! It was as if every person was with that flying dog and their dreams were still capable of happening despite hardships and tough times.

I had tears of relief and JOY and once again there was a reason we were on that platform. The naysayers were nowhere to be found but those who believed SAW it happen and now the stuffed dog was at the rim level of the stadium. Had that thing collapsed then it still would have been a success but there was no stopping that illustrative sermon now and I recall Michael Jackson departing on a jet pack at a Super Bowl halftime spectacular in the past and flying out of a stadium but half a world away and with next to no money we saw that stuffed animal soar out of the arena and the entire crowd was on its feet!

To say they went ballistic would be an understatement and the three of us were hugging each other and rejoicing that the bear not only flew but the sermon was a grand slam! Shortly after, the count down into the new year started and fireworks shot off for a full five minutes and for a third world country they sure spent some money on a finale that would have made America proud and the joy and jubilation from those sweet souls in Africa will be something I take to my grave. Once again, in America we have wealth, but they have worship, and it really is the truth that they are the richer because of it.

If the night could not get any better, I heard our names over the loudspeaker while we were sitting in a place of honor in front row on the stage. The Vice President of their Country had been quietly on the platform at the opposite end of the stage and unbeknownst to us invited our American delegation to come and meet the Vice President and pray over him and his country with the whole nation watching. What an honor that was and Chuck the year before prophesied that their President would win the election and he did! The Bible says, "Your gift will make room for you and bring you before kings and great men." The Lord did it again and regardless of if ministering to heads of state at home or abroad, everyone needs Christ, and it is humbling to be used by God.

We were all dead tired but a good tired and after taking in the festivities we were all hugging each other that night on the platform. We did not want to look rude and leave but very few could relate to how tired we were. We had already flown halfway around the world and ministered nonstop at various church services and conferences only to preach to the massive stadium on one of the biggest nights of our lives. The emotion and adrenaline that one expends at that level is exhausting but when you are in the front row you cannot just leave when you want. Everything must be weighed with tact and class. Finally, about three in the morning the celebration finally was slowly subsiding, and we were escorted to our awaiting car underneath the stadium. The crazy thing was that about 75,000 were still there as we humbly disappeared into the night.

Not trying to draw attention to myself but anyone that knows me realizes I was working the crowd and shaking hands with everyone while departing the platform. We were high fiving the janitor on the way out, saluting the security and taking pics with everyone with a camera heading to our van. No, we were not the Beatles but for a few fleeting minutes they thought we were Michael Jordan and the Bulls as they waved goodbye to us heading out with a small police escort.

One cannot help but recall all the folks who said you will never make it. One deacon at a previous church told me I would never make it as evangelist. At this juncture, we just gave it to the Lord but even Billy Graham's son in law would call me when I landed back home in the States and said, "Frank we all saw your sermon in Charlotte! We are so proud of you and loved not only how God used you but how you stayed humble." It meant so much for one of your heroes to call you and says, "Well done!" I am praying God says the same.

The host of the African crusade said, "Frank, everyone said that when you were up there preaching it appeared as if Dr. Graham was up there once again. Your presence and mannerisms resemble him and the anointing on him obviously has been placed on you." It is humbling but there is only one Billy Graham but glory to God!

The second person to call me when I landed in the U.S. was my mom. She was crying and she said, "Frankie you may recall when your Dad and I took you to hear Billy Graham in 1982, when you were ten. As we left RFK Stadium (home of the Washington Redskins) you just watched him preach to nearly 60,000 and you said, "Mommy, that was the most amazing thing I have ever seen. No one could be Billy Graham but if God just one time would do that in my life that would be one of the most amazing things." My mother with tears said, "Frankie, God can do above and beyond all you ask or think because God just doubled the crowd and used you and your friends to do it." We both were crying at that juncture and as my late friend Stevie Prather would say, "Look at God!"

Before departing Africa to head home we still had some unfinished business and there is an eight-hour time difference back home. The very next day after a couple hours of sleep we drove three hours to give out toys and free food in one of the poorest regions of Uganda. Our entire team from America loved on those precious kids in an orphanage and we played games and gave away hundreds of free clothes and toys. I took three suitcases of gifts I picked up from the Dollar Store and loaded up with candy, coloring books, crayons and all kinds of Nerf footballs, soccer balls, etc.

Chuck's church donated a couple thousand dollars' worth of free food and games and they loved it! We cooked beef, potatoes and gave everyone soda and they told us with tears of JOY that would be the best meal they would eat all year. What blessed me most was when some heard we were the group who spoke in that stadium the night before but the very next day we chose to be with them. Yes, we could have slept in, but Jesus would not allow us and besides, there was nowhere else in the world I would have rather been that day. Their beautiful smiles and expressions of joy and appreciation blessed us big time!

I learned much from Dad even when he did not know I was watching. When he retired at the pinnacle of his profession on Capitol Hill his retirement party was in the Cannon House Office Building and the hierarchy from Members of Congress to U.S. Supreme Court and Secret Service honored my father. We were all so proud of Dad and the next day he was in casual clothes on his first day of retirement when he stopped what he was doing and spent about ten minutes talking to a small young boy on his tricycle, making the child feel like the most special person in the world.

The night before, we had spoken to a hundred thousand but today we ministered to three hundred at an orphanage on the other side of Uganda. One told me I was the first white man he ever shook hands with but when we came with love in our hearts and bearing gifts days after Christmas it was easy to make friends. After a full day of ministering there on the way back to the hotel we saw a group in the middle of the street, and we showed up unannounced and Chuck and I preached with a makeshift microphone and we saw a couple dozen get saved in the middle of the street. I even met a man whose last name was Obama and souls are saved not only in a stadium but on the street and even a studio from time to time. The Gospel always works the question with time ticking are we willing to work? God calls us to be His messengers and the hands and feet of Christ.

That night on the way back it was now dark. Once again, we were spent, and someone offered to take us to a nice restaurant and truthfully, I had not had a really good meal since arriving in Uganda. We are so spoiled in the States, and we were on a long two-lane dusty highway filled with potholes. What was wild was we had pedestrians and donkeys on both sides of us as our car was slowly going five miles per hour. It seemed less than that and what I also recall was people walking beside our car and occasionally would shout and a two-foot ditch seemed to run parallel to our car.

It had almost been a full day since my sermon the night before in the stadium and I had my iPhone in my left hand and was in the process of trying to upload my thirty-minute message to Facebook so folks could watch it back home. Many were praying and until they saw the video some may still think I made the entire trip up. My driver was on the right side of the car and what looked like the driver seat back home was the passenger seat in Africa.

While I was minding my own business and en route to a nice meal after two long days of nonstop ministry, one of the two men walking adjacent to our slowly moving car reached inside our vehicle and grabbed my cell phone and tried to steal it out of my hands. The driver screamed, "What was that?" I said, "That guy just grabbed my phone!" To his surprise and mine as well we both were astonished that somehow the phone was still in my left hand. It was in my weak hand; I did not even see his hand coming to confiscate my cell and God's grace kept it secure.

Immediately the Lord showed me that the Devil was trying to steal my sermon. If my phone had been stolen, the video would have never uploaded to bless the thousands back home who eventually watched it and were blessed. God showed me that night in my hotel room that Satan often attacks after a promotion in life and ministry. Satan wants to not only steal our sermon but steal our platform. Remember this, dogs do not chase parked cars but only bark and try to bite those that are moving. Bishop TD Jakes said, "The only taste of success some will have will be those jealous folks who try to take a bite out of you." Lastly, Satan not only wants to steal our sermon or platform but silence our voice, too.

I was glad he didn't get my phone, but I actually felt sad and bad for the one who apparently thought he needed to steal to get something nice. Plus, it would be just like Satan to try to make me angry at an unidentified African when I just met nearly 150,000 of the friendliest people on the planet in the last five days while in country. That one poor soul then or still could not change my mind and I have often prayed for him that God bless him and maybe by now he has his own phone.

The next day would be our last day before heading home and I was invited to preach one more time to a packed crowd at another pastor's conference. It was the personal church and conference of the host pastor of the crusade, and I could not say no if I tried and besides, I prayed for years that God would use me and I could not stop now that the door was open. I was paired to preach with Dr. Hugh Osgood from England who overseas one third of all the churches in the United Kingdom. He has tea once per month with the Queen of England and he and the Archbishop of Canterbury together oversee two thirds of that entire region. Dr. Osgood was Dr. Billy Graham's host director for his London crusade years before and I was honored to share his stage twice while in Africa on this first trip. He was phenomenal at the stadium and equally has powerful in the pastor's conference setting.

I followed him that day and it was humbling with him in the front row watching my message for the second time in two days and I was wearing a grey suit with white shirt, teal blue tie and cufflinks. After pouring out my all to that packed crowd, I had left my all on the altar. As sports players would say, "I left it all on the field" and even Elvis at the end not only left the building but gave his all night after night even when it killed him. The Lord was all over that message and the anointing was extra thick but so was the pain excruciating up and down my back. I was soaked more than ever, and it had to be one hundred and ten in that church that day. They were hanging on my every Word, and I was dropping Truth bombs from God's Word and came too far to stop now although humanly speaking I should have. By the time I was finished my suit went from grey to when Dr. Osgood and I took a pic afterwards the suit appears black in the picture. No one would believe it was grey before and it was symbolic that once again I was spent in service to my Lord.

I was hoping to finally slip quietly into the awaiting car and crash early back in the hotel before the long flight home, but the pastor said to the capacity crowd, "Evangelist Shelton has a rare anointing of evangelism. If you would like him to lay hands on you and pray over, you then line up down front." I am not exaggerating when I tell you over one thousand Africans (both men and women) lined up asking me to impart unto them. I come from a Baptist background, but my friends have joked I am Bapti-costal for as long as I can recall.

One by one I slowly prayed and poured into each of them, and I was so fatigued that I could hardly lift my hands up. My suit was so soaked with sweat that it clung to my skin and truthfully, I smelled far worse than the sheep I was honored to minister to. I did resemble the compliment that a true Shepherd begins to smell like his sheep and indeed I had walked slowly among His people.

One by one, I laid hands on every single one and they touched me as if I were Jesus. One precious woman about ninety broke my heart. Through a translator she tried to give me an offering. She was a widow and God told me it was the "widow's mite" and she placed in my hand everything she had. I cried then and tears are streaming down my cheeks as I write this sentence. Not to be disrespectful but how do you take money from the poorest people on the planet and with a smile and hug I gave her back the money and thanked her for her generosity.

I was engulfed by hundreds of Africans and looking back, it was one of the most special moments of my life. We took one last group picture that you will see in this chapter, and I am the lone white brother in the mix, but these were now my brothers and sisters as kids of the King in the family of God. I like to think not only is my roommate in college George Odembo proud, but he was with me each step of the way in Spirit.

Almost like a prize fighter who was so tired in the ring I was almost helped with a person on each side of me. Barely able to raise my hands I was still shaking hands with everyone out the door. I had seen the American President work both sides of the aisle of a State of the Union and I was doing it exiting this church which may be for the last time. Indeed, I had left everything on the table, in the arena and on the altar. With sweat streaming down my face that was now appearing a dirt grime I was content because I had just preached and embodied grace. The moment I took two steps outside we encountered two women wearing African attire and they asked to have a word with me. I stopped on a dime and the one said, "Evangelist Shelton you have problems with your kidneys." Her words stopped me in my track because exactly ten years before with the U.S. Capitol Police indeed my kidneys crashed but very people on Earth knew that story. To say she had my attention would be an understatement.

She then said, "If you give me your tithe, I will cancel that attack." She had me until she demanded money and we had given and given until there was nothing left to give, and the two assistants assigned to drive me back to the hotel whispered that they both were witches. They were demonic and used by the Devil and no wonder why they were outside the church, and they happened to attack the man of God when he was completely exhausted. Once again, that would be just like the Devil to try to put a bad taste of Africa in my mouth when millions are the salt of the Earth. Satan always attacks after a promotion or when you are dead tired. I had experienced both and my handlers to their credit did not allow the Devil or these two lost souls mishandle me and finally like Elvis, I had "left the building."

Kids were running up to us and what few dollars I had on me I gave to them. Not to make a show but to try to let them know that America cares. One person asked me to sign their Bible and out the window I paused long enough to honor that request and the fact is I always felt unworthy to sign a Bible, but they asked, and I obliged and as I pointed towards Heaven, they understood that God not me is whom we must keep our eyes on. With a smile and one last wave we were through the gates and as the smoke cleared, I could still see the joy on their faces the day Jesus used me while in Africa.

As we rolled into the hotel for the last time on that trip, I was so tired I could barely lift my hands. I wanted to bless the driver that had been assigned to us all week and my African friend had his eyes on my Presidential cufflinks. Long before social distancing, I shook his hand, took off my cufflinks and placed him in his hands. His smile said everything, and Elvis gave away Cadillacs and the least I could do was give away my cufflinks. They were presidential but I told him he was royalty as my brother in Christ. He hugged me and I exited the car and walked through security, went to my room, took a hot shower and was down for the count with a full night of much needed sleep.

The next morning the team all met for breakfast for the last time, and we made the trip back to the airport to fly home. After changing planes in Ethiopia, we were walking on the runway to get on our jet and from the corner of my eye I saw two planes with UN on the tail. I knew immediately it stood for United Nations and the Lord whispered to me, "Frank you will see more of that in the future." I pointed to Chuck, and he acknowledged it as well and we finally were on our plane heading home. It was an amazing week, and we were blessed to minister to everyone from their Vice President to an orphanage to hundreds of pastors and a stadium crowd not to mention an entire nation on television. Not bad for a week's work and my accountant teased me for not making a dime on that trip but it may have not made me dollars, but it made tons of "sense" to bless that country. The widow gave all she had and how could I do any less?

God showed me two decades before it would happen and Habbakuk 2:12 says, "Write the vision down, make it plain. Although it tarries it will come to pass." The Lord is never in a hurry but always on time and God showed up. Thousands more were saved and their names forever in the Lamb's Book of Life. I often think if I never complimented Chuck that probably would have never happened, and it pays to be a blessing, but it is costly when rude. At the airport heading back to the States Pastor Chuck received a text that somebody from Uganda found "Maguja" the stuffed animal and we put Chuck's contact information inside the dog. We did it for two reasons to see how far the dog flew and we would have a prize for the person when they contacted us. Are you ready for this? That stuffed animal traveled not only out of the stadium but was found thirty minutes away when it landed. Those who resemble a doubting Thomas will rarely if ever see how far faith will fly! Chuck and I slapped five and we were now wheels up heading back to the United States of America with smiles on our face the length of the Nile River.

Honestly, like Chuck, I thought it was one and done but I was blessed to preach three consecutive years in a row to ring in the New Year at Nelson Mandela National Soccer Stadium in Uganda. In December 2016, 2017, and 2018, I kissed my family goodbye and went solo to help enlarge the Kingdom of God over the holidays. In just three sermons, I was honored to speak to over one third of a million people. Evangelist Reinhard Bonnke and Billy Graham could say the same but very few others could, and it is humbling but Frank from Waldorf, Maryland did, too. To put it in perspective, the average church attendance in America is two hundred per Sunday. With fifty-two weeks in a year would be 10,400 souls in a calendar year but to preach to over 360,000 people would take over 35 years to preach to that size crowd. We did it in three sermons in that stadium and this is the Lord's doing and He gets all the credit. Our desire is to reach the world ONE soul at a time and Dr. Adrian Rogers said it best, "You may preach the Gospel better than me, but you could never preach a better Gospel."

The fact is I believe the main reason God has used me over the years is that He knew that every time I preach that I would invite people to come to faith in Christ. Regardless of ministering to Presidents, prisoners, professional athletes, prostitutes, or to the poorest people on the planet, I would give an invitation after the sermon. God keeps inviting me to preach and I will keep giving an invitation.

Thank you Africa, thank you Pastor Chuck and thank you Jesus!

INDIA

(Taj Mahal)

WHAT a treat it is to sleep in your own bed and the truth is I almost was killed leaving Dulles Airport. After the third consecutive year preaching on New Year's Eve in Africa and flying all day home with next to no sleep on that plane I got to my own car. After hugging Chuck goodbye as we flew alone on this trip I jumped in my car and had not gotten on the main highway in Virginia departing the airport when I almost fell asleep at the wheel and an eighteen-wheeler hit the horn and had to go off on the shoulder to miss hitting me at full speed. The irony was I did not die in Africa but at my own fault was almost crushed by a tractor trailer minutes after landing back in America. Satan has tried to take me out more than once over the years and I keep reciting what the late Dr. Jerry Falwell, Sr said, "God's man is virtually indestructible until the Lord is done with him." I guess God's not done with me yet, but we have been close more than I can count.

As the ministry platform and profile got bigger not everyone is happy for you! Elvis Presley's stepbrother told me in my car, "most people want you to do good just not really good." I never forgot that and when you have preached in London and Los Angeles the folks back in La Plata, Maryland can get nervous. The Bible says, "A prophet is with honor everywhere but their hometown" and I had seen it for some time and God's favor may bring out the best in you but the worst of others and sadly, clergy can be some of the most jealous and insecure. I just continue to wish everyone well and even the pastors and local police who did not have our family law enforcement legacy. Winner's compliment but the wannabes criticize, and I am trying to be a cheerleader to all. Many want the platform, but most are not willing to pay the price and God called me to keep moving forward and fortunately by God's grace and that alert tractor trailer driver, we lived another day.

I had returned from Africa clearly exhausted, and the next month of sleeping in my own bed helped tremendously. When I am home, I try to help as much as I can around the house and often drive Andrew to school. My travelling is hard on him, too and I try to help him with his homework, shoot basketball with him out back or take him to miniature golf or the arcades to have fun, just the two of us. However, after less than a month at home I was invited to preach in India with my good friend, Dr. Sam Thomas of Hopegivers International. This would be my second long distance trip back-to-back in two months with Africa and India. The recent trips back-to-back to Europe was a walk in the park compared to this trek and I was reminded of an art class I took while a student at Gardner-Webb University in North Carolina. For the life of me I cannot remember the name of our kind art teacher, but she had a sweet smile and angelic disposition. She genuinely loved art and knew artists and artwork unlike very few others. She made the class fun because she was passionate about her art and made what could be a boring hour exciting.

One painting that had a profound impact on me while in that class was painted by Albrecht Durer and it was one of his masterpieces. It was an iconic work that was painted in the 1500s and it was titled, "The Knight, Death and Devil." I cannot explain it, but that one painting in that one class on a campus in Carolina got a hold of me. It was of a knight in full armor valiantly and confidently riding on a horse and both he and his transportation were focused like flint staring ahead while moving forward. This was no donkey or pony but a strong stallion that resembled a horse bred for war.

The day was turning to dusk and in the darkness was the Devil and death holding an hourglass and darn if the sand was not sliding quickly through the jar depicting either his time may be short or society as we know it almost up. It was if Durer could paint sounds that howled out of the forest and Satan snickering insults and lies to try to get him to abort his mission. The Bible tells the Christian to put on the full armor of God, but that brother had a mission, and he wasn't looking to the left or right to stop anytime soon.

Just as a movie a couple years before said, "Frank you may be considered an enemy of the state one day, the Lord at this Christian college was whispering to me to take a good look at the soldier on the horse because this will resemble you later in life. No pressure but I have looked at the picture more times than I can count, and it reminds me of the task at hand and that time is not on our side, but the Lord is.

After packing and kissing the family goodbye again it was off to Dehli, India days before my birthday in February 2018. Once again, on this trip I would be flying completely by myself halfway around the world. That is approximately 7,478 miles one way. To put in perspective, that is flying to and from DC to LAX roundtrip and back to Los Angeles. We were still dealing with some occasional fruit loops locally as the Lord was blessing our ministry nationally and globally, but it was par for the course. I recently saw a documentary that the FBI was targeting and following Dr. Martin Luther King, Jr and their former director called him the most dangerous man in America. When God starts blessing, the Devil starts messing and sometime people get nervous when the Lord starts promoting one of His own.

My father graduated from the FBI Academy and at one time I applied for a position of Deputy Director for their tour in Washington but after 9/11 they cancelled the program. At one time they had one of the most frequented public tours on Capitol Hill and the country. Some of our dear family friends served long careers with the Federal Bureau of Investigation but God obviously had other plans.

While driving to Dulles once again for another international departure the Lord was preparing my heart. Most folks have no clue the stress I had been under and for every clown that thought we were in it for the money should have sent me hazardous pay. Once you start ministering abroad and to public officials and stadiums with crowds more than 100,000 something surreal happens. Locally, some of your clergy friends pretend you don't exist and then you are on some government's watch list as you move about. Billy Graham had his spouse, staff, and security and lately, I had resembled Rambo more than the revered reverend and often flew in and out alone.

I am sure John Foster Dulles the former Secretary of State under President Dwight D. Eisenhower was a nice man but personally and professionally I have always despised that airport bearing his name. Most of my international flights originate out of Dulles but I always preferred both Reagan National and BWI. I had met Thurgood Marshall (BWI) in the Supreme Court and Dad protected Reagan but Dulles to me was aloof and out of the way. Lately, I had almost gotten killed leaving the airport and as you may recall flying to Romania, I was on all fours seeing if I had a tracking mechanism under my car.

It was only going to get worse, and I realized shortly after that the "Smart Phone" and "Smart Car" were probably two of the dumbest purchases Americans could make. The phones had already been tracking us all for years and the Patriot Act that initially was to protect us from terrorists lately deemed good, upstanding citizens as potential domestic terrorists. In the last days good would be called evil and the game was late in innings, time was ticking and now you know the cover of my book that the sands of time had been slipping faster than ever!

I found a place to park and the moment I got out of my vehicle I saw a man who was casually dressed standing on the curb about 200 feet away and the Holy Spirit whispered to me, "You will see him again." It is crazy but as the ministry grew my spiritual discernment grew through the roof. Just as God gives grace when you need it; I believe the Lord supernaturally extends discernment as well. Also, when you have a century and a half of detectives in your family not at the county but national level, you pick up on things before others might.

As I walked closer, I said "hi" and then walked by him and entered the airport. After checking in two and half hours early for my international flight, I left my bag at the counter and walked through security. Over the years, I learned to travel light and even RAMBO got "hung up" when he over packed trying to get out of the plane to do surveillance and rescue POWS in Vietnam.

From there with less than two hours until takeoff I made a few calls and went to grab a meal clear on the other side of the terminal. I had taken a tram a quarter of a mile away and was having my last supper at Carrabba's and I love that Italian restaurant and the fact there is one tucked away in one of their terminals is a plus for my least favorite airport. I joke when I called it my last supper because one it would be my last American meal for a while, and I ended up fasting the entire flight into India. Since airline food has steadily declined over the years and I was unsure what the food would be like, so I decided to load up now before my midnight flight east.

While I was on the phone talking to a colleague with the Billy Graham Evangelistic Association letting them know I would be out of town for a week, I looked up across the room and saw some guy staring at me. Perhaps you have been dining at a restaurant and while eating look up and clear across the room you catch someone awkwardly staring at you and then put your head down and are hesitant to look up for a while to see if they are still watching. When you look up a few minutes later it is fun when they are still staring.

I had already paid for my meal and was at my gate when this one gentleman was watching me. He was former military and while still on the phone I walked by him and decided to stand up clear across the hallway while leaning against the wall and sure enough, the same guy comes right up to me and stands next to me. I am not normally this bold but knowing he was listening to my conversation I said to my colleague on the phone, "These Air Marshals must be struggling to find talent because they are hiring them smaller and smaller lately." The moment I said that he disappeared, and I was voted the friendliest growing up in school but over the years I had to get bolder while doing the Lord's work. When your family has protected Presidents, you cannot be afraid of the fruit loops along the way.

As I got rid of one, I looked to my left and who do I see about five gates down heading my way but the same man that I saw on the curb two and half hours before that the Lord told me I would see again. There are at least four internal sections to this massive airport on 13,000 acres at Dulles and I was at gate 50 for an international flight and I saw him again around gate 45. He is getting closer and closer and sure enough, he is at my gate. No big deal and the Lord told me I would see him, and I pick up on things and we have nearly 300 souls boarding this flight to India. As we boarded the plane, I politely nod to him again because when you have nothing to hide you don't run but walk straight up and as I board the plane, I give the stewardess my ticket, I find my seat and throw my carry on above and sit down in my seat for the long twenty-hour flight.

Five minutes later he starts coming down my aisle and I already knew it, he sits next to me on my left on that outbound flight. Let me give you a math equation. With an international airport housing 113 gates and add that some planes have three hundred seats like this overseas flight but to make it conservative 250 seats would be a one in 28,250 odds that he would sit next to me, but I called it the moment I got out of my car heading to the airport. Not because I was wrong or living a double life but because in the last days "good" would be called evil and vice versa and Christianity and patriotism offended some and were too radical for other non-believers.

Over the years, I also picked up that Air Marshals often fly with just a carry-on bag and often don't go to the baggage claim but who in the world flies halfway around the world with just a carry-on bag? I travel light but these guys travel with next to nothing. Unless you know what to look for you may miss it. I politely thanked him for his service when he sat next to me and that rattled him. Most of them are often former military and some of them are childhood friends. The more casual they dress the more they stick out to me, but my family and I have a unique way to pick folks out of a police lineup. When I thank them for their service it reveals two things. For starters, I thank them genuinely for their past service and secondly if they are in fact a Marshal or someone assigned to monitor me it is a polite way to let them know I see you usually before you see me.

It is worth repeating that the TSA has a program called "Quiet Skies" that even some of their own think is worthless and a mismanagement of funds and one can be placed on a "watch list" for no infractions whatsoever. One said to the best of their recollection that he once got a parking ticket but was convinced he paid that five years ago. My dear friend and former NYPD told me to just look at it as a compliment that with me traveling alone you may have your own security detail, but I think more like the movie "Enemy of the State" with Will Smith and Gene Hackman that I saw decades before that in the last days some of the patriots would be viewed as terrorists to folks who really don't have America or God's best interest at heart.

As the stewardess came by three times on that long flight with entrees, I do not know who was more surprised her or my Marshal friend to my left when I was fasting from the food. Plus, I did not want to but had to learn to keep others on their toes. Most see the hour I give away Heaven on the platform, but most do not know the Hell I go through out of the pulpit. I had my "last supper" at Carrabba's in Dulles and plus as I was flying solo to India, I knew in advance that spiritual warfare would be high. Only three percent of the people in the nation of India are born again Christians and in a country with 1.3 billion only a small percentage have a reservation for Heaven. Plus, I heard about the "Dehli Belly" and did not want to get sick while on the ground preaching the Good News. I was starting to wonder what government was more hostile and very few love America as much as I do, but even the last few years, patriotism was under attack. Christians were labeled extremists and conservatives wanted to be banned by some, banished or both.

Very few had a resume or connections politically, policing or pastorally but add all three together someone or multiple folks were watching. When I joke about shopping at Walmart because "Target" was on my back was no longer a joke but a way of life. Was I selling arms to Iran, smuggling cocaine in Columbia or trafficking humans? Absolutely not! I was a man who was a pastor to politicians, a chaplain at Olympics, an occasional guest on television, a preacher of the Gospel to hundreds of thousands in soccer stadiums, ministering to high level celebrities and on staff with Franklin Graham's 50 states Decision America tour and it was obvious someone was praying we would fail and fall.

Who would think being a Christian or patriot was against the law, but it was obvious the "old America" was not going to fit in the New World Order and time was indeed ticking and the hourglass became a way of life for me as the sands of time were sliding quickly to reveal this life would be over and most were not ready to meet a Holy God only to be ushered into a Devil's Hell. After a few standard instructions from the flight deck, the door was closed, and the plane was now racing down the runway for a full day and all night in the air.

The moment the plane leveled out I noticed the guy to my left had the same matching carry-on luggage as the gentleman to my right. I was sandwiched between the two and another red flag was when I tried to have a friendly conversation with the guy next to me, he clammed up and did not want to speak and tried his best to sleep. I often found it interesting that the folks who get paid to watch you from afar pretend like they cannot see you when they are up close. My Dad always said, "Kill them with kindness" and his resume in the major leagues ran circles around them in the minor leagues and neither God nor I was going to strike out with them.

They both pretended to not know each other but I have an uncanny way to see things often before they happen while most miss things after they happen. When we changed planes some twelve hours later, I let them both deplane first and they seem agitated. Perhaps because I beat them at their own game and when we got on a train on the runway to go towards the airport for another flight, they both intentionally got on opposite ends of the train. It was comical because with their matching black back packs it was almost as if they were two lovers at night who were trying not to be seen together by day.

The hit song by Kenny Rogers started playing in my head, "Daytime friends and night-time lovers" and once again, I was in the middle of both of them on the train towards the terminal and when we arrived everyone got off and I intentionally hung back but knowing I had a two hour layover I kept my eye on the one and fifteen minutes later I intentionally walked in the opposite direction of my next gate only to find them both but this time talking like they were long lost friends. Out of the blue, a continent away I surprised them came up behind them and once again "thanked them for their service" and they turned white as a ghost. When you have been with the best you tend to pick up on the mistakes of the rest and I was off to catch my flight.

Babe Ruth and Michael Jordan both to fight against the boredom played a game within a game and going after souls was no game but sometimes you had to stay a step ahead of the opposition but both Babe and I were both swinging for the fence and trying to get people home. My dear friend Sam Glenn and I stayed in Tampa, FL on millionaire row visiting a friend of his for a weekend. We stayed at a lawyer's home which was incredible, and it was situated just feet from the Tampa Bay. He loaned us his brand new $114,000 Mercedes convertible while he went out of town and gave us the house free while in town. The owner's father played on the legendary New York Yankees World Series Champion Team and was a pitcher. On the team pic in the house framed on the wall was his father who was a pitcher that year and I believe a Cy Young winner. Standing next to him was the legendary Babe Ruth and the "Bronx Bomber" gave him a baseball bat with his autograph that was in the home we were staying.

Someone had offered two hundred grand for the bat and the son turned it down. We calculated that the home we stayed in had to have nearly one million dollars in sports memorabilia. It was the most impressive private collection I had ever seen. He had basketballs signed by Kareem, Bird, Magic, and Jordan. I held a New York Jets official helmet signed by Joe Namath and he had autographs from every Major League Baseball player that hit over four hundred homeruns. The house was incredible with the marble floors and elevator inside the home and mechanical blinds that could shut with the flip of the switch to protect all glass three story wall facing the bay to protect from high winds in a storm. However, the furniture and sports memorabilia he collected was over the top. It is surreal looking back how not only Satan has hit me each step of the way, but God allowed me to meet or loosely interact with some childhood heroes while fighting the good fight. I found myself holding the very bat that Babe Ruth swung with in a game and hand signed for the man's father that I am staying rent free while visiting one of my best friends in the Sunshine State. Indeed, God does order our steps.

Speaking of steps, I started walking towards my gate the other direction just to confirm my suspicion of the surveillance and I finally grabbed a slice of Pizza in Istanbul. Appropriate I was in that city because I just left a "Turkey" or two with matching back packs five minutes before. As soon as I devoured my meal, I found an abandoned gate and did my best to catch a one-hour power nap on those uncomfortable metal airport chairs and the alarm on my phone alerted me I needed to head towards my gate.

At one time, I had been in talks with producers at Trinity Broadcast Network (TBN) in Santa Ana, CA and other well-known Christian speakers and evangelists about possibly being in a television reality show featuring our lives on the road and speaking on stage. They were going to pick five or six diverse speakers and I was considered, and they were leaning towards naming it "Gospel Globetrotters, Road Warriors or "Rock Star Preachers." I get the first two but the third I had to shoot down and someone said, "Frank, we could possibly have a partnership with the energy drink, and we need an edgy name for shock value." That was the craziest thing I had ever heard, and I said, "No way! The problem with causing "shock value" is it is the innocent guys like me that end up getting electrocuted!"

The good news is they got my point on the name but for whatever reason the pilot for the show didn't materialize. Sometimes a denial is just a delay, but it also could be God's protection. Lord knows, I already had a TARGET on my back preaching and did not need to make the bullseye any bigger. Years ago, while working in the United States Senate at my first summer internship for the Architect of the Capitol, my nickname was "Inspector Gadget." He was the cool cartoon that was an undercover detective, and he had the gadgets to beat the bad guys. It was a popular show back in the day and it fit for two reasons. My Dad was an Inspector with the United States Capitol Police in the late 1980's like Inspector Callahan (Clint Eastwood) and I was tall and slim and could get in small places to get things done. My colleagues would sing, "Go Gadget Go!" just like the song from the show. It stuck and despite not being a Special Agent or Detective, the Lord still gave me incredible insight and traits to get the job done. I can still hear the kind compliment of the Special Agent in Charge with the United States Secret Service at an interview, and he said, "Frank you would have made one hell of an agent." High praise but despite going through some "Hell" lately at home and on the road, I was still trying to promote Heaven wherever I was.

Once more I am boarding another flight by myself and this time from Turkey and now, I am racing down the runway to connect with Dr. Thomas and the incredible ministry in Kota, India. After the equally long flight into Dehli we landed, and I was doing my best to navigate through their Customs. The first red flag was my bag had not arrived when I did. That is always a blessing. Fortunately, an hour later it arrived, and the second strike was when my dear friend, Pastor Jake Thornhill from North Carolina was to meet me at the airport I learned only after landing that his passport and paperwork was not completed in time, and he was unable to make the flight. Now the only other American that I know who I was excited about spending a week with is not coming! I had two strikes before and I had not even left the airport of India and Satan was once again trying to strike me out.

Dr. Thomas's son personally picked me up and we had met once before in Atlanta and that helped tremendously but I was used to flying alone around the world. I did not say I liked it, but it is often how we had to do it to get things done with the assignment God called me. Indeed, it is a team effort, and I was taken to a beautiful hotel and after a quick shower I was able to immediately go to sleep. Unlike my recent stay in Africa where I was forced to preach the moment my feet hit the ground, they genuinely encouraged me to crash and even though it was afternoon local time in Dehli I was down for the count. Fortunately, my Air Marshal friends were a distant memory, and I could finally rest.

After a nice rest I caught up with my assigned driver and after breakfast the next day we checked out of the hotel for the two-hour drive to Kota. I did not know but that rest the night before would be the last sleep I would have until my final night home. The tyrannical government had grown so violent and anti-Christian that they had threatened repeatedly to shut down the graduation at the Bible College where I was invited to give the commencement address. The President of the Bible College is a cherished friend, and his father was a legend in Christian circles before graduating to Heaven. My college friend Clayton King, who pastors one of the largest churches in America, told me that, "Meeting Dr. Billy Graham and Dr. M.A. Thomas were two of the greatest highlights in his ministry." Dr. Thomas was the father to Dr. Sam Thomas who was now in charge of the entire Bible College and orphanage. Both the late father and son had been arrested multiple times on fake charges simply because of their Christian faith.

Dr. Thomas told me in person and over the phone many times that his dream was to die and become a martyr for the cause of Christ. The hostility was so intense that you could feel it in the air and America is often welcomed with open arms world-wide but lately this white dude (me) was frowned upon in certain circles. The initial plan was for me to stay on the compound inside the Bible College, but the tension was so high, and the unceasing threats of the government wanting to return and raid the complex made it unsafe for me to stay within their walls.

To say I was not a tad concerned would be untruthful. A couple nights in a row I was told to grab my luggage and they checked me into another hotel to keep their government on their toes. For a guy who only preached about Jesus, it starts to mess with your head when you must be on the run for living right. This may disappoint some of my "friends" who think we are in the ministry for the money but now I have already dodged two governments watching me and I did not make a dime on this trip to India either. I recall an interview that Sam Donaldson did with Mother Teresa and after spending a full day with the respected nun he said, "Sister, I wouldn't do what you do for a million dollars" and without missing a beat she replied, "I wouldn't do it either for money, but I do it in service to my Lord." I never met her but had friends who did, but I was closer than ever to her Calcutta humble home in India.

Those times with Dr. Sam and his team are moments I will cherish forever but I could see the visible strain that was on his shoulders. Not only financially to provide for those precious children and college students but the nonstop threat of a government that would love more than anything to detain him and possibly kill him. The second day while in India, they took me to one of the Seven Wonders of the World and for my forty sixth birthday I celebrated it at the Taj Mahal. It was surreal being there in person and for a place built by Muslims, this Christian enjoyed being there and seeing it up close. It truly is a work of art and ministry is lonely at times; but it does have it perks and visits like this were a bonus despite the stress that comes with a global calling.

On the third day I was ushered to a leprosy colony and that would play a big part a couple years later when the Cov19 hit. When churches would close and cave like a deck of cards over a virus with a ninety nine percent recovery rate, I was reminded of diseases in Africa and leper colony in India that you either believe and preach that Jesus heals or you do not. I had seen God heal and I knew the power of faith and I could not stop believing now! India is a beautiful place with beautiful people, and I saw several weddings while in town and they are either always celebrating or mourning but I guess that is true in life for all in every city. That is why more than ever we must go after souls while time is still on our side. One day time will be up, and souls are either saved in Heaven with Jesus or banned forever in Hell with the Devil.

While in town I preached five times in three days to the pastors who traveled countless miles and some even came by foot to hear the messages. It was humbling that I have a few youth pastors that would not walk across the street to meet me and yet I have senior pastors so hungry for the Word of God that they would travel a full day to hear me preach. Indeed, a true prophet is with honor everywhere but their hometown. Sometimes I throw in their home church. In the Greek language the translation means, "The proper weight or value is not recognized in their hometown."

Jesus could not do certain miracles in his hometown because they were familiar with family and thought that is just Joseph and Mary's little kid. That little kid was no longer a child, but The Christ and the kid were now The King of Kings, and he was no longer just walking the streets of Nazareth but as an adult walked on the Sea of Galilee and was raising the dead. I am no Jesus, but the true term means "Little Jesus" and it is an honor to be his mentee and an Ambassador of Him. I certainly had not walked on water but had preached to nations, Hollywood, and heads of state both home and abroad. Part of the prophet not being recognized was twofold. One to protect the preacher from getting a big head because the only person God cannot use is the person full of himself and second it exposes those who cannot see what Ray Charles could see when God is using a person. Some have either so much pride or sin in their own life that they are BLIND to see when God promotes another.

It was a hundred degrees in Africa, but it had to be one hundred and ten degrees in India! Anyone could preach Hell because it was so hot in both places. I thought Alabama was hot and humid but that was a cold front compared to these two continents. Just in the last month I had traveled over 25,000 miles by plane, train, car, and boat and to say I was tired would be both respectful and misleading. For a guy preaching LIFE, I was dead tired and only halfway into this trip in India. God was all over me ministering to those precious souls in India and I say souls because that is the most important part of the body. Jesus said, "What would it profit a man to gain the whole world and lose his own soul?"

One day I was treated to a pleasant surprise and Dr. Sam Thomas and his team took us to a custom tailor to get fitted for a brand-new suit! In all my years, even working on Capitol Hill, I never had my own custom-tailored suit. They have some of the best linens and materials in the world in India and Dr. Sam allowed me to pick out the material and after they personally sized me and took my measurements, I was given the freedom to choose whether

I wanted a single- or double-breasted suit and whether I preferred it in wool or silk, in solid or pinstripes. In USD it would probably cost $800 for this suit, and he bought it for me for coming to speak.

The local price for the incredible handmade work of art was only about $140 per suit. I could not help but I bought five suits before flying home and on my last day the tailor personally showed up with six bags of suits for me to travel home with. For a guy who traveled with next to nothing I now had another suitcase on the return flight with my high-end suits at a fraction of the cost. They will last me until the day I die and lately I was wondering if that would be sooner rather than later.

It was a delight to meet many of the orphan children and hearing some of their stories were heart breaking but the love that Dr. Thomas and his team lavished on them was incredible. Many of these children never recall meeting their parents but they found a home filled with love and learned about the saving knowledge of Jesus when they arrived at the orphanage and Bible College. Many grew up to become preachers, evangelists, missionaries, to marry a pastor and/or serving the Lord in their own way.

Just like the poor kids I met in Brazil, or Africa I did my best to give money to some of the students while visiting India. I wish I were loaded with funds because I would have loved to bless them all but even Jesus said, "The poor you will always have." Dr. Sam and his team showed us the utmost love and hospitality while in town but once again we pivoted day by day with the government threatening to cancel the graduation in two days. Once again, I was relocated to another hotel and one can start to develop Post Traumatic Stress Disorder (PTSD) when you are told to grab your belongings and moved once again for security. Lately, I resembled a president without a security detail and a preacher on the run not because of private sin but because I publicly proclaimed Heaven's Son.

While visiting a missionary in his home who also was friends with Dr. Sam's ministry, talk about a small world, but he knew my friend from college. Halfway around the world we had a mutual friend back home and we were both brothers in Christ. While at his kitchen table I got a text that Billy Graham had died back in Montreat, North Carolina. My heart dropped and my childhood hero and earthly boss was now with the Lord. The one who preached to more people in person than anyone in history was now face to face with the One whom he preached so faithfully. My heart dropped but I recall something Dr. Graham said in an interview once, "One day you will read that Billy Graham has died. Do not believe it for a second because I will be more alive than ever before. I would only have changed my address." Dr. Graham was now at home and I was on the other side of the world away from home but soon after I learned that his body would be laid in honor at my former place of employment in the Rotunda of the United States Capitol and was excited to return after preaching to pay my respects.

I also recalled a story that he said for years that he thought he could live to be one hundred years old but multiple times as he was late in eighties and early nineties it was touch and go. He had a few scares before and was raced to the Mayo Clinic. He had said repeatedly and with passion that he would live to be one hundred. When he died on February 21, 2018, some scoffers mocked, "Well, the old minister fell short on that one." When I returned to the States, we had another staff meeting at the BGEA Headquarters and I shared that he did live to be one hundred and someone politely corrected me to say, "Frank, he was ninety-nine years and three months old when he passed on to Heaven." I knew that but said with a smile, "But he was nine months in his mother's womb and that equals actually 100!"

With the threats louder than ever while in India to shut the graduation down I was thinking we flew here only to not be allowed to minister but we had to trust that God would work it out despite the doubts. Satan also is like a junkyard dog with no teeth. All bark and no bite! The morning of the event we prayed that we would still have it regardless, what the government or their misguided police would do, and we prayed BY FAITH that it would carry on. Looking back, it was totally the Lord because the pastors walked from miles to attend, and the graduation transpired without a hitch. Before entering that evening where I would have the high honor to preach to over 600 Bible college graduates, I learned that leadership legend, Dr. John Maxwell had also preached in this same sanctuary on this same campus to this very same school. Dr. Johnnie Moore who was formerly VP of Liberty University and now on President Trump's spiritual advisory board had spoken to this school and on this same night I would be awarded an honorary Doctor of Ministry for preaching to this distinguished group.

The auditorium was packed to the gills and standing room only and the orphans were ushered up in the balcony to see the current generation's graduation. It was brilliant to have the young and old both present and gave the youth something to look forward to and many eventually would one day graduate too.

When those children sang it was hands down one of the greatest sounds I have ever heard. They sounded like angels singing at the top of their lungs and tears welled up in my eyes to see those that were abandoned by their parents found love in their Heavenly Father. The Brooklyn Tabernacle would have had a hard time keeping up with this children's choir. I have been around Grammy winners but the singing that night in India echoes in my mind to this very day!

With the news of Dr. Graham's passing the day before, I found myself now sitting in this gorgeous sanctuary filled once again. It was humbling but the month before at Mandela Stadium in Africa and now at Emmanuel Theological Seminary in India with folks standing wall to wall and others watching in an overflow room. Dr. Sam Thomas and I are on the front row side by side, and he is both President and host of today's graduation. Moments before I would be introduced to give the keynote address, I noticed a placard behind the pulpit filled with names. I leaned quietly towards him and inquired, "Who were the names on the wall?" and what he said next marked me for life.

With tears immediately filling his eyes and a look filled with both love and intensity he leaned towards me and said, "Frank, this school that you are going to speak to tonight has produced more martyrs for the cause of Christ than any place in the world." With a tear streaking down the right side of the face and sweat that was already visible on his forehead due to the intense India heat, he said while pointing to the board, "those names are former students from here who went on to graduate and have since killed for their faith in Christ." If that were not enough, he then said, "It is the dream of the graduation class and everyone under the sound of your voice tonight that they, too, would have the high honor to be martyred for our Lord. In America, your Bible college students dream of building a big church. Here in Kota, India our students' desire is to make the board with their name on it."

Dr. Thomas just dropped the mic and I had yet to pick it up to speak but my time was now, and as I was introduced the crowd roared with approval, but the truth is I never felt smaller in ministry than I did as I approached the pulpit. As I surveyed the crowd and with my Bible open and text before me, I found the eyes of my precious friend who just helped change the trajectory of my ministry. More than ever, I could relate to Charles Spurgeon who preached as a dying man to dying men. In the last year, I had preached on multiple continents and my messages had been interpreted in five languages while preaching, but at this solemn moment I gave no opening joke and went straight to Jesus.

Bill Gaither once wrote that if you live long enough, the words to the lyrics we sing will catch up to you. Lately, behind another pulpit speaking to another nation a half a world away and recently having been moved from hotel to hotel for security purposes, and now addressing a crowd whose dreams in life would be to die for the cause of Christ. With the government at our door and the repeated pressure of being monitored and followed both home and abroad it was starting to be taxing on my body and now looking at Dr. Sam Thomas in the front row knowing he could be arrested at any moment I was wondering how much sand was left in my proverbial hourglass? Not trying to make light of the moment but I had a couple brand new suits and anyone of them would look good at my funeral as I rested in my casket.

That night I preached on John the Baptist and if I ever recall have the power of God on me when I preached it was that night during the graduation in Kota, India. I had spoken to crowds most on my life and since eighth grade as Student Government President in junior high I would address 800 students daily giving the morning announcements. The crowds were a tad larger a couple decades later and I just preached in stadiums three years in a row in Africa but the intensity of this moment at the time was the most poignant and dangerous.

Despite speaking to crowds, I was always told to zero in on one, and President Reagan had an innate gift to speak to thousands but someone in the back swore "The Great Communicator" was speaking directly to him. At times as a former Congressional speechwriter, I had the rhetoric of Reagan and could impersonate our 40th President, but like Billy Graham, there was only one Ronald Wilson Reagan. However, at this juncture I was not only speaking to that great graduation but speaking and ministering directly to Dr. Thomas. Quite Frankly, I was also speaking to myself and we both knew intimately that the walls were slowly closing in on us. At any moment, the Indian government or their corrupt police force could barge in and disrupt the Bible graduation.

At that moment, I was no longer focused on the threat but the treat and task of speaking to these future world changers. John the Baptist knew Jesus before he was even birthed. He leapt in his mother's womb when Mary walked into the room while she was pregnant with Jesus. My message was that John Leapt for Jesus. He Lived for Jesus while alive and John Loved Jesus in death. You may recall the story, but John was beheaded for serving the Lord and as I surveyed that crowd and spoke life to those graduates with the martyr's Hall of Fame behind the pulpit as I preached, I knew that they and I could be next.

God's Presence was so thick that night and it was one of those surreal moments that it was as if I watched myself as I preached that message. It was truly the Hand of God on that sermon and Dr. Thomas said two things when I concluded, "We have had some of the greatest orators over the years come speak in that same pulpit you ministered tonight and not only were you arguably among the greatest speakers we have ever heard but that is bar none the greatest message I have ever heard on John the Baptist.

They gave God a standing ovation when my keynote was over and that evening, they bestowed on me just hours after Dr. Billy Graham's death an honorary doctorate degree. I have joked for years for all my friends who want to invest tens of thousands of dollars and countless hours in a doctorate that is fine, but I gave it to the Lord and said if He wants me to have one, they will just bestow one on me. The Lord works in unique ways, and I have been blessed to receive two honorary doctorates the last couple years. The first in India with Dr. Sam Thomas and my name is now inscribed next to Dr. John Maxwell at the Bible college and The River Church in Tampa, FL with my dear friend, Dr. Rodney Howard-Browne and it was an honor months later to give the keynote at their River Bible Institute graduation to over two thousand people.

That night in India I had the honor to shake the hand of every graduate and help pass out their much-deserved diploma, but I believe that what made the greatest impression was at the conclusion of the sermon we collectively took the "Martyr's Oath." Dr. Johnnie Moore who I mentioned at the beginning of this chapter after doing the same wrote a bestselling book and he was recently named by the President of the United States as an Ambassador to help persecuted Christians world-wide.

Dr. Billy Graham said, "You are not ready to live until you are willing to die" and on this night seven thousand miles from home more than ever I was ready to die for the Lord. In unison we all took voluntarily the oath that night and the only thing more angelic than hearing those children sing was that capacity crowd repeating the words of this oath:

"THE MARTYR'S OATH"

"I take a STAND to honor the Lord Jesus Christ with my hands to serve all mankind. I take a STAND to honor the Lord Jesus Christ with my feet to spread the Gospel to all the ends of the Earth, no matter the cost. I take a STAND to honor the Lord Jesus Christ with my lips by proclaiming the Good News to all who will hear and by edifying the body of Christ. I take a STAND to honor Jesus Christ with my mind as I meditate on His Word and His promises to me. I give my earthly treasures and all that I possess to follow the way of the cross. I commit to love my family, orphans, widows, lepers, the wealthy, and the poor the way Christ loved the church. I surrender my will and life to His will and life. I commit to the service of the Lord by being a good steward of my TIME. I surrender this body on Earth to the perfect will of Jesus and should my blood be spilled; may it bring forth a mighty harvest of souls. I pledge allegiance to the Lamb. I will seek to honor His command. I am not ashamed of the Gospel of Christ for it is the power of God unto salvation to everyone who believes. As a soldier of the cross, I STAND with the Apostle Paul in stating that, "For me to live is Christ and to die is gain." Lord Jesus, Thy Kingdom come, Thy will be done on Earth as it is in Heaven. I love my India and my fellow citizens, and I claim India for Christ. I have read this pledge and understood it completely. Being of sound mind and body, I do solemnly swear and declare this Martyr's Pledge without any persuasion or enticement."

Dr. M.A. Thomas & Dr. Sam Thomas

Founder & Son – Hopegivers International

Kota, India

(Frank received an honorary doctorate from Dr. Samuel Thomas)

I had no idea that in just over two years the oath to take a STAND and willing to put my life on the line would come back to help me become stronger at home and abroad during the COVID19 lockdown that would be coming to our shores. God indeed orders our steps, and we must follow His footsteps to be faithful.

The month before while shaking hands with everyone in Kampala, Africa I was exhausted and spent at the pastor's conference, but this time was a different tired in India. It was liberating and once you faced your greatest fears, it is a relief and now no matter what lie ahead, we are resting in the perfect will of God. We took hundreds of pictures and slapped hands with over a thousand new friends but despite the travel and stress it was time well spent.

Immediately following the graduation donors help purchase a Bible and brand-new motorcycle for each graduate. They are now officially "Holy Rollers" as they embark in their ministry, and it is wonderful how they bless the new preachers as they head off into their official service to Christ. My dear friend, Rex Thonkins from Oklahoma has been instrumental and securing hundreds of motorbikes over the years to these fine Christian men and women in India.

On my last day in Kota, we had a wonderful time of fellowship with Dr. Sam Thomas and his leadership team. We had a wonderful catered meal and indeed it resembled the Upper Room and we knew we had dodged a bullet and we didn't even consider it the Last Supper despite our last meal together in India. Our tailored suits arrived, and I found it interesting that the ministry that relies completely by faith were lavishly giving to us. Dr. Thomas and Dr. Rodney Howard-Browne have both helped me to become a more generous giver. It is a sin to be stingy as a Christian.

We prayed together one last time and we were driven to the train station where we would board a one-hundred-year-old train and ride through the dark night of India on a ten-hour trip only to arrive the next morning in Dehli. I must confess we encountered some unique folks at the train station and Steve Martin and John Candy were in a classic called, "Planes, Trains & Automobiles" and lately it had been the story of my life. Ever since childhood, I have been fascinated with airplanes and the Wright Brothers from Kitty Hawk, North Carolina indeed had "The Right Stuff" and I daydreamed early on about flying and traveling but I must admit there is something nostalgia about the old school train.

However, on this trip this train made the trek unique. For starters, it was old and with zero luxury amenities and when you add being in another nation in the midnight hour on a ten-hour trip it once again broke the mold that those that live for Jesus are "boring" and missing out. In my past political life, at times I resembled Harrison Ford on "Air Force One" but tonight halfway around the world it was more "Indiana Jones" but boring it was not.

It was blue and rusty, but it got the job done. I cannot make fun of it because it was faithful in service for years and the more, I think about it, I am not a spring chicken myself anymore and I pray to be as steadfast when my time is up. The train rocked nonstop which was both a blessing and burden, because after forty-five minutes in that small car for something resembling a bunk bed, I was able to curl up and try to sleep. The fact is I had been moved from multiple beds and hotels and after just preaching one of the greatest sermons of my life at the Bible college graduation completely exhausted in pouring into others one cannot be too picky where to crash. Jesus said that even He at times did not have a place to lay His head and sleep and while I was aboard this train, the rhythm of the train swaying back and forth on the tracks made this nearly half century old evangelist sleep like a baby in the cradle. Add that for brief respite it appeared that their government was not as intense on our trail helped somewhat but one can never be certain. The blessing was as much as I loved Dr. Sam Thomas, Hopegivers International, Emmanuel Theological Seminary, the orphanage, and staff plus the incredible Indian people I was inching or should say "rocking" myself closer to Delhi for my final day before heading home to the United States.

Within another fifteen minutes I would be out and there comes a time in your life that you just must trust God to watch you and faith allows one to sleep when the flesh is saying stay awake. It was almost one in the morning local time and after preaching eight times in a couple days it was good to finally sleep. The train pulled into the station and at the time I would say New York City was the busiest area per capita I had been, but I would venture to say it was even more congested in India.

After getting off the train I felt like the 1980's arcade game Frogger and it is putting your life in jeopardy just trying to cross the street. Finding the rhythm on the train required another groove crossing the street and I would dare say the horns were even more rampant than the taxis in the Big Apple.

After traveling all night, it was therapeutic to be placed in a nice, upscale hotel about a half hour from the Delhi airport. The hotel had to be five stars especially for overseas and I could relate to the writer who penned, "I have dined with kings and queens and ate pork and beans." To an extent that would almost be true, and the Bible does say, "your gift will make room for you and bring you before kings and great men." I had stayed in motels where I had to keep an eye on the door and take a shower with my shoes on because it was so filthy. Over the years, the Lord allowed me to stay in Beverly Hills and on rare occasion stay at some of the nicest hotels in the world.

This hotel was first class and everything that Dr. Sam and his team do for others is incredible and their generosity is a blessing. My prayers then and now remain with Dr. Sam and not only will his reward in Heaven be huge, but the fact of the matter is also I often pray for him and am concerned for his safety. I have tried unsuccessfully for our own government to investigate easing some of the harassment against him and his ministry. Lord willing, that will change but with time ticking and the Lord's return closer than ever, I am not certain that things may get any better for the born-again Christians. Jesus made it clear that they persecuted Him and will do the same towards us but be of good cheer because God has overcome the world and greater that is He in us than he (Devil) that is in the world.

Dr. Sam Thomas often prayed for those that abused and accused him and taught us to do the same. As this whirlwind trip in India was ending, I realized it had also been one of emotions resembling a roller coaster ride. I not only had to fly solo to and from since my dear friend from North Carolina did not make it, and then shortly after arriving I learned that my boss and mentor from afar, Dr. Billy Graham was now with the Lord. Several times I had been in touch with colleagues in Charlotte to learn more about his funeral arrangements and was happy to learn God had worked it out providentially that the flight home that I purchased from the beginning was going to arrive in Washington with just enough time to shower and return to the United States Capitol to pay my respects. Add in the emotional duress of back-to-back trips to Africa and India in one month halfway around the world to preach only to feel on the run and look over your shoulder wondering is this the day everything stops. I'm not referring to the day the living stops but rather the day that freely preaching the Gospel stops. In these days with the world's value system upside down perhaps we were more than ever considered a threat.

After a restful sleep it was time to be taken to the airport to return home. Once more I navigated alone through the airport and boarded another jumbo jet for America. As the plane raced down the runway my mind quickly reviewed the past week in one of the most amazing countries in the world. From spending my birthday at the Taj Mahal to shaking hands with almost every graduate and orphan and that by God's grace, no one was arrested, beaten or detained. Christianity is not a spectator sport and Theodore Roosevelt's "Man in the Arena" speech came to mind more than once over the years.

"It is not the critic who counts; not the man who points out how the strong man stumbles, or where the doer of deeds could have done them better. The credit belongs to the man who is actually in the arena, whose face is marred by dust and sweat and blood; who strives valiantly; who errs, who comes short again and again; who spends himself in a worthy cause; who at the best knows in the end the triumph of high achievement, and who at the worst, if he fails, at least fails while daring greatly, so that his place shall never be with those cold and timid souls who neither know victory nor defeat."

Indeed, I was in the game and too far in to turn back now. Southern Gospel legend sang, "I wouldn't take nothing for my journey now" and those lyrics still say it all.

"Well, I wouldn't take nothing for my journey now
I'm, gonna make it to Heaven somehow
Though the devil tempts me and tries to turn me around
He's offered everything that's got a name
All the wealth I want and worldly fame
If I could still I wouldn't take nothing for my journey now

Verse I

Well, I started out a-travelling for the Lord many years ago
I had a lot of heartaches, I've had a lot of grief and woe
But when I would stumble, then I would humble down
And I can say thank the Lord I wouldn't take nothing for my journey now."

As our Boeing 777 lifted airborne I whispered another prayer for my new friends and with contentment of a job well done, I was heading home as I took one last look at the Indian skyline.

After an uneventful landing, a day later back in America, with no time to spare, I was able to shower, shave and put on a clean suit and race to the U.S. Capitol to pay my respects to the world's most beloved preacher and evangelist. Dr. Graham had pastored over a dozen U.S. Presidents and my father had met him twice in that same building. My father had not returned to the People's House since retiring two decades before, but when he heard Billy Graham had passed, my father also put on his Sunday best and we met as a family, stood in line to circle around the Beloved Preacher's casket in the Rotunda.

It was a special family moment for us all and Deputy Chief Shelton was back in the building. We were able to say hello to Will Graham (Billy's grandson) and hugged him and offered our sincere condolences for the loss of such a great man of God.

EL SALVADOR

LATELY, the doors of ministry were swinging open wider, and the platform was growing bigger both at home and abroad. God has been so faithful, and He showed me years before that I would be traveling and preaching to crowds, and it was indeed happening. Satan taunted me relentlessly for years as if I was in the ministry because of me. I joke I certainly wouldn't be in the ministry if it were for me, I think opening up for Van Halen in the 80's or trying to break into Hollywood would be a better route.

In high school, when I was not daydreaming about playing sports outside, or hoping to date a pretty girl or drawing hot rods and sports cars in class I would often doodle a stick figure on a stage speaking to a sea of people. The man was holding a microphone in one hand and holding up a Bible in the other and speaking to a capacity crowd as far as the eye could see. For two decades Satan would mock me repeatedly and try to make me think that the ministry was for me or to feed my ego when in fact it was always for the Lord. Frankly, I did not pick the ministry God picked me and I would have loved to run for office and serve God and constituents. It is a powerful privilege to represent others and serve them while honoring the Lord.

Perhaps you have ever struggled with the thought of serving the Lord and Satan the sick snake and accuser of the brethren would insinuate that our labors were not pure. One night, God gave me a breakthrough and I was awake at three in the morning. I would come to learn much later that the "witching hour" was at that time and much happens in the supernatural late after midnight and before sunrise. The Devil was once again harassing me about the ministry, and I had long graduated from high school, and I was tossing and turning with no sleep.

The Holy Spirit whispered, "Frank do you recall when you drew that picture long ago of that stick figure representing you?" I said in my mind, "Absolutely!" God hinted take out that picture you drew long ago. The fact is, I still had it folded in the bottom drawer of my nightstand next to the bed and the Lord inquired in my spirit, "what is that you are holding in your right hand?" I said, "The Bible." God replied with a resounding, "Yes!" It was as if the Lord were telling me, "Frank, if it were all about you than you would not be holding up the Bible preaching to a crowd of people if you were trying to make a name for yourself." From that point on, I put the drawing back in the drawer and never looked back. Satan had lied to me for years and serving God was not about me but honoring Him.

Since then, I was blessed to speak on Christian cruises on five trips to the Bahamas, preach in Jamaica with some of the most recognized pastors and Grammy winners in the world. We traveled to over two dozen nations and had since been invited to preach on five continents. The past three years to over a third of a million Africans at Nelson Mandela Soccer Stadium in Uganda and ministered to gold medalists in both London and Rio. Now I was on staff with the Billy Graham Evangelistic Association and leading a Bible study to lawmakers in the state capitol while my supervisor at the time was leading the weekly White House Cabinet Bible Study. In the last few months, we had preached twice in Europe and just last month was ministering in India half a world away.

Indeed, God was blessing, and Pastor Rodney Howard - Browne had just had me return and preach four days during his winter camp meeting in Tampa, FL. I still had some little league critics at home, but God had strategically placed some Major League mentors in my corner. While ministering at The River Church, the Lord was blessing in a powerful way and I also was invited back to minister on live television at Christian Television Network in Clearwater, Florida one day while in town. My good buddy Pastor Jayson Williams who is an assistant to Pastor Rodney came with me that day and we had a blast! It was super reuniting with Bob D'Andrea again with his lovely bride and we laughed and hit it off like my last visit to their world-wide studio.

After a nice meal, we raced back to Tampa to be present for the evening revival service with Pastor Rodney and his church family. After preaching again the next morning to a packed crowd in their gorgeous sanctuary my wife, Ruth and I were summoned up to Pastor

Rodney's office and his quarters are second to none. After taking the elevator to his private suite we were ushered back inside, and his office resembles both Animal Kingdom and the West Wing of the White House.

It would be hard pressed to find another who loves America as much as Dr. Rodney Howard - Browne and he is a brilliant, creative, historian and powerful preacher. Some folks have a deer or two on their wall, but this brother has an elephant with ivory tusks mounted to the wall. The head of that elephant is almost as big as me and I am still trying to figure how they got that not only up on the second floor but into his office quarters. He also has the exact replica of the Resolute Desk that President John F. Kennedy had in the Oval Office.

This brother is at another level and Ruth, and I adore both him his incredible wife, Dr. Adonica, their family and amazing church family. He is the Billy Graham of the Pentecostal denomination and for almost my entire life friends joked I was "Bapti-costal." While my wife and I were seated in two plush blue chairs facing Pastor behind his presidential desk he asked me point blank a question that I had been asked many times before, "Frank, how many times have you been to El Salvador?"

My head dropped as I stared almost in shame at my shoes on the floor as my wife watched and he waited for my response. I said, "Pastor Rodney, I have wanted to go but have yet to visit." Over the years, I have had many people ask out of curiosity how many times had I visited my wife's homeland before she became a United States citizen. If you do not know her testimony it is powerful and in the middle of a Civil War in the late 1980's armed guerillas were going door to door destroying property, attacking citizens and murdering families on the spot. Ruth and her sister literally ran for their lives and with less than one hundred dollars made it to the United States of America after being temporarily detained in Mexico.

When Hispanic people inquire of me, "Mr. Frank, how many times have you been to El Salvador? I take it as if they are suggesting that I loved Ruth enough to marry her but apparently not enough because I have not been back to her hometown thirteen times since." I shared with Pastor Rodney that money was one of the main reasons as an evangelist who lives "by faith" and relies mostly on love offerings. Another legitimate excuse was between my traveling schedule and my wife with limited personal leave, El Salvador was just not a reality. It is less expensive to take a cruise to the Caribbean than it was to fly to her home-town. It is not the most frequented tourist spot in the world, but I did eventually hope to visit where she grew up.

I was expecting Pastor to tease me for failing to "man up" and have already been to El Salvador and the man who is as bold as a lion on the platform can be gentle like a lamb at times behind the scenes. It was almost like something I had seen in a movie, and he picked up the phone on his Resolute desk and the next thing I know a door opens behind me and a secretary with a note pad and pen sits down on the couch. He pressed another button, and another assistant came through another door asking how we wanted the coffee I did not even order.

Pastor then looked at Ruth and me and then said, "This is what we are going to do. The

Lord just impressed on me to pay for you, your wife and your son to send you for two weeks on vacation with all expenses covered for you to see firsthand her native El Salvador." He continued, "Frank, I will pay for your flights, hotel and even throw in a rental car and you have been to Israel and followed the footsteps of Jesus, but you need to go to El Salvador and walk where your wife grew up."

At this juncture, tears are streaming from Ruth's eyes and my mouth is on the floor. Dr. Howard-Browne in one single motion of goodwill was both presidential and pastoral. Pastor is hands down one of the most generous men I have ever met, and many pastors are kind but very few give personally like he has invested selflessly and sown into others. I was told "give until it helps" but Rodney and I believe give until it hurts. My motto is if it does not hurt you it may not help anyone else. Honor and generosity are dying attributes these days, but we have them in spades and those without them are often failing to play with a full deck.

We were touched so much by this incredible gift plus it was a private prayer of Ruth's heart. Later that day, we were having a private lunch with pastor and his bride at their table with other distinguished guests and Rodney looked at me and said, "What are you doing on the eighteenth of May?" As I have grown in the Lord I can sense when God is moving, and the Holy Spirit is speaking, and I knew to check my calendar and not inquire "Why?" Fortunately, it was clear, and Pastor said, "Frank, your messages have been phenomenal all week and our people love you and I want you to be the keynote graduation speaker at the River Bible Institute." Once again, I was floored and humbled and I just recall thinking "Thank you Jesus!"

Within a few short months, I flew back solo and preached that night to a packed sanctuary and over five hundred Bible students graduated that night in their caps and gowns. Approximately two thousand were present and you can see that sermon on the homepage of our website. Folks from across the country were texting Pastor while I was on the platform and he told me afterwards, "Frank in over a quarter of century we have had some incredible commencement speakers but that was hands down arguably the greatest ever." It takes a big person to compliment others and within ninety days I had just preached in India and now Tampa and received two honorary Doctor of Divinity and Ministry degrees respectfully from two generals in God's Army. In addition, both Presidents said the message God gave me was pound for pound some of the best preaching they ever heard.

What was intriguing to me was a few local leaders could not compliment the gifting on my life, but the heavyweights could not stop. Less than a month later, my wife, son and I were racing down another runway and this time heading for San Salvador, El Salvador. Pastor and his team really know how to bless and roll out the red carpet when lavishing love on others and he not only paid for three airfares but had us at five-star hotels throughout the trip.

After arriving and going through Customs we were able to retrieve the rental car that they graciously provided and got a quick ice cream on the road adjacent to the airport. For starters it was HOT in El Salvador and secondly, preachers love "Sundaes" and Sunday too!

After a couple hour drive, we were staying in these beautiful huts overlooking the ocean and we were right on the beach. We had our own villa, and it was something you would see in a magazine and El Salvador does have some beautiful spots.

Our hut was surrounded by six other similar two-story huts that you had to take private stairs up to your room. Each wrapped around the pool with palm trees and then a few steps later you would be on the sand. We had dinner right on a beach and it was nice meeting other folks. I noticed shortly after arriving that some undercover detectives were doing their best to blend in but when your family has deeper roots at the national level in law enforcement you can see the mistakes of those who have been in the game much less.

We pick up on patterns and I had been trained to also see suspicious behavior and sometimes it is government folks that are not on the up and up. One flag was since very few people were at that upscale resort when those working or trying to be "undercover" they would relieve the other at the same spot. If there were fifty chairs along the perimeter the one coming on post would sit in the same chair. These were not lifeguards taking a seat from their perch or security canvasing the compound, but it was clear they were providing surveillance and once again the American seemed to be in their sights.

As I mentioned previously, I noted when God is blessing the Devil starts messing and now the snake was not only harassing me at home but on vacation abroad. A dear friend who retired from NYPD told me to take it as a compliment from the Lord that your influence now was on the Devil's radar. Consider having your own free security but I had been flanked my entire life with the best law enforcement security in the world, but they were family and friends. Lately, I have had fruit loops that had neither God's or my best interests at heart.

I have had one beer in my life and do not advocate drinking, but Babe Ruth would show up to the game drunk. For him, it became a game within a game, and he could still while impaired smash a fastball four hundred feet over the center field fence. He would toy with the opponents and sometimes this "young gun" had to beat the older crowd at their own game. It not only exposed them watching but their ineptness while on duty. I knew what my motives and assignment was for the Lord but when you interact with professionals and politicians at a high level not everyone loves God and Country.

Despite the gorgeous view we cut that first part of our trip a day early and left our "security" friends behind. No, I was not guilty nor running from them, but our departure was twofold Ruth was dying to drive closer towards her childhood home and despite it resembling paradise she was thrilled to go see her Mom and Dad. I could not blame her, but I did want to send a subliminal message to those "watching" that I saw them first and like Babe Ruth had to beat them at their own game.

While in town I was invited to preach at two large churches while in El Salvador and God used both sermons powerfully. One renowned Christian preacher in America years before helped donate towards the gorgeous sanctuary that I found myself preaching in that day. The other church I preached while in town was packed and was standing room only and they treated us like I was a visiting head of state while in town.

Ruth was smiling ear to ear to be back in her native country in a church like the one she attended while growing up. The worship was great, and the atmosphere filled with joy and excitement. My translator assigned to me is a dear brother and he was fantastic, and they can make or break you, but God was on the sermon out of the gate. When I gave an invitation literally hundreds responded to the altar call. God used this visiting preacher to speak to a crowd that resembled my beautiful wife and yet most did not understand my English but when translated to Spanish the Lord moved mightily in our midst.

Many see the one hour of Heaven on the platform but are not familiar with the twenty-three hours of Hell that at times had surrounded me personally and professionally. When you start speaking to stadiums, minister on worldwide television and interact at times with national leaders, you would be mistaken to think everyone is happy. The Devil is not going to give any of God's servants a free pass to take back territory especially as multiplied thousands get born again and snatched from the pit of Hell to now being saved by the blood of the Lamb and have their reservations in Heaven. The Hyatt has nothing on Heaven, or the Sheraton on the Savior and I kept pressing on and the Lord kept saving souls.

I mentioned before but it was said that the FBI was irate when Dr. Martin Luther King, Jr rose in prominence and his platform grew wider. Sometimes governments at home and abroad can be tainted and witchcraft and sinister back room deals not only happen in cloakrooms and barstools near Congress but smoke-filled halls that do not glorify God. After slowly working the crowd and shaking hands and taking pictures with every single adult and child desiring once again, I exited slowly towards our awaiting car. The pastor and members of his family and staff treated us to a nice meal and life on the road is always a roll of the dice. I took many chances but rarely gambled in life, but faith must beat fear daily.

After a couple days making our way towards Ruth's childhood home, we enjoyed the scenery and connecting with the citizens of her native country. They are hardworking and humble people and Andrew enjoys meeting different folks and experiencing other cultures. The fact that he is part his Mom and part like me makes him at home even when he is away. God has also given him great discernment and he not only detects when God is speaking but when the Devil is lurking. He told me twice while in the pool back at the plush huts on the beach, "Dad, those men trying to dress casual are not right."

We were able to take in a few tourists stops but if you see one you have seen them all and Ruth could not get enough but more than ever, she was dying to see her parents. Who could blame her and after one more delicious meal at a steak house overlooking a mountain we finally descended and were just a couple hours from her parents. The next day we arrived, and it was an honor to retrace her childhood footsteps. It was a nice home built by love and her parents are precious people. Her father has preached for over sixty years and beloved in his native El Salvador. He has preached all over that country and walked countless miles at times just to bring the "Good News." He had planted dozens of churches as well and like Jesus, his fame had started to spread in various countries including America and Canada as well as all over Central and Latin America.

Ruth shared with me years before when her Dad had preached a weeklong revival and the only compensation, he would get would be a bag of oranges or mangos. Everyone that thinks we are in it for the money but realize that at times no money was involved. When the dust settled, we now found ourselves in Ruth's childhood home and my Bible, faith and feet had taken me halfway around the world several times but now finally standing in the kitchen of the house she grew up in. Tears of joy ran done her cheeks as well as her parents and thanks to Pastor Rodney and Adonica's generosity, little Andrew and I might have had a tear or two as well. Truly, there is no place like home.

Inside their home there were a few small bedrooms, but several hammocks suspended from the beams and Andrew lived in those and loved it. They played video games while swinging in them, he took "siesta" in them and a night or two bypassed the bed and that hanging cocoon was his bed. He was about nine or ten on that trip, but I recall knowing we were making memories that would last forever.

The house is nestled on a humble farm and one specialty was that they had plenty of ice-cold Coca-Cola in bottles stocked in their refrigerator. There is nothing like a cold Coke out of a bottle on a hot summer day! Particularly a home with no air conditioning and I bet I drank a dozen a day. If Forrest Gump could drink seventeen Dr. Pepper's in the White House waiting to meet JFK I could down a dozen drinks from Atlanta while visiting my in-laws in El Salvador!

Ruth's Aunt and Uncle lived around the bend and a cousin or two more lived up the dirt road. We had a reunion while in town and it was festive, and everyone was having fun. While in town we also walked the dirt road from her childhood home to her school that was less than half a mile walk. We finally got to go on the school campus and visit the classrooms and met several of the teachers and students. Two of her childhood educators were still there but most were long gone, either retired or deceased.

I was asked to give an impromptu speech to the students and Ruth translated and when we were finished all of them were crowding around us. Kids really want love and when you take time to connect more likely than not, they will respond. Sometimes teens get involved in gangs because deep inside they are dying for affirmation and attention and sadly, they will "kill" to get those needs met. We must be intentional in beating those with impure motives to help mentor this next generation no matter what their skin color or religion.

The soccer field needed repair and most classrooms were clean but could use some TLC. The wheels started running in my mind and I was already assessing the condition of the campus and was already contemplating how one day we may be able to return and do some renovations. I am no Eagle Scouts and three of my cousins beat me to it but we all would agree to try to leave a place better than we found it. Lord willing, we can do just that in the days ahead, but I knew the clock was ticking and the sand in the hourglass was not going backwards but racing forward.

After trying to encourage the educators on the way out the door their smiles and service were a big blessing to us. Our culture for far too long has celebrated the wrong things and it is selfless servants like my new friends and family in El Salvador who are super special. Their work ethic was inspirational to me and after waving goodbye and one last long at the school campus we made the trek back towards Ruth's childhood home. The road was dirty and dusty but their love for God and each other was a clear and clean as a Colorado spring of freshwater cascading down rocks with a sound of peace in the air.

Peace is a good and precious gift and considering one of my wife's last visits to her country was when she was running for her life in tears sprinting towards freedom (America).

President Ronald Reagan was right and this quote hangs on the wall of our foyer, "*If we lose freedom here, there is NO place to escape to. America is the last stand on Earth.*" In a chapter or two I will expound on my trips to communist Nicaragua. On my last visit, everywhere I went we had television crews and reporters interviewing me as I went city to city preaching revival. One reporter of a large television network asked me with the Mayor of that city over my shoulder, "Evangelist Frank Shelton, why do you preach peace when in our country?" I replied, "My office was evacuated on Capitol Hill on 9/11, my father served in Vietnam, my wife was almost killed by armed guerillas in El Salvador, and you as well have seen war. Those of us have seen firsthand war tend to find peace more attractive." I concluded, "Jesus is the Prince of Peace and tonight I bring Good News. God loves Nicaragua" and we saw scores get born again into the Family of God while in that Central America nation.

Andrew had a great time and despite my living on the road so much and too often with him and Ruth behind, it is crucial that he can take in the sights and sounds of another culture. We ate from grills on the side of the street and dined at some humble restaurants with good cooking. While in town, I was even able to wash the rental car and the contraption that used for a car wash was almost as primitive as an Elephant in Africa spraying you with its trunk. The crazy thing while in El Salvador at the car wash one of the attendants told me through my brother-in-law translating into English that he had seen me a couple times preach on television. It is humbling when you are thousands of miles away from home in a remote place and they recognize you. That is why it is so important to be nice to all because you may not know them, but they may know you! I knew something was brewing when the man kept pointing at me when we got out of the car and God is good.

We found a waterpark less than half hour away and Andrew was in Heaven with his cousins swimming in the pool and eating ice cream and drinking Cokes in the hot sun. One of the highlights was another reunion while in town at Ruth's relative's house just around the bend and over eighty family and friends were present. Many of whom I met for the first time but every single one of them were accommodating, loving and gracious. Plus, all of Ruth's family can flat out cook! The party lasted late into the evening and after being in the sun all day I politely excused myself and called it an evening in a bedroom that we were blessed to stay while in Ruth's childhood home with her parents and siblings.

The next morning, we did some shopping in town and navigating through the stores was an adventure, but my globetrotting had prepared me for the hustle and bustle. I do not fear for me but as a husband and parent I must always be vigilant of Ruth and children. Sadly, our society is not safe like it was when we were kids and for the last six years, I have served on a national task force helping educate, expose, and eradicate human trafficking particularly when children are involved. We love the precious people of El Salvador and having been invited to Guatemala, Honduras, Ecuador, and other nations I sensed similarities between them but deep inside they are hardworking, humble, and happy with a desire to love God in Heaven. I thank the Lord often for giving me my wife and I am a better man for her upbringing, and we make a great team.

God has used us together to reach both cultures and her ministry of running the three

Christian radio stations in DC, VA and PA has been a great asset. Heaven only knows how together we have been able to multiply the Kingdom of God with our respective relationships and backgrounds. Later that afternoon after returning to pack and load up the car for our last few days in country we had to say our goodbyes. Because of Pastor Rodney's generosity, the last four nights we would be staying closer to the airport and our reservation was at the Sheraton Presidential Hotel of El Salvador.

As we were saying good-bye, Andrew really touched our hearts. As Andrew hugged Ruth's parents, he looked at his grandparents with tears and said with all sincerity, "I know where we are going the next few days are where heads of state stay when they visit, and I have been told it is very fancy, but I prefer to stay a few more days here." When they him asked, "Why?" Andrew said with huge tears, "This place is nicer because love is in this place." We were all crying, and the fact is the Presence of God is in my in-laws' home and our boy was exactly right that the Spirit of the Living God who embodies love was in their house.

We seriously considered arranging for Andrew to stay, but with a four-hour drive back towards the capital city knowing our trip was coming towards an end we had to head back. The huts were gorgeous on the beach and the hammocks were a blessing at Ruth's childhood home, but we were finishing up at the Sheraton. As we approached the hotel, I spotted the massive blue and white soccer stadium where their national team plays. I had preached at the Uganda soccer stadium in Africa and was already daydreaming about returning to preach in their venue. I knew intimately that time was ticking, and we didn't have forever to swing for the fence, and I had made up my mind to allow my father-in-law to preach a bit before my sermon. If anyone deserved to speak to that massive crowd would be him.

Ruth's father is a humble man with a respect from countless people in his home country and abroad. I am certain he had dreamed to preach to big crowds but if you brought in all those, he ministered to throughout the decades most stadiums would be too small. However, I would love for him to preach to his home country on that stage before God calls us home should the Lord make it possible. We finally found ourselves at the majestic Presidential hotel and I felt like we were in Beverly Hills. It lived up to its name because the first thing I noticed other than the marble floors in the massive foyer were the portraits of our former Presidents hanging on the wall. One of the bellhops saw this American staring at the framed pictures of President Bill Clinton, George W. Bush and Barak Obama, respectively and he confirmed what we already knew with a smile and excitement in his voice, "Your Presidents stay here with us when they visit El Salvador." Only God and Pastor Rodney could pull this off and I knew if it were good enough for them it will certainly be fine for us. One night we are swinging in a hammock and the next something resembling the Taj Mahal, but the fact is both were fun and first class. Plus, the bonus with family involved I was a "rich" man, not in my bank account but in blessings.

The hotel was incredible, and we played in the pool a couple days and then met friends for dinner and Ruth's longtime friend was running for President of El Salvador. Ironically, the previous president was at The White House and Ruth had been invited by President

George W Bush to attend a Cinco de Mayo event and she and the El Salvadorian President took a picture together. It did not take long for me to spot some of our "friends" again poolside and strategically placed watching from afar. I have learned that those watching you from afar are hesitant to look you in the eye up close.

On the next to last night in town I pointed out the team that seemed to always appear after we arrived and then leave right afterwards. Like Babe Ruth, I had a little fun with them and kept them on their toes. It was interesting in public they acted like they did not know each other yet sat fifty feet apart conspicuously watching and I waived to the waiter to get a check they would quickly do the same. Better agents would be trained to not be as obvious but after a while it was interesting to know what government was watching more, mine or theirs? Once again, when God is blessing the Devil is messing and after having relationships with high level leaders not everyone is happy and more than ever it is imperative to live honorably because people are watching but most importantly God is watching.

Thirty minutes later, Andrew and I were in the lobby playing while Ruth was saying her good-bye to one last Aunt and as I looked in my peripheral vision, I saw one of those same men that were at the pool was now aiming his cell phone camera at my son and I laughing in the lobby of that presidential hotel. Two days before I had a young man at an old school car wash thrilled to see me, but I got some undercover man filming me and I do not think he was wanting an autograph or a word of encouragement. Since my youth, I have been a nice, non-confrontational guy, and have never been one to thrive on out-debating people. However, God had given me more boldness as my assignment and platform expanded. Without missing a beat, I immediately stood up and approached the guy and he collapsed like a deck of cards and almost dropped his phone. He scurried off like a scared cat for a guy packing heat he was exposed, and his ops were finished.

We had been in the hotel now for three days, but I noticed a door leading to a lounge that I did not ever consider darkening. But it was as if the Lord could allow me to see through the walls and I resemble Clark Kent more than Superman, but the anointing of God enables one to see things others overlook. I told Andrew to stay with his mother who was eight feet away and that door led to a private bar inside the hotel. Most preachers don't frequent night clubs or bars but, on this night, the Holy Spirit prompted me inside and who are the first three people sitting on the couch, having a drink and laughing like long, lost friends were the same trio that had been watching me since I arrived. The same group that acted like they did not know each other were now off duty and their mouths dropped when the preacher with the police lineage dating a century and a half once again out detected the detectives. I did not have to say anything, and their reaction was priceless and after giving a friendly wave I was back through the door retrieving Andrew. Sometimes you must confront the opposition and like Babe Ruth beat them at their own game, but the difference was I was not showing up to work impaired.

It was empty in the morning when we departed to the airport and God allowed me to shut down whatever surveillance they were doing, and I had to take comfort that Heaven was watching me even if at times it felt like Hell was right behind me. The old hymn reminded me that indeed two were following me but not two government agents but "Goodness" and "Mercy." The chorus was, "Surely goodness and mercy shall follow me all the days of my life."

We were now at the airport, checked in, through security and after boarding we were once again wheels up heading home to the States. As I looked out the window, I could see the stadium and recall thinking, "Lord willing, we will be back and preach to those wonderful people and my prayer was my father-in-law would preach, my wife, Ruth testifies, and thousands would be born again before its eternally too late. Hell is too long to be wrong." As I leaned closer to the window looking down over the bowl of that beautiful but empty stadium, I daydreamed it would be filled and overflowing, and I even prayed that the three "friends" following us may come and if they watch a little longer, they may see Jesus and get saved. The Bible says, "Bless those who curse you" and sometimes your critics are confused fans. They know a lot about you while studying your every move but are too small to compliment. Either way, time was ticking, and fear must take a backseat to faith if you are going to move forward serving the Lord.

Thank you, Pastor Rodney and Adonica, for the incredible trip and indeed it was a privilege to follow the footsteps of Ruth and we have been walking closer together side by side because of that trip. Thank you, El Salvador, and thank you Jesus!

ENTERTAINING ANGELS UNAWARE

AFTER adjusting to being home and ministering nonstop my duties called me once again to a staff meeting at the Billy Graham Evangelistic Association headquarters in December 2018. As a husband and father, my priority must be at home first, and as my own ministry was expanding professionally, it was a tug of war on me personally.

The Lord had strategically used that incredible season on staff with BGEA to help grow me in multiple ways and it was an honor to connect with thousands of pastors and wonderful people. My duties as mentioned before covered a lot of bandwidth and I was the state coordinator for Washington, DC / Delaware, and my beloved Maryland. One state would keep you busy but juggling three regions was almost inhuman, but God gave grace, and I was doing what He called me to do.

Returning to BGEA was always a thrill and therapeutic for me and the setting and atmosphere was both beautiful and Biblical. Just being on the grounds you could almost feel Dr Graham's presence but more importantly sense God's Presence. Plus, being with likeminded colleagues and clergy with an intense passion for soul winning and evangelism was always a shot in my arm to keep moving forward. I must admit that the training sessions were sunup to sundown, and it was like "drinking water from a fire hydrant" trying to absorb all the information. It was nothing for us to put in twelve-hour days and the hotel accommodations were always comfortable and clean and they do everything with excellence as well.

Despite a business week of nonstop ministry, I was once again like a pigeon programmed to fly home and looking forward to it. After shaking hands goodbye, I was being chauffeured to the Charlotte-Douglas Airport in a fifteen-passenger van and was sitting up front in the passenger seat with my one carry-on bag. I had mastered traveling light both home and abroad and to be "frank" with you I graduated past the vans a long time ago but the fact it said "Billy Graham Evangelistic Association" on the side made it appear more impressive and I gladly made the exception.

The van pulled up to the airport and after a hug goodbye to one of my colleagues and wave to the rest still on board I grabbed my bag and threw it over my shoulder and the sliding doors opened to enter the terminal and now I was leaving "The Queen City" (Charlotte) while in service to The King. Within minutes I would get my boarding ticket, clear security, and grab a coffee at Starbucks and head towards my American Airlines gate.

After a quick pit stop in the bathroom to wash my hands and throw some water on my face, with coffee still in hand I noticed that the gate was packed to the gills. One seat remained and I was able to finally sit back and get as comfortable as one can in those metal airport chairs. I had boarded this flight dozens of times over the years and it would be just under a one-hour flight from Charlotte to Ronald Reagan in Washington, DC. I loved both cities and with my Dad's mother originally from the Charlotte area, both were home away from home to me.

After another sip from my five-dollar coffee (we joke Starbucks is really 'Five Bucks') and I scanned the gate to see who was on this flight. Looking in front of me it appeared to be mostly businessmen and women. Over the years, I met some interesting folks and recall having a conversation with a former White House counsel to multiple Presidents on a previous flight home on this same flight and airline from Charlotte to Reagan while I was still a college student heading home for a break. Everyone is important to God, but I was always on the look out to bless others and lately more than ever had to keep an eye out on my surroundings.

At this juncture, I took another sip and surveyed the bustling crowd and to my left about two rows away were several business professionals dressed to the nines and were happy to be heading home after a busy week on the road. I could relate and to their right I saw a few children talking to their parents asking them a thousand questions and I had been there, too, and just smiled and a nod to enjoy that season of parenting. I took another sip and dead center about fifteen feet away I saw a few senior citizens chatting and one of them had no teeth, but his mouth was moving a thousand miles an hour.

About the final swig of my coffee, I noticed that the gate that was full when I arrived was now standing room only and it was frenzied with activity with less than thirty-five minutes before departure. At that time, I picked up on an African American woman that was to my right and struggling to find a seat and she was heading in my direction. She was about twenty feet from me but coming fast and the Lord said, "Get up and give her your seat!" Part of me was thinking I just sat down. The Holy Spirit prompted with greater urgency, "Get up and give her your seat." I am going to be honest with you, but I had this image of the cartoon as a child with one angel on a shoulder and a red Devil with pitchfork on the other and I now have a war going on between the two in my head.

She was now about seven steps away and the Devil of course was running his mouth and said two things, "Frank, you have been doing ministry all week for God and the Billy Graham Evangelistic Association and if anyone deserves to sit and relax its you!" The second thing that snake said in my ear was, "Besides, Rosa Parks got a seat half a century ago so just sit still." The woman was now two steps before me and not a seat to spare and the Lord said it one last time and despite worrying about what others may think, I stood up at the last second and said to her, "Ma'am my mother raised me to think of others and she would be disappointed to learn if I didn't offer you my seat."

She had the sweetest smile and looked relieved but the least I could do was honor her, God, and my mother in the same swift action. Sometimes the greatest sermons are out of the pulpit and for a guy who at times was made fun of for not having his "own church" I could relate to a fellow evangelist and world changer, Dr. Charles Spurgeon who said the world was his parish. The moment I stood up the man seated next to my left automatically got up and took off. I had not met him because I was decompressing while sipping my coffee and scanning for any of my Air Marshal "friends" and the lady said, "He left so why don't you to take a seat next to me!" I was not sure if he had to use the restroom one last time, perhaps he wanted his own five-dollar cup of Joe or the slight chance he struggled with 'race relations" I don't know but I do know she didn't have to tell me twice to take a seat! My mind muttered, "Thank you Jesus!" After a quick greeting we both sat down, and I felt like Abraham when he was willing to sacrifice his son on the altar in obedience to God. The blessing was he was "all in" and willing to give up his son and God allowed him to keep his son in the process. On a much smaller test, God told me to give up my seat in Charlotte and by doing so I got to keep it in the process. It is true, you cannot out give God and besides, I made a lifelong friend in the process. Pull up a seat yourself because this is where the Lord showed up!

The Holy Spirit whispered, "Frank you are a preacher, but this time don't say much. Let her speak and listen." That was fine by me because I was still exhausted and was just trying to zone out daydreaming about my own bed and hug my family once more. It has been said, "God gave us two ears and one mouth for a reason." Pray for me, I am sincere but still a work in progress.

As she continued to speak, I was listening. I noticed a few people around us were listening to our conversation. Perhaps it was because I had just offered her my seat. It may have been she was black, and I am white and regardless of what the news reports, we can get along fine. About five minutes later she mentioned Chuck Colson. Some of you may know that name but I knew immediately that he was a Republican who was senior staff to President Richard Nixon. Colson was caught up in the Watergate scandal and went to prison.

I had the honor to attend Chuck Colson's 75th birthday party in Ashburn, VA and he was a changed man. He had political power while working in the White House but was bankrupt spiritually and he gave his life to Christ in jail and started the greatest prison ministry since the Apostle Paul. It is amazing how fast your brain works, and I am usually so slow it takes me two hours to watch "60 Minutes" but I was tracking and the detective lineage flowing in my veins instantly made me curious. I recall thinking to myself how could she know who Chuck Colson is unless she has been to prison?

The moment I thought it she immediately said, "I was incarcerated for twenty-one years and was just released from prison." She continued, "I accepted Christ while in jail." Several more folks surrounding us at the American Airlines gate were listening to our conversation. One they were bored and two it was refreshing to see two individuals totally different having a friendly conversation and unlike the 24/7 false news narrative from every media source and television in the world, most people are not racist.

I knew now the Lord was up to something and when I heard she gave her life to Christ my reaction was "Praise the Lord!" When I said that her eyes grew wide, and a big smile came over both our faces and we slapped five right there and had Church in the Charlotte airport! Initially, I was going to title this chapter, "Church in Charlotte" but entertaining angels will make sense soon. The Bible says, "Be careful how you treat strangers because some have entertained angels unawares (Hebrews 13:2)." We were no longer strangers but now friends and even better, she was my sister in Christ, and I was her forever brother from another mother but with the same Heavenly Father! Somebody say, "Amen!" At that juncture, half the gate was listening to us and our conversation.

Despite being exhausted and away from my bed and on the road all week, I am now wide awake. God and she have my full attention. I proceeded to ask since she just got out of prison and she was on the same flight as me heading to Washington, DC where she was coming from? She said, "I was just in Beverly Hills last night?" My eyes were bigger than offering plates in church and I said, "Awesome! You just got out of jail, but you were in Beverly Hills last night?" I have friends who have never been to the West Coast much less Rodeo Drive and she gets out of the prison and already near Pacific Palisades. I said, "Praise the Lord" again and inquired, "What were you doing in Beverly Hills?'

Now we have about two thirds of our gate eavesdropping on this conversation, and she said, "I just had dinner last night at Kim Kardashian's house with Kanye and their kids." I come from a Baptist background but turned Pentecostal at this juncture and almost "fell out" on the floor. It would be safe to say three quarters of that gate was now not only listening they were looking. Nobody was trying to hide it anymore that the only conversation happening in that gate was the one God orchestrated between her and myself.

She looked at me and said, "We just filmed an episode of "Keeping Up with the Kardashians" and presently I am trying to keep up with Christ. My new friend then said to me, "I am the woman that Kim Kardashian flew to the White House earlier this year and had a private meeting with President Donald Trump in the Oval Office and helped me get out of prison. My name is Alice Marie Johnson, and it is good to meet you."

You can see where this is going. EVERYONE and I mean everyone were now listening and I speak worldwide for a living, but I was smart enough to do what the Lord told me to do when I first offered her my seat and let her talk while I listened. I did not want to break protocol now and quench the Holy Spirit and after sharing my name it was off to the races. She said, "Frank, we had the best time at dinner and all Kim and Kanye's kids wanted to do was talk to me about Jesus." Alice shared, "Kanye is growing in the Lord and has a passion to follow God and he is leaning towards coming out with a Gospel album in the fall."

I was stunned not about Kim or Kanye but The King's touch on her life. When we genuinely find freedom in the Lord the places, He can take you and the people you meet are second to none. She went from a prison cell to Beverly Hills faster than a Ferrari and I am smack in the middle of this conversation hearing of God's grace and goodness. After another ten minutes talking side by side about life, the Lord, and several other random topics we were getting close to the time for folks to begin the boarding process.

As our conversation was ending, I know we live in a culture that says if you do not have a picture to prove it then it probably did not happen. It is also interesting if you have a picture some would suggest that it is photo shopped. It is hard to satisfy clowns who are clueless and only live to criticize from the cheap seats. Plus, as God over the years had opened unique doors for me to minister to prominent people and powerful politicians or professional athletes including celebrities from Hollywood, I quickly had to learn two things. One, I had at times to pretend like the meeting never happened with no "selfies" and never betray their trust or something said in private. Second, I like what one said that we need to resemble the sports star who scores a touchdown and opposed to doing cartwheels in the endzone should act like we had been there before and humbly give the ball back to the referee and go back to the sidelines while the stadium is erupting with applause.

Everything inside me was wanting a picture but I felt like God was whispering not this time and if it is meant to be perhaps down the road. By the end of our conversation, it slowly came out that I was on staff with the Billy Graham Evangelistic Association, and she put two and two together with some quick investigative work of her own and pieced together why I was flying home from Charlotte. She shared she loved the Graham Family and his ministry blessed her while incarcerated. What was funny was she did not know who Kim Kardashian was while in prison but certainly knew who the world-famous evangelist was who was now with the Lord.

Folks were now standing in line to board the plane and it was just like our conversation it was just us when it started. God gave me a word to speak into her life and I gave her my business card and a hug and boarded the plane. On that short flight from CHA to DCA my mind was spinning thinking what would have happened if I disobeyed God or let pride get in the way from me standing to offer her my seat? The Lord strategically made that happen and I was like a pawn on God's chess board, but He moved me around to bring about an unforgettable meeting.

I have flown in and out of Reagan Airport a hundred times in four decades while living near the Nation's Capital. I have met some interesting people and witnessed some unique things but what floored me more was after deplaning the first picture I see to welcome me to Washington was a HUGE banner of Alice Marie Johnson on some campaign she was involved in. My initial thought was there is my new friend and secondly it dawned on me I was so glad I had been obedient and offered her my seat because I would have really felt like a loser to see her larger-than-life face and smile if I had been too small to bless another or to be obedient to God. Praise the Lord that I passed that pop quiz back in Charlotte!

Eventually I found myself back at the American airlines baggage claim and there was my new friend, Alice with her sister patiently awaiting their bags. Once again, we reunited, and the chat and smiles resumed, and we had a time! My roommate in college was from Kenya and now in Washington it was obvious that Alice and I were family. We laughed and had them in stitches, and I learned that the reason she was coming to DC was for Alice to meet with the President at the White House. This sister in the Lord who was just shackled went from prison to the president, from the big house to The White House, from shackles to celebrities and was now flying high without drugs!

I told her I had been working on a faith global initiative at the United Nations and would she be interested in attending a future meeting? She smiled, "Frank, I am getting an award at the UN next month!" You had to been there to appreciate it, but it was comical to say the least because those that truly know me realize I live to privately promote others behind the scenes. Too often many are too insecure or focused on getting to their next rung on the ladder that we do not pause to help others. With Alice, I was trying to bless her, and God had once again beat me to her. We both laughed and smiled because anyone else may feel as if someone was trying to one up on the conversation but with two Christians celebrating the goodness of God, we both had already won.

We finally did in fact take a picture by the baggage claim in Washington, DC and I felt I passed the test in Charlotte without looking like some fan or groupie, but after two conversations in two cities and our sides hurting from my jokes, we were now forever friends. The picture with Alice is something I will cherish for a lifetime and after another hug I wished her and her sister well and like Elvis, I left the building (airport). Looking back, some of our best sermons were not on a Sunday in a church pulpit but in venues like an airport, waiting to catch a flight during the week. Indeed, the greatest sermons are not always preached but lived.

About a week later, I got an email from Alice out of the blue and it was a pleasant surprise to hear from her again. Some may see someone that was incarcerated but I saw one who was liberated by grace and the irony is the stigma or stain of prison was not on her, but it was evident to me that promotion was all over her and she resembled royalty to me. God's grace goes a long way. Fast forward two months later when I was home on the couch with my family as the State of the Union Address was coming on the television. The pageantry of a president's speech would bore some people, but it was fascinating to me. Perhaps it was because of our family history in DC and my life experiences in that same building and in that very room. Very few could say that sat in a Members of Congress' seat during a special joint session of Congress when I watched a visiting head of state address our House of Representatives.

For decades I had watched up close and from afar our chief executive of both political parties speak to the nation and on this night our forty fifth President was working the room on his way to the rostrum as the House Sergeant at Arms belted out the iconic phrase to the world watching, "Madam Speaker! The President of the United States!!" Ten minutes later, love him or loath him, President Donald Trump was sharing his accomplishments and halfway into his speech he paused, pivoted, and then pointed to the balcony. As a former Senate Doorkeeper, I had worked in those galleries, and had watched during the speeches of every President since Reagan as they shined the spotlight on average Americans who displayed ideals that were unique and extraordinary.

President Trump then said, "I would like to highlight my new friend, Alice Marie Johnson who has recently been released from prison and is currently helping our administration with prison reform." The chamber erupted with applause and my wife, Ruth hit me in the ribs and her and Andrew were shouting in unison, "That is your friend and the lady you recently talked with at the airport in Charlotte!" My eyes were bulging out of my head and my heart after started beating again was not only proud of her but another confirmation that I am so glad I honored God when His small voice told me to "get up and give her your seat." Regardless of your political preference, it would be embarrassing if the leader of the free world is honoring her in the United States Capitol with the world watching but I had been too small to honor her at a packed American Airlines gate in North Carolina.

Truth be told, I did not even know who she was then but was trying to honor another because it was the right thing to do. The pain from Ruth's shot to my left ribs from her excited elbow paled in comparison to the pride I was feeling with my new friend once again being elevated to new heights. The very next day, we texted after another meeting she had in the White House and all I could think of was the prison may have been Satan's past, but the promotions were God's will for her in the present.

Less than two weeks later, I was racing to Union Station to take an Amtrak train to Penn Station in New York to preach that night at an all-African American church in Brooklyn, NY. This was the third time in three years that my dear friend, Apostle Robbie Germain and his beautiful bride and church family had this white brother preach revival at their all-black church. His people are the salt of the Earth and some of my best sermons were with this type of crowd. Folks have joked for years the way I play with words that I am a white Jesse Jackson and throw him and Billy Graham in a blender it was safe to say that if it were a milkshake that Frank Shelton would pour out.

I just dined alone (once again) while on the road and finished a pizza at Uno's inside that iconic train station and after paying my bill, I grabbed my carry-on bag and was heading towards the gate to catch my train and my cell rang and the caller id read, "Alice Marie

Johnson." I smiled while walking quickly to the gate knowing they were now boarding and answered on the second ring and said, "Hello my friend!" She said, "Frank, I can't believe you picked it up so quickly!" I said, "Alice, you are a legend and would not dare have it go to voicemail." She said, "Frank I woke up thinking of you early this morning and God laid you on my heart."

No joke, despite being in a full stride to catch my train on the other side of the station I recall almost coming to a complete stop long enough to hear her exact words. The irony is we had met in an airport and now she is calling me at a train station, and she said with excitement, "My life story has been picked up by a large, respected publishing company and it is scheduled to be released in the next month or two." She added, "You were thinking of me in Charlotte, but I am now thinking of you!" All I could think of was two things, one 'Thank you Jesus' and secondly, I bet those folks eavesdropping on our conversation back in Charlotte at the airport would die to be listening to it now!

She said, "Kim Kardashian is writing the foreword, but would you be willing to write an endorsement as well? It would mean so much to me and besides, it would be in bookstores across America." Without missing a beat, I said, "Absolutely! It would be an honor!!" I could not help but think on how much I would have missed if I were too preoccupied to help another or if I had ignored the urging of the Holy Spirit. Write this down, the doors you open for others God may open for you!

After catching my breath, I assured her I would work on that endorsement immediately and thanked her for the huge privilege and told her I would be in touch. While simultaneously hanging up I was now boarding the train and finding my seat and after tossing my carry-on luggage above, it seemed like within mere minutes we were pulling out of the station heading north to the Big Apple. Once again, time was ticking, and "urgency" had become a way of life for me and today was no exception.

I called my mother who I still share many of my victories with and she was excited to learn of Alice's request for me to work on the endorsement that would be featured in the book. My mother is great at grammar and has saved me more times that I can count on various projects so after conversing with her before the train had reached Delaware an hour and half later, I had already sent Mom a rough draft that I typed on my cell phone, and this is what we submitted to Alice for the book.

"After Life" is not just the incredible, almost fairytale experience of a person who found a pardon from prison by a President but is a reality for all of us as to where we will spend eternity after this life.

What looked like the end for Alice was just the beginning that God had in store for her and for all those seeking mercy and a second chance. Every single soul in life has dropped the ball and has made less than flawless decisions and a sentence awaits us all in death. One prison sentence in the afterlife leads to death and despair hosted by the Devil, and the other is an open prison cell door of light, liberty, and love by the Lord. Not everyone can relate to being pardoned by a president but to find a home in Heaven you need a pardon from the Prince of Peace. God and Alice picked freedom and you can, too!"

Frank Shelton, Jr
Maryland State Coordinator @ Billy Graham Evangelistic Assoc. & Chaplain at 2020
Olympics - Tokyo, Japan

When the train, racing at eighty miles per hour, was just rolling into New Jersey, I could finally kick back and contemplate my sermon that evening in Brooklyn. Long before BLM, I had been privately and publicly intentional on race relations and I was excited to return and preach to an entirely African American congregation for the next two nights. I always had a pep in my step coming to New York but after just connecting with Alice I was like a race car waiting for the light to turn green! The Lord blessed that night and God shook the church service in Brooklyn and just like in Charlotte it was safe to say, "We had church!"

The next two years, Alice and I kept in contact on various issues and one time I called her, and she was back in Washington, and she said, "Frank, I mentioned you yesterday to some officials in the White House. I love your heart and I just know we are going to be doing more projects together in the future." Everything Alice shared with me on our first meeting in North Carolina had come true and Kanye did in fact release his Gospel album and sure enough it went Number One! Praise the Lord!!

I was able to open a door for Alice to help with a panel I serve on combatting human trafficking and she was able to record a video for us lending her voice to this much needed initiative. If anyone understood slavery and serving time it was her and once, she tasted freedom, she became a powerful advocate to help others to be liberated, too. The night of President Trump's first debate against Vice President Biden, I got a text from Alice out of the blue with two pictures sent to my phone. It read, "Frank, guess where I am?" It took me a nanosecond to realize where she was and where she was heading. The President of the United States had invited my friend to fly as his personal guest on the world's most recognized plane – Air Force One. She had sent me a pic with her standing next to Ivanka on the plane and while watching the debate that night in Ohio there was my friend Alice sitting in the second row watching the two most powerful men on the planet debate for the highest office in the land.

Satan prefers the prison, but God prefers promotion, and I could not help but smile wider because my sister in the Lord had just been to Beverly Hills the night before I met her while the Kardashians were now keeping up with her. The day after meeting me, she is back at the White House with the President and less than a month later she is being singled out at a State of the Union Address only to be awarded in New York at the United Nations. On this night, she texted me as she was flying on the President's plane. Regardless of your politics you must admit that God was blessing, and she was not only a mover and shaker, but grace will move you forward while guilt keeps you down.

With God, His blessing resembles an upwards staircase and with each step we advance higher and higher. However, with the Devil each step goes downward, and the million-dollar question is we are all on a staircase and are you on the Stairway to Heaven or Highway to Hell? When Jonah in the Old Testament had an assignment from God, he first rebelled and ran the other way. The Bible says that had he obeyed the trip was already paid for, but sin is more costly than you can imagine. When he went the other direction, he had to PAY for his ticket to another city. When God guides, He provides and when you are in His Will it is on God's bill.

After BUYING the fare Jonah had to take a step down to get in the boat. Then he went to the bottom of the boat. That was another step down. When the storm came folks realized that the culprit who brought on the tempest was in their midst and found Jonah and threw him overboard and that was another step down. He is now drowning in the sea and that is another step down only to be swallowed by a great fish (whale) and now in the belly of that beast which was another step down. As you can see with the Devil the snake promises the penthouse only to bring the eviction notice. He promises a Cadillac only to mock you when you are left hitchhiking. Millions are looking for love in all the wrong places only to be discarded and thrown overboard on an inverted staircase going down nowhere fast.

Consider Alice in the last few years. She does a crime and while doing time is forgiven of her sins and God sends one of the most famous celebrities in the world to petition her plight before the sitting President of the United States and she is given a pardon. Alice is now: dining in California; she landed a book deal; was an invited guest to meetings at the White House; was recognized at State of Union; was awarded at the United Nations; was flying on Air Force One; was featured in a Super Bowl commercial at half-time; and spoke behind the Presidential podium both inside the White House and on the South Lawn. Absolutely incredible! Look at God!! Stevie Wonder and Ray Charles could both SEE that God was elevating Alice Marie Johnson and only someone who was clueless, racist, or too small to see another elevated had to agree that the Lord was allowing Alice to climb the ladder fast!

We are still in touch, and I smile every time I think of Alice. She called right before the book came out and said, "Frank your remarks for my endorsement were perfect for the book but at the last second our publisher chose to only run with Kim's foreword. However, your endorsement will be on all the press releases promoting the book distribution and helping secure potential radio and television interviews." Although neither my name nor words ended up being in the book, I was thrilled to know somehow I could help push and promote her life story to executives who would consider bringing her on. Plus, you cannot subtract the fact that she had asked me for it to be featured for which I am forever honored. To a small degree, I was just selflessly trying to give up a seat to help another along the way and no, you cannot outgive God.

The Bible verse is true, "*Be careful how you treat strangers because some have entertained angels unawares.*" I have met a few angels in life and Alice Marie Johnson is one of them. The Devil imprisons but the Lord liberates and where Satan prefers prison God promotes. You go girl!

I started this chapter in an airport and I will close with another airport. A few weeks later after meeting Alice, I had been in New England preaching and promoting Franklin Graham's rallies that were coming to Vermont and New Hampshire. I was also invited to preach at a church in Vermont and at a Bible camp in New Hampshire. You absolutely must try a maple creamy ice cream because they are amazing! After non-stop ministry I was driven back to Manchester, New Hampshire airport for a short Southwest flight home. Since my childhood, God has given me an incredible memory but the eyes of an eagle. Some of my friends from high school are Air Marshals today and we have tons of friends in the law enforcement community at every level.

However, the last few years I sensed that I was being watched and followed more times than I could count. It was coming with the territory and end times. Those who are asleep in bed or clueless on the couch have no idea how late in the game we are and neither my followers nor I were playing games. The loudest insults come from the cheapest seats, and I had to step up my game if I was going to finish the assignment God gave me early on. The old song I sang in church resonated in my head, "Onward Christian soldier, marching as to war; with the cross of Jesus, going on before!"

Elvis Presley had the famous "Man in the Arena" speech by Teddy Roosevelt framed in his private bedroom. It inspired me for years since childhood and even more knowing that Elvis had a copy at Graceland and for a guy that sang in stadiums across America it resembled being in the arena in a way that 'The Big E" could relate.

> "It is not the critic who counts; not the man who points out how the strong man stumbles, or where the doer of deeds could have done them better. The credit belongs to the man who is actually in the arena, whose face is marred by dust and sweat and blood; who strives valiantly; who errs, who comes short again and again, because there is no effort without error and shortcoming; but who does actually strive to do the deeds; who knows great enthusiasms, the great devotions; who spends himself in a worthy cause; who at the best knows in the end the triumph of high achievement, and who at the worst, if he fails, at least fails while daring greatly, so that his place shall never be with those cold and timid souls who neither know victory nor defeat."

While saying goodbye to my host in New England I grabbed my bags and was now inside the airport, checked my bag, got my ticket, smiled to the agent, and went through security. The moment I put on my shoes coming through the x-ray machine, I saw a man literally one hundred feet away with his eyes locked on me. Perhaps you have been at a restaurant eating a meal and look across the room and find the uncomfortable setting of someone staring at your while dining. Maybe you have been there, too, only to be hesitant to lift your head a few minutes later to wonder if they are still staring. It is fun when you look up and they are still watching. That will bless you!

The irony is for those that have been watching from afar it was almost as if God allowed me to see them first. I came out of security and my gate was right there and it was packed, and no, Alice Marie Johnson was not on this flight. As a person who is in the public I love to connect with people and work the crowd, but I like to also decompress quietly in the corner. Intentionally, I elected to sit at a neighboring gate that was completely empty. With fifteen minutes before boarding, I was checking emails on my phone and finally trying to catch up and out of nowhere I felt this shadow hovering over top of me while I was sitting down.

The funny thing he resembled in tactics my neighbor who welcomed me to the neighborhood a few chapters before, but this guy was dressed business casual. What was odd was he was not facing me but had stood right in front of me with his back to me. The Lord impressed on me instantly that he probably had a colleague on the other side of the neighboring gate implying whoever I stand next to is the guy to watch. Me!

This clown could have done it thirty feet away and got the same results because I was the only soul sitting in that gate. I pick up on patterns and he did not even go back and sit at the same seat from which he came and my friends from childhood will tell you that arguably most would suggest I was the friendliest guy in school, but I also had to stand tall for the Lord and take back territory both foreign and domestic.

Despite the gift to speak I am not an in-your-face type of guy that must win or debate every person, but God had been stretching me and strengthening me and I figured two could play that game. Immediately, I got up from my seat and walked straight up to him and did the same thing but this time hovering over him in my assigned packed gate. It rattled him and then I calmly without saying a word walked over towards the counter as we were getting close to boarding. Ironically, on that Southwest flight home I was "A1" and would be at pole position number one flying home.

Just as the Lord warned me about the snake the night before my neighbor visited my driveway, this gentleman was now coming to get in line and what are the odds, he was A31. That means we are shoulder to shoulder in line to board, but my row was first. Satan always over plays his hand, and he was holding a book and the first words out of his mouth to me were, "What do you think of the FBI?" I got a neighbor talking to me about one three letter agency and this guy is now referencing another. The Holy Spirit whispered, "Be careful how you respond." Billy Graham was gracious to all, but we were in a different day and he did not travel alone. My initial thought was, "My father graduated from the FBI National Academy in 1978 but his class and generation would have run circles around some of them today." I did not say it and we have some dear friends employed with them in the past. I simply responded to his question, "I wish them well."

The man immediately twisted my words and said, "Did you say you wanted to throw them in the well?" I looked him in the eye, and I was six inches taller than him and replied, "No. I wish them well." He then said, "You don't look like Billy Graham!" I was wearing a black polo shirt and I forgot I was wearing it with his name embroidered on my shirt. I thought to myself, "He's been dead for nearly a year now and I am half his age so of course I don't look like the revered evangelist." I smiled and replied, "No sir. There was only one Billy Graham." He then scolded me, "How did you get A1? Did President Trump get you the first spot?" The fact is, I have boarded Air Force One several times before on a private tour of the famed 747 airplane, but I like Southwest, but they are far from resembling the world's most impressive airplane. This brother questioning me who was employed or impersonating a government agency was also few fries short of a Happy Meal and Fruit Loops must be his favorite cereal. I noticed the book he was holding was the biography of FBI Director Robert Mueller. At that point I just killed him with kindness and the Bible says to let your words be few and I wished him well and I showed the gate agent my boarding pass and left him behind looking for answers.

Nothing new is under the sun and the Pharisees tried to trap Jesus but once again He slipped through their hands and plots and lived another day. Yes, Walmart was looking more attractive by the day because *target* was on my back but quit was not in my vocabulary and in the words of Rocky Balboa I had to "keep moving forward." Once again, God was blessing, and Satan was messing, and the Lord just shook New England, and they are not the Bible belt, but some wonderful friends live there who love God. The Lord was on the move, and I had a couple misguided minions that were moving, too.

I called a few of my friends, detectives, special agents, and my old Sunday school teacher was an Inspector with DC Metropolitan Police. They all agreed that there are different types of surveillance and a person of interest who was really being watched most likely the folks watching would not want you to know you are being detected. However, some are novices and when you have been with the best in the world you can see their amateur mistakes. There is one tactic that is intimidation; but they are frustrated because nothing is on you and they must let it go and it may be their warped way to say we are watching you just to see my response. Jesus beat them at their own game, and I thanked them for their service and wished them well. At the beginning of the chapter, I met an angel unawares and just now met one of the Devil's minions and fully aware but like Durer's painting, "The Soldier and Truth", I must keep marching on. God bless them both. Nine times out of ten I am flying coach class but honoring the Lord and kindness to others resembles First Class or today in Southwest terms, "A1."

RUBBER MEETS THE ROAD

FOR those still tracking with me you can see that airports and airplanes have played a role in my life. We have had Divine Appointments and delays along the way. However, when God is calling us higher, we have a Devil and adversary trying to ground us. Late in 2019, right before the holidays I had the honor to fly west once more and speak at Dr. Luis Palau's three-day conference in Portland, Oregon. It was a privilege to be asked to speak at one of the breakout sessions on evangelism and my message then spoke on the urgency of our call and we must redeem the time to win souls.

Before boarding the plane that afternoon to fly across the country, I preached that morning at Southern Maryland Christian Academy in White Plains, Maryland and God was all over that message. It was like a Biblical bomb went off and God shook the place. I also sensed and had seen through the supernatural that a couple colleagues were misdirected, and religious spirits get nervous when God is in the House. When some get their marching orders from the wrong team or misleading intel the Lord allowed me to see who was with me and who was not. More importantly, I could see who was with God or not.

Once again, when God is blessing the Devil keeps messing but you cannot keep a good man down. With ministry doors continuing to blossom and you have preached in Los Angeles and London, the locals in La Plata can get nervous or jealous. The FBI got nervous with Dr. King and those callous in the county can get jealous when you are moving across the country. With a friend that was willing on this rare occasion to drive me to the airport because I did not have time to park, we stormed out of there like a student at the end of the school year! Billy Graham said while dealing with critics or those confused, he just out-loved them and out-lived them, and I was going to do the same.

While exiting, I saw one of our disgruntled teachers who still needed a fresh touch from the Lord and just waved and prayed for them as I left riding shotgun to catch my flight. With four minutes to spare I made it passed TSA, found the gate, boarded the plate, buckled my seatbelt and with a sigh of relief waited for the last few people to sit down. While flying towards Portland, Oregon for the conference I had a layover in the Midwest, and we were late coming in. I had not eaten anything all day and knew it would be a long night and grabbed a bite to eat at the world's favorite Christian Chicken. After hearing, "My Pleasure" I washed my hands in the restroom and took a call and started heading to the gate.

On one of the rare times in my life while traveling I miscalculated, and the gate was not next door but much further at the far end of this terminal. My phone had not updated with the correct local time when I landed for some reason and with the delay arriving and my Chick-Fil-A sandwich and sweet tea was brewing for the perfect storm. The irony is we made record time with my friend driving me to get to the airport departing Maryland but inside this airport in the middle of the country I was behind the clock.

With a twenty-one-pound backpack I was running and this chaplain to the Olympians was now trying to qualify in this unexpected indoor trial. No, I was not in tip top shape and with no time to spare I rounded the corner, headed to the finish line and was literally forty feet from the gate and this woman is standing between me and the door. I was looking at her and she was looking at me and she knew that was my flight and opposed to "helping a brother out" with a Cheshire cat grin, she through her insincere smile seemed to enjoy shutting the door as I was now seven steps away. Jesus had a Judas, and I am now staring at my Jezebel. With time ticking, I missed the flight and had to wait an additional three hours for the connecting flight and that delay hindered my first night into Oregon.

Two wrongs do not make it right and I knew God was in charge and she needed prayer, so I took the high road, did not say anything to her nor give her the satisfaction that she tried to sideline me or the Gospel and slowly walked away until the next flight out. I have learned that man's disappointments are often God appointments, and I was just trusting that God would work it out.

Looking back, she would represent what the globalists are trying to do to those who travel for a living, particularly the Global Globetrotters. Where Meadowlark got the runaround in his day because of race, lately I was getting it because of my faith, but Meadowlark, now in Heaven and me still on Earth were on the same team in more ways than one. It was great re-connecting with my childhood friend, John Schlaefli who graciously picked me up at the airport. We had a blast at dinner; and he allowed me to crash at his house. Just like old times and although the delay was inconvenient to me, John said the extra few hours was better for him.

After a restful sleep, I went to the conference and preached the stars down in that conference. Dr. Palau was well up in his age and struggling with cancer and that would be his last conference before the Covid-19. Regardless of your profession, the next time the Devil holds you down or man (Jezebel) tries to hold you back, more than ever Lift up Jesus!

Robert Frost penned the words, "It was the best of times and worst of times" and 2019 could indeed be summed up in that one statement. The Lord was indeed blessing, and no doubt Satan was still messing, and I am confessing that the next year was wild. Initially, I was going to name this chapter "Wipe Out" and I can hear the Beach Boys sing it as I type this.

The year started out great like it had the past New Year's Eve, and I was just flying into Dulles International Airport after my third consecutive year preaching to over 120,000 at the Nelson Mandela Soccer Stadium in Uganda. In three years, we were able to address a third of a million souls in just three sermons and when you add the national television coverage, nearly 100 million may have watched those three celebrations. It was extra special to share the stage with Pastor Chuck Balsamo, Coree Balsamo, Eric Newberry and my college buddy, Dr. Clayton King. I knew the day I met Clayton that God would use him to impact the world with the Gospel and it was an honor to help open the door for him to preach to that massive crowd. Just as Chuck opened the door for me, it was an honor to help open the door for Clayton and he said later, "Frank, you helped open the largest door in the history of my ministry and I am forever grateful." We all win when we open the door for others and let them shine for God's glory.

Lately, I had been doing a leadership podcast and teaching on class that some did not learn in class. Too many are insecure to bless others and I am of the persuasion that God smiles when we promote others. Those who are territorial are trying to build their castles but those who are building God's Kingdom open doors for others. The blessing is the stadium service was another huge success, but those trips were also taking a toll on my body and family. For three years in a row, I would kiss my wife and family good-bye and fly two days after Christmas halfway around the world on my own dime and miss New Year's Eve at home while bringing in the New Year in Africa. More importantly, I was there to help usher thousands into the family of God. The last year after we all preached on that platform, Clayton was told that nearly thirty thousand souls were born again into the family of God. That is not embellishment but evangelism and not arrogant but accurate of what Christ did in our midst and all glory to Him!

When my plane touched down on U.S. soil on that return flight; Chuck and I flew alone together on that trip home. Our friends remained in Africa for another mission, but we had to get back as soon as possible. Chuck's wife Emily was waiting at the airport after a long day in the air and they were able to get away for a much-deserved week in West Virginia for rest and relaxation. He was exhausted too, but she drove to the mountains, and he crashed in the passenger seat. Once again, I did not have the luxury of an assistant, spouse, personal security, or chauffeur to drive me home and to say I was exhausted would be an understatement. After sleep walking to my car, it was freezing cold and I climbed into my Lincoln SUV and once again, "Honest Abe" started up and I said a brief prayer and pulled out of the airport. We just flew all day and through the night and the sun just rose about an hour and half before.

The fact is I was exhausted. Less than four minutes later leaving the parking lot, I had not gotten on the interstate with Dulles Airport in my rear-view mirror when I almost dozed off to sleep and I heard a massive eighteen-wheeler hit the horn and brakes and not sure in what order and then had to swerve around me from not killing me or him. The irony is we just saw thirty thousand saved and I almost killed myself and some innocent trucker. The irony was Chuck crashed in his passenger seat to get some winks and I almost crashed in the driver's seat and nearly permanently went to sleep.

God spared us both that day (trucker and myself) and my accountant joked about some of my international trips, "Frank, you didn't make any DOLLARS preaching in Africa" and I replied, "but it makes sense when going after souls" but the fact is I probably should be getting hazardous pay along the way.

The sun had just come up over the Virginia skyline and I was racing to try to get back to Southern Maryland Christian Academy by 9:30AM to preach at chapel. Time was ticking and after finally getting home I was in bed for a full day. I had felt like I had been hit by a truck and the fact is I almost was! Similarly, to an aging boxer even if he won the fight, the recovery time for healing is slower as one ages. Yes, I was still in my late forties; but the nonstop travel was wearing on me fast.

Just two weeks before flying to Africa, I was at home on the couch in Maryland with my family and we were watching television. An interview on CBN News grabbed my attention. It was a man in pilot's uniform talking about a ministry he had to take missionaries, pastors, church planters, evangelists and leaders to various countries doing the Lord's work. Plus, bags fly FREE and lately the harassment I had experienced on occasion was growing old. My heart was racing, and this brother was speaking my language and the Lord impressed on me to reach out to him, tell him I exist, and we are supposed to work together!

Other than getting my wife's cell phone number before we first dated; I was racing online and googled to see if "Judah 1" had a website and did Everett (the man in the interview) have an email or office number? They had some planes, but could I find a phone for him and while the interview was continuing, I was a detective on steroids and by the time the segment was over I located his address, office phone and email. We were cooking and I emailed him while still on the couch, "Mr. Aaron – I just saw your interview on Christian Broadcast News! Your mission with JUDAH 1 Airlines is incredible. I have been on staff for over four years with the Billy Graham Evangelistic Association. I am an evangelist and am called to minister around the world. I feel like we are supposed to meet" and included my contact info.

One week went by, two weeks went by and an entire month went by, but I figured he was busy and trusted Christ to make the connection and prayed for his ministry and was trusting God to bless us as well. The next month, I was to be awarded by an Ambassador at the United Nations in New York for a faith global initiative I had been helping for over a year. I had already made several trips there in a couple meetings and being born in DC was one thing, but New York is larger than life. One of my previous luncheons with the Ambassador and his assistant as we were eating, I told him that I saw a vision. While dining, he was listening and then I said, "Sir, I see jet streams crisscrossing across the continents bringing relief by day and revival at night." His eyes grew big, and you know you have a man's attention when he takes his fork out of his mouth. He then showed me with excitement his cell phone and he showed me a promotional video with an initiative he had in his head and planes were crisscrossing the continents bringing relief. This Baptist preacher was turning more prophetic and Pentecostal by the month and God was supernaturally equipping me as the weeks and months passed and the ministry grew.

I was tasked to bring seventy-five Christian leaders in the next calendar year to subsequent meetings at the UN per their request. I had also attended the last couple winter camp meetings at Pastor Rodney's church in Tampa and those services were both therapeutic and valuable teaching lessons that I was not learning or gleaning from any other place. Pastor Rodney graciously had me preach several different times the year before including the keynote graduation address at their River Bible Institute. To this day, folks still talk about that sermon and praise the Lord and I am so thankful for the invite of Pastor Rodney. It takes a big man to open doors for another, and we are about the same height, but he is ten feet tall to me.

One of his senior staff, Pastor Jayson Williams called me out of the blue as I was about to go on the air in Washington, DC. I was at the radio station where my wife Ruth is the station manager of a Hispanic Christian radio network. He said, "*Dr. Frank are you coming to winter conference next week?*" My mind raced because I was to be ON AIR in three minutes and my first thoughts were "Yes, I just landed from Africa. Yes, I was extremely fatigued, and Satan was teasing me to not go but the Lord impressed on me to attend. Satan is such a loser, and he was mocking me, "Well you spoke last year but most likely not this year so just stay home." I made a point a long time ago that regardless if on the platform, behind the pulpit or not, I wanted to be in the church and taking notes. It is too tempting to only show up if you are on some poster or platform, but ministry is so much more than that.

Pastor Rodney and Adonica are two of the most generous people I know but I felt strong of the Lord to pay my own expenses and go by faith. I shared more than once that others may out finance me, but most will never out faith me! Faith is all I have known, and I have come too far to stop now, so I flew to Florida by myself. Ruth was a saint to let me go but she knew the Lord was in it and God bless her for being so selfless. When I arrived once again, they gave me the VIP treatment and rolled out the red carpet and no one does ministry like The River Church. After the first powerful session of camp meeting, I was invited to a private luncheon with Pastor and some respected leaders from around the world. Out of the 1,500 who attend the camp meeting daily only about 80 are invited to a private lunch and once again I find myself at one of the head tables with my name next to my plate and assigned seat. Satan is still running his mouth, but I had to turn a deaf ear to the Devil and what happened next silenced him on a dime.

While seated and awaiting the five-course meal that their staff are the epitome of hospitality. Their talented chefs could be employed at the White House or Buckingham Palace. The atmosphere and food are second to none! While talking to a few friends at the table I inadvertently dropped my fork and it fell to my left on the floor. To retrieve it, my left knee accidentally hit the leg of the man seated next to me.

He was the one person I had not gotten a chance to introduce myself to, and since first impressions are important this was not the signal I was hoping to cast while playing accidental footsies under the table! In my mind, I was trying to dig myself out of this mess and apologize to him and as I grabbed my silverware and now leaning back up, I came eye to eye with a man who instantly I recognized! He was Everett Aaron, the founder of JUDAH One Airlines that I desperately was trying to get ahold of just two months before! With seven billion people on the planet, what are the odds that God would strategically place him next to my seat? I thought instantly of my Air Marshal "friends" were impressive at Dulles heading to India with those odds of being seated near or next to me, but God just blew my mind again with one and seven billion odds while in Florida! Go God!!

What if I had let Satan talk me out of going? What if I let pride keep me home in Maryland? Sometimes our best opportunities from the Lord come not from being on stage but being on post. Everett and I hit it off instantly and we ended up having lunch, dinner, and breakfast while in town that week and he invited me to come to his airport hangar the next month when I was already scheduled to be doing ministry in Dallas and Houston. That week at Pastor Rodney's winter conference was life changing and the Lord was already aligning up ministry dots that only God could connect.

During that first meal after putting my best foot forward (accidentally), I looked at him and told him of my conversation with the United Nations Ambassador. I told the owner of the world's first and only Christian airline while looking him dead in the eye and with goosebumps on my forearm, "You sir, are the Jetstream in the vision God gave me to crisscross the country and continents bringing relief by day and REVIVAL at night!" His eyes grew wide, his mouth dropped, and he said, "Frank, this is a God thing and everything we live and fly for. Count Judah One in!" If I would have packed up and left, then it would have been over the top, but Pastor is like the Lord that things just keep getting better.

It was funny because right after saying that I told him I had this inaugural meeting the following week with the Ambassador in his office next to the United Nations with faith leaders that I handpicked across America. I said to the man who owns an airline, "Everett do you think you can get from Texas to New York next week to be in our meeting?" He laughed and said, "Frank I may be able to pull it off." We both laughed and God was moving, and the trip made perfect sense while attending by faith that incredible winter conference.

It was humbling to receive an award at the United Nations in front of all my peers and it was a powerful group assembled at that all-day meeting in the Big Apple. I had brought a Hollywood actress, the pastor of a mega church in Los Angeles, a NY Times bestselling author, the chaplain to the New York Knicks, the minister to Members of Congress, and staff members from the Billy Graham Evangelistic Association to name a few and God was moving. The ambassador had tasked me to reach out to a prominent Christian band about possibly doing a concert on the lawn of the United Nations and within 24 hours I was on the phone with the drummer of Casting Crowns about them possibly playing at the United Nations.

When Chuck and I saw that UN plane in Africa, the Lord made it clear that I would be seeing more of them in the future. God was moving rapidly, and I now felt like I was on one of the supersonic trains in Europe and when the Lord moves, He often moves at the speed of light. After all, He is the Light of the world. Still running on adrenaline and anointing it had been next to nonstop since returning from Africa and after just returning from Florida I had to leave for a flight to Dallas the next week.

For the past six years, I have served under the radar on a national task force combatting human trafficking and we were having meetings with the front office of the Dallas Mavericks, Dallas Cowboys and Dallas Stars while in town. It was wonderful that the NBA, NFL, NHL, and MLB have all been open to assisting us fight this evil epidemic and economic empire. Billions of dollars are exchanged with stealing children for sex and slavery, and I believe it is pure evil. Anytime you are pushing back the darkness you can expect the enemy to come fighting back, and the Devil not only threw the sink at me, but he picked up the entire kitchen and almost knocked me out.

While in the parking lot to go into our meeting with the Mavericks, I got a call from a dear pastor friend in North Carolina and this brother is the best of the best. He said, "Frank, the Lord put you on my heart and I wanted to tell you that I know it is still March, but we raise money every October to bless three local or national ministries. We take one offering and last year we collected $100,000 on one Sunday and we send one third of the offering to each of three organizations. Last year, we gave $33,333 to each group and you will be one of the ones we bless this year!"

The first reaction I had was thank you JESUS! I had somewhat of a pep to my step walking into that meeting and normally I would be walking on air, but my body was still suffering from that trip to Africa. The meeting was good, and it is kind of surreal being inside the office talking with leaders of professional sports teams face to face about fighting a noble cause. I have several friends both past and present who are pro athletes, but the Christians will tell you it is a game, but the bigger game is honoring the Lord with the platform He loaned them. The real fight is for those who are defenseless and who are held against their will. Scoring a touchdown, hitting a jumper, or smashing a fastball over the left field fence is impressive but rescuing a kidnapped child is life and death.

After that meeting, we raced over to the Dallas Cowboys practice facility and met their staff there discussing trafficking. My friend and I were in awe of the display of Super Bowl trophies, and their practice field and office space were immaculate. Since childhood, I have been a lifelong Redskins fan being from Washington, but I admit they do everything big in Texas! I was starting to see "stars" and you cannot but help to when looking at the big blue star on the fifty-yard line and everywhere you go on the property.

After back-to-back meetings with the biggest names in sports, we headed to reconnect with my buddy Everett at his hangar about an hour away. It was surreal to reunite with the man I just met but I knew two months before I absolutely had to meet him. I am now in his office, touring his airplanes that I saw on television and am now standing on the same runway! Fear will keep you on the couch, but FAITH will get you in the game and at times, in the air.

We filmed a video on the runway with the jumbo jet behind us and it went viral considering my viewers with folks excited and commenting. The funny thing was it rained earlier that day and I am standing on the runway with holes in my black wing tip dress shoes. No one knew it but I now have water seeping into my socks as we shot that video. I did not mind because I was a kid in the candy store and just then a Gulfstream jet flew by landing on the runway, and I learned it was the owner of the Texas Rangers who parked his planes next door.

I know the Lord walked on water, but I am standing in it with holes and despite my socks soaked I heard the Lord whisper with the Judah One jet behind me, "Frank if you trust me, I can help you fly on this jet more often." I about did cartwheels on that runway in Texas and that was an answer to prayer because the occasional monitoring at airports and in the air was adding to the emotional and physical tiring of my body. Most people have no clue how stressful it had been the last few years and not because one is living a double life but because in the last days what is good will be called evil. The Lord was expanding our territory and the enemy, and a few local haters were not pleased. God was blessing and Satan started messing. Again!

We got back into the hangar, and I was unusually fatigued and who would not be after having flown tens of thousands of miles and speaking to millions on television just in the last few months? As we got back inside the hangar to Everett's office, I got a call from my supervisor with the Billy Graham Evangelistic Association. I could tell instantly with the tone in his voice that something was off. I knew all the state coordinator positions were up for contract renewal at the end of the month but with the fifty-state tour now behind us they were not keeping everyone on the payroll. I had been let go before only to be picked back up, but this was now the second time they were not renewing my contract with them, and my heart dropped.

Very few loved the Graham family as much as I do, and I did get a monthly stipend while serving and what an honor it was! However, I just went from the top of the mountain with nonstop ministry and learned that my days with BGEA were up at least on the payroll. It almost knocked my breath out and after sitting down I shared with my two friends what had transpired, we said a prayer and knew God was in control.

A good meal always helped, and it was now dinner we had not eaten since breakfast so

Everett and my friend and I had a nice meal at Cheddars about fifteen minutes from the airport. I had lost most of my appetite, knowing my contract was not going to be renewed. I had to give it to the Lord and thanked Him for the honor to serve while I did and to learn firsthand with a front row seat from my heroes of the faith. After all, how could I complain when what was supposed to be a three-month contract turned into just shy of a five-year run? The Lord used it abundantly to train me and prepare me for what was in store.

After saying goodbye to Everett, we headed an hour back to our hotel and with each mile my body was fading fast. By the time we got to the hotel I was feeling punk, and the color had gone out of my face. I was slow walking into the foyer and found myself getting weaker by the second.

We had front row seats reserved to us by the Dallas Stars for our work with the human trafficking issue and I politely turned down the hockey game and stayed in the hotel room that night. My friend went, met the goalie of the team and they even featured him on the Jumbotron that night and I was like a car on empty and lying-in bed. The pain around my waist and back was intensifying and later that night after my friend returned to the room, I went up to use the bathroom and my urine was brown. I am no physician but knew that was not good.

The next morning, I could hardly stand and when I went to the bathroom my bowels were white and urine was brown. I must be sick because it was reversed, and I could hardly stand. We already had a lunch date with a dear friend from Houston and we met halfway as we were in route that night to be at Lakewood Church. Our mutual friend was the guest preacher that night at one of America's largest churches and they reserved two seats for us in the second row to hear him preach and spend time together afterwards. The irony is I have a couple senior pastors or youth ministers in my hometown who are too busy to return a call or grab lunch but some of the biggest ministers and ministries across the country want to hang out or have me preach for them. Leadership is lonely and ministry will keep you humble. That is not a bad thing but as we left our hotel near Dallas temporarily, we started heading to Houston. On the way we grabbed lunch with our dear friend who has also been instrumental with multiple ministry projects and the three of us were scheduled to eat at a nice restaurant for lunch.

During our meal with my friend next to me and the lady we reconnected for lunch and a member of Lakewood said, "Frank, you don't look good." We met ten years before in the Bahamas on a Christian cruise and friends can keep it real. The funny thing she is always beautiful, and she is dropping truth bombs that I did not look well. The truth hurts but helps and heals in the long run and the fact is she was right.

My buddy was telling her my symptoms and I was 47 that day in lunch but you would have seemed by the way I was slowly moving that the numbers were reversed. I was born in '72 but Lord knows I wasn't seventy-four! The food was delicious and for one not having much of an appetite I did devour it and even picked up the bill for our table but as we were leaving, they both knew something was wrong.

As we made our way to the car, cooler heads prevailed, and they both agreed I needed to go to the Emergency Room. We went five miles to a hospital that just happened to be located around the corner and when we slowly walked in, I felt like I had broken ribs. I felt like the fourteenth round of the original ROCKY when Balboa tagged Apollo with two consecutive rib shots and in fact cracked the ribs. My breathing, like the movie champ, was difficult, breathing was painful, and my legs were wobbly.

My mind reminded me that the proverbial clock was ticking, time was running out, we still had an engagement in three hours at Lakewood, a preacher I wanted to reunite and minister to and kids needed saving enslaved in trafficking. As we entered that hospital we were denied, and it was standing room only and packed to the gills. As I walked out, I was doing my best to stand erect and make it back to the car. At least on this Texas trip my friend Matthew was doing most if not all the driving.

Volkswagen has spent half their marketing life looking for drivers but with all the miles I have racked up on planes, trains, and automobiles I was content to let others drive so I could zone out occasionally. We were told that another hospital was around the corner and would not have a wait and after gingerly sliding into the passenger seat we were to find hospital number two. When we arrived, I thought we either have the wrong address or the hospital is closed or not completed. In a massive parking lot, there were only two cars on the side of the building. That should have been a red flag of caution there.

As I walked in looking worse than the compliment at lunch, I was grateful to be flanked with both caring friends and two nurses raced to meet me in the lobby. They gave me the VIP treatment and I was not sure if I were in a country club or hospital but immediately, I was put in a room, told to take off my shirt and was on a bed and faster than I could say my name ten times. I had two other people in gowns checking my vitals, sticking me with a needle and installing an IV in my veins. Immediately, I now have wires fastened to my head, chest, arms and half my body. I loved the Six Million Dollar Man as a kid, and I was resembling him now as an adult. The problem was he was worth six million and I did not even have that in Monopoly money!

Another nurse with a clip board said, "Mr. Shelton, we are going to wheel you down and take some x-rays and an EKG." At this juncture all I could think of was Tom Hanks' line in the movie Apollo 13, "Houston, we have a problem!" It takes an awful lot for me to postpone an event or cancel an appointment but my two friends that just dropped me off knew I would be there awhile, and Lakewood was not going to happen as I am now on my back undergoing multiple tests.

This was only the third time in twenty years that I can recall being admitted to a hospital. The first was to get my tonsils removed in early thirties. The second was when my kidneys crashed while training with the United States Capitol Police and now in Texas the day after I learned I was no longer on the payroll with the Billy Graham Evangelistic Association. It is amazing what dances through your head when you are on your back in the hospital and most visits are not cheap.

My kidneys were the issue during my last hospital visit was now it was my liver in Houston. Despite having all the required shots for my trip to Africa, I picked up a disease while ministering on the most recent trip to Uganda. I never publicly shared this, but my liver was functioning seven times less than a healthy one and before where doctors feared I may be on dialysis with my kidneys after they crashed the numbers scared them from my liver being contaminated doing the Lord's work.

The urine was a dark brown and at first resembled blood and that would explain the excruciating pain, the back and ribs sore like Iron Mike Tyson had a few free shots to my side and back and the legs weak now make sense. We learned halfway through my stay the reason no one was there was because it was a private hospital for the rich, but the other hospital told us to go, I was from out of town and the country club vibe and empty parking lot explained a lot now. After five hours of testing and me telling them to allow me to not stay the night because after losing a job the day before and knowing the tab was not going to go backwards with me spending the night, I was finally released.

I must admit the care and kindness of that staff was first rate, but I would hope so for the bill that came less than a month later and being arguably the only patient in that entire wing on a Saturday. After getting dressed, I was able to have my friend return with the awaiting car and felt like I was sneaking out of prison, but I was released but despite walking slow I moved a tad quicker just in case one of the staff changed their minds! It was still tough for the next two days in Texas and even more uncomfortable flying home sandwiched between two adults in coach class on a commercial plane. That was one of the longest three-hour flights of my life and it is bad enough being sick and weak but being stuck on a middle seat on a plane with no chair to recline it was purgatory for even a Baptist.

Immediately, I was instructed to see my local physician and his eyes almost came out of his head when he saw the numbers and damage done to my body. He was worried that recovery could take a full nine months and he was right. The good news is the liver finally grew healthy but once again my body, mind and soul had taken another shot. The bill did come in and for my six hours stay in one of Houston's finest hospitals it came to $15,000! Good night, even all my friends who despised President Trump would have opted to stay a couple weeks at his gorgeous hotel on Pennsylvania Avenue and still saved money! It is amazing that folks who despise folks cannot even think straight.

Our health is often a private matter and the more public the person or ministry some things you want to try to keep under cover. Folks who are clueless can hold stuff against you that was not your fault or worse, make up a false narrative just to cause trouble. Plus, I did not want to dare blame the beautiful people of Uganda for me getting a disease on my last trip with them. You may recall I had a witch doctor try to curse my kidneys on the first trip and my liver was attacked on the last trip.

I never even told my teammates in Uganda what happened, and I sure did not want to tell my friends at Billy Graham Evangelistic Association that I was in the hospital because I did not want anyone to feel bad or they think I made it up for some sympathy. I just knew that things would get bumpy, and the wheels almost came off the cart for a while and we were only a third into the new year of 2019.

The collective one two punch of nonstop ministry advocating for fighting for others, preaching coast to coast and around the world only to pick up a disease that I had been carrying for three months and did not know it; and then to lose the paid contract with BGEA and to receive another hospital bill all within half a day was a sucker punch from the Devil. Satan does not play fair, and I was hit with a cheap shot, but they say, "What doesn't kill you make you stronger." I was either dying or would die trying to glorify God and grow stronger. My Mom told me years ago when things do not go your way, "Don't ask God WHY but ask Him WHAT do You want me to learn and do from here?" That has been a great lesson and the Lord has honored that and to this day we love the Grahams and they have still asked me to collaborate on a couple of projects in the past.

Perhaps you are also seeing a pattern in this book and once more the moment I was partnering with and programming the world's only Christian airline I was grounded. Just hours before talking about flying, and now skydiving in a spiral and admitted to a hospital. Indeed, "Houston, we have a problem!" Add the fact that nearly the same day that I was not having my contract renewed in North Carolina I would get a massive bill mailed to my home in Maryland for the brief hospital stay in Texas.

Where Satan may have been knocking me down, God was just setting me up. Two months into the healing and still only five people on the planet knowing exactly what I picked up at no fault of my own in Uganda, I was slowly recovering while still holding all my ministry responsibilities. For Memorial Day weekend, my son Andrew and I wanted to surprise my parents and we were going to have a brief Daddy-Son weekend in Ocean City, Maryland.

You may recall the 1992 Corvette we have that I rarely drive, and my friendly neighbor hoped to acquire. Well after removing the cover, washing it, and throwing in two small carry-on bags, we were heading off to see my parents who live east of the Bay Bridge. We had not gotten ten miles from my house, and we were in the center lane of a three-lane interstate on 95N doing about 65 mph when my car got bumpy. This is a car that is wide in the rear and low to the ground with massive thick tries to keep it snug and secure.

When I say bumpy it was now shaking and I am in the center lane on arguably one of the busiest days to be driving and before I could assess or diagnose what that noise was, my right rear tire not only had a blowout but literally blew off! Trying to navigate across two other lanes and then safely find the shoulder I think NASCAR would have been impressed how I weaved in and out of traffic on a Saturday while on the interstate. However as other cars are whizzing by at 70 plus it was wild to say the least. Eventually, I was able to pull over on the side of the road and what I saw next floored me! When I got out to look at the tire as you can see in the picture is all that was left on the massive 285/35/18 rim. The complete tire was missing - talk about where the "rubber meets the road."

A tow truck came up no less than a minute later and the narrow strip of rubber around the rim is what I had to drive two miles an hour on the side of road because there was not enough room on shoulder. How the rim did not get destroyed is another miracle and God had His hands on us before, during and after. Once at a stop with my hazard lights on, I found one of those large four-foot-tall construction cones behind the guard rail and placed that about 100 feet from the rear of car and some vehicle still managed to hit that. Motorists don't always pay attention nor care when someone is sidelined. NEWS FLASH: Don't be in such a hurry to reach your destination that you run over someone struggling to get by. #ThatWillPreach I am thankful for the Maryland law that requires drivers to get in the other lane when you see the police or tow truck assisting others because it's dangerous out there.

Neil, our friendly tow truck driver, put a dolly on it and towed us back home. The tow truck driver said "It's a miracle you both are not dead! How did your car not roll, or do a 360, or get smashed by other cars as your quickly changed lanes? And it is amazing that when your tire blew off it didn't cause severe damage to the quarter panel!" Indeed, God's Grace is amazing, and it was not a mystery but miracle! Satan had been trying to take me out for some time now. 🐱 More importantly, Andrew and I were safe, but he was a tad shaken up emotionally and after calling nine tire shops no one had that size tire, but God worked it out being towed back to Waldorf, Maryland.

A few hours later, we made it to my parents with four new tires and were most thankful for God's protection. The moral of the story is this - On the road of life even when you BLOW it – God, in His grace, can still lead you safely Home in this life and in the life to come. The Lord is good! I used to drive the Congressman as his fulltime driver and never had an accident but when God is blessing the Devil starts messing and he does not seem to take a day off. Part of the problem may have been that those high dollar tires had dry rotted from the inside out and sometimes the worst thing you can do is not drive a car. The car did sit outside under a cover under a semi enclosed driveway, but the problem was it had spent all those harsh summer and cold winter months on a black top.

When we were blessed with the new house the first thing, I did was get that car but despite it being immaculate sometimes the car just sitting did more harm than not. Satan will use anything or anyone to try to derail you or God's assignment on your life. Corvettes are fun to drive and a little bumpy but even with four brand new tires, Satan has an uncanny way to mess with your head while rolling down the highway in God's service. Praise the Lord that we lived another day, but I can see a pattern once again. You may recall when God was promoting me to get on staff with the Billy Graham the first time our Lincoln stopped dead in its tracks and Satan tried to sideline me. After not preaching in Pakistan the car died on top of the bridge going to Virginia and sidelined me again. What I did not know then but realize now was that my sermon was getting ready to air to multiplied millions the next day in Pakistan and Satan was pleased and tried to halt me at home. As we were going to preach on the air, the Devil wanted to stop me on the ground and where thousands may have been born again into the family of God, my Dad and I would come to a screeching halt in the car.

Now with the most recent car problem I knew I was already less than four days from our first official visit to minister in Nicaragua at the invite of President Daniel Ortega. This trip would possibly become one of the most powerful dates in the history of our ministry when you consider all the politics, history and add Communist country while trying to minister to this world leader and his people. Many liked the board game "Risk" but the stakes where much higher in life and ministry. It was evident when you see all God did in the visit how Satan tried to wipe my son and me out in the Corvette.

If you could see a video footage of the tire literally blowing off on the interstate there is absolutely no way how our car did not roll over, flip several times, get smashed between the two cars that were side by side with me or how as we were losing speed the entire tire blew off that we did not get hit by cars coming behind us. Why didn't the car veer violently to the right with no rear tire and why didn't that rim get destroyed when I navigated it to the side of the interstate? All I can tell you is that Jesus took the wheel that day and fortunately the call of God is irrevocable, and God's man is virtually indestructible until Almighty God is done with him.

NICARAGUA

(Even Communism needs Evangelism)

FOR several years now I have been leading a Bible study to legislators particularly in Dover, Delaware. My supervisor and his wife are co-founders of the national political ministry I was serving under at the time, and they invited me to dinner at an upscale restaurant the day before my birthday in Washington. During the conversation at the table with just the three of us, I shared that a dear friend of my wife's and mine was also an evangelist and had connections all over the world.

He mentioned to Ruth and me that my name had just come up in Nicaragua at a private meeting with President Daniel Ortega. He told the communist president that I had many years on Capitol Hill and was now leading a Bible study and Ruth was originally from El Salvador. We now are leading a weekly bi-partisan Bible study to politicians and my supervisor leads the White House Cabinet Bible study.

President Ortega immediately said, "I want to meet this man" and I am now being invited to this Central American nation. At the dinner I asked the couple since Nicaragua is on the table and their president is interested in meeting is that something, they thought we should pursue, and they both said, "Absolutely!" When God moves, He can move fast and within a few weeks Ruth and I were now packing for the trip, boarding another plane and touching down in Managua, Nicaragua. I was familiar with the Iran-Contra news as a child; I loved President Reagan and my Dad and I briefly met Colonel Oliver North and now I am asked to try to bring ministry to this country.

This was not a walk in the park going into it and Bible college does not have a class teaching you how to handle situations like this. The Holy Spirit must be your guide and I had already received two honorary doctorate degrees but more than ever taking notes from my Teacher (Jesus). They gave us the VIP treatment when we arrived and Dr. Antonio Bolianez and Pastor Monsogo who both had a huge hand in that visit accompanied Ruth and me flying from Miami to Nicaragua. When the four of us landed at the airport we were met by staff from the Vice President's Office and were whisked into a VIP reception area and were invited to sit on a plush couch and served fresh, piping hot coffee in that hidden terminal lounge.

After clearing through customs that we did not even have to wait in line for, we received our passports and then climbed into an awaiting SUV to take our small delegation to our hotel. The hotel was first class and in the capital city of their great nation. Our intention all along was to represent Christ and serve as an Ambassador to Him knowing we were "unofficial" representatives of America and minister to their people and public servants. The focus was to see if in fact it was possible to implement a Bible study at the highest levels of their government from the President on down.

God exceeded every expectation, and, in my Spirit, I just knew that the Gospel deserved a chance. It was a quiet mission heading in, but much was at stake and God had positioned Dr. Bolianez and Pastor Mansogo for their relationship with President Ortega and their citizens. Dr. Bolianez was born in Nicaragua but moved to Texas years ago and is a powerful evangelist and even considered a career in government, but God led him to preach. Pastor Mansogo is from Africa and his family all have high levels in his government including a Cabinet level position. We did not take for granted our friendship with them over the years or forget about their relationship with the Ortega's and with many ministers and politicians in their country. Ruth and I knew we were on an assignment from God and went there by faith to make a difference.

From sun-up to sundown, they had us meet pastors of large churches, mayors of various cities and top leaders in their government. The first day we were blessed to have a meeting with the mayor, politicians, and their Ambassador to Israel. God really blessed our time of fellowship together and we met several of their Cabinet Members. It was an honor to hear their hopes and sympathize with them in their hurts. We took an inventory to see how we can partner and bless them in a future trip. At dinner with these prominent politicians and the Ambassador, they shared their dreams and we talked about faith in God and their Secretary of Education shared those sports were also popular in their nation and was a great tool for learning. I shared the global initiative that we were working with back home and hope to return with a plane load of gifts and goods to help foster goodwill between our two countries.

We took a boat ride and saw several of the 365 islands that are part of this majestic country and they also have volcanoes, and the landscape and views are breathtaking. During our trip we also had a meeting with several area pastors and politicians and met the man who owns the TBN studios for all of Nicaragua. The Ambassador to Israel and some other Cabinet Members were present and I was asked at the conclusion of the lunch to share the Gospel and with no notes or notice I recalled the verse, "Be instant in season and out of season." Immediately stood to my feet and whispered a private prayer that the Holy Spirit would use my brief words to touch hearts. I proceeded to speak Truth to power in love and preached the simple Gospel message. I shared how the RED blood of Jesus could take our DARK sins and wash us as PURE as new- fallen snow. God gave me confidence to extend an invitation on the spot with dignitaries present and it has been said, "You have not preached the Gospel until you invite others to respond." Despite Satan teasing me during my remarks that no one would respond we had THREE professions of faith and one of those receiving Christ as Lord and Savior was one of their high-ranking officials. Glory to God! The Gospel is the power unto salvation!

We were taken from there to have a private hour meeting with the President and Vice President of their Congress along other leaders, Ambassadors, and officials. They had me sitting next to their President at the table and through a translator we were able to encourage them and offer hope. It was surreal sitting at the table with the hierarchy of their nation and God arranged for the whole thing to happen. The Lord indeed used all my years on Capitol Hill to prepare me for a seat at the table. Two decades before, I was a Special Assistant to one of the most powerful Members of Congress and was also his driver and occasional speechwriter. One day I went to get the boss lunch and when I returned to his private office on The Hill, he had some high-level leaders there in an impromptu meeting. He was sitting on the couch, and everyone was around him and to his credit he said, "Frank go ahead and sit behind my desk and you can eat your lunch with us." That was gracious of him, but I felt awkward sitting behind his Congressional desk and after a minute or two I humbly dismissed myself and retreated to my cubicle in his DC office outside the room and down the hall. That was his desk and our district voted for him and not me and despite his kind gesture I wanted to honor him and his position. The timing was not right then but now sitting next to their nation's leadership I had peace because I knew I had been positioned there by God like a pawn on His chess board and I was doing the Lord's work.

Around the table were the President and Vice President of their Congress. They would be equivalent to our Speaker of the House. They are each powerful leaders indeed as Nicaragua has two presidents. One is for the Congress and other one is for the Country. President Ortega and his wife, who is the Vice President and First Lady, oversee the country and I am now sitting side by side in a conference room in their Capitol inside the Congress with their President, a few Cabinet leaders, and the Ambassador to Israel. The Christians have been persecuted immensely and the pastors and politicians alike both told me they want to honor God, they desire peace, they long for revival in their land and they are open to implementing a Bible study to bless their government and their public servants.

When it was my turn to speak, I had been listening to them but also trying to listen to Him to hear what God would have me say. A translator was kneeling to my left between the

President and me and I was once again at the table with some heavy hitters. The President and Vice President of the Congress were so gracious to us and to start off the meeting, the Vice President presented Ruth with a beautiful basket with various gifts, and she was moved to tears (picture above).

As we sat back down, it was obvious the politicians present were tired from the hostility thrown at them the last year, but I am pleased to report both their faith in God and desire to lead their country is stronger than ever. During our discussion I noticed that our small delegation was the same in number as the group of public servants of their government leadership in the room. The Lord impressed on me to have each of us stand behind them and I asked them to pray specifically for the ones in their presence. Before petitioning God, I shared that this will be symbolic long after we leave the room that we as Christians stand BEHIND you in prayer and until our next return, we will be BESIDE you in your journey with Jesus and never forget most of all that God is IN you both now and forever. You could feel the Presence of God in that place and when we concluded we were hugging one another. I shared with them that I wish we had a basin of water in the room because Jesus taught us that servant leadership is the best. Even Dr. John Maxwell would agree, and he is beloved around the world on leadership. I told them the "greatest among you is the servant" and it would be my high honor to wash their feet. We came as servants not celebrities and we are ambassadors of Almighty God. Their leadership had tears in their eyes, and they hugged, and some did not want to let go. The Lord blessed that meeting between a couple preachers and their president and leadership. After a group picture was taken, we waved goodbye and wished them God's blessing personally and professionally.

As we left, TV reporters were waiting for us outside in the hallway, but I told my wife, Ruth to have this moment alone. She has selflessly stood by my side all these years and she is a leader long before meeting me and **true leadership not only delegates but sometimes steps aside to let another shine**. With her Hispanic background and formerly living in El Salvador she was the perfect one to address the media. She was incredible! I smiled just outside of camera range and let her have this moment and besides her Spanish is perfect and she so valiantly serves behind the scenes and this was a great chance for her to be front and center.

Immediately following that meeting we were taken across town and then learned we had a private meeting with their Secretary of State and Supreme Court Justice at a table with them in his office. They were most hospitable to us and they also relayed their desire for peace and longing for hope and better days. I have been invited to speak on six continents and their streets were clean, safe, and peaceful. Sadly, many other places like the Dominican Republic, Haiti, Mexico, Jamaica, and other nations are extremely dangerous specially to visiting Americans. We are living in violent times and our only refuge and safety is in the shadow of God's grace and protection. We were scheduled to meet President Ortega, but it was rescheduled because he attended and spoke the eulogy at the funeral of a citizen who was murdered. We heard his remarks on the radio and when we met him the next day, I thanked him for his remarks, and he was both presidential and pastoral in his address. That evening we were invited to another dinner with much of their Cabinet present and what an honor to break bread and interact with each of them. The hospitality and generosity were both first class and second to none. Our son Andrew was having his fourth-grade awards ceremony on the last day of the school year and Ruth flew home by herself to be present with our son as he received his awards. There is nothing like a mother's love and I am so proud of my family.

The very next day the three of us remaining were summoned to the private residence of **President Daniel Ortega** and his wife, **Rosario Murillo**. She is both the Vice President and First Lady of Nicaragua and I had driven through the gates of the White House a couple times for work and the United States Capitol Building when the barricades would be lowered so we could enter, but now I am doing the same thing but in Nicaragua. We were temporarily stopped at the security check point with armed guards who now cleared us through to proceed to their President's personal home.

While walking into the meeting it was just three of us and it was something like out of the movies. At one point I felt like Harrison Ford in "Clear and Present Danger" and then felt like Forrest Gump getting ready to meet JFK. As we stepped closer towards the residence with armed guards watching our every move from the side, I recall countless times on television seeing heads of state meet with world leaders at Camp David talking peace but the last remaining steps before entering the house I felt like Dr. Billy Graham as an Ambassador of God and His Gospel. One of my favorite pictures is of the newly sworn in President George W Bush as he walked into the Oval Office for the first time as Commander in Chief. All the furniture was missing but the carpet with the embroidered eagle and presidential seal was present and the first few steps he looked small, overwhelmed and a tad scared walking in the room, but once he was behind the desk, he grew into the job quickly. I do not care what one's resume was in the past; the presidency has a weight that very few could comprehend much less handle but there is an anointing for those appointed. With each step I could sense the Lord strengthening me and it was as if my spine grew taller once I was in the house. Not arrogant but on assignment and some folks strike out in the majors and others were waiting for the opportunity to smash it over the center field fence.

We were welcomed into a private reception area with massive windows and a spread of fruit with flowers and they were gracious and kind to us. We met privately with Mrs. Ortega first and she enjoyed catching up with my friends who made the meeting possible. Over the years, they have been doing a lot of ministry and missions to bless their nation.

About ten minutes later, President Ortega walked in and we all stood to meet him, and Ruth and I had brought him gifts. After introducing me to him I think it was obvious because I was the lone American on this trip and delegation and I presented him a biography of Dr. Billy Graham in Spanish. We presented him a Bible and a copy of one of our political Bible studies for him and his staff to consider implementing in their nation. After a few pleasantries while standing once again I was asked to sit next to the President. Two days before I was at the table with the President of their Congress on my immediate left but now, we are in the President of the country's house and I am seated with him directly to my right.

Once again, I prayed silently with my eyes open that God would bless this meeting, that I would be a light for Christ in this communist country and that they may see the Lord in me. My prayer was as we have a dialogue about the importance of honoring God personally and politically and that the Bible would in fact be adhered among their people. The Vice President sitting next to her husband shared, "*we don't want more politics. We want peace, revival and the Word of God.*" We talked about several faith initiatives and how we desire to bring relief to help their citizens but also see REVIVAL transpire during and after our departure. The pastors, politicians and people long for better days and desire to please God.

With our meeting almost up and I knew time was ticking we asked if we could close in prayer and the three of us were now in a circle with arms on each other's shoulders were now praying with President Ortega and his wife while in their residence. I was asked to conclude the prayer and with a translator the Lord gave me words from a direct line from Heaven. All the previous meetings that I prayed under my breath that God would show up and touch hearts before each meeting was answered then but particularly now. The Presence of God was in that room! We had a wonderful conversation and time of fellowship and as we were exiting, the Vice President invited us back for further ministry opportunities.

In my ministry, I had prayed with prostitutes, professional athletes, politicians and presidents and it was an honor to close in prayer with this power couple and President Daniel Ortega personally walked us to our awaiting car. I noticed a couple of armed guards outside and made a temporary beeline from the president and approached them and shook their hands while thanking them for their service and providing protection. I shared my Dad and family have been in law enforcement in our Nation's Capital for over five generations and "Blessed are the peacemakers.' In God's eyes, the police are just as important as heads of state, and I thought of our family and countless friends who despite being around power may have felt left out and I wanted to leave power to include them through a translator. Friends have called me Rambo without a gun, and I approached them with their machine guns but after our conversation they were smiling.

What a way to close this historic trip, as right before climbing into the awaiting car to take us to the airport. The President was standing outside to the right of the car, and I approached him again, shook his hand and thanked him for receiving us. I felt compelled of the Lord to hug him, and the gesture touched him. I know protocol doesn't allow folks to hug their leaders often, but grace trumps the law and when representing God sometimes you have to flip the tables. This may surprise some, but I felt like what the Lord might have felt while holding him.

As we jumped into the car and with a final wave to the President and Vice President, we were whisked off to the airport with a police escort and sirens blaring. They had already taken our passports to clear us for departure and that is the way to travel with no bags or worries and only board the airplane. When we arrived at the VIP reception, I noticed the

Chief of Staff to the Vice President had a large, wrapped package. He said, "Frank – this is for you from the President and Vice President." My heart skipped and my mouth dropped, and my eyes almost popped out of my head. I was so touched, and we came to give, and they gave. You cannot out give God. The picture below is the hand painted picture of a lighthouse, and the irony is it closely resembles the one in our front yard. You will notice a fisherman who caught a fish, and it encourages me to continue to be a light in a dark world and keep fishing for the souls of mankind. Everyone from the custodian to Commander-in-Chief needs Christ.

Once again, it was wild having a police escort racing to the airport with senior staff from the president in the car accompanying us. It was like we were in our own motorcade and on that trip, We did our best to show the best of America while representing Christ and sometimes politics and ministry can mix. While racing to the airport in that hot summer sun with no time to spare a call came in. During our visit when a certain ring tone chimed, I realized after the second call that it was the Vice President calling our friend assigned to us. She said to him to tell us, "Please tell Evangelist Shelton that we are so grateful for his visit to our nation." She continued, "We have had many people pray for my husband and me over the years, but we have never felt the presence or power of God on them like you did today in that beautiful prayer. We are deeply touched!" Those words touched my heart and praise the Lord! The Bible says, "Your gift will bring you before kings and great men" and I was trying to be a willing vessel to bless others. The song I sang as a child at church still held true, "Red, yellow, black and white, we are all precious in God's sight."

Days before our departure to Nicaragua some folks were complaining at home that a pastor in Virginia prayed for President Trump. The Lord gave me a word, "**If we only minister to folks who look like you, dress like you, talk like you, think like you or vote like you then you are not LOOKING like the Lord.**" Paul was all things to all men that some would be saved and the picture they gave us will be special to us and today is in our home. The Lord set the table for us to have a wonderful relationship with this great country and their President and political leaders and please pray for them, that the persecution across the board stops and if you would like to assist with resources to bless Nicaragua please reach out to our office. We are so thankful to God for making this trip possible and grateful for Dr. Bolianez who selflessly opened the door. President Reagan was correct when he said, "It is amazing what you can accomplish if you don't care who gets the credit." We are hoping to return soon and encourage all in their walk with Christ. The Answer is not in any government but in God Almighty. It is Jesus alone who changes hearts, transforms lives and can better a society. Saul had an amazing "Damascus Road" experience and was converted and became the Apostle Paul. Lord willing, with God's grace and willing hearts, we may see thousands saved and millions drawn closer to Christ. The Gospel compels us to look for a way in not out and the first two letters of Gospel spell GO! To God be the glory – great things HE hath done!

We arrived at the airport and flew through security but when you just came from the president's house things tend to speed up. One last cup of coffee in the private reception and one last hug to our host whom we have come to admire and love, and like Elvis, not only left the building but boarded the plane and left the country. The three of us were heading back to the states and God moved in a great way! That would be the first of several trips in the next year to that nation and now halfway into 2019, I had a greater urgency that time was of the essence. Most folks were clueless of the storm brewing as the clock raced towards the end times. I had been on local and national radar for several years now, but it only intensified after this trip. The moment you start speaking in stadiums, appearing on radio and television, and ministering to powerful people not everyone will be happy. The Bible says, "We cannot be ignorant of the Devil's devices". More than ever, I was trying to resemble the knight in armor fighting the good fight with Satan, snakes and with time slipping through the hourglass that Durer depicted a half century ago in his famous painting.

While on one of those early visits the Vice President's office was touched by our ministry throughout their country. They had arranged meetings for me to preach at various churches both indoors and outdoors and television crews covered what God did. Scores were born again, and political leaders were both saved and inspired and some for the first time in a long-time, were considering living for Christ. We met countless pastors who had a heart for both peace and revival, and I was honored to inspire and minister to them and their people. God gave me great favor with their leaders and over one meal I was invited to return and possibly preach at their annual summer festival where a reported 700,000 had congregated in the past. They saw the three times I had preached to over 120,000 in Uganda to a third of a million souls in three sermons but now Nicaragua was inviting me to preach to nearly three quarters of a million people in one sermon.

If we were not willing to take the risk, go in and give the Gospel a chance that plate would have never been on the table. A few weeks leading into the big celebration which I was invited to speak I humbly gave the speaking opportunity to my supervisor who led the national political Bible study and the biggest sermon of my career never happened because I deferred to another. However, the entire endeavor trying to bless their nation was not to elevate me but exalt Christ and further the Gospel. Reagan was right, "It is amazing what you can do if you don't care who gets the credit." In golf, you must tee up the ball and Ruth and I with our friends indeed put the ball on the tee and the plate on the table and talks immediately started to begin the Bible study for their government leaders. Praise the Lord!

About three months later, I got a call from an excited Ruth saying the Vice President's office called inviting me back to minister. Once again, I was wheels up flying to Nicaragua on a moment's notice but this time no spouse, no staff, no security, no salary and just God and me. Like Han from Star Wars, I was flying "Solo", and I don't know too many preachers nor politicians would have flown in all alone, but God graced and equipped me for this opportunity. Plus when you met Rambo as a kid you caught some traits as an adult. I am not talking violently but serving faithfully and my buddy Dr. Tim Lee and former U.S. Marine said, "You don't need a lot of Marines to get the job done." My cousin is in the United States Marine Corps but we both are in the Lord's Army.

My ancestor, Officer Joseph Gales Shelton who was a friend and bodyguard to President Abraham Lincoln was recorded in his obituary by The Evening Star, October 25, 1907, that he resided in Washington since his birth in 1829 and "Was identified with nearly every movement for the advancement of the interests in general and East Washington in particular. He was appointed a policeman October 18, 1861, soon after the old Auxiliary Guard had been merged into the first Metropolitan Police Force, he patrolled the duty of a patrolman in the exciting and trying period of the Civil War. He had many thrilling experiences with deserters, bounty jumpers and desperate characters who flocked to Washington during the war period. There was a saying among the policemen in those days of the fire and smoke of war that there was on any average one murder a day in the capital city. The policemen were therefore required to perform heroic service. It was said Mr. Shelton was one of the officers who responded to the call of Patrolman Clements when he arrested single-handedly nearly an entire company of Zouaves near the Capitol in 1862. He was stationed at the White House and was frequently detailed as one of President Lincoln's bodyguards and his sagacity and bravery won for him high esteem about the city and among the police force where he had many friends. He was on terms of personal friendship with Mr. Lincoln as the result of his position at the Executive Mansion and was also acquainted with many famous men of the day."

Between my Dad's family who were linked to Queens in England and protecting presidents in America and Mom's family having a hand in planting the world-famous cherry blossoms around the Tidal Basin, the Lord used all of that in my lineage for me to minister to the powerful and poor. Plus, the Shelton bravery as policemen for the last century and half in one of the most dangerous times in American history propelled me to walk in God's authority and take back territory today. One of the most important aspects of an officer's job description is not only integrity and kindness but being on post.

Once again, I was on post and landing all alone on this trip. It was another whirlwind trip and God gave me great favor. The Lord allowed us to do more in a week than some could do in decades and God has a unique way to make things happen and I could not let fear or politics keep me home on the couch. I can live with trying and not winning and was willing to die trying but I couldn't be content to sit on the couch wondering, "What if?" Personally, the four words, "What might have been" scared the daylights out of me and I had a friend whose father played with Babe Ruth and my friend, Deidre is married to Albert Pujols who is the top five homerun hitter in MLB history and trying to follow their lead, I was going to swing for the fence!

While in Nicaragua we had many meetings once again and the pastors had shared that their nation was ripe for revival. Once again, they rolled out the red carpet for me while in town and I was happy to hear the Bible study was moving forward and they were already bringing a pastor up to speed for him to start leading the weekly devotion. After preaching at various events, I was able to make some great progress with creative ways to bless their nation literally and spiritually. Now with my affiliation with the Christian airline being established, we in our mind and heart were already looking forward to returning on one of the jets to bring help and hope with some Heaven on Earth!

As a chaplain at several summer Olympics, I have been blessed to make some special friends. My buddy Bill for twenty-five years was the chaplain to the Boston Celtics and was considered at one time the Dean of NBA chaplains. While having a working lunch meeting in Nicaragua I shared to the president's staff that I could arrange for Bill and his ministry working with former NBA ball players and possibly bring them to their nation and we play a goodwill exhibition game between their current players. Their eyes got bigger than the plate and we had a verbal *carte blanche* from their leadership that they would allow us to use their 12,000-seat stadium in Managua and pack it out. We would have the two teams play and then they were going to allow us to preach at half-time to that packed crowd and share the Gospel. I had already envisioned in my head that thousands would have come forward to receive Christ as Savior.

I excused myself from the table, stood outside and told them I would try to get Bill on the phone to share the news! While standing outside in Nicaragua I am calling his home in America, and he answered on the second ring!! I shared with him the news and only God could do this because he said, "Frank, this is incredible! You will not believe this, but my son is flying to Nicaragua next week on a mission's trip and I didn't want him to travel alone so I am going with him." Only God could write this script and I was able to connect the president's office with him when he flew in just days later! When God moves, He moves quickly!!

Between that meeting we were then in the process of praying, preparing and already planning between our respective calendars to bring the former pro basketball players to come and play while building relationships between the nations and preach the Gospel. I have seen the Lord use sports as a tool to bring folks together and come to faith in Christ. Alexis Arguelo was a native of Nicaragua and world boxing champ and they built a brand-new stadium bearing his name. The leadership gave us permission to not only use that state-of-the-art stadium, but we began to think out of the box advocating that we should do more than one game. Opposed to just one game in the capital city perhaps spread them out and they agreed! We were going to plan to do three games in five days in three different cities spread out all over their country. This would allow us to minister to over 30,000 citizens of Nicaragua in just three games! Plus, they agreed to air it nationwide to their nation on LIVE television.

Folks have joked when I preach and play with words at times, I sound like a white Jesse Jackson, but I am also part promoter like Don King. A preacher who does not promote the greatest message of all time is problematic. We must look for creative ways to reach souls with the Gospel because time is ticking. Business as usual is killing the Church and I felt compelled to wake up sleeping saints. Too many were overweight with big buildings and bloated budgets but could not afford to help a struggling single parent with a light bill.

God was on this effort, and I even reached out to a well-known major league baseball player and that is their number one sport, and we could fly him in to do a teaching clinic to bring families together. Plus, we were reaching out to see if we could get bats, balls, bases, hats, and shirts donated to bless their people. We would use sports to get them to the Savior and my recent trips to the United Nations got my mind thinking how we could bring relief by day and then set up a crusade to usher revival at night. The Lord had allowed me to meet some incredible ministry contacts both as singers and speakers and my tenure with the Billy Graham Evangelistic Association and saw how Samaritan's Purse could fly in and lift morale instantly was something we were hoping to emulate.

The Lord had me make a few calls and we have a Bible study in play for their government. Even communism needs evangelism! We were blessed to make another phone call and get a fellow Olympic chaplain friend on the line, and he was in talks of bringing former NBA players and another call was using the Christian airplane to fly in like Santa bringing gifts but more like a future scheduled "Christmas in April."

At the conclusion of that second trip, I was invited to preach on the floor of their Congress. It was on occasion of the 450th anniversary of the Bible being translated into Spanish and while in town unbeknownst to me I would be asked with no notes, no preparation, and no time to get nervous to address their entire Congress.

God had me work on the floor of the United States Senate in 1995 as an appointee by the Sergeant at Arms as a bi-partisan figure to serve all 100 U.S. Senators daily. I had also worked on the floor of the House of Representatives assisting Senators, Members, Supreme Court Justices to their seat during a special joint session and even worked on the James S Brady press room floor of the West Wing at the White House on occasion as a visiting correspondent covering daily press briefings by both the Obama and early Trump administrations. Up close and in person I was tasked to serve there but where I had "home court advantage" in DC, I was playing on the road in Nicaragua.

Literally mere minutes before the celebration I learned I was the only American that would be invited to speak to that capacity crowd and it would be filmed LIVE on national television with the President, Vice President, and my new friends I had met on subsequent trips over my shoulder on the floor of their Congress. Once more I said a silent prayer and as a former speechwriter to a Member of Congress, I wrote the remarks as if one day I would give them and years later I am now standing up and speaking out.

God gave me a message downloaded from Heaven and for years I knew how to even write applause lines in a speech and sure enough the crowd erupted at that very moment. It is true, you must see it before you see, or you will never see it. After that first applause, God and I threw it into second gear while hitting the second paragraph and the place erupted again and now with time ticking and not the place to downshift in a speech or moment in time, I threw the speech intro third gear and God took it straight to fourth and that crowd came unglued! They began to clap as I was already heading into fifth gear and for more consumed with delivering God's mail than basking in any applause, the Lord took us faster than a Ferrari and went to overdrive knowing overtime was not an option. We were on all cylinders and the place almost gave a standing ovation. When you speak another language and are from another nation, but God allows one to transcend culture and politics, it is a humbling but powerful thing to witness the Lord touching hearts.

Behind the podium it was part presidential and preacher delivering the mail and I watched Dr. Graham a million times in person and online via films and social media. I recall him speaking behind the presidential podium at a prayer breakfast in Washington, DC in the early 1960's and President John Kennedy was to his right sitting down while the reverend was up speaking. Every single eye in that room was not on President JFK but the King's ambassador who like Jesus at age twelve held the lawyers and doctors in the palms of His hand. He was barely a kid but already The King and not, yet a teenager was the Trinity wrapped in One. Even President Kennedy was moved by Dr. Graham's speech. It was humbling, but even the President and Vice President of Nicaragua were over my shoulder hanging on to every word. The fact is they were not my words but God's and after praying for peace, wisdom, grace, and the hope that they would honor God and His Word not just on the historic day but every day of their lives. I mentioned in my message that nations have thrived who honor God, but countries have collapsed when the turned their back on Almighty God. After closing the prayer in the Name above all names, Jesus Christ I said, "Amen" and the Congressional crowd cheered more!

Within an instant the Lord reminded me of how God used Dr. Bolianez and his connections to set the plate on the table. My wife, Ruth would be from neighboring El Salvador and spoke their language even though she was not on this trip she was my biggest fan. Plus, marrying her and meeting people from her nation gave me a love for this group of people that at times may have felt overlooked or underappreciated. The seed was planted the night before my birthday at the dinner at Trump Hotel when a respected Bible teacher wanted to continue to reach this region and their leaders and urged me to go to Nicaragua. So I was obedient and made that first trip with no guarantees of success. Amazingly, in just a few months of friendship and trips, I had met with their nation's highest leaders, preached at revivals across their country and had now spoken on the floor of their Congress. Look at God! Plus, if I was not willing to risk going in, I wasn't worthy to speak standing up to preach the Gospel and promote unity.

A reporter asked me while in town, "Pastor Shelton, why do you promote peace?" I smiled my office was evacuated next door to the United States Capitol on 9/11 and we were told "Run for your lives." I looked her in the eye while the camera capturing my response, "I promote peace because when you have seen war up close you tend to find peace more attractive. Plus, Jesus is the Prince of Peace." God truly gives you a word to say in due season and after shaking hands with many of the leaders, clergy, and politicians we made our way outside the Capitol and back into an awaiting vehicle.

That was an incredible trip and once again they were extremely hospitable to me the entire time. After returning a couple times I was even contacted by the Vice President's office to encourage them Biblically and getting things ready for the future crusade. Despite God's blessing I just knew the walls were closing and this may sound arrogant but, in this season, very few in ministry had gone as fast and far on a shoestring budget. One cannot be this passionate if you were not called or could not see the signs of the times. More than ever, the Holy Spirit was warning me of things to come and objects coming around the corner. Plus, He was alerting me who was on God's side and who were just pretending while playing games. The following year would show who was legit and who should repent or quit.

Later that year, I was disappointed to learn that the sizable donation from a pastor friend's church that I was told to expect in the fall, would not be coming after all that year. When I kindly called him, he paused and said, "Frank, I am so sorry, but we ended up going at the last second in another direction and that $33,000 check went to another ministry. My heart dropped but when you are counting on a check of any amount much less that amount your heart can skip, go south, or quit!

Once again, it was one step forward and two steps back. The blessing is my insurance paid $11,000 of the $15,000 hospital bill from Texas and my parents graciously wrote a check to cover the difference. Debt can be heavy, and I had taken some shots, but praise God we were still standing. Once again, we had to trust God and I knew my pastor friend is literally one of my favorites on the planet and we just had to keep trusting God. Plus, two wrongs do not make a right. A friend of mine said, "People get funny when playing with money" and I needed to model Christ in all situations. Bishop T.D. Jakes said in a sermon, "A full calendar doesn't mean a full checking account" and just because you are ministering to prominent people does not mean you will not encounter problems. In fact, you may come across more, but the Lord is faithful!

ROGER STONE – LEAVE NO STONE UNTURNED

IT was getting late in the year 2019 when I received a call out of the blue from Randy, a dear friend in Florida. He said, "Frank are you still on staff with the Billy Graham Evangelistic Association?" I said, "No sir, I am no longer on staff but still friends. We have since formed our own ministry and am preaching nonstop at home and abroad."

I said, "How can I help you?" Randy replied, "Do you know Roger Stone?" I said, "I certainly know who he is, but I have yet to meet him." He said, "You are probably familiar with his predicament and looking at possible prison time and I have been able to encourage him and grow as friends and minister to him." He added, "Franklin Graham is coming to town in Florida for his DECISION AMERICA tour and he was hoping to go to the outdoor service in the Sunshine State. Roger wanted to go as well and asked me if it were possible for me to connect them?

I knew the situation from the news, and you cannot always believe what you hear, read or see and the public controversy surrounding the issue but also knew how the FBI sent two dozen agents to arrest him on national TV with a helicopter hovering over his house before sunrise. I also knew the eerie feeling of someone "hovering over me" and despite no longer being on staff with BGEA or on their payroll, I knew the heart of **Dr. Billy Graham** and that was to minister to others in the good, bad, and ugly. Long ago, I was taught to under promise and over deliver and I reached out to a dear friend and former colleague and asked if Franklin would have a few minutes to offer hope one on one with Roger at the Florida service should he come? Billy would counsel heads of state but also the homeless and everyone in between. I knew he loved on those shackled in prison and ministered to those in the news under less than stellar circumstances.

Ministry and leadership must look past self and try to help others, especially when they are hurting. I wrote a post years ago called "**The Hinge**." A hinge is a small (often hidden) part of a door. Ironically, they are not expensive and often out of sight, but doors don't open without them. *It is worth noting that the design of a hinge is the same whether it's in a janitor's closet of a public school or on the five-inch-thick doors that open into the Oval Office.* While Randy was on the phone asking me to try to make the connection, I felt the Lord leading me to be "a hinge." The very next day Franklin's team responded, and he obliged, and a week later Roger with the weight of the world on his shoulders, went to the Florida service by faith. I prayed that God would touch that capacity crowd but also do a great work in Roger's heart, too.

That night just before the service, to Franklin's credit, he met with Roger Stone privately for ten minutes and prayed with him. Later that evening, during the service Roger Stone with tears streaming down his face, made a public profession and re-dedicated his life to Christ at the Decision America rally. That pic is posted above, and I believe the Associated Press ran with it. I was texted a pic that night afterwards of seeing Roger's hands raised in worship and it touched my heart. After hearing the Gospel, Roger Stone indeed found **FREEDOM in Florida**. The Gospel sets us free! Both Randy and Roger called me that night while leaving the prayer event from their car and they thanked me for the connection. I spoke with Roger for about ten minutes that night on the phone. It was kind of them to call and say, "Thanks."

Many people may not agree, but Jesus often left the crowd to go after ONE. It was a privilege to speak life that night on the phone with them both and I have been praying for him and asked God to do a great work in his heart. Fast forward a couple months and Randy asked me to have a private meal in Washington in early 2020 while he and Roger were in D.C. It was on the eve of Roger's sentencing with he, his wife and a few of their friends at a small table in a nice restaurant on Capitol Hill. It was surreal to be at the table and I was just trying to be a blessing. I did not share anything on social media that night and as I left, Roger thanked me again and shared that Franklin had just personally mailed him a Bible. He was beaming ear to ear and was so appreciative and enjoying reading God's Word.

As I left that night, I told him I have no idea what will happen in that court room but stick with Jesus because He stuck on the cross for you and mankind. God is faithful and His mercies are new each morning. Accepting Jesus was the greatest decision of his life and no matter what happens, press into the Lord. I had met Chuck Colson and he was also connected with a past White House and God used him to touch tens of thousands with the Gospel. The Lord is in the redemptive business, and I know some are reading this now and suggest, "I despise Roger Stone!" You must realize that God made, loves, died and cares for Roger and his family. Plus, you must remember at the beginning of this book I drove six hours round-trip all alone to minister to Vice President Biden at the time in 2015." If you only pick and choose who you feel is worthy of God's grace you may not be born again. Read that again!

Plus, I went to Nicaragua multiple times not because I was a closet Communist but because I was an evangelist. People need Jesus and sometimes the worse sinners become the best saints. You cannot hamstring or handcuff Grace. The next day, Roger and his team went to the court room and his bride, lawyers and Randy were over his shoulder and the cards were stacked against him and they threw the book at him. When Covid-19 would hit a month later they were allowing convicts to go free for fear of them getting the released virus but were adamant that a sixty-seven-year-old man be forced to go, and hopefully die, in jail.

Folks continued to pray and as a minister of the Gospel our job is to try to represent Christ in each session and love on everyone regardless of color, class, or politics. Doctors take a Hippocratic oath to help those hurting and ministers of the Gospel are no different. I received a call a few months later and learned that the President had just commuted Roger's sentence and he was not going to jail after all. When ministering to him I was not talking legally or politically, but pastorally trying to speak LIFE not death. I know I am not perfect, and the fact is all of us have dropped the ball and facing conviction to an unpleasant **cell called Hell** and we all need forgiveness, mercy, and a pardon. Yes, I love ministering to public servants and lawmakers of both parties, but looking way past politics and more at the heart, we all need the grace of God and forgiveness found only in the Gospel. Looking back on the last few months and leading up to this almost Presidential pardon several people had a small role. Randy has been HUGE and has continually been in Roger's life and I just a small hinge and Franklin Graham sharing the Gospel reminding me of the Bible verse, "**one planted, one watered but THE LORD brought the increase (1 Cor. 3:6)!**"

Recently, I have been asked to lay hands and pray over a communist President from Nicaragua and minister privately to this Republican commuted recently by this current American president, but we all need grace and second chances. I am praying again tonight for Roger and his family. **The Gospel is "Good News!"** The catch is it is only good news if it arrives on time. Proud of my buddy, Randy who had been with Roger each step of the way and discipling him still today. Some of you know I have the honor to lead a weekly Bible study to politicians in the Dover, Delaware State Capitol when they are in session. I have shared for years that the Church has been great ministering to the poor, but Christ also would have us to minister to the powerful. Ministry is not always glamorous and sometimes it gets muddy, but the Living Water washes clean. May we all realize Jesus is our only Hope for our nation and our world and true freedom is found in the forgiveness of God. An adage says, "Leave no stone unturned" but thanks to God I am thankful that this **Stone was overturned**. #JesusSaves!

HOLY LAND -- ISRAEL

EARLIER in 2019, I saw that my favorite Christian singer and friend, Grammy winner Michael English was going on his first trip to the Holy Land. The trip would be around Thanksgiving 2019 and I reached out to one of his managers who have been friends for a long time and inquired about pricing and specifics. She called back and said with excitement, "Why don't you join Michael on the trip, and you can preach at one of the events!" That was all I needed to hear, and I could hear Rocky's trainer Mickey Goodmill with his earpiece dangling out of his ear and when Adrian told her husband to win against the upcoming second fight to Apollo he screamed, "What are we waiting for?" Once again, the Rocky theme and trumpets began to blow in my ear, and we were off to the races.

I began to promote the trip to the Holy Land, and I said, "If you have ever wanted to go to the Holy Land this is the time!" One reason, it is not every day and very few trips to Israel accommodate a Christian concert on the trip. To add, a ten-time Dove Award and multiple Grammy Winner was icing on the cake but like the cover of this book you must give me the benefit of the doubt when I say that "time was almost up!" My schedule coincides with my calling, and you cannot go that fast and that far if you do not believe God or His assignment and the Bible depicting end time prophecy before our eyes daily. Reading the Bible was more accurate than the daily newspaper and where they promoted "fake news" I was preaching Good News!

The Lord was on it from the beginning and when we boarded that trip to Tel Aviv, we had ninety-four on our trip with Michael and I brought fifty-two of them! We had friends come from over fifteen states coast to coast and they loved it! It was incredible walking where Jesus walked with my family and friends and one of the highlights was not only spending time with Michael privately and publicly but the honor to baptize over a dozen friends in the Jordan River. I had the honor to baptize Tommy Smith, a retired U.S. Capitol Police officer and longtime family friend. I love both Tommy and his bride Melody. He was also an incredible basketball coach and now in his sixties, he can still shoot the lights out of basketball. He has become a cherished friend and his new blue Corvette is beautiful but takes a back seat to his lovely bride. They are the salt of the earth and I do not know of another couple who have more fun than they do.

The greatest blessing for me was the privilege to baptize our ten-year-old son Andrew in the Jordan River where John baptized Jesus. While in that same body of water and wearing a white gown with a red cross on our chests, I had the honor to baptize my son "In the name of the Father, Son and Holy Ghost." Indeed, I am well pleased with him! It was a special and sacred moment for me, and I have seen tens of thousands respond to Christ in person and God alone knows how many responded via radio and television over the years but to share this moment with my son was something I will cherish forever.

We had about sixty on the seashore celebrating all the baptisms that day, but they too were happy for what transpired for me personally. As most were now walking to the bus, Andrew said, "Daddy, I want to go back in the Jordan River." My initial thought racing silently in my mind was Andrew once is enough, and we need to get on the bus, but the Lord impressed on me to zip and trust what my son was saying and not interfere. Christ said, "A child shall lead them" and I gave him the green light to get back into the river.

Adults can relate to kids wanting to jump in the pool one last time after they had already toweled dry, but this was the Jordan River, not the pool at the YMCA. Andrew, wearing his white gown had not taken three steps back into the water and with God as my witness, a white dove flew out of nowhere and nearly landed on Andrew's shoulder and perched on the guardrail next to him. Ruth was able to somehow capture that one-in-a-million picture and it looked like the dove indeed was going to land on Andrew before touching down next to him.

When Jesus was baptized by John, when Christ arose out of the water a white dove out of nowhere landed on Jesus' shoulder and God in His booming voice from above that James Earl Jones or Morgan Freeman would not have enough bass to capture said, "This is my Son in whom I am well pleased." For a guy who speaks for a living and who rarely does not have something to say, I was speechless, and God met with us once more. We both had a pep to our step as we headed back to the bus, and I almost missed it had I quenched the Spirit. Thank you, Jesus, for that moment in the Son with my son under the Holy Land sun!

That eight day and seven-night trip in Israel was EPIC! We went to where Jesus fed the five thousand, we went to Bethlehem and yes, something REALLY GOOD can come out of Nazareth! He wasn't just good, but He alone is God and grace has a face and He's named JESUS! We became a big family on that trip with tourists and friends from California to Maryland, Texas to Florida and several states in between including a seventy-five-year-old handicapped lady who flew solo from Minnesota. She had as much faith as me and she loved Michael and wanted to see Jesus. I pushed her for two days in the wheelchair, but those cobblestone streets were both hard on her and me. However, she had the faith to make the trip and God gave me the fortitude to try to make it worth her effort. I did work on my forearm muscles while pushing her several miles, but the greatest are the servants and some of our best ministry moments are not in a pulpit Sunday but pushing a wheelchair on Monday.

The closing night, we arranged for Michael English to give an hour concert at the Jerusalem Pavillion, a state-of-the-art theater. He was on all cylinders that night and the crowd loved it! When I preached in London during the 2012 Olympics, I became good friends with a big band called the "Joshua Experience" from Dallas, Texas. Their founder, Dr. Larry Randall, was an incredible musician and showman, and for years he did all the entertainment on big cruise ships. We hit it off in London and became good friends with his wife, Orlano and their band and have stayed in touch. Dr. Randall was an encourager to me and was constantly complimentary of my preaching ministry and he died a couple of years after the Olympics.

God gave me an idea while driving down the road and since I am part preacher but part promoter the Lord allowed me to put the pieces together. All artists who sing are used to singing to tracks but the greats would rather sing with an orchestra behind them. Elvis was incredible but what really set him apart and complimented his God gifted voice was the twenty-piece band behind him. I made one phone call to Orlano in Dallas and one call to the owner of the Christian travel company and the next thing I knew God used me to bring a band halfway around the world to open for and compliment Grammy Winner Michael English's concert. It was a WIN-WIN for all and most of them had never visited Israel much less played in concert there. It was a privilege to connect the dots. On the last night, if the Lord tarries we shared about following the footsteps of Paul to a future trip to Rome and the crowd cheered with excitement. Plus, everyone was now friends, and we wanted a reunion sometime in the future.

The backstory to that incredible trip in 2019 transpired a quarter of a century before, in 1994. I was at the Bi-Lo Center in Spartanburg South Carolina assisting with concerts as a financially strapped college student. While at Gardner-Webb University I would often set up and tear down when some of the biggest names in Christianity came to town. It was a treat to see 4Him, Twila Paris among others live. One of the perks was a FREE Chick-Fil-A combo and a soda. Some things never change! The second perk was a courtesy ticket to watch the concert and the best part was meeting many of the artists before the show when they got off the tour bus. During those events, I met George Younce, Glen Payne, Jake Hess, Janet Paschal, Ernie Hasse, Scott Fowler from "The Cathedrals" and Bill Gaither among others but a highlight was when the Gaither Vocal Band came to town.

For several years (since 1989), I was a huge Michael English fan, and he was in town that night with the GVB and I would have worked for free! Looking back, other than the lunch and concert ticket, it was for free! I am a cheap date, and that night Michael was not on the bus when it came in and I did not see him either at the sound check but then I recall thinking "when you are that good maybe you don't need to practice."

A few hours later, the concert started and in my spirit something was off. He was gone the second the concert was over, and I began to pray. Yes, I was a tad sad I did not get to finally meet him and hoped to be able to maybe down the road. No less than a week later, the check in my spirit was revealed. After winning a record amount of Dove Awards, among them male vocalist of the year, song of the year, album of the year, to name a few, it was announced that he had had an affair and the bottom fell out. He lost his marriage, ministry, and record label almost all over night. Very few had been so high and crashed so low but none of us could walk in his shoes. To make matters worse, I was working part-time at Christian bookstore and was instructed to "take all of his music off the shelves." I CRIED that day and too often Christians have been known as the only army to shoot their own when they lie wounded on the battlefield.

God had me pray around the clock for him. I found a fan mailing address and began to send handwritten notes of encouragement to him periodically over the years telling him God was not done with him. I was not even sure he was getting them, but God told me to write so I did. He slowly began to sing solo dates periodically and I drove thousands of miles to attend his concerts up and down the East Coast and it was the best of times and worst of times. From a fan's perspective it was great because before I was in the nosebleeds when he sang to 7,500 each night but now sitting towards the front of a country church.

It was a blessing to see him up close but a burden as well because there was always someone from the Pharisee police that would stand up in the middle of his singing and bring up the past. We finally met in 1998 and I told him I was praying for him and then we connected a few more times in early 2000. Around 2005, I drove several hours at another concert to hear him and told him I felt led of the Lord to bring him to my hometown for our first "Celebrate Jesus! Crusade" in Charles County, Maryland in 2006.

He was a tad reluctant because people had promised the moon, but no one delivered! He had been wounded by so many and to honor my promise I told him when we do it he was going to be my main singer. As I went to work with posters and promoting his visit, excitement spread in the air quickly, but a few fruit loops came out of the woods and sadly some of the critics were clergy. One preacher called me and said, "Frank, I was coming to your event but cannot now knowing Michael English is coming!"

I already knew where he was going and then I said, "Do you believe in forgiveness?" The pastor caught off guard said, "Yes." I said "Sir, you may preach it from the pulpit, but you need to give it off the platform." He then said, "He may hurt your ministry." I cut him off and said, "Sir, I don't have a ministry. The Lord is the One with the ministry and Michael sang to millions over the years in concert and via television specials and night after night to multiplied thousands and I prayed to God to meet him but for the last few years been ministering to him from afar and now the chance to share his stage. If God used Michael to minister to millions, then maybe God will use me from Waldorf, Maryland to minister to Michael. If that means hurting my ministry well praise the Lord and sign me up!"

The pastor told me no one would come but come they did, and God packed out Thomas Stone High School gym with standing room only and nearly 1,200 were in attendance. Not bad for a guy with no church and another that some said God was done with! It was the talk of the town and that pastor was one of the few who did not make it. At least he told me where he stood but I still saved a seat for him should he show. God rocked the house and in front of everyone that night I gave Michael the replica ROCKY boxing trunks. I was just with Sly Stallone as an extra in Rocky Balboa filming in Vegas. That night in my hometown in Maryland I told Michael that millions loved "Rocky" not because he never lost but because he never quit. After a hug I gave him the boxing trunks in front of that capacity crowd, and he hugged me and the next few years we ministered in several states and in a couple countries together. Write this down: "*Who you respect is who you attract.*"

A few times I gave him all the money in my pocket but not because he asked but I wanted to resemble Jesus who gives when others were out to get. Let us fast forward now to being invited to preach in Israel with him in Nov 2019. I prayed with him in the green room before he took the stage in Jerusalem and then once again shared the stage with him and preached a sermon and gave an invitation for folks to receive Christ. It does not get much better than that! He mentioned in front of the crowd halfway around the world about how the night I gave him the ROCKY shorts had really touched him and he still had them. He said, "I will never forget that gesture."

Before leaving Israel, he told me about his admiration for NFL great John Riggins. Michael and I both loved the Washington Redskins, but he shared he had never been celebrity struck but he always wanted to meet the Hall of Fame running back. Michael shared after midnight in our hotel lobby in Israel with just us and two friends at a table that he saw "The Diesel" in an airport years before back in the US and started to approach him to get an autograph. Right as he got to Riggins, Michael turned back and did not ask for the autograph. When we all shouted, "Why?" He said, "I felt like a kid, didn't want to bother him and was not sure I could it handle if he said "No."

Michael is a Grammy Winner and at 6"4 a very handsome man and my heart dropped when he did not reach out. Just like He did with the Rocky shorts before in 2006, the Lord gave me another assignment in 2019. I said, "Michael in my home on my fireplace mantle is an autographed Washington Redskins helmet signed by Super Bowl MVP John Riggins #44 himself. The Lord told me that when you come back to sing at my home church next week in Maryland I will give it to you!

He almost cried and thought I was crazy but God's love is radical and generous and after hosting him at my home church the next week in Maryland after returning from the Holy Land - Ruth and I were able to host him and his two family friends for lunch in our home at our dining room table. Following the meal, I took the signed Riggo helmet out of the glass case as promised and gave it to him. Now we are toe to toe, and I am 6"1 and he three inches taller I looked him in the eye and certainly not trying to preach to him I said, "Michael you are entering the fourth quarter of your ministry. What made John Riggins so special was when the game wore on he got stronger. When most running backs were dead tired in the third quarter, he was waking up and warming up."

As I handed him the helmet and he was like a kid in the candy store, inspected it and holding the authentic pro helmet signed by the man himself and Hall of Famer, I said to him standing dead center in my family room, "Michael many would love to see you get tackled one more time and stay down but not God, me or those who really love you." I gave you the Rocky shorts in 2006 to remind you to "get up" but I am giving you the Riggins helmet now to remind you keep running! Do not quit and you are a winner not loser!

He hugged me and to see him back on TOP of the charts today reminds me of God's goodness and grace. I'm still the college kid hoping to get a peek of one I admire and never dreamed I would go from a fan to friend, and he wrote years ago a testimonial on my website,

"In the darkest days of my ministry when many mocked me - Frank Shelton ministered to me. He's the real deal!" It broke me reading his endorsement then and does all these years later tonight."

Years ago, I was told if you can't SIT with someone in their valley you don't deserve to STAND with them in victory. Nearly 30 years later, Michael is back to number ONE on billboard charts. Look at God! We love you, Michael and praise the Lord! Some today would say I still do not have much of a ministry and God alone keeps score but ministering to Michael has been one of the greatest privileges of my life. God does not throw us away when the bottom falls out. His specialty is revival, restoration, and redemption. We are never more like Jesus than when we are giving and forgiving.

Here is Michael's post on February 2021

—-

I woke up with this text from my manager Kevin today. WOW!

#1 debut on Billboard Top Christian/Gospel Album Chart
#1 Best of Michael English
#2 Lauren Daigle
#3 Zach Williams
#4 Brandon Lake
#5 We The Kingdom

Yes, thank God for grace and second chances and we resemble Christ when giving and forgiving. That trip to the Holy Land was phenomenal and only God could weave a story for us both that started in college with me setting up chairs for the concert to preaching for him as an adult. God does all things well in His time and the Lord took me from the back row to center stage and not in the crowd but with the microphone preaching. He is one I admire and love with all my heart and I couldn't be prouder of him, and he will always be TEN feet tall to me.

Lord willing, we are planning two other trips to Israel for 2022 and would love to have you join us!

TURBULENCE LEADS TO TURBO

THE month before Christmas 2019, I was resting on the couch at the house when I heard a boom! The irony is I heard it both to my right and left. I detected the one to my left first and when I went outside my next-door neighbors' front tree snapped and fell just missing our house but causing great harm to their house. For over an hour I helped them remove the debris, but I learned the boom to my left was in my house.

At first, I thought it was in the garage, but it was in the dining room. When I walked in our forty-pound chandelier had fallen from the ceiling and smashed unto our cherry dining table and was thrown in a thousand pieces! I called an accountability partner in Indiana who used to work on staff with me at the Billy Graham Evangelistic Association and I mentioned him in the first chapter of this book. Stan is one of my best friends and both anointed and filled with wisdom. He said, "Frank, no doubt that was spiritual warfare and secondly the chandelier crashing down was not related to you but another that is not on the up and up and will be falling in the future.

You may remember when we first moved into our new home with all the hostile welcome surrounding my house and when that one neighbor ran across my lawn only to stare at our security signage and when he had read the label, ran back across the yard only to speed off and for two years never come back to say hi. I had World Champions visit and stay at our house but those in little league sometimes get inspired and others intimidated. I have also learned that even those trained detectives who stare at your from afar are often afraid to look you in the eye up close. Interesting that once the cameras were in place some of the behavior kept everyone honest.

One afternoon I took a walk down my street and I was surprised to see that same neighbor walking his dog and he was about three houses away from me but the second he saw me he did not even try to hide it, but he made a u-turn so fast it was as if someone screamed more burgers are done on the grill and come and get it! That brother from another mother turned on a dime and started walking back when he saw me. I needed the exercise, so I put some pep in my step and just like when Washington Redskins Darrel Green tracked down Dallas Cowboys Tony Dorsett on national television on a "Monday Night Football" game and tackled him on the one-yard line, I caught up to my distant "friend" and said, "Howdy neighbor! I haven't talked to you in two years since you came to check out my security system" He was retired from DC and connected with the police department in the past where my grandfather was a Captain and among the chief of detectives and with a smile I had to "thank him for his service." He was speechless! Nor did he want to speak, and I just had to laugh. The righteous are as bold as lions but the rest flee when all is well. Praying blessings on him and the rest of the non-conformant at the end of the street and hoping they experience more of God's grace and less guilt.

Fast forward a few weeks and this would be my first time not boarding a flight to preach in Uganda in four years to minister in that massive stadium. I had just gotten a clean bill of health and since being contaminated exactly the year before and after going to the hospital in Houston it took the full nine months to recover. What few would know was what in my spirit was preparing for years now while full throttle on faith crisscrossing the country and a couple trips around the globe. That would be the last big stadium event before the COVID-19 halted the world.

The week before Christmas I was driving our son to school when the car's engine shuttered and was struggling. Indeed, something was indeed wrong, and the car RPM shot up, and it was a fight to go 40 mph and when we finally made it on the highway just two miles to his school, I prayed earnestly that we could at least get him safely to school. I love Lincoln as a president but as a car this one was a love/hate relationship. I had almost been killed in it twice before and now we are crawling to Andrew's school. We limped our way in and dropped him off and I parked at the school, and it died on me right in a parking spot. After further inspection, we got it going another three miles, but it was on its last leg. The irony is just as my liver had finally recovered, the Lincoln received its knockout blow and was down for the count. The car blew a couple cylinders, and the timing chain came off and destroyed the engine. The car was extremely clean both inside and out and despite sixteen years old it had only 165,000 miles it was done.

We prayed for grace and the bill not to be high, but two estimates came in at $6,000. That was the week of Christmas! The day before Andrew's school let out for the holiday, I drove my wife's Nissan and it is extra clean and only four years old. It was crazy I drove him to school and already had one car down and when I pulled into the same parking lot to drop him off, I had to run into the school to pass out a few Christmas cards to some friends. When returning to our car would you believe the car would not start? The engine would not turn, and the battery was dead. It was surreal and you had to be there to believe it. This was two cars in three days that were both dead and the irony is I was in the same parking spot!

Your resistance determines your distance, and your adversity today is preparing you to make God's Varsity tomorrow. It was inconvenient but I was able to get a jump to buy enough time to purchase a new car battery and the bills were piling up the week of my favorite holiday. On Christmas Day, we opened presents and it was relaxing knowing I did not have a plane to catch and around lunch time the Lord put the Ortega's on my heart. I went upstairs and penned a one-page letter and told them we were praying for them and their nation and forwarded to them to our friend in their office. One more time I prayed for them and whispered a silent prayer for them and reunited with my family downstairs.

The day after Christmas like any good parent, I find myself in Target so my son can exchange a gift and utilize a gift card. Honestly, I really did not want to be there but because it was with him and for him, I was in the house. My wife called me while walking out of the store and she was so excited and she said, "Vice President Ortega just had her senior staff contact me to tell you they were so touched by your Christmas letter and they want you soon to return to preach a five-day, five city revivals in Nicaragua at the personal invite of her and the President. Wow! Praise the Lord!! I would have really felt bad if I were too tired, lazy, or indifferent to take Andrew to get some items and the call came while I was at the house. True ministry is first at home.

In the coming weeks preparing for the trip much happened. I still had one car that was dead and would not move. We did replace the other and was as good as new, but Ruth and I shared one car for about three weeks. Truly, you do not know what you have until it is gone. On January 10, 2020, I was thrilled to leave at four in the morning and drive in a rental to Ocean City, MD at the invite of my new friend, Darryl Strawberry. Darryl is a four-time World Series Winner and one of the greatest baseball players to swing a bat. God had radically saved him from drug abuse and a stint in prison and today he is redeemed, restored, and rolling all over the world as one of the greatest communicators of the Gospel. Both he and his beautiful wife, Dr. Tracy Strawberry are powerful preachers.

My longtime friend, John Luppo who works with Darryl on many projects connected the two of us together. We had talked on the phone once or twice before thanks to John, and Darryl shared that he was invited to speak at the annual Ocean City Mayor's Prayer Breakfast, and he said we can finally meet there. Again, who you respect is who you attract, and Darryl and I connected at seven in the morning in that beautiful hotel on the beach facing the ocean. It was indeed cold in January, but that brother brought the HEAT sharing of God's love for the world. Darryl referenced me from the stage, and it was humbling made me feel like a million dollars. We took pictures before leaving and I walked him to his awaiting car. We were already in preparation to bring Darryl to my hometown in May 2020. The Lord made it clear that his powerful message on overcoming opioids would be much needed and received in our community. Plus, I wanted to be intentional on diversity and together we were Ebony & Ivory. Add his stellar career in the pros playing with the Yankees, Mets and Dodgers gave him great star power and name recognition to bring folks together. Just a few months later with the senseless George Floyd murder I was once again way head of the curve. Darryl played in MLB and when the BLM became front and center, I had already lived it and promoted unity between the races.

My tenure working with the Congressman in the past and state coordinator for DC, Maryland & Delaware with the Billy Graham Evangelistic Association gave me many tools to not only bring folks together, but I had a gift to get a crowd to assemble. We had just entered a new year and just mere weeks this would be a season that no one could ever forget. This may sound self-congratulatory, but the fact is I knew time was of the essence and the sand had almost emptied out of the proverbial hourglass. Urgency had been the silent alarm that had sounded in my head long before and most were either asleep at the wheel or in bed and I was not sure what was worse.

God has been faithful, but I would be lying if I said there have been no challenges along my journey: my kidneys crashing, a serious liver ailment, our cars dying, my 235-page book deleted days before going to print, losing a job contract, and the $33,000 promised donation to our ministry had gone to another. There were times I did not know whether to cry or die but I knew I had come too far not to keep trying while swinging for the fence. That was another reason I was bringing Darryl to my hometown and that brother hit one ball over five hundred feet above the scoreboard and it landed on the roof of the stadium! Over the years, I cannot explain it, but I had some little league haters but major league helpers in my corner.

The next week I was ready to go to Nicaragua and once again I was flying all alone on this trip to preach to more of their country. I recently had a local leader hint that I did not know what I was doing in ministry, but the crazy thing was I had heads of state and respected pastors privately seek out counsel or sermon notes. The Bible says, "Be careful when all men speak well of you" and I was just trying to love God, love others and lead the lost to the Lord. Over the years, I realized that if we just focus on those three things that will keep us busy and out of trouble. Too often we get into skirmishes because we have taken our eyes off Jesus and start fighting among ourselves.

This was going to be a unique trip and before landing in Nicaragua I would stop for three days and reunite with my good friend Dr. Rodney Howard - Browne at his winter conference. For the past several years I have grown so much and learned incredible truths that would not only propel our ministry but help me teach others who were still in the dark. On previous trips to Managua, I would fly from Ronald Reagan National Airport (DCA) in Washington to Miami to Nicaragua and repeat the flight pattern home. The Lord impressed on me to start the trip in Tampa and Ruth gave me her blessing to go and plus I needed as much spiritual support as I could possibly get before flying into that nation.

Even at the prayer breakfast with Darryl, I did not eat. Over three hundred folks were enjoying an incredible breakfast with eggs, cheese, bacon and succulent sausage and I was fasting and drank nine glasses of water and two cups of black coffee to help curb the head-aches. I knew in my Spirit that we had to press into God during this season and I figured if I could forgo food with my childhood hero, I would have momentum to turn the corner and get rolling. Starting at the beginning of the year I just went THIRTEEN days with NO FOOD except for water and couple cups of coffee. On two occasions I went to Chick-Fil-A and paid for just broth soup with no chicken and drank it for nutrients. Heading to Tampa, Florida I was still on the fast and in eighteen days I had dropped thirty-one pounds!

Many folks want the platform, but they will not pay the price. New levels equate new devils and I had to step up my game because we were at war. I knew the Lord wanted to take me to the next level and I had to press into God to be fit for this new assignment. Fortunately, after another uneventful flight to Florida when I retrieved my bag, I went to the curbside to wait for my ride. I have had Lex Luger – The Total Package and former World Wrestling Champ, drive me to the Atlanta airport; I have dropped off Nikita Koloff – The Russian Nightmare and five-time World Wrestling Champ at Baltimore-Washington International. I took Elvis Presley's stepbrother and Harlem Globetrotter legend Meadowlark Lemon to the Reagan National Airport in DC and was picked up by a Kardashian in a Benz in California but this trip in Tampa was hilarious.

While lined up outside waiting for my ride, I spot a silver Prius pull up to the curb. The car stops and a guy jumps out wearing a baseball jacket with the Presidential Seal on the chest and American flag patch on his shoulder and he is none other than President George W Bush impersonator John Morgan. He is smiling ear to ear and he hugs me, and everyone's mouth is on the ground. Their eyes are bulging out of their sockets and after throwing my carry-on into the back seat of his car while everyone is watching and with us both waiving as if we might be boarding Air Force One, we jump in the car and the "president" and I drive off in a Prius. The irony is if we were in anything but a Prius, they really would have thought he was "W."

I thanked John for picking me up and laughed saying this sounds like the name of a reality television show, "The President & the Prius." He laughed and honestly, John is a dead ringer for our 43rd President. We have become good friends and with no time to spare we are racing to attend Pastor Rodney's packed conference which is already in progress. Pastor does everything big and no one but the three of us knew but when we arrived, we both would be escorted into a private entrance to meet briefly with Rodney as the praise team was already worshiping to a packed crowd on that evening service. It was great for us to fellowship, and the irony is Pastor Rodney's office resembles the Oval Office and John is a dead ringer for President Bush and wearing my Washington suit, tie and presidential cufflinks I resembled the Secret Service leading the way with him in tow.

After laughing and catching up, I went down, and it is humbling but they had two front row seats reserved for me while in town at The River. They always roll out the red carpet to make their visiting friends feel special and no one does hospitality better. About forty minutes into the service Pastor shares some opening announcement and greeting to the audience and then through their top-of-the-line surround sound speakers it sounds as if a helicopter had just landed. The crazy thing is it is very possible because Pastor Rodney rolls and flies at another level. Plus, he was in the Oval Office with President Trump laying hands on the Chief Executive while praying for the most powerful person on the planet.

The crowd is on the edge of their seat and then no less than sixty seconds later, "Hail to the Chief" starts playing throughout the auditorium and it appears that President Donald Trump just walked unto the platform and the crowd went wild! John comes out wearing a Trump wig that he paid big bucks for and from ten feet you start wondering is it really 45 in our midst? When he opens his mouth and begins to speak the crowd believes indeed it might be him. The irony is Rodney has met so many people you would not be surprised if it were President Trump, and about six minutes into his opening monologue John said in his Trump accent with matching mannerisms, "You know that I know that I am not really President Trump." It was fun while it lasted, and people loved every second of it and before you think it was sacrilegious it was good, clean fun with mixed races and denominations in the house. John then with no time wasted grabbed his high dollar Trump toupee and ripped it off tossing the blonde locks to the wind and screamed, "I'm George W Bush!" The place went NUTS! The crowd fell on the floor and people were gasping for air because their ribs hurt.

For another seven minutes he went into his President Bush spiel and not one soul thought it was not "W" in the house. He not only resembles him, but his voice and eyes are exactly like his and he went in with his good natured, family values and love for God speech and the place came unglued. It had to because Trump's hair was detached moments before and still lying on the floor, but John (Bush) was on all cylinders. When he was finished, they gave him a rousing applause and the former president who just picked me up in the Prius sat next to me on the front row for the rest of the service.

Even while out of town, we still run into some leaders on the road. We had the best time that service and Pastor Rodney preached the stars down as he lifted Christ that night. Scores raced to get a picture with John on the way out and we had the best time slowly departing the sanctuary. We snuck back upstairs to pastor's private office for half an hour and then after saying goodnight the two of us headed out for a late meal.

Where else could you go to eat at during the midnight hour but where every president would go? We went to WH!! No, not The White House but WAFFLE HOUSE!! When John and I pulled up there were about ten people scattered in that rectangle box of a restaurant while two cooks were making some smothered and covered hash browns. Once again, I was leading the way and the "President" was over my shoulder and those cooks and customers didn't appear to go to church but almost turned Pentecostal when we walked in because they almost "fell out" on the floor. Several came over to take selfies and one felt comfortable enough to sit down next to him at our table and John not to disappoint while kept on delivering the goods. We stayed until one that morning just the two of us and then John dropped me off at my hotel and he headed home towards Orlando. I love that brother and he is a Godly man who has a passion for Christ and His Church and shares a deep love for our country.

Our trip to the Holy Land was scheduled for October 2020 and it was right around the corner but something inside me was thinking it may not happen. Since childhood, I knew the Lord was returning or my time on earth may soon be up, but I was like Darryl Strawberry "swinging for the fence" and as the Bible says, "Redeem the time." Some waste time and I was trying to make the most of what time we had left.

The next night in Florida, Pastor Rodney knew I was on an under the radar mission to Nicaragua and he called me up on the platform and he allowed me to testify and briefly preach the night before following John as the former president. This time, he wanted to pray for me before the entire church. They have become a family at The River and Ruth, and I love them wholeheartedly. No football player would play an NFL game without his uniform, shoulder pads, helmet and cleats and I could not show up in Nicaragua ill-prepared or not properly dressed. The Bible talks about putting on the "full armor of God" and more than ever I am suited up and resembled more than almost any time of my ministry, the image on Albert Durer's iconic panic. With my trip the next morning I needed all the prayer I could get, and most ministers would not fly alone but God had called me and like Rambo,

I was going in without a gun but loaded with my Bible that had more miles on it than five hundred Uber drivers.

Pastor laid hands on me and his prayer equipped me. In the past, God used me to minister to President Ortega but the same man that prayed for President Trump was now praying for me. After the service, I thanked him and said, "See you later" and went to my hotel. It would be an early morning with a way too soon wake up at 3:30AM. I was at the airport at 4:15 and on the plane just after five in the morning and once again racing down the runway towards Nicaragua. Many want the platform but not disciplined to pay the price.

I had dropped weight, been fasting for nearly three weeks but Pastor encouraged me to break the fast because one, you do not want to start eating food your body is not familiar with much less overseas is always a gamble to begin with. After a fast it is imperative to go slowly back into food and you do not want to eat something heavy or spicy. He added, "Frank it is hot down there and with your nonstop preaching schedule you will need to have food for energy." My body had shed thirty pounds, but I had little gas in my tank physically and he gave me the green light to eat again. Even at Waffle House the previous night I ate a little and eggs and wheat toast with my water was me slowly returning to some type of normalcy.

The Vice President of Nicaragua had graciously arranged for me to preach five times, in five cities in just five days and I needed all the prayers and stamina I could get. With my friends in Florida below and my heart with my wife at home in Maryland, my head was now in the clouds as I prayed in the pre-morning sun that the Son of God would use me in Nicaragua. While you were sleeping, God and I were preparing to shake a nation for His glory.

WELCOME TO WASHINGTON

MANY people see the platform publicly, but most do not see the price privately paid to make it work. After next to no sleep the night before and another pre-dawn departure and zero sleep on the plane, we were now making our descent into Managua. I say "our" because two hundred other souls were on that flight, and I had the Trinity with me each step of the way.

While on final approach I could see the terrain and beautiful skyline that had become familiar to me in past visits while landing but coming into foreign soil is never a cake walk. This is particularly true when you are arriving all alone. At times, it is like riding a tiger knowing full well it could turn on you anytime and life is like the game of golf. Once you think you have it figured out the next two balls are in the woods! For the novice it takes a lot of balls to play golf and it can get expensive if you do not know what you are doing.

The plane touched down with no problems and it was comforting that I flew in on American. As the aircraft taxied to the terminal, I was looking out my window the whole time and my heroes as a kid were part Rambo and Billy Graham and I would need a little of both on this goodwill tour but the only heat I was packing was the Holy Spirit. I knew that I have come to love the precious Nicaraguan people.

My entourage was smaller than ever, as it was only me, myself, and I, and after going through the VIP reception area this time I politely waved off the complimentary cup of coffee. They have delicious coffee, but I would get some of that later in the trip. Ruth made it clear to bring her back some FREE home-grown java juice. Stallone once said in an interview that he was Rambo before a cup in the morning and resembled Rocky after one. #Yo

Immediately, I met the smiling friends who came to get me and seeing a familiar face was always a blessing. They offered to grab my bags and the fine folks in Nicaragua have always made me feel extra special, but I had to remind them and myself that I was coming as a servant not a celebrity. It is nice to have folks occasionally carry your luggage, but I learned long ago to travel light and plus I needed to remain low.

My mother told me to "dance with the one that took you to the prom" and I made an intentional effort to minister to the ones assigned with them and bless them with an occasional gift or tip during the trip or before leaving. On a trip like this I am representing both the best of God and America even though it is "un-official." I was taken to the beautiful hotel where I had stayed on previous trips and it is right in the capital center and literally just a few miles from where President Ortega's residence is located.

They took me straight to grab brunch and I was still easing my way back off the fast, but they could tell I had dropped weight and more than ever I am trying to be the best billboard for Jesus. Most folks will make an opinion of you before you even speak a syllable. The more I can put the fork down the more credibility I will have when I pick the mic up. It was great to reunite with my friends and it was a treat to have a few eggs, fresh pineapple, and couple of mangos. Washing it down with a fresh glass of orange juice was just enough and they told me to crash and get a few hours of sleep. They did not have to tell me twice because with most trips including Africa, India and Paris the moment my feet hit the ground we were on full throttle from sun-up to sundown.

We all knew that the next five days would be both a sprint and marathon and nonstop meetings and I was so thrilled to be there. I have come to deeply admire John Matamoros and he serves in the Vice President's Office and he is a Godly man, and the Lord is using them greatly. I have had the chance to have dinner on a couple occasions with his beautiful family and they remind me of my wife's family. They are happy, humble, and hardworking people with a deep respect for God and Country.

Surprisingly after arriving to my beautiful suite on the top floor, I was able to climb under some clean sheets and fall straight to sleep. Anytime I am with Pastor Rodney it is like running a decathlon and one must build up almost superhuman endurance to keep up with his pace. Plus, back-to-back nights at the WH with the "president" and the three in the morning wakeup call made sleep a lost but loving commodity. I slept the rest of the day and it was an answer to prayer, and I was most grateful for the space to regroup before taking off in the morning. However, I did have to preach that night at one of the largest churches in the region and that was going to officially kick of this tour.

Some folks have no clue what they are doing but I must admit that they not only rolled out the red carpet but most importantly had their act together. The Vice President and her staff not only had doors open but the news media was there to report each step of the way. After a great rest and hot shower, I was now putting on my navy suit with white French cuff shirt and solid red tie with the dimple I was taught in the middle. God already blessed me with two on my face and now had an extra one on my tie.

Before leaving my hotel room with a beautiful two-sided view of the city and a walk out balcony, I got on my knees and asked God to use this entire trip for His glory. My prayer was that He would give me favor with the citizens of Nicaragua and help me minister to all whom I came in contact and that they would see Jesus in me. I hoped to speak life to pastors, police, and politicians while in town and God answered that prayer a hundred times. Most importantly, I asked that God bless my family at home and have his way with my life and that souls would be saved. I hoped the Ortega's would also hear good reports while I was traveling and that they would be drawn closer to Christ in the days ahead. After closing in Jesus' Holy Name, I whispered "Amen" and grabbed my Bible and was out the door, on the elevator and now heading down to the lobby.

When I walked out some said I looked presidential and pastoral and at times both. Since birth, God and country have been the hallmark of my life and the heartbeat of my soul. As I exited the elevator, immediately to my right were my friendly bell hop acquaintances and I greeted them in broken Spanish, and they smiled and gave me props for trying. I saw my two chaperones on loan from their government to graciously accompany me everywhere we went and after a hug, handshake and fist bump we were exiting the hotel and now outside climbing into the awaiting vehicle. As we pulled out, I waved to one of the grounds crew who was wrapping up after a long day in the sun and I wanted to let him know regardless of whether he knew me or not that I saw him as my equal, not as someone inferior. He smiled, I smiled, and we were off to the races.

It was an honor to be invited to preach at Revival Waters Church in Managua and I had heard great things about them, and they were exploding with great growth. As we approached that large church to kick off the first celebration, one never really knows what to expect but all doubts dissipated when we turned onto the street that housed the church. Folks were jammed packed in line waiting to get into the building. Others were carrying their children and Bibles heading towards the church and most were holding both. They were smiling and happy and it was my honor to be there. They dropped me off right our front and two other doors opened, and my buddy John and his assistant followed us in.

Especially when in another nation, many see America as the land of great opportunity, and I wanted to make folks feel comfortable in my presence. I stopped to shake hands and say hello, but time was ticking, and they politely reminded me that the senior pastor and news crew was waiting for our arrival to film before taking the pulpit. A few bystanders were inside the bowels of that big church and they were looking, and I just had to wave and connect with a few more while still moving forward.

We turned a corner and before I knew it, I was inside the pastor's office and he was most gracious. We hugged each other and it was as if we had met many times before. I was intentional to compliment him on his ministry and the beautiful building and they had grown so much they were already in the process of building again. He showed me the humble church that they started, and he was smiling as he pointed to the picture on the wall to the right of his desk. Deuteronomy says, "Don't despise the days of small beginnings" and without hesitation he immediately showed me the blueprints of the architectural drawings of the massive mega church he was building. This brother was a visionary, and he had the crowd following him to prove it. After a few minutes together conversing, another door opened and in walked the reporters from the six o'clock news and within a minute the two of us were now on air talking about the service getting ready to start and the schedule of my week's visit in the country.

After the interview, I immediately shook hands with everyone in their group and thanked them for their service and they aired it across their region later again that night. Pastor and I said a brief prayer before entering the sanctuary and asked that God would get all the glory and that lives would be touched. After closing with "Amen" I followed his lead and then I was ushered on to the platform and could see firsthand that the sanctuary was packed. Flags were flying, balloons were in the air and it felt like a party and for a Sunday night service it was ALIVE! The worship was off the charts and the atmosphere was electric and after fifteen minutes I was now introduced and met my new translator. After a brief greeting, I switched gears and lifted Christ and told them the soon coming Savior not the visiting American is the

One worthy of our attention and admiration. That night I went from first to overdrive and asked them to give the Lord a round of applause and the place went WILD!

America can take God for granted but when you are struggling financially but know your wealth is in the Lord then you can truly let loose and worship. After a prolonged applause they sat down and that night I preached on the family of God. The Lord was on that sermon out of the gate and when it was over, souls were saved, and hundreds of lives were touched and encouraged. My hosts came around me and once again I was trying to shake every hand. If a United States president could work the crowd coming and going at a State of the Union address then this evangelist should do it, too. It has been said, "People don't care how much you know, they want to know how much you care." A sermon or speech is worthless if we are too arrogant to connect on the way out the door and sometimes my greatest moments are not on a stage speaking but off the podium hardly saying a word.

My suit was soaked but my heart was full as we slowly headed back in the tunnel towards the car. Several folks were already congregating and asked to take pictures, shake hands, or sign a Bible and it is humbling but I did all three heading to the awaiting car. I was always taught to walk slowly among the people, and one is not much of a shepherd if you cannot smell sheep on your clothes. After connecting with a few more people, we were back in the car and with help from a cop in the street we were back off to the races and had just finished night number one. The Lord was in that place and God shook the place and I was told it received great reports both from the church members and the positive reports on the evening news.

We grabbed a light dinner that night and retreated to my hotel knowing the first full day on the ground would be busy. After waving goodnight to the nightshift crew at the hotel I was back up the elevator by myself and back in my hotel for the night. After locking the two security levers on the door I took off my suit coat and tie, ran the hot water in the shower and within ten minutes was back down for the count in that comfortable bed.

It was not too early the next morning (compared to three the morning before) with a seven thirty wakeup call and within seventeen minutes I would be showered, shaved, and suited again to have a nice breakfast downstairs and then off to our first meeting that Monday morning. I genuinely love my new friends in Nicaragua, and they are first class. After the meal we were back in the car and would not be back until fifteen hours later.

Thanks to their invitation and detailed planning, I would be in five cities in five days ministering to folks in meetings by day and preaching at night at festivals, churches, and city-wide outreaches. As an evangelist, it was a preacher's dream because not every host is organized and at times, I have found more politics in the ministry. It was so humbling that each city had a lunch in my honor and the mayor of each city welcomed me with the right hand of fellowship extended to me and around the table would be both local Christian and political leaders.

Our first stop we met with the Mayor of Managua and she is a wonderful woman and we have met several times before and she is both beautiful and smart but most importantly, she is kind. The two of us always have a great time and a dozen well respected pastors were at the lunch. The food was delicious and the hospitality second to none and moments before I was to give some remarks to the pastors and politicians present with staff from the Vice President's office accompanying me, the deputy mayor showed me a text from his phone. My heart skipped and had to read it twice and I was praying it was some crazy Hollywood lie that another celebrity died. I quickly googled my phone and sure enough CNN, Fox News, ESPN, and other national sources had confirmed that on January 26, 2020 basketball legend Kobe Bryant and his daughter with a few friends were all killed in a helicopter crash outside of Los Angeles.

The color went out of my face and I am already white, but my heart sank, and I had just ate and my appetite was gone and now not trying to be graphic, but almost lost my lunch. The person to my right whispered it was my time to speak and it is hard to address a crowd after getting bad news. The Holy Spirit directed me as I stood to speak that I would relay the bad news to those assembled and I called for a moment of silence. Someone once said, "You say it best when you say nothing at all."

Kobe was a household name and very few are known around the world by their first name only. Cher, Elvis, Madonna, Meadowlark and Kobe were among the rare ones known by their first names. My chaplain friends Randy Shepherd and Jamie Johnson of Crossfire Ministries were able to meet and minister to Kobe while we were at the 2012 Olympics in London. What few knew but my friend Bill (who was a chaplain during a couple of the World Champion Boston Celtics) had already reached out to Kobe about possibly joining us in Nicaragua. Bill was currently the chaplain for a Top 3 former NBA basketball season that was gaining great reaction and fanfare.

He was already in the process of getting his roster of former NBA players and they were in final talks about Kobe potentially joining us to play during our three game, three city outreaches in Nicaragua. Losing Kobe was more than great talent, but his fame and smile resonated with multiplied millions. It appears he was really open to the things of God and he had just left a church service the morning of the crash which happened in route to his daughter's basketball game. He learned from his mistakes and was a family man now, more than ever.

At this lunch with local officials around the table after honoring the moment of silence for his death I switched to an impromptu sermon on "Living in light of eternity." I shared that tomorrow is uncertain and it is imperative that we are right with God so that we nor those around us may be left out. The Lord was on that message and I started with Kobe's death but took them to God's resurrection and we all will encounter death and then give an account to God at the judgement. Following the remarks, the Ambassador to Israel was present and we had met a couple times briefly in meetings and over meals and I have great respect for him. He also has a pastor's heart and in ministry as well in addition to that powerful position.

Some of the clergy had already opened about their earnest desire to see revival in their land and were praying for peace among their people. The Catholic Church was at odds with the protestants, and it was contentious in the land. The Ambassador said two things in front of everyone that really touched my weary heart and in front of his colleagues he pointed to me and said, "Our American friend, Evangelist Frank Shelton reminds me of a modern-day John the Baptist." What a compliment! I had just preached about John baptizing Jesus in Israel and that was the message I preached in that hostile environment while in India with Dr. Sam Thomas. He said my message on John was the greatest sermon he had ever heard preached on the great man our Baptist denomination was named in honor of.

Then the Ambassador while still pointing to me adding icing to the cake, said at the table with the Mayor and other dignitaries present, "The country wide revival we are looking for I believe will be preached by you!" After a two second pause the entire audience agreed in affirmation and it was a momentous time. The urgency with Kobe's passing only enhanced what I had been feeling and sensing for years -- that time was short and now, more than ever, we had to give our all in God's service. The meeting was adjourned, and I spent the next twenty minutes encouraging every pastor in attendance and one pastor oversaw some 30,000 members across the country and he had approached me, hugged me and invited me to preach at his church. He was so emphatic it was not verbal hyperbole with the standard "The next time you are in town" but can you come this Wednesday to speak at our main service?

The aide to the Vice President said in Spanish, "Pastor this is most gracious of you, but Frank will be in another city that night some three hours away but perhaps next time promoting the event." He was sad but understood and I would have loved to and I recalled the times that some pastors or youth ministers would intentionally hinder me from coming to their church of a hundred, but here was a mega church pastor running several thousand that was adjusting their schedule for me to preach. Truly, a prophet is with honor everywhere but in their hometown and when you have preached in London and Los Angeles sometimes those in LaPlata or Waldorf get a little nervous, jealous or both.

I thanked him for the gracious invitation, hugged him and after connecting with all before leaving I caught up with their Ambassador to Israel and thanked him profusely what his endorsement meant and how God used him to set the table. We hugged and I told him I look forward to reuniting with him the future. Heading out I ran into to the chef and thanked him personally for a great meal and those behind the scenes deserve as much respect as those on the scene. It is a team effort, and I was going to refrain until a later chapter, but should I forget I thought it safe to share here.

When the pastor of that massive church invited me to preach, and I had to decline because of a previously arranged and full schedule, and he genuinely looked sad. Looking back, I now know why for two reasons. First, like me, he understood in advance with eyes of faith the URGENCY of the hour and if we ever needed revival, it was now. Secondly, when the COVID-19 hit weeks later, I would sadly learn in a couple months that the same pastor had succumbed to the virus. My heart dropped when I heard this news, and for ministers who lived to bypass me, this brother was dying to give God, the Gospel and me a chance to bring Good News! God bless his family and that precious man of God is now in Glory and I know the Lord is pleased with him. Well done, thy good and faithful servant!

He was the National Treasurer for the Assembly of God for the entire country and his ministry aired weekly on over 300 radio stations. When he visited the United States the year before, I heard he preached at the Hylton Memorial Chapel in Dale City, Virginia and he was loved by many. I recall a story that Dr. Billy Graham shared of an account that happened in the fall of 1963 while he was in town ministering to lawmakers on Capitol Hill. Dr. Graham received a phone call in his hotel room from the youthful and charismatic president. JFK was calling Dr. Graham to see if he would have time to come over to the White House that evening and he was inquiring to learn more about the second coming of Christ.

Dr. Graham had a massive migraine headache, and it was one of the rare occasions that Billy politely declined a request to meet with a U.S. President. They had just golfed together months before and were growing as friends. Dr. Graham thought at the time he just knew that he could reschedule for another time to reconnect with the youngest president in American history. After politely declining due to the massive headache, Dr. Graham said he could sense the sadness on the other end of the line when JFK learned that Billy Graham would not be able to make it. Less than six weeks later, President John F. Kennedy would be assassinated in downtown Dallas. It haunted Dr. Graham for years and the fact that Kennedy, a Catholic, was interested in end times was a moment that the evangelist wished he could try again.

The blessing is the pastor that invited me was totally ready to meet God and I didn't cancel because I didn't want to but this schedule was set in stone to try to bless their nation. Lord willing, it will happen in the future to return to his church and love on his family and congregation. After finally heading to our next assignment, we had a good time being with my new friends and each night we ministered somewhere, and God met with us each step of the way.

All those years shadowing Members of Congress paid off and it was almost like running for state or national office crisscrossing the country. We met with thousands of folks that week and each day the news media came out and a delegation of pastors and politicians. Souls were saved every night and the thought of bringing revival to their nation was catching quickly in the hearts and heads of the precious citizens of this great country. After another restful night's sleep, we were back at it again the next morning and back out the door to build morale, encourage people, strengthen friendships, cast vision for the future revival and minister both privately and publicly to whomever God put in my path.

The next city was two hours away and once again they rolled out the red carpet for me. The fine people of Matagalpa are wonderful, and I fell in love with their humility, hard work and kindness. The Mayor of every city was there to greet me and gave a lunch in my honor. It was incredible then and still is, thinking of it now. When you have been rejected locally it keeps you humble in a place of honor nationally and more than ever, we are to model Christ. I forever will cherish my time with these public officials and pastors and with each passing day, the lunch by day and crowds at night grew. Excitement was in the air and Billy Graham had an entourage, but I was the Lone Ranger and God used us both.

That night at the revival in the second city the Lord shook the place, and scores were born again and just as impressive was the fact that everyone was happy, joyful, and talking revival in their native language. The news at night were running glowing comments about what God was doing in our visit and you cannot pay for this publicity even if you had the money to market, but promotion comes from the Lord. The irony is the man with next to no finances had a wealth of faith and God was honoring us each step of the way.

One minister from the region outside of Nicaragua was convinced that they did not deserve God's grace or revival, but I knew the Lord told us to go and preach the Gospel and give it a chance but either way I would die trying to leave them better than I found them. On the third day I was brought to beautiful Masada and once again welcomed by my friend and Mayor. We had met several times before on previous trips and this time the table was shaped in a large square and we probably had twenty people sitting in the meeting.

Their national flag was behind us and both pastors and politicians were in the mix and after their gracious introduction, the Lord impressed on me to honor both respective occupations. I shared if your country is to truly turn the corner it is imperative that the pastors and politicians must work together. I mentioned two oars row a boat and you both represent an oar in the water. If you allow pride to get in the way and only one set of people are rowing then the nation would just go in circles but if you row together, you can move forward by faith. Plus, we are "All in this boat together" and let us honor God and do what is best for the nation.

God gave me great boldness in front of that distinguished crowd and the Lord impressed on me to pick both a politician and pastor from the crowd as a visual illustration. I grabbed the Mayor and a local pastor and sat them both down with all watching and already arranged with an aide to have a basin of fresh water and a towel. I proceeded to get on my hands and knees and following the model of the greatest servant leader of all time I took off my presidential cufflinks from a past White House and rolled up my shirt sleeves to my elbow and one by one began to wash their feet.

It touched them profoundly and it was my honor to minister, and both had tears. God showed up and what someone said later to me after that act of humility and honor that if the American could serve us we have no excuse to not help and honor each other. Bible college does not really prepare or teach that, and it is crucial that we hear from God because methods do not work apart from Christ. We had another delicious meal and that really set the tone and was a game changer. The mayor was visibly moved, and he was touched profoundly and once again they gave me a homemade bag of coffee. I was now three for three with receiving a fresh bag of coffee from their town and it was a privilege to meet the mayor and hand selected delegation at each of my stops to neighboring cities.

That night we had another city-wide revival, and it was packed and overflowing. The mayor was in attendance and several other prominent leaders came as well and the news covered the service. I preached on Hell that night and was drenched in sweat and hundreds made decisions for Christ and it was a packed altar call. On a previous visit, I was blessed to learn three politicians were saved including a cabinet member and the Gospel works! Several reporters approached me and with help from a translator together we were interviewed and despite being exhausted, I knew the power of the media to help us share the Good News once more to the many watching via television. Intentionally, I thanked each reporter, camera man and assistant with their team. Jesus was both professional but never lost the personal touch and I wanted to make sure they each felt valued. Plus, if you are rude to them, they can halt the message later from not airing or with a biased and unfavorable spin. It pays to be kind but costly to be a jerk.

Before heading to the hotel for the night after another marathon day of nonstop ministering and campaigning for Jesus, I was able to reunite with the Mayor of Masaya, Nicaragua (sounds like Messiah) and thank him for his hospitality and he was still touched by the foot washing earlier in the day. I am 6"1 and he is a big man and was probably two inches taller than me, but we hugged and told him I was proud of him. I waved "Goodbye" and after shaking another dozen hands as I walked towards the car, someone brought a man who was just delivered from drugs and I was asked to pray for him as he just made a profession of faith. After I slapped five with three more teens to my right and paused to thank a couple police who provided security that night and I finally made it to my awaiting car.

Exhausted but in a good way climbed in the back with the aide to the Vice President sitting next to me and our car rode off into the night for another hour drive to our next hotel. I do not normally skip ahead but two months later when the world as we knew it would be shut down, I got word that the mayor of that city whose feet I washed had died due to COVID-19. That would be the last time I would see him on Earth, and it was almost as if he did not want me to leave. I am not Billy Graham, and he was not JFK, but it appears that he genuinely made his peace with God and I believe I will see him again in Heaven.

We were now already more than halfway into this five-day, five city tour and thousands had already come out and hundreds had already been born again and the Lord was moving. As always, the accommodations were wonderful and hospitality second to none. Late that evening, we arrived at our hotel, and it did not take long for me to check in, take a shower and crash into bed. After a restful sleep, we hit the ground running and on Thursday I was blessed to have lunch with another mayor and local pastors from their region. Once again, they were most kind and we had a dialogue about life, ministry, and the upcoming revival we hoped to be part of. During lunch I sat next to the police chief for lunch, and he was so impressed with my words and our family's history in law enforcement he immediately lined up for me to speak later than afternoon to nearly two hundred police officers.

Before doing so, we took a private tour of the farmland owned by the mayor and he showed me how they grow their coffee. Ruth did ask me to bring home some coffee and I was now four for four with each mayor of each city hand delivering a bag to me. Lately, I had visited Nicaragua so frequently someone hinted that one day I may get the key to the capital city! God is so good and that afternoon I showed up to meet some of the rank and file of the police department and that was not initially part of our tour but the unscripted are often the best times for God to move in our midst. When I turned the corner, a dozen reporters and camera crew were present with bright lights, and I sat next to the Assistant Chief and after sharing my appreciation for law enforcement I wove in the Gospel message, and we had a dozen sworn officers give their life to Christ.

Dr. Billy Graham had a unique gift, whether ministering to world leaders, middle class citizens or members of the military to preach the Gospel while lifting morale and their spirits. Souls were saved and the police officers loved both my remarks and the Gospel message. We shook hands and took pictures and after connecting with each person we headed out. For a guy who flew in all alone with no security it was nice to be surrounded by two hundred of Nicaragua's finest knowing they were appreciative of your visit.

After a brief break in route to our next visit, we grabbed something light to eat and drink and the countryside of Nicaragua is gorgeous. The people are very friendly, and I have been to El Salvador, Guatemala and invited to Honduras and my visits to Nicaragua were safe and the people most friendly. The event that evening was standing room only in a community center and folks were lined up outside and around the block and with my background of part politics, part police and part ministry I could not help to tap into all three with showing the love of God. Most pastors are extremely nice people with caring hearts, but they probably are not shaking hands with every single person in the door.

We were ushered to the head table and with a local talent opening in some music and a praise selection to worship I now had met more distinguished guests and on this night my friend, John who serves on staff with the Office of the President introduced me and God rocked the house. As always, I prayed that God would transcend customs and culture and may the words of my mouth be straight from the Lord's heart and my translator was excellent. God touched many hearts and I noticed to my left in the front three rows were local police and first responders who came to hear my speech.

Afterwards, the Mayor of Jinotega and their first responders presented me with a beautiful hand painting that now is in the dining room of our home and after another picture I enjoyed thanking each of them and no one wanted to leave. Ruth's request was to bring home a bag of coffee, but I now had four fresh bags from each of the cities I had visited, and they were making me look good coming home to fill up our kitchen and our morning cups.

While in town, I was invited to speak in the middle of a street with a stage with lights and speakers that was well designed. They had about four hundred chairs in the middle of the street and had blocked off traffic and with many dignitaries in the front row I was invited to get up and preach to that crowd. Any evangelist or missionary worth their salt would look for a way in not out and after whispering a prayer that God would use me once more, I preached with a special anointing that night and even with the translation they were receptive and hanging on every word. That night we had about sixty-five people repent of sin and trust Christ as their personal Lord and Savior.

Just as folks brought people to Jesus, they were bringing people to me. One who just got saved and came to the event high on drugs but now appeared sober by the transforming power of God and now high on the Highest. Crack has nothing on Christ! We prayed for an entire family, a father who wanted to be a better husband and I met two American missionary couples who live fulltime in Nicaragua, and they became a big help and stayed with me the rest of the tour across the country for the next couple days. Having them nearby was both a blessing and a gift to communicate with them without an interpreter. They are both pastors with wonderful wives and little children. God has blessed them and is using them in a powerful way.

While leaving, the news crew circled me, and we did another impromptu interview that would air across their region. On the way out I saw six police officers and felt compelled to approach them. One asked for prayer, and we all held hands and I prayed that the Lord would protect them and their families and two had apparently received Christ that night while they were on post and I preached. The Word does not come back void! After shaking hands like a politician looking votes and a pastor desperately trying to convey that God loved them, I found myself once again in a car driving for another two hours towards the next city.

After another nice rest, the night before and wrapping up a fourteen-hour day we hit the ground running. After another delicious meal with the Mayor of Estelí, and local leaders of that city I shared with them my appreciation of their work and upcoming revival. When I mentioned the basketball games that would be coming with former professional players and then the revival attached to it they were excited. Several of them came with me and I just learned another addition to the schedule that I was to speak at the main headquarters to the Nicaragua national police department at one of their precinct headquarters. Soon as I saw the stars and the brass on many of the shoulders, I knew that I was surrounded by many of their leadership. After being greeted by their Assistant Chief; we had a nice time encouraging those in his circle. A door was opened and when I followed His leads this time it was packed once more and light bulbs were flashing as cameras took pictures of us walking up to the podium. Flanked with the number two police official out of their 5,000-officer strong department and my new American missionary translator to my right and friends from the President's office two seats down it was quite an event. Once again, I was handed the microphone and after already whispering a silent prayer that God would use me, I came out swinging like Balboa after the bell in the rematch with Clubber Lang. The difference was the bombs I was throwing were rapid fire, not of violence, but of faith and Truth laced in love.

Within an eight-minute message I switched gears from our testimony and history with my family in police work for over a hundred and fifty years I went to the Gospel and gave an invitation in that communist country. We had two dozen police officers bowed their head, repent of sin and trusted Christ while in uniform. Go God! Before leaving, I intentionally shook hands with every single person in that room from the rookie officer to their top brass and everyone was smiling.

Later that evening, I had another sermon to preach to close the five-city tour and scores were born into the family of God. Not to be outdone, I was hand delivered my fifth and final bag of coffee and I started smiling and my carry-on bag would almost be bursting coming back home. With all that the Lord did this week and me holding my fresh coffee, indeed I was standing on "Holy Grounds." It was Biblical what the Lord did in our midst, and it was humbling to learn that from the previous trip with ministries working together, the Bible study was in play to lead a weekly devotion to their powerful politicians.

The next day would be my last day to wrap up the trip and after that final service it was John's birthday and we reunited with his wife, kids, and extended family for pizza at a local restaurant. Those two hours with them celebrating will be a memory I carry with me forever. He has been such a blessing and great asset to their country, and he was nonstop going with me accompanying me, racking up hundreds of miles away from his family. I felt compelled to pick up the tab that night for our party of sixteen, but the missionaries were a big help and John and his family had become extended family to me. One's politics can be totally different and still learn to respect and love one another. It was therapeutic for him and me to be reunited with their family.

That night I crashed and on my last day I had a television appearance at the largest Christian television network airing across all of Nicaragua. I was able to once again for thirty minutes look into their camera and speak life and preach Jesus to an entire nation. On a previous trip, I did it on their floor of Congress but today on television to millions and everyone needs the Lord. On the last night at the hotel, John and I ate alone at a restaurant adjacent to the hotel and it was refreshing with just him and me. It is humbling to have lunch with all the mayors, and I had dinner with their Ambassador to Israel and met privately with their Secretary of State, but my mother told me a long time ago to "dance with the one that took you to the prom" and John was the very first person I met on our inaugural trip and had been with me each step of the way.

On this last night it was just him and I and that was fine by me. I used to be a driver to a congressman and there are times we talked and other times I knew he needed to unwind. John and I had been together so much for two guys that did not speak much of the other's language we could almost read each other's mind. We had a great time and he walked me to the hotel lobby and watched me get on the elevator and he has always been a blessing with his friendship, counsel, and presence. He loves the Lord and is an extremely hard worker and I am honored to call him friend.

After another quick shower and my bag already packed for a four thirty in the morning departure to the airport for a six o'clock flight, I called Ruth to say "hello" and "goodnight" and was in bed about ten that evening. While finally scrolling through my phone to catch up on a few texts and emails I was reading through all the comments on my Facebook page. Hundreds of folks back home were tracking what God was doing on our trip and ninety percent were so encouraging. The Bible says, "Be careful when all men speak well of you" and praise God for the dissenters and fruit loops who always think they know what is best while sitting in the basement of their parents' home while on the couch eating potato chips. You cannot help but smile and wish them well.

Right as I was placing my phone on the nightstand and charging it throughout the night to keep up with me flying from one country to the next my cellphone rang. It was approximately 10:30 PM local time and John was calling me, and he said, "Frank, I know we are planned to meet you at four thirty tomorrow morning to take you to the airport, but President Ortega and his wife have been getting daily updates of your visit and everyone is most pleased. He is hoping you will intentionally miss the flight for you to tomorrow after breakfast and spend time with the president and his wife. They are hoping you will pray for them and lay hands on them."

It was surreal and something right of the movies. I was touched and grateful but after already a week on the road I really needed to get back home because my flight was to depart Managua, Nicaragua and then change planes in Miami only to land to Reagan where my flight originated. My flight was to land at 2 PM local time and then I had to drive three hours to Delaware and spend the night and preach at not one but two churches at 9AM and 11AM in the First State. I would have ministered in two countries and two churches in less than twenty-four hours and some folks cannot find time to drive six miles to attend a local church service.

Like the title of my book, I knew time was short and my schedule was packed and by missing the flight they were proposing I would fly out at six that evening. The catch is that instead of landing at two on Saturday afternoon to drive three hours with no rest I would now be landing at two in the morning Sunday only to drive three hours to preach at two churches that same morning. Very few have gone so fast, so far in these last days. Pastor Rodney and Billy Graham were never lazy, and neither could I.

After hearing the new opportunity, I called my wife, Ruth but our calls had been limited and I was not dumb all our calls were not guaranteed to be secure, so I walked outside in a t-shirt and shorts that night in the parking lot of the hotel and called my wife for nine minutes to run the idea by her. Plus, her Spanish background was a great help and she called John to speak directly to him in their native language and I was going to intentionally miss my flight at the request of the president of their country and slept in two extra hours. Opposed to out the door at half past four I was showered and eating breakfast in the restaurant for the last time at quarter to seven. Once again, I was in a navy suit, white dress shirts with cufflinks and silk blue tie. My last visit with the President I was wearing a red tie to match Old Glory wearing red, white (shirt) and blue (suit). If you name a city at times, I can not only remember the sermon I preached but the outfit I wore and did not want to repeat the outfit, so I had to mix it up.

The late, great political author Tom Clancy once penned after his first meeting with President Reagan, "Waiting to meet the President in the West Wing is kind of like waiting to meet God. The only difference was the angels (Secret Service) often carry 9mm." It was a little political humor to that, but truth be told that neither President was God, and the Oval Office is not Heaven but the "hurry up and wait game" is the same.

With the shuffle and getting a new flight itinerary I would not only have a different flight route home but different time and to make matters more interesting departing and arriving in a different city and airline. I had peace to an extent honoring the request to miss the flight to try to minister to the president because Jesus left the ninety-nine sheep to go after ONE. However, this switch was really going to take a toll on me, my family and schedule. My flight was no longer on American to Nicaragua to Miami to Reagan but now on a totally different aircraft departing Managua to El Salvador with a layover and fly into Dulles airport two hours after midnight! In precious chapters I shared Dulles as not my favorite airport and this return trip home would really help solidify why.

Like Superman still in his Clark Kent attire I was finally heading to the airport and I knew that time was ticking and could sense in advance things would get interesting coming home. For next to nothing I upgraded at the last minute to a rare first-class seating from the short flight from Nicaragua to El Salvador. One sitting in a suit for any length of time can wear me out and I sat up front in the front seat of the first row in First Class. It had been a long week and now longer with my schedule being pushed back a full twelve hours.

When I boarded the plane immediately, I recognized an Air Marshal, and he was out of place. The fact I had just crisscrossed Nicaragua I was wondering was he watching me or protecting me, and I already knew the answer. When you have been with the best law enforcement leaders in the world you can see the mistakes of everyone else below. As always, I thanked him for his service but that was a friendly nod to let him know if he is looking, I saw him first. After putting on the seatbelt we were racing down the runway and with one last look to my left out the window I whispered a prayer for the president, his wife and all those below that they forever would look to Him who is Most High.

After landing in El Salvador, I am always looking for God's hand in things and although that was not my original flight plan it was a reminder of being back in my wife's native homeland. I made the most of that ninety-minute layover and with the clock ticking on my wrist, on the wall, displayed on my cell and the internal clock in my head I was trying to speed things up. It was going to be brutal coming into Delaware and Clark Kent would need more than his reporter suit to switch into a cape to make tomorrow "fly." The fact is I knew that Jesus alone is the real Superman and Judah 1 Airlines was looking more and more attractive by the second. While waiting at my gate I noticed another marshal that would sit at my gate, and he was a tad flustered when I waved to him. My heart genuinely is to build people up, but niceness is not weakness.

Finally boarding the plane, I had already checked in my lone luggage and did my best to rest and relax now in my coach class chair and would not dare recline until we were at least thirty thousand feet in the air. You may recall on the flight to London that folks do not hesitate to bump into me, but I often am willing to be uncomfortable out of respect to the person seated behind me. Leadership is not indulging what is yours but being considerate of others and that will preach.

I do not recall sleeping a wink on that late flight into Dulles and when we touched down just outside of two that morning about thirty miles from Washington, we slowly deplaned. While going through Customs I talked to the agent at the window, and he asked me some standard questions and did I have any agriculture or cash above $10,000 with me. I told him, "No" and it is mandatory if bringing in any cash above ten grand it is required to report it. It is not wrong to have cash but to not claim it is a problem.

Just like in Africa, India, France, and this trip to Nicaragua I did not take any money for preaching on those recent trips. It is perfectly fine to make a difference and make dollars, but I went on assignment from God to bless their respective nations and God would reward me in Heaven. I shared with the man I had about $150 USD in my wallet and a couple bags of fresh coffee that my wife requested. After wishing him a good day and it was now two thirty that morning, I went to retrieve my bag.

Interesting enough, the man I saw at the gate in El Salvador was looking suspicious in Dulles and after grabbing my bag off the carousel of the baggage claim I sped up my walk because Ruth and Andrew were waiting curb side at Dulles at quarter to three in the morning. Even before sunrise police at the airport since 9/11 do not like cars to be parked exceptionally long in front of the terminal. I was already twelve hours late coming in and did not want to inconvenience them and plus I had a long drive in the dark before arriving in Delaware to preach.

Right before entering the silver doors to leave the baggage area and exit the airport I noticed two large U.S. Customs men in uniform stand between me and the door. The tall one on the right was kind but the shorter one was agitated. I read people extremely fast, and he began to rattle off some questions that he already knew the answers to. One of my dear friends was the number two official for US Customs in the past and I was in the wedding of a high school friend who today is part of their management team.

Just before three in the morning the shorter man to my left said, "Were you in Tampa recently?" I said, "Yes sir." He said, "What were you doing there?" I told him I was attending a winter camp meeting and was asked to preach briefly while in town. He then said, "What kind of Nissan do you have?" Before I could answer he said, "Do you have a Maxima or Pathfinder?" I replied, "Neither, my wife has a new Altima." The fact is the computer already told them a few key things about me and all those traveling. Simple questions but if I would have lied on something elementary like my car or why I was in Tampa then they would know I was up to no good at a higher level.

After passing the questions to the pop quiz he was still not satisfied, and he said follow me. An African American was detained next to me who I saw on the plane but did not know. We both were now entering a steel door and a holding area with steel tables. The man next to me said, "I'm going to call my lawyer." I was thinking this must not be his first rodeo because this brother had seen this before. I am now no longer surrounded by two agents wearing blue but five and a large man with my one black carry-on luggage in hand says at seven minutes after three in the morning and all I can think of is two things in my head, "WELCOME TO WASHINGTON" and Lionel Richie's classic chorus to his hit song, "Easy Like Sunday Morning."

The man said, "Are you responsible for everything in this bag I am about to open?" I remember saying, "God, I hope so." He said, "That doesn't sound so promising," but it is amazing what runs through your head in a situation like this. I have said before that when God is blessing the Devil is messing! Indeed, the Devil was now working overtime. Satan is never happy when souls are saved, and light is exposing the darkness and taking back territory. The Lord just saved hundreds in person and no telling how many on radio or television while preaching revival. Satan was not a happy camper and despite no sleep he was not going to throw the sink at me but was aiming to toss the entire kitchen on me! The agent then proceeds with his colleagues surrounding him and me to rip my bag open and throw all my clothes on the table while wearing his blue latex gloves. The irony is I had just ministered to that long line of blue in communist Nicaragua but was now getting the treatment from the police in the city of my birth.

When the debate has been defunding the police as of late, it would be hard to find a stauncher advocate to promote and protect the police and I now have a few of our nation's finest at the entry level welcoming me to Washington. Not to be moved or shaken just like before a speech to a crowd or one on one I wanted my words to be gracious, kind and the Bible says, "let your words be few." They looked like they hit the jackpot and now holding one of my coffee bags. However, pride goes before the fall, and they resembled Geraldo in front of Al Capone's vault on national television.

He grabbed a steel rod and now jamming it in my coffee that was given to me from the mayor of that city as a gift for my wife. Any extra credit I would get now was not only out the window but all over that steel table inside Dulles International Airport. I knew my heart was pure but then the thought was "Dear Lord, what happens if cocaine was placed in that bag!" I could see TMZ running my mugshot now, "American Pastor arrested in nation's capital for smuggling cocaine after preaching revival across Nicaragua." I knew my motives were sincere, but much can happen when dealing with different governments and nations. Looking back, I had one beer in my life and never held a cigarette but what happens if I am arrested for Coke, and I am not talking the bottle manufactures in Atlanta. Bible college did not prepare me for this happening at half past three in the morning!

One by one and for a man who knows time is of the essence, these men were methodical in taking their time. They did not destroy one bag but all five of them checking for cocaine and now cash. The same short fellow with the smirk on his face when I arrived said, "Where is the money?" I said, "Excuse me." He said more intently, "Where is all the money?" I said, "Sir, I told the man coming in I had $150 on me, and they really got nervous when I pulled out my wallet from my back pocket." Sure, enough that was exactly what I had on me, and they proceeded to go through every pocket, nook, cranny and checked for secret pockets. I learned later that day that a pastor had landed in Dulles recently with $90,000 USD in his carry- on luggage coming in from another nation. Again, it is not wrong to have money but against the law not to record on the form coming back into the country where you have been and what you have on your possession.

The fact is being a pastor, politician or policeman does not mean as much anymore because too many have abused their position for personal gain and have done some unethical things. However, my family taught me character was more important than cash and Dad did not get to the top of his profession by compromising, cheating, or cutting corners. I honored God and them as much as any law and did not want to break their heart or the law and embarrass the family name. My dirty clothes are now in a pile resembling a mountain and praise the Lord the ones who thought they had something resembled Geraldo on national television with an empty vault.

An African American gentleman was to my right, and he was the nicest man of the bunch. I could sense and see that he was a born-again Christian, and he told the short white agent, "He is clear, and you need to let him go." Amen! This man reminded me of what Moses said to Pharaoh, "Let My People Go!" Plus, it was now ten to four in the morning and if they were not going to arrest me, I was now worried that the airport security out front would detain poor Ruth and Andrew at curbside. They knew something was wrong, but I was not allowed to call them to tell them where I was or what the holdup was!

The "friendly" agent who started the whole procedure was still not satisfied and pride has one struggle with defeat. He grabbed my passport and was now seeing all of the nations I had travelled in the last few years. Yes, I have racked up more miles than a few Uber drivers or Air Marshal friends at times and he said trying to sound sincere, "So what were you doing in Nicaragua?" I told him I was invited to preach revival. He then inquired, "Why didn't you come back on the same flight, same airline or same time?" I said, "Good question." I did not want to drop names on him but all I have was the Truth and I better to stick with that. I said, "Sir, you probably hear some crazy things periodically; but I was invited by President Daniel Ortega to intentionally miss my flight, come to his house and pray for he and his wife."

The interesting thing was that was the one thing he did not try to debate. He then said, "So you preached all week in that country and didn't receive a dime." I said, "That is correct, but I did receive five bags of fresh coffee as a gift for my wife" but now that was spread all over the stainless-steel table and I do not think we will be enjoying it anytime soon. What was interesting I know they were doing their job, but no one even apologized for being wrong. The African American said more sternly to his white colleague, who was smaller than him in both size and resume, "You have held him up long enough. Give him his passport and he is free to go." Thank God for race relations because that brother was the sharpest one of the bunch plus it was evident to me even on the midnight shift that he had his act together. The Bible says, "Don't touch thine anointed" and before him finally handing me my passport barked, "So what were you doing in Uganda?" At fifteen after four in the morning now I said, "The last three years I preached to a third of a million people on New Year's Eve at the iconic Nelson Mandela Soccer Stadium." I asked him if he wanted to see a picture and he said with a sneer, "No! I don't have time for pictures." I thought that was interesting because his failed detective work and people skills had just held me and wife and son up an hour.

He then looked at me with some of his colleagues leaving said, "So let me guess you didn't get paid for that trip either while in Africa?" I said, "Not everyone in ministry is in it for the money." Further, on the tip of my tongue I almost said, "Plus, not everyone you meet dealing with foreign nations are receiving millions of dollars illegally under the table" but the Lord reminded me less was more and I did what I wished they would do to my luggage and "zip it."

After finally getting my passport and forced to pick up all the debris from their search as I was walking away more worried about Ruth and Andrew outside at the curb, he inquired why I was wearing an American Flag lapel pin on my suit. I said, "Sir, just because I was preaching in a communist country doesn't mean I forgot where I came from." He asked about the Secret Service logo on the lapel, and I replied, "My family is five generations of Washington DC police at the highest level dating all the way back to President Lincoln." The color came out of his face and when your family were detectives for over a century and half sometimes like Babe Ruth you had to beat them at their own game and concluded the conversation with compassion, "not everyone you meet is bad" and I looked him in the eye and despite being dead tired after now being in three countries in half a day with no sleep thanked him for his service and like Elvis, left the building.

It is amazing what one thinks and how fast the mind moves when you are faced with unique situations. The Customs officer was lecturing me, and I was reminded Dad protected multiple U.S. Presidents. He stood next to **President Ronald and Nancy Reagan** during both his terms and hearing him at the DC Convention Center in 1982 made a huge impression on me as a ten-year-old. I always said if you had the "rhetoric of Reagan" and "charisma of Clinton" you could go a long way. My father protected **President George HW Bush** and he was the last person to shake his hand before entering the House Chamber on his final State of the Union to hear the famous words, "Mr. Speaker! The President of the United States!!" My third summer internship in 1989-1990 I worked in the US Capitol and flew flags over the roof and often put the American Flag on the Senate side to signal to the world that we were in session.

Very few are allowed on the roof, and I joked that most start at the bottom in Washington but over 150 feet up in the air with the Capitol dome behind me I was at the top. Without question, I knew it was God and a gift my family was entrusted but the view I had on the roof of the DC skyline was unrivaled, overlooking the matchless Mall with the monuments glowing in the morning sun or lit up after dark when I lowered the flag.

I proposed to **Ruth** on the steps of the **Lincoln Memorial** on the exact spot Martin Luther King gave his "**I Have a Dream**" speech and Andrew was born the hour **Obama** became President on Jan 20, 2009. On rainy days, early in my Capitol Hill career, I was tasked to assist and set up in the Rotunda for President Bush Sr. appearances when employed with the Architect of the Capitol at the time and would polish the brass elevator railings with Brasso. I also polished the statues in the Rotunda and Statuary Hall and when I ran into my tour guide friends with the US Capitol Historical Service, after seeing me they would pause with their groups tour and say, "Frank, you take it from here and show us around!" It is wild when you are giving a guided tour to the tour guides. They always walked away and said, "I learn something every time from you that we had no clue." When you have 150 years of the Capital city and walking the corridors of the US Capitol running through your veins you catch a few tidbits.

My mother was with the U.S. Capitol Historical Society employed in that majestic edifice. My father helped run the entire security for the world's most powerful symbol of our Republic and tour guides often deferred to me while giving tours. I am now with a guy working the midnight shift doing his best to welcome me to the city of my birth. I am far from Christ, but He came to His own and they received Him not. A prophet is with honor everywhere but his hometown and the revelation of one day being deemed an enemy of the state was no longer a distant vision but on my doorstep. However, God called us to be welcome mats but not a door mat.

Exiting Dulles and throwing my bag in the backseat and said hi to my son and kissed my wife who was scared to death gladly let her drive while I crashed comfortably in my own passenger seat. It was four thirty in the morning and it dawned on me that while in Nicaragua their country rolled out the red carpet for me but upon arriving back in our Nation's Capital and city of my birth I was detained, harassed, questioned but finally released and all I could think of was "Welcome to Washington." It is okay because they were doing their job to an extent and my last second change on the flight, time, airline switch and totally different airport certainly probably threw up a red flag or two or three but add to that I was coming back from Nicaragua and dealing with their leadership may have a couple folks watching from both governments.

The Lord told me a couple decades before that some God fearing and American loving citizens in the last days would be one day deemed an enemy of the state or a person of interest on some watch list. The Bible says, "In the last days what is good will be called bad and bad will be called good." The game was getting late and the morning was extremely early and we finally made it to Delaware at six thirty, checked into our room graciously reserved for us by the host pastor and with one eye on the alarm clock and the other trying to stare at the back of my eyelid for some type of resemblance of rest or sleep the alarm clock buzzed at seven forty five and with less than an hour sleep I was up again, jumped in the shower, got dressed and off to preach my first of two sermons in two churches back to back.

Why do I do it? God called me to preach, and this evangelist knew intimately what the world would soon learn is that time is ticking, the sand is sliding quickly through the proverbial hourglass and souls hung in the balance. Though I was completely exhausted, I preached my heart out at both churches and the Lord moved in a mighty way and souls were saved at both churches. In less than a day, I had been in Nicaragua, El Salvador, Virginia, Maryland and preached in Delaware but returning to Washington was growing discouraging and disappointing. My mother was a tour guide for the United States Capitol, my father, Uncle, and ancestors practically lived inside the Capitol for decades and very few knew its history like I did. More than ever, this native was feeling more like a foreigner by the second and the Bible is true, "a prophet is with honor everywhere but home."

America had changed in front of my eyes and the New World Order was not on our shores or doorstep but already forced itself in our nation's home. Despite our respect for the law, our government and its foundation and architecture, our trust was always in God. More than ever, we needed the Lord corporately and I needed Him personally. Pastor Jentezen Franklin was correct, "Christianity can survive without America, but America cannot survive without Christianity." Lately, I had been harassed in my neighborhood a time or two in my own hometown and Washington was not as welcoming, but Heaven was looking more attractive by the second.

GLOBETROTTER

AFTER climbing into the car at Washington Dulles Airport just after four in the morning on February 2, 2020, we were off to the races and heading to Delaware. After being in three countries in one day, I was now preaching in two churches at nine and eleven A.M. in the First State. The Bible says, "When we are weak that God is strong" and I was completely exhausted after preaching in five cities in five days and then asked to privately pour into their president only to be interrogated by Customs upon my return to U.S. soil.

That first sermon I preached at Millville, Delaware United Methodist Church at 9AM –and found myself pressing into God like never before. The fact is I was running on empty literally, physically, emotionally, and especially financially. I did not receive any compensation the entire week while I was in Nicaragua. What a pleasant surprise to see my dear friend, Dale Dukes who had invited me to preach a couple revivals for him in the past and who had me preach at the Sussex County, Delaware Prayer Breakfast in between the back-to-back trips to Romania and France. Heaven only knows what it meant to me personally to see his smiling face in the crowd that morning and he had driven there support me. After preaching that morning, I also went to the altar and I resembled a bruised and battered boxer barely hanging on to the ropes, completely exhausted and I was now clinging to the wooden altar trying to catch my breath. Souls were saved that morning and then after thanking Dale for coming and saying "goodbye" to the pastor I was off to the second church to preach at their 11 AM. service.

For a man without a private jet, very few had traveled so fast and so far, the night before to make it to preach on time when some are too lazy to drive nine miles to church. Leadership comes with a price, and I could not quit now if I wanted to, and lives hung in the balance suspended between Heaven and Hell and I just knew that time was running out. Ruth drove me with Andrew in the backseat and I got up to preach at St. George's United Methodist Church in Frankford and the Lord met with us in a powerful way. One of my Dad's retired colleagues from the U.S. Capitol Police was in attendance and it was great seeing him and his wife. I have the utmost respect for them, and some souls were saved again. God strategically placed those men in both meetings to be a boost to my batteries.

For the past eight months, I had made over a dozen trips not just leading the Bible study in Dover but connecting with pastors in preparation for a tent revival I was invited to preach in October 2020. I had been invited by local clergy to preach under the same 2,000 seat tent that we ministered under in Alabama, and I made reservations to bring it by eighteen-wheeler to Delaware. My father had a work ethic almost second to none and lazy was never a word labeled on any Shelton that I knew.

God impressed on me something I learned long ago that it is much easier to promote something or someone the second time around than it is the first time. It is one thing to hang a poster around town or wall of a church or coffee house promoting an event but once they experienced a visit you now have built-in press secretaries willing to promote the next stop. Plus, it not only allowed me to connect with the crowd but reduce walls among pastors once they could trust me and realize I was not competition. Some churches were a couple hundred or more, but most were a hundred or less, but they all add up. However, despite the countless miles logged I just knew time was not on our side.

After driving another 170 miles home, I was finally in my own bed for the first time in nine nights and after getting our son to school the next morning before eight o'clock, I did come back to bed and slept nonstop until three that afternoon. In the last week, I had preached at an almost inhumane pace in Nicaragua, ministered twice to their national police department, spoke life into half a dozen mayors and multiplied thousands in person and over a million on television and radio interviews. Flying home alone, navigating through security and being delayed in Dulles, only to preach the paint off the walls in both churches in Delaware the following morning and praise God, I lived another day back home in Maryland.

After spending one full day trying to recover, I was invited on the radio LIVE for two full hours on American Pastor's Network with my good friend Pastor Dave Kistler on February 4, 2020. He has an incredible ministry on Capitol Hill and the irony is his program is called "Stand in the Gap." I had been a guest several times before, but this time we were talking about Ortega, White House and revival and ministry when done right includes politics and religion.

On February 6, 2020, I was doubled-booked in both Annapolis, Maryland and New York City. My plan was to meet with a state senator in our capitol that morning and then pick up my good friend Pastor John Love who is the chaplain of the New York Knicks. It is rare that I cancel but I had to politely cancel my scheduled meeting with the senator and needed all the time I could muster to drive 250 miles each way to the Big Apple. It is always a treat to be at Madison Square Garden and even more fun to be at the team chapel led by my friend. John has met everyone in the NBA, and he is first class and loved by all. This was the second time in two years that he had allowed me to accompany him and "The Garden" is arguably the world's most iconic sports venue.

That night the Orlando Magic was in town and my dear friend is their director of security and it was great to reunite with him before tip-off. It was surreal being on the floor while they were warming up and while in one of the locker rooms for chapel, players from both teams were present. Pastor John had me close in prayer while holding hands with players from both teams and Jesus poured into twelve disciples and Pastor John does as well. These guys are just a tad taller! In my closing prayer I prayed that they would never forget the dream they had as kids was now a reality. The Bible says, "Whatever your hand finds to do that we do it for His glory." I prayed that they would break ankles for the Lord, play to their full potential and never forget it was God and hard work that made it happen. After closing in Jesus Name and a hearty amen it seemed that the players played with a greater urgency that night. Interesting enough, the same players that were in chapel that night were key to the win at home, and I have always said when you promote the Lord – He will promote you.

After a few high fives and hugs with the men seven to ten inches taller than me, we walked out and I did not dare ask for any selfies while in their midst. We were just minutes from an NBA game to a capacity crowd, but I had to honor the NFL mantra, "Act like you have been in the end zone before." While walking out, I ran into the Harlem Globetrotters and my heart stopped. Only God could write this script and I met Curly Neal as a kid and Meadowlark, but I did not know the present Globetrotter team was in the house for halftime that evening! Pastor John graciously introduced me to them and the next thing I know they were spinning the red, white, and blue basketball on their finger and on the spot made up a "Pastor Frank Shelton move" and we did get that on tape. It was crazy and this forty-seven-year-old was a kid all over again and I could not help that Meadowlark was looking down smiling on the whole thing. After saying goodbye to them we were now leaving the tunnel that is restricted only to players and personnel and thanks to John, we found ourselves being spoiled with this all you can eat spread reserved for family and staff.

With no time to spare we found our seats and this DC native is once again feeling like a country bumpkin in the larger-than-life venue in New York that Elvis, Sir Elton John, Michael Jackson, countless basketball games and heavyweight boxing championship fights with the whole world watching. That night at the game I walked by both Rev. Jesse Jackson and Fox News Bill O'Reilly and after the game started, they honored my new friend, Darryl Strawberry who was courtside. Right when you could not think it could get any better, it did! I immediately texted Darryl and he had just taken me the month before as his guest when he spoke in January at the Ocean City Mayor's Prayer Breakfast and now, he graciously met John and me out in the hallway in Madison Square Garden. Darryl was beloved as both a former Yankees and NY Mets player and with four World Series Championships under his belt, he was a fan favorite.

Pastor John over the years had met Kobe, Lebron, Bird, Magic, and Michael Jordan on numerous occasions but he was just as excited when I introduced Darryl to him, and I was able to take their pic together. It was nice being able to bless John for selflessly taking me to his team's chapel. He is not only a phenomenal preacher but a super nice guy. What is interesting despite living near Baltimore, he still has his childhood Boston accent.

Despite being fatigued from all the travelling since landing earlier that week, I found myself driving us all the way home that night and did not find my pillow until two in the morning. Driving up and back to NYC on the same day will wear you out and that Amtrak is often a blessing and can usually kick back and relax despite the tossing and turning of the train on the tracks. I was invited to speak the next day at lunch in Norwalk, Connecticut which is close to New York but once again my heart is bigger than my head and to get John home safely, I was more worried about him than I was myself. With two and half hours to sleep (I do not recommend this) I was back up, showered and out of the house for a six in the morning departure on the train from Washington's Union Station to Norwalk, Connecticut to speak at one that afternoon at a pastor's luncheon in talks regarding a potential revival and then stay the night and preach both morning and evening services on February 7-8, 2020 at Parkview Assembly of God.

After grabbing a cup of Joe once again I was boarding the train and was able to close my eyes for a tad as the train rolled passed the DC skyline glowing in the pre-dawn setting. I had been in and out of DC a thousand times and the buildings were always beautiful to me and now I am finding myself once again racing north while the sand in the hourglass was slipping south. While rolling about eighty miles per hour we flew past Delaware, New Jersey and the irony is I was just in New York hours before and once again heading past Penn Station just beneath Madison Square Garden.

We joked about Lark making my friend Ronnie Dean and I honorary Globetrotters and despite us being white we blended with all, and as a child I played on the court with the Harlem Globetrotters but as an adult I was part of Heaven's Globetrotters. We racked up some miles while delivering a smile but because we had a mission to populate Heaven it was worthwhile. While many passengers did get off the train at Penn, I knew I would be continuing northward and for the last few years that would have been my stop for visits to the Garden, meetings at UN or appearances on Fox News.

Just six months before I spoke in Long Island, NY and that kept me on the NE Regional, but this was also one of those rare occasions I was still on board moving my way towards Connecticut. Speaking of moving forward, I made my way towards the food cart to get something to eat and after grabbing a snack and drink I elected to sit at a vacant table while looking out the window as the scenery passed by. About five minutes after sitting down what was odd was a man chose to sit down next to me at my table when he had three other empty booths to choose from. He seemed kind and was talkative and inquisitive and we had a good conversation, but I could sense that he was off. The Bible says, "To keep your words few" and loose lips sinks ships, and I was sensing he was either with our government or a contractor to monitor me.

Just a week before I had finally purchased my ticket to fly to Pakistan and it was looming both at the back and forefront of my mind. Most folks would not fly to the Middle East, Communist Nicaragua, Africa, India, Romania all alone and I do not advocate it. However, when you are rolling with foreign nations, powerful politicians both home and abroad, someone is always looking. While the train was rolling, I was careful when he inquired about politics to make sure I could speak well of both Dems and GOP. It was not speaking out of both sides of my mouth but sincere that I learned and served in the past on both sides and if I was being profiled like Jesus, I flipped a table on their assessment. After thanking him for his service I went back to my coach class car and the following stop had grabbed my bag and departed.

We had a great time in Connecticut and the Lord was moving. Despite the mounting pressure around me, the Lord gave me great liberty preaching and God moved. The pastor was already talking about bringing me back to speak at a pastor's retreat with local clergy and

I was happy to be their guest speaker but in the second week of 2020 I knew something was amiss in the air and would not hold my breath. As a child, I recall the trash compactor scene in the original Star Wars movie released in 1977 and I could sense innately that the walls were closing in fast. While in town at a diner having dinner with the pastor and his wife, he also shared his experiences of being watched up close and from afar from various governments while serving the Lord. Not because he was living a double life or making millions from foreign leaders or embezzling funds, but simply for serving the Lord.

Two years before, my buddy Randy had met a woman who had dated former Russian President Mikhail Gorbachev and he led her to the Lord. She had lived in both the USSR and now on the East Coast visiting and was in her mid-sixties and she had stayed in touch with Randy periodically. She was trying to arrange a meeting for both Randy and me to fly with her to the former Soviet Union to share the Gospel one on one with their former leader Gorbachev. Make no mistake, this would have been no Russian collusion; rather we would have gone with hopes of witnessing a <u>Russian conversion</u>. God had given me a burden for both the powerful and poor and all those in between but the Lord had given me a unique grace and favor with notable figures.

The opening chapter in this book I talked about Rocky IV and I was willing to fly alone to Pakistan but what you are just learning now was I was invited to fly with Randy and Gorbachev's friend to Moscow to try to talk peace relations. Not in a governmental capacity but tell him in love but point blank that there is no peace apart from a personal relationship with Almighty God. In 2014, I could have gone to Sochi, Russia as a chaplain for the Winter Games but didn't feel led of the Lord on that trip but we had already been working with a Member of Congress in Randy's hometown of North Carolina to try to secure a VISA for us to fly into Moscow. Once again, I can hear Adrian's brother-in-law, Paulie at the press conference when he learned the fight with Drago would be in Russia he looked to Rocky Balboa and screamed, "Are you nuts?"

While waiting and praying for the potential Visa to be issued, I did in fact have the privilege to meet with the former Russian president's friend while visiting North Carolina. We had the opportunity to connect and pray with her, encourage her and talk further about what the trip to Moscow would look like. Shortly thereafter, I received the news that her son had died unexpectedly while living in the Washington, D.C. area. My heart dropped, and just like I had raced to Dover to try to be a light at Beau Biden's funeral, I felt compelled to try to minister to her and offer comfort during her son's tragic death. At the cemetery in our Nation's Capital, it was a small crowd of predominantly Russian Orthodox family and friends. What was surreal to me was seeing three presidential helicopters in formation flying over the gravesite during the service. I do not think it was part of the program; I am sure it was a complete coincidence, but it was in fact that three presidential helicopters known as Marine One (HMX-1). I found it interesting that I seemed to be the only one who noticed the helicopters and while I am paying my respects to the woman who was very close with the former Russian president, I am now staring at three Marine Green choppers with the white tops linked to the American presidency fly above my head almost directly over the grave. The Apostle Paul was all things to all men to win some and once again I was on post, standing in the gap and trying to represent God as an ambassador of Hope and Heaven. After the funeral, I did get to pay my respects to her personally at the grave. She was understandably visibly shaken and broken and was weeping uncontrollably. I reminded her that God is good even in our darkest hours. She thanked me for coming to the funeral. I have since learned that she is currently at a Monastery and is studying to become a nun.

At times, maybe I was just a tad nuts, but I have preached for years one may not be emulating Christ if folks do not think you are a tad peculiar or off your rocker. Zacchaeus went out on a limb to the see the Lord and half the crowd thought he was nuts but that is where we find fruit at the end of a limb. Question – When is the last time is you went out on a limb for the Lord? In a world where most of the church was playing it safe, God was imploring me to preach, "Jesus Saves!" This may sound self-serving, and God knew I had some help from family and friends, but very few had accomplished or attempted more with a shoestring budget and next to no paid staff.

Once you add meetings with presidents in Nicaragua, praying for the Vice President at Mandela Stadium with Pastor Chuck and our delegation, leading a weekly Bible study to state lawmakers, and building friendships in both Annapolis and Capitol Hill it was not only exhilarating but taxing. I shared with a local pastor over lunch, "Most in ministry will out finance me but very few will out faith me." Faith is the currency of Heaven and without it you cannot please God and where some mega churches had finances, I had incredible trust in the Lord. I am no Rev. Billy Graham, Luis Palau, or Reinhard Bonnke but they had enormous budgets and donors with deep pockets and a security detail that would impress the Secret Service. For most of our ministry, it had been me, myself, and I.

However, when you send the United States Marines or Special Forces, in the words of my friend Dr. Tim Lee who lost both legs in Vietnam, "You don't need a lot of them to get the job done." Plus, some of the places I was going to were dangerous but it sure was lonely on the road. After the pastor took me back to the train station early on Monday, February 9, 2020, I grabbed a coffee in the station, and I picked up on patterns and people. About half hour before my train was to depart back to DC, I noticed a man out of the blue who was alone with no luggage, no carry-on bag, no coffee, nada.

That was red flag number one and when I made my way to head towards the other side of the terminal to look out the window about eight minutes before my train was to arrive, I noticed he followed me. I had been getting used to it and I reminded myself that those following me even if where "friends" in the alphabet soup couldn't compete with what the Psalmist shared in Scripture that surely, "Goodness and Mercy shall follow me all the days of my life." They were two sheep dogs on loan by The Shepherd who would follow me. While at the United States Capitol I had my Dad's friends or colleagues at times shadow me and even protect me but now I have some following me. However, if they only knew I was not part of the problem but was hand delivering the Answer both locally and now world-wide.

When your family were detectives at the highest level you not only pick up on tools and tricks of the trade, but you can sense and see the mistakes of those around you. Intentionally, I went up to the glass window that overlooked the track to watch for my soon incoming train, but also to allow me through its glare to now monitor the man who is monitoring me. At that juncture, I was able to beat him at his own game and then he hesitantly left and I with coffee in hand exited with my loan carry-on bag over my shoulder and exited the dreary yet warm terminal to be met once again with the freezing cold Connecticut weather.

My friends at Washington Dulles tried to destroy my coffee and I was not going to allow him or someone on this trip to mess with my cup now. Stallone said, "He was Rambo before a cup of coffee but resembled Rocky after one." I sure did not sign up for this lifestyle but when God called me it just happened and now you know why I find Walmart more attractive than Target. Those who think Christianity is boring, you do not know the Lord or me and if you want to join me, I would love to mentor you and show you the ropes. I could use the company and you would see up close that any child can live like the Devil, but real men love Jesus.

After descending the stairs to the platform, I read that my train would be arriving in two minutes. I cannot explain it, but the Lord warns me in advance as of lately things not only while they happen but often before. I just knew my new friend would be returning and I would bet that he would appear and board the same train. With not a minute to spare, darn if my friend did not appear and sure enough, he was about five people behind me boarding and I grabbed a seat and throw my luggage above and gingerly put my remaining coffee on the tray table attached to seat in front of me. He sat three seats behind me to my right and I noticed his eyes were fixed on me the moment he sat down.

Forty-five minutes into my trip home I went to throw away my empty cup and use the restroom and he about broke his neck to see where I was going. I made a call or two in the car before me while the train was racing and rocking heading south. Another interesting flag was that an Asian woman that had been sitting behind me suddenly wanted to sit directly next to me. What was odd was she was aiming her laptop with camera towards me and when you have been around God's General you can see "Captain Obvious" probably needs to be demoted. A call came in from a retired friend who was with the United States Capitol Police and the conversation turned towards him protecting Presidents and my recent ministry travels and where some tend to talk louder to impress strangers I on the fly heard the Lord say, "Frank leave now" and immediately got up in mid conversation and could see the depressed look on her face.

I had just taken my wife to see Kenny Rogers in concert right before he died months before and his smash hit "The Gambler" was right and you got to know when to hold them, when to fold them and when to walk away. That I did and now both she and my friendly follower with no luggage were feverishly looking even more. With the phone to my ear and talking to my buddy I gave him a little nod to keep him on his toes and once more headed towards the beverage cart. After about half hour towards the front of the train I came back and sure enough the female with the laptop retreated to her original seat and I sat back down.

All I could think of was that movie "Enemy of the State" and America was under attack in more ways than one and multiplied millions had no clue. President Lincoln was correct that if we collapsed as a country, it would not be from outside but within, and some had already sold their souls for power, pay and pawns to the New World Order agenda. A couple of hours later and a few phone calls in between, I stood up to stretch and sure my friend was still seated and fixated on me. To play with him I grabbed my bag as the train rolled into the station one stop short of my destination in DC and to really test him, I wanted to see his reaction. I headed as if to disembark a stop early and he knew I was going to Washington and when I did, he almost came out of his chair but after temporarily going into the next car I came back.

I had nothing to hide nor needed to run but was just toying with the one who for whatever reason was shadowing me. Plus, the Bible says, "The righteous are as bold as a lion and the wicked flee when no man chases." I was not guilty and not going to flee when Jesus already made me free! That will preach. As the train finally arrived back in DC, I quietly grabbed my bag and since ladies are first, I wanted to wait and allow him to go before me and sure enough he has nothing on him. What person takes a five-hour train right in the middle of winter with absolutely nothing? Only him and as he walked by, I thanked him for his service, and it rattled him. The funny thing in writing this book I almost named a chapter "Thank You for Your Service" not because I am insincere to those who are legit but for the fruit loops who should quit.

Once again, I was back in the city of my birth and where Dulles airport detained me the week before I was monitored in the Nation's Capital. After waving to a homeless brother and trying to give him both hope and a dollar or two I kept rolling to my car which was parked in the garage. It was good to be heading home but unfortunately not for long because three days later I would be boarding another plane to Birmingham, Alabama. Once again, the trifecta was planes, trains and automobiles and I should have been earning hazardous pay in service to the Lord.

It was a race to the finish and on February 12, 2020, I was now landing in "sweet home Alabama" and more than ever it was ROLL JESUS! It was raining when I arrived at the airport, my friend picked me up at the curb and like bats out of Hell, we raced through the rain to preach that evening at the Wednesday night service at Union Hill Baptist in Oneonta, Alabama. We had no time to spare to get there and we had to forgo dinner to help deliver the hot message from God's kitchen. I was so elated to see a packed church parking lot in the pouring rain on a Wednesday night an hour from Birmingham and after saying a quick prayer in the truck, we ran in between the rain drops.

I was not successful because the rain soaked my shirt, but I was getting ready to bring the Heat. The second man I met walking into the church was Pastor Bill Barnett and his smile was as wide as the Alabama Football Championship rings, and he could not have been any nicer. The service was now underway and after one song they pitched it to me after a kind introduction and I preached the stars down that rainy night in Alabama, and we had THIRTEEN souls born again on a Wednesday night service. Pastor was beside himself and I am trying to remember if his feet hit the ground leaving that evening and he baptized a dozen of them the next Sunday. He understood urgency too and did not waste any time.

The pastor and I grabbed dinner at a Mexican restaurant that stayed open a tad late just for us and I felt like we were long lost friends and who does not love authentic food cooked to near perfection? He booked me on the spot that evening to return in two months and preach a four-day revival and was going to get me in several public schools to do assemblies to their students. The very next day I was whisked to speak to the Alabama Baptist Convention to many of their leaders and dozens of clergies to help train them on how to prepare for the upcoming world games that were scheduled to come to Birmingham the following year in the summer. It was an honor to speak to peers and respected leaders but like many groups they can be so busy in the classroom learning that they never truly implement out on the street what they learned. Leadership and life lessons are often caught more than taught and at times we can, regardless of profession, be so professional that we lose the personal touch.

My experience serving as chaplain at already two Olympics enabled me to speak with credibility and confidence on how to reach a region for Christ. This is by no means an indict-ment on this trip but over the years at times I felt like a dentist more than a preacher because it was like "pulling teeth" to get some clergy excited about evangelism, revival or saving souls. Too often we are so busy looking in that we failed to look out like Christ weeping for a city as if they were sheep without a Shepherd.

Rarely had I been so bold that day in Birmingham and I could sense some really were not excited reaching their community for Christ while the world class athletes came to town. Some preach to be invited back but I knew that time was of the essence and was not sure if there would ever be another chance to return. With love but boldness I said to that capacity crowd of clergy, "If I am willing to fly next month to preach in Pakistan, I am hoping you will be on post in Birmingham when the World Games comes next summer." It was basically a "drop the microphone" moment and it stirred some hearts and stepped on some toes, but I was not in the ministry for a popularity contest or seeking a position in the denomination. After decades on Capitol Hill, I had been around power my entire life and now had a higher goal. It was an honor to share meals with various ambassadors, but Billy Graham said, "He was an Ambassador of Heaven" and despite Donald being president, I was reminded that God trumped the United Nations, Congress and the President.

After scarfing down some delicious barbeque that was prepared, I got a text from Southwest Airlines that a storm warning was expected that evening and my flight later that afternoon was cancelled. In my Spirit, I felt compelled to have my driver race to the airport and I would walk in "by faith" to the counter to see if I could fly stand by on perhaps the last flight out as the Alabama sun was now nonexistent and skies were grey. Fortunately, I already had my carry-on bag and I learned long ago to travel light. It is hard for God to use us if we are holding on to this world.

My friend dropped me off and I am now like O.J. running to the counter. Some whistle while they work but I was praying as I ran, and a mentor told me it was wise to put feet to your prayers so like Forest Gump, I was a running fool while having a front row seat daily to watch God outsmart the Devil. After arriving at the ticket counter, I was blessed to get on the last flight of the day, and it was only three that afternoon on a flight that was boarding in eleven minutes! After going through security, surviving the pat down by TSA while recollecting the old hymn we sang in church, "He Touched Me" I was once again racing to catch a plane.

What I love about Southwest is you can pick your seat and at this juncture I was thrilled to just have a chair and right after I boarded it was no less than three minutes later, they shut the door and we were now taxiing on the runway. As the rain began to beat down on that plane resembling a sunrise over the plains somewhere in the southwest of our nation we were rolling once more gaining speed and took off towards the sky.

Despite the gloomy clouds as we hit several thousand feet the sun was still there and no matter how dark our culture is, the Son of God is still present, on the scene and in control. However, in my heart the storm clouds were symbolic of what was to come in less than thirty days. Less than one day later I was invited to be a guest speaker on a conference call in Denver, Colorado, and the day after that was racing back to Delaware across the Bay Bridge to preach at an all-African American congregation church in Dagsboro, Delaware. The church was named "Spirit of Excellency" and some of my favorite ministry moments are with my friends of a difference race. The Human Race is where it is at and this chaplain at a couple Olympics was now sprinting spiritually in a race of his own. Superman was one of my heroes as a child, but he had a cape to help save the world, but I was preaching the cross to help spread the Good News before time stood still.

GO WEST YOUNG MAN

THIRTY years before, I saw Michael W. Smith in person when he was a guest on the Johnny Carson Show. It was the famous night show host's last year before retirement and that night Jay Leno was filling it and my godmother Judy was in the studio audience in Burbank, California. Michael's new album was "Go West Young Man", and he sang the title song that night and one verse says, "Why must I wander like a cloud following the crowd? I do not know. I am asking for the will to *fight* to wear the crown of *Life* and you say, 'Go West Young Man' when the evil go east. Follow the heart that is golden and go west young man!"

As a child I asked God for favor for some reason in Washington, Hollywood and New York and He honored that prayer again and again by allowing me to minister to a couple celebrities in Los Angeles, to ministry in the Big Apple and to serve a couple of decades on Capitol Hill. God blessed me with flying to Los Angeles at age thirteen to meet Sly Stallone in 1985 and again the summer after graduating from high school in 1990 and both times were with my Godmother Judy. The Lord has used her repeatedly in our lives and we are forever grateful, and I am thrilled to say we are still in touch after all these years.

However, it is now February 22, 2020, and this young man is racing down another runway on yet another Southwest Airlines flight that is heading west! In the past I had flown into Los Angeles, San Francisco, San Jose, John Wayne Airport, Oakland, but this time I am going back to beautiful Orange County, California. My dear friend Pastor Danny Daniels is at Ann Arbor Christian Church in Lake Forest, and he served twice at Saddleback Church and was the best man in Pastor Rick Warren's wedding. Danny and I had been friends for years and he also pastored in Las Vegas and had me preach multiple times for him.

Once again, like Han I was flying "Solo", but I was living Star Wars because spiritual warfare is real and those who do not get hit on occasion by the Devil are either on his side or are no threat to him because they are asleep or inconsistent in their walk with Christ. Once you have been on Air Force One on a couple private tours and flown on the plane known as "Air Force Two" it is not quite the same flying on anything else. However, this late in the game I was willing to fly almost on anything to get to anywhere if it was to help reach another soul before time expired.

Ruth, my son, and I had just celebrated my forty eighth birthday two days before on February 20, 2020 (02-20-20) and it was hard to believe I was almost half a century old. I have never regretted serving Jesus, but I do despise wasting time. The Bible tells us to 'redeem the time' and I was doing my best to make the most of it. After another safe touchdown on West Coast soil, I was happy to see my buddy, Pastor Danny. We gelled the moment we met over the phone and have become good friends ever since. God always moved in our midst with his precious people, and I love the fine folks of his church and their native California. Anyplace with palm trees is a home away from home to me! While in town we had a blast, and I was receiving calls for my upcoming trip to Pakistan, and I will confess it was a tad concerning.

My bride Ruth had been tossing and turning in her sleep about the upcoming trip and I had stood toe to toe with Ortega but staring down the Taliban was at a whole other level. I saw "Death Wish" as a kid, but I was no Charles Bronson, but I related more to Rambo, The Lone Ranger and Mr. Rogers all rolled into one. If I were a fruit roll up it would have made for one wild flavor! Plus, add Elvis and Evil Knievel and with Billy Graham sprinkled on top you would have gotten the freckled face kid with dimples from Waldorf, Maryland.

While in town I was passing the time sitting and relaxing in the hotel lobby (a very rare occurrence) when the flat screen on the wall was interviewing fans at the Staples Center in neighboring Los Angeles as they were in line to start the public service honoring the late great Kobe Bryant. I mentioned in a previous chapter that I was sitting next to the Mayor of Managua and Ambassador to Israel while in Nicaragua when I got word that Kobe died. I now find myself in California watching the coverage of his funeral.

Some fans said while I was out west that Kobe had a pending lawsuit with a big pharmaceutical company and hinted that despite the poor weather conditions, the helicopter may had been more at play. South Park cartoon even predicted in advance that Bryant would die in a helicopter crash. By no means am I insinuating there was a correlation with the fatal accident killing half a dozen precious lives, but it is true that we live in a culture of death. Michael Jordan, Shaq, and others were phenomenal sharing their personal friendship with the gifted athlete and if it were true that he may have played with us on a future team of retired NBA players that Bill was assembling, it would have been incredible.

Watching his funeral service, it was even more apparent that time was of the essence and plus I now had to divert from the funeral in the lobby to meet out back for a scheduled meeting. Pastor Danny and I met by the pool of the hotel sitting at a chair in the corner all by ourselves and had a phone call with my good friend, Everett from Judah One Airlines. For the past year and a half, I had been dreaming, planning, and strategizing in my head about a global tour. In private prayer it was becoming more evident that time was escaping me. The Church had become more focused on entertainment than on evangelism. We talked about being on mission but were failing with the Great Commission and wondered why we were out of commission.

My years recently with the Billy Graham Evangelistic Association and my past life as a Special Assistant to a Member of Congress have taught me directly and indirectly how to assemble a crowd for an event. God had since allowed me to work on a national tour, volunteered on a Presidential campaign and spoken in stadiums with over one hundred thousand in attendance. Regardless of whether preaching or promoting, I had a God-given gift to do both and since I am in the people business I had to move swiftly and methodically if I were to help reach more souls stranded in life's sin sick sea.

Pastor Danny is both a dreamer and doer and you need both. Between calls with him and sharing my vision with Everett at Judah 1 we were finally at the table together casting vision, crunching numbers, and counting the cost literally and spiritually. For those in ministry who for the last two decades had discounted the value or competence of an evangelist, the Lord impressed on me that in these last days it would be the evangelist whom God would use in incredible ways. In the next months when many clergy were sitting out, we would be the ones to STEP UP and go toe to toe with tyranny and the Devil while reaching the masses for Christ in person or online.

With Danny's experience serving two different tenures on staff at one of America's largest churches, he knew a thing or two about church growth and he also shared an evangelist's fire and urgency. My time with BGEA had taught me how to assemble a crowd, and as an evangelist would allow me to preach the Gospel while sounding the alarm and reminding people what I knew intimately all along -- that the clock was ticking! When 28 of 32 local pastors were too busy to help me on my first crusade in my hometown of Waldorf, Maryland back in 2006 we still had 1,200 attend the event in my former high school. When we brought the two thousand seat tent to Alabama in a town of six thousand, we had one third of the town under that tent nightly for almost a week and 1,800 showed up on opening night. While on staff with the Billy Graham Evangelistic Association and I was tasked to go to a non-Bible belt state knowing hardly anyone much less not a resident and the crusade team shared if you could get a thousand people to show up at the state capitol the day Franklin's bus comes to town we will be thrilled. With prayer, perseverance and assembling an incredible team of volunteers and with the help from my friends, we had over four thousand at that rally! After preaching at Mandela Stadium in Africa to over 300,000 in three sermons and recently invited to preach to 700,000 in Nicaragua, the crowds came. By faith and prayer, I had no doubt what my next assignment would be, but I knew time was not on our side.

I have shared for years that the church in your hometown around the corner running more people than yours is not your enemy. We must realize that we are colleagues not competition, because our foe is Satan, and we are running out of time. Go back and look at the cover of this book and perhaps you will get a glimpse that if we are going to do anything for the Lord with eternal impact IT. IS. NOW!

The plan would be to take a private chartered jet around the world in one week and hold SEVEN teaching celebrations on SEVEN continents in SEVEN days. It would be including worship, teaching, and mobilizing leaders with a fresh fire and holy urgency to reach their communities and region for Christ. I had all the faith in the world but not much money, but it is better to have God's favor than man's finances, but both are important.

Initially, I considered bringing a praise team of five or six but with a Gulfstream, Leer or slightly larger jet holding a maximum of about a dozen people that may not be possible. The Lord revealed that we would use a praise team locally from that area where we were ministering on that leg of the trip. They would be dressed to match their culture, sing in their native language and we would have it translated on the screen. We would assemble about 800 to 1,000 pastors, church leaders and their spouses in one room and praise music would fill the atmosphere with about half hour of glorious worship.

In each city our service would be held at a hotel either attached or adjacent to the airport. Most large hotels house a good-sized conference room, and we would direct the leaders there. After the praise music then Pastor Danny and I would welcome them and thank all for coming. When I was a speechwriter for a Congressman, I wrote applause lines in the speech that he would read. While drafting the remarks I not only knew the content I wrote a sentence with a "zinger" knowing where the applause would come. Sure enough, it was always there, and you must see it before you see it.

Pastor Danny would share with pinpoint accuracy his experience working at a mega and local church with a global reach. He would teach and train on mobilization and he speaks with clarity and confidence as a statesman in ministry. I would then close and preach the Gospel message to a room full of pastors but would also incorporate Hell in my message. Most ministers have preached for months and years without ever mentioning the horrors of Hell in a sermon for not wanting to scare or offend anyone. Many of those same pastors would cave and close in less than a month after the planned demic hit.

Once they saw a modern-day Moody, Spurgeon and Wesley preach with great power and paint a picture of the urgency of our times I know that it would ignite a fire inside them that for far too many had becoming dying embers. We would then deputize them to evangelize and mobilize with one last shot at terrorizing the Devil while depopulating Hell and populating Heaven. With the three of us met in California at the hangar where Everett's planes were parked on the runway. He agreed that now was the time to set the plan in motion.

The plan would be to start in New York and perhaps kick it off with nearly a thousand pastors at a hotel next to JFK airport. We would start on night one on our soil and watch God shake the place while releasing His Spirit on the saints and after receiving their marching orders would return to their churches never the same. Most evangelists and missionaries are hot hearted and on fire for the Lord, but the cares of shepherding have made some pastors weary and burned out. That night as everyone was heading back to their homes from the Big Apple our team would immediately fly to Heathrow Airport in London and host the same event in England. We would have hit the US one night and UK the next! After the fire would fall there, we would fly through the night to Brazil and host a third event in Rio de Janeiro. With the convenience of a hotel next door to the airport the crowd would already be waiting for us and after each event we would have a room to quickly shower and change clothes into something more comfortable only to find ourselves back on the plane racing down another runway.

The fourth stop would be in either Uganda or Kenya while in the massive continent of Africa and then on to Delhi, India to hold the same event on night five. Then off to Australia and lift up Jesus while "down under" and then close out the world-wide tour in Antarctica. We would bring the heat of the Holy Spirit in the frigid cold but that would have enabled us to hit all seven continents in one week. Joking with Pastor Danny, I said "since you live near Anaheim, we could hit Disneyland while heading home to drop you off and we get on the ride and sing, 'It's a Small World After All." Danny laughed and while too many in the church world where asleep, God was dispatching us to wake up the slumbering saints.

We would closed the meeting in prayer and if the Lord allowed, would spend the next year sharing the mission and raising the monies needed to pull off such a large endeavor. My friend does the flight travel for the President of the United States but Air Force One had the entire U.S. Air Force to help with logistics, schedules, and flight patterns not to mention money from our government. We literally were on a WING and a prayer. Jesus and Judah 1 were on our side and now we wanted to link arms with clergy to let them know we stand shoulder to shoulder with them to help us reach souls while time was still ticking.

We had two more nights of the revival and God blessed us. On the last evening, I was standing next to Pastor Danny when a call came in and I could hear the conversation, "Can you tell me if Evangelist Frank Shelton is speaking again tonight at your church?" He said, "He sure is!" To be frank with you, at one time that would have encouraged me thinking I am clear across the country and folks are coming to hear a word from the Lord, but there had been so much spiritual warfare it was now nerve-wracking wondering who was in the audience and just because someone is in your crowd does not mean they are in your corner. With some of our alphabet friends in attendance on occasion it was interesting being under the microscope, but I had to give it to the Lord and prayed if they keep watching and listening, they may get God in the process.

God shook the House that night and no one wanted to leave. Pastor Danny attributes a past revival I preached for him a couple years before in being instrumental in the life of his church and his ministry. It is humbling when some of your heroes are touched and inspired and after shaking hands with every soul before leaving that night, I gave Danny one last bear hug and thanked him for everything. While in town one of his deacons had a brother, who was also a pilot to the stars and who had access to one of Hollywood's biggest name private jet. We also had coffee the night before leaving, and he was excited about our proposal to go around the world in a week.

I had a three thirty in the morning wake up for a four in the morning ride to the airport for a 6:15AM flight heading home. I was go west young man but now was an adult flying east. Pastor Danny had already done so much for me, I didn't want him to have to get up in the middle of the night to take me to the airport, so I insisted that Danny sleep in and I took an UBER to the airport instead. With little sleep but a fresh shower I jumped in the backseat of the car and my driver was sharing about the COVID-19 that was making headline news. It was now February 26, 2020 and the first reported case was the month before.

Dr. Fauci had just shared in a press conference that social distancing was not paramount and wearing a mask was not necessary. The female driving me to catch my flight was sharing how several folks in Orange County were getting sick and some were already hospitalized. Preaching was a privilege, but it came with a great price on the body and family and when you throw in the spiritual warfare it was almost unbearable. Preaching a Sunday sermon is taxing enough but when you are preaching extended revival meetings it is at the next level and the demons of Hell are not only throwing fiery darts at you but the Devil at times throws the kitchen sink, too. Sometimes it misses and other times it can take you out. Constantly aware of my surroundings, I went through security and once again was racing down another runway and fortunately this time I was going east and home to my family after by God's grace, I had just helped to increase the family of God.

STRIKE OUT

UPON returning after a long flight, I noticed I was starting to feel weak and tired. It was now the last week of February and I had a great weight on my chest, and I felt like I had flu-like symptoms. I was in bed for about three days and just stayed home resting but could sense in my Spirit what we were up against, and I loaded up on zinc, Vitamin D and prayer and rest.

I had certainly been fatigued before, but this was different. I just pressed into God and was trying to decipher while once again in bed and flat on my back whether I was ill or simply weary due to the last few weeks of nonstop coast to coast and international travel and ministry. Yes, I had just turned forty-eight which is still considered young, but my body did not adjust as quickly as it did when I was thirty. Michael Jordan playing at forty was still Michael Jordan and he still dazzled crowds on occasion, but he was not leaving from the foul line anymore. Plus, the crowds still came, and I love MJ but even the wide-open dunk was not always guaranteed anymore this stage of his career. Plus, he had dozens of assistants, world class athletic trainers, a billion-dollar shoe company in his corner and he flew on private jets. The seats in these commercial class planes were getting too close for comfort and were making rest almost impossible for me.

More than ever, Pakistan was looming at the back of my mind and the trip was coming towards me quickly like a train almost out of control. Ruth was worried more than ever and unlike any time in my ministry, things were uncertain about this trip. After feeling better in three days there really was not much rest for the weary and I preached on February 28, 2020, in Dover, Delaware. We were officially sliding into March, and I would be in five states in seven days preaching and once again I would resemble Steve Martin and John Candy in "Trains, Planes and Automobiles."

After returning from California, I was back on my feet and traveling to Delaware, Pennsylvania, New Jersey, New York, and Connecticut, and on March 4, 2020 ministering in White Plains, Maryland at Southern Maryland Christian Academy. As the ministry had grown both across the nation and at times globally, true service is still at home, and I always felt honored to invest in my backyard. We had been planning for several months now about bringing four times World Series Winner Darryl Strawberry to my hometown.

Drugs had always been a problem, but it is more rampant than ever before. Several of my friends had buried children prematurely to this unforgiving addiction and epidemic and I just knew we had to do something. Darryl and I had known each other for about two years and thanks to my dear friend, John Luppo who assists with some of Darryl's schedule was able to connect us on a couple phone calls in the past.

Darryl had just had me as a guest in Ocean City in January and then running into him in February at Madison Square Garden and the buzz was spreading like wildfire that he was coming to town in May. God had me bring him as both a magnet and messenger. His resume and baseball accomplishments are legendary and his bout with drugs, rehab, and prison was almost as public as his career. My desire was to bring the community together and unite the races, economic status and even churches together.

We designed a color flyer promoting his visit and the response was phenomenal. God was allowing me to combine my past experiences in both the Congressional community and as a clergy to bring folks to the table literally. We hand selected two dozen leaders to convene at the Charles County Government Building in La Plata, Maryland, our county seat, and around the table we had a representative from my congressman's office, an aide to the Maryland Governor, a deputy from our Sheriff's office working with the opioids task force and seven clergy from different denominations and the President of our county commissioners. Plus, I had four parents who lost their children to drugs and they all had some serious skin in the game.

We had to add chairs and Frank Shelton Global provided Chick-Fil A box lunches and drinks for everyone and what was to be an intimate two dozen was thirty-six people around the table and some standing in the back of the room. The Lord was in that place, and I was bringing the secular and spiritual together. Darryl's message was going to have a powerful impact on those in it now, encouraging those to stay sober and clean and hopefully prevent others from trying drugs in the first place.

I was going to give an award that night to Darryl along with we had a verbal commitment that the governor of our state may attend along with our congressman, possibly Sherriff and honor the county commissioner president. My intention was to honor both pastors, police and public servants and we must all be in this fight together. A heard a statistic once that startled me that a funeral director of another area said they were burying as many if not more teens and young adults due to drug overdoses than senior citizens dying of natural causes. How tragic!

My good friend Keith Elkins in the Karate Hall of Fame is a very respected leader in my hometown and an incredible mentor to countless students in our region. He has a black belt but even better, a big heart and he lives to help others. He was instrumental in helping us get a meeting with the front office of our minor league baseball stadium. About a week before I had a vision of seeing if we could get Darryl right before our big event to speak about ten minutes at the minor league baseball game. In my mind, I saw him on the jumbotron while holding a microphone and sharing his story to a packed crowd. While at that initial meeting at the stadium with two of their personnel they said, "You are not going to believe this, but it is Charles County Public Schools appreciation day for our students. We rarely have a game at ten in the morning, but we are expecting four thousand to be in the crowd that day! Do you think Darryl would want to speak before the game?"

Keith and I both looked at each other and smiled and that was God! I then hinted only if he speaks from home plate. I said that for two reasons. One because that is what I saw in the vision and two what better place would a four-time World Series winner talk from? He was known to not only smash a couple balls nearly five hundred feet with massive homeruns, but his message would help many find their way home. Darryl could hit the blistering fastball but cocaine through a curve and the demise dropped faster than a breaking ball when the bottom fell out. However, Darryl was restored, redeemed and a man with a message and on a mission.

After checking back with Darryl's camp, he was going to speak to a packed minor league baseball stadium that morning and we anticipated eight hundred that night in the gym of our local Christian school. We were looking for a neutral venue and churches can be both competitive and territorial, but I resembled Reagan who believed you could get a lot done if you did not care who got the credit.

In Dover, I was able to steer four thousand to Franklin Graham's Decision America event and did not even live in their state. By God's grace and my faith, we already had nearly five thousand before I had a poster printed. The ninety-minute meeting was electric in that governmental building, and we closed in prayer with politicians, pastors, parents and concerned citizens. Once again, God was using me to bring the secular and spiritual together. A great time was had by all, and I thanked the Commission President for graciously granting us the open room and honored to have his presence at the meeting. I was intentional with bringing a bi-partisan effort to the table and the races together and my VIPs were not going to be just the leaders from our state but also a local drug rehabilitation and were in talks to have those turning the corner towards sobriety would be front and center to hear a message of Hope from one of the greatest baseball players of all time.

I was the first in the room and the last to exit that day and someone in the hallway came up to me and thanked me profusely for including them on such an historic and much needed event. Her husband and I had been friends since elementary school, and they too had recently buried a child who died of an overdose. I just knew she needed to be present, and we could learn from her pain and sense God wanted to use her to help others. Someone chimed in, "Frank, what do you need and how can we help you?" My mind was thinking I need about ten thousand dollars to pull it off and our non-profit was knowing, and the Lord told me to do our first big event not in Los Angeles or London but more like LaPlata, about five miles from my home.

Like Darryl, I was going to swing for the fence and faith was all I had, and I was used to not having tons of finances, but faith is the currency of Heaven, and I was willing to put it all on the line to bless our community. As we continued to walk outside of that building after that incredible inaugural meeting when they pressed again how they could help. I stopped dead in my tracks, looked them in the eye and what I said next floored her. I said on Friday, March 6, 2020, at 1:45pm EST, "The truth is, I don't even know if it will happen." Her eyes were bigger than an old school offering plate at a country church, her mouth hit the floor and she for the first time in our friendship thought I had lost my mind.

I told her when God is blessing the Devil will start messing and I am nervous that things have fallen this fast into place and something is off. She really thought I was crazy, but she couldn't completely rule against me because thanks to my friend, John Lewis, Keith Elkins and shout out to two board members Terry and Cindy Barnes, very few could get that many people around the table in such a short notice. As we continued to walk, I encouraged her to keep praying and reminded her how proud I was of her and could sense God was calling her to be used in a greater capacity in the future.

Looking back, I said that for two reasons. One, I just knew that I knew that the walls were closing but anyone that may have doubted me to date could not help but admit that I was right with what would happen the next week when the world as we knew it would be shut down. Secondly, I was 72 hours away from boarding a flight all alone from Dulles to Lahore, Pakistan and preach to the largest crowd of ministry. Only five people in the world knew I was preparing to fly on that undercover mission in the Middle East with no guarantee to come home. For a guy combatting drugs in our community, some may think I was on some type of narcotic myself, since I was willing to risk preaching in the Middle East. The irony is only one person around that table knew I was heading there and for a guy who God previously told to go west, I was now open to His leading me east.

The Lord could use me to help get crowds at minor league stadiums because I already preached with the major leaguers and all glory goes to Him. It is neat how God uses all our past experiences -- both the good, bad, and indifferent -- to bring things together in the future. The Lord does all things well in His time. Without question, this was an Esther moment, and I am not a woman, but some ladies have more guts than a lot of men! We both left to go to our respective families, and I prayed heading home to mine that God's will be done.

Leadership will never ask you to do something that they have not done or would not do themselves, but I have learned that folks will follow a leader who is bold and knows where they are going. Neither complacency nor laziness described me and regardless of whether I lived or died, I would at least die trying while swinging for the fence. The next day I was racing to Wilmington, Delaware to spend the night with our dear friends, Mike, and Lisa with whom we went to Paris and the next morning I had the honor to preach at their home church in Philadelphia, Pennsylvania.

The day before I had helped conduct that incredible meeting preparing for Darryl's upcoming event, and I was now speaking to a packed crowd at In the Light Church in the City of Brotherly Love. It always intrigued me that the city of love produced many fighters and Rocky's statue was not only around the corner at the base of the iconic steps of the famed Art Museum, but I had a fighter spirit deep inside of me. Kenny Rogers also sang about the "Coward of the County" but that brother was overlooked and perhaps the boldest of them all. You cannot judge a book by its cover.

It is hard to describe in words exactly how much stress and strain I was under, but the anointing of God breaks the yoke and His work, when done right, is light. However, carrying the cross can get heavy and as I stood on the platform it was an honor to preach to that diverse crowd. It was comforting once more to see Mike's smiling face in the crowd, and he helped connect me with his awesome and anointed pastor. It was one of those services that from the word go, it was all God and the Holy Spirit was in the House.

What no one knew was I was less than twenty-four hours from boarding that plane to Pakistan. I had done Africa, Brazil, Canada, Dominican Republican, Europe, Guatemala, India, Israel, and two dozen others but Pakistan was not going to be a walk in the park. Just like in India the year before, it was one of the times when I could relate to the evangelist of yesteryear who said, "I preached as a dying man to dying men." When I gave the Gospel, we had dozens respond to Christ for salvation and over two hundred come to the altar. It was a powerful move of God, and the Lord literally shook the place during that Sunday service in Philadelphia. I was a marked man and God had done a great work in me. I was weary but right where he needed me to be. It reminded me of a poem that has blessed me repeatedly over the years.

THE FELLOWSHIP OF THE UNASHAMED

I am part of the "Fellowship of the Unashamed."
The die has been cast. I have stepped over the line.
The decision has been made. I am a disciple of
Jesus Christ. I won't look back, let up, slow down,
back away, or be still. My past is redeemed, my present
makes sense, and my future is secure.
I am finished and done with low living, sight walking,
small planning, smooth knees, colorless dreams,
chintzy giving, and dwarfed goals.

I no longer need pre-eminence, prosperity, position,
promotions, plaudits, or popularity. I now live by
presence, lean by faith, love by patience,
lift by prayer, and labor by power. My pace
is set, my gait is fast, my goal is Heaven, my
road is narrow, my way is rough, my companions few,
my Guide reliable, my mission clear. I cannot be bought,
compromised, deterred, lured away, turned back,
diluted, or delayed.

I will not flinch in the face of sacrifice, hesitate in the
presence of adversity, negotiate at the table of the enemy,
ponder at the pool of popularity, or meander
in the maze of mediocrity.

I am a disciple of Jesus Christ. I must go until
Heaven returns, give until I drop, preach until all know,
and work until He comes. And when He comes to get
His own, He will have no problem recognizing me.
My colors will be clear.

The Author of this work is a Rwandan man in 1980 who was forced by his tribe to either
renounce Christ or face certain death. He refused to renounce Christ, and was killed
on the spot. The night before he had written the commitment "The Fellowship of the
Unashamed" which was found in his room. Bob Moorehead had written this in his book
"Words Aptly Spoken"
c. 1995

Paul had said: I am not ashamed of the gospel . . . Romans 1:16

Honoring the mentor who reminded me to walk slowly among the people and I didn't want to be a Shepherd who couldn't smell sheep on his clothes, I intentionally shook hands with as many as possible. Many looked at me with respect and others could see and sense the power of God and some after learning at the end of my message of heading east were watching as if they may not see me alive again. After a few hugs, fist bumps and high fives Elvis had left the building and Mike and I were once again heading out while time was ticking. After a great meal with the pastor and his family I was heading back on the three-hour trip home and very few have racked up more miles on a shoestring budget than me.

The flight would be less than a day away and for a man who embodied faith, some doubts were creeping in. Jesus at the Garden of Gethsemane sweated drops of blood, but He had the whole world on His shoulders. The pressure I was carrying as an evangelist was almost suffocated for these mere mortals completely spent in service to the Lord. Urgency was at an all-time high and I love the Biblical admonition that in the multitude of counsellors is safety and wisdom. Ruth and I called two cherished pastor friends to get their counsel regarding my trip the following day to Pakistan. Ruth was exhausted, restless and all cried out about me leaving and I just knew those Muslims needed Jesus.

My dear friend, Stan Lovins, II who I mentioned on the first page of this book was my former colleague with BGEA and he is a cherished friend, incredible counsellor, wisdom beyond his years and has a prophetic anointing that most in Baptist circles have no clue exists. Plus, as a former minor league baseball player, he not only knew about "The Heat" but could swing for the fence too! Faith could be his middle name and to his credit he connected me with Anwar and his team who invited me. I had now dropped nearly forty pounds since starting that fast at the beginning of 2020 and I just knew that God was preparing me for something in this season late in the game.

Stan was at home in Indiana, and he said, "Frank, I don't think you are supposed to get on that plane tomorrow." For a guy who was clocked throwing it in the low nineties, that was STRIKE ONE! We prayed together and I was confused with his prophetic word but knew he was hearing from the Lord and had my best and God's best interest at heart. I would trust Stan with my entire family, and he is a dear brother.

I reached out about nine that evening to Dr. Dave Kistler who is a great guy, respected friend and has a phenomenal ministry on Capitol Hill to lawmakers. We have done several events together and I was blessed to be on his national radio show multiple times, and we went to the United Nations together for meetings. His son is one of my dear friends and I love their family. Many say we resemble each other, and he is first class and when he answered he had me put the phone on speaker so Ruth could hear. He knew some of the backstory and he also is a phenomenal evangelist who has preached at large events and can really sense the big picture with a shepherd's heart.

He said to us both, "The longer I was in marriage and ministry I learned early on to really seek not only the Lord but ask my wife what she thought." He paused and said, "Frank the few times I really made a mistake is when I went against either God or my wife."

I thanked him for his time, friendship, and counsel that evening and it was as if the Holy Spirit who is the official Umpire said sternly, "STRIKE TWO!" Later that evening, as we crawled into bed, I was reading a book and still thinking about what to do before tomorrow's flight, just about midnight I got a text out of the blue from Dr. Rodney Howard - Browne. It was short, sweet and succinct basically implying, "Frank, do not go to Pakistan at this time. America needs help at home."

This was totally God! These three men are not only some of the best in the world and been with the top one percent of those in active ministry today but are beloved by countless people around the world. They all three minister at a high level and are true evangelists at heart and are trained to go in when others run out, with the DNA of bonified soul winners. Pastor Rodney has preached in eighty-five countries, killed an African elephant with a rifle, seen millions saved and been an eyewitness to watch the diseased healed and some near death come back to life. For not one, not two but for all three respected evangelists in a span of less than eight hours on the same day to say "No!" That was a clear and resounding "STRIKE THREE!

On one hand, I was disappointed, really disappointed. But to a small extent, I was relived. I am not sure so much for me but for Ruth and the family who had no peace from the start. It was only the fourth flight in my entire life that I missed. The first two were by accident over a fifteen-year span and now the last two ironically were intentional back-to-back in just over a month of this same year. The first intentional missed flight was while in Nicaragua in February 2020 at the president's request for prayer in his residence to now with three generals of the faith saying stay home, don't fly to the Middle East now.

Ruth had peace with me staying and to say she was relieved would be an understatement. Part of me was relieved, too, but while staring at the ceiling before falling asleep I was still trying to process what just happened. I certainly did not 'chicken out' and did not want Pastor Anwar to think I bailed, and I had to notify him despite the time change that I would not be boarding the plane. He knew me well enough to know something was serious if I was not heading his way and he was a true gentleman and he thanked me for being discerning and listening to the Lord.

The next day I kept watching the clock but before another trip to my least favorite airport in the Capital region it felt odd not leaving the house to drive to Dulles. I am sure he was a fine Secretary of State and on rare occasions I felt like an unofficial ambassador representing both God and our great country. At one time, I applied for a position two decades before with the Department of State for a unique job to greet Heads of State and visiting foreign dignitaries when arriving to the United States of America. The job would have been to be positioned on the runway at Joint Base Andrews AFB and I would have been a real-life Eddie Murphy saying, "Welcome to America!" I received a handwritten letter from a United States Senator's son who was head of that department of the time saying despite the resume and impressive references they went with someone else.

That would have been a great job and I always loved to make folks feel welcome and loved honoring God and the red, white, and blue but God had other plans. Instead of welcoming folks to America all these years later I was now welcoming citizens who just got born again and now were going to be permanent residents of Heaven. God does above and beyond all we ask or think. President Eisenhower said that my former boss, Dr. Billy Graham was one of America's best ambassadors, but Billy said it was a higher honor to be an Ambassador of Heaven. Most do not know this but both political parties at one time begged Billy Graham to run for United States President, but he turned them both down.

Even though the trip was off, I could not help but to be curious about what "friends" may have been on this trip to Pakistan. When I was on the train to Connecticut the previous week and that man had inquired about my trip, he was probably trying to get all the info he could. On the train coming back to Washington when I was tempted for the first time in my life to exit the train a stop before my destination to play with him, I now found God ditching them all now that I would not be boarding that international flight. Jesus flipped a table or two to keep them on their toes and He knew better than anyone in history the value of timing.

The Messiah was known several times in Scripture when to wait, when to go and when to stop. The moment we stop listening to His voice we cease to be effective in delivering His mail. On this rare juncture God said, "Stay home." Now, for the second time in thirty days another plane left without me, I almost on the hour contemplated where I would be in the world on that leg of the flight. The itinerary was to change to another plane in Dakar with a brief layover and it would have been an entire day in the air.

About the time the plane was scheduled to land in the Middle East, we got word from my son's school that administrators were following orders to close school in person for two weeks to "slow down the curve." I knew immediately that was suspicious and governors across America were jockeying for position with press conferences and in my spirit, things did not add up. Two days into this "lockdown" it was obvious we heard from the Lord and the counsel proved right. The large church event at Pastor Anwar's church never happened and the massive crusade was already cancelled more against the Taliban than the virus, but either way nothing happened.

The fact is when I bought my plane ticket by faith, both events were on and in my mind, I was already there. Again, if you do not see it before you see it you will not see it. One of the most frustrating things for a person of faith is to see it in advance and then be in a holding pattern in the present. Sadly, the multiplied tens of thousands of Muslims who would have heard the Gospel and possibly been born again were left in the dark, too.

Pastor Anwar and I talked the following day and he said, "Frank you truly heard from the Lord and did the right thing by not coming." He said, "Lord willing, we will do it again" but both of us knew as evangelists that we did not have forever, and the walls were closing in fast, not counting the sand evaporating from the hourglass. It was a blessing to know I did not waste an entire day of my life flying east only to be stuck in the Middle East. Later, I was receiving reports of tourists who were stuck or detained in airports around the world.

It is terrible to circle the airport on a plane, but it is not much better walking in circles in an airport, but Jesus did say, "Lo, I am with you always" and this time I was stuck on the ground.

The reports were coming in at record pace concerning the news and instructions with this shutdown and on the fourth day in, major colleges were already cancelling public graduations for fear of this pandemic. I knew immediately somebody was not telling the truth nor telling the entire story. I pick up on patterns and people and when folks start coming off script I detect in the Spirit when others are in the flesh. During that flight returning from Orange County, I was weak and wiped out but now the event we were putting on with Darryl was officially cancelled and some would say we struck out. However, it was not because we did not try, and Lord knows we did not swing and miss.

A few weeks later, my childhood friend whose wife for a split second thought I missed it said in a later conversation, "Frank, I told my husband that night how incredible that lunch was and your leadership to help bring it together but thought what in the world could happen to stop this event?" She continued, "You absolutely called it and were right!" President George Bush, Sr. said, "It takes a man of God to see in advance the hand of God" and the Lord told me to put the event on, but He had also been whispering for years to and to those awake and now with greater urgency to go after souls because time was about up.

This chapter was almost entitled "Straw Man" because that was Darryl Strawberry's nickname but unrelated to him that name often resembles someone that easily collapses when times get tough. The world, including the church would soon see and reveal who was legit and who should quit. Who was real or those who were just playing games and I already knew what I was made of but niceness isn't weakness and the "nicest in the county" was getting ready to come out of the closet as arguably among the boldest in the country.

Desmond Doss was considered unfit for battle by his own battalion, but he helped save countless souls with uncanny bravery in the war. Make no mistake, our world was at war and most people, like too many in ministry, were asleep at the wheel and on cruise control. They were apart from Christ, clueless to the signs of the time, complicit or could not care less and I was not sure which was worse. Looking back, despite naming the chapter "Strike Out" it was actually more like "swing and a miss" but God knew we were swinging for the fence. Deidre Pujols is an inspiration to me, and she is a modern day "Wonder Woman" and her philanthropic work is incredible. Her husband, Albert is among the best to ever swing a baseball bat and she has been an encouragement to me and many others the past few years. Like her husband, I could not help but try to go yard and use our platform for God's glory. They do it as well as anyone I know.

Praise God, I survived the wipe out, I knew we did not truly strike out but with time running out I was up to hit, and God was next on the on-deck circle. When you are down to nothing Jesus is UP to something! #PlayBall

PANDEMIC OR PLANNED DEMIC?

ADDED - During slavery slaves were forced to wear masks as to symbolically mark them as not having a voice and to be owned and under the control of another person.

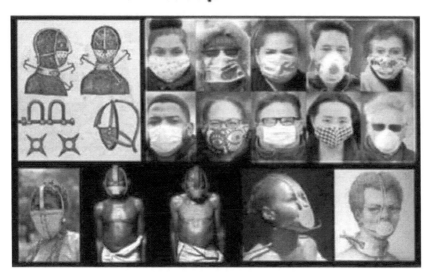

IT had been said that according to the Chinese calendar, 2020 would be "The Year of the Rat." Some speculate that the rat is the most common rodent to spread diseases in the world. This is not an indictment on China or their millions of friendly, upstanding citizens. Just recently I had the honor to lead one of my best friends to the Lord who was born in China. We have been friends since fourth grade and loyalty could be his middle name. Regarding rats, I do know that the people would have endured the politization from both Democrats and Republicans on this issue. Truth be told, I do not read astrology, horoscopes or dabble in the occult but it is intriguing that this disease released from China would harm so many around the world, particularly those with poor immune systems or underlying health issues.

Pastor Danny Jones of Northlake Baptist Church said in a sermon, "*For the last one hundred years billionaires, bankers and businessmen have been trying to sell the world on a one*

world government. After World War I, they tried to establish the League of Nations and that failed.
After WW II, they established the United Nations and dumped billions of dollars into trying to
build their New World Order and we are almost there. Do I think that the Covid-19 is a sign of
the end of the world? I don't think so, but I do believe it is a drill, simulation, dress rehearsal to
work out the bugs to get all the nations prepared for this final one world government." He went
on to unpack truths that the globalists tend to cause a <u>problem</u> and wait for society's <u>reaction</u>
and then conveniently offer a <u>solution</u>. Those that create the crisis and grab the popcorn
to enjoy the chaos have the cure so those that are sinister at the start play savior at the end.

Pastor Danny continued, "When President Trump shocked the world and won the presidency on November 8, 2016, the globalists, socialists and never Trumpers went nuts and the
powers to be threw everything they could to stop our imperfect president. God has always
used imperfect people, but our forty-fifth chief executive was working hard in that window
of time to genuinely try to protect, promote and watch America prosper. He put America
first, ceased financial support towards the UN and NATO, stopped those illegally crossing
the borders and began promoting fair trade. Trump tried to stop the globalists' agenda and
advancement, but his opposition turned on him immediately and they unrelenting tried to
impeach him." After three years of being unsuccessful they had to pull out their biological
weapon from the Far East.

David Rockefeller for decades had been known to pull the strings of this global puppet
cast but he died in March 2017 at 101 years of age. George Soros is up in age but still deep
in funding pet projects and pharmaceuticals that tend to harm more than hurt. Today, Bill
Gates appears to have been 'the chosen one' in this Ponzi scheme at humanity's expense.
Former Secretary of State Henry Kissinger has been a player for years and proponent of
NWO. He wrote an opinion/editorial piece on April 3, 2020, rejoicing how the corona virus
would lead us to the New World Order. The virus that would go viral would bring victory
in their eyes and Kissinger even complimented Gates on his expertise.

To know Gates today you need to consider Rockefeller from the past. Gary Allen in
1976 wrote in The Rockefeller File, "To the Rockefellers, socialism is not a system for redis-
tributing wealth – but a system to control people and competitors. Socialism puts power in
the hands of the government. And since the Rockefellers control the government, government control means Rockefeller control. You may not know this, but you can be sure they
do! When the Rockefellers join the United Nation's World Population Conference in calling
for the "promotion of a new economic order by eradicating the cause of world poverty,
by ensuring the equitable distribution of world's resources, by eliminating the injustices
of existing world trade systems and exploitation perpetuated by capitalistic corporations,"
something smells as fishy as an unwashed tuna boat. Curbing population growth is just part
of the Rockefeller war on the American family. According to John H. Knowles, president
of the Rockefeller Foundation and one of America's foremost promoters of the slaughter of
the unborn, the goal of the foundation is to achieve the capacity in America for <u>1.8 million</u>
<u>abortions</u> every year." #GodHelpUs

Population control and Depopulation go hand and hand and the sooner we wake up the more we can speak out before time runs out. Pastor Danny in that sermon, "*Every January over three thousand wealthy power players assemble in Davos, Switzerland to cast the vision and roll out their future agenda. In January 2017, at the World Economic Forum Bill Gates rolled out CEPI (Coalition for Epidemic Preparedness Innovations) which is a collaboration with the Gates Foundation that partners with countries like India, Norway, Japan and two big pharma one of them being Moderna. Sound familiar? They began to work on the next pandemic in 2017 and Gates released a video airing on Netflix in 2017 called "Pandemic" that was released in November 2019 and the plot included a coronavirus that was developed in a wet market in China and millions of souls would die.* Is Bill Gates a prophet? Was it a coincidence or was the pandemic planned?

Fall - October 18, 2019, *a pandemic simulation was conducted called Event 201 by the Gates Foundation along with World Economic Forum and Michael Bloomberg School of Public Health at Johns Hopkins University and they tried to run Bloomberg against Trump for the highest office in the land. This exercise predicted that the corona virus would have the same death rate as the Spanish Flu of 1918 that caused 65 million deaths. On the same day as Event 201, October 18, 2019, the World Military Games were playing with ten thousand athletes partici- pating and where was the event?* Wuhan, China.

January 7, 2020 *news reports that a coronavirus escaped Wuhan, China. Following the world military games, the elites reassembled back in Davos, Switzerland two months later on January 20-24, 202. At the Gates-led event he announced with excitement a new coronavirus vaccine program with a partnership with Moderna and the U.S. National Institute for Allergies and Infectious Diseases led by* Dr. Anthony Fauci." If I may quote again Dana Carvey who played the Church Lady on "Saturday Night Live" – "Isn't that special?

Pastor Danny continued, "*Dr. Fauci wrote a piece featured in the New England Journal of Medicine in March 2020 that this Coronavirus would be nothing more than a seasonal flu but when he went on camera he said, "its ten times worse than the seasonal flu! May kill two million Americans and even if we shut down Americans, we may still lose 200,000." Where did he get those numbers? The model came out of the University of Washington that is funded by the Bill & Melinda Gates Foundation.*

On March 11, 2020, *the World Health Organization officially declared a global pandemic. The first stimulus check you received in March 2020 was from a bill that was drafted back in January 2020. Once again, we have some quick-thinking prophets who were already bringing relief to throw trillions of dollars to mostly folks not related to corona relief.*" President Reagan said the scariest eight words ever strung together, "I'm from the government and I'm here to help."

Pastor Danny went on to say, "*This novel coronavirus (COVID-19) is a manufactured crisis designed to deceive people to accept a radically different world than you or I are used to living in. According to the CDC, every year 39 million cases of the flu and upwards to 60,000 flu-related deaths and we never once shut down the country and our economy. For some reason, the powers-to-be shut it down even knowing their books have been cooked and we are being deceived and manipulated.*"

Most people on the left revere Bill Gates, while most on the right esteem Billy Graham. Bill Gates' father was at one time on the board of Planned Parenthood. He heard a phrase as a child that was music to his adolescent ears, "depopulation." His father went on to be at the helm of Planned Parenthood and I love what President Reagan said, "It is interesting to me that all those who are for pro-choice forgot they had parents who were pro-life."

Gates in a Ted talk several years ago allegedly said regarding vaccines, "If we do them correctly, we can eliminate ten to fifteen percent of the population." He was not talking about reducing debt or deficit but depopulation people around the world. In his own words he was intrigued to depopulate the Earth while Dr. Billy Graham lived to populate Heaven. One gravitated towards dollars and death while Dr. Graham promoted life and the Lord.

The Gates Foundation gave an astonishing $80 million to Planned Parenthood and yet God gave His life that others could have a chance and second chance. The third week of March I was on a national conference call, and I spoke for eighteen minutes. I said respectfully the only thing Gates and Graham have in common are their initials and we closed in prayer for the one who has been accused in the past of creating viruses for computers only to sell a program later to restore them.

Laura Ingraham of Fox News said, "One out of every ten bucks that the World Health Organization receives is from the world's second wealthiest man." When Cheryl Chumley of the Washington Times was asked if Gates' gifts to the WHO were concerning, she replied, "Definitely. Bill Gates wields tremendous influence at the World Health Organization." Politico in 2017 called Gates "The WHO Doctor that when he wanted some policy pushed, the World Health Organization bureaucrats caved to his wishes." Chumley added, "This is an unelected guy who really has no political affiliation with America and has been given a huge platform to push what I view as anti-American policies based on coronavirus figures and this is something that he won't be held accountable for by voters."

Pay to play? Chumley closed, "Here is an interesting tie. Bill Gates, for the longest time, wanted the WHO to declare coronavirus a pandemic but they did not want to do that. A day after Gates via his foundation gave $50M to the therapeutic accelerator to help fight the coronavirus and find a vaccine, the WHO Secretary General declared the coronavirus a pandemic."

Coronavirus Timeline: Let the events and dates speak for themselves in context:

4/25/2003: CDC files for patent #7776521 for SARS-CoV "coronavirus isolated from humans" and the means to test for this virus

https://youtu.be/C2CsNqHFx68

2004: Dr. Shi Zhengli and team of researchers begin to study coronavirus pathogens in bats in China

https://news.cgtn.com/news/2020-05-25/CGTN-Exclusive-The-story-of-COVID-19-told-by-a-Wuhan-lab-expert-QMsRNq9Bde/index.html

8/22/2005: US National Institutes of Health (NIH) under Dr. Anthony Fauci finds chloroquine a "potent inhibitor" of SARS coronavirus infection and spread: "Chloroquine has strong antiviral effects on SARS-CoV infection of primate cells. These inhibitory effects are observed when the cells are treated with the drug either before or after exposure to the virus, suggesting both prophylactic and therapeutic advantage."

https://pubmed.ncbi.nlm.nih.gov/16115318/

2014: NIH under Dr. Anthony Fauci places moratorium ban prohibiting research intended to create novel pandemic pathogens with gain-of-function capabilities that could increase transmissibility and virulence of pathogens in influenza, MERS and SARS due to concerns over risks from the research

https://mbio.asm.org/content/5/6/e02366-14

https://pubmed.ncbi.nlm.nih.gov/25505122/

2014: Dr. Shi Zhengli continues work in bat coronavirus "gain-of-function", conducts research to create modified "gain-of-pathogenesis" with Dr. Ralph S. Baric at UNC Chapel Hill NC, finding SARS has the potential to re-emerge from coronaviruses circulating in wild bats

2014-2015: After funding is halted at UNC, Dr. Shi Zhengli takes research back to Wuhan China

https://en.m.wikipedia.org/wiki/Shi_Zhengli

https://youtu.be/AJjaQJTBTGU

2015: China opens Wuhan Level 4 biowarfare lab in Wuhan China, gives grants for talented students to work in American university labs, and donates funds to those universities. Students then take the intellectual property back to Wuhan

https://en.m.wikipedia.org/wiki/Wuhan_Institute_of_Virology

2015: NIH under Dr. Anthony Fauci's NIAID awards $3.7 Million in grants to EcoHealth Alliance for bat coronavirus research at Wuhan Institute of Virology to study "risk of future coronavirus emergence from wildlife using in-depth field investigations across the human-wildlife interface" at wet markets in China

https://www.dailymail.co.uk/news/article-8211291/U-S-government-gave-3-7million-grant-Wuhan-lab-experimented-coronavirus-source-bats.html

https://www.washingtonexaminer.com/news/paid-for-the-damn-virus-thats-killing-us-giuliani-rips-fauci-over-grants-to-wuhan-laboratory

2015: A team including two scientists from Wuhan Institute of Virology engineers a hybrid virus, combining bat coronavirus with SARS virus adapted to grow in mice and mimic human disease. The hybrid virus was able to infect human cells. The team published research on bat coronavirus that could be made to infect HeLa

https://en.m.wikipedia.org/wiki/Wuhan_Institute_of_Virology

3/2015: Bill Gates does TED Talk on the "Next outbreak" of a viral pandemic

https://www.ted.com/talks/bill_gates_the_next_outbreak_we_re_not_ready/

4/2015: Pirbright Institute, funded by Bill and Melinda Gates Foundation, holds patent #10130701 for coronavirus and is published in coronavirus book for conducting coronavirus research in Wuhan China

https://www.pirbright.ac.uk/our-science/avian-viral-diseases/coronaviruses

https://www.pirbright.ac.uk/news/2015/03/institute-scientists-contribute-new-book-coronaviruses

11/9/2015: Research by Dr. Shi Zhengli on "SARS-like cluster of circulating bat coronaviruses shows potential for human emergence" published in Nature magazine

https://www.nature.com/articles/nm.3985

11/9/2016: Donald Trump elected 45th president of US

1/10/2017: Dr. Anthony Fauci predicts there is "no doubt" Trump administration will have a "surprise outbreak" of a global virus pandemic

https://twitter.com/susanstjames3/status/1246525709947940864?s=12

https://youtu.be/fe-cbMLJZzU

1/20/2017: Trump inaugurated 45th president of US

5/4/2017: Bill Gates becomes second largest donor to WHO

https://www.politico.eu/article/bill-gates-who-most-powerful-doctor/

11/2017: Dr. Shi Zhengli, head of Wuhan SARS research project, leads team studying horseshoe bats in China, publishes findings indicating genetic components of SARS coronavirus exist in bat population in cave in Yunnan 1000 km away, most likely same bat population behind first SARS coronavirus in 2003

https://en.m.wikipedia.org/wiki/Shi_Zhengli

https://www.foxnews.com/world/state-department-cables-coronavirus-origin-chinese-lab-bats

12/19/2017: NIH lifts moratorium ban on controversial research intended to create novel pandemic pathogens that could make deadly viruses even worse

https://www.nytimes.com/2017/12/19/health/lethal-viruses-nih.amp.html

https://www.npr.org/sections/health-shots/2017/12/19/571744856/nih-lifts-ban-on-research-that-could-make-deadly-viruses-stronger

1/2018: US investigators find Wuhan Institute of Virology "not in compliance with safe operating procedures for the level of severity of the biohazards of that laboratory"

https://youtu.be/C2CsNqHFx68

3/27/2018: American officials visit Wuhan facility multiple times, send two official warnings to Washington about "inadequate safety" at Wuhan lab researching coronaviruses in bats

https://www.washingtonpost.com/opinions/2020/04/14/state-department-cables-warned-safety-issues-wuhan-lab-studying-bat-coronaviruses/

https://www.dailymail.co.uk/news/article-8281083/amp/Wuhan-biosafety-expert-admits-widespread-security-maintenance-concerns.html

https://www.dailymail.co.uk/news/article-8281085/amp/Wuhan-virus-lab-cover-up.html

1/16/19: Dr. Tedros with WHO tweets: "WHO & #China have enjoyed a long & productive partnership. WHO is proud to have supported the overseas training of more than 2000 Chinese #HealthWorkers. Grateful for China's commitment to strengthening health systems in other countries through its Belt and Road Initiative"

https://twitter.com/drtedros/status/1085559977597636609

1/24/2019: The Coronavirus Aid, Relief and Economic Security Act HR, also known as the CARES Act, was introduced in US Congress as HR 748 (Middle Class Health Benefits Tax Repeal Act of 2019) by Joe Courtney (D-CT), although the bill was amended before it was passed.

https://en.wikipedia.org/wiki/Coronavirus_Aid,_Relief,_and_Economic_Security_Act?wprov=sfti1

1/28/2019: Dr. Shi Zhengli is elected as a fellow of the American Academy of Microbiology

http://english.whiov.cas.cn/ne/201903/t20190308_206697.html

2019: Researchers continue to study horseshoe bat at Wuhan Center for Disease Control and Prevention, 300 yards from Huanan wet market. Horseshoe bats were collected from Yunnan province 1000 km away, but are not sold at Huanan wet market

https://youtu.be/Frx3YjMT1_I

9/1/2019: Trump imposes 10% tariff on $300 Billion of Chinese imports

9/5/2019: China retaliates by halting import of US goods

9/18/2019: China holds exercise/drill for novel coronavirus in Wuhan China

https://thefreedomarticles.com/chinese-government-foreknowledge-coronavirus-drill-

30-days-wuhan-games/

10/18/2019: Bill Gates, Johns Hopkins and UN hold "Event 201" coronavirus exercise in NYC

http://www.centerforhealthsecurity.org/event201/scenario.html

10/18/2019: China holds Military Olympics with 10,000 athletes and 250,000 volunteers from 110 countries in Wuhan China

https://thefreedomarticles.com/chinese-government-foreknowledge-coronavirus-drill-30-days-wuhan-games/

11/15/2020: CDC advertise job positions for Pandemic Public Health Advisor Quarantine Program in 19 Cities

https://jobs.cdc.gov/job/dallas/public-health-advisor-quarantine-program/250/14136286

11/20/2019: Pirbright Institute, funded by Bill Gates, receives European Patent EP 3-172-319-B1 for CoronaVirus vaccine

11/2019: Breach of containment occurs at Wuhan Institute of Virology

https://youtu.be/AJjaQJTBTGU

12/1-10/2019: Patient 0 and other patients present onset symptoms in Wuhan China. It is believed that "Patient zero" worked at Wuhan Institute of Virology lab

https://youtu.be/Gdd7dtDaYmM

12/8/2019: Chinese citizen Chen presents onset symptoms of Coronavirus in Wuhan, recovers and is discharged from hospital

12/10/2019: Wuhan Huanan market vendor Wei Guixian presents onset symptoms of COVID-19, goes to clinic for antibiotic IV drip in Wuhan

12/12/2019: 4 people in one family unrelated to Wuhan Huanan market present symptoms https://www.wsj.com/amp/articles/how-it-all-started-chinas-early-coronavirus-missteps-11583508932

12/13/2019: Trump negotiates $50 Billion trade agreement with China

12/13-29/2019: First cases of outbreak reported in Wuhan

12/18/2019: Under Nancy Pelosi, House votes to impeach President Trump

12/21/2019: MIT research funded by Bill and Melinda Gates creates invisible quantum dot tattoo to ID vaccinated kids

https://www.sciencealert.com/an-invisible-quantum-dot-tattoo-is-being-suggested-to-id-vaccinated-kids

12/29/2019: Growing indication of person-to-person transmission in Wuhan China

12/30/2019: Chinese doctors share concerns of contagion with colleagues, spurring reprimands and censorship in China

12/30/2020: Dr. Li Wenliang posts warning about new unidentified coronavirus resembling SARS. Dr. Li is forced to sign statement denouncing his warning as unfounded and illegal rumor. Not long after his reprimand, Dr. Li contracts the virus from a glaucoma patient

https://www.nytimes.com/2020/02/06/world/asia/chinese-doctor-Li-Wenliang-corona-virus.amp.html

12/30/2019: Wuhan Health Commission issues private internal memo: "There has been a continuous occurrence of cases of pneumonia of unknown cause at Huanan Seafood Market"

12/30/2019: A "pneumonia of unknown cause" is first officially reported to WHO Country Office in Wuhan China

https://www.who.int/emergencies/diseases/novel-coronavirus-2019/events-as-they-happen

12/31/2019: Wuhan Health Commission officially announces "pneumonia outbreak" related to Huanan market

1/1/2020: Wuhan Huanan Market closed and scrubbed

1/5/2020: WHO attempts to identify virus

https://www.who.int/csr/don/05-january-2020-pneumonia-of-unkown-cause-china/en/

1/6/2020: CDC issues travel advisory for Wuhan China

1/7/2020: Virus first identified as novel Coronavirus

https://www.nytimes.com/2020/01/08/health/china-pneumonia-outbreak-virus.amp.html

1/8/2020: WHO praises China: "Preliminary identification of a novel virus in a short period of time is a notable achievement and demonstrates China's increased capacity to manage new outbreaks."

https://www.foxnews.com/politics/from-new-york-to-canada-to-the-white-house-initial-coronavirus-responses-havent-aged-well

1/9/2020: Wuhan China maps genome

1/11/2020: 1st death from virus in Wuhan China

1/11/2020: CDC tweets about corona related "pneumonia outbreak in China"

1/13/2020: 1st case identified in Thailand

1/14/2020: Wuhan health officials and WHO report no evidence of human-to-human transmission: "Preliminary investigations conducted by Chinese authorities have found no clear evidence of human-to-human transmission of the novel coronavirus (2019-nCoV) in Wuhan China."

https://twitter.com/neuro7plastic/status/1251597728791949313?s=21

https://link.theepochtimes.com/dr-fauci-china-misled-the-world-virus-erupted-in-mid-december_3308635.html

1/15/2020: US-China trade deal signed

1/15/2020: 1st infected Wuhan patient travels to US

1/15/2020: Pelosi delivers impeachment papers after inexplicable 28-day delay since House impeachment vote Dec 18, 2019

1/16/2020: Trump impeachment trial begins

1/17/2020: CDC and DHS start health screenings of travelers from China at LA, SF and NY airports

1/18/2020: Wuhan holds Lunar New Year potluck banquet for 10,000+ in Wuhan

1/18/2020: 4 new cases reported in Wuhan China

1/19/2020: WHO reports "Not enough is known to draw definitive conclusions about how it is transmitted, clinical features of the disease, extent to which it has spread, or its source which remains unknown."

1/20/2020: Wuhan officials officially acknowledge virus outbreak

1/21/2020: 1st US case of Coronavirus of traveler from Wuhan reported in Seattle WA

1/21/2020: China's Wuhan Institute files to patent use of Gilead's remdesivir for the treatment of novel coronavirus

https://en.m.wikipedia.org/wiki/Timeline_of_the_COVID-19_pandemic_in_January_2020

1/21/2020: Chinese President Xi Jinping asks WHO to not call the virus outbreak a public health emergency.

1/22/2020: WHO claims the virus outbreak is not a public health emergency.

1/23/2020: Dr. Shi Zhengli claims source of virus was "probable bat origin" in Wuhan (even though no bats sold at Wuhan market)

1/23/2020: Beijing locks down Wuhan, cancels plane, train and bus travel

1/23/2020: Vox publishes article stating that travel bans to fight viruses "don't work" https://www.vox.com/platform/amp/2020/1/23/21078325/wuhan-china-coronavirus-travel-ban

1/23/2020: Dr. Fauci says US wouldn't implement shutdowns of cities like what was occurring in China

1/23/2020: WHO again claims no human-to-human transmission outside of China, not a public health emergency

1/24/2020: Politico reports Trump held coronavirus briefing for senators that was "sparsely attended" because it "was held on the same day as a deadline for senators to submit their impeachment questions."

1/26/2020: Dr. Fauci says "The American people should not be worried or frightened by this. It's a very, very low risk to the US. It isn't something the American public needs to worry about or be frightened about."

1/27/2020: VP Joe Biden receives inside intelligence on virus outbreak, but does not share information publicly.

1/27/2020: WHO raises alert level but says China has virus contained

1/27/2020: CDC issues updated travel guidance recommending travelers avoid nonessential travel to all of China

https://www.cdc.gov/media/releases/2020/s0128-travelers-avoid-china.html

1/28/2020: CDC: "While CDC considers Covid a serious situation and is taking preparedness measures, the immediate risk in the US is considered low."

1/28/2020: FBI arrests Dr. Charles Lieber, chair of Harvard's Department of Chemical Biology, for lying to the Department of Defense about unreported payments of $50,000/month and millions more from China to set up chemical/biological "Research lab" at Wuhan University. Two Chinese research assistants arrested, one a lieutenant in the Chinese CCP Army, the other caught smuggling 21 vials of "Sensitive Biological Samples" while boarding flight to China

1/29/2020: Trump creates White House Coronavirus Task Force despite WHO downplaying the threat

1/30/2020: WHO declares public health emergency, but says countries should not restrict travel or trade in response to the new virus

1/30/2020: US State Dept. issues travel advisories against traveling to China

1/30/2020: Bill and Melinda Gates Foundation pledges up to $100 million to WHO, Chinese frontline responders and others at national and global levels for coronavirus research

https://www.gatesfoundation.org/Media-Center/Press-Releases/2020/02/Bill-and-Melinda-Gates-Foundation-Dedicates-Additional-Funding-to-the-Novel-Coronavirus-Response

1/31/2020: Trump declares a "public health emergency" and issues restrictive travel ban from China after 6 cases reported in US. Democrats and media slam his decision, calling it racist/xenophobic

https://www.theverge.com/2020/1/31/21117403/trump-coronavirus-ban-travel-non-us-citizens-china

https://www.washingtonpost.com/us-policy/2020/01/31/trump-weighs-tighter-china-travel-restrictions-response-coronavirus/

1/31/2020: Nancy Pelosi proposes a "No-Ban Act." Pelosi tweets "Trump Admin's expansion of its un-American travel ban is a threat to our security, our values and the rule of law."

https://twitter.com/speakerpelosi/status/1223414098614018057

2/2/2020: US State Dept. issues Level 4 travel advisory restricting travel to China

https://travel.state.gov/content/travel/en/traveladvisories/traveladvisories/china-travel-advisory.html

2/2/2020: Trump defends closing borders to fight Coronavirus

https://www.nytimes.com/2020/02/02/us/politics/trump-super-bowl-interview-coro-navirus.html

2/2/2020: China agrees to allow American scientists into China as part of WHO team https://link.theepochtimes.com/coronavirus-live-updates-south-korea-quarantines-800-soldiers-as-precaution-for-coronavirus_3225132.html

2/4/2020: Trump warns about coronavirus in State of the Union address. Pelosi tears up speech, calling it "lies"

2/5/2020: Trump acquitted of impeachment

2/5/2020: Chuck Schumer tweets that Trump's travel ban from China is "premature"

2/7/2020: Dr. Li Wenliang dies from coronavirus in Wuhan at 34

2/7/2020: White House Coronavirus Task Force gives press briefing

2/9/2020: White House Coronavirus Task Force meets with governors regarding virus

2/11/2020: WHO names virus COVID-19

2/12/2020: CDC awaits Chinese approval for CDC team to travel to China

2/12/2020: Dow Jones hits all-time record high closing at 29,551.42

https://www.investopedia.com/ask/answers/100214/what-dow-jones-industrial-average-djia-alltime-high.asp

2/13/2020: Harvard, Yale accused of failing to report hundreds of millions in donations from China

https://www.npr.org/2020/02/13/805548681/harvard-yale-targets-of-education-department-probe-into-foreign-donations

2/18/2020: HHS announces partnership to develop vaccine over 12-18 months

2/19/2020: Democratic presidential debates: COVID-19 coronavirus is never discussed

2/21/2020: CDC tweets it is working with states on preparedness

2/21/2020: 1st case identified in Italy

2/24/2020: Trump sends letter to Congress requesting $25 B for virus effort

2/24/2020: Pelosi makes a stop in Chinatown encouraging people to "please come and visit and enjoy Chinatown."

2/25/2020: CDC tweets still no reported community spread in US

2/25/2020: Trump sends 2 warships to South China Sea

https://www.express.co.uk/news/world/1247180/south-china-sea-disputed-spratly-islands-us-warship-donald-trump/amp

2/27/2020: Trump appoints VP Pence to coordinate coronavirus efforts

2/27/2020: 1st community transmission in US reported

2/27/2020: WHO warns coronavirus has 'pandemic potential'

https://abcnews.go.com/amp/International/latest-american-infected-coronavirus-1st-case-community-spread/story?id=69251035

2/28/2020: WHO does not expect a coronavirus vaccine to become available in less than 18 months

https://www.sciencealert.com/who-says-a-coronavirus-vaccine-is-18-months-away

2/28/2020: Dr. Francis Riedo, EIS (Epidemic Intelligence Service) expert at Evergreen Health, Kirkland WA, and EIS Dr. Jeff Duchin, top public-health doctor for Seattle/King County, learn of COVID-19 cluster at Life Care nursing home in Kirkland, WA

https://www.newyorker.com/magazine/2020/05/04/seattles-leaders-let-scientists-take-the-lead-new-yorks-did-not

2/29/2020: Dr. Fauci on CNN: "No need to change anything that you're doing on a day-to-day basis"

https://twitter.com/steph93065/status/1247340325389164545?s=21

2/29/2020: 1st US death from COVID-19 in Seattle, WA

3/4/2020: With only 12 COVID-19 deaths in the US and no diagnoses among Microsoft workers, Seattle-based Microsoft and Amazon tell employees to stay home

https://www.newyorker.com/magazine/2020/05/04/seattles-leaders-let-scientists-take-the-lead-new-yorks-did-not

3/10/2020: Italy locked down

3/11/2020: Trumps bans EU travel

3/11/2020: WHO declares COVID-19 a 'pandemic' after over 118,000 cases spread to 110 countries on every continent but Antarctica

https://time.com/5791661/who-coronavirus-pandemic-declaration/

3/11/2020: Mayo Clinic offers drive-through specimen collection for COVID-19 testing

https://newsnetwork.mayoclinic.org/discussion/mayo-clinic-offers-pre-screened-patients-drive-through-specimen-collection-for-covid-19-testing/

3/13/2020: Bill Gates steps down from Microsoft to focus on global health issues

https://www.nytimes.com/2020/03/13/technology/bill-gates-microsoft-board.amp.html

3/14/2020: Spain locks down

3/16/2020: Imperial College London model predicts 81% infection rate with 2.2 Million deaths in US, 510,000 deaths in UK

https://www.cato.org/blog/how-one-model-simulated-22-million-us-deaths-covid-19

3/16/2020: Trump urges Americans to practice social distancing. Governors begin issuing stay-at-home orders to maintain order and public safety under US law, as decisions on closing businesses, shutting schools and ordering people to shelter in place are made by governors and local officials

https://amp.cnn.com/cnn/2020/03/23/us/coronavirus-which-states-stay-at-home-order-trnd/

3/19/2020: CA issues stay-at-home order

3/20/2020: Trump urges looking into more research on using chloroquine hydroxy-chloroquine with Z-Pack after proving 91-96% successful in clinical trials, in Australia, France and other coronavirus areas, with quinine was successfully used against malaria over 75 years. (see 8/22/2005). Democrats and media attack Trump, calling him irresponsible for promoting unproven drugs, accuse him of giving false hope, and claim nothing is approved to treat the virus

https://www.nytimes.com/2020/03/20/health/coronavirus-chloroquine-trump.html

3/21/2020: IL, NJ issue stay-at-home orders

3/22/2020: NY Gov. Cuomo says NY is set to begin clinical trials for malaria drugs as possible treatment for coronavirus. Democrats and media immediately praise Cuomo: "This is what great leadership looks like."

https://dailycaller.com/2020/03/22/chloroquine-hydroxychloroquine-trials-corona-virus/

3/22/2020: NY, OH issue stay-at-home orders

3/23/2020: CT, LA, OR, WA issue stay-at-home orders

3/24/2020: DE, IN, MA, MI, NM, WV issue stay-at-home orders

3/24/2020: Bill Gates does TED chat on coronavirus pandemic with Chris Anderson

https://www.ted.com/talks/bill_gates_how_we_must_respond_to_the_coronavirus_pandemic/details

3/25/2020: HI, ID, VT, WI issue stay-at-home orders

3/26/2020: CO, KY issue stay-at-home orders

3/27/2929: MN, NH issue stay-at-home orders

3/28/2020: AK, MT, RI issue stay-at-home orders

3/28/2020: FDA issues Emergency Use Authorization (EUA) allowing providers to request a supply of chloroquine/hydroxychloroquine for hospitalized patients with COVID-19 who are unable to join a clinical trial

https://www.goodrx.com/blog/coronavirus-medicine-chloroquine-hydroxychloro-quine-as-covid19-treatment/

3/29/2020: FDA issues Emergency Use Authorization for donated hydroxychloro-quine, chloroquine; HHS accepts donations of medicine to Strategic National Stockpile

https://www.hhs.gov/about/news/2020/03/29/hhs-accepts-donations-of-medicine-to-strategic-national-stockpile-as-possible-treatments-for-covid-19-patients.html

3/30/2020: KS, MD, NC, VA issue stay-at-home orders

3/31/2020: AZ issues stay-at-home order

4/1/2020: NV, PA issue stay-at-home orders

4/2/2020: ME, TN, TX issue stay-at-home orders

4/3/2020: AL, FL, GA, MS, MO issue stay-at-home orders

4/3/2020: Pelosi tweets "We're up to 90% of Americans being under shelter-in-place orders. It should be 100%"

https://twitter.com/speakerpelosi/status/1246192803316740096

4/3/2020: Henry Kissinger writes op-ed article in WSJ: "Coronavirus will alter the new world order," encouraging people to "safeguard the principles of the liberal world order"

https://www.wsj.com/amp/articles/the-coronavirus-pandemic-will-forever-alter-the-world-order-11585953005

4/7/2020: SC issues stay-at-home order

4/9/2020: Mark Levin: "President Trump hasn't shut down a single business. The Governors did."

4/9/2020: Bill Gates claims mass gatherings may not return without global vaccine

https://www.theburningplatform.com/tag/bill-gates/

4/10/2020: China donates $86 million to WHO vs $893 million from US. China vows to add another $36 million to WHO

https://www.foxnews.com/world/coronavirus-us-china-who-world-health-organization-china

4/13/2020: US Surgeon General Adams plans to reopen economy, dumps Bill Gates' predictive contagion model for real data

https://www.fort-russ.com/2020/04/major-plans-to-re-open-u-s-surgeon-general-adams-dumps-gates-predictive-contagion-model/

4/13/2020: SD Gov. Kristi Noem announces SD will be the first state to conduct a **hydroxychloroquine** trial to test against Covid-19 #YouGoGirl

https://www.cnn.com/interactive/2020/us/states-reopen-coronavirus-trnd/

4/13/2020: NY Gov. Cuomo, along with the governors of NJ, CT, PA, RI and DE, announce a regional effort to reopen the economy in a "coordinated way" amid the coronavirus crisis

https://www.foxnews.com/politics/cuomo-governors-coordinated-regional-effort-to-reopen-amid-coronavirus

4/14/2020: Trump announces US to withhold funding from World Health Organization over coronavirus response. **Bill Gates becomes largest donor to WHO, followed by China**

https://www.foxnews.com/politics/trump-announces-funding-to-world-health-organization-who-halted

4/15/2020: Trump says latest data suggests US has 'passed the peak' of coronavirus cases

https://www.foxnews.com/politics/trump-argues-us-has-passed-the-peak-on-new-cases-teases-forthcoming-guidelines-for-reopening-economy

4/15/2020: Reports surface that coronavirus may have originated in Wuhan Institute of Virology labs as China tries to compete with US

https://www.foxnews.com/politics/coronavirus-wuhan-lab-china-compete-us-sources

4/15/2020: Dr. Oz: SD to implement hydroxychloroquine HCQ drug trials for up to 100,000 patients

https://video.foxnews.com/v/6149275790001/

4/16/2020: Infectious disease specialist Dr. Stephen Smith on using hydroxychloroquine and azithromycin to treat #COVID19: "It's an absolute game changer... I think this is the beginning of the end of the #pandemic."

https://twitter.com/lotusoak2/status/1251043604728029184

4/16/2020: G7 Leaders call for review and reform of WHO amid "lack of transparency and chronic mismanagement" over coronavirus

https://link.theepochtimes.com/g7-leaders-call-for-who-review-reform-white-house_3315548.html

4/16/2020: CDC: As coronavirus is blamed for more deaths, number of deaths from influenza decreases from previous years

https://www.cdc.gov/nchs/data/health_policy/Provisional-Death-Counts-COVID-19-Pneumonia-and-Influenza.pdf

4/19/3030: Some US states to begin lifting restrictions

https://link.theepochtimes.com/trump-some-states-to-begin-lifting-ccp-virus-restrictions-in-coming-days_3317985.html

4/20/2020: CDC's failed coronavirus tests were tainted with coronavirus, Feds confirm

https://arstechnica.com/science/2020/04/cdcs-failed-coronavirus-tests-were-tainted-with-coronavirus-feds-confirm/

4/21/2020: Dr. Shi Zhengli claims coronavirus was not created in her Wuhan Institute of Virology lab

https://www.wsj.com/articles/chinas-bats-expert-says-her-wuhan-lab-wasnt-source-of-new-coronavirus-11587463204

4/23/2020: NY Gov. Cuomo: New study shows as many as 2.7 million New Yorkers infected with coronavirus, 13.9% have recovered, bringing death rate down to 0.5%

https://www.cbsnews.com/amp/news/new-york-coronavirus-13-9-percent-coronavirus-antibodies-covid-19/

https://www.cnbc.com/amp/2020/04/23/new-york-antibody-study-estimates-13point-9percent-of-residents-have-had-the-coronavirus-cuomo-says.html

https://www.nny360.com/news/publicservicenews/study-reveals-state-has-13-9-virus-infection-rate/article_58263eb6-2fbc-5706-85bf-7c5d5df6eed0.html

4/27/2020: CDC adds 6 new coronavirus symptoms to list

https://apple.news/AEhVfoe59RNS09zOaZo_Mag

4/27/2020: Dr. Fauci challenged to explain giving "$3.7 million to Wuhan laboratory"

https://m.washingtontimes.com/news/2020/apr/27/anthony-fauci-should-explain-37-million-wuhan-labo/

4/29/2020: AHA Journal publishes report on benefits of Hydroxychloroquine, Chloroquine and Azithromycin on corrected QT interval in patients with SARS-CoV-2

https://www.ahajournals.org/doi/10.1161/CIRCEP.120.008662#.XrG-i8LBjDA.twitter

5/1/2020: 16 states reopen

5/1/2020: CDC reports Covid-19 deaths showing 65,735 reported "confirmed and probable deaths" to 37,308 "provisional" deaths

https://www.cdc.gov/nchs/nvss/vsrr/covid19/index.htm

5/1/2020: FDA approves drug Remdesivir for emergency use for coronavirus

https://apple.news/A1WtJTdgPRMaPFFGfZAOh1g

5/1/2020: Doctors group urges AZ Gov. Doug Ducey to reverse his ban on drugs used to successfully treat the coronavirus because studies show they work. AAPS, Association of American Physicians and Surgeons, points to research on 2,333 cases treated with Hydroxychloroquine in studies in France, South Korea, China, Algeria and US

https://www.wnd.com/2020/05/doctors-group-asks-governor-back-off-ban-experimental-covid-19-meds/

5/2/2020: Intelligence reports China lied about origin of coronavirus

https://nypost.com/2020/05/02/intelligence-report-says-china-lied-about-origin-of-coronavirus/

5/3/2020: Dr. Eric Berg compares 91.7% success rates and other benefits of Hydroxychloroquine (HCQ) to more expensive Remdesivir

https://youtu.be/iBma_0oAiMI

5/3/2020: US Sec. of State Mike Pompeo says there's "enormous evidence" coronavirus originated in Wuhan lab

https://www.axios.com/pompeo-coronavirus-wuhan-lab-5f305526-9ceb-49af-943a-fd8291a6d5d9.
html?utm_source=twitter&utm_medium=social&utm_campaign=organic&utm_content=1100

5/6/2020: NY Gov. Cuomo: 66% of new CV-19 patients in NY stayed home

https://www.msn.com/en-ca/news/world/shocking-e2-80-99-66-25-of-new-coronavirus-patients-in-ny-stayed-home-cuomo/ar-BB13HKJO

5/7/2020: Russia approves use of HCQ to treat Coronavirus. Russian medical research center to distribute 68,600 packs of hydroxychloroquine donated by Shanghai drug company to Russian hospitals for free. Russian doctors in Moscow are to test HCQ on themselves.

https://www.themoscowtimes.com/2020/04/17/russia-approves-unproven-malaria-drug-to-treat-coronavirus-a70025

5/20/2020: CDC says coronavirus does not spread easily on surfaces

http://nypost.com/2020/05/20/cdc-now-says-coronavirus-does-not-spread-easily-on-surfaces/

5/25/2020: China's "bat woman" Dr. Shi Zhengli warns CGTN deadly coronavirus is "just the tip of the iceberg" faced by the world without a global effort to prevent more outbreaks. "If we want to prevent humans from suffering from the next infectious-disease outbreak, we must go in advance to learn of these unknown viruses carried by wild animals in nature and give early warnings." Dr. Shi, China's top scientist special-izing in viral transmissions from bats, is deputy director of the Wuhan lab suspected of unleashing the virus on humans. China has been accused of not revealing the danger soon enough and lying about the virus's toll on its citizens. Shi denies her lab was involved in the pandemic, saying the strains it is researching are different.

https://news.cgtn.com/news/2020-05-25/CGTN-Exclusive-The-story-of-COVID-19-told-by-a-Wuhan-lab-expert-QMsRNq9Bde/index.html

5/26/2020: Australian scientific study concludes that the coronavirus causing the global pandemic contains unique properties suggesting it was manipulated in a Wuhan Chinese laboratory and was not the result of a natural occurrence.

https://www.washingtontimes.com/news/2020/may/21/australian-researchers-see-virus-design-manipulati/

It is proven if you slightly alter a virus, you can in fact patent a virus. The Lord made it clear that those that would create the virus would also conveniently have a vaccine. April 2020, a friend in California called and told me that her neighbor had already had a stash of the Covid-19 vaccine in their possession. That was months before it was officially announced publicly and confirmed what the Lord told me in advance privately. In my spirit I knew some role playing of "good cop – bad cop" would be acted out. I knew deep down folks could not roll it out too quickly because that would look too obvious, but for millions whose discernment was out the window it was obvious to those with eyes of faith.

Some of the world's most powerful people had gathered and this reset had been in the works for some time. It had been reported that the CIA had been pitching Hollywood scripts for decades. The three-letter agency coined the term "conspiracy theorist" in 1967, because they tried to shame those who did not believe the conclusion our government gave society over the assassination of President John F. Kennedy. Noah was a conspiracy theorist until it started to rain and once it started to rain and his boat began to float the one that was considered clueless, and crazy was proved to be accurate all along.

It was reported that during the Obama administration Dr. Fauci received over three million dollars towards the virus in China. Some of the same folks counseling the Republican President were donating to candidate Biden in the process. The same expert telling POTUS not to wear a mask for nearly a month and half before the lockdown, now insists that even after an unnecessary vaccine for a virus with a 99 percent survival rate without it, should still wear one better yet two masks. While the Apostle Paul, saw the Light while on the road to Damascus, we were told to keep wearing one while in the dark. Those who are free want it off! Personally, I started preaching we need to all be on the road to DE MASK US.

I still think that it is interesting that Dr. Fauci was boasting before Trump was in office that the next administration would certainly deal with a virus that America was ill-prepared. These folks are not prophets, and some suggest not much of a physician either. On January 15, 2020, two interesting things happened almost simultaneously, three thousand miles apart. Despite several sources and individuals complaining in hindsight back in late fall 2019 with similar symptoms, the first Patient Zero known to land on United States soil touched down at Seattle-Tacoma International airport. Approximately at the similar time on the same day the House of Representatives clear across the country in the other Washington officially filed Articles of Impeachment against President Donald J. Trump.

Some believe that the virus was to intentionally cause death to countless lives, cripple small business and America as we knew it only to have the audacity to eliminate the sitting president politically. When power becomes your god, then you can be so blinded by ambition that you become a pawn on Satan's chessboard. I am not accusing anyone, but President Lincoln was correct when he said, "Sir, my concern is not whether God is on our side; my greatest concern is to be on God's side, for God's side is always right." A statesman is thinking of the next generation while politicians tend to think only of the next election. One is thinking the big picture and the other is for political expediency. God grant us more statesmen and women in these last days! I am happy to report I have several of them in my respective Bible studies in the state capitol. Those who fear God want the best for their constituents. Those who follow Lucifer could care less and you are basically on your own.

The released virus would send the nations of the world in a tailspin, and it would lock unnecessarily millions of healthy, innocent taxpaying citizens on house arrest while convicted felons would be released from prison to go free. For those who need to be reminded that quarantine is when you monitor and detain the sick, but tyranny is when you lock down the healthy. The intentionally released virus from China would neutralize their political opponents, clamp down on God-fearing citizens, create fear, destroy small business, and leave multiplied millions gasping for air literally and financially.

Public and private school students would go into deep depression while being isolated from their classmates. The Devil promotes death and destruction while the Lord is life and liberty. One student committed suicide on a class zoom call in front of his peers because he could not handle the stress that was forced on our nation. The virus was created to depopulate the globe with mass deaths and set up the reset towards the end as prophesied in the Bible.

While visiting the United Nations you can visibly see Lucifer in the hallway of their massive foyer. Those in the dark used to hide their actions but now they have gotten bold, and they are unapologetically showing their cards this late in the game. I was told about their sustainable growth plan four years ago and that it was already in the works to fundamentally change the world and usher in the New World Order. What most are missing is that we are in the battle of the ages, and it is no longer rivalry against sports teams but Good versus Evil, Light against Dark, God against Satan and all of Hell coming against Heaven.

During my recent trip to Israel in November 2019, I stood in the very vicinity where Jesus told Peter, "Upon this rock I will build my Church and the *gates* of Hell will not prevail against it (Matthew 16:18)." I have been praying for the son of the former head at Planned Parenthood and Gates needs God before it is eternally too late. The fact is all of humanity need to come to Christ before the clock runs out.

The lockdown is not a science-based approach and in fact, seasoned professionals and experts were completely against it from the start. The fact is the vaccine was not made for Covid-19, but the opposite is true. Covid-19 was made for the desired "forced" vaccine. This vax is the Trojan horse utilized to push a demonic agenda to not only wreak havoc on the world but usher in the end times.

It was reported that Microsoft on March 26, 2020, filed a patent for a body-interfaced crypto currency. Some speculate it contains a human body implanted microchip connected to a cloud computer system. What is the patent number? 060606. In early April 2020, I reached out on social media to a senior White House official sharing my concern against anything related to this vaccine and had reservations against some of those standing next to the President in press conferences. That very same week, the White House suspended funding to the World Health Organization and split half a billion dollars between the American Red Cross and Samaritan's Purse. On April 15, 2020, Bill Gates tweeted at 1:17AM, "Halting funding for the World Health Organization during a world health crisis is as dangerous as it sounds. Their work is slowing the spread of COVID-19 and if that work is stopped no organization can replace them. The world needs @WHO more than ever." Didn't mean to burst your bubble Bill but when we are talking the global family's well-being I had to stand up and step out. Keep in mind my family come from a century and half of law enforcement lineage taught to protect others.

I am not implying that I saved the day or that the message was even read, but a year ago last Spring I already knew that pandemic was planned, and the globalists' plan was not in the best interest of society. Someone joked, "Frank, if the White House just re-directed half billion dollars to two other respected organizations you should at least get a finder's fee for seeing the handwriting on the wall." I laughed but once again, I did not get a dime, but I was able to connect the dots in real time while most were asleep on the couch, I was already doing some investigative work. The reason that I went so fast, so far at almost an inhumane pace the past decade and half as an evangelist was because I knew that this day was coming. A twelve-year plan was in place to ultimately destroy America, and some speculate had Hillary won the 2016 election, it may have been the proverbial nail in the coffin. Personally, I still believe that God intervenes in the affairs of men and God to this day can turn things around on a dime. I have been praying for the Clintons for years we all need God's grace. We never once told anyone who to vote for on that Decision America tour, but the left did not take Trump seriously and when 82 percent of evangelicals finally voted it helped grant a space to disrupt their plan temporarily.

Make no mistake, Trump is not the Trinity nor the Savior. My family has been about as bi-partisan as one can be with respect to others individually and has provided protection, prayer, and kindness to all in authority, but it is imperative to be aligned with God in these last days. It is a dangerous thing when folks put their trust in anyone apart from Christ. In politics when done correctly, it is both a noble calling and respected profession. Some of the finest people I know are in the political arena. I want to be clear that we are all human and at times you will meet the absolute of the best in public service and the worst, and it is worth saying that is true on both sides of the aisle. This book is not intended to bring guilt but with time ticking no matter where we have failed or dropped the ball, we can begin anew with God's grace.

The second week into the lockdown my dear friend, Pastor Rodney Howard-Browne was arrested. Not for selling crack but honoring Christ. Not for smoking cocaine but simply for having church. He was on my heart that morning and I texted him to tell him I was praying for him only to learn he was indeed arrested by the Hillsborough County Sheriff in Tampa, Florida. Pastor was willing to turn himself in and was booked. Once again, the Holy Spirit is the greatest detective and alarm system, and it alerts in advance before things happen. The irony is when I finally saw both video footage and still clips of his arrest, the first thing that was obvious was the same county police who handcuffed Pastor Rodney were not wearing masks when they apprehended him. That is the only time I agreed with their actions when the same folks saying he was recklessly endangering lives for not wearing a mask was arrested by county officials failing to wear masks themselves! Not only the irony but hypocrisy, but I give them a pass today because the home I grew up in we were taught only doctors, nurses, or the guilty wear the mask. The folks who knew the virus was coming want to hide behind every press conference wearing one but when you can see through the scam and sinister plot of the enemy you do not want to play their game.

Senator Ted Cruz was right recently when a reporter demanded the national public official to wear a mask because he felt unsafe and uncomfortable. I love what the son of a preacher and senior senator from Texas said, "Not while I am before the cameras and take a step back if you need to." That was quality for those who are sick or feel unsafe feel free to step back, stay home and quarantine yourself but no need to have shut the entire world down while misguided media, Members of Congress, and money hungry, power grabbing, god-playing souls who want to call the shots at humanity's expense. Not today!

The irony is Pastor Rodney had just given the same Sheriff an award less than a month before and his ministry and church's involvement had helped reduce crime in Tampa by several percentage points. He was verbally told he was fine per the Sheriff's Office to have church and then the next thing you know his mug shot was plastered on TMZ around the world. Pastor felt sorry for the Sheriff because he was stuck between a rock and a hard place. Pastor Rodney resembled and preached "The Rock" and even the county sheriff who at the time seemed to enjoy for the moment some national news attention, everyone has superiors. Everyone has a boss no matter how high you are in a particular profession. The fact is we either must decide now to honor Christ and The Constitution as public officials and do what is right for America or knowingly or ignorantly bow to the winds of change, cancel culture and communism. The legit stand for the Lord and do not twist laws to fit a demonic agenda.

The Lord told me three things a couple years ago and they have all proven true. The Confederate Flag was a diversion and folks were really coming after the American Flag. The red, white, and blue is offensive to those who do not love God or America. When million-dollar female athletes walked off the basketball court in the middle of the national anthem before the start of a WNBA game, they showed their cards and disrespect. Actions speak louder than words and too many have showed their hand and revealed allegiance to a sinister plot to destroy America.

The second thing that would come to pass was that "soul winners" would be called murderers. The <u>false</u> narrative was that the pastor/evangelist who preached to 85 countries and saw millions repent of sin and trust Christ as Savior, wanted to see people die. Not a single person in Pastor Rodney's congregation at the time of his arrest was sick, hospitalized or had died because of the intentionally released virus. However, he was labeled and libeled as a murder. I rest my case.

Lastly, the Patriots would be called un-patriotic if you did not immediately fall in line to take this unhealthy vaccine. The Bible talks about a cashless society in the last days and some stores had signs saying NO CASH. Just days before where cash was king, it was now a pauper or obsolete for fear that the virus could be transmitted by paper. The same doctors at the helm in this fiasco lied about the transmission of HIV (AIDS) decades before. Only some skirt the system and with a terrible track record get promoted up for failing. One reason the masks are still encouraged today because some doctors have attested that the vaccine does not really help. The problem with herd immunity is that when following the masses, you are a letter away of following the wrong crowd. Drop the "m" in *masses* and you get the picture. From a pastor or pasture perspective at times sheep can be dumb and even fall off a cliff if the Good Shepherd is absent to lovingly steer them in the right direction. When a pastor is blocked, muzzled, or neutered, it makes it difficult trying to minister from the outside looking in. Plus, God created humans to have community and intimacy but lately thanks to the global agenda fallacy folks, many are depressed and dying for fellowship. Even at the local Christian school where I am a chaplain some teachers were so paranoid with my traveling ministry insinuated that I would automatically get folks sick or worse die. The one who embodied faith was sidelined by those in fear.

I found it interesting that it was our beloved Abraham Lincoln who helped free the slaves and the cancel culture crowd was not only trying to re-write history but cut out the one that carved a space for them. President LBJ didn't even want to sign the civil rights bill and his words where he wanted to use them for political purposes and he said, "These Negroes, they're getting pretty uppity these days…Now is we've got to do something about this; we've got to quiet them a little something, just enough to quiet them down, not enough to make a difference. I'll have them n*gg*rs voting Democrat for the next two hundred years." That language is offensive!

In the 1960's we had a white Democratic president that wanted to use black people to extend his political life, but by contrast a century before in the 1860's, a white Republican President Lincoln was assassinated and paid with his life for his belief that all people are precious to God and should live in freedom. Sadly, many in politics on both sides of the aisle are more concerned with political power than liberating lives.

Vince Everett Ellison is an African American and was born on a cotton plantation in Haywood City, Tennessee. His father worked in President Gerald Ford's White House. In 2000, Vince became the Republican Congressional nominee to run for the sixth Congressional district of South Carolina. He wrote the greatest book I have read on how the left use race to divide Americans in their thirst for power. The Iron Triangle is a book that every single soul should read but the only hope for America and the world is Christ not Congress. Ellison in the overview of his book penned, "*Not all black preachers, politicians or civic organizers are bad* – just the vast majority." That is a bold statement, and I am not agreeing with everything that was said and no question some of my best friends are black pastors, business leaders and conscientious and caring souls. Quite frankly, I have learned from and leaned on many for their wise counsel.

Ellison's experience and some have shared with me over the years that like with any race sadly some who were gatekeepers or leaders who truly could have made a difference and help foster change were "pimped out." They were willing to sell out and be bought out by the dollar more than the Divine. He references some sparse groups of black clergies not only hindered the Holy Spirit but blocked the blessing to their own community for the preacher to gain personally while in or out of the pulpit. Several over the past decades sold their souls to shackle their own peoples' chance for growth and additional success just for some clergy to get a kickback. They will have to give an account to God for failing to do right. Dr. Martin Luther King and Dr. Billy Graham worked too hard together and individually to improve race relations for folks to be more greedy than gracious in standing up for Truth. While God's Truth was marching on, some members of their own congregation were held back and in the dark because of deceitful pastors and public officials.

Gunner Mydral stated in that same book, "The Negro in America will always be used for either entertainment or exploitation." Like the plantation owners, drug dealers, and pimps throughout history, the Iron Triangle has attached itself to the black community, sucking away its strength but never giving anything in return."

The successor to Dr. Martin Luther King, Dr. Ralph Abernathy, after seeing the devastation the Civil Rights Movement had wrought on the Black community, went to black democrats to consider a plan to get black families off government assistance and to help them stand on their own and be self-sufficient while supporting their family. In his book, And the Walls Came Tumbling Down, he wrote: "I discovered a curious thing…they liked the idea of a huge, economically-dependent population. The fact that there were third generation welfare families pleased them." The Book Iron Triangle noted that it was all part of a plan and Ellison said, "I submit to you that the Liberals are getting exactly what they pay for: The Black vote. They have been retaining more that ninety percent of the Black vote for the past forty years and over eighty percent for the last sixty years – all due to the Iron Triangle. Lose ten percent of that vote and they lose all their power. Why would they be motivated to change a thing? Members of the Iron Triangle live like kings during abject Black poverty. They do not care about Black murder, Black crime, the Black Family or Black people. They care only for the Black vote. As it was in the past with their Democrat forefathers, it remains now: Black death is collateral damage in the new slave trade." God, heal our land!!

Regarding the disparity in education, the book reveals that in past years approximately 93 percent of Loudoun County students graduate in Virginia while in neighboring Prince Georges Country, Maryland, graduation rate that same year was a dismal 57 percent. Ellis wrote, "For Liberals to explain the educational disparity, they had to describe Prince George's County as 'high poverty' which is an absolute lie. In 2017, poverty was described by the US Department of Health and Human Services' poverty guidelines as a family of four earning less than $24,600 annually. As stated before, Prince George's County's median income was $79,185. Recently, it was discovered the school system was worse. On November 3, 2017, WUSA9 reported that an audit by the State of Maryland found grade inflation and irregularities in grade changes and the manipulation of transcripts after graduation." It sounds as if not the students were all failing but some professionals were dropping the ball.

Ellison further elaborated, "The argument that race is a precursor to poverty and crime was debunked in an article written in OZY.com I was illuminated to find that Nigerian immigrants are the most successful ethnic group in America (read that again). If race or color were a factor when determining success in America, how could this be? It is simple. These first-generation Africans have not been infected with the disease of the Democratic Party's liberalism. The June 7, 2018, article written by Molly Fosco explained that today 29 percent of Nigerian Americans over age twenty-five hold graduate degrees and have a median household income of $62, 351 per year. According to Quor.com, 41 percent of all Black Ivy League schools came from an immigrant background (Africa/West Indies) even though black immigrants constitute only 8.7 percent of the population of Black people in the United States."

America is certainly not the best in everything, and we can learn a thing or two from those excelling in education and other noble endeavors around the world. Ellison concluded, "The Iron Triangle remains effective in America because they have convinced most Black Americas that racism and poverty are the cause of every Black problem. Liberals are not stupid: They believe you are. They know the truth and will consistently hide the <u>three deadly diseases they have planted in the Black community</u>. <u>I call it F.I.P = Fear, Incompetence and Pride</u>. Fear: Most blacks are so insanely afraid of racists and racism that the mere accusation causes hysteria and paralysis. Incompetence: The inability to enjoy life, build a family, build a relationship with God, recognize evil or make a living. Pride: Too stubborn to change or admit error."

The race issue is not as bad as the 'lamestream' media would have you believe. Meadowlark Lemon told me more than once while we ministered together, "Frank the tables have flipped. The white folks love me but some of the black pastors and my own people don't want nothing to do with me." One reason may be because he was a success and did it without selling out to the system. Nancy Reagan loved him and gave him *carte blanche* at The White House; but he was boycotted by other administrations.

Apostle Fred Berry is a dear friend, and he pastors the historic Azusa Street Mission in Los Angeles, California. We preached together in London and Rio during the Olympics as chaplains together and he had me speak at his New Year's Eve event with Sean Feucht on New Year's Eve 2020. I returned there to speak on April 9, 2021, at the 115th anniversary of the revival that broke out at Azusa Street which started the Pentecostal Movement. Fred was just a guest on my radio show, and he said this recently while in another message, "Martin Luther King, Jr. is my hero in terms of what he accomplished as a man of God," said Pastor Fred Berry of Azusa St. Mission, who recently visited a local church. Berry, a child of the Civil Rights Movement, now ministers to the African American community in downtown Los Angeles.

"MLK, Jr.'s legacy as a pastor is about someone who was bold and courageous about the gospel, and who demonstrated it," according to Berry. "We can judge the movements we've been seeing, such as BLM and Antifa, (and recently, the extremist invasion of our Nation's Capitol), by MLK, Jr. and his response to the same kind of repressive atmosphere we see now." MLK, Jr. preached and practiced peaceful protest and conducted civil disobedience to the unjust laws.

"Their revolution is a Marxist—take by force—approach, which is dangerous to our country." Berry continued, "MLK, Jr. would 'roll over in his grave' and say, 'that's not what I preached.' When you are looting, threatening, and attacking, that is another form of revolution—that's socialism and anarchism. None of that is from God. We have to reject it." Berry noted that Rev. Warnock, who just won a Georgia Senate seat and is the pastor of King's former church, "is promoting all those things. … We're seeing a blindness to the righteousness and holiness MLK, Jr. talked about."

The African American community, Berry continues, "has been hijacked" by sexual-identity politics and socialism. "They've gone back to judging us by the color of our skin, not by the content of our character," as MLK, Jr. spoke so eloquently against. Those movements are "essentially selling us out, like the people who sold us out of Africa to be slaves. Their leadership is being bought and paid for, and there's a judgment coming on it."

Berry expounded that "there's a war against the African American community that was part of the plan behind the eugenics activism of Margaret Sanger [founder of Planned Parenthood] providing abortions in their communities." "We're seeing it happen: the disintegration of our families," he says. "And African American men are not being promoted, even by the Democratic Party. Most of them are either incarcerated, or if they're working, most aren't part of the ideology of the Democratic Party -- they became Republicans."

On April 4, 2021, Charles Barkley said on television while covering the Final Four Show, "Politician's fuel hatred between 'Whites and Blacks' to keep their grasp" on "money and power." The former NBA star and "Inside the NBA analyst alluded, "That system is designed to foster hatred and to "scramble the middle class." One of the greatest rebounders in the game bounced back and scored with this, "Man, I think most white people and black people are great people. I really believe that in my heart." For a guy who went to Auburn, this Alabama fan would agree his comment just helped win the game. Dr. Willie Montague is a pastor, a PhD in Religious Studies and an African American said, "Critical race theory is not more than racist critics spreading their theories."

The race relations war that was on the news 24/7 the past two years is also stoked to divert what is happening today. Unfortunately, some are convinced the African American community is once again being played for another's pleasure and profit. Barkley is correct when he talks about a "system" because those who have been clueless for the last year need to learn that is a planned agenda to unequivocally alter America and the world permanently on this planet. I am so glad that God in Heaven is not taking architectural cues on how to run the show in the afterlife. What we are seeing are Devilish protégées inflicting their desires on us all. The diabolical agenda has ushered untold billions and trillions of dollars to a few pockets while we were told to shut up, mask up and sit down and maybe, just maybe, they may throw another few stimulus crumbs for us to nibble on. All the while financing their pet projects and aiding foreign nations with no relation to the virus at all. Perhaps this is because the pandemic was a lie to begin with. Sadly, some elected officials then basked in the media limelight as if that miniscule amount saved the day or the Republic. No wonder they insist on wearing a mask on camera because how can you lie with a straight face?

Make no mistake, we are so late in the game that the mask today will lead to the future mark tomorrow. If you cannot enter the store now, wait until you cannot buy from them next. It intrigues me that those who scream racism and want to be "free" somehow swallowed the lie of being shackled with a mask that does not work but promote an ungodly agenda around the corner with the bridge out. Once again, it is some pastors who promote it about being safe. It is extremely hard to follow a leader with no backbone or courage and God in this season is exposing counterfeits in our midst. Pray for them now because repentance is still a prayer away.

I shared with Pastor Rodney that I made the connection that I met him at Constitution Hall and how appropriate that he we would be the one arrested for taking a stand for the Constitution. In 1987 my father, while part of the command leadership of the United States Capitol Police, was tasked with planning the movement of Members of Congress from Washington, DC to Philadelphia by train to participate in the Bicentennial of the Constitution celebration. My Dad helped protect those honoring the Constitution and Pastor Rodney was arrested for standing on its principles. In this hour, we need men and women who are standing for Truth and who are not sitting down or backing out!

Rodney is white but from South Africa and joked he was really an African American, but the fact is both he and my father love America almost as much as anyone I know. Some pastors were trashing him on social media, but we all owed him a debt of gratitude. His bold stand and arrest resulted in two governors within forty-eight hours declaring that the Church is essential. Sadly, some of the biggest churches in America caved like a deck of cards. Will the real church stand up because most have been sitting out! Pastor Rodney was arrested, released and his actions gave him permission to return to church and pastors nationwide were still not back inside for services. Why? They had already arrested <u>themselves</u>.

Pastor got arrested and it helped the Church go forward and yet some pastors dropped the ball and decided to lock themselves up. Twelve months later as they are still hiding behind "keeping others safe" opposed to preaching with passion that JESUS SAVES! If your congregation was preaching more about vaccination than salvation, then your church dropped the ball. Pastor Rodney was not only gracious to the sheriff after the arrest but treated him to lunch to reconcile their friendship. The Sheriff called him saying, "I miss my friend." In these days, we must not just preach grace Sunday in the pulpit but extend it during the week. Pastor Rodney has an amazing sense of humor, and he got the last laugh as he sold coffee mugs bearing the image of his mug shot that TMZ had plastered around the world.

Someone recently spotted John Kerry on a plane with no mask. Speaker Pelosi went to get her hair cut without a mask. Biden at the Lincoln Memorial was not wearing one while the California governor was at an upscale restaurant without one and the Hon. Lori Lightfoot was caught celebrating Biden's win without one. Unless the cameras are on or they are promoting the demic that was planned, the science just does not add up.

When President Trump sent a floating hospital in New York to help infected Cov19 patients their governor because of his disdain for the Donald sent thousands to infect healthy senior citizens only to multiply needless death. When two years before a bill enabled for more babies to be murdered the co-signers and folks in attendance gave a standing ovation that a bill could pass and babies die, we are on dangerous ground. Gov. Cuomo also wanted to deflect any success from God and had the audacity to take the credit for it, but the Bible says, "pride goes before the fall."

The same politicians that are for killing babies are also for death to small business. One African American said it best, "Planned parenthood has killed more babies than any police department ever could or would." I have learned that those yelling racism the most are often the most racist in the bunch. Our hope comes from the Lord, but most are either clueless or complicit to where we are in America. The reason some of us have been tracked while on the road the last few years is because some agencies, groups and individuals were paying money to try to find any dirt to ensnare those with a voice of reason, truth and not aligned with the false agenda not of God. I am not perfect but more than ever I live to promote the One who is. Plus, if anyone knew the pressure on one would hopefully want to cover them in prayer not kill them.

We are praying for all our public servants on both sides of the aisle, but it is hard to trust a party that cannot fight for the unborn and expect them to have your best interest at heart when alive. God was booed off a national platform two elections before and we are seeing a culture of death, despair, and destruction. Eventually you must ask the hard question are you aligned with a person, platform or program pushing death or life? Death and the Devil are synonymous, but the Lord is light, love, liberty, and life. #DropTheMic

Not every clergy is doing the Lord's work. Some are silent because they are not listening to God or others have the fear of man, but the Bible proves that to be a snare. True Shepherds STAND UP not sell out. Department of Homeland Security has been recruiting clergy for several years and infiltrating churches to control America. Pastors and police are often the friendly face in the community but those not sold out to the Lord will sell out those under their care. Even sheep when interviewed would say, "That is BAAAAAD!"

God gave me a word that if you were in the public arena of some capacity and did not display a backbone in 2020 than you would probably not be listening to if you were holding a microphone in 2021. The line has been drawn clearly on the ground and the seeker friendly churches have been closed for far too long.

Some were prophesying that Trump would remain in office, but I did not have the liberty to go that far out on a limb. I knew that Biden was in his basement and Trump had crowds that would give Elvis a run for his money but the Bible I read talked about the demise of America and as much as I love her, would die for her, and try to embody the best of her I knew our real home was in Heaven not here.

The virus would also halt large gatherings. I predicted on the radio three days before the lockdown and said on air, "What will they do next? Tell us we cannot go to church?" I then quoted with passion and urgency, "The Bible says in Hebrews, do not forsake assembling together as some do, particularly in the last days." Within hours of that statement, they shut churches down! Liquor stores and strip clubs along with Planned Parenthood could be open for business but the church was threatened to be shut down permanently.

The left was burned with Franklin Graham's tour and Trump's crowd and by hamstringing the church and trying to cease the president's popularity status as if a rock star they would do their best to even the playing field. There is no way on God's green earth that Biden had more votes than Barack Obama. Kamala Harris only had one percent of Democrats votes while running for the highest office in the land. The moment she called Biden a racist, she steps out of the race only to be picked back up as his running mate and with the Biden's questionable health she could very well slide into the office that is Oval. Today, I am once again praying for them and us all. The fact is this is not about who sits behind America's desk but about Who is still on the Throne. We do not need a reset but repentance and revival.

The forced mask also resembles the Muslim garb worn by women around the world. 2300 years ago, long before Islam, Arabs discovered that forcing people to cover their nose and mouth broke their will and individuality and depersonalized them. It made them submissive. That is why they imposed on every woman the mandatory use of a fabric over her face. Then Islam turned it into the woman's symbol of submission to Allah, the man owner of the Harem and the King. Modern psychology explains it: "Without faces we don't exist as independent beings. The child looks in the mirror between the ages of two and three years old and is discovered as an independent being. The mask is the beginning of deleting individuality. He who does not know history might help repeat it. We must honor the Almighty and not Allah.

An African American woman with a doctorate degree testified in support of HB 248 "In slavery, blacks were masked for several reasons. To dehumanize, to shame, to silence, to isolate, to punish and incite fear. Blacks had to show papers to prove that they had freedom of movement off and on plantations owned by their masters. How are the Cov19 masks, social distancing, tracking, and tracing, vaccine passports of today any different than the tools of their oppressors of yester year? They are not! Fear and intimidation were used on blacks then and being used the same on society today. Fear is psychological warfare. When the mind is controlled by fear than one's movements and body can also be controlled. President Roosevelt was right, "the only thing we have to fear is fear itself." Lockdowns, masks, tracking, tracing, and the idea of mandatory vaccines in order to keep their jobs are abusive because they are systematically stripping away the freedom of citizens the best course of action for their health. These are all forms of medical apartheid. Some of my friends shortly after taking the vaccines have gone into adverse shock and sickness. Any student of history clearly sees the distinct parallels between segregation due to race and segregation due to vaccine status. In here in this discriminatory practice is the understanding that what is happening in Cov19 or next 'fear driven narrative' connected to illness will become the next battle for civil rights. Government sanction discrimination based on skin color is no different than government discrimination sanction based on vaccine status. The unvaccinated will become second class citizens just like blacks once were. During the Civil Rights Movement blacks fought against unjust laws. Today, citizens are fighting against the tyranny of government officials and the bullying from people in their daily lives who expect them to relinquish their God given freedoms upheld in the Constitution to the state and to obey mandates, mere words of men which are not laws."

The mask also reveals the eyes only. Will the "eyes have it" and they are the window to the soul and the government has installed technology that cameras only need to see your eyes to track you in a crowded airport, busy hotel lobby or walking down fifth avenue in New York. The 5G towers are not your friend and the mask is demonic in nature, and it was used to suppress the vote and silence the voice of truth tellers. Some would get less of a frantic death stare for walking in a grocery store or bank holding a machete or pistol than failing to enter an establishment without the mask. Some warnings on the side of the boxes containing the masks clearly state, "This mask doesn't protect against COVID-19". On Halloween, millions of kids could not wear a mask on October 31, 2020, but multiplied millions of adults choose to wear one to this day. In the words of Biff from "Back to the Future" while knocking on the main character's head, "Hello, McFly! Anybody home?" Saul became the Apostle Paul when He saw The Light on the road to Damascus. I submit to you, "We the People" and the global community will see the light, too, the moment we by faith take off the mask on the road to De MASK us.

The Devil promotes division and isolation and who would have thought that I would put on a mask, walk into a bank, and come out with some money? When I preached on July 4, 2020, I said, "The only folks who wear a mask are sick or guilty. America is sick of the overreach but most of us are not guilty." Therefore, why hide behind a mask? It is not to show respect to your neighbor it is to be complicit in an agenda that is un-American, un-Constitutional and will usher in a global reset on the fast track to the New World Order. When folks would scream about the four hundred thousand souls that died, I would be the first to tell you one death is too many but when you applaud nearly 70 million abortions and then refuse help and turn your back on floating hospitals and exaggerate by counting nearly every death as COVID-19-related, until that number hits seventy million you don't have a leg to stand on. Candace Owens would make an excellent national public servant and she tweeted on May 4, 2021, "Masking children is not "trusting the science". It is psychological child abuse."

The same group that does not want you to have guns have no problem with babies being crushed and killed in the womb. Everyone that says the "right only votes on one issue" fail to grasp the fact there is no other option if you fail at getting the first one right. The vaccine is not to protect you but correct you when you get out of line and eventually detect where you are always. The first month of the lockdown all the false gods collapsed. Even mega churches were not as mighty and what was appeared to be a force was a farce. NBA, NFL, MLB, NHL all ceased, and NCAA brought "March Madness" to an entirely different meaning.

To make matters worse, "Humans Are Free" posted this on April 1, 2021, "BOMBSHELL: Disposable Blue Face Masks Found to Contain Toxic, Asbestos-Like Substance That Destroys Lungs." Ethan Huff wrote in the same article, "Health Canada has issued a warning about blue and gray disposable face masks, which contain an asbestos-like substance associated with 'early pulmonary toxicity." I have said since day one that wearing the mask all day is not healthy. Many friends complained of getting asthma and the air restriction is slowly evaporating health. Gym teachers were forcing their students to run at recess overseas wearing the mask and were confused when they collapsed and several died. My goodness even a sightless Helen Keller could see that wasn't healthy.

The Olympics in Tokyo were cancelled after a billion dollars invested and finally folks were starting to see that since their idols fell maybe they could finally see that the Lord was the only one still standing and worth staring at. In the 1950's, we loved people and used things but lately too many love things and use people. Some find the symbolism of the Apple logo interesting. The chunk out of the Apple may be capitalizing on Eve eating the forbidden fruit and they have been promoting and profiting from the demise of mankind since.

My first role as a chaplain at the Olympics was in London in the summer of 2012. On the opening ceremony was a dark, demonic creature with a syringe and chasing children and they had corona-like images dancing around the stadium. What looked like misguided art then may have been those behind the scenes showing their cards in advance. One of those in that skit with the world watching resembled their now Prime Minister and he was among the early ones to catch the Covid-19.

It would drive me nuts when marketing, media and even clueless ministers would espouse the term the "new normal." That is just code for New World Order, but Jesus reminds us we are NOT of this world. If you are still living in fear, do not be! The media, global organizations, the government, and its agencies misled the public. The CDC just confirmed that the death rate for the flu shot is TWICE as high as the Covid-19 death rate! The folks who lost their minds and kept verifying with the 'fact checkers" failed to do their homework to learn News Punch wrote on April 15, 2020 that "George Soros and Bill Gates fund Facebook's Fact Checkers." How convenient! Just because folks have dollars does not mean they have SENSE or your best interest at heart.

While rolling out their plan we have since added $6 trillion to the national debt. Did you enjoy your $1,400 stimulus? The fact is we did not want a handout but wanted to go to work. The Bible says we must earn a living by the sweat of our brow. Fifty million workers were either furloughed or laid off. A reported 60 million people were on food stamps and what was three and half percent on unemployment saw a surge to nearly fifteen percent! The tourism industry tanked, petroleum was on fumes, literally! The service industry (hotels, restaurants, etc.) took a nosedive. Business owners and even pastors were arrested, harassed, and threatened. Church goers were even ticketed for parked at a drive-in service. Mental health problems were multiplied because of the pressure and shortage of food was at play for the first time in a long time.

Schools and colleges were either shut down or forced to reconsider how to educate students but that also fit along the globalists' desire to "reimagine education." Imagine that! Enormous over-reach was now on the table with power hungry public officials and the Lord allowed us to see who is for God and the people or who is for power and are sold out to the future one world government. Countless civil liberties were violated while medical care and surgeries were often delayed or hindered all together. Finally, over three hundred million (300M) Americans were on house arrest while some convicts could leave free. Read that again!

Bill Gates was now the face and the philanthropist who somehow was elevated to continue to kick this agenda like a can down the street. However, they were punting forward from every Main Street and small side street around the world. I tip my hat to them that it is not that their goal was not big, bold, or brash but dumb, depressing, and demonic. It will make some loads of dollars but makes no sense (cents). This entire agenda roots back to greed and ungodliness where dollars is the name and depopulation and dominion is the game. The same guy who believes the Earth is overpopulated wants to "save" your life with a vaccine. God help us all! Interesting enough that Locks News Network on February 7, 2018, wrote, "Bill Gates' Former Doctor Says Billionaire Refused to Vaccinate His Children."

In the book, "The Phantom Virus" both Dr. Rodney Howard - Browne and Paul L Williams revealed, "In 2002, Gates shelled out $70 million to vaccinate children in the sub-Saharan African continent against meningitis. The vaccines were manufactured by GlaxoSmithKline and were administered with disastrous results. Within the 5,949 children ranging from ages five to seventeen months, 151 died and 1,048 were left severely para-lyzed. Despite this outcome, the researchers maintained that these were "normal" risks to be expected from vaccinations. The South African newspapers did not agree and used editorials to complain, "We are guinea pigs for the drug makers." The outcry against the vaccination campaign eventually caused Professor Patrick Bond, former senior economist for Nelson Mandela, to condemn Bill Gates and his philanthropic practices as "ruthless and immoral." Praise the Lord! Someone called out this atrocity and while some trust the science and not trained scientist, I will stick with the Savior.

Furthermore, thanks to a gift of $450 million from his foundation, Gates and his "Vaccine Alliance" wanted to graciously help more of humanity. On page 183 of the book, The Phantom Virus notes, "Gates gained control of India's National Technical Advisory Group on Immunization (NTAGI). In conjunction with Gates' instructions, a government program was initiated that mandated up to fifty doses of an anti-polio vaccine to children five years old or younger. The vaccine contained an active polio virus, known as the cVDPV. The results of the vaccine program in India were even more horrifying than the vaccinations in Africa. The vaccines gave rise to a non-polio flaccid paralysis (NPAFP0 epidemic that left 480,000 Indian children severely paralyzed. In 2011, an extra 47,500 new cases manifested. Indian physicians gradually realized that the incidences of NPAFP were directly proportional to doses of oral polio that had been ministered." It was noted that those children vaccinated and ill during that program were more than twice as likely to die during the acute phase of the illness as non-inoculated children who developed a similar disease. Trust the science? Think again.

The book of Revelation has warned the world of this for thousands of years and there is nothing new under the sun. For those that know intimately the Son of God can discern and decipher what is real and what is counterfeit. Only those on the side of the Devil would think depopulation, depression, isolation, and house arrest was a good thing. God wired us for freedom and liberty and those that want to place shackles on you do not have the Father's heart.

Pastors who either intentionally or accidentally followed this lie need to repent when their Boss is The Truth. While you and I were told to trust the science, I sought the Savior, and It was clear that one side was pushing a lie. This recess on house arrest enabled folks to install thousands of high voltage 5G towers that would do more harm than good. I come from five generation law enforcement not at the local level but national and among the best in the world. But this type of policing is not normal, but it is lockstep with the globalist agenda. Who needs "Big Brother" when they want to introduce you to a brand-new family that will destroy?

Indeed, in the last days what is good will be called evil and now public enemy number one are Christians, conservatives and conscientious citizens who promote truth and respect their neighbor. While we were forced to remain at home, they ushered in steps on the ladder towards the 'promised land" of a great reset, surveillance state of control, nothing is sacred or private anymore. What were freedom breathing people before would now suck in the polluted air of an open-air prison where you are tracked and followed.

For the first six months of 2020, I could relate to the Little Dutch Boy back in the day who saw a dam breaking and he started to use his fingers to try to plug it but eventually he ran out of fingers, and it burst. We are so late in the game and my job as an evangelist is to love God, others and deliver His message while hoping others will repent and receive it before it is too late. We have had good public officials on both sides of the aisle both past and present and scandals on both political parties. Every one of us has dropped the ball and I thank God for grace and forgiveness.

Franklin Graham was correct when he said, "The answer is not in the Republican or Democratic party" but our only hope is in Jesus Christ. The Gospel is the only thing that can turn our nation around." The fact is those that are content cancelling culture and demanding a Utopia on Earth most likely do not have their reservation in Heaven. That is why the hostility towards people of faith is atrocious because Jesus said, "They hated Me, and they will hate you (John 15:18)."

I want to ask you today to pause and pray for Speaker Pelosi, Bill Gates, Dr. Fauci and politicians on both sides of the aisle. It is still not too late for folks to genuinely repent and get right with God. I have heard stories of powerful politicians who asked ministers privately for prayers and their request was not asking for forgiveness but asking that they would keep their power. That petition is a dead prayer because they are worshipping a false god and not the living Lord. You will never hear me bash Asians and I do not fault China's people for the virus; but we are dealing with a demonic regime that does not care about anything other than control as if We the People were pawns on their chess board. Make no mistake that the Vatican, Pope and China are big actors in this end time drama. It is interesting that one of the venues that Pope has preached in before from the inside is shaped as a serpent and the "great white whore" may look pure on the outside but needs Jesus on the inside.

I knew from the beginning the vaccine was a joke, but I was not laughing. Dr. Steve Hotze of the Health and Wellness Center from Houston said, "The so-called Covid-19 vaccine is not even a vaccine at all. It is a dangerous experimental gene therapy. The CDC gives the definition of vaccines on its website.

"A vaccine is a product that stimulates a person's immune system to produce immunity to a specific disease."

Immunity is the protection from an infectious disease. If you were immune to a disease, you could be exposed to it without being infected. This so called Covid-19 vaccine does NOT provide any individual who receives the vaccine with immunity to Covid-19 nor does it prevent the spread of the disease, nor does it meet the CDC's own definition of a vaccine. That is why it is a deceptive trade practice under 15 US Code Section 41 of the Federal Trade Commission for pharma companies who are producing the experimental gene therapy claiming it is a vaccine. These companies are lying to the public and government bureaucrats are lying as well."

Dr. Simon Gold and many other doctors shared that hydroxychloroquine, Ivermectin, doxycycline, zinc and Vitamin D are great deterrents against Covid-19. Dr. Peter McCollough, Professor of Medicine said, "Hydroxychloroquine works and is the most widely used thera-peutic to treat Covid-19 in the world. The chances that it doesn't work are calculated to be one in 17 billion," he told Sky News. Even more powerful was this knockout statement, "There's no controversy over whether or not hydroxychloroquine works. The controversy is on the public health approach to Covid-19. Sadly, in the United States and I know in Australia this happens all the time, patients get no treatment whatsoever. They literally are told to stay at home until they are sick enough to go to the hospital. I think that honestly is atrocious. History will look back on that and think it was the worst way to handle potentially fatal illness."

The truth is that Trump and his doctors did their best to warn and share insight that hydroxychloroquine could help save lives and they were mocked, ridiculed, and censored. Jim Hoft wrote, "The latest international testing of hydroxychloroquine treatment of coro-navirus shows countries that had early use of the drug had 79 percent lower mortality rate than countries that banned the use of the safe malaria drug." The title of the article in bold said, **"After 440,000 Americans are dead – Facebook and American Journal of Medicine Admit their Stand on HCQ was wrong – The people should be prosecuted."**

No wonder the globalist, left leaning politicos and CNN discouraged the off-patent hydroxychloroquine for a couple of reasons. One, it works wonders and two, this entire shutdown was about dollars, death, domination, a new narrative and defeat of anyone that stood for truth and justice. The price point alone should make folks take note what I have said for over a year now. Dr James Todaro tweeted #Cov19 Treatment options in USA:

Hydroxychloroquine: **$0.63 per pill** – generic – 11 US Manufacturers
Azithromycin: $0.84 per pill – generic – 12 US Manufacturers
Remdesivir: **$1,000 per pill** – ON PATIENT – One US Manufacturer (Gilead)."

The 'trust the science' camp wants you to chase what is more expensive. The Lord impressed on me to take the Hydroxychloroquine in advance last year to get it in my system and it works! When you shoot it straight you can get ahead of the curve. #DropTheMic I encouraged my family to take it and it was a game changer. God is good!

It begs the question if the very folks that have the patent to a particular vaccine are conveniently pushing the vaccine, you must wonder is it for your benefit or theirs? Robert F. Kennedy, Jr the nephew to President John F. Kennedy, U.S. Senator Edward M. Kennedy and son of the former U.S. Attorney General and presidential candidate is not your card-carrying Republican. RJK Jr. has been heroic against this global planned demic and vocal against Gates, Fauci & Inc. He is adamantly against the vaccines they are proposing and pushing for this global reset, and he went on record as saying, "The Center for Disease Control (CDC) is not an independent agency. It is vaccine company. The CDC holds over 20 vaccine patents, and it sells about $4.6 billion dollars of vaccines every year."

Dr. Leana Wen slipped on national television with guest Chris Cuomo and showed her hand that this is about control and compliance not for the protection of our health. In a recent CNN interview, the good doctor said, "The vaccine is the ticket to pre-pandemic life. The window to do that is a very narrow window. With all these states opening at 100 percent and we have a very narrow window to tie re-opening policy to vaccination status. If everything is re-opened, then what is the CARROT going to be? How can we encourage people to take the vaccine and that is why the CDC and Biden Administration need to be much bolder and say, "If you are vaccinated you can do all things and here are all these freedoms you will have? Otherwise, people will go out and enjoy these freedoms anyway." Perhaps (without the vaccine)?

When the President of Pfizer was to tour Israel, it was reported that he was not able to visit because he had not received the vaccine. Think about that for a second. As of April 1, 2021, reports reveal those 40,000 injuries and more than 3,500 deaths have been attributed to the Covid-19 vaccine. On March 30, 2021, I received a call from an old friend in South Carolina and his brother got Covid-19 immediately after taking the vaccine and then his body shut down and was rushed to the ER. The vaccine apparently attacked his immune system, and it almost took him out. We are living in a culture of death and many need to wake up, turn off the television and get right with God because soon and very soon the game on Earth will be over and it means nothing what your political affiliation is, or whether you have money in the bank but most importantly, are your sins forgiven?

Dr. Carrie Madej was invited to a World Congress meeting with a scientific theme on transhumanism and the keynote speaker was Dr. Craig Binter who was linked with human genome project and his opening statement was, "What is God? God creates and now we can create and so we are gods." They can now manipulate human genomes and now uploading them into the cloud they were downloading them in China, and he believed everyone's genome should be altered. In that meeting they talked about "designer babies" and synthesis things in the genome that part can be patented. Read that again! If something is synthetic in, you then you have a new owner and you are literally branded. We are not talking Adidas or Gucci but try to play God.

For those who have asked who died and made these globalists, elites, and mad scientists in charge? I can assure it was not Jesus, The Christ. The answer is that the Lord alone is Almighty and unless they repent, heads will roll, and Hell is waiting for these misled souls.

Dr. Madej said these vaccines have three proposed variables. One is a software code that goes into your cells that goes into making part of the virus on our own. Bill Gates in his own words said, "At least 700,000 will die but that is for the good of the whole." So "the good doctor" said it was a good thing for lives to die. Yet, his ambition was to receive the Nobel Peace Prize. Some of us need some work. While this evangelist is trying to save souls, we have a "philanthropist" that is trying to reduce the population. The second is modified DNA or RNA can become permanent although they hint it is temporal, but it cannot be controlled. You cannot put your life in the hands of anyone but the Great Physician and regarding the virus or vaccine He would not consult with the Surgeon General. It has not been reported but the deaths from the various vaccines are escalating drastically and where they exaggerated numerically the Covid-19 deaths, they are downplaying all those numbers who have been damaged and/or killed by the vaccine. All those who always just had to have the next best thing may realize too late that the vaccine was your last thing before visiting a morgue. Mike Yoder tweeted, "People who haven't been sick all year, are lining up to get a shot that'll make them sick, just so they don't get sick." Folks, some of you are being played!

One Israeli female just said, "We woke up to a nightmare. Our life has been destroyed. We have been kidnapped by our government which sold us to be guinea pigs to an experimental vaccine that they want us to donate and give up our bodies and souls with no questions and we have become the biggest clinical trial in history on the scale of an entire country. Usually, you have the right to accept or reject but we were told if you don't participate then you are a criminal in your country." #EnemyOfState

Brian Shilhavy, Editor of *Health Impact News* wrote, "Stop fearing the Coronavirus, the new COVID "variants" are a hoax, let the children go back to normal activities, take off your mask, and avoid the experimental "vaccines." The headline screamed in caps, "CANADIAN DOCTORS SPEAK OUT AGAINST GOVERNMENT COVID RESTRICTIONS – MASKS and VACCINES NOT NEEDED." Doctors for Truth: Tens of thousands of medical professionals suing and calling for an end to COVID tyranny. A Wyoming medical doctor who is manager for Wyoming's State Public Health Department says, "Covid-19 vaccines are biological weapons of mass destruction". Dr. Judy Mikovits and Dr. Sherri Tenpenny: "A new Covid-19 vaccine could kill 50 million people in the United States." Censored Dr. Kaufman who said, "They want to genetically modify us with Covid-19 vaccine" loses his job and is willing to go to jail to resist. Doctors around the world issue dire warning: Do NOT get the COVID vaccine.

Dr. Hilde De Smet – Medical doctor from Belgium said, "Due to the excuse of the global "pandemic" that vaccines typically run trials on animals first has been bypassed straight to humans and are using people as guinea pigs." Dr. Elizabeth Evans from the United Kingdom said, "The vaccines are not proven to be safe or effective. We believe it is reckless and unnecessary using a new MRNA and no long-term effects like cancer and other diseases." Dr. Kelly Brogan, a medical doctor in the United States, "Vaccination is penetration of the body, mind and spirit by The State. The Covid-19 vaccine is not proven safe or effective and this is NOT a real medical pandemic. Will you trust 5G, Pharma subsiding eugenic technocrats with your health, or will you see through their claims to a transhumanist agenda that aims to dispossess you of trusting your body of any agency around your own life and even the fabric of your own humanity?"

Once this technology is in your body, they are telling us "That you will have a healthy body or more strength to combat cancer and disease" but in fact it could cripple, maim, and kill. We are made in God's image and these clowns with a god complex are not your savior but could be your downfall. Bill Gates allegedly wants to protect humanity and wants you to prove that you have been vaccinated. That proof is called Luciferian and it includes your data, medical records, passport, banking information and for all of you who did not see where this coming, welcome to the party. Read the first seven letters of Luciferian and not only are they no longer hiding their cards, but it is in your face, and you must choose are you with the Lord or world? The Luciferian injected gel will also have a glow in the dark capability to reveal who is marked and not. Satan is an imposter, fraud and imitator of the highest order and he tries methodically to be what only The Light of the world is.

Dr. G. Vanden Bossche, "You lose the most precious part of your immune system every protection against any viral, variant of Coronavirus. Your immunity has become nil. It is all gone!" General McInerney (RET) said that President Trump got bad intelligence on the vaccine and shared, "Do not take the vaccine! *I just learned this less than a week ago. I had one shot a week ago and was scheduled to get the second at Walter Reed but did not get it. The danger is I just learned that the Cov20 and Cov21 you will not have the immunity built in. Look, all our first responders, military, medical personnel have been encouraged to take this shot. Most of them already have it*! (That is attack on our forces).

We have some Deep Staters that wanted to lock everyone down, steal the election, and the third phase is to get everyone vaccinated and eliminate us. It is a power broker deal between the DEMS and CCP." Then we see public officials bragging and posting on social media that they got the shot. God help us! NEWS FLASH – Rip Van Winkle woke up a long time ago and yet some of you are still sound asleep.

The irony is one person shared those that took the jab are becoming super spreaders. It was not Pastor Rodney, Franklin Graham, Sean Feucht, or me preaching coast to coast before and during the pandemic but the one who sheepishly failed to follow The Good Shepherd. The fact is many clergy are clueless or complicit and at this stage of the game I do not know what is worse. The Devil placed the lie on God fearing, conscientious citizens but it was the other camp causing the damage. The Devil is a LIAR! He always overplays his hand and what we accuse others of is often where we are guilty. The socialist crowd is playing right out of the Devil's age-old playbook!

Sean Feucht in a tweet on April 6, 2021, "Secular humanism, moral relativism and "virtue signaling" has been around a long time. It is not new. It is powerless to change the human condition. It will NEVER lead to eternal salvation. This is why we must "PREACH CHRIST CRUCIFIED." It is the only hope for the world."

Prescription – Dr. Sherri Tenpenny said, "If you have family or friends who have taken this injection, they need to get powdered Vitamin C and build up their immune systems. It will help with your brain, heart, and mitochondria. What can we do to reverse it? To my knowledge and all my medical circles of people is NOTHING! The best we can possibly do is to get your vitamin D level up to 80, iodine level to 80, large doses in a gel cap of vitamin C." Dr. Judy Mikovits was slammed on news narrative, but she predicted upwards of 50 million souls could die, become seriously sick or ill in America alone." Some have speculated within two to three years those fully vaccinated may not make it.

Moderna has been known to mean modify DNA. Charlie Kirk said an eight-year-old girl holding a sign at a recent rally stopped him in his tracks. From the mouths of babes her sign simply but profoundly read, "Not your DNA – not your choice!" We are fearfully and wonderfully made the Bible says and when we try to alter our DNA, we not only disrespect God but say we know better. Shame on us for believing that lie! This vaccine is putting in aborted baby matter from another human in each jab. It is unwise and unhealthy to comingle DNA.

Bill Gates is already talking with excitement today about another wave of the planned demic virus. Some get excited over Good News and others tend to get excited and passionate when crisis comes. The Washington Post on May 17, 2021, acknowledged through a spokesperson that he had an extramarital affair with a Microsoft employee shortly before he resigned from the board the year before. His ties to Jeffrey Epstein did not help and after leaving Microsoft he began to work on his "philanthropic work" more than ever. If Gates would have worked on his marriage, he may have had less time to hurt the global family.

Emerald Robinson covers the White House and she tweeted in May 2021, "Bill Gates: I'm the victim of conspiracy theories! Also, Bill Gates: I have no idea why I flew on Jeffrey Epstein's plane! Or why I funneled money through Epstein to MIT! Or why my wife is divorcing me! Or why Epstein named my science advisor as the executor of his will!" Some take 'pay to play' to another level.

Pro IP Patent is a law firm and on their Turkish website wrote this, *There are many plot theories today such as beverages which produced by Coca-Cola contain the blood of Christian babies, reptiles rule the US government. Certain technological events are interpreted by prophecies in the Bible. There are some reasonable facts that cannot be denied such as the presence of the Bilderberg Club, the CIA's MK-Ultra project, and George Soros' funding for suspicious political activities.*

Patent WO / 2020/060606 relates to officially recorded facts. It was registered on March 26, 2020. It was made by Microsoft Technology Licensing LLC under the presidency of Gates and gained international status on April 22, 2020. " Cryptocurrency system using body activity data " is the title of this patent.

The online patent application can be summarized as follows: The human body activity associated with the task provided to a user can be used in the mining process of a cryptocurrency system. A server can provide a task to a user's device connected to the server. A sensor attached to the user's device or positioned within it can detect the user's body activity. Body activity data can be generated based on the attained body activity of the user. The cryptocurrency system connected to the user's device can verify whether the data generated by body activity meet the conditions set by the cryptocurrency system and can issue cryptocurrency to the user whose body activity data is verified."

In other words, thanks to the crypto money, the chip that monitors the daily physical activity of the person will be placed in the body. If the conditions are met, the person receives certain bonuses that can be spent on something.

In a detailed description of the invention, it explains how to use the device with 28 concepts.

It also provides a list of countries for which the invention is intended. There are several regional organizations with all members of the United Nations, which are separately mentioned. These include the European Patent Office, the Eurasian Patent Organization and two African intellectual property protection organizations.

Although it is not new to insert microchips into the body, the Masonic Youth Child Identification Program has been used in the USA for a while and people who call themselves cyborgs exhibit various implants because of these practices. Microsoft gave the patent code number 060606.

Bill Gates's name is constantly referred to today for his keen interest in pharmaceutical companies, vaccines and WHO financing. The global media try to highlight Bill Gates as a great philanthropist and try to protect him from attacks and criticism, but it is unlikely that they will hide an entire network of connections.

Bill Gates' company is also involved in the ID project ID2020 Alliance, a digital project that has addressed digital rights. The Alliance actively supports the Rockefeller Foundation, design studio IDEO.org, consulting firm Accenture and various vaccines. and Gavi, a company that distributes these vaccines around the world. This alliance Secretariat is in New York.

The Vaccine Alliance covers countries mostly in Africa and Asia. In Europe, the organization operates only in Albania, Croatia, Moldova, Ukraine, the Caucasus, Georgia, Armenia, and Azerbaijan. and all of them are listed as founding partners.

Since February 2020, Gavi has been focusing on the Vaccine Alliance coronavirus outbreak. The CEO of this organization is Dr Seth Berkley.

Theological interpretations of patent numbers are probably best left to religious experts, but they have strong links between organizations and companies such as the Rockefeller Foundation, Microsoft, the pharmaceutical lobby, and the World Bank Group. National governments are responsible for epidemics, diseases, and famines. They are constantly trying to play the role of government, focusing on the fact that they cannot deal with it alone.

However, the idea of realizing China's stance on this issue is not accepted by the West and they do not want to do so because they do not want to share their power, so the globalist media will continue a campaign where the blame is placed anywhere outside the West. As new information about the coronavirus begins to emerge, he says, false stories about China's role in the epidemic are increasing and statistics are being manipulated.

Let us pray for Gates and his family now. We are all in the dark when we have not been born again by the Light. Some have speculated and recent Hollywood movies show hardship, detainment, encampment, and death for those not with their agenda and program. Dr. Madej went on to say, "This was never about a virus but world domination and control. Shut down your television because you are being lied to and turn of your smart phones because they are dumbing us down."

This is not only a tracking device of sorts but recording everything you do and even record your intimate moments. Only those dead to Christ would think this beast mindset sounds liberating. We are dealing with folks who salivate for death and dominance. The smart phones we bought into was the dumbest investment because to a large extent we have sold our liberties away for a pot of porridge and some have already sold their souls. I was not being tracked by a GPS, but the phone and local and national police have abused their authority to target folks that do not align with their ungodly agenda. Mark my words – we have NO normalcy to look forward apart from grace from God. Pause now and look at the cover of this book and realize time is ticking and are you going to trust Gates, the Globalists, Government or God?

The answer is not VACCINATION but SALVATION! It is possible that a food shortage can come into play very soon and they can hold that over your head that you cannot get food until you get the vax. Those injected with this devastating technology can become irate, moody, and even destructive. Plus, with transhumanism your thoughts may no longer be yours. For those that saw Will Smith's movie "A.I." that was conditioning us years in advance for social distance now and acting like part human and half robot but that is not God's Plan.

As a kid, I liked Circuit City or Best Buy, but God did not create me to be a walking microwave or flat screen television. If your dream was to become a human ATM machine, then you are not *banking* on God. I am convinced the reason I could sense that I was being followed through God's supernatural discernment is that these fruit loops were trying to catch someone failing or see who would be a problem for them today.

Picture the likeable and Twinkies loving off duty copy in the original 'Die-Hard' starring Bruce Willis. Sergeant Al Powell was played by Reginald VelJohnson in the iconic theatrical smash hit that went number one in 1988. Sgt. Powell while loading up on some late-night calories in a convenient store got the call to check on a potential hostage situation at the neighboring Nakatomi Plaza in Los Angeles. After first inspection appeared to be a false alarm but open further review it was more than he and the entire LAPD bargained for. I love when Sgt. Powell told his superiors in advance that the terrorists were trying to "take out the lights" and they not only did not believe him but failed to respect him. His insight proved right, and these past seventeen months has been no different. Big Tech borrowed the same playbook and they have been intentional trying to *take out the bright lights* and voices of reason to not only suppress them but silence those who stand tall and are part of the resistance. YouTube has cancelled some platforms, Facebook and Twitter have given others the boot and Amazon has hindered some authors from getting the Truth out. Keep in mind, the one financing the 'fact checkers" are George Soros and some of his associates. I will stick to the Truth of God's Word and the last year, countless preachers were DE platformed, truth tellers were ridiculed, a sitting President of the United States was kicked off social media and Christians, conservatives and patriots were muzzled. No wonder they want us all to wear a mask. More than ever, I love the t-shirt, "Unmasked, Unmuzzled, Unvaccinated and Unafraid!" For those who late to the game and are just now seeing what we saw from Day One let me quote Bruce Willis in that original "Die Hard" movie, "Welcome to the party, pal!" My friend, Anna Khait who was on "Survivor" a former poker champion and a sold-out sister for Christ was right when she said, Wicked people hate the people of the Light."

Part of my job as an evangelist is part preacher but also protector and opposed to taking a bullet for a president; I am preaching that Christ died in your place, Jesus is the only way to Heaven, and I have gone through a private Hell to warn you DO NOT miss salvation. The Bible says, "He that has ears let them ear." You better listen up, confess up, and wake up if you desire to go up because Hell is too long to be wrong.

Enjoy this statement from the book, "Verbatim" written in 1981 by Bilderberger Jacques Attali. This statement reveals his heart and their demonic plan and remember what is in the well eventually comes up in the bucket. The Bible says, "Out of the abundance of the heart that mouth speaks." Here is this astray man's words, "The future will be about finding a way to reduce the population…of course, we will not be able to execute people or build camps. We get rid of them by making them believe it is for their own good…We will find or cause something, a pandemic targeting certain people, a real economic crisis or not, a virus affecting the old or the elderly, it doesn't matter, the weak and the fearful will succumb to it. The stupid will believe in it and asked to be treated. We will have taken care of having planned the treatment, a treatment that will be the solution. The selection of idiots will therefore be done by itself; they will go to the slaughterhouse."

Those were his words not mine. He called you stupid not me. The elites, globalists and demonic players do not care about you or me. I was correct when I said from day one that those who unleashed the virus already have the vaccine and what they are selling you is not "the cure." Can you hear me now? For those trusting the globalists, government or Gates over God how are you doing? The Bible says, "Look up! Your redemption draweth nigh (Luke 21:28)."

In response to the March 31, 2021, editorial in The Wall Street Journal that Pfizer-BioNTech Covid-19 wants to start vaccinating all 12–15-year-olds by May 2021 was aptly rebutted by Ezra Levant of Rebel News, "Twelve- to fifteen-year-old children have a negligible risk from Covid-19. Last I checked, not a single death in Canada. But Pfizer will make billions off this, and that is what counts. I bet they start advertising on kid's cartoons. Maybe co-brand with McDonalds in Happy Meal or something." Well known, fast food restaurants are giving away free food and donuts from a popular chain if you can show proof of your vaccination card.

The government is giving away candy to grown children (adults) as if it were Halloween and what is *scary* is the older crowd loves it! We sold our nation's soul for a pot of porridge like Esau in the Bible, and he lost his inheritance. Honest working, God fearing, patriot loving small business owners who would rather die than be forced to stop working, lost their hard-earned dreams, income, and stores while people clapped like a dog getting a treat not for doing good but for being content with the forced house arrest. Prisoners were set free while taxpaying citizens were emotionally and internally incarcerated.

Patrick Henry screamed, "Give me liberty or give me death" and the mantra for millions of misguided souls lately whispered, "Give me another stimulus and I will sit silently on the couch." Globalists pocketed trillions while our economy tanked, and we clapped when another stimulus check worth peanuts finally came in the mail or was deposited directly into your bank account. If there is any "shaming" that would be appropriate, it should fall in the lap of those bragging about being vaccinated and wearing a masked muzzle as if it were a badge of honor when it is a symbol of death, deception, and indoctrination. The individual's worth celebrating are those who could cut through the crap and saw through eyes of faith that this pandemic was planned and who did not feel in fear, compelled to wear a faux mask. The joke is on those fooled by the socialist left not those who live right day and night. I shared with a teacher who drank the Kool-aide on the week returning from the lockdown in March 2020, "When you know where the virus came from and who is behind it and what is at stake, you don't have to play by their rules." Her eyes about popped out of her head but in the words of my friends from the streets, "Homie don't play that!"

This prepared, well-thought-out scheme and scam used artists, celebrities, and professional sports stars to jam their narrative down our throats. Just where ungodly political leaders in the past have used and misused three letter agencies (CIA, FBI, IRS) among others to harass those different than them, the irony is they have been using three letter sports agencies (NBA, NFL, MLB) with the global reset, vaccine, and future passport. The reason many of the stars are vocal is being they were still getting PAID while you were being "PLAYED" and no wonder viewership tanked because after putting two and two together, no one wanted to watch. What the NBA did not realize is they got dunked on by the viewers who turned them off and the globalists that used them like pawns in their chess game.

Allen Iverson would be impressed by the way the white elites broke their ankles with a cross over and even Jordan jumping from the foul line could not dunk the way these million-dollar stars will get dunked on in the end. Make no mistake, if the globalists get their way, they will dunk on all of us and hang on the rim above us while doing so. I am so thankful that as a child of God I have a Daddy who plays "Above the Rim!" What too many do not understand is that with depopulation and death eventually they are after all of us. This war was never about racism but the reality that a small club of wicked people do not want you alive. It is all a diversion and distraction to depopulate the globe and worship the Devil. In the movie "Frankenstein", eventually the monster turned on the one who helped create it. The fact is while we are in the corner playing checkers the elites are at the chess table, but God will flip the table one more time. #Checkmate

We have seen tens of thousands of children in Africa, India among others that have been used as guinea pigs on these dangerous, untested vaccines. While a "race war" was created and fabricated at home we have seen far too many dies abroad. If only more of our society would learn that we are being played right into their hands and today, artists, entertainers and pro athletes are still today enslaved. The only difference is they are no longer picking cotton or shackled in chains but given multiplied millions of dollars to push an ungodly narrative that would further enslave to our detriment emotionally and devoid of liberty. The Devil isolates but the Lord unites.

Dr. Madej said, "World leaders at the G20 meeting often talk about depopulation and that is their agenda on how they can get rid of us. Canadian Prime Minister Justin Trudeau does not believe you should own anything, you should be eating plant-based items, and that we need the great reset and start over with crypto currency. UK Prime Minister Boris Johnson speaks about how one day you cannot hide from anyone because your thoughts will be known twenty-four seven. Until you get in the Bible and read Good News you will die because of the lamestream media's Fake News. Get right with Jesus or you will be LEFT out. Sadly, many will take the vaccine due to ignorance or fear.

Over forty nations have stood up with protests, but the great America is behind the ball. The WHO, United Nations and some Members of Congress are already completely behind this. Children can be taken out of their homes, and this will haunt you when proven true. A true prophet is not always in it for profit. I have preached in stadiums for free but delivering you the Truth with no ulterior motive but to warn, encourage and get right with God because time is ticking.

For those who think you are turning the corner you better think twice. Christ alone has your best interest at heart. Governor Cuomo chose the first week of April 2021 Christian's most Holy Week, to start implementing the Global Vaccine Passports in New York. It is not accidental that this roll-out is the time we celebrate the resurrection of Christ. For far too long we have had some suggest that science was our Savior, and this reset would revive us as a people and protect us when in fact Christ alone saves the soul. South Dakota Governor Kristi Noem tweeted on March 29, 2021, "The @JoeBIden #CovidPassport proposal is one of the most un-American ideas in our nation's history. We as Americans should oppose this oppression. #Freedom

Regarding the Covid Vaccine Passport, Dr. Naomi Wolf who is a Democrat but sees the big picture was on Fox News on March 29, 2021, and she said the following day that this agenda is happening at warped speed and, "This is the most dangerous tool that humanity has faced in my lifetime regarding personal liberty." She elaborated, "With the vaccine passports if you don't get let into the supermarket, dine at a restaurant, you cannot board a plane or travel on a train or meet a friend at the pub. The vaccine passport platform is the same platform as a social credit system like in China that enslaves a billion people. The CCP can fine any dissident within five minutes because of the 360 surveillances of the social credit system. When you act like a "good" system you get a boost but when you do something considered a "bad" citizen opportunity get closed to you. Your child may not get in college, a prep school, you don't get that job, miss out on the promotion."

People thought I was a tad off when I said the week after the "stay home for two weeks and slow the spread" that the virus was a biological weapon. A few thought I lost my marbles when I said the mask today will lead to the mark in a future tomorrow. The mask was not only to silence you but enslave you. The same camp that forever screamed, "My body, my choice!" demands that you do not have a choice if they fear you could hurt them. The fact is, the mask has made some get sick, develop asthma and trouble breathing and what is mind boggling too is how may so-called people of faith fell for the deception of the Devil. In Revelation chapter eighteen, the Bible talks about sorcery in the last days fooling the globe. In fact, "And the light of a candle shall shine in you any longer, and the voice of the bride-groom and a bride shall never be heard in you any longer. For your merchants were the great ones of the earth, because by your sorcery all the nations were deceived (Revelation 18:23)." Can you hear me now?

The goal is not to slow the spread of an intentionally released virus but slow the roll of your liberties to travel, be free and they desire that you be lockstep with their Luciferian new way of life. This beast system is created by folks who are lost souls, and you must realize that the only freedom you will ever have is repenting of sin and coming to faith in Christ. This ungodly agenda is slowly phasing in card-carrying Christians on Earth but without Christ, the Lord will permanently phase them out of Heaven.

Some pastors are clueless to the reality of a cashless society and despite their smarts they were not wise when it came to evangelism, redeeming the time and understanding end time prophesy. Dr. Wolf reminded us that, "The U.S. is proposing a digital currency. Many groups are already working for China, and they are in alliance with big tech. Their desire is to weaken our society, not allowing grandparents to hug their grandchildren, not speak freely, not able to congregate or assemble in prayer and desire to weaken America and subversion is their desire. China wants to be the global superpower. The vaccine will create a way for China to take control. They own Zoom and many media companies. Microsoft sales force rolled out an alignment of the vaccine passport with Apple Pay and Google Wallet. With a digital currency, you know what is next and one day if you are not deemed "a good citizen" your revenue stream can be cut off or taxes can be boosted, or your PayPal doesn't function in order to get it back you may be asked to disavow any renegade positions you may have." Dr. Wolf had already been de-platformed multiple times and the CCP is already putting on the pressure. One doctor eloquently said, "Covid-19 means the certificate of identification of vaccination with artificial intelligence." You may recall in the first book of the Bible the moment Satan tempted Adam and Eve to become smart like God was the dumbest trick in the Devil's playbook.

Gov. Kristi Noem (R-SD), "A vaccine passport is 100 percent hypocritical coming from those who oppose voter ID. But it is entirely predictable after the overreach that we saw this past year. When leaders overstep their authority in a time of crisis, that's how they break our country."

Trump was mocked for wanting to put America first; but the sheep missed it; Trump was never the Savior but despite his flaws he did try to promote and protect our nation. However, this is way bigger than Biden and way above Trump and the Bible told us this two thousand years ago that time would be ticking and one day it would be over on Earth. Those trying to build a utopia down here (Earth) most likely will not be up there (Heaven) when they die. You may recall in 2014, I preached a sermon in Phoenix, Arizona and said in my sermon with the cross of Christ behind me, "*There is a tidal wave coming to America. It is a wave of persecution not promotion and the United States are ill-prepared.*" I pleaded with them then and with all now to get your house in order because it may get bumpy; but we must seek the Lord before time runs out. You see, it is not just the sands of time siding through the hourglass but the American Dream and all her ideals that are evaporating before our eyes. On the cover of this book, I almost had the designer have the grains of sand colored red, white and blue going down the drain and slender neck of the hourglass, but this is much greater than America. President Trump, despite all his flaws, was right on some extremely critical issues and he was spot on when he said, "They are not only coming after me but YOU!" If America topples then the world falls like *dominoes,* and I am not talking Pizza. Respectfully, they are coming after everyone, and these globalists want the globe! I have Good News! God, not Gates, holds the "Whole world in His hands."

You may recall the story while in Paris my friend relayed about trains and what role they play in the future and Amtrak on December 22, 2020, received $1 Billion dollars and $25 billion of those trillion dollars from stimulus bill for transit. Dr. Simon Gold said on March 29, 2021, "The government and private companies will soon try to enforce unconstitutional "vaccine passports" to require inoculation for a pathogen with a 99.7 percent survival rate. This is not about public health. This is an attack on civil liberties and human freedom."

Some have aptly suggested that one reason the first responders, teachers, doctors, military, and police were encouraged to take this vaccine with side effects, reported deaths, without fully being familiar what exactly is in it and with the knowledge you could not sue should one get sick, impaired or die -- could be this sobering thought: If depopulation and control while ushering in the global reset should be the key to the front door of the New World Order, then many of our brains and brawn could die and leave our nation weaker than at any time in our history. Those behind these vaccines promote death and dollars and far too many are anti-God and anti-American. The vaccines are known to cause infertility, too. Once again, that not only makes sense because depopulation and "population control" are part of the global reset agenda. It is not only re-distributing wealth but marginalizing people who see through their sinister plan. The bottom line is this train is heading to a dead end and the "New World Order" is paved on the Highway to Hell.

Eventually what will happen is this agenda is threatening to shrink the world. @ Braveheart_USA nailed it on a tweet on a tweet 4/1/21, "We have a nation that is locked down, but a border that is wide open…it defies logic." This demonic plan is not for opening commerce or lavish more liberties but the opposite. You are either lockstep with their plan or a menace considered a threat to society not because you are violent but because you can see through the lens of God's truth with end time prophecy. Those who continually will be harassed are those who honor the Bible not the beast system and it will be the children of God that will be mistreated by those aligned with the Devil.

Dr. Vernon Coleman, a trusted voice in a time of chaos said, "The vaccines can kill more people than the virus. I have always believed the Covid-19 fraud was planned on purpose to kill as many of the elderly, frail, and those with weak immune systems as possible. Then, introduce mandatory vaccines. Add to that, the plan to destroy and then reinvent the economy to satisfy the requirements of Agenda 21 and the Great Reset. Days after dropping the truth bombs, he was demonized and discredited and folks who live a lie cannot stand truth and try to eliminate their credentials or comments. Sometimes if they cannot stop the message, the messenger mysteriously is found dead. Despite the attacks on his content and character, the good doctor is still speaking up and out. God bless Dr. Coleman and he concluded, "The politicians and advisors did everything wrong and those that questioned were silenced. The fact is that immune systems of healthy people are boosted through interaction with others. The world's politicians and advisors deliberately led us into a mass vaccination program. The public were originally assured that only through a huge vaccination program could they possibly win back some of their lost freedoms. This was always dangerous nonsense."

I love what Ian Smith wrote and he is in the ministry and a Christian business owner and dropped a Truth bomb, "They've offered free money, lottery tickets, booze, weed, reduced prison sentences, VIP and lap dances at the strip club, donuts and fast food to get you to take the *Fauci Ouchie*. I am just a dumb gym owner, can someone explain to me the public health policy behind this?"

The cherry on top is when a former Vice President of Pfizer pharmaceutical, Dr. Michael Yeadon made headlines on the release of the Coronavirus vaccine saying there was no need for any vaccines to bring the COVID-19 pandemic to an end. According to an article published in "Lockdown Sceptics, Dr. Michael Yeadon wrote, "There is absolutely no need for vaccines to extinguish the pandemic. You DO NOT vaccinate people who are not at risk from a disease. You also don't set about planning to vaccinate millions of fit and healthy people with a vaccine that hasn't been extensively tested on human subjects." He dropped the microphone with this truth bomb, "The pandemic is effectively over and can easily be handled by a properly functioning NHS (National Health Service). Accordingly, the country should immediately be permitted to get back to normal life."

Drum Roll Please – that article was published in the National Herald on November 27, 2020. While millions were told to stay at home for the Holidays, Christmas, and New Year's, we were on house arrest. Not me, I flew to Los Angeles to preach on New Year's Eve and on the flight over felt like I was in a communist country. I will forever have etched in my mind the Mayor of New York dancing on the empty streets of Times Square with his wife. Rather than watching the iconic ball drop ushering in the New Year, the only ones having a ball as of late were tyrannical lawmakers and the globalist elite espousing "Rules for Thee but Not for Me." The Federalist wrote, "Your political leaders hate you and think you are stupid," headlined an article by Federalist Political Editor John Davidson highlighting the hypocrisy plaguing this year's liberal lockdowns. For months, left-wing liberals have fined, shamed, and arrested all who dared reject their tyrannical orders closing churches and schools in the name of public health over a virus with a 99.98 percent survival rare while defying their own edicts. Many, including beltway reporters masquerading journalists, even excused, or participated in massive social justice protests after condemning Trump rallies as homicidal super-spreader events poised to erase all progress on viral mitigation. Their promise of "Two weeks to slow the spread" turned into "wait until there is a vaccine," which could have been a lifetime. Now American liberties have been forfeited to power-hungry elites reluctant to give it back. In November, Supreme Court Justice Samuel Alito made rare public remarks calling pandemic restrictions "previously unimaginable" suspensions of constitutional liberty. "We have never before seen restrictions as severe, extensive and prolonged as those experienced for most of 2020," Alito said in a video address to the Federalist Society."

The Lord's message to me in advance was true. The Holy Spirit impressed on me that the "soul winners would be labeled and libeled wanting to murder people." Satan is the Father of Lies. While the devil and his minions want to keep us in the "dark" the Lord is the epitome of Light, life, love, and liberty. Read that again slowly. The released virus would cause death, neighbors would be fearful of each other and encouraged to turn folks in for breaking orders on a false narrative and the innocent and healthy would be both sidelined and shackled. As born-again believers and evangelists, we are all super spreaders. Our task is to sow the evangelism seed into the sin sick soil of society to reap an end time harvest of newly converted Christians to graduate from Hell to Heaven before time runs out.

The goal of the New World Order can be summed up in four key points. One World Government (Revelation 13:7). One World Leader (Daniel 7:4-7) & Revelation 13:2. One World Religion (Revelation 13:8). One World Currency (Revelation 13:16-18). Having been to the United Nations and familiar with some of their plans for the near future below is a proposed list of NWO UN Agenda 21/2030 Mission Goals:

One World Government
One World Currency
One World Bank
One World Military
The End of National Sovereignty
The End of All privately owned Property (No wonder Bill Gates went on a spending spree
and is now one of the top owners of farm acreage in USA)
The End of the Family Unit
Depopulation, Control of Population Growth & Population Density
Mandatory Multiple Vaccines (#NoThanks)
Austerity (Universal Basic Income)
Microchipped Society for purchases, travel, tracking & Controlling (Big Bro on Steroids)
Implementation of global Social Credit System (China already has it)
Appliances hooked into 5G monitoring system.
Government Raised Children (Try Again)
Government owned schools, colleges, and Universities
End of Private Transportation, owning cars, etc
All businesses owned by Govt/Corporations.
Restriction of Air Travel
Human beings concentrated into human settlement zones, cities.
(read the word concentrated again and think of camps)
End of Irrigation
End of Private Farms and Livestock
Restricted Land Use that serves Human Needs
End of Fossil Fuels
Ban of Natural Non-Synthetic Drugs & Naturopathic Medicines

Only folks who do not know the Living Lord would think this entire planned roll out sounds safe, fun, or liberating. I cannot expound with any more urgency that this is not of God and is of a beast mindset. Write this down, it will not get better, but God is coming soon and now is the time to get our house in order.

One friend posted on Facebook, "Will life insurance policies cover those who took the experimental jab for the pandemic that's coming? Asking for a friend." A friendly reminder that you waive all rights to sue if you get sick, hurt, or die from the shot. The proposed required two jabs remind me of the two fangs of a snake. I had them in my feet when that snake bit me last summer writing this book. Satan's fingerprints and teeth marks are all over this, but God is still overseeing everything. He alone not secret societies is the "all seeing eye."

Brian Shilhavy wrote on May 26, 2021, "**12,184 Dead** and **1,196,190 Injuries**: European Database of Adverse Drug Reactions for COVID-19 "Vaccines." Someone aptly stated, "The Most Evil Plan Ever Hatched in THREE Easy to Understand Steps." Step One: Trick people into being afraid of a fabricated threat for an entire year so they give away their rights and freedoms in exchange for a perception of Safety. Step Two: Trick people into taking poison that they believe will protect them from the fabricated threat and will follow them to regain their rights and freedoms that they gave away. Step Three: When people start getting sick and dying from the poison, trick them into believing the fabricated threat was mutated so they take more poison and permanently give away their rights and freedoms." Friends, we are not going back but Jesus is coming back!

Keep in mind that regardless of whether talking virus, vaccines, or abortion on demand, that Hitler did all his atrocity in the guise of being legal. The shaming for folks choosing not to get a vaccine has been both incredible and intense. If in your mind you feel like you absolutely need to be protected by getting an untested vaccine known to alter DNA in your body only to still according to Dr. Fauci wear not one, but two masks go right ahead. Why mock or make fun of those who can see through the lies? If you feel safe and secure behind the science do not be offended by those protected by the Savior.

Andrew Cohen, PhD in a story posted November 9, 2020, ICD10 Monitor – "False Positives in PCR Tests for COV-19" wrote, "The prevalence of misinformation coming from the most trusted form of coronavirus test may be more significant than previously expected. Three types of tests are used to diagnose current, active infection by the COV19 virus: PCR tests, rapid molecular tests, and antigen tests. PCR tests are generally held to be the most accurate and are often used as 'gold standard' against which the other types of tests are measured. Medical and public health professionals have generally treated positive results from the PCR-based tests for COVID-19 as if they are completely reliable. We are told that if we test positive, then we are infected with the virus, and that positive results in PCR tests are rarely if ever inaccurate. In fact, however, false positives occur in PCR tests for COVID-19 often enough to be a significant problem. What is PCR? It means Polymerase Chain Reaction. This is a chemical reaction that repeatedly duplicates certain targeted segments of the virus's RNA, until there is enough of it to be detected. The targeted segments are carefully selected to be unique to the COVID-19 virus, and thus absent from other genetic material – human tissues or other pathogens – that might be present in human respiratory samples. This means that with a well-designed test, we can be highly certain that any reaction and duplication occurs only with genetic material from the COVID-19 virus, and that no false virus are produced."

Dr. Kary Mullis wanted to debate Dr. Fauci, but it never happened. Who is Dr. Mullis? He received the Nobel Prize in Chemistry in 1993 and he invented the PCR method and let us hear his thoughts on Dr. Fauci: *Fauci doesn't know anything about anything, and I'd say that to his face. The man thinks you can take a blood sample and stick it in an electron microscope and if it has got a virus in there you will know it. He does not understand electron microscopy and he does not understand medicine and he should not be in the position he is in. Most of those at the top are just total administrative people and they do not know anything about what is going on at the bottom. They all have an agenda. They make up their rules as they go; they change them when they want and like Fauci smugly go on television and lie directly into the camera. You cannot expect the sheep to respect the best and brightest. They do not know the difference. Most people do not have the ability to judge who is and who is not a really good scientist. The President of the University of South Carolina asked Fauci if he had come and debate me in front of the student body, and he refused.*

Dr. Kary Mullis, 1944-2019. If he had not inconveniently died last year right before the release of the virus, he would have been calling fraud on this entire PCR "testing" scam just like he had done since it was used in the same way to inflate HIV cases." It has been noted that the PCR test cannot properly identify HIV or COV19 and the doctor who created it before his sudden death was telling folks that truth. Former boxing heavyweight champion Tommy Morrison had an incredible career and like us all certainly had his ups and downs in the ring of life. When he turned the corner, got his life on track, and repented for past mistakes his career was stopped abruptly. Tommy was on to the demonic lies of culture, Deep State and was exposing them one by one. He quickly found himself isolated and became the poster boy for having AIDS.

He was ridiculed relentlessly and said to have allegedly died of HIV. He was a born-again Christian, and his career was ruined, and he was harassed and yet his autopsy showed no signs of HIV in his body. None! Nada and no trace whatsoever. You may recall he was the protegee to Rocky Balboa in "ROCKY V" and they fought in the street at the end of the film in that final fight. Tommy's promoter George Washington Duke, who portrayed a Don King role stole him away from Rocky and then had the audacity for them to fight each other said, "Tommy Gunn only fights in the ring!" Sly in his trademark snarl said, "My ring is outside." Then the war was on! When the movie was first released it was a disappointment to many ROCKY fans for a few factors. One, Balboa lost his wealth, fame, told he suffered brain damage and add to the mix for the first time in the franchise the film's final fight was outside, away from the glitz and glare and in the street. However, I knew then thirty years ago at its initial release that despite some of the fan's critics initial disappointment it had some powerful life lessons tucked in there. Tommy did a superb job playing this part and upon further review, Tommy Morrison's life and death leads us to some powerful lessons and clues too.

It is a fact that HIV was not detected in his death, but they did find previously a roll of twelve-foot surgical gauze tape that was left inside him in surgery. That negligence caused septic to fill his body and forced him to fight multiple surgeries and suffered intense pain and appears to have started the downward spiral to ultimately knock out the champ. Was it accident or intentional? The good news is "The Duke" had made his peace with Christ and with The Lord now in Heaven. Tommy Morrison was a truth seeker and when he found Truth, he was willing to speak out. Sometimes those that stand tall get knocked down by those who do not play fair or respect God. He may have lost in the film but won in the afterlife.

Before he passed in 2013, he said in several interviews that he knew his life had a higher purpose than just boxing. He was indeed a fighter and defender of the faith but his life and death both are encouraging and educating millions now about his wrongful   death. The

Bible says, "Even in death, he still speaks (Hebrews 11:4)." Like Rocky, Tommy Morrison could also attest that his ring was outside, and he did a phenomenal job going toe to toe with the demonic agenda in our culture today. Yes, Tommy was a bonafide world boxing champion at one time, but God alone will ultimately defeat death and the Devil. This final fight is bigger than us and we do not wrestle or box against flesh and blood but principalities, powers, and darkness. However, quoting Rocky, "Yo, I didn't hear no bell!" Until the trumpet sounds, and the Savior splits the sky we as Christians must continue to stand strong, hold our ground, fight the good fight of faith, be on post and Jesus told us to, "Occupy, until He comes."

The Bible says, "nothing new is under the Sun" and the same tactics that kept others away from visiting him due to "HIV" two decades ago were the same draconian measures to keep loved ones away from seeing their family with coronavirus in hospitals. Sadly, many died alone and did not have to die. Interesting some of the same "experts" are still calling the shots today. Some was on deck for both the HIV debacle and today calling erroneous plays from a misguided playbook. Now, you wonder why I do not take the bait on "trust the science" when some of the scientists are wrong.

Bill Maher is not "Captain Conservative", but I couldn't agree with him more on his "Show Me the Science" segment related to Covid – April 18, 2021. The show was called, "Bill Maher Blasts Covid Panic Porn." The host came out swinging after Congressman Jim Jordan grilled Dr Fauci on failing to be consistent despite being the highest paid person in the United States Government. Maher nailed it when he said, "What about liberals. You know the high information buy the science people. In a recent Gallop poll Democrats did much worse than Republicans in getting the right answer to the fundamental question what are the chances of someone getting COVID needs to be hospitalized? The answer is between one and five percent. Yet, 41 percent of Democrats thought it was over 50 percent! Another 28% put the chances at 20 to 49%. So 70 percent of DEMS are wildly off on this key question. They also have a greatly exaggeration view of danger of immortality rate among children which explains why all the schools are still closed are blue states. Shouldn't the liberal media have to answer for how your audience believed such a bunch of crap about Covid? Michael J Matt on Remnant TV said, "Governors like DeSantis (R-FL) and Gov Abbott (R-TX) looking like geniuses – no forced vax, no mask mandates, businesses open, stadiums filled to capacity yet no spikes in the cases. No hospitalizations or deaths increases. Are you not seeing this our you still buying this while driving alone in your car wearing a mask?" Maher elaborated, "Texas recently released their Covid restrictions, and their infection rates went down partly because the sun and wind did their thing. This cannot be right because both Texas and Florida are run by Republican Governors! The Florida Governor did a much better job protecting his elderly constituents than the New York Governor (Cuomo - D)." Wow! That was coming from a Democrat blasting another's failed leadership in the Empire State.

Matt concluded, "Personally, I trust the science. I am not worried about COVID in the least. What I am worried about is the Covid cult trying to abolish the Constitution and turning our homeland into a Gulag. What I am worried about scientism posing as science and worried about "junk science" put on mask it will save your life." Senator Rand Paul said, "If you look at all the mask mandates throughout the country when we instituted them the incidents of disease went up particularly in December and January as we went up exponentially as rise of infections occurred everyone was wearing masks. So, there is not a great deal of evidence that masks mandates or economic lockdowns changed the trajectory." Matt put the icing on the cake, "If you were not in a cult, you would see as we are seeing that this has nothing to do with your health but power and control."

The word of the year in this planned exercise was this, "The vaccine wasn't made for COV19 but COV19 was made for the vaccine." For a free refresher, COVID literally means Certification of Vaccine ID (Identification). When I said last year that they were desiring to trace and track you I was not misleading you. I am hoping you will start tracking with God. The Devil marks his own, but the born-again believer has already been bought with a price. Our bodies are His holy temple, and we must glorify God with everything we do with and put in. If I can quote the current White House press secretary and 'circle back' to Mr. Matt he summed it succinctly, "I am not anti-vax. But you are saying we have to be forced to be vaccinated?"

On Memorial Day 2021, I received this email from a respected group indicating, "A recent example of this is Facebook data technician, Morgan Kahmann, who leaked internal company documents to Project Veritas that detail Facebook's efforts to secretly **censor vaccine concerns**. For Kahmann, sharing the TRUTH about Facebook censoring what could possibly be life-saving information was worth the risk he knew he was taking.

But wait...why wouldn't Facebook and our government and the media and the pharmaceutical companies want us to share information and let each other know if people were being injured or killed by the vaccine so that people could make an informed decision about what they are putting into their bodies?

According to another brave person who chose to speak out, Dr. Peter McCullough, MD, "this whole pandemic from the beginning was about the vaccine."

He says there's a global goal to "mark" people with this vaccine so that the global elitists bent on running the entire world know who you are and where you are so they can force the entire world into compliance. The number of reported deaths and injuries from the COVID vaccine continued to climb this past week on the government's Vaccine Adverse Event Reporting System (VAERS). (And according to a Harvard study only 1% are actually reported.)

The media and Big Tech probably won't share this information with you, but there are brave people who are speaking out despite the backlash they will receive. You just have to find them.

On this Memorial Day let's honor those who gave the ultimate sacrifice for our freedom by doing something brave. Speak out. Educate others." The same fired Facebook whistle-blower boldly said in a sit-down interview, "The Facebook narrative is to get the vaccine, the vaccine is good for you. Everyone should get it. And if you don't, you will be singled out… as an enemy of society."

It takes guts to stand on principle and a fist bump to Mr. Kahmann. Interesting enough when I typed in the former Facebook employee's name nothing came up. Imagine that. It is as if he does not exist. In fact, it appears that some are cancelling their own. He started a GoFundMe campaign and nearly half a million dollars was raised to help provide for his family. I will note it is also a Christian site. The Lord takes care of their own! God bless you sir and blessings on your family.

Friends, what the Holy Spirit told me in that movie theater in the early 1990's about "enemy of the state" proved true. The former Facebook employee just said it what we knew all along. The Holy Spirit is always the best detective and even the Deep State is not deep enough to outmaneuver God. The Lord does not lie. Our only hope is not Obi-Wan Kenobi but Christ, Almighty. I realize this is a very personal decision and in love, I am just on assignment by God to share with you information that you need to weigh and decide. I have two honorary doctorate degrees but do not suggest or imply I am a medical doctor, but I am friends with the Great Physician. My prayer is that you will press into Him in prayer even more in these dark days and seek Him for not just this issue but every area of your life.

I will wind down this chapter with a quote from Senator Paul's wife in a tweet in May 2021, "I'm old enough to remember when Fauci told Rand (my husband) that he was 'completely and entirely incorrect' to question whether the NIH was funding Wuhan lab bat research. Now he says, "it would have been a 'dereliction of our duty' not to'? #Shamless."

When you are not walking in Truth it is easy to fall for the lies. If you have already been vaccinated kindly be respectful of those who are still on the fence or set against it. I would also encourage you to load up on the wisdom of those earlier in this chapter to try to fight against the ingredients and potential side effects. Vice versa to those abstaining from the vax but what we can all agree is we need more love and respect for one another. Furthermore, if you are still listening to Frank Sinatra's MY WAY than maybe you should get real and start doing things God's Way because time is ticking. I am certain that the lockdown was a space of grace from the Lord for you to start getting your house and hearts in order. We find no extra innings in Hell.

What the globalists failed to see is that we honor God more than we honor the government. We value friendship more than fame or fortune and we would rather die in freedom than live long incarcerated or shackled to a scam not worth living for. I am praying that the globalists will repent and come to God because despite their billions and trillions, without Christ, they are the ones most poor. Hell is too long to be wrong, and I knew the walls were closing and the sand is almost out. #WakeUp

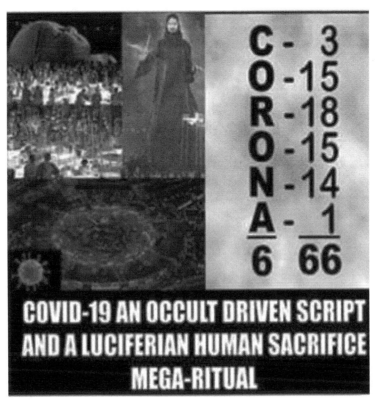

Corona spells 666

THE STAND

THIS year was going to be the most traveled of my ministry. Entering 2020, I was
booked in TEN countries and my dear friend World Wrestling Champ Nikita Koloff
and I were scheduled to tag team and minister in eight of them together. We were both
invited to speak May 25-29, 2020, on a Royal Caribbean Cruise Ship on leadership while
sailing at sea and were going to room together for five days at sea to Bahamas, Honduras,
and Mexico. In July 2020, we were scheduled to fly side by side to Tokyo, Japan serving
as chaplains during the XXXII Olympiad only after the Olympics to fly straight to the
Philippines and minister at a couple churches and large pastors conference. We had a trip to
Israel together in October among others and then the curve ball came.

When I shared to my friend that the event with Darryl Strawberry may not happen, I
was right and more than ever I had to stand up when most were just now sitting down. The
Lord told me three things at the start of the lockdown in March 2020. God impressed on
me, "Get CREATIVE in the CRISIS. Just because you are STILL do not STOP serving Me.
Lastly, Frank you have been in my Army (Lord's Army) but pivot because I need you in the
Air Force."

Instantly I knew what that meant that the Lord wanted me to take back the airwaves
for His glory and we began to pray and press into how that may happen. Beginning in the
second week of March and for the next two months were the most surreal times in my life.
The darkness was so evident in the air and I revealed in a sermon that I had to look outside
more than once to see if the American flag was still flying because our nation had been
hijacked by an invisible agenda. Frankly, I could see it and sense it miles away. Some were

scared out of their mind; others I was appalled at how cavalier and quickly they enjoyed "the new normal." What planet are these folks from? Bless their hearts, Lord knows the majority were not heading towards Heaven while adopting a way of life created in Hell.

You could sense a dreariness in the air and depression was at an all-time high. The thirty plus pounds I had just shed since January after starting that fast would return quickly. The stress and strain were almost too much for me and for a guy who rarely quits I admit let my weight slide while I was boxed in. That will never happen again!

On March 15, 2020, I was scheduled to preach at New Covenant Presbyterian Church in Lewes, Delaware and Pastor Robert is a great guy and he has been a big help while I was leading the Dover Bible study. One of the lawmakers in our study attends his church and is a dear friend. I tip my hat to all the law enforcement and lawmakers who get up every day to honor God and represent their constituents and protect their community. Most churches had already switched to online services, and I went to preach a message that Sunday morning to a nearly empty sanctuary that would be streamed LIVE for their parishioners. Over a thousand watched it online and some said it was pound for pound one of the best sermons they ever heard. Praise God!

You must keep in mind when I gave Michael English the John Riggins helmet I loved "Riggo" since a child, too. He inspired me and many others to run stronger when the game was late and on the line. When most caved and were sidelined, Riggins was running for a touchdown. Just because I generously gave my Grammy winner friend the autographed helmet worth nearly a thousand bucks did not mean I also gave away the inspiration learned by the Hall of Famer and Super Bowl MVP. I was watching pastors quit, throw in the towel or align intentionally or unconsciously with the dark side but I was now not only standing up but stepping out and walking in to preach with greater passion and urgency.

The Lord was allowing me to see through the media lies and it was disconcerting to see how many people, including pastors, were not only coming off message but derailed in discernment. The same group that missed this was also closing their church doors. Yes, every single soul matter to God and only Christ can heal the hurting heart.

BLM founders at heart push a Marxist agenda and recent reports revealed that some of their leadership has been buying multiple houses and some with cash. The New York Post blasted with an article released on April 21, 2021, "As protests broke out across the country in the name of Black Lives Matter, the groups co-founder went on a real estate buying binge, snagging four high-end homes for $3.2 million in the US alone, according to property records." It is bad enough when another race uses and misuses a particular group of people for their agenda but when pastors and insincere neglect their own, it is disappointing. Yes, we have a few bad apples in any line of work and those that abuse authority or derelict in duty must be held accountable. I want to share with all our friends regardless of color that it is never wise to be disrespectful to the police, do not try to run when at a traffic stop and brandishing a firearm is never helpful when dealing with the police. You exponentially put yourself and others at risk when you are disrespectful, resist arrest, disobey initial instruction and act arrogant or violent.

Law Enforcement Today posted in May 30, 2021, "MINNESOTA – a former Black Lives Matter (BLM) activist who now serves as executive director of the Minnesota Parent Union revealed he "learned the ugly truth" about BLM, including the fact that the group has little concern for rebuilding black families and even less for improving education for black children. In a recent video published by TakeCharge, a Minnesota-based, black-led movement that rejects Critical Race Theory (CRT), Rashad Turner described how he became a founder of BLM in St. Paul, but after only a year on the inside of the organization, came to realize that caring for black lives, black children, and black families was the least of the group's concern." God help us! It seems that my friends, including clueless "Christians" and so-called clergy who lacked discernment to see through the Marxist BLM mission are the same crowd who caved to the virus with a 99 percent survival rate and shut their church doors and almost gave up America's rights. They turned their churches into vaccination centers opposed to salvation hospitals and missed Jesus in the process. I have also seen the same camp that has been off on evangelism over the years too. They do not have a heart for souls, discontinue revivals, mock evangelists and were more enamored with building their kingdom than enlarging His. When you are off on all four one must ask the question are they genuinely born again? #Hello

My parents are the salt of the Earth. Everyone loves Mom and Dad, and your heart or head are not right if you don't appreciate Frank & Sharon Shelton. Mom posted this on her Facebook page several years ago and worth repeating today. She is among the kindest souls you could meet but sometimes you must STAND up when folks are wrong.

"Fifty-One years ago tonight, May 31, 1969, Frank and I went to my senior prom at Suitland High School. My English teacher Miss Griffith was at the door checking names on the guest list. Guest list? I had not heard there was one! It turned out everyone who was attending the prom and who was not a Suitland student needed to be pre-registered on the guest list!

Not usually one to challenge a teacher, I did not hesitate that night when Miss Griffith pointed out that since Frank's name wasn't on the guest list he would not be allowed into the prom!

He might not be on YOUR list, Miss Griffith, but he was on the LIST of graduates of this school in 1965; he was on Uncle Sam's LIST when he got drafted into the Army, and he was on the LIST of soldiers who got sent to Vietnam.

Since he just returned home from Viet Nam three weeks ago, we have become engaged to be married, and Frank has been added to the LIST of men who are members of the US Capitol Police,

As you can see, Miss Griffith, we have had more important things going on than making sure his name got on YOUR LIST! She let him in! Sometimes you have just got to speak up and STAND UP!"

A week before I was going to preach to nearly 150,000 Muslims in Pakistan. I was now content to preach to an empty church. If you cannot give your all when next to no one is watching, then you are probably unfit to preach when everyone is watching. For me, it is still an Audience of One but when you get that one right you may stand before millions before it is all over. The next weekend I was scheduled to preach revival at Dunkirk Baptist Church, and it was my first sermon back there in twenty years. It meant so much to return because I served as their youth pastor and Minister of Evangelism from 1999-2001 and at one time, we were one of the fastest growing churches in the Great State of Maryland. Ironically when I left their church and stepped out "by faith" to enter evangelism, one of their deacons said I would never make it as an evangelist. It was therapeutic for me to return.

This revival had been on the calendar for several months and I was really looking forward to it and so thankful Pastor Ben did not cancel. Instead of a packed house I showed up preaching several nights in a row to nearly 700 hundred empty seats while everyone was locked down at home. I knew the evangelists were now stepping up and I felt like I was carrying a chunk of the country on my back. We came too far to quit or slow down and just because Satan wiped ten countries from my calendar did not mean I was going to roll over and die.

It was crazy that I needed a letter on the church stationary proving should I get pulled over that I was "essential" in driving to preach while everyone was emotionally shackled at home. At 48, as I needed a hall pass to drive on the road and the guy who used to drive a congressman daily now had to be chaperoned by Big Brother. When your godmother was part of the hierarchy of the world's most infamous three letter agency and your family lineage was at the top of the food chain in law enforcement, I was God's man, and nobody's boy. That is not arrogant but accurate and sometimes we need to walk in authority while taking back territory.

The Lord was telling me to move forward in faith while the Devil and his minions wanted me stuck in reverse or worse on the couch! Try again Satan but not today. It was wild preaching to an empty room, but I had done both before and during the pandemic so I was used to it but what no one can deny is the same passion was just as strong and possibly stronger. Elvis, Michael English, John Riggins and even Jordan with the flu gave their all every single night and I was not going to let off the gas or run out of it now either.

A true running back will look for any hole to run through to advance the ball and a fireman worth their salt will run up buildings into harm's way while everyone else was running down only to put their life on the line that others may go free. Unfortunately, many of the meetings that were scheduled in advanced got cancelled and that is hard for a man and ministry who lives completely by faith and love offerings. One of the services scheduled in April 2020, was for me to return to Alabama and preach with my dear pastor friend and it was cancelled. Within a few months I would get the news that he passed away due to Covid-19. I never once said the virus is not real but the agenda pushing it was not right and many good people would die and what a legacy he left. My heart ached for his family, and I recalled the Lord telling me to get creative, do not stop and fly above their heads in the proverbial preaching Air Force.

Out of the blue, I was contacted in May 2020 by my friends at Trinity Broadcast Network and they asked me to co-produce a national youth special that would be aired across America featuring some of the biggest names in Christianity. While TBN is based out of Tustin, CA near Santa Ana and I was planning it from my house in Maryland and the Lord really blessed. I could have easily inserted myself to be the main speaker, but I felt like God implied, "bless others" and I picked my dear friend, Tony Nolan to be the guest speaker. We had other well-known leaders and I personally handpicked seventeen youth leaders from coast to coast and let them get some television time and shine. I often wonder could others given the chance in that capacity, have removed self to promote others? I did not even ask that my name be in the credits, and it was an honor to co-produce the show. It was as if I was not even there, and no doubt one of the most rewarding moments in our ministry.

It is imperative to sow a seed before you can reap a Harvest. You need to promote God and others before you get elevated in the process and by being willing to die, we truly live. Two days after it aired, I preached a Mother's Day sermon outdoors at a drive-in service and God moved in a powerful way. The next Sunday I drove one hundred miles to preach at an outdoor event on the water shoreline of Cambridge, on Maryland's Eastern Shore.

It was still volatile and news reports showed almost weekly of another pastor arrested for having church and my cousin was named Maryland Trooper of the Year once but every time one of our state's finest was behind me I could not help but wonder is today the day I go to prison for preaching the Gospel? One of my best friends in ministry had already been arrested in Florida and the same clueless crowd that kept saying they did not see any persecutions towards Christians had obviously never met Christ or were following Him so far behind that they no longer knew Him or could hear His voice.

I had met Chuck Colson at his 75th birthday and my friend Alice Marie Johnson had been released from prison for less than a year, but I was starting to think I would give Chuck, the Apostle Paul and Silas a run for their money with possibly having the next best prison ministry soon. Not for doing wrong but more than ever for living right! Jealousy makes one blind to other's gifting and those who do not know God, cannot stand His associates or kids. Without question, I was a 'kid of the king' and royalty not just because of our connections to presidents at home and a queen across the pond but simply because my sins were forgiven. I had been inside the Pentagon, but the most powerful person is the one used by God. Our society was shifting so quickly, and the sands of time were sliding faster, and police, military or government may try but I was going to keep running until God called me Home or said, "Stop."

While preaching for my dear friend Pastor Abraham Lankford at Gerry Boyle Park in Cambridge, Maryland to a congregation listening intently from nearly two hundred cars, I said in the middle of my sermon with no notes and completely off the cuff, "The Lord said we will see a riot, revival and rapture." Those that know me could vouch I do alliteration in my sleep, but my points are often in alphabetical order. To share those three "r" words in that sequence was God and once again proved right. Within forty-eight hours of saying that in the outdoor sermon near the water on the Eastern Shore, several cities were looting, rioting, and burning to the ground. It is true that if you do not see it before you see it you will never see it.

During that season I was on several faith leader calls with the White House and on one call was POTUS; another call was with Dr. Ben Carson; one call was the Surgeon General and the Secretary of State. I was on another faith leader conference call with the Vice President, but keep in mind I was doing my best to minister to Biden and Ortega, and you do your best to play with the cards you are dealt. On May 30, 2020, I was invited for two hours with my friend, Caz Taylor on his popular "Come Together San Diego" radio show and we were on air LIVE the entire time. We talked about the Deep State and the deep sleep the Church had been in and how I was adjusting while ministering online, in person and on the road. God was indeed faithful, and I am so thankful to all our supporters and partners who continue to help. Ministry is a TEAM effort and we closed out the show praying for Governor Newsome. Ironically, his winery was open on the weekends, but lawsuits were already stacking up against California churches for holding Sunday services.

Governor Cuomo in New York was yelling during press conferences, threatening to shut down churches personally and we have added him and his brother to the prayer list, too. We have no ill will towards any of these who have been extremely excessive in overreach, but you cannot hinder God's anointed and expect to be blessed in this life or the one to come. Let us pray that he comes to faith in Christ before it is too late.

The next day after the radio show in California I was preaching both morning services at Oak Grove Baptist Church in Colonial Beach, Virginia. Pastor Randal Snipes is literally one of the most amazing ministers in America and I am blessed to call him, and his church family friends. They had booked me for several revivals in the past and Randal was one of the rare brothers who was not only standing up to this nonsense but inviting me to preach FAITH > FEAR. When I gave an invitation, we had souls saved and the entire altar slammed with folks praying to God and seeking His help for our nation. One precious woman told me later that the sermon I preached on faith over fear was not only a game changer but a lifeline to her family and in saving her marriage.

Afterwards he asked me over lunch to share with another two dozen leaders exactly where we were as a nation, and they could not get enough of it but obviously had enough of the planned exercise enforced on us by the globalists and misguided government leaders. Yes, the Darryl Strawberry event came and went without happening that same month but where Satan thought we both struck out, God was getting ready to hit a grand slam.

I had worked for an entire year planning a group trip to Israel for June 4-12, 2020, and it was cancelled. I looked for Plan B and another open hole and door. On June 7, 2020, I was blessed to return and preach for my dear friend Pastor Todd Felkel at Bethlehem Christian Church in Altamahaw, North Carolina. I love that brother, and his church has on more than one occasion been a great source of encouragement to this weary traveler. I forever will love him, his family, and that awesome Carolina congregation.

Since Nikita and I were not able to travel the globe as planned, he invited me to go on a men's retreat with him and former World Wrestling Champ Lex Luger at the lake in Kannapolis, North Carolina. Both Nikita and Lex are Godly giants to me and when the three of us get together it is wild! Two champs and this chump, but we are all champions because of Christ. Lex and I wrote a book together in the past called, "The Blessedness of Brokenness" and I love those guys and am humbled to go from being a fan to a friend to now part of the family of God. I stayed five days with them as we chased the heart of God and for folks who think serving Jesus is for losers, try hanging out with some winners in the Lord.

Iron sharpens iron and I needed some additional strength to face the fight before me and who you hang out with is what you become. Now you can connect the dots from the opening words to my first chapter and more than ever I went through Hell while marching forward in faith for Heaven. Durer's painting was etched in my mind more than ever and I was suited up with my armor and marching daily past the Devil, Death and the dreaded hourglass reminding me time was about out. My car had just died on top of the bridge the last week of June and my father and I were stranded between two states above the river waiting for a tow truck.

Where Satan sidelined me once more with the **$6.66** receipt for bottled water, God smacked him in the mouth the very next day when my sermon aired LIVE on television to millions of Muslims in Pakistan. Despite not preaching in person, I was able to preach on television and did not have to fly to the Middle East to do it! Write this down, repeat after me and take this truth to heart: "When you are down to nothing – Jesus is up to something!"

Three days later, my son Andrew and I drove over 900 miles to Tampa to be with Pastor Rodney Howard - Browne's outdoor services. Pastor started an outdoor revival and God gave him a vision to take a Stand. The Bible says, "Having done all to stand!" Not sit, not sulk nor stop but STAND. To know Rodney is to love him and he is the most creative clergy I will ever meet. Everything he does is with excellence, over the top and he could have given tips to Walt Disney because he may not be a mouseketeer, but he is a visionary in every sense of the world. I also love him not only because he is God and generous, but he is spontaneous and hears from the Lord.

He has ministered around the world countless times and preached in some of the world's largest churches and in packed-out arenas and to his credit he was nonstop. The Lord told him two years before the lockdown to go on a 300-city tour coast to coast and around the world. The crazy thing is I think he only missed four Sundays total out of two calendar years from his home church as he was ministering world-wide. Yes, I was on staff with the Billy Graham Evangelistic Association and linked with Luis Palau's young evangelist program and met some other generals of the faith but the last six years since meeting Pastor Rodney not only helped prepare me but strengthen me when the bottom fell out.

Pastor Rodney and his team were on city 185 when the lockdown happened. He knew as well, as both a pastor and evangelist at heart, that the walls were closing, and time was escaping. Then came clueless clowns mocking him (and I am talking clergy) who could not compete with his relentless schedule to see souls saved. You cannot but take an inventory of what they and folks like me were doing prior to the Covid-19 scam to see how they pivoted quickly and excelled during the crisis. It is worth repeating but LOL used to mean "laugh out loud" but lately it meant lack of leadership. Those that did not have a backbone in 2020 did not deserve a microphone in 2021 and I am still getting private messages from folks who are deeply disappointed in their church and are never going back. Some of the biggest churches had the smallest spines or discernment and praying for them but we are not looking back. Some churches are still closed over a year after the lockdown. They preach about a God who is triumphant, yet they missed the mark and His mandate to, "STAND and OCCUPY "until He returns!

Let me park the car here and brag on God and how He used and continues to use Pastor Rodney and his staff at The River. Liberty Counsel wrote on April 7, 2021 "Pastor Who Was Arrested Ignites Revival." Liberty Counsel Founder and Chairman Mat Staver said, "Despite the discrimination and punishment from local officials, Dr. Rodney Howard-Browne has taken a courageous stand and not allowed government oppression to stop the incredible revival that is happening at The River at Tampa Bay Church. The church underscores what we have said from the beginning. The Church is more than a podcast. Churches should be so essential that when the lights go out and the doors close, the community groans in its absence. This is certainly true of The River at Tampa Bay Church."

WHILE YOU WERE SLEEPING (or sitting) read the rest of this story penned by Liberty Counsel, "As a result of a pastor experiencing arrest and criminal charges from local officials who were discriminating against houses of worship during COVID-19 lockdowns last year, his church has not only thrived but flourished. On March 30, 2020, in Florida, Dr. Rodney Howard-Browne, pastor of The River at Tampa Bay Church, was the first pastor in the world to be arrested because of government restrictions on churches during COVID-19. Pastor Howard-Browne was arrested for holding a church service on March 29, 2020, regarding the Hillsborough County Executive Order that went into effect the previous on Friday, March 27, at 10:00 p.m. The two charges were second-degree misdemeanors that carried a maximum penalty of two months in jail and a $500 fine. Following this arrest, Liberty Counsel began preparing a federal lawsuit that was set to be filed on April 2. However, on April 1, 2020, Gov. Ron DeSantis issued a statewide executive order declaring that attendance at churches and houses of worship was an essential activity. He also preempted every local order to the contrary. On April 2, 2020, Hillsborough County officials met and voted to reverse its order from law. The charges against Pastor Howard-Browne were later dropped.

Since the date of Pastor Howard-Browne's wrongful arrest on March 29, 2020, the church has reached people in 168 countries with the gospel through their broadcasts, had 50.8 million views and 186.2k new followers/subscribers. In addition to their Sunday services, they broadcast live to 250 million homes worldwide by television six nights a week. As a result, 6,913,464 people have embraced a relationship with Jesus Christ.

After Pastor Howard-Browne was arrested, he laid Astroturf on part of the parking lot the size of nearly two football fields. He began outdoor revival services on Pentecost (the last Sunday in May 2020) that have continued six nights a week for three and one-half hours each night. This is in addition to a four-hour Sunday morning worship service. Attendance at The River has grown so rapidly that the church has decided to permanently cover the portion of the parking lot used for these outdoor services.

Locally, during this one-year period since March 30, 2020, the church has fed over 13,000 families with its full-scale aquaponic garden center and tilapia fish farm. Church members harvest and package the food and deliver the boxes to needy families throughout the highest crime areas of Hillsborough County. Each week, The River provides free food to 900 people who attend the Sunday service. In addition, over $114,000 was invested into families in the inner city and twenty families and/or ministries were presented vehicles.

In one year, the church has transported 21,211 men, women, and children to church services and baptized more than 1,200 people. In the week between Palm Sunday and Easter, its six-day missions in Honduras and the local soul winning team saw over 2,000 people trust Jesus Christ for salvation. The River Church has also equipped thousands of people with educational opportunities which include scholarships to attend River University in Tampa."

As humiliating as it may have felt at the time, Dr. Rodney Howard-Browne's arrest was the best thing that could have happened as it motivated many of his friends including me to step up, take a stand and strengthen our spines. The Church and authentic leadership excels in the storm not the sunshine and when it begins to rain down here, we must remember who reigns up in Heaven.

Over the years, Pastor Rodney had invested in so many lives around the world that they were starving for leadership and started to come to his home church after his arrest. People do not want someone perfect, but someone who will have a spine and who is not corrupted to the core or a false narrative. His staff initially tried to rent a fair ground or property where they would put up a tent. Instead, God gave him the vision to buy artificial turf and erect a stage, state-of-the-art sound system, jumbo screens and place chairs socially distanced as far as the eye could see. He did not crisscross the country and travel the globe to stop when the planned demic hit the fan, but he would proclaim the Gospel message and be winds to many sails. For nearly three hundred nights they are still meeting on what he named "The Field of Dreams." The Son was shining more than ever in the sunshine state! When many in ministry were cloudy and confused, his brief incarceration brought a clarity and laser -like focus to reach the lost at any cost while precious time was ticking.

Truth be told, and I told him later in person that his arrest may have been the best thing that could have happened to our country and countless clergy like myself. His arrest gave us freedom to preach with greater passion and urgency. His brief incarceration loaned liberty to us and what was to be his shame brought glory to God's Name. Billy Graham said when one make takes a stand it strengthens the spine of everyone around him. My Dad taught me not to back down and Pastor Rodney did as well. I am so thankful for Pastor Marvin Harris and all those past and present men of God who have mentored me and played a huge role in my life.

While in town for the July Fourth celebration, I ran into my childhood friend Brian Collins. He is the Vice President of a Christian television network, and I am so proud of him. Several years before, I had a television ministry called BY FAITH with Frank Shelton and we had twenty-seven half hour programs. We were gaining traction and touching lives on television, but we had to temporarily stop airing due to lack of the funds needed to purchase the airtime. We had the funds for the first season but had to pause after the second. However, the Lord told me to trust Him, and He would work it out. When we force something, it is usually not of God. That is why Pastor Rodney and Adonica named their church "The River" because when it is of the Lord it flows. For four years, somehow the files that contained those twenty-seven programs were lost and nobody at the television network could find any of them. At the time, our television show was airing to 15 million homes weekly and on Dish Network. It was disappointing that those shows were missing but even if I had them, I didn't have any money to put them on the air.

This is the work of the Lord! Say this with me again: "When the Devil is messing, God is blessing." It goes both ways because I used to only think the Devil came after a promotion but the next time you hit a wall it may be God fixing to bless your socks off! That is more than prosperity but a REALITY! Plus, what you do for others God may do for you. The TV show that I just helped produce start to finish with TBN and felt led of the Lord to not be featured even though I could have or tried to get my ministry out there, I wanted to honor others. Basically, I sowed it away and God as my witness, no less than two weeks later I got a call from the station manager where I used to film my television show in Fort Myers, Florida. He exclaimed, "Frank, you are not going to believe this! My wife was cleaning up in our studio and we just found ALL twenty-seven of your shows!"

When you give something away, the Lord has an amazing way to bring something back! The good news was they found the recorded shows, but the bad news was I was still running on faith spiritually and fumes financially with no budget to air them. That was in May and early June, but now the first week of July during that lunch in Tampa with my friend Brian, he asked me over our meal and out of the blue, "Frank, do you have any of your old shows?" I about fell off the stool at Cheesecake Factory and said, "As a matter of fact, I do." He said, "I feel the Lord wants me to help you and if you get them to me, I would like to start airing them four times per week on our network to nearly 50 Million homes on DirecTV, Dish and cable across America!"

This Baptist turned Pentecostal and almost fell out and off the chair! Somebody say, "AMEN!" It was not an accident that my giving away television time for others allowed an entire television show to come back to me. What I was trying to bless others with, the Lord resurrected for me to be on multiple times per week on a major network. Worship is often letting GO and you can really sing His praises when you find Him faithful. Like I told the pastor years ago, "Most may out finance me but very few will out faith me." When you are linked with God you will do things that money cannot buy, or agencies cannot market.

Sadly, most churches and Christians have no clue how to honor others or be generous. Until we give unselfishly, we will be stuck without joy or progress. After returning from lunch, it was back at the Stand and what a treat to bring my son on this trip! It was an honor to bond with him on that long trek and it was good to have my wingman with me.

It was an honor to sit or stand with Pastor Rodney and just like his evangelistic crusades, he was packing them in as a preacher but either way he would take the crowd to the cross, Christ and His coming again. If more pastors would get past pride and be willing to pay the price personally, they too could be more effective professionally. Until we can complement others, we will be a complaint to those around us.

While I was still in Tampa, Pastor texted me while I was at the hotel with my son and out of nowhere, he said, "Frank, I want you to preach for me tonight on the Fourth of July." The tyrannical public officials across the country had suspended America's birthday but the man originally from South Africa loves our land as much as anyone and he would not be deterred from lighting up the sky with the Gospel or fireworks! To my knowledge, they were shooting off the biggest fireworks display in all of Tampa and no prior arrest or threat would stop my buddy.

My friend John Morgan the presidential impersonator was able to join us, and we are good friends and had a trip that was scheduled that October four weeks before the election, but Covid-19 sidelined that trip in 2020. John brought the house down even though we were outdoors, and I had the honor to tag team preach with Evangelist Jonathan Shuttlesworth who also stepped up tremendously during this crazy time. FACT: The ministers who were both Biblical and bold saw God's favor exponentially and just like the fireworks soon to shoot upwards, both Jonathan and Pastor Rodney's ministry skyrocketed.

After a gracious introduction, I took the mic from Pastor and preached my heart out. I preached how we must stand for Christ, The Church and Constitution. I said that Christianity is not a spectator sport. That capacity crowd was right with me and I reminded the audience and viewers at home around the world that guilty folks and sick folks wear the mask but the rest of us were not guilty but were sick and tired of the charade that ran its course. I learned immediately afterwards that the sermon I just preached was airing live to over 100 million homes around the world! I was glad they told me after and not before, but God honors those that speak Truth.

Pastor is one of my dearest friends and it was after the near thousand-mile trip home with Andrew that the next day the book that I had been writing was deleted from my computer. I had written 235 pages in three months and was just two chapters away from the editing process last July and it was gone! The only file missing was the brand-new book, and I will let you try to guess where it went or why it went missing but Microsoft Edge automatically downloaded an update that I did not request and the only file to disappear was the file containing the book. I did not dare share on social media what happened because I did not want to give the Devil a premature victory. Having to re-write this from scratch was one of the hardest things I have ever undertaken. However, I knew we had to press on and this preacher does not quit.

The late Jerry Falwell had a sign in his office that read, "How do you stop the man that won't quit? You can't!" God's child is very indestructible until the Lord is done with them. After a car died on top of a bridge one Saturday and the book was deleted the following week, the very next Saturday for the trifecta is when I started to re-write this book I was bitten by a snake in my garage. You cannot make this stuff up and it was evident the Lord wanted you to read this, and the Devil did all he could to stop it, but the truth always come to the top and I am just delivering the mail.

On July 25, 2020, I preached twice in Aurora, Indiana and not many were flying but I never dreamt that America would feel like a third world or communist country, but I could see it and feel it and this patriot did not even feel welcomed at home. However, some people only play well at home but when you are linked with God you can be good at home or away. The enemy of the state was being fulfilled but I am just a pilgrim passing through and we still had some work to do. However, the more Satan played games, or I was harassed at home or the road I just made the Devil pay. If he were smart, he would know when to let others alone but the faithful just pick up their game to another level.

After flying home from Cincinnati, it was apparent that my trip to the Philippines was cancelled and once again resembling an open door I called my good friend, Pastor Randal Blackmon at Faith Baptist Fellowship in Cambridge, Maryland. They are precious to me and though their church may seem a tad small from the outside, they love God and their community in a BIG way. God does not waste a trial and had I been in the Philippines I would have missed out on the miracle the Lord was getting ready to pull off.

They were excited to hear about my program airing every Monday on DirecTV and Dish, but I told them another network mentioned for under $10,000 per year I could reach another 180 million homes on several continents. With social distancing in place, I preached a message that I had not ever recalled preaching and God was on it out of the gate. I asked a question after I gave the invitation, and we had a couple souls saved. I asked of those precious saints in that church whom I have fallen in love with and preached revival before, "How many of you believe evangelism is important?" They all raised their hands. I said, "How many of you believe God could come back real soon?" They all raised their hands and then I gave them a proposition.

The Lord just opened a potential door that I could air my television ministry to 180 million homes weekly. The church of under one hundred that day grew excited. Their eyes looked like they were going to pop out of their sockets and then I said, "If I had an address for 180 million homes do you know how much that would cost with a normal first-class stamp?" I said approximately $90 million dollars! If I were mailing a postcard once it would cost an ungodly amount of money to promote God only to be glanced at and tossed in the trash. However, we just were offered a chance to air the half hour show every week for an entire year with me preaching the Gospel including the cost of airtime and production of new shows for $10,000.

Faster than a Ferrari I shifted gears and said if you could buy a house that was worth $180 million dollars only to find out it was reduced to not $90 million but $10,000 how many of you would think that was a great deal? EVERYONE'S hand went up and when they took the love offering, that country church led by one of my heroes of the faith collected $7,800! Thanks to Brian Collins on Monday and that Maryland church on the Eastern Shore, we are now reaching millions of homes on multiple continents. When you are down to nothing – God is up to something!

The very next day my television ministry aired on DirecTV and Dish and then on Tuesday, August 10, 2020, I had a busy day. That morning I had a conference call with the U.S. Department of Education talking about drugs and at noon I was a guest on Total Christian Television out of Marion, Illinois sharing Christ in a Crisis to their world-wide audience. On August 12, 2020, I was a guest for half an hour with my dear friend Brenda Epperson who is a Hollywood actress and an amazing Christian wife and mother. She rocks and it was a pleasure to reunite with her on the show. We went to the United Nations for a meeting the year before and her discernment is through the roof.

On August 16, 2020, I had the honor to return and preach morning and evening service at Everett Assembly of God in Pennsylvania and they are some dear friends. God shook the place and pastor was so complimentary of my message and ministry. It is a high honor to minister to minsters privately while in town and that month God still had me preach in multiple states. Things were picking up for those standing up and too many ministers were muzzled, and I am not just talking about the mask.

On August 27, 2020 I was a guest for half an hour on Nikita's national podcast and we had the best time, and that message went across the country and several countries. It is interesting over the years at a sports or toy store, and you see posters, jerseys, bobbleheads of athletes or stars that you are friends with or are contacts in your cell phone. It is humbling, but surreal at the same time and I was told long ago that who you respect is who you attract.

When Satan tried to lock us down, I was going to help shut him up and was getting ready to do more damage. No, it would not be at the Olympics or Israel, or cruise ships or stadiums like in the past or as planned during 2020, but I was going to pivot to the times and come out swinging like Balboa after hearing the bell. On August 29, 2020, I spoke at New Heart Ministries in Newark, Delaware pouring into their leadership. Then on August 30, 2020, at 9AM I preached at Experience 447 Church in Cambridge, Maryland and God was all over that service and several called on Jesus for salvation, including a millionaire. I then raced across town and preached at Jesus Church International Church at 11AM. Once again, that was two churches in one Sunday morning and like John Riggins I was not slowing down but warming up. The very next day our "BY FAITH with Frank Shelton" TV ministry was airing four times on two networks to 50 million homes across America. Satan's plan to try to stop the Gospel was foiled again big time. Praise the Lord!

On September 5, 2020, I was invited to officiate the renewal of the wedding vows of my dear friends Bob and Rebecca Forgy in Bedford, Pennsylvania but had to reschedule. They have been a huge comfort to my family and ministry over the years. Their counsel has been priceless, and prayers mean more than all the gold in Fort Knox. Becky had a hand in helping get Steve Perry at the helm of "Journey" during a transition and they soared to top of the charts. She reminded me more than once directly and directly, "Don't Stop Believing!" Thank God for friends and family who cheer you on and wind to your sails.

On September 6, 2020, I was invited to preach the morning service with my good friend Pastor Chris Dito at Parkview Assembly of God in Newark, Delaware. On September 9, 2020, I spoke at the funeral for my dear friend Mike Saul at Grace Baptist Church in Bowie, Maryland. From weddings to Sunday sermon to funeral in a couple days, I know what Paul meant when he was all things to all men to win some. We weep with those that weep and rejoice with those who rejoice. September 10-13, I was invited to be the keynote at ELEVATE Global Leadership Conference in Los Angeles, California, but that event was temporarily postponed due to Covid-19.

Since that door closed at the last minute, I had to do what any good running back would do, and that was to pray and then once again to look for the open door to advance the Gospel ball. It was a joy to reunite with my good buddy, Pastor Dennis at Bethel Tabernacle Church in Frankford, Delaware, and God shook the place! We had been working relentless on that city-wide tent revival with local pastors, but it was cancelled due to the corona but Pastor Dennis and his bride, Kathy were serving nonstop, and I was thrilled to stand with them as we prayed to reschedule.

On September 15, 2020, I was on another flight heading west to Seattle, Washington and invited to preach at THE STAND hosted by Pastor Debbie in Olympia. Pastor Rodney's personal stand encouraged many others to start their own across America and I ended up preaching with Pastor Debbie and Greg Locke and other well-known ministers. John MacArthur was not my cup of tea theologically but one I respected and when he took a stand, I was willing to stand alongside those who were not sitting down. In war, you tend to fight with folks you never thought you would but praise God we are on the winning team.

Those two nights I preached in Seattle were a blessing and despite the cooler temps outdoors the Lord warmed hearts and saw souls saved and delivered. After returning on September 17, 2020, I had a meeting at the U.S. Department of Education as my friend and I serve on a national task force helping to combat human trafficking. Afterwards, we had another private meeting with a retired Lt. General in his office combatting trafficking and there is nothing like being in the trenches with some soldiers who are not afraid to stand up to the enemy.

By God's grace, prayer warriors and financial supporters, we were able invest in another television ministry and we were now not only on television four times on Monday on two networks and Thursday to 180 million homes but now an additional network starting every Saturday at 7AM across the US, UK, Africa, and part of Asia. One channel had me right after Jim Bakker, another right after Billy Graham classics and the other after Pastor Steven Furtick from Elevation.

We also began to invest in radio and thanks to Wilkins Radio in South Carolina, Salem Radio Network in Dallas, Texas and WWGB in Washington, DC, our BY FAITH Radio show was now airing across America in seventeen cities. We also run our show every Sunday morning at 10AM out of Nashville, Tennessee on Worldwide Christian Radio and that goes to 80 nations. Someone asked why my radio show is only fifteen minutes and my initial answer was because I could not afford thirty! I also knew that God gave me a gift to say more in fifteen minutes than some could say in an hour, and some called me the human Twitter feed. Plus, Elvis always left the crowd wanting more not less. #ThankYaVeryMuch

Yes, the trip to Pakistan was cancelled in March 2020 but Eternal Life TV Network graciously called and wanted to start airing my thirty-minute television ministry every Friday at noon and midnight to multiplied millions to the precious people of their country. Just like I prayed for the Taliban then, I now believe that God will save them by the precious blood of Christ before it's too late. Only God could write this script and despite not preaching in person to ten countries in 2020, our ministry is now reaching over 250 million homes on four networks and four continents every day of the week somewhere on the globe.

God honors those who take a stand, and I was doing my best to take the airwaves back for His glory. I love that song as a child, "I may never march in the infantry, ride in the Calvary or shoot the artillery. I may never zoom over the enemy, but I'm in the Lord's Army." Thanks to God's grace, the generosity of God's people, and good old-fashioned determination and perseverance I am also now in the Lord's Air Force!

On September 21, 2020, I had a meeting with World Wrestling Champ STING and NFL Hall of Famer Ray Lewis as we both serve on a task force against human trafficking and Lord willing, planning for a trip to Israel in Easter 2022. On September 24, 2020, I did a LIVE radio show with my good friend and fellow Olympic chaplain Randy Shepherd and on September 25, 2020 was invited to be part of a pastor's VIP luncheon in Virginia. The next day, September 26, 2020, I was back at the National Mall for Franklin Graham's Prayer event and even though I am no longer on the payroll it was a treat to reunite with some of the Graham family and staff. That night I was invited to speak at a fancy hotel on Capitol Hill for a well-respected pro-life organization and the Lord promotes life while the Devil promotes destruction.

October 4, 2020, I was blessed to return and preach for my good friend, Pastor Paul at North Glen Community Church in Glen Burnie, Maryland, and God moved in a powerful way. Thank God for those who support your ministry, and they are first class! Another trip to Israel I was diligently working on was cancelled for October 5-12, 2020, due to Covid-19 and travel restrictions, so I pressed on and preached October 9, 2020, at a local Christian school in Southern Maryland and then preached October 11, 2020, at The Fellowship Church in White Plains, Maryland. Just the year before, I had the high honor to be asked by Dr. Billy Graham's son-in-law to co-lead the evangelism summit in Montreat, North Carolina in Dr,Graham's office.

Our second event was cancelled for October 12-15, 2020, but we hope to try again soon. October 23, 2020, I had the honor to officiate my double cousin Stephanie Shelton's memorial service and October 25, 2020, I preached at Bible Fellowship Church in Newark, Delaware and God rocked the house! On October 25, 2020, we helped lead chapel online with Southern Maryland Christian Academy and on November 1, 2020, I preached three straight services at Soul Quest Church in Jackson, Tennessee. I love Pastor Ronnie Coleman and they are doing BIG things there! Early the next morning I caught a flight to Atlanta and preached that night at a large church in Roopville, Georgia with some Grammy winners and the place went nuts!

You may recall the awesome church in Jamestown, North Carolina that had hoped to give the $33,000 the previous year but with all that was happening in our own ministry they at the last second gave to another worthy group. It hurts and when you were told it was coming it was another curve ball with a swing and a miss. Their pastor is one of my heroes and God does all things well in his time. He assured me the next year they will designate the gift to us but when the Covid-19 hit, church attendance was hit, too. As we got closer to their annual giving in late October, he shared in the summer the truth is our attendance is nowhere near what it was the year before. However, I have good and bad news. I recall thinking what could be worse than getting nothing the year before and he said this year we want to help six groups instead of just three. The good news you are one of the six, but we are not dividing the offering by three but by six. My heart dropped again but God is our source and no one else, but He certainly uses others to help.

He went on to also share that although our attendance is way down our giving is up! He is a phenomenal preacher and leader and then I was praying if the Lord could feed five thousand with a lad's lunch maybe the He could double their giving from the previous year in a pandemic. That next week when they gave would you believe that generous church raised over $170,000 in one offering? Someone suggested that since we were evangelists with a heart for souls and living completely by faith, they added a little extra to our gift, and the check was not $33,000 like the year before but was $35,000 in the pandemic! Truly, God can do above and beyond all we ask or think. Praise the Lord and what the Devil meant for heartache blessed us in His perfect time.

On November 7, 2020, I was invited to preach at an event with a well-known artist and Judah 1 Airlines in Nashville, Tennessee, but that got cancelled. Instead, I flew into Johnson City and preached for my dear friend Dr. Todd Holmes and for two nights was guest evangelist at THE STAND in Tri-Cities Tennessee. I love Pastors Todd and Katy and they are doing phenomenal things and he used to be the Dean of the River Bible School with Pastor Rodney in Tampa.

After returning to Washington, DC for one full day I was back at the airport the following day for a flight to Pensacola on Thursday, November 12 to preach at the Men's Barn Meeting in Molino, Florida. Two local real estate moguls host an incredible evangelistic outreach the second Thursday of every month and nearly five hundred men show up weekly. It is nestled on a gorgeous water view property, and they even have alligators on the premises. Inside this massive barn the men are treated to a steak dinner, and they come in by the busloads. They cook the food on the property and fathers, sons and even some homeless show up to be treated to some incredible praise music, testimony and they fly in a guest speaker almost monthly. Over the last couple decades, they have seen thousands repent of sin and trust Christ as their Savior. That evening we saw thirteen souls give their life to Christ and Florida had begun to open before many other states and their governor has done a fantastic job.

Pensacola is "home of the Blue Angels" and with all my traveling it would be nice to sit in the back of one of their F18 hornets. Getting to work and worship would be quicker than ever and you could certainly make up for some lost time in those planes. After a great lunch with the founder of that event the following day on the water of a popular restaurant it was time for me to head back towards the airport for my flight. We did talk to two Navy pilots that were dining a couple tables away and thanked them for their service. They represent the best of America and were flying high. It was sad that some of the government was playing low and could use a fresh touch from Jesus.

Despite our massive tent revival postponed because Cov19 I was invited to preach a two-day revival in Frankford, DE and with time ticking I did only what God called me to do and that was keep moving forward, get in and lift Jesus and we had more souls saved! On November 21, 2020, I was back at The Fellowship Church in White Plains, MD and I love Pastor Marvin and Dona Harris. They are incredible!

Local governors were encouraging to remain at home for Thanksgiving and sadly many families were still afraid to congregate. It was a sad time in America and millions of families did not make it home to be with loved ones either because of restrictions, fear, or finances tight. President Abraham Lincoln made Thanksgiving a national holiday and despite the craziness in the air and tension on the ground we went by faith had Thanksgiving at a friend's beautiful log cabin on top of the mountain in Upper Tract, West Virginia. The log cabin was named The Evangel house and was nearly two hundred years old but with state-of-the-art appliances inside. Ironically, each room was named after evangelists from the past including Spurgeon, Wesley, Moody, and others. You could say we were right at home, and it reminded me of the classic TV show, "The Walton's."

Very convicting read by Charles Spurgeon: "*Today, as aforetime, you stand idling. Some of you, indeed, were in a more hopeful condition thirty or forty years ago than you are at present. What account can you give of yourselves? What has become of those intervening years?...*

O sirs, 'the time is short,' the business urgent, the crisis imminent! 'Tis madness to be halting between two opinions. If God be God, serve Him, and if not, take the alternative and serve Baal. Let your mind be made up, one way or the other, without another moment's delay. How long halt ye between two opinions?"

The greats know exactly what time it was and that mountain top experience away with my family to be rejuvenated and reconnected what just what the Great Physician and for that I did not need a national holiday to remind me to be thankful. My friend, Steve Wingfield owns the property, and he for years has been a chaplain to NASCAR. We agreed on the mountain to try and return the following year and celebrate Thanksgiving again. It overlooked two ponds and on 530 acres you can really connect with nature and the Lord. John Denver was right to sing about Colorado and West Virginia and the mountains and beach are good for the soul.

Our third trip that was scheduled for the Holy Land in 2020 as we were to initially fly to Israel on November 30 – December 7, 2020, and despite the tyrannical leaders and fear paralyzing the world I was still marching on in God's Army and flying in His Air Force. Regarding fear, I found it interested that the same people who a decade before boasted big bumper stickers on their trucks and car, "NO FEAR" were now scared out of their minds.

Jesus said when He returns would He find faith on the Earth? Sobering words from our Savior in Scripture. He will with our team and since departing the Graham organization the year before we finally started our own nonprofit ministry. Despite the pandemic, church doors limited, received no PPP or unemployment we pressed onward and upward. I do not think I worked harder in one year and it was not just traveling while others were stationary, but we poured into thousands daily on social media with content encouraging folks across America. We did Facebook live, even had communion online and prayer meetings to minister to friends and strangers and scores watched.

Between recording new radio shows and editing television episodes for our television ministry we went from the twenty-seven original episodes that were lost and now found to creating another eighteen-half hour shows to be aired world-wide. My dear buddy, Caleb in North Carolina is a video genius and since most television studios were not taping due to COV19 we pieced together past sermons, added content, and packaged them as if we filmed in a million-dollar studio.

In addition, I was still helping lead the Bible study in Dover and already in talks of assisting in Annapolis weekly. I had now been on about a dozen White House, Department of Education and other faith leader calls and was privately ministering to ministers. Thankful for our generous partners and our ministry led of the Lord to sow into others. Some clergy and Christians have a hard time parting with $50 but we had given nearly forty thousand dollars away in missions and ministering to others in the middle of a lockdown like Riggins we were running for a touchdown. Once again, opposed to worrying about me I was blessing others. Dr. Luis Palau's the world-famous evangelist was battling cancer, but his ministry asked me to lead a once a month zoom call to mentor and minister young leaders across America.

One week, I taught integrity, another responsibility and flexibility. Until folks can grasp faith and generosity, they will never make it or go to the next level. It is by giving your all to God and others that you experience victory, and most are stuck in a rut opposed to advancing the Gospel and taking back territory from the enemy.

On December 5, 2020, my son accompanied me to Elkton, MD and we connected with Pastor Brian at River of Life Church of God. After a great dinner that Saturday evening we stayed in a hotel and reunited with his church family and preached both morning and evening services on December 6 and God shook the place. The altar was full, soul saved, and congregation thrilled, and Andrew even prophesied to the church that evening a word the Lord gave him. I was so proud, and the pastor invited the child not yet a teen to return and preach. Jesus was twelve in the synagogue teaching and holding lawyers in the palm of His hand. Some things never change.

After returning around eleven that evening it was a late night for a school night the next morning and I left at four the next morning to drive three hours to co-lead a meeting with Delaware lawmakers as we advanced and grew our Bible study. It was great to see some new faces in our midst and my friends, Rev Morris Webster and Pastor Robert Dekker have been invaluable in that ministry with me from day one.

On December 12, 2020, I was back in the air once again and this time to Jacksonville, FL and would be in town for two days of meetings for helping create Christian television network and then on Sunday morning preaching at Cedar Bay Baptist while in the sunshine state and after a delicious lunch with Pastor Jeff and his friends I was flying back north. My friend, Dr. Paul Pitts is a world renown tenor and he sung the stars down as I lifted the Son (JESUS) up that morning in Florida and I am so thankful for him, his wife, Annette, and our dear friend Jonathan Goodwin who is connected to everyone in Nashville. It was a treat to have all three of them in attendance that morning.

Two days before Christmas, Andrew and I left with excitement in the pouring rain at four in the morning and drove eight hours to Myrtle Beach, SC to give our daughter her gifts while she is at the community college. We are so proud of her, and God does all things well in His time. After eight hours up we stayed the night in the same hotel that Andrew and I had stayed when I preached both years at the Big God Conference. While in the room that night I learned my dear friend and former colleague who led the Bible study for lawmakers in Nebraska had just died from Cov19. My heart dropped and without question the virus is real and it targeted those with weak immune systems.

We are up against a culture of death and knowing it was released intentionally we as Christians were not going to cower to the enemy. The Bible says, "it is appointed once for man to die and then the judgement" and it was time for my dear friend to go Home. He ran an incredible race and I cherish his wife and their family. He was the real deal and looking forward to reuniting soon.

The next morning, Andrew and I grabbed breakfast and I was back on my diet. I had one egg and one piece of wheat toast, three glasses of water and one cup of black coffee. As I pulled out the parking lot, I got a call from an old friend who was now a Special Agent with the United States Secret Service. We graduated from high school and played basketball together and I always knew he would do well.

During that forty-five-minute call he shared to me before closing, "Frank, I am so proud of you and know at one time you were up here and considered joining us, but God has you right where He wants you and you are doing the big work and don't stop." Coming from him meant so much and on that day my special agent friend ministered to me and after a long trip home we were celebrating Christmas at home.

This year, I would not be returning to preach to 120,000 in Uganda but was invited to preach in Los Angeles. My good friend, **Apostle Fred Berry** and his wife, **Wilma** for over a decade have been pastoring at the famed church that God sent revival in **1906**. The Lord used that extended meeting to not only birth a Pentecostal movement but bring racial unity that was fractured previously. Pastor Fred and I served as chaplains at the **2012 Olympic s** in *London* together, **2016** in *Rio* and were scheduled to have been in *Tokyo* for the **2020 summer games** but Cov19 threw a curve. Fred is both a preacher and evangelist but also a true visionary and he has his pulse on the present, finger on the future but knows his history from the past. He graciously invited another cherished friend and fellow evangelist **Randy Shepherd** to also come minister and he has been at six Olympics. The three of us were on hand to be part of this incredible move of God and Fred invited **SEAN FEUCHT** to some lead worship on his **"Let Us Worship"** tour that culminated the last day of the year in Los Angeles.

I knew that trip and invitation would not be a cakewalk and only someone who had preached around the world, stood in stadiums in Africa, ministered in Nicaragua and was willing to go toe to toe with the Taliban could see and smell similar obstacles. I must confess flying into Los Angeles was intense and it resembled a flight into a communist country. Our country had changed so quickly that I almost did not recognize her anymore. Pastors were arrested, church doors locked, and the spirit of the anti-Christ was breathing in the air.

In the last days what was good was now evil and Fear Factor was not only a past popular show but a way of life for billions on planet Earth. Faith and fortitude could also have been my middle name and it was daunting preparing for that trip. To the clueless citizen of callous Christian, you could not comprehend what I was up against the last few years but particularly the last nine months was almost suffocating. Walmart was more bearable because indeed the bullseye from Target was on my back.

Prior to departure I was getting updates that the airlines were threatening to do manda-tory testing either arriving or departing while in the United States and LAX was on the list as hot spots. I prayed that I would be unseen to those looking for anything and for a guy who embodied grace it was easy for the over-reaching government trying to make the conscien-tious feel guilty. The tests had also been proven inaccurate and while others were trusting science, I was going to trust the Savior.

Even at the baggage claim I could pick out my two new "friends" who were on the flight and one who happened to sit in the next row to my left. They both stood at different ends of the baggage claim, and I could see I was in their sights and once again I could sense in the supernatural "Target" was both on my back. It is no longer a complaint but compliment and in the last days good will be called evil and some of our own government is corrupt. I had seen this game before in my recent travels and just to keep them on their toes I went up to both on my way out and thanked them for their service. Once again, while they stood hundred feet apart publicly at the baggage claim with me in their sights as I waited for my ride at the curb they exited together. It seems that those that watch from afar are afraid to get eye contact with you when you confront them up close. Cowards run but the righteous can lovingly but boldly walk up. Today, it a badge of honor to be on the Devil's watch list and when you have been with the best you can see the flaws of the rest. That includes both national and local levels and they better pick a side soon because time is running out.

Most people have no idea how intense it has been to bring the Good News in these turbulent times. The thought of folks like me now considered an enemy of the state to some was looking like a dark cloud but I still promote and certain the Son still shines and if folks keep following my prayer is that they may find Jesus in the process.

Los Angeles was no longer near as clean as it was when I was child on that first flight out west to meet Sly Stallone in 1985. You know it is bad when he just moved two weeks later in the new year and put his drop-dead gorgeous Beverly Hills mansion up for sale at $110 Million. I never thought he would leave but the Governor's harsh restrictions, massive tax proposals and disrespect for the normal American way of life led to many leaving in droves. It is not that Rocky, or Rambo did not put up a fight but sometimes you must move on to warmer climate and clean air leaving and the Stallone Family are now living the dream in the Sunshine State.

A local realtor in Tampa told me on the phone that they were considering naming New York Governor Cuomo the "Florida Realtor of the Year" because his lack of leadership forced and encouraged tens of thousands of New Yorkers to fly south not for the winter but permanently. Notice that those craving freedom are heading to a state with a governor that is about opening society not controlling it or running into the ground.

Had I not answered the call to preach I may have very well run for office, but I assure you it would not be to sell out, get rich, or piously be a dictator at my fellow friends and citizen's expense. True leadership thinks of the next generation not the next election or popular polls and we need more statesmen not politicians. After saying goodbye to my two entry level friends that watched me afar and stood miles away on that Southwest flight the moment, I turned the corner to catch a ride by my fellow Olympic chaplain friend it was evident the community resembled more of the city of death more than angels. It is so true that everything rises on leadership and the people rejoice when Godly leaders are in place.

The second thing I noticed is not what I saw but could smell the heroine could be tracked a block away before coming to tent city and the glamor of Hollywood in the distance resembled the grit and grime of New York city streets. I kept thinking that Speaker Pelosi's San Francisco and we were getting ready to swear in Kamala Harris from Los Angeles and both these powerful leaders were running our nation and could not even clean their congressional district and respective state. Let us pray for them and their families personally and all of us collectively. If you are a professing Christian but politically line with death to America, babies, Constitution, small business and closing churches following Science more than the Savior and prefer a reset over revival and lockstep with globalists more than God you better look long in the mirror. It is more than being right politically but not left out spiritually.

A special shout out to my friend Pastor Matthew Barnett who is the eternal energizer bunny when it comes to serving his Los Angeles region. This brother and his team at the incredible L.A. Dream Center fed over one million meals during the lockdown and they even beat Chick-Fil-A when it came to service with a smile. Another thing I will never forget about those few days in California for the New Years' service was while in town we stopped at Rodeo Drive. Stallone used to frequent a popular restaurant frequently called "Café Roma" and I had dined once or twice before hoping to reunite with my childhood hero only to find out his house was already on the market and they were flying both east and south.

Governor Newsome made it next to impossible to eat and not only did he block folks from dinning in due to a planned demic that medical organizations declined for years to justify it as a "medical pandemic", but his tyrannical orders wouldn't even allow dining on the street. Nearly all tables and chairs were removed, and I will remember this as long as I live. We finally found a Cheesecake Factory opened on Rodeo Drive arguably the most expensive street in the world in downtown Beverly Hill with the Hollywood sign suspended in the hills not far only to pay full price and get a carry on bag with plastic plates, forks and water and he sat on the curb. After saying grace my buddy and I along with others are eating many sitting down on the curb while looking at the palm trees lined up in perfect unison and despite the Lamborghini, Ferrari, Porsche, Mercedes, Range Rover and Bugatti parked near me we all resembled being homeless as far as the eye could see. That is not leadership but lack of leadership and no wonder folks with a brain and can see through the charade are jumping ship and leaving town.

Hollywood was always fake to begin with and so happy some stars are seeing the light and Gina Carano may have been cancelled by Disney, but the Mouse will regret it in the long run because when she succeeds for standing for truth the rest will be "Goofy" for letting her go. She is not only beautiful but bold and she is a fighter both in and out of the ring and more than ever kudos to folks like her who stand up not shut up or sit down. Rock on Gina!

Speaking of a wild man with the heart of a champion and faith fueled in the fire. God has used Sean Feucht and his praise team greatly while boldly but lovingly preaching the Gospel and praising Him during a pandemic. The boldness comes from being right with God and understanding the urgency of our times. Sean had run for Congress in the past and thought maybe that was his mission but where he thought he may have a *seat* in Washington the Lord wanted him to make a **STAND** across America.

Sean wrote, "If I were to ever pick up a guitar or speak publicly again, I would need to find some ground to stand on. Like Jacob in the book of Genesis, I was willing to wrestle with and not let go of God until I was wounded at the hip. It was far better to live with a limp the rest of my life and be authentic thank fake it and walk straight." Faith > Fake and Fear all day long and stand tall he did! After the tragic death of **George Floyd,** the Lord impressed Sean to show up in select cities with his guitar and turned the riots into revival. Prayer and praise extinguish problems and protests all day long. What George Soros help fund Sean showed up by faith on a mission from God and wanted to shine a light in a dark time. Antifa cannot compete with the Almighty and yes "black lives matter" but the song still is true, "red, yellow, black and white" they are ALL precious in God's sight.

On Memorial Day (2020), I was preaching an outdoor service in Maryland and said, "God showed me we would see **riots, revival** and then the **Rapture**." Three days after that statement cities were literally burning to the ground. I was booked to preach in TEN countries last year but the "planned demic" tried to halt our mission but you cannot stop The Message. After just preaching in five cities and five days in Nicaragua in February and invited to preach to 150,000 Muslims in Pakistan and then Tokyo cancelled the Olympics, I was not going to sit idle and do nothing. After prayer and praise and nonstop preaching on radio, TV with multiple "drive in" worship and occasional indoor service when the invite came to spend New Year's Eve in California, I was in my mind already on the next flight. That day last week was EPIC at Azusa Street, and I had the honor to minister there once before a couple years ago while still on staff with the **Billy Graham Evangelistic Association,** but I knew Los Angeles was where I needed to be. Pastor Fred and Sean planted a tree to display racial harmony and then after a couple pastors prayed the PRAISE kicked in. God showed up and the streets were packed! Folks were atop a neighboring building worshipping with us below while a CBS News Helicopter circled above to film for their television audience that night. Souls were saved, addicts delivered, and the hurting found Hope.

Pastor Fred made a great point, "**We are so concerned about being six feet apart when we should be more scared of being six feet under dead without Christ**." The virus to date as a 99% recovery rate but you have ZERO chance apart from salvation in Jesus. It has been aptly said, "Hell is too long to be wrong!" In my sermon that night I preached, "Last year, I preached in Nicaragua at the invite of President Ortega's wife. I did not go because I am a Communist but because I am an EVANGELIST. In March 2020, I was invited to fly alone to Pakistan and preach with the Taliban on the roof tops, but Cov19 cancelled the outdoor crusade. If you think I was going miss preaching in Los Angeles tonight you are wrong! Regardless, if at home or aboard we preach the Gospel saving message, "Jesus loves you and He's the only way to Heaven." I then concluded, "**Los Angeles, I have Good News! God loves you!**" The crowd erupted with applause. God showed me the lies of the Devil in advance and as you can see by the picture below that Wuhan China where the virus was released had capacity crowds for New Year's Eve while America was shut down. While our Congress is debating on *gender pronouns* and tyrannical leaders demanding *lockdown,* we figured it was time to watch God score a *TOUCHDOWN*!

Thankful for Pastor Fred's leadership and Sean's worship and it is a privilege to be in partnership with likeminded ministers who are willing to against the grain, reject the status quo and stand in the gap with a guitar and God's Word. I was voted the nicest in my class as a kid but lately been one of the boldest as an adult. People need Jesus and while most of the world play it safe, we are sharing **JESUS SAVES**! The Holy Spirit showed me a year ago that 'soul winners' would be labeled as murderers for meeting. The Bible says, "Don't despise the assembling of yourselves in church especially as the Lord is closer to appear" and where we get falsely labeled as wanting to kill people in fact, we have a front row seat to watch God save souls." Lately, some of the biggest churches have the smallest spine and if we cannot worship God in the lockdown, we may not be used to preach as an ambassador for God with or without a microphone in days to come. We are praying for all those in authority, but God and His Gospel are essential and if you must wait for the government to say you can worship than we may have a long wait. People are hungry and hurting but HELP is on the way because we preach Jesus is The Way, The Truth and Life." **We do not need a vaccine made by man but preach salvation and healing found in the Blood of the Lamb**.

Ironically, on a building in the alley where the worship was held on Azusa Street was a mural of Michael Jordan. Randy has been friends with MJ for thirty-five years and in town where everyone as of late has been doing it for KOBE we are doing it for The King of Kings. Happy New Year praise the Lord and God bless California, our country, and the citizens of all continents. People need the Lord and let us roll!

More than ever the Church must take a stand for Christ and the Constitution. We have the right and privilege to assemble, and God wired us for community and fellowship. It is not healthy to humanity to lock them up. Shepherds need to be with their flock and people are starving for touch and hungry to live free. This new proposed, planned and diabolic roll out neither honor God or will help society. The Church hiding behind the eight ball will continue to rack if not out front. In these late hours, I am imploring every pastor to get back in their prayer closet until you have found the power of God to return a renewed minister. Of course, the elderly or that sick can stay home but you do not advocate shutting down the church or country for a few. Do not throw away the Gospel Truth because of a lie you have failed to see. A.W. Tozer said, "Outside the will of God, there is nothing I want. And in the will of God, there is nothing I fear." Perhaps some of your stress is because you are trusting science more than the Savior. You are enamored with "Fake News" and not meditating on the Good News. Stop looking down and look up where our Help comes from. We find peace when we ponder The Prince of Peace.

Professor Klaus Schwab at the World Economic Forum said, "The pandemic represents a rare but narrow window of opportunity to reflect, reimagine, and reset our world." #GlobalReset #Planned the Church is not to play dead but stand strong and love loud. We are a welcome mat but not a door mat and you cannot change culture comfortable on the couch. We need to get up, stand up, roll up our sleeves and show up and look up because God will soon split the sky and too many are failing to no longer try.

FACT: The Federal law prohibits employers and others from requiring vaccination with a Covid-19 vaccine distributed under Emergency Use Authorization. The problem is some folks do not believe that the rules apply to them. Politician's blood thirsty for control and dollars would sell their mother to dominate the world's brother and sisters. Consider guns. Those who commit crimes with or without guns do not adhere to the law and outlaws are not deterred with what is or not on the books. Our only Hope is in Almighty God.

One of the saddest things etched in my mind during all this is our amazing son, Andrew. When school was gearing up in the Fall of 2020, we were on campus the day before school started. The next day, he would start his first day of middle school. I remembered when I was moving up to junior high and it was daunting, and I knew he had some fears too. The Governor and other mandates were strongly forcing a mask, but only guilty or sick people wear one. I have been so proud of my son's faith in this entire ordeal. He was with me while we were on campus, and he was not wearing his mask but keep in mind the school year would not start until the next day. The two of us were walking through one of the trailers when one of the teachers saw us and opposed to say with a smile, "Welcome Andrew!" or "Are you ready for the big day tomorrow?" She scolded, "Andrew where is your mask!!" I mentioned in this book about my "welcome to the neighborhood" and "welcome to Washington" but bless his little heart this was his "welcome to junior high." To make it worse it was a Christian school, and I can now see why Jesus asked, "Will I find faith when I return on the Earth?" Those who taught faith were now struck with fear and Andrew told me after with tears because he did not want the teacher to have the luxury to see she hurt him with that disrespectful greeting, "Dad, I knew I would be stuck wearing that stupid, Satanic mask the next day, but I just wanted a little bit of freedom before tomorrow." That little kid has more faith than most adults today.

The demonic forces behind this planned demic will not only have to apologize to God when they bow before Him and confess, He is Lord before burning forever in Hell, but they owe billions of children world-wide an apology for causing great havoc to their world and well-being. Countless students who hoped to get a good look at college sports scouts did not have the chance to receive a scholarship and the opportunity of going to college may have slipped through the cracks. Many have grown into a deep depression, isolated from their friends and Andrew's fifth grade graduation was cancelled for the first time in the schools near forty-year history. He received his awards in a brown cardboard box. The fact is that his school is amazing, and the leadership is first rate, and they did their best under the circumstances but when you are getting your marching orders from the CDC and county it is tough.

I have had to remind myself repeatedly that this Earth is not our home, we are just pilgrims passing through and Heaven is looking more attractive by the day. Plus, God will soon pass out all the awards and it will not be rushed in a cardboard bus through a car drive in line. One of the teachers on staff who often publicly said to my son in front of his peers that he may get them sick had something interesting happen to them. What was egregious is when teachers start encouraging young students to take a trial vaccine and when she boasted of getting the shot, she got the COV19 symptoms and had to quarantine for two weeks and my son never once had to self-isolate. The Bible says, "the thing Job feared the most came upon him" and I do not believe in Karma, but I do believe Christ settles all scores and faith is greater than fear all day long. I am praying that the rest of us will grab on to a measure of faith because millions are missing it. Without faith it is impossible to please God.

A couple years ago, my family was invited to attend the advanced screening of the movie "I Can Only Imagine." MercyMe is one of my favorite Christian bands and at the event was Bart Millard and the entire band and we were standing in line, and he walked by and that was one time I wanted to grab him, say hello, and thank him for his ministry but everything happened so fast it did not happen. The movie was incredible, and the song is arguably the most played Christian song in modern history, and some suggest all time on radio.

I love many of their hits! I spoke at an event called ATLANTA FEST with them the following year but did not get to connect. Often one artists or group is exiting from one end of the stage and another artist or speaker is coming up the other side and do not always get to connect. That was the second time I was close but like the hourglass the sand slipped through my fingertips. One of their more recent songs "Almost Home" is one of my favorites and Galatians 6:9 reminds, "Let us not to grow weary in well doing for in due season we will reap if we faint not."

"Almost Home" By Bart Millard and Mercy Me

Are you desperate for help?
You know what it's like to be tired
And only a shell of yourself
Well, you start to believe
You don't have what it takes
'Cause it's all you can do
Just to move, much less finish the race

But don't forget what lies ahead
Almost home
Brother, it won't be long
Soon all your burdens will be gone
With all your strength
Sister, run wild, run free
Hold up your head
Keep pressing on
We are almost home.

Well this road will be hard
But we win in the end
Simply because of Jesus in us
It's not if, but when
So take joy in the journey
Even when it feels long
Oh, find strength in each step
Knowing Heaven is cheering you on

We are almost home
Brother, it won't be long
Soon all your burdens will be gone
With all your strength

We are almost home
Almost home
Almost home
We are almost home."

Sister, run wild, run free
Hold up your head

Keep pressing on
We are almost home

I know that the cross has brought Heaven
    to us
Make no mistake, there's still more to
    come
When our flesh and our bone are no
    longer between
Where we are right now and where we're
    meant to be.

When all that's been lost is made whole
    again
When these tears and this pain no longer
    exist
No more walking, we're running as fast
    as we can consider this our second
    wind.

Almost home
Brother, it won't be long
Soon all your burdens will be gone
With all your strength
Sister, run wild, run free

Hold up your head
Keep pressing on
We are almost home
Almost home

SECRET SOCIETY

THE HIDDEN HAND
The Masonic hand gesture

George Washington — Karl Marx — Friedrich Nietzsche — Baron von Knigge — Pope Francis

Masonic Sign — Frederic Bartholdi — Joseph Stalin — Napoleon — Barrack Obama

Lafayette — Edgar Allan Poe — Mozart — Robert E Lee — Charles Darwin

I‍T is hard to stand up to something if you do not know why you are standing. Furthermore, it is even more difficult to stand up and face something if the enemy is invisible. The first page of this book I intentionally wrote Scripture. My words are something, but God's Word is everything.

> *"For we wrestle not against flesh and blood, but against principalities, against powers, against the rulers of the darkness of this world, against spiritual wickedness in high places (Ephesians 6:12)."*

Everyone believes in something. Atheists have a belief in the false commentary that God does not exist. The same Being they swear is not real and yet they use His holy name in vain on a frequent basis is the same God that they spend multiplied millions of dollars taking to court and trying to keep out of school. Why? Their conscience is pricked, emotions infuriated and lose sleep at night tossing and turning over a Supreme Deity they are certain does not live. If they really believed that to be true, then why fret, toss and turn and spend gobs of money trying to disprove God's existence? Intentionally I ended with a question mark to their question because Christ lives, and He is The Answer. Notice how no one ever takes Buddha or Confucius' name in vain? Do you know why? Because they are dead, and their name has ZERO power. The name of Jesus is the Name above ALL names.

Since the beginning of time and the fall of man, a dark, demonic force has been present, and a war has been raging ever since and the final fight is coming soon. I have said for years that it was not the fruit in the tree but the *pair* on the ground that wrecked it for humanity. When Satan the snake tempted Eve, sin was birthed into the world through a woman who was yet to be pregnant. Instantly Adam and Eve's sin became our sin and that same sin separated us from a Holy God. I have said before, but I believe it is worth repeating that I often wondered if the Apple logo bearing the bite out of it was not a tip of the hat towards the enlightened or educated but to when Eve ate the forbidden fruit.

While researching this book I came across this fact. Mr. Stephen Wozniak priced the first Apple computer. Their marketing slogan for the advertisement was, "Byte into Apple for $666.66." They did not even hide it! God opened my eyes to see that just as the born-again Christian has an anointing on them there is a demonic counterfeit that tries to copy on Earth what God in Heaven made. Satan is a copycat, but Christ is the Lion of the Tribe of Judah. Satan is a wannabe, but the Savior is King. Lucifer is a loser, but the Lord wins forevermore!

God revealed to me that one of Satan's primary conduits that have wreaked such havoc on the world is a *secret society*. The Bible says, "What is done in the darkness will be revealed in the Light." Indeed, we do not wrestle against flesh and blood and *principalities*, powers, and darkness. You will soon see that the secret club is not only Satanic at its core but demonic in its duties and brings ultimate death.

In 1961 President John F. Kennedy gave a powerful speech exposing the secret society. He said, "The very word secrecy is repugnant in a free and open society, and we are as a people, inherently and historically, opposed to secret societies, to secret oaths, and to secret proceedings." In just two short years, the youthful and charismatic leader of the world would be gunned down in downtown Dallas. President Kennedy also vowed to dismantle the CIA into a thousand pieces and yet he had multiple bullets blow off part of his skull. Many Americans believe that he was the last true Democrat. Despite his imperfections he did want the best for America.

Counter-culture Mom, Tina Marie Griffin has been studying the occult for three decades and she said recently, "FREEMASON – A member of an international order established for mutual help and fellowship, which holds elaborate secret ceremonies. It is a fact that that Freemasons help rule and own the entertainment industry. If you want to go UP, then they insist you must be "down" with the Devil. Did you know that fourteen out of the first forty-three United States Presidents were Freemasons? They are a cult with connections to the

Illuminati or with the fabled Elders of Zion as part of anti-Semitic claim that Jewish bankers control the world's governments. The symbolism we see in our culture associated with this cult are hands over the eye, the triangle sign that many celebrities form while on stage and on TV shows, and specific handshakes. We must continue to stay awake to the demonic, satanic cults that are being shoved in our face."

I have learned those that are 'woke to culture' are asleep to Christ. #Boom The Freemasons and other cults parade by day as a charitable group wearing women's aprons, jewelry, and funny customs but a recovering and rogue Mason who forsook the oath, repented of his sins by the blood of Jesus received Christ as his personal Lord and Savior attested on record these startling observations. For starters, the Masonic Lodge is a veiled filtering system that leads to full blown Satanism. Secondly, consider a farm team developing baseball players you have the minor leagues (A, AA and AAA) and a select few will one day play in the Major Leagues.

It is no different with those who climb the ladder or pyramid in route to selling their soul to become part of the hierarchy of the Masonic Lodge. The truth is there is an invisible side and public aspect of this secret club, and they are known to at times be a band of brothers but also withhold information from one another. They will also lie, if need be, to others and one another. The entire structure is built on a lie because they do not collectively know the true Christ, who is Truth and all powerful. They have bought the lie that Satan is all powerful, but it is Lucifer who is a weakling and far inferior to Jesus, The Christ.

Sadly, we have corrupt cops, judges, attorney generals, politicians, athletes, religious leaders, businessmen and entertainers who have sold out to a Satanic system. My friend in Texas called with me while researching this and said, "Frank, I was taking a tour of a courthouse near my home one day and the man was boasting about all the Masonic symbols in the courthouse and courtroom. He must have thought I was a Mason, but he elaborated with passion and in great detail with pride how the certain dimensions of the court room was done in accordance with the Masonic measurements." If you have ever wondered why there seems to be little justice in a courtroom this would explain some of it when you have folks who do not seek truth, blinded by their own ambition, linked with Lucifer, and can be paid off and bought out. Even Pontius Pilate tried to wash his hands of Christ, but all the crooked attorneys, judges, pastors, politicians, and mankind past, present and future will have to give an account for every idle word before Almighty. The Bible says, "it is a dangerous thing for sinners to fall into the hands of a Holy God."

Nearly gone are the days when an innocent boy or girl with a dream can go to Hollywood and with talent and integrity intact, reach the pinnacle of their profession. Hollywood stars, NBA, NFL, heads of state to name a few are part of this dark society and by pimping out, they got promoted up. Frank Sinatra and Sammy Davis, Jr were Freemasons. No wonder old blue eyes signature song was "MY WAY." I was told that is the national anthem of Hell. Those who boast in life they did it their way will realize they missed God's way and are on the fast track on the highway to Hell. Even Jay-Z has been wearing a Luciferian shirt promoting "Do What Thou Wilt." It is the motto of the dark society and the aged old song with a modern twist.

The irony is that those who think they are free are enslaved. Half of the Freemasons name implies a stone, but they are not building on the Solid Rock of Jesus, The Christ, and Master Carpenter. They are still playing in Little Leagues and striking out for not being with Christ in the Major Leagues. They thought they were swinging for the fence only to realize they struck out on God's genuine salvation of grace and faith. Satan is the father of lies. Countless celebrities both past and present have been seen with the "hidden hand" or covering one eye to reveal the all-seeing eye. Dr. Anthony Fauci at several White House Press Conferences could be seen with his hand in coat revealing this symbolism. No wonder their motto is, 'trust the science" when in these perilous times we need to trust the Savior.

Katy Perry, Justin Timberlake, Jay Z, Brad Pitt, Lebron James and Kobe Bryant throughout their careers sadly at times had prominently revealed their worship for the dark one. Not saying you cannot change but the cult and Satan's grip is strong. Timberlake said, "Satan is my Master." My heart breaks for them all and Heaven is still a prayer of repentance away. God still allows U-turns! The finger over the mouth is also a tell-tale sign and Confucius wrote, "*Signs and symbols rule the world, not words or laws.*" Look on countless magazine covers and once you know what to look for you will never miss what was in front of our eyes all along. In their mind, particularly those who reached the thirtieth level up {with thirty-three being the highest), grow darker and more demonic as they climb in the Masonic misguided club. They take an oath to stay secretive and never share points or tell strategy that would expose or undermine their devilish ways.

In this Christ-less cult, you could find politicians on both sides of the aisle. Some of the biggest names in media and movies are not only dabbling in but are deep into the bowels of it and find false satisfaction from it. It is true some good folks still exist in the world and political arena but too many in politics are contaminated and feel stuck. At times we are dealing with a two headed snake. One former Mason said, "**Masonic Lodge = Satanism**." He elaborated they read from a sinister script and have sold their soul to Satan, and they believe they are not only superior to others, but they are above the law. If need be, they are trained to mislead, malign and even murder to further their agenda.

The power that they possess and promote is powerful. The satanic stronghold on them is incredible and the success Satan is willing to lavish upon them is almost intoxicating. We have folks who earned millions, billions and heading towards a trillion dollars. Do you think they got there without demonic help? The Bible is clear, "what would it profit a man to gain the whole world and lose his own soul?" Even if you had wealth and fame for a few, fleeting decades why trade that for guaranteed endless torment in a lake of fire? They failed in the game of life and took the bait while Satan ate the cheese.

A story recorded centuries ago in Africa where someone could be picked from obscurity and rise to the level of king. For two years, he would live in a palace, have the finest clothes, scrumptious food, lively parties, and women galore. The only caveat would be exactly after his two-year term, regardless how much the community loved him; he would be executed. Do you know there was never a shortage for folks "waiting to be king" and they would be willing to lose it all after selling out and kissing the ring of the enemy? I submit we find a similar proposition that is older than time itself and Lucifer is still playing from the script and scores are willing to line up before they die down.

On President George Washington's monument, it mentions that he was a Freemason above the fact that he was Commander in Chief. President Harry S. Truman said, "Although, I hold the highest civil honor in the world, I have always regarded my rank and title as Past Grand Master of Masons the greatest honor that ever came to me." He took the picture wearing his apron. It is brainwashing and idol worship to put anything above God.

The aprons are part of the Mason's uniform. It protects the Mason's private parts. Behind closed doors some in the top tier have enjoyed sexual acts and they value the male penis. The erected monuments in cities across America and around the world and the seeing eye is to be symbolic of both being "all knowing" and the tip of the penis that shoots out sperm. Their compass with the G in the middle is to portray both man and woman having sex. The "G" has been known for 'geometry" but some suggest it stands for sexual generation. Their compass and *ordinances* play a big part in charting date, time and some believe the fate of their followers without God's intervention and their followers finding God's saving redemption. Keep in mind about compass and ordinances when we unpack Kobe Bryant's death later in this chapter.

Thomas Paine, who despised Christianity, wrote a book entitled <u>Age of Reason</u> that is beloved and worshipped by the Mason community. In fact, it was his desire to <u>exterminate</u> Christians. He also was a Free Mason and Adolf Hitler was a thirty third degree mason as well. It is no accident that we are dealing with an agenda of death. Interesting enough that Hitler was named TIME magazines "Man of the Year" in 1938. The man that killed millions of innocent people was celebrated and it will be curious to see what globalist they pick this year. Paine desired to usher pain on all his opponents, and he wrote about the New World Order.

The Georgia Guidestones are large blocks standing in the middle of nowhere and they record that the world's population should be reduced from over seven billion to a mere 500 million. The elites, globalists and demonically possessed see humans as trash but Almighty God sees the world as His treasure. Satan wants to discard you, but the Savior died to deliver your soul.

Walt Disney was a thirty-third degree Mason. Peter Pan could be seen as horny and what was disguised as a cute cartoon was grooming grounds for pedophilia and every evil thing. Mickey Mouse wore white gloves and the Masons often do as well. Just because hands may be clean on outside doesn't mean their hearts and minds are clean on the inside. When you spell MICKEY upside down it looks like WICKED. I always thought it was tragic when so many in church circles and Christian leaders bragged on Disney and often mimicked their leadership model. I knew as a kid they were off and often the same folks bragging about the Mouse did not have their HOUSE in order. They were wrong on evangelism and often dead wrong on discernment. No wonder too many of our churches are closed during the pandemic because they were not truly open to the Living Lord.

The logo of the World Economic Forum with their three O's reveals the veiled 666. Google has the Satanic triple six in their logo and when you look at the dollar bill under the pyramid with MDCCLXXVI we find Satan at work. M=1000. C=100. X=10 and that equals 1776 the year America was founded. When you subtract 1000-100-10 from 1776 that total is 666. DC=600. LX=60. VI=6. They also add up to <u>666</u>.

The United Nations logo has thirty-three segments to represent the 33 Mason and Satan is their god. They have a picture of their god Lucifer in the hallway at their headquarters in New York City in their large edifice pointing to the sky. I have been in the building! Referencing thirty-three, keep in mind that a <u>third</u> of the angels fell from Heaven following Lucifer and the thirty third are symbolic of the Devil's angels. Freemasons believe they are free of guilt, free of sin and free (void) of Jesus, the Christ. Some pastors are deep into this as well and they are no different than a store front church pretending to be an authentic preacher of the Gospel and House of God. No wonder during the planned demic they caved like a deck of cards because they were either complicit, compromised or do not truly know Christ.

The United Nations has been linked for years with 'Lucis Trust' and in short it stands for Lucifer Publishing Company. It was founded in 1922 by Alice Bailey and it is no surprise she was a Free Mason. George Orwell's best seller, <u>1984</u> had a seeing eye on the cover of the book and he wrote, "If you want a vision of the future – imagine a boot on your face." We have had Presidents, Vice Presidents, Popes and even royalty across the pond deep into this demonic culture. The Bible talks about a cashless society and in 2021 *Business Insider* wrote, "Releasing its annual global payments report, FIS noted the trends towards a cashless society only accelerated during the Leadership pandemic. Ninety-eight percent of all payments nationally projected to be cashless in 2024." For my clueless friends who do not think a cashless society is coming, well it is.

David Spangler, United Nations Director of Planetary Initiative, Lucis Trust Member, Outspoken Luciferian and no surprise here, Freemason said, "*No one will enter the New World Order unless he or she will make a pledge to worship Lucifer. No one will enter the New Age unless he will take a Luciferian Initiation.*" The Devil tried to get Jesus to bow the knee to Him and said, "I will give you the whole world if you worship me." Christ turned him down on the spot and this world has nothing on the goodness, grace, and glory of God! Earth is not our home! Wake up slumbering saint! Wake up those who are sleepwalking the past year the Lord has granted the world with one last wakeup call, and we conveniently hit snooze or worse waltz through our day apart for our directions from the Divine. We are sheepishly following a wolf dressed in sheep's clothing to the slaughterhouse. While you trust the Science, Dr. Fauci's track record during this storm is weak at best. Plus, it is proven that more people have died from this un-tested vaccine than all others combined in last twenty-five years. Why not trust the Great Physician who has not lost a patient yet? How can you trust a team that worships Science when they don't even respect the Savior who created science? #Boom

Yes, Kobe was in the middle of a big pharma lawsuit, but *Gematria News* noted, "Kobe Bryant death predictive programming. Legends of Chamberlain Heights, November 16, 2016   https://gematriaeffect.news/kobe-bryant-death-predictive-programming-legends-of-chamberlain-heights-november-16-2016-kjv-1611/

Los Angeles Times – The helicopter, a Sikorsky S-76B built in 1991, departed John Wayne Airport at 9:06 A.M. Sunday, according to publicly available flight records. The chopper passed over Boyle Heights, near Dodger Stadium, and circled over Glendale during the flight. The crash occurred shortly before 10 AM near Las Virgenes Road and Willow Glen Street in Calabasas. Authorities received a 911 call at 9:47AM, and firefighters arrived to find that the crash had ignited a quarter acre brush fire in steep terrain, said L.A. County Fire Chief Daryl Osby. Responders included 56 fire personnel – firefighters, a helicopter with paramedics, hand crews – sheriff's deputies.

According to the *LA Times*, Kobe died at age 41, 41 minutes after his helicopter took off, in LA, which has a Gematria of 41 (LA = 15+26 = 41). It was reported the helicopter took off at 9:06 and crashed at 9:47.

As for the 9:06 AM takeoff, that connects to 'Lakers' and 'LeBron'.
"**L a k e r s**" = **96** (Reverse Ordinance)
15 26 16 22 9 8

"**L e B r o n**" = **96** (Reverse Ordinance)
15 22 25 9 12 13

"**F r e e m a s o n**" = **96** (Reverse Ordinance)
6 18 5 5 13 1 19 15 14

About Freemasonry and the chopper crashing at 9:47, on a date with <u>47</u> numerology (1+26+20 = 47), the Masonic Compass is set at 47-degrees in tribute to the 47th Problem of Euclid, and it is a number that many masonic rituals are conducted around."

Right now, there is much chatter of Kobe the Legend. They even have a special on Hulu about this subject within hours of his death. Notice 'Legend' has Gematria of 47.

"Legend" = **47** (English Ordinal)
L e g e n d = **47**
12 5 7 5 14 4

Keep in mind Kobe's most well-known teammate, a man who is a Freemason himself, Shaq, is 47-years-old right now, and Kobe died a span of 41 days from his upcoming 48th birthday. *Freemason = 48 / 96

Read about the death of Shaq's sister October 25, 2019, in a "47 ritual": https://freetofindtruth.blogspot.com/2019/10/25-47-74-97-233-shaqs-sister-dies.html

Coming back to the word 'legend', it turns out a cartoon titled 'Legends of Chamberlain Heights' predicted in advance Kobe Bryant's helicopter crash on November 16, 2016, The specific episode was named 'End of Days.' Legends of Chamberlain Heights is an American adult animated sitcom and aired on Comedy Central from September 14, 2016 to August 20, 2017. https://en.wikipedia.org/wiki/Legends_of_Chamberlain_Heights#Episodes

The cartoon showed the world in advance and predicted that Kobe crashes in a helicopter in the *8th episode of this show, which released November 16, 2016. Keep in mind his Lakers jersey was the number <u>eight</u>.

Watch the clip here: https://www.worldstarhiphop.com/videos/video.php?v=wshhvZiWANr4zpEG2Byx

Notice it emphasizes Kobe's 5 rings, as they come off his fingers in the accident, and the two trophies. At the time of Kobe's reported death, along with his 13-year-old daughter, this image with the 5 behind both is being shown. Interesting, it had the Masonic Lodge logo on side of the chopper.

The initial reporting was 5-dead but has since changed to 9-dead. 5 to 9?

*Black Mamba = **59** *Negro = **59** *Slave = **59** *Freemasonry = **59**

The writer for the episode was Grant DeKernion, summing to 74, and here we are in the 74th NBA season, 2019-2020.

"Grant DeKernion" = **74** (Full Reduction)

"G r a n t **24** D e K e r n i o n **50** = **74**

7 9 1 5 2 4 5 2 5 9 5 9 6 5

Kobe is the latest 74-33 ritual. **Kobe = 11+15+2+5 = 33**

Jesus = 74; Cross = 74; Messiah = 74; Gospel = 74; Parables = 74

The episode was called End of Days, and this death comes just before Super Bowl 54, Super Bowl LIV (150).

"End of Days" = **150** (Reverse Ordinal)

E n d **58** o f **33** D a y s **59** = **150**

22 13 23 12 21 23 26 2 8

"Super Bowl LIV" = **150** (Reverse Ordinance)

S u p e r **56** B o w l **56** L I V **38** = **150**

8 6 11 22 9 25 12 4 15 15 18 5

"Kobe Bean Bryant" = **54** (Full reduction)

K o b e **15** B e a n **13** B r y a n t **26** = **54**

2 6 2 5 2 5 1 5 2 9 7 1 5 2

"Freemasonic" = **54** (Full reduction)

F r e e m a s o n i c = **54**

6 9 5 5 4 1 1 6 5 9 3

The cartoon released on Kobe's <u>86th</u> day of his age, and he died on a date with 67 numerology, after leaving from an "86 airport"

Kobe Bryant's Date of Birth – August 23, 1978
From and including: Tues, August 23, 2016

To and including: Wed, Nov 16, 2016
Result: <u>86</u> days
It is 86 days from start date to end date, end date included.
Or 2 months, 25 days including end date

Alternative Time Units
86 days can be converted to one of these units.

7,430,400 seconds
123,840 min
2,064 hrs
86 days
12 weeks 72 days
23.50% of 2016

Word or Phrase Full Reduction Reverse Full Reduction
Blood Sacrifice 67 86

They are reporting the 'legend' departed from John Wayne Airport, having a gematria of 86. And when you think John Wayne, think Hollywood…

The helicopter that crashed amid foggy conditions Sunday in California, killing all nine aboard, including basketball legend Kobe Bryant and his 13-year-old daughter, looped around several times and rapidly decelerated and accelerated during its chaotic final flight, air traffic records show. The Sikorsky S-76B lifted from John Wayne Airport in Santa Ana at 9:06AM local time, ascending into fog so dense that even the Los Angeles Police Department and county sheriff's department had grounded its helicopters.

https://nypost.com/2020/01/27/
inside-the-final-flight-of-the-doomed-helicopter-carrying-kobe-bryant/

"John Wane Airport" = **86** (Full Reduction)
J o h n **20** W a y n e **23** A i r p o r t **43** = **86**
1 6 8 5 5 1 7 5 5 1 9 9 7 6 9 2

For more helicopter predictive programming read about this 2011 Nike short film, The Black Mamba, where Kobe Bryant takes out the villain, Kanye West, on a helicopter, with a basketball bomb.
https://bleacherreport.com/articles/620757

Kobe Bryant is, "The Black Mamba". Directed by Robert Rodriguez.
"<u>NBA</u> superstar <u>Kobe Bryant</u> of the <u>Los Angeles Lakers</u> made his return to the big screen

last week February 19, with the world premiere of "The Black Mamba," directed by Robert Rodriguez.

Bryant, who previously starred in "Kobe Doin' Work," an ESPN documentary movie directed by Spike Lee in 2008, found himself for the first time faced up to the challenge of projecting a fictional script.

The movie's main objective is to promote Nike's Zoom Kobe VI shoes, which more than any other in the Kobe shoe series epitomizes on the image of The Black Mamba.

The Black Mamba movie revolves around the very character and essence of Bryant's alter-ego, The Black Mamba—a moniker for the legendary side of the five-time champion fans and players alike claim reveals itself when Bryant is at his fiercest and deadliest mindset.

The nickname Bryant has been bestowed with, is derived from the large, venomous and swift African snake with a likewise name.

The movie takes to the theme of switching to and from between and within the imaginations of Bryant and Director Rodriguez to form mental images of each scenario they visualize.

The Black Mamba begins in an office like setting, with Kobe Bryant getting up from one of the present lounge chairs to greet the approaching Robert Rodriguez.

The two share a customary handshake, and each take a seat on their respective sides. Bryant wastes no time and immediately inquiries about the word of Rodriguez's idea for a movie. Rodriguez then proposes his thought of making a film about The Black Mamba—Bryant's alter-ego.

The imaginative scene begins at nightfall, with Bryant getting off the Los Angeles Lakers' team bus on a supposed game night. Unlike the usual routine he has grown accustomed to in his experience as an NBA athlete, Bryant is left to wonder about his particularly chilling situation and why there is nobody aside from himself around the town or on board the bus.

Bryant's common sense leads him to understand that the safest thing to do would be to re-enter the bus and await assistance, but before he is able to execute the task, the possibility of it is immediately compromised, as the bus suddenly explodes without warning.

Bryant is luckily left unscathed and thus forced to venture deeper into the town—in search of potential help—in the middle of nowhere.

As he walks on, he finds a rather large figure of a man facing the other direction, wearing a black leather coat, with long hair.

Director Rodriguez dubs the said man as "The Crippler," whom he mentions that hopefully actor Mickey Rourke would portray (The Crippler is instead played by action star Danny Trejo).

The mysterious figure turns back to reveal the man with unexpected monster-like arms and tells Bryant that a man named The Boss wants his Nike Zoom Kobe VI shoes. Bryant promptly responds by saying he is still using them, but the intimidating man reveals himself to have a hostage—a little Jack Russell Terrier dog that is blindfolded and leashed to a pole on the street.

Bryant is not pleased with the immoral hostage taking and decides to put up a fight.

Unfortunately for him, The Crippler is pure aggression, and begins to relentlessly swipe and claw at Bryant with his inhuman arms.

Thanks to Bryant's elusiveness and a number of The Crippler's futile attempts at ripping Bryant's head off, The Crippler finally gets a taste of his own medicine as The Black Mamba—who is narrated to have a killer instinct that is unmatched—retaliates by picking up a basketball that happens to be lying around on the side of the road and throwing a superbly strong and accurate chest pass at The Crippler, propelling the antagonist onto a cement pillar, causing the structure it supports to collapse and ultimately put an end to The Crippler's life.

Bryant then turns back to save the canine hostage, he unleashes the dog and finds a piece of paper around its collar with the words "GAME ON" written on it. To Bryant's surprise, the seemingly innocent dog turns on him and attacks his new sneaker.

After escaping the situation, Bryant discovers that The Boss wants to end his reign as the best player on the planet and NBA champion. He wants to defeat Bryant, and after which collect his shoe as a trophy.

Bryant, being himself, doesn't back down from the challenge and takes a jeep to make his way towards the rendezvous point. Bryant then meets a bald man at a back-alley basketball court wearing a respectable looking suit.

The formally dressed man is dubbed by Director Rodriguez as Mr. Suave, whom he again hoped would be played by the person of actor George Clooney (Mr. Suave is played by Bruce Willis).

The outline of the back-alley court then catches fire, creating an eerie and intimidating surrounding for the approaching Bryant, who despite the occurrences looks as unshaken as always.

Mr. Suave, holding a basketball, utters the beginnings of what sounds to be a lengthy monologue but is interrupted by The Black Mamba's nature to strike first—Bryant quickly snags the basketball away from him, only to find that The Boss was counting on his actions exactly.

The ball releases a metallic contraption that captures Bryant's right hand.

Mr. Suave then explains to him that The Boss wants to meet him. When Bryant asks Mr. Suave what the Boss wanted, the calm lackey says that while some take souls and scalps, The Boss, takes shoes.

He leads Bryant to a tall tower, topped with a basketball court with no rails to keep one from falling over the ledge, illuminated by two patrolling helicopters.

There, Bryant finally meets The Boss—who is played spot on by music artist, Kanye West.

The Boss then initiates the battle by asking Bryant if he is ready to join his trophy wall, while putting out five muscular genetic freak athletes to play against Bryant in a full court game of 5-on-1.

As the contest commences, Bryant's alter-ego takes over, beginning the game with a steal and a slam at the other end. He continues the intense game play, understanding that his life is at stake.

He resumes to eliminate the bigger thugs one by one, despite their continued efforts to push him off the sky-high court.

Later on, with Bryant down to one last opponent, The Boss gets involved and out of sheer desperation, pushes Bryant off the ledge, in what seems to have sent The Black Mamba plummeting to his death.

With Bryant gone, The Boss commands his final playing subordinate to complete a fast break score and finish the game—but Bryant was not to go away that easily. Bryant never fell, he simply hung on to the side of the penthouse ledge, and with a rush of adrenaline; sprints, jumps and blocks what was to be an easy basket for The Boss' team—sending The Boss into a fit of profanities.

With a look of fear on his face, the final henchman jumps off the side and completes a suicide, leaving The Boss unguarded.

The Boss runs off to one of his helicopters and swears to Bryant that their encounter isn't over.

Bryant then hears a beeping sound resonating from the basketball in his hand, which he discovers has a bomb implanted into it. Thinking fast and true to himself, he sends the ball into the air and towards The Boss' ascending helicopter, causing an infernal explosion that leaves no one aboard the helicopter alive.

To bestow a fitting conclusion to his rough night, Bryant sternly bids his enemy goodbye in his signature Italian, "Arrivederci" (Bryant learned Italian when he was a child as his father Joe Bryant played professional basketball in Italy).

The scene then switches back to the conversing Bryant and Rodriguez, with Bryant asking how the movie should end. To this, Rodriguez toasts the idea that The Black Mamba doesn't end, because heroes come and go, but legends are forever." *This article was brought to you by: The Carlo Chronicles.*

Nike Basketball's Kobe Bryant: "The Black Mama' Movie Recap – Joseph Carlo Herrera (February 26, 2011)

"The Boss runs off to one of his helicopters and swears to Bryant that their encounter isn't over. Bryant then hears a beeping sound resonating from the basketball in his hand, which he discovers has a bomb implanted into it. Thinking fast and true to himself, he sends the ball into the air and towards The Boss' ascending helicopter, causing an infernal explosion that leaves no one aboard the helicopter alive."

"The Black Mamba" = 79 (Reverse Full Reduction)
T h e **12** B l a c k **34** M a m b a **33** = **79**
7 1 4 7 6 8 6 7 5 8 5 7 8

"Helicopter Crash" = 79 (Full Reduction)
H e l i c o p t e r **57** C r a s h **22** = **79**
8 5 3 9 3 6 7 2 5 9 3 9 1 1 8

The poster with the exploding helicopter on Kobe's right shoulder, CLASSIC, like CALABASAS, CALIFORNIA. Use that gematria.

The caption at the top sums to 157…

"You lose this road game, you don't go home" = **157** (Full Reduction)
Y o u **16** l o s e **15** t h i s **20** r o a d **20** g a m e **17** y o u **16** d o n t **17** g o **13** h o m e **23** = **157**
7 6 3 3 6 1 5 2 8 91 9 6 14 7 1 4 5 7 6 3 4 6 5 2 7 6 8 6 4 5

"Accident" = 157 (Reverse Ordinal)
A c c i d e n t = **157**
26 24 24 18 23 22 13 7

"Kobe Bryant" = 157 (Reverse Ordinal)
K o b e **75** B r y a n t **82** = **157**
16 12 25 22 25 9 2 26 13 7

The Grammy's were the day of his death.
"Staples Center" = 157 (Reverse Ordinal)
S t a p l e s **92** C e n t e r **65** = **157**
19 20 1 16 12 5 9 3 5 14 20 5 8

His dad's nickname was 'Jellybean'.
"Jellybean" = 157 (Reverse Ordinal)
J e l l y b e a n = **157**
17 22 15 15 2 25 22 26 13

Kobe died on his **157**th day of his age

(August 23, 1978) DOB
From and including: Fri, Aug 23, 2019
To and including: Sun, Jan 26, 2020

Result: 157 days
It is 157 days from the start date to end date, and date included.
Or 5 months, 4 days including the end date.
And for another 157..connect he and his daughter…

"It's devastating to watch videos of Gigi now, knowing she'll never have a chance to become the person she wanted to become. Here she is swishing a turnaround jumper on her

11ᵗʰ birthday in May 2017, wearing a Nike t-shirt with her father's No. 24 on the back and "RISE WITH GIANNA" across the front."

"RISE WITH GIANNA" = 157 (English Ordinal)
R i s e **51** W i t h **60** G i a n n a **46** = **157**
18 9 19 5 23 9 20 8 7 9 1 14 14 1

Get a load of that caption! "*You lose this road game, you don't go home?*" The Lakers lost to Philly &76'ers), in Kobe's hometown, the day before his death, with LeBron James passing Kobe for third all-time (in the 33k range), dropping Kobe to 4th, the number associated with death from the Far East (read about Mandarian Chinese and 4, as well as Japan and 4).

Read more about the ritual of LeBron passing Kobe on January 25, 2020, with the 54th points scored by the Lakers, while Philadelphia was stuck on 74. Search "Kobe LeBron" in the top right. You can't miss it. * Remember, the Russian helicopter 76 he was on and the Lakers just lost on the road to the Philadelphia 76'ers. With Satanist, illuminati and those deep in the occult numbers are everything to them.

And notice this connect with Kanye West. Kobe's death came a span of 135-days before his 43rd birthday. Notice Kanye is 42 right now and the chopper crashed on the 4200 block of a street that sums to 81...

"Kobe Bean Bryant" = 135 (English Ordinal)
K o b e **33** B e a n **22** B r y a n t **80** = **135**
11 15 2 5 2 5 1 14 2 18 25 1 14 20

"Central Intelligence Agency" = 135 (Reverse Full Reduction)
C e n t r a l **44** I n t e l l I g e n c e **65** A g e n c y **26** = **135**
6 4 4 7 9 8 6 9 4 7 4 6 6 9 2 4 4 6 4 8 2 4 4 6 2

"Gina Cheri Haspel" = <u>135</u> (English Ordinal)
G i n a **31** C h e r i **43** H a s p e l **61** = **135**
7 9 14 1 3 8 5 18 9 8 1 19 16 5 l

And here's the evidence Kobe is dead, along with 8 other people, in a helicopter named S-76, the day after the 76ers ritual with LeBron passing Kobe in his hometown, Philly, which makes me think Fresh Prince, but we'll save it for later. It was interesting or not so ironic that before his passing toys were made of Kobe with a flying helicopter and one as him as a flying chopper in purple and gold.

And let us go back to the name of that film 'Black Mamba'.

Kobe died 211-days before August 24, 2020, what is now known as Kobe Bryant Day in L.A. because he wore the jersey numbers 8 & 24. They also add up to 32. One level away from 33ʳᵈ Mason. The same folks who falsely promote you on the fast-track up do not hesitate to bring you down with no remorse.

"Black Mamba" = <u>211</u> (Reverse Ordinal)
B l a c k **106** M a m b a **105** = **211**
25 15 26 24 16 14 26 14 25 26

Word or Phrase English Ordinal Jewish
Mason 62 **211**

From and including Sunday, January 26, 2020
To, but not including Monday, August 24, 2020
Result: 211 days

It is 211 days from the start date to the end date, but not including the end date. Or 6 months, 29 days excluding end date.
The location and date tied with "Black Mamba" as well
1/26/20 = 1+26+20+20 = 67

<u>Word or Phrase English Ordinal Reverse Full Reduction</u>
Black Mamba 59 67
Calabasas 59 67

This article below shouts out <u>113</u>, and gives a nice photo of Kobe Bryant Day, from August <u>24</u>, 2016, when it was declared. "NEWS – For LA's leaders, Kobe Bryant's death is 'a dark and sad day for Los Angeles." Bryant's death immediately brought flashbacks to his glory years, and that day when Bryant got his own day at LA City Council." L.A. City Councilman Curren Price was in church Sunday, Jan 26, when the word came. The pastor gave the news to the congregation at Phillips Temple CME Church, which was celebrating its **113**ᵗʰ anniversary. Kobe Bryant, <u>41</u>, the athlete would help define LA for a generation – and, in the process, bring 5 NBA titles to the city of The Angels – was dead, along with his daughter Gianna."

Word or Phrase	English Ordinal
Kobe Bryant	113
Michael Jordan	113

You know the meaning of 113 right… Talmud.

"The National Basketball Association" = 113 (Full Reduction)
T h e **15** N a t i o n a l **32** B a s k e t b a l l **22** A s s o c I a t i o n **44** =**113**
2 8 5 5 1 2 9 6 5 1 3 2 1 1 2 5 2 2 1 3 3 1 1 1 6 3 9 1 2 9 6 5

Remember when Jordan retired on January 13, or 1/13???

Read about the first Scottish wrestler winning the 33rd Royal Rumble, the day that Kobe Bryant (Kobe = 33; Masonry = 33) died. Gematria News reported, "On the same day Kobe Bryant died, his 157th day of his age, and on the same day of the Grammy's in the Staples Center, where Kobe was remembered, Drew McIntyre won the Royal Rumble."

Scottish spelled in English Ordinal = 113
K o b e spelled in English Ordinal = 33
11 15 2 5

Word or Phrase	Full Reduction
Masonry	33
Federal	33
Secrecy	33
Order	33

Or another parallel to the NBA, McIntyre became the first Scottish Wrestler to win the Royal Rumble, and on January 23, 2020, the only Scottish NBA player, Robert Archibald, died at age 39.

Read about Archibald's death here:

https://gematriaeffect.news/robert-archibald-only-scottish-nba-player-dead-at-39-january-23-2020/

Archibald died 67-days from his birthday and Drew McIntyre won the Royal Rumble on a 67 date numerology.

1/26/2020 = 1+26+20+20 = 67

Drew Mcintyre spelled in Full Reduction = **67**
Kobe died in Calabasas. "Calabasas" in Reverse Full Reduction = **67**
Alicia Keys paid tribute to Kobe @ Grammy's – "Alicia Keys" in Reverse Full Reduction = **67**

"Blood Sacrifice" in Full Reduction = **67**

And for clincher, that part about him being the first 'Scottish' Wrestler, when it is the Scottish Rite that runs the show. "Scottish" in English Ordinal = **113**

And about that 113... read here:

https://freetofindtruth.blogspot.com/2017/04/47-93-113-youtubes-12th-birthday-april.html

Since 113 is about the morality of lying, there is a point that must be made about Kobe Bryant dying on the 37-year anniversary of Bear Bryant, January 26, the 26th day of the year.

Recall, God sums to **26** in Hebrew and English.

The point to be made is, you can play God with lies, if you can reach enough people, and have enough persuasion.

Word or Phrase	English Ordinal
Lie	26
God	26

YHWH (Jesus name = sounds like 'Yah weh' or Yah-Way
*26 = "nin' (Hebrew Official) = 26
"YHWH" = 26 (Reverse Single Reduction)
Y H W H = **26**
2 10 4 10

Remember, mankind is made in the 26th Verse, Genesis 1:26, where later in the book, mankind is deceived by the serpent, with the lie. *Kobe died on 1/26, January 26.

Genesis 1:26
King James Version

[26] "And God said, Let us make man in our image, after our likeness: and let them have dominion over the fish of the sea, and over the fowl of the air, and over the cattle, and over all the earth, and over every creeping thing that creepeth upon the earth."

Notice the first man Adam sums to 26.
"Adam" = 26 (Reverse Full Reduction)

A d a m = **26**
8 5 8 5

And there is a lot more to this 26 business, which the first chapter of my is about, speaking on its meaning, and why there are 26 letters in the English alphabet. For many in the modern world, the 'game' is 'God', and players like Bryant and Jordan are treated as gods or living LEGENDS.

"Bryant" = 26 (Full Reduction)

"Jordan" = 26 (Full Reduction)
"Game" = 26 (English Ordinal)
"Ballgame" = 26 (Full Reduction)

Keep in mind LeBron passed Kobe the day prior, 26-days after LeBron's 35th birthday, December 30, 2019, and LeBron came into the game with 33,626 points scored, emphasis on the '26' at the end.

*Philadelphia = 101 (26th prime)
*Philadelphia is named in Revelation, the 66th Book of the Bible, when referencing the Synagogue of Satan.
Revelation 3:7-9
King James Version

[7] And to the angel of the church in Philadelphia write; These things saith he that is holy, he that is true, he that hath the key of David, he that openeth, and no man shutteth; and shutteth, and no man openeth;

[8] I know thy works: behold, I have set before thee an open door, and no man can shut it: for thou hast a little strength, and hast kept my word, and hast not denied my name.

[9] Behold, I will make them of the synagogue of Satan, which say they are Jews, and are not, but do lie; behold, I will make them to come and worship before thy feet, and to know that I have loved thee."

"Philadelphia" = **223** (Reverse Ordinal)
"The Synagogue of Satan" = **223** (English Ordinal)
"Philadelphia" = **101** (English Ordinal)
Properties of 101
Octal of: 65
Duo of: 145
Hex of: 257
Sequence Position
Fibonacci (11th) 89 – 101 – 144 (12th)
Triangular (13th) 91-101-105 (14th)
Prime Yes – 26th
"In light of this being the 74th NBA season, don't forget the meaning, in light of those who manage the league."
Word or Phrase English Ordinal
Masonic 74
Jewish 74
Occult 74
English 74
Gematria 74

Recall, the Zion Williamson sweepstakes were May 14, 2019, the anniversary of the establishment of Zion Israel (Jewish nation), May 14, 1948.

"Zion Williamson" = 74 (Full Reduction)

Z i o n **28** W i l l l a m s o n **46** = **74**

8 9 6 5 5 9 3 3 9 1 4 1 6 5

Word or Phrase English Ordinal

Jesus 74

Cross 74

Messiah 74

Gospel 74

Parables 74

Remember when LeBron said he was getting that 'Jewish' money on the 74 date, then he sat out with a fake injury for a chunk of last season, his first with the Lakers (that was all for lining up the Kobe ritual)?

Read here if you forgot: https://freetofindtruth.blogspot.com/2019/01/34-35-lebron-james-to-return-against.html

Another name associated with God is the 'tetragrammaton' (or YHWH), which connects to the fact that real King James died at age 58, and he was a Rosicrucian and a Freemason. He also died unexpectedly. Praying today's "King James" will truly find King Jesus.

Word or Phrase Full Reduction Reverse Full Reduction

Tetragrammation 58 86

"Los Angeles Lakers" = 58

"Kobe Bryant" = 58

Word or Phrase Full Reduction

Freemasonry 58

Rosicrucian 58

Solomon's Temple 58

Secret Society 58

All of this knowledge goes back to the Crusades, when the Knights Templar occupied Jerusalem, for God, calling Temple Mount, what is now al-Aqsa Mosque, 'Solomon's Temple', where the Mason's secrets are

"Jerusalem" = 58 (Reverse Full Reduction)

J e r u s a l e m = **58**

8 4 9 6 8 8 6 4 5

About the 86 part of Tetragram Maton, the alternate value to 58, recall the cartoon of Kobe crashing in the helicopter from Chamberlain Heights, released on Kobe's 86th day of his age, and then when Kobe supposedly died in a real helicopter crash, he departed from John Wayne Hospital, summing to 86. Well, let us not forget that King James Bible, published in 1611, not unlike the release date of the cartoon, November 16, or 16/11. Again, "King James" passed Kobe, and pushed Kobe to 4th place in points, the number associated with death, and reminding of the 4th book of the Bible, which is titled NUMBERS. The King James Bible was published in 1611."

The Bible is clear to stay away from the occult, witchcraft, and sorcery. Over the years, I have had friends tell me that the security code names for particular "legends" or larger than life figures are "Yahweh" or Black Jesus. That is pure blasphemy! I have heard that attributed on a select few basketball players and Hollywood A-list stars. God is not mocked, and we tread on dangerous ground the moment we try to take his Glory or desire worship to ourselves. Just because the devil lies that you can become like god or greater than Him you will pay a price when you sell your soul to Satan. I would encourage all my friends who may be linked or dabbling with this demonic force to repent and plead the blood of Jesus.

Rewind a decade ago, interesting read featured on NBC Sports by Rob Mahoney on July 26, 2010 with headlines, "**LeBron's rooting interest in the Chris Paul order. <u>Also Freemasonry</u>**." He writes, "If we've learned anything from free agency this summer, it's that NBA superstars are a part of some secret, underground, **<u>Freemason-esque</u>** society. LeBron James, Dwyane Wade, and Chris Bosh have been conspiring to team up for the last 15 years, and only now, with all of the planets in perfect alignment in their orbits and all three stars unrestricted free agents, could their vision finally be made a reality.

Of course, Chris Paul was in on everything. He too is a part of the superstar fraternity, and as such, LeBron has fully endorsed Paul's decision to attempt to force his way out of New Orleans, with a caveat. It seems that even relationships formed in super secret underground lairs have their limits, and **<u>according to Brian Windhorst of the Cleveland Plain Dealer</u>**, James would prefer it if Chris Paul stayed in the Western Conference, to make for a better rivalry.

I'm sure this has absolutely nothing to do with the possibility of Paul ending up in Orlando (**<u>improbable though it may be</u>**), and teaming up with Dwight Howard to cut James, Dwyane Wade, and Chris Bosh down in the conference finals. Nope, nothing to do with that at all.

LeBron just wants to make a better rivalry by putting Chris Paul miles and miles away rather than in his own backyard, by playing him two or three times a season rather than four, and in a completely different division that would not have the two highly competitive stars battling it out for regional supremacy. This all makes perfect sense. There is no question that having Chris Paul, regardless of what team he is on, in the NBA finals against LeBron, Wade, and Bosh would make for a fantastic show. However, there is plenty more to James' wish than simply wanting to meet Paul on the league's biggest stage, and to ignore his more selfish interests here would be foolish."

While at the Olympics in London during the 2012 games my friend and fellow chaplain, Randy Shepherd was able to connect with Kobe and asked him point blank, "Kobe, have you ever put your trust in Jesus Christ as your personal Lord and Savior?" Kobe with his million-watt smile said, "Yes" and I pray that is indeed the case. Only God knows the heart. They took a picture together and Randy shared him promotional material with his basketball ministry and had the Gospel message on it and Kobe was reading it as he was on his way. May we all know that Jesus is The Way, Truth and Life and no one gets to the Father except through Him (John 16:6)." My heart breaks for his beautiful wife and family and may His eternal presence comfort them always.

Tupac's Killuminati Soldiers of Truth posted September 9, 2020, on Facebook – "Kobe Bryant "Illuminati Sacrifice" and Corona Virus.

1) Kobe was sacrificed or 'disappeared' and beside the headlines it says the US government is coming up with Cov19 vaccines.
2) The Lakers were originally from Minneapolis…
3) Kobe Bryant is trying to hash out a settlement in the battle with a pharma company Hi-Tech Pharmaceuticals over "Black Mamba" before heading to trial.
4) Kobe and George Floyd both had daughters had daughters named Gianna. * Kobe wore a t-shirt to practice saying, "I Can't Breathe" several years before the world knew who George Floyd was. #PredictiveProgramming
5) Both were linked to Freemasonry, the Boule and were friends with high level Masons and some were in their family.
6) Both died under "strange circumstances" and both had closed caskets.
7) Kobe's 666 Workout. Six hours of work, for Six days a week, over Six months. He breaks down each six-hour workout into two hours of track running, two hours of shooting and skill conditioning and two hours of weightlifting.
8) His most memorial game was scoring the most points (81) happened in his 666th game. Scoring 66 percent of his team's points. His number was 24 at the time. 2+4=6." The author to this referenced Facebook post above went on to speculate that the helicopter crash was a hoax.

The same author also notes, "Background of the Boule Secret Society or the Black Illuminati." He writes, "On May 15, 1904, nine African American men created the Black Boule Secret Society, the oldest black charter in the world that has 126 chapters, over 5,000 members worldwide and is essentially the Black counterpart to the Skull & Bones Secret Society. The order was found in Philadelphia, Pennsylvania, the home of Kobe Bryant. Boule is also known as the Greek Letter Fraternity, Sigma Pi Phi. Henry Minton and eight others created the Divine 9 of the Greek Letter secret society and went on to create, The Talented

Tenth. This meant one of ten blacks of a certain wealth and pedigree would be selected to be part of the Boule. Boule means "gatekeeper" or an advisor to the King. The gatekeepers or the Boule are the "Lower House" that protects the "Upper House" or the upper Echelons of Society. They are the 9 knights of the Round Tables – Meaning 9 families of the 13 control 99% of the world's wealth and are the "Money" the actual Elite families. The Knights of the Roundtable include, the Council on Foreign Relations, The Trilateral Commission (Barbara Walters), The Club of Rome, The Committee of 300 and each are assigned one of the nine Boule chapters to protect the Knights of which former President Barack Obama was a member. The Boule Chapters, aka, The Divine Nine are:

Alpha Phi Alpha
Kappa Alpha Psi
Omega Phi Psi
Phi Beta Sigma
Lota Phi Theta
Alpha Kappa Alpha
Delta Sigma Theta
Theta Phi Beta
Sigma Gamma Rho

The same author continued, "The nine Black letter societies comprise the world-wide "Boule Secret Societies" or a Black Illuminati Society, which was started by the Rockefellers. Their job is to protect the Rothschilds or the Council of 13 Families or the wealth of managers. The system is in place to keep other people of significant influence in line all over the world. In terms of the average person's world that would be equivalent to the censorship we truthers experience on social media every single day. Fortunately, at our level, the danger is quite minimal compared to the upper crust players. Book – The History of Sigma Pi Phi by Dr. Charles H. Wesley University President reports:

75% of Black Attorneys are Boules
85% of Black Accountants are Boules
75% of Black Doctors are Boules

These people are designated and selected by the system to protect the current system of which Oprah is a member. She serves as a high-level designated gatekeeper. In this Boule fraternity is LeBron James, Barack Obama, Al Sharpton, Gayle King, Jessie Jackson, Shaq, Jay Z and Beyonce (Boules). The insignia of the Boule is a beast (referred as a Griffin, Gargoyle or Sphinx). Half man and woman with its right hand on an Urn, as a sign to the Boule that any people are not initiated are dead and they are committed to keeping them dead or in other words without knowledge or true illumination. Simply put, the Boule are caretakers of the one percent.

Male boules are called Archons, which means King of Principality, which is also Demon. Females are called Archiess or Demonesses. The Demon Abraxas is also referred to as a Griffin, which is a beast consisting of half man and half fish and/or half woman and half fish which is the logo of Starbucks. #Hello The Boule held a conference in 1941 in Los Angeles and two men attending worked at the Tuskegee Institute and were responsible for the syphilis experiment. It was said they killed Booker T. Washington, whose autopsy was a threat to the Boule and members of its secret society, and they made certain his influence would no longer be an issue for them.

Ray Charles could SEE that those who align with this group tend to promote a pattern of death. The writer of that post mentioned, "Another man Ron Brown (Cabinet Member), who worked for President Bill Clinton was a Boule and he died in a plane crash, but autopsy showed a bullet to his head. He no longer wanted to protect the system and when stakes are death high, death is inevitable. Robin Williams was said to have been deep into the dark society. The world loved his humor but if it were true that dabbling with the Devil is no joke or laughing matter. Did he die of depression or was his time up and he taken out?

It was believed Marcus Garvey who was a Black conservative was killed by J. Edgar Hoover via the Boule black secret society. Hoover started the FBI in 1918 and was specifically known to target black movements such as the Black Panthers that again were never organic movements as popular belief claims but in fact were created and funded by subversive non-black Illuminati connected associates. The organization was created by the establishment and was intended to be no different than Black Lives Matters, which was created by Nazi Zionist George Soros. However, when the leaders went against protocols and began to unite and empower the black community, they were quickly taken out and/or imprisoned for life by Hoover through the weaponized. #NoWonderMyDadLostHisRespectForTheFBI

The author continued, "Even Martin Luther King, when he learned of the true nature of politics, said he felt he was integrating the black population into a burning people. Singer Harry Belafonte shared MLK'S sentiments and began to denounce the Democratic Party shocking both Hillary Clinton and Barack Obama at the 2005 Democratic National Convention. What people do not realize is that many, if not all of the black interest groups were started by Zionists, whose sole goal is not to promote the well-being of special interest groups but to foster division between races in order to keep the public divided." Let me park the car here and shout from the hood, "Satan divides and destroys but Jesus came to bring life and love."

That source elaborated, "Julian Mack is the perfect example. He was a Zionist, who founded the NAACP and was the judge who sent Marcus Garvey to jail for embezzlement, which was an obvious coup Garvey, a black conservative who was not in compliance with the notice of making American Blacks dependent." Albert Pike was recruited to be the face of the Ku Klux Klan and in addition, the Civil Rights movement was created by Rothschild Zionist.

Decoding Greek Letters of the Boule:

Greek letters of the Boule secret society, "Sigma Pi Phi." <u>Sigma</u> is the 18th letter of the Greek alphabet is the 18th star in constellation. Sigma means to conjure a spirit. <u>Pi</u> is the 16th letter of the Greek alphabet and is the 16th star in constellation. Pi means "hypnotic solution" or osmatic pressure. Refers to magic or spell. Phi is the 21st letter of the Greek alphabet and the 21st star in constellation. Phi means to control a plane or dimensional reality. Sigma Pi Phi means to conjure a spirit to offer pressure through hypnotic solution to have an effect on the earth plane."

Consider Kobe, "he was born in Philadelphia. Home of the Boule. Kobe's father was a pro basketball player for the Philadelphia 76ers. The logo has 13 stars. The pyramid on the dollar has 13 stairs, which are 13 levels of Freemasonry. Kobe's helicopter was Sikorsky 76B. In 1985, Kobe's family moves to Italy when Kobe is 6 years old and remains for 7 years. They return to the United States when he is 13. There are no coincidences. The Sikorsky helicopter was created by a man named, Igor Sikorsky, the Helicopter King, born in 1898 from what would now be Kiev, Ukraine, formerly the USSR. Sikorsky's bloodline dates to Court of Peter the Great, Russian Czar of the 1600s. In the book titled, "Freemasonry and the Occult at the Court of Peter the Great" by Robert Cowlis – if you bring up Wikipedia, it shows Igor with his right hand in his left jacket pocket, which means he was a high-level Illuminati.

The Sikorsky name is also rooted in Russian Occultic Freemasonry through the Czars of Russia who had to flee Russia when Leo Trotsky Stalin took over Russia. Sikorsky is now owned by Island Express Holdings Corporation in Van Nuys, California. Kobe attended Lower Merion high school. The term "merion" means to be immersed in the dark arts according to Larry Gaiter. In the book, "The Word A Monthly Magazine Devoted to Philosophy and Science' page 302; volume 6; Merion who is a demon who marries a woman found within a stone and the woman is called Granity. Kobe Bryant opened a studio in 2013, called Granity Studios.

Kobe's daughter Gianna is also 13 years old. Symbolism on top of symbolism on top of symbolism is what we see here. In 2000, Kobe meets 17-year-old Vanessa Cornejo Urbieta. Vanessa Bryant's one-eye symbolism. Her family is involved in Santeria witchcraft, which by the way is what Jennifer Lopez and Cardi B are alleged to also practice; where Beyonce is a practitioner of Voodoo and is allegedly related to Madame Laveau out of New Orleans on her mother's side. Madame Marie is one of the most famous Hoodoo practitioners in the world and Beyonce's hit song "Lemonade's" was an homage to her long deceased relative of the 1800s, whom she has depicted in several of her videos. Actress, Angela Bassett depicts Madame Marie Laveaux in the TV show, "American Horror Story."

Back to Kobe, he is sent by the Lakers to Eagle, Colorado, to see a doctor named Dr. Richard Steadman who is a member of Phi Beta Kappa, an extension of the Elite secret society, Skulls and Bones." Phi Beta Kappa represents the education and legal aspects of the Illuminati system. The doctor convinces Kobe to go to a hotel and spa for rehabilitation where he meets the 19-year-old desk clerk who claims Kobe raped her, however and Kobe suggests the relations were consensual. She never calls the police and then leaves and has sex with her boyfriend the same night. It wasn't until her parents got involved that the 19-year-old makes rape allegations against Kobe who seems to be blindsides and confused by her allegations. The questions beg exactly what went on at the hotel and spa in Eagle, CO? Was Kobe compromised at the time the Elite?

Was Kobe initiated unto the Boule, or was he blackmailed into cooperating with the Cabal now that he was earning a certain type of money? Kobe is subsequently arrested and is gifted an attorney named Pamela Mackey by his doctor of all the strange things. Pamela is also a Phi Beta Kappa member connected to Harvey Weinstein. However magically, one year later, the charges against Kobe are dropped and the victim's attorney claims no money was exchanged. Was it then Kobe gave in to Deep State pressure, joined the Boule secret society and all charges where then dropped? Kobe, in 2003, changed his jersey number from 8 to 24. 8+24=32 symbolizing 32 degrees of Freemasonry. Was Kobe a 32-degree Mason of the Boule secret society?

It is during this time, in 2004, that Kobe allegedly begins his induction into the Luciferian 33rd-degree levels of Freemasonry and adopts the alter ego called the "Black Mamba." To get into the million-dollar range of Freemasonry and adopts the alter ego called "The Black Mamba." To get into the million-dollar range of Freemasonry, all must be initiated into the homosexual order of the Baphomet initiation levels of Freemasonry. This goes all the way back to the time in Moses in the book of Exodus. When a person wanted to gain access into the Court of the Pharaoh, he or she had to sleep with the head magician within that court. Same with today's music industry, they must be initiated into the homosexual ranks or have sex with the leadership of that industry. Did Kobe that sells his Soul to the Boule secret society? The ritual of the Boule, like the Skull & Bones, is that one must sleep with a same sex inside a coffin while other members watch. To move to higher ranks within Boule society specifically, one must initiate into the Freemason Order of the Golden Centurion of Germany, ironically where Kobe used to frequently travel to have work done on his knee when he was still playing with the Los Angeles Lakers."

I would like to interject here and the next time you see someone walking with their pants halfway down their backside with their underwear showing that not only shows a lack of parenting or discipline, but it is a public code and came from prisons. It means you can violate me from the back at any time. Symbolism means everything to these misguided souls, and I pray more teenagers pick up their pants or they may pick up more than they can bargain for.

The author from that post alluded, "The second layer of this initiation process in order to get to the 33rd degree level there is the rite of bestiality, whereby the person must have sexual contact with an animal or entity they choose to embody." This goes back to John Dee, the wizard who taught Queen Elizabeth 1 about Dionysm, the Greek god of wine, hedonism, and transgenderism, which spawned what is known today as "Dianetics," which is considered a book about witchcraft and is the religion attributed to Ron L. Hubbard as Scientology. Was Kobe Bryant a Satanist and member of the Illuminati? Was he sold out?

Now as the 'black mamba" spirit relates to Coronavirus, the active ingredient or poison is the venom of the Black Mamba serpent. Jesus, during the days of the crucifixion, was given a sponge by the Roman Deep State that contained vinegar infused with the blood and venom of a Black Mamba snake of which Jesus refused, knowing what they had planned. We can absolutely liken that to today's Deep State offering of vaccines, I can assure of that. However, Jesus defeated the Deep State of His day, which gives us the hope we live and act today.

You may wonder how all this is relevant to what happened to Kobe. According to the Golden Order of the Centurion, a lodge founded in the 1800s, one of their requirements was that one must have been previously initiated into an existing magical order before being considered to join this upper level of secret societies. We believe this happened to Kobe in 2004. However, this order strictly limits the members of society, and those few numbers are rigidly maintained as shown below. Similar to Russian Roulette (also practiced by the order of assassins which also existed at the turn of the century (19th and 20th) in Central Europe, every five years (if at that point of time no other lodge member had died) a balloting for "death certificate" took place on the evening June 23rd) before John's Day. This death certificate served as "lodge-sacrifice" for services for the transcendental powers in which the lodge believed. The dead-certificate was determined by the draw of a lot or ballot. In the latter case, there were 98 white and 1 black ball in the ballot box. Whoever drew the dead-lot became, according to the constitution of the order, property of the supposed lodge daimon (i.e. he had to consume deadly poison during the lodge meeting.

When Kobe scored 81 points it was his 666th career game. Notice Baphomet head.

All rituals had as their goal to attain high and highest levels of initiation, but it was always their intention to obtain on that level the most possible influence, power, and wealth. Strict observance was the rule. The hierarchical structure required the enviable acknowledgement of the word of the master. It was demanded that every neophyte who was to be admitted was a member of a red masonic lodge as well he was required to hold a high degree in a purely magical knowledge lodge. It was also demanded that he be influential in public life, that he was economically independent or at least have some influential close friends. One can see it was nice easy to enter this circle. Kobe has been connected to the Clintons, The Clinton Foundation, Jeffrey Epstein, Wall Street, Celebrities, Barack Obama, Nike, The Brain Initiative that was started by the Obama administration, which deals in the industry of furthering transhumanism, and other highly influential brain-trusts, and think tanks and by all accounts Kobe Bryant was the Black Illuminati's "Golden Child."

To summarize, for new members to be initiated, an existing member had to be sacrificed. There were no exceptions. If you tried to run, they would find you and kill you. If no brother had died in a year, a "lodge sacrifice" had to be chosen. The chosen initiate would be forced to drink a poison draught to complete the sacrificial act. In case the initiate refused, the sacrifice could still be fulfilled using the German "tepaphone" - a machine which when coupled the will of a magician, could kill anyone no matter where they were. New initiates would be assigned a demon/entity and embody the required essence associated with it, with the hopes of gaining even more power and influence. #TheBlackMamba

The neophyte was provided, after his actual admission, with a demon-helper. In reality of course, this was nothing else than a mutually created and enlivened imagospurinus. Franz Bardon wrote a book called, Initiation into Hermetics" and discusses the technique. Something completely different was the blood-pact with lodge-daimon which was required. Here, the total bonding to the transcendence is clearly expressed. However, it can be stated with certainty that there were two daimons which were ritually worshipped I the FOGC lodge. First, was the demon Belphegor and other was Asmodi, which is identical with Aschmunadi, mentioned by Rah Omi Quintscher. Ever evocation-magician knows it is not easy with these two fellows when you evoke them, they are extremely clever, brutal, and yes nothing less than blood-thirsty in the true sense of the word.

The first thing the neophyte had to learn was the adoration rituals of those two beings as well as the practice of how to call or evoke them. Lebron James, also a Boule, passed Kobe's record of 33,000 points, as 3rd top scorer in the NBA and it is at that time Kobe was rendered obsolete in the world of basketball. Was this the needed Masonic sign communicated worldwide that Kobe Bryant's time was up and that LeBron James would now take Kobe's place?

Remember, when it said you will lose on the road, and you can't go home.

Notice how LeBron is referred to as King or in other words, an Archon in the Boule secret society; Archon again means King or Principality or Demon. He also commented on his accomplishments one day before Kobe's passing. LeBron James also met with President Clinton two days before Kobe's helicopter accident. Did he take over Kobe's place with the Clinton Foundation?

The Freemason Order of the Golden Centurion, founded in 1840 in Munich, Germany, lasted for three years and then entered the life of Adolph Hitler, of Rothschild blood, and becomes the template to the 3rd Reich. This the Masonic Order of which Kobe became a part of with his early travels to Germany at age 6 with his family and then frequently traveled to throughout his career; and thus, the place that no doubt began to hastened Kobe's death.

So many questions remain:

1. Did LeBron sacrifice Kobe?
2. Did Kobe, under Order of Centurion draw the short straw and simply accept his fate?
3. Did Kobe know he soon must die?
4. If he did, did he escape and fake his death to his daughter's life?
5. Or did his sacrificed faked like has been alleged about so many Hollywood celebs and he only died in name alone?"

You may recall, I was in California preaching revival the very day that Kobe's life celebration memorial was hosted at the Staples Center. My heart ached for him, his family and fans. The top of the headlines on the newspaper depicted "Kobe's death and service" and top right of the same paper talked about the Coronavirus sweeping across America. What is interesting that the word "**Covid**" in Hebrew translates back to English, Google Translate comes to "*Kobe.*" Both he and his daughter were laid to rest in **Corona** Del Mar, California on February 7, 2020. Another connection was on that same day is when Coronavirus whistleblower Dr. Li Wenliang died. His age? 33. The doctor while dying was still warning about the coronavirus outbreak and it spread anger and grief in China. Just months before he sent a message to medical colleagues warning of the virus but was told by police to "stop making false comments" and was investigated for "spreading rumors." Even in death the powers to be silenced him! Keep in mind, the Devil hates the Truth. Is it purely coincidental? Was it predictive programming from the demonic forces who love to show their hand in plain sight? Do the two events have something in common in that Kobe's superstar death represents the multiplied hundreds of thousands that too would soon die? Keep in mind to the Cabal and demonic the *bigger the star* the *greater the sacrifice.* God only knows but we truly don't wrestle with flesh and blood but principalities, powers and darkness. It is imperative that we don't lose heart and must remember that God wins in the end!

Bishop Larry Gaiters on a podcast, "Boule – Secret Society" shared some powerful points. For starters, there is a big pharma company in Davos, Switzerland but they have another in Siena, Italy. That was Kobe's childhood hometown and interesting enough a massive COVID-19 broke out there. Kobe was most likely controlled and consider Bill Cosby, he wanted to buy NBC but when the powers to be said, "no" they took out his son and he was killed. Then he's in prison. Boule is created by nine black scholars, but they don't play with black money."

Rockefeller helped build it and no surprise that Jay Z new motto is ROCKA FELLA" Immediately after Kobe's death and half the world was on lockdown, Gaiters said, "9 Illuminati = Li family from Hong Kong helped finance (bankrolled) the Covid-19." It is a global Luciferian Deep State, and it appears they took out Kobe. Those who dance with the Devil are never smiling when the music stops. Gaiters dropped the bomb with he said, "The NAACP founders were not even black and the KKK were NOT founded by white people. In fact, it was a Rothschild agent." Just as some African American pastors had been paid off to pimp off their own people, we have artists, athletes, academia, and powerful politicians who were paid off at the detriment of their own race and then have the audacity to blame us for being racist.

If you ever see LeBron with his shirt off the Boule symbol his on his chest. He is a marked man and David Rockefeller said, "Some even believe we are part of a secret Cabal working against the best interests of the United States characterizing my family and me as internationalists and of conspiring with others around the world to build a more integrated global political and economic structure; one world if you will. If that is the charge, I stand guilty, and I am proud of it."

Ruslan Abdullah referenced some staggering Satanic symbols in our Nation's Capital, "When the architect, Pierre Charles L'Enfant was a Freemason, laid out Governmental Center of Washington, D.C., in 1791, he planned more than just streets, roads and buildings. He planned to use the layout to hide certain occultic magical symbols, which, when they were instituted, became on large Luciferic, or occult symbol. An occultic magical symbol is defined as "…an image which hides an inner meaning. This meaning is usually cunningly hidden behind a form." (Frederick Goodman, Magic Symbols, Brian Todd Publishing House, Ltd, London, 1989, page 6).

Most know that the 555-foot-tall Washington Monument was erected to honor the first Masonic President. What is eye opening for many is that Ruslan stated, "The Washington Monument was designed so that both the White House and the Capitol Building face toward it, so the leaders of both branches have to face the spirit of Lucifer thought to be residing in it. This is typical occultism. The Washington Monument was placed directly on a straight line, precisely 900 West of the Capitol. Thus, the inhabitants of the Capitol could face the obelisk daily. However, note the Washington, DC, obelisk does not lie in a straight line 900 South the White House. Why? Because it was lined so that it lies in a straight line 900 from the House of Understanding, the headquarters of Freemasonry!! In the mind of the occultist, the true political administrative power resides in this Freemasonry headquarters, not in the White House. Therefore, President Andrew Jackson considered himself to be the subordinate to Albert Pike, the leader of North American Freemasonry.

Clearly, the power of leadership to drive this country towards the New World Order, leading the rest of the world, lies in Freemasonry, not in the White House or the Congress. These symbols, built into the physical layout of Government Center in D.C., represent the extent of that power. Think of the many years these symbols have remained from most people's knowledge; think of the millions of tourists who have walked on these streets during this time, without having any idea of the existence of these symbols, not to mention their meaning! And, if you have ever driven a car in Washington, you will now understand why these streets are laid out so weird. Driving in DC can be a nightmare. Now you know why." Plus, Satan is the author of confusion, and everyone gets lost on DuPont Circle as well as DC in general.

The House of the Temple (Masonic Building) in Washington is intentionally located 13 city blocks north of the White House. From the first city block of Lafayette Square and you a baker's dozen streets later you end up at the Executive Mansion. Coincidence? NO! It was intentionally planned. It is worth noting that 13 represents rebellion against God's authority and is generally regarded as Satan. We have had over a dozen presidents who were Mason's and although George Washington is the most famous it is a fact that Franklin D. Roosevelt did more to further the New World Order than anyone in American history.

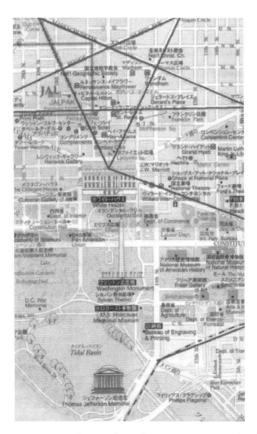

The layout of the monuments forms the Christian Cross and adjacent almost near the same land the Mason's not to be outdone placed their shrewd, Satanic symbols and we have had a war going on in plain sight for centuries in the Capital City and most did not even see it in broad daylight. The secret societies like to mock us before our eyes, and it makes them feel superior. Once you know the symbols and how they operate you can pray and ask the Great Physician to do some much-needed open-heart surgery in these misled men. Pride and rebellion are the two oars that row Lucifer's boat and while we were distracted on the Redskins vs Cowboys or Yankees at Fenway Park, we now must take inventory that the biggest and only game in town is the feud from the beginning of time. Today, you are either with Team Satan or Team Jesus, but you cannot be playing for both.

The city of my birth is special to me on Capitol Hill, but I knew it was oppressive and almost suffocating at times. The Satanic presence is thick here and across the pond too. True royalty is in King Jesus not the Queen of England. Prince Phillip who recently died said, "When I die, I hope to come back as a virus to kill as many people as possible." No wonder the day he passed that former President Obama praised him. Look carefully at those that praise you and birds of a feather flock together. I flew with Meadowlark Lemon, and he was a labeled an "Uncle Tom." I did not detect a racist bone in his body.

Our Facebook friend went on to articulate, "The United Nations flags shows the globe divided into 33 sections encircled by olive branches. The flag happens to also be blue just like the first 3 "blue degrees" of Masonry. 33 is the highest degree of Scottish Rite Freemasonry. There are 13 degrees of York-Rite Masonry. Our measuring system originated in Masonic France in the 1790s which explains why 13 standard inches is equal to precisely 33 metric centimeters. The Grand Orient de France of Freemasonry was founded in 1733. Harry S Truman, a 33-degree Mason, became 33rd President of the United States. In 1933, Adolf Hitler became Chancellor of Germany. #33

The Masonic Great Seal with the Latin "New World Order" was added to the dollar bill in 1933. Walt Disney was a 33-degree Mason and founded the "Club 33." During WWII 33rd degree Winston Churchill gave us the "V for Victory" two finger salute which since the 1960's became "Peace." Before it stood for Victory or Peace. It was a symbol of the 33rd degree. There are 3 joints to the knuckle on two fingers making 33 then held apart like a V is about 33 degrees. Where did Churchill learn of the satanic powers of the "V" sign? Few are aware that Winston Churchill was a Freemason. Stephen Knight wrote an explosive expose, The Brotherhood, that rocked the British Isles when it was published some 15 years ago. In it, he unmasked many British nobles, police, judges, and politicians who were all Masons. Among them Winston Churchill who was documented in 1903 at Lodge No. 3000 of the United Lodge of Great Britain. He was not only a Mason but a witch druid." Dr. Stanley Monteith, occult and secret society researcher and host of Radio Liberty out of California, states: "Churchill was an adept of the occult, having been inducted into the Druids in 1908, and having pledged the occult oaths required of those who have entered into the world of Freemasonry.

33rd degree Mason Buzz Aldrin and the son of a 33rd degree Mason, Neil Armstrong, Jr supposedly performed a Masonic ceremony (ritual) 33 minutes after arriving on the moon, held the Masonic Flag, and took pictures of each other. "Aldrin also carried a handmade silk Masonic flag with him on his space journey, embroidered with the words, "Supreme Council, 33-degree, Southern Jurisdiction, USA." Brother Aldrin visited the House of the Temple in Washington, DC, and presented the flag to Grand Command Luther Smith. The flag is now located in the House of Temple archives." Progress could be Masons middle name and they are also willing to go to the ends of the Earth and beyond to spread their mission and message. The Church needs to wake up and not allow cults to beat them as their own game. Master Number <u>33</u> is generally called the number of the Master Teacher and resonates at a highly spiritual vibration. Superdome goes dark during Super Bowl XLVII. NEW ORLEANS – The power went out for <u>33</u> minutes in half of the Superdome, not long after Beyonce finished her 'high powered" halftime show.

LeBron James became the fourth player in NBA history to score <u>33,000</u> points also known as the 33K Club. Kobe Bryant's high school would have <u>33</u> seconds of silence at the first game following his death. It was also the same number he wore in high school and the team retired. Keep in mind that Jesus was 33 when he died, and the anti-Christ spirit tries to not only mimic but steal God's glory. Luciferians despise the Lord. God works in mysterious ways because I was finishing up this book this article appeared today on May 21, 2021, by David Wysong on Sportscasting, "**Kobe Bryant Made $<u>323</u>.3 Million in the NBA and Wouldn't Go to Dinner Without Saving Seats for his Alter Ego: "There Were Drinks Sitting All the Way Around**."

Many NBA players become wealthy, but guys like Kobe Bryant and Michael Jordan reached another level in terms of money. Their play on the court made them superstars and allowed them to spend cash on almost anything and everything – this included taking an alter ego out to dinner. Bryant is known for his alter ego, the Black Mamba, but that did not just impact his play on the court; he also took his alter ego out to eat with him, according to his former trainer Tim Grover.

Grover who trained both Jordan and Bryant, recently appeared on The Complex Sports Podcast to discuss his new book, and he shared a Kobe story no one had ever heard before. "We finished a game, Kobe and I decide to go out to eat in a restaurant … and he goes, "I need a table for four." I am like, "it's just the two of us." I did not ask, Grover said on the May 18 episode. Grover then said that two men came up and asked if they could sit with them since there were two free seats, but Bryant would not let them.

Kobe said, "These seats are taken." Grover said to Complex. "I'm like, "Man, am I working this guy too hard?" He's starting to hallucinate a little bit." Bryant's former trainer then added that the two men probably thought Kobe was just being a jerk, so he finally decided to ask about the two open seats. I said, "Kobe, who are those seats filled with?" Grover said, "He goes, 'Wherever I go'…where they say, 'everyone tries to hide their skeletons,' he goes, "I bring everything and all of them with me. The good, the bad, the indifferent." And those seats are for those individuals because they (demons) make me who I am.' So, he's talking about his alter ego, the mamba mentality."

Respectfully, I want to remind you that mamba is snake, and that serpent is symbolic of

Satan. Recently, I saw a video of United States Senator Chuck Schumer talking to his empty seat on the floor of that prestigious body. Someone said, "It was as if he saw a demon in his chair and asked it to move." When you start dabbling in the dark the Lord exposes it with His Light.

Some may not want to believe it but keep in mind that most of society communicates verbally with words but those aligned with the Devil speak via symbols. We are playing in Satan's playbox every day and if you don't believe me check this out. Tony Hines wrote on Facebook on March 4, "Now people don't believe Satan is taking over your planet.

James Naismith was a Canadian and invented the beloved game of basketball. He moved to the United States of America and became a legal citizen and traveled extensively across the country and in Europe. He was quite good at the game himself and the sport he invented touched the world. What are the odds? Naismith was a member of Russell Lee Lodge in Springfield, Massachusetts. Later he affiliated with Lawrence Lodge No. 6 in Kansas. He was deemed "Worshipful Master of Lawrence Lodge from 1927-1928. He died on November 28th, 1939.

It is worth repeating but the reason the 33 is so prevalent with the occult is because they are mocking and trying to sabotage God's deity referencing Christ was thirty-three years old when He was crucified. The beauty is where the Devil thought God is dead what they don't realize or want you to know is that Satan and his team are on a fast track with a dead end. We know since childhood that acting class and drama included "theater" and over the years realized some power brokers a time or two have been known to engage in political theater. It is possible that same stream and agenda has permeated many major sports and turned adolescents with talent to become men swimming in money and worshipped as if a god in arenas and stadiums around the world. Perhaps when the planned demic hit, the Lord was bringing low the idols who falsely elevated them. The Lord has a unique way to knock folks down.

It has been reported in several documentaries that the CIA has been pitching movie scripts to Hollywood for decades and unfortunately has trickled into other three letter government agencies. FBI Director J. Edgar Hoover was a full-blown Freemason, and it was said he ordered the assassination of Black Panther Spokesperson Fred Hampton as part of the Cointelpro Program.

The prince of preacher's, Dr. Adrian Rogers (1931-2005) in more modern times in his book, "In a Twinkling of an Eye" also had something to say about the Federal Bureau of Investigation. The former President of the Southern Baptist Convention and late pastor of the historic Bellevue Baptist in Memphis, Tennessee said, "Now, we're thinking about living on the edge of eternity, the soon coming of our Lord and Savior Jesus Christ. It is not only the Church that is interested in the Second Coming of Jesus Christ; the FBI is interested in the Second Coming of Jesus Christ, because they think that many who believe in the Second Coming of Jesus, as we believe are dangerous. They think that we're part of the lunatic fringe, and they've said to the FBI, "Keep your eye on those kinds of people. They're nuts!" Well, I may be a nut, but I am fastened to a good bolt. His name is Jesus." It was refreshing to hear he also had a problem with them. We are in good company when the three-letter law enforcement agency of the world is monitoring us. Keep watching because Hell is too long to be wrong.

This secret society is rooted in Satanism and driven by the Devil with an agenda of death. The problem is they will help raise you up and then bring you down. This entire battle is greater than awards or money but blood. Jesus, the Christ offered His perfect blood to give us a chance to be forgiven of our sins. For those that want to play on Lucifer's team not only drink human blood (adrenochrome), shed innocent blood (murder) but will use your own blood as a sacrifice to Satan. Get out while you can! The number "22" is a big number for the demonic and deranged. It would be interesting in what they have in mind for the year 2022. I am thankful that God wins this final war but if you do not know Christ, now is high time to get your house in order. Are you ready to meet a Holy God? It is a scary thing to be on the wrong side of the Living Lord. Lucifer has power but is powerless when it comes to the Almighty.

Keep in mind, the word pharmacy is a Greek word derived from sorcery. That is where we get the word 'pharmaceutical' and I am not completely anti-vax but have zero peace about this agenda. Of course, those who are not in tune with Christ would want you to follow their plan and churches pushing vaccination more than salvation and missed Jesus in the process. It bears repeating -- If your personal beliefs and political affiliation are fine with death to babies, death to small business, death to the Constitution, death to Christianity, death to the family, death to entrepreneurship, and death to America -- you need to ask the hard question, "Why so much death?" The Devil comes to steal, kill, and destroy and the Lord is Light, love and liberty. Plus, if your friends are aligned with death, do not be surprised when death knocks on your door. They do not have your best interest in mind at all.

With my birth almost in the halls of Congress, I have been employed with both political parties over my career on Capitol Hill, but we are so late in the game I am not recruiting anyone to a particular party. The real party is going to be the one to come and not on this Earth. The true party will be in Heaven not Hell and I am still giving away free invitations as an evangelist. Hawaii is nice but Heaven is over the top and Hell is too long for you to be wrong! Those who miss Heaven will find no party in Hell and all the rock stars, professional athletes, politicians that had power on Earth will be powerless in Hell and even religious leaders who had a form of Godliness but denied the power thereof will be wailing and gnashing their teeth in a burning, bottomless pit forever and forever with no relief and the worm die not. My prayer is that Jay Z will come to the saving grace of JC, Jesus Christ. That Timberlake will find repentance from the Trinity and that Freemasons will get out of the bondage of the Devil. Cher needs Christ, DeNiro needs the Divine and all of Hollywood's stars need the Son. The next time this cancel culture society demands that you "say their name" why not instead whisper the Name Above All Names, Jesus who died for us all. This will rattle some wrong but repeat after me – Jesus, is Lord! Lucifer is a loser, liar and damned in the Lake of Fire. #Boom

My friend, KrissAnn Hall is a former prosecutor and Constitutional Scholar and she recently posted in May 2021, "Do you know what I think is the saddest thing in America today? That there are so many Americans that still believe it is all about the Democrats versus the Republicans (or vice versa). If your entire conversation is about how your political party wants to save the world or how the other party wants to destroy it, you are sorely deceived and you make BOTH parties rejoice! You maintain the power brokers. You empower the deceivers. You take from others for the profit of the few. Your political party does NOT give a royal crap about you." #DropTheMic

Society does not need a new world order but needs to cling to the old, old Story. The Holy Bible is the answer and riches to our dilemma. It warned us that this day would come, and your only Hope is in Christ alone. It is time we dupe the Devil and be delivered by the Divine! I can speak with clarity and boldness because I have seen close enough the division that the Masonic Lodge places between family, friends, and folks in the marketplace. You cannot serve two masters and our allegiance must be in Christ alone.

I have friends who thought they would get inside and on the fast track to further their career and be enlightened only to be blinded and mislead. My father did not take the Masonic route and I am so thankful he did not. He climbed the top of the law enforcement ladder as Acting Assistant Chief of America's police department with the United States Capitol Police and he did not sell his soul to do it. Newsflash – young officer, community leader, elected official, promising businessman, musical artist – DO NOT sell your soul, make a pact with the Devil, take an oath to an occult or sell out to Satan. Anyone can fall and follow Lucifer to Hell fire, but the real soldiers take a stand for Christ and His cross. Be like Durer's onward Christian soldier and keep marching forward in faith. It takes a true man or woman to serve the Lord and who does not bow to the lowly Lucifer.

No wonder some of the world loves certain folks because they are already linked with them directly or indirectly. It was said President William Jefferson Clinton has ties with the Masons. Hillary is a 16-degree, Grand Dame. Many on the far-left politically love Karl Marx's writings and his demonic ideology. The Clintons and the Obamas love the Dalai Lama, and he is a Free Mason and former President Gorbachev is as well. They perceive Christians as inferior and weak, but Jesus said, "They hated Me, and they will hate you, too."

On occasion I would visit the White House on a volunteer basis covering some of the daily press briefings for a Christian news outlet. I did it for a couple years during the Obama administration and just a few months into the Trump presidency and left to preach nonstop as an evangelist. One time I was outside the northwest gate at the White House and was waiting to be cleared to cover one of the press conferences in the West Wing and one of President Obama's aides on the phone laughed at me when they realized I was with a Christian news outlet. It was disappointing and hurtful, and I recall thinking if I was linked with any other affiliation in the world, it may have been a lawsuit. The audacity to mock and make fun of Christianity is nothing new and praying continually for them to know true Power and that is the Lord not Lucifer. I have heard stories of some friends who asked some in the occult if they know Jesus Christ as their Lord and Savior and their face becomes distorted, their countenance changes, eyes grow dark and begin to foam at the mouth. Demons tremble at the name of JESUS! Indeed, there is something special in that name because His is the Name above ALL names.

When you start seeing these celebrities over the years die often at the peak of their career you must reexamine the death of one of our biggest stars called the "Queen of the Night" and that leads us to Grammy Winner Whitney Houston. My friend was in the Beverly Hilton Hotel staying in the same building the night leading into the Grammy's on the very evening that Whitney was mysteriously found dead in her bathroom suite. Numerology and occult numbers were prevalent all over once again in her death. The Beverly Hilton Hotel management and security asked the LA County Coroner to NOT remove Whitney's body from the hotel room until Clive Davis' pre-Grammy party. Her daughter, Bobbi almost drowned the night before in the same hotel. Some suggest the Illuminati came after her daughter first as a 'blood sacrifice" and when she survived, they came after her mother next. In these demonic players' minds, they believe the bigger the star the better the sacrifice to their god.

Go back and watch the awkward video of Whitney the day before she died when she came out with soaking wet hair, and she interrupted unannounced a gathering of a trio sitting on bar stools. The powerful trio were Hollywood mogul Clive Davis, Brandy and Monica. When Whitney unexpectantly walked in they almost passed out and she told them she almost drowned and the look on their face is priceless. At first glance she appears to totally disregard Brandy. When she exits and asks her daughter to kiss "Dad" Clive Davis, who helped promoted her to fame. When Whitney finally acknowledges Brandy, she gives her a note and appears to grab her by the throat. #HowDoesThatGrabYou?

One person said, "Two things are odd. For starters, the drowning comment since she was allegedly drowned hours later. Secondly, When Whitney gave a note to Brandy, who seemed incredibly surprised by the gesture and Whitney interrupted their interview did Whitney put two and two together and hinting at Brandy that she knew what was happening behind her back?" Literally. Since Satan and his minions love numerology, here are a few more for you. Whitney Houston died on the same day as Brandy's birthday on the 11th of February on which Brandy was turning 33. 11 is number of death / 33 freemason numerology. Ironic or not that the Century Plaza Towers have in the lawn landscaped that is clearly visible from above "all seeing eye" pyramid shape near the Beverly Hilton Hotel.

Numerology: Whitney Houston was born in the day 9 died in the day 11 stayed and died in the hotel room 434. Those three numbers 4+3+4=11. Her funeral occurs in the day 18 = 9. dead body was ordered by Clive Davis to stay in the hotel room for another 11 hours. The Whitney Houston Illuminati video (4/52) that was on YouTube said, "So nobody can use Bobbie Brown as a scapegoat for her downfall. The Satanic industry was her real problem, and she knew that already."

9, 11, 434 = 11, 18 = 9, 11

9, 11 is written all over Whitney's death signaling a ritualistic sacrifice by the 'black magicians." It was the 54th awards 54=9. Nicki Minaj 54th annual Grammy Awards on Sunday, Feb 12, 2012. The Pope elect 22 Cardinals the same day as Whitney Houston's funeral. Nicki arrives in a red cloak embroidered with the image of 'Versace' or is it Whitney the sacrifice? Nicki had a fake pope with her on the red carpet, and both the cardinals, the pope and Nicki had red robes. They represent both "Whore of Babylon" and "blood sacrifice" symbolism. The Pope elected 22 Cardinals the same day as Whitney Houston's funeral. Sadly, over the years, the Catholic church has the inverted cross behind the pope on some of his public appearances. The 'inverted cross" suggests that the Vatican is the throne of the dark Lord – the anti-Christ's gateway to Hell. Jesus said, "You must be born again!" We find only one mediator between God and man and that is Jesus, The Christ.

The Queen of England began her ran in 1952. It was said the Pepsi Super Bowl commercial released just weeks before Whitney's death may have been more advanced foreshadowing what was to come. Sir Elton John (the grand wizard of Oz) represented the royalty link. That same commercial feature a Whitney look-a-like and Whitney's middle name is Elizabeth. For those that did not know, Whitney Elizabeth Houston. Another royalty link is Whitney's middle name which is "Elisabeth." Five days after Queen Elizabeth's 50th Anniversary. Was Whitney sacrificed as a gift to QEII? Indeed, it is evident for those awake to the demonic symbolism that a case could be made of Masonic Monarch and Papacy symbolism present. Brandy and Monica perform a song "It All Belongs To Me" as a tribute to Whitney on the night of her death. It is a story about the rise (birth) and fall (murder) of a star. The old-style Porsche represents Whitney, and the red BMW is the entertainment industry. The constant reference to "Black" refers allegiance to the Devil and destroyer. The signature bright light in the background represents Sun-Ra/Black Sun. The end of the YouTube video says, "You decide whether this is a fitting tribute or an insult/backstab?" What a terrible song to pay tribute to one of the world's greatest voices. The closing picture at the Grammy's that night they selected resemble Whitney in a sacrificial pose as if on the cross. That would not only be sacrilegious but showed their hand in how she died. Indeed, she was a blood sacrifice.

The interview of all three acted as if they saw a ghost or a dead man walking when Whitney walked in. Some speculate they thought she was already dead to secure the sacrifice and shocked and almost mortified that she was still standing erect and keeping folks in check. Some believe that they already knew that their mentor dying would pave the way for the next generation to climb up the ladder. The music video the duo starred in showed an old Porsche and it insinuated that the older car was symbolic of Whitney who was the older model. Unfortunately, out with the old and in with the new. Sadly, we are all replaceable, but nobody had Whitney's voice but when her voice had deteriorated some in the system thought it was time for her to go. The Satanic Club used to use and abuse talent but now they are after their money. Is it coincidental that she died the eve of the Grammy's? In their minds, with Whitney struggling to hit her iconic notes they thought she was worthless and knew she would be worth more dead than alive.

With friends like these who needs enemies. Clive Davis has come out as bisexual in his memoir but that would make sense with the Baphomet symbol, idol, and ideology. It is half woman and man, and they must partake in some demonic behavior to go to the next level. Again, they believe by going up they must go down. His net worth is reported to be just shy of a billion dollars. The Bible is clear, "What would it profit a man to gain the whole world and lose his own soul?" My prayers are with him, and it is not too late to get right with God. You may be down, discouraged, divorced, have a disease and be in debt but if you are not dead than the Lord is not done. It would be sad to have a billion bucks on Earth and be bankrupt in the afterlife. Hell is too long to be wrong.

The show must go on and how evil that Whitney Houston's body had not even been removed from her hotel suite while her "friends" partied like it was 1999. If you ever thought the Grammys, Oscars and Super Bowl halftimes were growing darker and darker and obviously more demonic than you would be correct. What never ceased to amaze me when mega church pastors would tweet during the half-time shows that the demonic spectacle was both artistic and creative were obviously blind to see the deceptions of the Devil. It would make you wonder if some of these 'pastors' were indeed children of the living God or wolves in sheep's clothing aligned with Lucifer? The same churches that boasted about their big buildings and capacity crowds displayed ZERO backbone in the planned demic. They paraded as a force only to be exposed as a farce. Will the real Church, Christian and clergy stand up because too many of you are still sitting out! #Lame

The same camp that says Christian's shove Christianity down their throats are the same clueless clowns in Lucifer's cult that promote witchcraft, idolatry, Satanism, pedophilia on a world-stage to a world-wide audience. The Bible says, "Many who are first will be last and the last first." These poor souls have sold their soul for peanuts to be famous for a few fleeting years only to burn forever in eternal damnation in the lake of fire without redemption by grace and the blood of Christ.

Prince was trying to get out. Do you recall how he died? Plus, he was trying to get control of his own musical catalog worth multiplied millions. Michael Jackson was the same way. The gloved one feared for his life. One insider said in a "Sun Report" interview, "There were serious concerns for his mental health near the end – so much that he was seeing a psychiatrist. He said he was being pushed into a corner and had an irrational fear that he would die or be killed if he didn't perform in London." Do you recall the name of his tour? It was, "This Is It" and sure enough it was. Sadly, once again we see predictive programming and he did not live to talk about it. How about Kobe's death? I think you are starting to connect the dots.

It is worth revisiting but sadly more than not to make it in elite circles these days almost must sell their soul to the Devil to become a celebrity at a high level. It has been documented that in the entertainment industry if you want to operate in the $20 Million and above level it is necessary to make a human blood sacrifice. In Hollywood, there are two different types of sacrifices 1). Blood Sacrifice for Fame 2). Human (Solstice) Sacrifices. I am not accusing anyone but if you watch a YouTube video "Whitney Houston Illuminati - 6/52) You will see Kanye West. Unfortunately, his mother died shortly after a routine surgery. Tupac was killed and the media said it was a "drive by" shooting but did he in fact die because his number was up, and they took him out as a blood sacrifice. Jay-Z nephew died in a car crash. Eminem close friend and colleague was killed outside a nightclub. What was wild was his "Like Toy Soldiers" video showed it in advance. Once again some would say "predictive programming" but only God knows and praying for all involved. In the video his best friend was shot and killed outside a nightclub. Dr. Dre lost his son, Andre Young Jr because of an apparent overdose in 2008.

Bill Cosby's son was killed. Some say that Cosby who at one time was the face of NBC tried to buy the network but the folks at the top would not let him. Some say he was trying to break away from Freemasons and then after murdering his son they brought out testimony that has him behind bars today. What is interesting some are saying some of the alleged victims appear to be transgender. Mike Tyson's daughter Exodus died because of a mysterious hanging accident in May 2009. She either slipped or put her head in the loop of a cord hanging under a treadmill's console and was suffocated.

Jennifer Hudson's family went on record implying her nephew's death was intentional and part of a more sinister plan. The father of Jennifer Hudson's murdered nephew expounds on his allegation that Hudson sacrificed her son for fame and fortune as a Freemason ritual. The video continues and notes "shortly before Lady Gaga arrived on the music scene, her friend Lina Morgana died after plunging ten stories from the roof of a Staten Island Hotel.

Shortly after Lina's death, her mother accused Stefani Germanotta (Lady Gaga) of not only sacrificing her daughter but also stealing her image and style."

Back to Whitney and I love her music. In fact, her mother sang back up for Elvis Presley and Whitney met Elvis backstage when she was a teen. Here is something to consider. Why in God's green earth would two Egyptian mummy caskets have been strategically vertically placed on the side of funeral home that hosted her funeral. Only family, friends and Hollywood elite walked past those two erect caskets. Some said her casket was already closed and one implied her deceased body may have been in one of those Egyptian vaults. Those two vertical, erect Egyptian coffins also represented the presence of the Masonic Lodge. They always have two vertical towers or columns.

The Cross and Crown is a Christian symbol appearing in many churches (particularly Roman Catholic). The symbol is associated with Freemasonry, specifically the Knights Templar branch of Freemasonry. That symbol of the cross passing through the crown was present and prominently placed for the world to see on the pulpit as Whitney was being eulogized. They like to leave their mark for all their "brothers and sisters" to know while they mock the rest left in the dark or by God's grace in the Light. They believe it was a tip of the hat to the demonic realm and many are convinced she was a blood sacrifice. Mark this down, those that dance with the Devil are not smiling when the music stops.

Randy Quaid was the loving, "Crazy Eddie" in Christmas Vacation but his career has been shut down from working in Hollywood or Hollyweird as some would call it. Why? For not having the "chops?" Absolutely not! Because he has been telling the truth and exposing their lies. He went on record saying several of his friends were taken out or "whacked" as he calls it. Consider Hollywood heartthrob Heath Ledger who played the JOKER and he was killed right before the Batman release. Was he offered as a sacrifice? Those awake agree he was taken out and you must keep in mind that this industry claim to make you, control you and dispose of you at their discretion? You automatically begin to play "Russian Roulette" the moment you want to roll the dice with the Devil. Ledger's powerful portrayal of the demonic joker needed to tap into something dark and sinister to play that character. He nailed it but sadly it may have nailed him apart from Christ. My heart breaks for him and his family. Hollywood does not care about those they enslave. They have a demonic track record of taking you up and watch you crash and burn. #Literally

Enter Paul Walker of Fast and Furious fame. His very first movie was "The Skulls" and the subtitle on the movie poster read, "A *secret society* so powerful it can give you everything you desire…At a price." When you play with the Devil folks get seriously hurt. In that movie Walker is in a red Porsche, and he dies at the end of the movie. Did Hollywood predict his fate a decade in advance? After a string of Hollywood massive success and sequels following Skulls the handsome Hollywood hunk was last seen climbing into the passenger side of a rare red quarter of a million-dollar Porsche and he was killed. Coincidence? Many now think it was another Illuminati blood sacrifice. Does art imitate life or life imitate art but make no mistake the Bible says we will all die and then face the judgement. Those that don't get right with the Lamb of God that takes away the sin of the world will face coming judgement by the Lion of the Tribe of Judah and no one enjoys swimming in the lake of fire. You cannot win with the Devil.

Funnyman Martin Lawrence was not joking when he said, "The Illuminati …they are trying to kill me!" It was no laughing matter when comic Dave Chapelle left $50 million dollars on the table and moved out of the country for a while. To his credit, he was trying to live with integrity. Hollywood also encourages their own desiring to get to the next level to wear dresses or cross-dress on occasion. That is symbolic of emasculation and the Devil wants to neuter and negate what the Lord created male and female. Folks dabbling in this are both confused and pawns on the Devil's chess board. When you see A-list stars cross-dressing usually mean despite how much they can lift or how prominent they are in their field were not "man enough" and sold out to fit in this Satanic scheme.

Consider Princess Leia herself, Carrie Fisher. She died while wrapping up the latest STAR WARS film and take note how the secret societies and Freemasons give names like "King," "Prince," "Princess," "Queen" and "Legend." They are names of respect and almost godlike status. Once again, but their intent is evil because they steal the glory of Jehovah who alone is Almighty God. It is said Fisher was not only revered as royalty, but she boasted she did inappropriate things to get to the so-called top and various pictures reveal her linked with the Masonic Lodge. Folks literally worship their idols and almost collapse when they receive news of their death. I loved STAR WARS as a kid, but we need some Jedi's for JESUS in these turbulent times.

Tom Brady is incredible and one gifted athlete, but he joked recently saying his wife is a witch. He was laughing when he said it but if not joking, I would love to spend a day with them both and just love on them sharing Christ is the Way. For all my athlete friends, what is it worth if you lived with bling and championship diamond rings but died without salvation from the King? A winner on the field but we lose in the game of life apart from forgiveness from the Lord. God help us! Soon the Lord will return, I can assure that not a single soul will be asking who won the Super Bowl, received a Grammy in 1984 or was the best politician the world ever known. One nanosecond in Hell you will realize you were duped for Lucifer's lies and we focused on the temporal and lost on the eternal. The only thing that will matter is the holiness of Christ and we reign forever and ever with Him in Heaven. Hell is too long to be wrong. It is fact, you are either saved or lost. I have been a chaplain to world class athletes and Hollywood stars on occasion and would love to minister to anyone who feel they are in too deep with the Devil. God's middle name is grace, but we must repent before time runs out. The big battle is the blood war, and we are either redeemed by Jesus' red, royal blood or still under the curse of Satan, the Father of Lies and Deceiver of the brethren. The real brotherhood is in the Savior not secret societies.

Have you ever noticed some stars seem so angry? It could be because when they look in the mirror and frustrated with themselves that they disobeyed God, their parents moral code and sold out they realize they failed. The drug abuse could also be in their vain attempt to curb the torture of the demons that ravish their soul day and night. Opposed to genuinely seek the Lord for forgiveness and repent they feel stuck and in prison and to a large degree they are. Bob Dylan on a 60 Minute interview said, "He made a pact with the Devil." One anonymous person said, "If your ultimate goal is to be famous than you will do a lot to get there. Like sign your name in blood and make a contract with the Devil. Like you are going to end up on a one-way street going nowhere and that is truth. I have seen so many forsake their value systems just for a little bit of fame." She said it all in three sentences!

This chapter we have referenced numbers, the occult and witchcraft and I am not glorifying this demonic practice. The reason it doesn't add up for those on the wrong side need a refresher in basic math class that **666 < 777**. We always lose when with Lucifer. Put that in your pipe and smoke it because it is high time we graduate from Little League and join Jesus in the Major Leagues. Today, is the time to get right with Christ. My prayer is that you will not dabble in the occult, secret society, or witchcraft at all. In fact, stay far away. For the living artists who may still be involved I would encourage you to repent now and find freedom in the blood of Jesus.

Over the years, I have noticed another fraternity that is often 'oil and water" with authentic born-again Christians, and they are Greek organizations on college campuses. Initiations are based on "works" and are often dark, sinister acts that involve shaming, guilt, and violence behind closed doors. Some have been tortured, raped, and even murdered. Mark this down, true brotherhood and sisterhood is found solely in a personal relationship with Christ and the family of God. You are either under the blood of Christ or the blood of the Devil.

Satanic practices include drinking out of human skulls and drinking human blood. Microsoft's former PR person, Maria Abramovic has been known to host house parties to drink the blood of humans. The Devil is dark, deadly, demonic, and disgusting but best of all he is already damned. @DavidDelArt2 tweeted, "I cancelled my Microsoft office package after Microsoft used Maria Abramovich as their mascot. I do not want my money to support a satanic cult. Bill Gates is also a criminal with crimes against humanity. They are all Satanic. #BoycottMicrosoft"

Ms. Abramovic has been seen wearing an upside down cross making a mockery of the death of Christ. Rock stars like Lady Gaga and Jay Z have been photographed with her. Melinda Gates has reported as of late one of the reasons for wanting a divorce from Bill was her uneasiness with his reported relationship with Jeffrey Epstein. Some reports indicate he may have been on his private jet to that island while inappropriate behavior was going on with minors.

Witchcraft is prevalent in Satanism and the Masonic Lodge and Steve Wozniak who first sold the bytes for Apple at $666.66 was also a thirty third degree Mason. The Beatles were knee deep in as well and no wonder John Lennon penned, "Imagine There is No Heaven. It is easy if you try. No Hell below us, above us only sky. Imagine all the people Living for today."

Louis Armstrong was a Mason and so is Lebron James and countless others, but we all need JESUS. Over the years, Karl Marx, Friedrich Nietzsche, Pope Francis, Joseph Stalin, Napoleon, Charles Darwin are all said to have been linked with or appreciate this "all seeing" organization. What they fail to see is that Almighty God sees all, and I have read the back of the Bible and not only Jesus wins but the born-again children of God do, too! Some are convinced that Freemasons were under the hood as racist Klansmen. The KKK has no place in God's Family, because He loves diversity. Some believe that the Freemasons had a hand in murdering Dr. King and Malcolm X. Some have said that Freemasons were tied to the Wuhan virus. The virus was banned in North Carolina for being studied but President Obama's administration and Fauci helped fund it overseas in China. President Abraham Lincoln was not a Freemason but John Wilkes Booth who assassinated him sure was. Are you tracking yet? Those that embody light, love and liberty are despised but the dark side. #CanYouHearMeNow?

ABC News reported on May 6, 2015, that an aide to Kamala Harris was arrested for impersonating a fake Masonic Police department. The headline read, "Kamala Harris aide, 2 others arrested for allegedly running fake Masonic police department."

https://abc7.com/free-masons-masonic-fraternal-police-department-california-of-justice-fake/701005/

SANTA CLARITA, Calif. (KABC) -- Three people, including an aide to California Attorney General Kamala Harris, were arrested for impersonating police officers, and creating a fake law enforcement agency called the Masonic Fraternal Police Department.

On April 29, Los Angeles County Sheriff's Department detectives served search and arrest warrants in the 28000 block of Linda Vista Street and the 17000 block of Sierra Highway, both in Santa Clarita. Three people were arrested and identified as David Henry, 46, of Santa Clarita, Tonette Hayes, 59, of Santa Clarita, and Brandon Kiel, 31, of Los Angeles.

Badges, identification cards, weapons, uniforms, police-type cars and other law enforcement equipment were found in the searches at both locations.

Henry, Hayes and Kiel were all arrested for impersonating a peace officer and booked at the Santa Clarita Valley station. Henry also faces charges of perjury under oath. Kiel, who worked as deputy director of community affairs at the California Department of Justice, faces charges for misuse of government identification.

He is on administrative leave and the department could not comment on an ongoing personnel matter or criminal investigation.

Near the end of January, chiefs of select law enforcement agencies throughout Southern California received letters stating Henry had been elected as chief of the so-called MFPD.

Shortly after the agencies received the letters, many started receiving phone calls from Kiel, who identified himself as the chief deputy director of the organization. He began requesting meetings with agency chiefs.

A meeting was scheduled between members of MFPD and Capt. Roosevelt Johnson with the Santa Clarita Valley Sheriff's Station on Feb. 4.

During the meeting, the group claimed they were descendants of the "Knights Templar" and that their police agency was created in 1100 B.C. The members also claimed their department had sovereign jurisdiction in 33 states and Mexico.

The meeting raised red flags, and LASD detectives began an investigation into the group.

"They couldn't answer basic questions about the MFPD's jurisdiction and the overall department mission," Deputy Amber Smith said. Detectives conducted their investigation in collaboration with several other law enforcement agencies and found that MFPD was not legitimate. Detectives also believe the three suspects were attempting to deceive citizens in the community and that other people may be associated with the fictitious organization." No wonder some political "leaders" want to defund the police because their agenda is not in the best interest of the Almighty or of America. While in Los Angeles two months ago, I met two of L.A.P.D.'s finest and I asked one officer did his cruiser have 300,000 miles on it? He dropped his head almost in shame and said, "No sir, I only have about 80,000." I said, "How is that possible." The hood was faded, the rims were missing, it looked like it had been in a war-zone and truth be told it had." He said, "When they started to defund the police budget, we cannot afford to keep our cars looking good."

My heart dropped and this preacher wanted to take an offering on the spot not for me but them! The irony is the folks running the nation now are misguided and need God's guidance. Praying blessings on them and we need to stand up and look up because our redemption is close at hand.

Write this down, it is hard to trust those who are not only playing on the wrong team but who are being paid to push a false narrative. I had the chance to be an extra a decade ago in Batman's "THE DARK KNIGHT", but the Holy Spirit told me to stay away, and I refrained from showing up. When the trailer came out, I realized I heard right because of the diabolical mask that they were wearing in the movie and that is where we are today. It was another example of predictive programming. The guilty and misguided wear a mask and Jesus believe in transparency while the Devil delights in secrecy. Read that again!

Do you know what fifteen percent of 7.8 billion is? I will help you the answer is 520 million. So, when the massive Georgia guide stones reveal they believe society's population should be half a billion and you factor in Bill Gates talk indicating if you do the vaccines correctly, we could reduce the population down to fifteen percent that would be 5.2 million. This entire planned demic is about dollars, domination, and depopulation.

My twelve-year-old is a genius. He said, "Dad I heard recently the United States has approximately 410 million people." He said, "A report said that one third of our country already took the vaccine." He grabbed his phones calculator and beat Apple at their own game, and he divided a third into 410,000,000 and the answer is 136,666,6667. He then said, "Look at all those sixes and you have seven straight!" He then multiplied that number times two to compute those that had yet to take the vaccine and that answer was 273,333,333 and that is seven straight numbers of three. Six, Six, Six is symbolic of Satan but three is God's perfect number. Keep in mind that a third of the angel (even elect) fell out of Heaven and the threes are God's providence protecting His own.

What breaks my heart is how many Christians and decent citizens had both no discernment as of late and trusted the government and science more than God and the Holy Spirit. The same folks that promised to save you do not have your best interest at heart. Today, we have three letter agencies that are not only deep state but demonically used. You may recall that I shared the government has allegedly housed 40,000 guillotines in warehouses across the country. Why would we need them you ask in 2021?

Altijan Juric is a past winner of Australia's X-Factor. He became a born-again Christian and saw the Light and left to live right and severed ties with his past connections with the "brotherhood." The recovering Mason shared with boldness knowing he could get killed. He said on video that they (Freemasons) intend to play a pivotal role in carrying out beheadings in the future unless the Lord intervenes. On some of their white aprons have the all-seeing eye, compass and some in leadership will help perform the decapitations. In a kitchen, women wear an apron when their hands get dirty. The devils at the top wear one to not only hide their privates but they don't want you to know they are "nuts" for following the Devil.

He went on to divulge that the guillotines already made and stored and are manufactured by CHANEL and you ask why would a perfume company be linked to death? Their logo has the seeing eye and the moment you finally realize society is not really for you, the better off you will be. I am certain that most countries do not want to look like the bad guy so they will wash their hands like Pontius Pilate and allow complicit corporations began to phase out all those deemed inferior, who are linked to Christ or who are against their demonic scheme.

President George H.W. Bush (41) was the first modern chief executive to mention New World Order in a speech at the United Nations in 1991. He also signed the Noahide Laws in the Oval Office with some Masons surrounding him. They called that Education Day, and, in the future, we will quite possibly have court trials for folks who will not renounce the name of Jesus Christ. In fact, worship to Him is considered blasphemy by the demented and demonic and the punishment for worshiping Christ will be execution by death.

In 1995, the House of Representatives passed a bill called HB 1274 that enabled guillotine provisions. To this day, those laws are still on the books and in effect. What is interesting, the Bible predicted this in advance before the guillotine was created. That shows you right there the Supremacy of Christ and the accuracy of His Word. Satan is a Liar and Jesus said, "I Am the Way, the Truth and the Life. No man gets to the Father but by Me." Guess who made the infamous, deadly guillotine? His name is Joseph Guillotine and what are the odds? He was a Free Mason. Are you starting to see a pattern?

The Bible says in the last book of the Bible, "And I saw thrones, and they sat upon them, and judgement was given unto them: and I saw the souls of them that were beheaded for the witness of Jesus, and for the word of God, and which had not worshipped the beast, neither his image, neither had received his mark upon their foreheads, or in their hands; and they lived and reigned with Christ a thousand years (Revelation 20:4)."

We have put so many stars on a pedestal for far too long and worshipped them as gods. Looking back, we have been watching a script too often penned from the Dark side and now realizing as the sand of time slips through that we have been fooled and fed a lie. Let us stop making idols of those who were imperfect, compromised and sold their soul when we need to get back on our knees collectively and worship The One who alone can save our sin sick soul and that is Christ, the Lord. Everyone loved Star Wars as a kid, but most are clueless that we are in the final battle of "Good vs Evil" now. As a child, I resembled C3-PO who was a true diplomat, but we need some fearless Jedis for Jesus and I had to grow up and praise God we did! In these last days, I am happy to resemble John the Baptist even if that means losing my head for it.

Albert Pike is one of the most respected Masons of modern history. He is adored and admired by many misled in this group, and he rose to the highest level – 33rd Degree Freemason. I will wind down this chapter with a quote from him and it is sobering, sad and should be a wake-up call to all in this demonic craft that dabbles in witchcraft indirectly and directly.

"I tell everyone that high level Mason's worship Lucifer. But nobody believes me. I was the head of the Masonic Lodge."

If you have friends, family or neighbors linked to this group let us pray now and around the clock for their soul. The compass and ordinances of Satan and secret society promise the penthouse but leave you homeless in an eternal Devil's Hell. Satan wants to devour you but only Christ is willing and able to deliver you. Heaven -- not Hell -- is the greatest party ever and it is appointed for man to die and then face the judgement. We must get right now with the Lord, or we will be left out with Satan.

The Bible says it is better to enter Heaven maimed than split Hell wide open whole. Again, this demonic group has two sides to the same coin and some of them could be initiated and completely clueless but despite what some suggest these brothers need to find Christ's forgiveness sooner rather than later because time is ticking and to be frank with you it is almost out.

It is no secret that I have had a burden for Hollywood since childhood. God allowed my godmother Judy Henderson to win a Rambo II contest with all expenses paid to Hollywood to spend the weekend with Sly Stallone and Ralph Napier who played the villain, "Murdock." Judy generously took me to Hollywood with her. We gave Stallone a Bible and God allowed me to start off sharing the Gospel with one of the biggest stars in Hollywood at age thirteen. When you have been toe to toe with Rambo as a kid it made the other battles today not as tough. Make no mistake, we are in a war now and will the real Church, Christians and clergy rise up, wake up and look up because the King is coming soon, and I am not talking LeBron or Elvis. Sly, if you are reading this I want to say, "Thank you, God bless, and I love you!"

I love in the last RAMBO that he told the villain, "If you want to live you must run to the light." It is true, we must run to Jesus, the Light of the world. John J Rambo wounded and bloodied took that massive machete and performed opened heart surgery on the bad guy at the finale of the film. God also must take out our old heart of stone and replace it with a new one filled with grace, love and truth. The Truth hurts at first but heals and brings hope at the end.

Over the years, I have considered flying to Hollywood to host a monthly Bible study to celebrities, and we are still open to doing so now. For those who are reading this and think you am too far gone or too deep with the Devil, I have Good News! <u>The blood of Jesus can still conquer and cancel the entanglement and your pact and past with the Devil</u>. The remedy? Repent of your sin and trust Jesus as your savior! We don't need to cancel culture but cancel the stronghold of the Devil on society's soul.

I got a call this week from a pastor in California who served courageously in battle in the Vietnam War. He said, "Frank, as you know I was in the United States Marine Corps, and I am calling today to thank you for standing so strong and being so bold on social media." He then said, "I was thinking about giving you one of the medals I received in war because you are being bold in this end time battle." Wow! It does not get much better than that and glory to God and praise the Lord!

Satan is always a step behind and for those still duped by the Devil I want to remind you that 'the all-seeing eye' misses the fact that the two eyes of Emmanuel alone sees all but misses nothing. In fact, He is looking on you now with eyes of love and He is encouraging you perhaps for the last time to come home to Heaven. Respectfully, let me beat the Devil at his own game and give you some predictive programming. In the wise words of Ronnie Dean, "The Preaching Machine" who was also the third bird who flew with Meadowlark Lemon and me as the black and white tag team trio. His trademark phrase that he made popular in his hometown of Missouri and has since spread world-wide, "Devil, back your wagon up and get a load of this…"

JESUS > Lucifer

OCCUPY

Sean Feucht

ONE of the commands the Lord gave us in Scripture and particularly when it is late in the game of life was "Don't forsake the assembling of yourselves as some do as the Lord draws near" but He also said four words that should encourage every Christian, church, and clergy. The Son of the Living God said, "Occupy, until I come."

To occupy *space* is to be in <u>place</u> when the Boss shows His <u>face</u>. We do not want to be AWOL when the Almighty returns nor missing in action when the Messiah splits the sky! Military and police personnel can literally be written up, reprimanded, court marshalled, fired and on rare occasions killed for failing to be on post.

It is imperative to be still and on duty until you have been relieved. At the tomb of the Unknown Soldier in Arlington, Virginia when the sentry is replaced when his shift is over, he will whisper three words to the one relieving him, "Orders Remain Unchanged." Our Commander-in-Chief has not changed our mandate or marching orders and for two thousand years they are the same today. The Great Commission was not the good suggestion and now is the time to have the foot on the gas, the Church in drive and to throw the rear-view mirror out the window because we need to be moving forward by faith not stuck in fear.

My friend's first position with the United States Capitol Police two decades ago was guarding the massive Christmas tree on the West Front during the midnight hour. He had dreamed of guarding Members of Congress, Heads of state, Hollywood celebrities and tourists from around the world; but in his inaugural year on the job, he was guarding a Christmas tree with no one watching. However, with the Capitol behind him and the Washington Monument before him, he with his 9mm beside him was guarding a tree. However, he was standing tall while on post and he was not vacant, MIA or AWOL but was ensuring that his assigned space was OCCUPIED.

Another friend shared a story about standing post in the Midwest while a Special Agent with the United States Secret Service. His assignment that night, in the pouring rain, was guarding a dumpster that was leaning near the wall of a massive hotel with beautiful architecture. Early in his career he, too, daydreamed of guarding the most powerful person on the planet but on this assignment, he was on post and guarding a trash bin not the POTUS. Why was he in the pouring rain? Because the next night the leader of the free world would stay in that same hotel, and he had to OCCUPY that area so no one could hide a bomb in there before the presidential arrival. They felt it an honor to be both employed with one of the best law enforcement agencies in the world, but in that moment, on that shift, their respective assignment may not have been glamorous, however, to their credit, they both faithfully remained on post and their space was occupied when their boss showed up.

As the sand slides through the hourglass ever so quickly as I type this, and you are reading this, the Boss could come any minute and now is not the time to be vacant when He comes. In every lavatory on an airplane or port-a-potty on the street you will find a bathroom door with a knob indicating one of two possibilities. It will either read VACANT or OCCUPIED. As you know, I have been known to travel a time or two and one time while I was on the plane and in the air, I had to use the restroom. The long flight was killing me, and I was stuck in the middle of two complete strangers who somehow could sleep and snore in flight. Not to disturb either one when the moment arose while they were waking up, with no time to spare I had to go right now!

Let me ask a question of you. If you are born in the United States of America but you must genuinely have to use the bathroom, are you truly an American? Your answer?? Wrong! You are RUSSIAN because you are rushing to hit the bathroom! #LOL

Next question, once you are finally inside and lock the door are you still RUSSIAN? Your answer?? NO! You are officially EUROPEAN!! Can I get a witness?? You are a peeing!! In the words of Ric Flair, "WOOOO!" Lastly, trick question. When you are finally done are you American, Russian, or European? Neither because you are FINISH! #Finland I don't care who you are that is funny!! #SlapYourNeighbor

Joking aside, you will find on that door a sign indicating the room is either empty and vacant or it is occupied, and someone is taking care of business. Hello! Typically, if the restroom has been frequented often and occupied continuously it stinks to high Heaven because folks "are taking care of business." With exception to predominately elderly congregations I felt the Lord saying, "Frank, do you know a stench on earth that smells all the way to Heaven? The churches that for the past year that have been so shackled in fear and they remained mostly vacant. That stinks to high Heaven but what is actually a sweet aroma to Me is the Church that has still been OCCUPIED and taking care of business."

The vacant symbol on a bathroom is red and occupy is in green. The first two letters of God spell "Go." The first two letters of Gospel spell "Go" and first two letters of Good News spell "Go". We have the green light from God to get going but the restrictive red tape imposed by others has threatened to arrest, fine, harass and permanently shut down His Church. I love what Evangelist Jonathan Shuttleworth said, "Churches who caved to lockdown orders. Churches who require masks to worship. Will require vaccines to gather." #ChurchOfTheState

News flash we get our orders from God not from government and from Christ and the Constitution not from Caesar. Dr. John MacArthur shared his response to L.A. city officials trying to use COVID-19 as an excuse, "*The latest threat was two weeks ago. They called and said they were going to put a homeless encampment in our parking lot. They are going to gather homeless from everywhere…they said they will fill up our parking lot with homeless people to try to shut us down. My response was*, "Perfect. We'll have our seminary students evangelize them all day long."

That is what I call getting creative in the crisis and sticking with the stuff and God gave him a word to beat them at their own game. It is a perfect example of misguided public officials using people as pawns on their crooked chess game of political domination and financial success. Michael Jackson sang, "They don't really care about us" and sadly many do not, but GOD CARES!

After the 'insurrection' at the United States Capitol, I watched with an aching heart like almost everyone else. The slight difference is I was literally almost born in that building unlike the seven billion on the planet. My parents were both employed while Mom was pregnant with me and very few know the inner workings like Dad and my family. Yes, our society has demonic activity on both sides of the aisle politically and despite me co-leading a Bible study to lawmakers our Hope is in Christ alone. Our family was trained to die for folks regardless of if we voted for them or not but despite my shortcomings, I am going to shoot it to you straight. Intel did confirm that Antifa entered that building and not everything you see or hear is true. The truth always comes out but as beautiful as that building is, it is not the Kingdom of God. One of my friends is among the longest serving U.S. Marshals active in America today. He shared that on that day of the insurrection what you did not see or hear from the news were the dozens of Antifa, BLM and Proud Boys arrested while President Trump was still speaking blocks away on the other end of the Mall.

I was contacted about ten days after January 6th by someone in the leadership offices of the United States Capitol Police and they said, "Frank we have a private Facebook page and many of our officers are hurting and grieving. We have received some wonderful messages from folks all over the country and that means so much but none of them to date have offered a prayer. Would you film an impromptu prayer and post it on the page to encourage our department?"

My heart dropped and this was totally the Lord. What are the odds but the day before Christmas 2020, I have Special Agent with the United States Secret Service calling me to thank me for my ministry and now two weeks into the New Year 2021 I have the United States Capitol Police seeking me out to minister to them? God writes a better script than Hollywood or the CIA ever could.

Over the years, I have been so blessed to have the heavyweights in my corner but those who are still in little league had a hard time acknowledging the anointing and gifting. Lincoln believed that big events stretched people to grow to the occasion. Whether receiving an award at the UN, speaking on the floor of Congress in a Communist country, serving all 100 United States Senators, working in the office of the Assistant Chief of the United States Capitol Police, writing remarks, or giving a speech in the absence of a Member of Congress, or preaching to over 100,000 in Africa, it was the Lord using big moments and little ol' me. Glory to His Name.

After church two days later, I recorded a seven-minute message of hope in one take. Immediately after it was posted, over a thousand rank and file watched it and I received glowing comments from Deputy Chiefs, former Assistant Chiefs, Special Agents from the Dignitary Protection Detail, and public and private notes from officers both thanking me and asking for additional prayer or counsel. A portion of my prayer that day was this:

"The USCP has had a tough week. Just like my leg was torn some of you are torn tonight. We lost two of the best and I want to tip my hat to the new Acting Chief, and you are in our prayers. My leg was torn while in training with the USCP. Now my leg is now stronger than ever. What is torn and tiring now with God's help and you moving forward, you will be stronger as a department. If you feel like a zero after what happened, you are still my HERO. Millions of Americans are not only proud of you but praying for you and pushing for you.

Father God, I am thankful for what the men and women of the USCP mean to me and they are not the best in the county but among the best in the Country. I pray for them what my pastor would always pray for me and that you would go before them, behind them, beside them, above them but best of all as kids of The King you are in them. Where they have spent their lives protecting others, I pray they will feel your Presence and our prayers and that you will protect them.

Lord, I pray you will bless their families. Lift up morale and give the chiefs wisdom and I know that you will make the crooked straight, the cloudy clear and give them double for the trouble. Bless the new transition, bless America, and bless the United States Capitol Police. In Jesus Name, Amen." I love you but God loves you more!

Only God could allow my injury in 2007 and leaving the department "by faith" to use me an un-official spokesman of hope in 2021 after one of the darkest days since the conception of their department in 1828. The Lord does all things well in His time and my dear friend, The Rev. Dan Cummins for the last five years has been a constant source of hope to "America's Finest" and even gave the heartfelt eulogy in the Rotunda of our Nation's Capital at the funeral of Officer Brian Sicknick. You may recall my mother, Sharon who was adamant about me trying again and she was right it would have been a huge honor to have made a career with the U.S. Capitol Police. God had another assignment but looking back I had the best of both worlds, and we are helping behind the scenes more than can be elaborated now to try to minister to some of America's Finest. Mom, to her credit, is the most loving and loyal friend you could ever have, and she has been the glue to hold much of the ministry together. For the last several years she has assisted with my bookings, travel, and she is the queen of administration. Truly behind every good man is a great woman and Mom made Dad and me look good for a long time.

It is now Spring 2021, and we have been one full year into the lockdown and our world is still in a tailspin. Had the book never been deleted in July 2021, this would have come out the month before the November election, but God is always on time. This is much more than the White House and are you heading to God's House should you die tomorrow, or if He should He return tonight?

People are hungry for hope, are hurting from isolation and dying to live. The Illuminati has been around for over 300 years and originated in Germany. Some of the most powerful families have been linked with this occult. Household names like Rothschild to Rockefeller just to name a few have been associated with this demonic force.

Without question, it is more than a group of individuals, but it has become an institution with an assignment from the enemy. At the heart of their existence is for power, control and it is fueled out of fear to push an agenda. Make no mistake, that assignment promotes death. Long before the Illuminati were formed, a battle has been waging and a war has not ceased since the Garden of Eden. When Satan made Eve doubt God's command, the subtle snake made her fail to recall God's purity, power, and plan. The moment she had a dialogue with the Devil her communion with God began to suffer. She took her eyes off the Eternal and was sidetracked by the temporal. The Bible reminds us that we do not wrestle with flesh and blood but principalities, power, and darkness (Ephesians 6:12).

The Illuminati has caused enormous havoc to our country and on continents world-wide. Those involved have not only attained additional massive wealth but have accumulated enormous political and cultural power. The pyramid with the "all seeing eye" at the top depicts not only surveillance but a hidden master controlling public people like puppets on a string. Many of the folks at the pinnacle of professions ranging from the arts, government to Hollywood have been involved in this demonic structure.

Similar to some underground groups, the Illuminati is a secret society coveting power and prominence. The Deep State in our culture is deadly and dangerous as well. Some of the three letter alphabet soup agencies in our government today have literally sold their souls to obstruct Justice, promote ungodly values and attempt to not only control but rule the world. One premiere law enforcement agency in some areas compromised character and one retired special agent said, "they are among some of the most lawless in the nation today." When you go from patriots policing evil to partisan, political sell outs, we have a problem. They are not as noble as they used to be.

When another three-letter agency intentionally targets Christians or conservatives because of their faith and unleashes relentless, unnecessary audits to not only hinder but harass innocent individuals, they do both a disservice and resemble the Devil. When another government agency monitors born again believers and places them on a watch list and labels them terrorists, they are part of the problem, not the solution. They are partners of the New World Order and are hostile and not helpful.

Hollywood actors, actresses and producers too often had to sell their soul to Satan to get screen time and multimillion dollar salaries. Rumors have floated for decades about sin, sex and Satanic scandals that elevated careers. Pedophilia is rampant and human trafficking is a delicacy to these Devil worshippers. Rituals including drinking blood of children and eating human flesh have been the demonic delicacy to their ungodly hunger. The Playboy mansion is tame compared to the unthinkable evil that happens behind closed doors.

In the past, public figures tried to hide their wayward actions but now they flaunt for all to see. Sadly, many (including Christians) are asleep and are blind to what is before them. Super Bowl half-time shows are filled with demonic symbols and rituals exalting Satan instead of our Savior. The media lectures born again believers for "cramming religion down our throats" but with over 70 million viewers watching the biggest sporting event of the year they are honoring Hell not Heaven at half-time before our eyes.

For years Disney has promoted an alternative lifestyle contrary to God's Blueprint and the common denominator that the Illuminati and Deep State have is a twofold agenda promoting control and death. For too long millions looked at our culture through the lens as if it were political, but the truth is we must view through Biblical binoculars. Society is racing towards the end times faster than a Ferrari with no brakes and more than ever what is most important is not if one is Republican or Democrat but that they are linked to Heaven not Hell.

Heaven promotes LIFE, but Hell promotes death. Jesus promotes INTIMACY but Satan promotes isolation. God promotes FAITH but Satan promotes fear. Heaven is the Truth, but Hell is full of lies. Last year when the Governor of New York signed a bill that millions of babies would die so that legislation could live we are beyond a slippery slope. That day as he signed the bill, he received a standing ovation. Last week, the same governor said "God didn't bring the Coronavirus death numbers down but he took the credit, and that moment is on dangerous ground. God will not be mocked! I am praying tonight that Cuomo comes to Christ because Hell is too long to be wrong.

On 9/11 my office was evacuated as I worked one block from the U.S. Capitol. On that frightful day we were hijacked by planes but two decades later we find ourselves hijacked by an intentional plague and sinister plan to destroy our nation, cripple our country, and try to hinder the Church. From the first fall in the Garden, it was not "The apple in the tree but the pair on the ground" that succumbed to Satan's scheme. Today, the Devil continues to use the Illuminati and Deep State to hijack life and our liberty.

The Lord told us that this time would come. While some want to de-populate the earth, I am living and willing to die to help populate Heaven. It used to be in the past follow the money, but more than ever we would be wise to watch who promotes life. Remember, Jesus saves but Satan came to kill, steal, and destroy. Four months ago, my family and I returned to Israel and while visiting we stood near the spot where Jesus told Peter, "Upon this Rock I will build my Church and the <u>Gates</u> of Hell will not prevail against it."

The first page of this book contains a single Bible verse. I wanted to start it off right with not my words but His Word. The problem is not people but Satan using some people as pawns, but God wins the game. We are dealing with not just communism and socialism but Satanism. It is principalities, powers, and darkness. Yes, the mark of the beast and Anti-Christ is on our doorstep, but I have good news! The Illuminati, the Deep State, nor the Devil will prevail. I have read the end of the Book and the born-again Christians win! In the interim, let us pray for those who persecute us, and I am reminded of Christ's words on the cross, "Father forgive them for they know not what they do." It is now the week of Easter as I am writing this, and we just celebrated Palm Sunday. Crowds can be fickle, and on the first Palm Sunday they went from hailing Him King to nailing Christ to the cross five days later. Stick with Christ because He stuck on the cross for you and while He was on the cross you were on His mind.

"I'll Be Back!" Arnold Schwarzenegger was not the first to say, "I'll be back!" Two thousand years ago, the Lord conquered sin, death and the grave and on that first Easter morning arose victorious. <u>Christmas brought God to man, but Easter brought man to God</u>. Today, Jesus is on the throne at the right hand of God, The Father in Heaven and soon the trumpet will sound, and the Savior will split the sky! Indeed, The King is coming, and this Easter may we be reminded that it isn't about coloring eggs, chocolate bunnies or new clothes, but about Christ crucified on a cross for the sin of mankind. He was buried in a borrowed tomb and arose on the third day, and He is returning very soon! Several years ago, I had the honor to be a guest with Lauren Green on Fox News in NY and the segment was on the second coming of Christ. I shared on the show "Spirited Debate" that it is not if Christ is coming tomorrow but if He returned now would you be ready? **Jesus** said, "Today is the day of salvation." #Easter

NO FEAR! Jesus asked when He returns would He find FAITH on the Earth? These are sobering words from our Savior in Scripture. Praise God, He will with our team at Frank Shelton Global! God has given me a generous measure of faith since childhood. I have been to a leper colony in **India**. I have preached to stadiums in **Africa** where disease is rampant. I Stood toe to toe with a drug Lord in **Rio de Janeiro, Brazil** armed to the teeth with an AK-47 and 9mm while sharing the Gospel with him and watched my buddy, Randy led him to the Lord. The irony is the man we witnessed to in the most dangerous region of that city was out gunned with God and two soul winners. My friend, Ronnie "The Raven" and I led a Muslim Priest to Christ in **London, England** while in town for 2012 Olympics. My godmother, Judy and I shared the Gospel with RAMBO at 13 years old in **Hollywood, California**. I preached alone on the floor of Congress in Communist **Nicaragua** with no security detail and was willing to fly by myself to the Middle East and preach to 150,000 Muslims in **Pakistan** inside Taliban territory near Osama bin Laden's compound with no guarantee to return home last year two days before lockdown.

Let us pray for **President Biden**, if I could fly solo with no security to preach to a packed crowd in Congress of a communist nation last year, the American President could hopefully ride in a motorcade sixteen blocks from the White House with protection from the 10,000 National Guard, Secret Service, US Capitol Police, FBI, US Park Police, DC Metropolitan Police, and a few others for "State of the Union" at the United States Capitol. Leadership is not in a basement but out front. All the preachers with "armor barriers" in the past are MIA in the present. I've never advocating drinking; but the meme was "hold my beer" and yet millions sat silently waiting for a stimulus check, but I grabbed my Bible and logged thousands of miles and preached indoors, outdoors, on street corners, radio stations and in television studios. Praise God! We will not let up now!

Sometimes the "nicest guy in the county" was among boldest in the Country. When some of America's largest churches folded like a deck of cards, I traveled coast to coast to not only expose government overreach but call out the planned demic. Many were either clueless or complicit and neither are fruits of the Spirit. There is a boldness when bathed in the Bible and fear honors the Devil, but FAITH pleases God.

Yes, we must take precautions, but God's people are virtually indestructible until He is done with them. It is interesting that the same folks that had big bumper stickers and wore t-shirts "NO FEAR" a couple years ago are scared out of their mind today. We have PEACE, power and protection with the Lord and **Psalms 91** is still in The Book. The Bible says in

Hebrews 11:6, "It is impossible to please God without faith." The Lord told me during the lockdown to get in the Air Force and I am asking you to get in the Lord's Army.

On April 9, 2021, I was invited back to fly to Los Angeles to speak at the 2021 Azusa Fest two-day conference. The topic of the conference was "Redeeming the Time." How appropriate and those that are still hosting events and meeting in person know what time it is, and I prayed for favor in Los Angeles as a kid and the Lord had me fly back into LAX as an adult. A state senator is also on the program along with Pastor Caleb Cooper from New Mexico who also took a stand and was threatened by their State Police about being arrested for having church last year. Apostle Fred and Wilma Berry are the salt of the Earth and Pastor Fred was just a guest on my radio show. Evangelist and worship leader Sean Feucht returned once again to be with us leading worship and would receive the William Seymour Courage Award. April 9, 1906, is the anniversary of when revival broke out and it is a beautiful thing when races and denominations unite, worship, and STAND together.

It is my honor to be the guest evangelist on the closing day of the two-day conference and people need the Lord. On June 6, 2021, my wife Ruth and I will fly together to Albuquerque, New Mexico. Pastor Caleb whom I met because of the event in Los Angeles has since written a book together and over a phone call we are co-creating a day honoring the law enforcement. The New Mexico State Police threatened to arrest the man of God in the House of God while some were overzealous and tempted to follow the wrong orders. The local Sheriff stood at the door blocking the Troopers from arresting the pastor.

Pastor Caleb felt compelled to "BACK THE BLUE" and is going to have a church celebration that Sunday evening by hosting a BBQ dinner outdoors on the grounds for law enforcement and will give the Sheriff an award for his courageous leadership to the community. Caleb shared they have thirty-three counties in New Mexico, and he is inviting all thirty-three Sheriffs to attend this incredible event and will award everyone that night in front of a capacity crowd. A Member of Congress, State Senator and other dignitaries confirmed to come, and I am honored to be the keynote speaker.

Only God could write this script because the exact town of the church is Truth or Consequences, New Mexico and that town's name will preach. No doubt the local Sheriff has great authority, but it comes with greater responsibility. One of my favorite movies is Arnold Schwarzenegger's "The Last Stand." He is a small-town Sheriff who is up in age and no longer the Terminator but loves his county and country. He is the last line of defense standing up for Truth to arrest the lies and misdeeds of the enemy. The villain of the show is running to the border for safety and the only thing standing between prison and freedom is the Sheriff.

He single-handedly tackles and apprehends the bad guy who was cocky and dead wrong. The United States of America has approximately 3,200 counties meaning we have that many Sheriffs. I tip my hat to all those who lead in that noble profession and do it right with integrity and honor. A line has been drawn and if we learned anything during this last year's lockdown, it is that God is coming soon, and we are now seeing who is with God and who sold out to a misguided government. Churches, Clergy, Public Officials, Police, Scientists, local teachers, and next-door neighbors are aligning with both sides.

Anyone with their eyes open can see we no longer have grey areas but are back to black and white and I am not talking race relations but right and wrong. Pastors, Police and Politicians who you thought were legit got compromised and now, towards the end, are part of the demonic agenda. However, some obscure people stood up to tyranny, promoted justice and love God and their country more than their own lives.

Pray for all those in authority and particularly your local Sheriffs because one day soon you will see with your eyes who STOOD for Christ, our County, and the Constitution or who sold out to communism and a counterfeit agenda dishonoring God. I am flying over two thousand miles to honor, applaud and stand with the ones still wearing the white hats regardless of the color of their skin or uniform. I loved the Lone Ranger as a kid and the good not only win in the end, but they had two hats on the show and like the cover of my book is black or white. We all have dropped the ball, made mistakes but with the game on the line this Riggins wannabe may have given away his prized helmet but did not forget his fortitude and perseverance still running to the end while gaining yards when the game was on the line.

Today, we are seeing corruption across America in our Mayor's office; power-hungry States Attorneys who have already adopted this Demonic agenda are in some pockets nation-wide. When a misguided Sheriff, States Attorney and judge are in cahoots, that is a dangerous combination. However, true Justice is in Jesus and unless folks start repenting nation-wide and around the globe it will not be pretty.

Yes, I loved Mister Rogers and would race home daily after school and wanted to emulate him and Satan and society says, "Good guys finish last" but the blessing is at least they finish and in God's economy the last will be first. Evil Knievel took some chances and despite landing more on his back than bike he was still in the air BY FAITH. John J. Rambo took on the Afghanistan government and lately I went toe to toe with Nicaragua and was willing to preach next door to Osama bin Laden's compound and have been scrutinized by my own beloved government on occasion. The Shelton's that were friends with Lincoln are now harassed by folks that President John Kennedy would not respect or recognize. True leadership is not about amassing power for self but selflessly giving it away to benefit others.

All of us most stand for Truth or we will face consequences. In this life those who stand for Truth indeed will face persecution but better to die for what is wrong than live prematurely longer for a lie. The Bible is clear, "As for me and my house we will serve the Lord (Joshua 24:15)."

An anonymous source shared some nuggets with me that will interest every Bible scholar, laymen, concerned citizen or open-minded atheist if you want to make a better decision for your future. Buckle up because this will take you for a spin. This trusted source has allowed me to share some of his opinions from his unpublished private journal and it paints a powerful picture that Albrecht Durer or Van Gogh would struggle with, but nonetheless here is the truth and nothing but the truth. When the Democrats once again filed for the Articles of Impeachment on the same day as Patient Zero landed on U.S. soil in January 2020

Two weeks later Trump announces the Deal of the Century Middle East Peace Plan. It was then I realized why the Democrats had launched impeachment against the President. This is all about Israel. You cannot understand God's prophetic timeline until you realize it is always about Israel. Trump was the Head of the Eagle whose two wings (House and Senate) were sustaining Israel. To destroy Israel, you must cut off the head of the Eagle.

My next chapter of this expedition started with the death of Justice Ruth Bader Ginsburg on the eve of the fall feast of Trumpets. But ten days later, the day after Trumpets, when Trump announced her replacement, Judge Amy Coney Barrett, I knew this could be no coincidence either. What I then began to chronicle was the mathematically impossibilities of every major event regarding the election, leading up to, throughout and to the present, were all happening on God's calendar of the Jewish Fall feasts. And now, the Italy Gate affidavit was released on the Christian feast of Epiphany. Any serious student of the Bible knows the importance of understanding prophetically the Seven Feasts of Israel. They are one of several keys we must have to unlock what is ahead for Israel, the Church and America.

The most fascinating of overlapping political events of the election and the Fall feasts of Israel was the Electoral College falling during the Feast of Hanukkah. The historic feast is the celebration of Jewish religious liberty with the liberation of the Temple by a band of guerrillas led by Judah "The Hammer" Maccabee in 166 BC. Who could have known in 166 BC, that 2000 years later the fate of the free world and religious liberty would revolve The Dragon, the Woman & the Great Eagle 3 around a computer program called "the Hammer and Score Card." It is beyond the impossible. But God!

<u>China, the Pope, and the Vatican all have roles in the globalist's agenda</u>. The historic city of Rome has always been known as The City on Seven Mountains. In the book of Revelation chapter 18, John reveals that the identity of this Scarlet clothed Whore of Babylon is Rome. There are <u>two women</u> in Revelation that John describes. The first is the Sun-clothed Woman of Revelation 12. She primarily represents God's Woman Israel. She is the focus in Book I. The other is the great Scarlet Whore of chapter 18. The former represents the Kingdom of God and the true Israel of God. The latter is the apostate one world religion that is resurfacing in these latter days. She is the woman of Books II and III. The end time Antichrist Kingdom is threefold: economic, political, and social (religious). The Whore rides and manipulates the Beast until it turns and devours her. This is Rome's fate. China, the red dragon, will destroy Rome. This is John's prophetic word, not mine. In a nutshell, two current articles best summarize the events of John's Patmos Revelation. The first is "Planet Lockdown" an interview of former high-ranking leader explains with specificity the interlocking pentagon pieces of the plans of "Mr. Globalist" in enslaving the world's population. It is by far, the most comprehensive expose of a five-tiered master plan of the globalist's agenda for the world. I have renamed it, "Revelation at 30,000 Feet." It exposes the Babylon "system" of Revelation.

The other event that is developing, even as I type, is "Italy Gate" and the affidavit released on the Feast of Epiphany, a Christian feast, of the whistleblower who uploaded the computer program that switched the votes from Trump to Biden. It explains why the globalists Democrats are so eager to impeach Trump with just ten days he had left in office. In over forty-five years of studying, writing, and teaching the book of Revelation, I can honestly say never have the words penned by the Apostle John on the isle of Patmos literally leaped from his papyrus through our computer's screens and into our living rooms. We are watching and living through what the prophets of old desired to see.

A word of disclaimer. I am not a prophet, or the son of a prophet. If at all, I am a teacher. That is my gift. I connect the dots of the past and present current events with biblical patterns and principles I have studied most of my life and then see if they point us in the direction God is moving. In Book I, I outline the effects of the COVID invasion upon society, the economy and government. That they concur with Scripture to be the providential hand of God in the affairs of Israel and the Church. I outlined the major events of the 2020 Elections falling on the Fall Feasts of Israel beginning with the death of RBG up to the affidavit released in Italy on the Christian feast of Epiphany, the feast of light and revelation.

First, according to the Center for Disease Control (CDC), the initial case of the Wuhan virus (Patient Zero) arrived in America from Wuhan, China, landing in Washington state at the Seattle-Tacoma International Airport on January 15. The same day, 3,000 miles across the continent, a major political event was just taking off in the Rayburn Room of the U.S. Capitol, in Washington, DC. So how are these atypical events even remotely related? I believe they had been set into motion months prior. It might be more accurate to say they were set into motion 6,000 years prior by another pandemic event of sorts recorded in Genesis 3 that created a new normal for the earth and humankind. Could it be possible that millennia later we find the same three entities - a dragon, _a woman_, and an eagle - struggling for world domination?

Are we witnessing the biblical pattern of an ever-expanding conflict between good and evil throughout the ages coming to a head? Is the pandemic a symptom of something greater, something on a cosmic scale? Let us see. It was also on January 15, that Speaker Nancy Pelosi surrounded by her Democratic House leadership, held a press briefing in the Capitol and signed legislation to officially begin articles of impeachment proceedings against President Trump. Coincidence? Not for me. I do not believe in political coincidences or any other kind for that matter. So, I went to sleep that night pondering if there were any connections between these two occurrences. I would begin exploring the timeline around them first thing in the morning. At 5:30am, while drinking my first cup of coffee, I was checking my texts and came across a week-old video link about Passover. I clicked on it.

About 15 minutes into the teaching, I discovered my next clues to the links surrounding January 15. On January 28, two weeks later, President Trump announced the Deal of the Century — the once in a century peace plan for the Middle East and Israel. On January 31, President Trump closed the borders for travel with China and the UN World Health Organization (WHO) *announced that the Wuhan virus was now at a world pandemic stage level. That was it! That is why the launching of articles of impeachment in DC and Patient Zero landing in the US occurred on the same day. They are connected. How so?*

They are both connected to Israel! How could I make the leap from impeachment to pandemic to Israel in one bold move? I am glad you asked. (Think chess not checkers.) Let me explain. I am not saying Israel is to blame for the COVID-19 pandemic. No, the Jews were responsible for the Black Plague of Europe, the Great Depression, WW2, and most other world calamities. (Sarcasm! My beloved Jewish friends know my sense of humor. I love Israel.) But according to the Bible, that is who Satan is ultimately after. Israel. Read the back of the Book! Israel is God's woman. You cannot understand world events today, political, or otherwise, if you leave Israel out of your equation. That is like trying to find the circumference of a circle and leaving Pi out of your formula. Understand this. That is who the Great Red Dragon in Revelation chapter 12 wants to carry away with the flood – Israel – God's chosen people. This is the primary application of this prophecy in Revelation chapters 12-13.

God is preparing Israel for Messiah's coming! God is preparing the world for Messiah's coming. And this is Satan's nightmare. Today, can we see a red dragon, a woman and an eagle embroiled in warfare and turmoil? Yes. And that is why they are coming after President Trump. The impeachment really is not about Trump. It is about Israel. To stop Israel, you must stop Trump. Is not it an irony that the three main congressional leaders coming after Trump are Jewish – Nadler, Schiff, and Schumer. And today, May 18, the same Democratic House committee members announce to the Supreme Court that they are still investigating the president for more possible impeachment proceedings before year's end. Why are they so vehemently after Trump? The Dragon, the Woman & the Great Eagle. There has never been a president as pro-Israel as Trump. He recognized Jerusalem as Israel's eternal capital, moved the US embassy to Jerusalem, recognized the Golan Heights and now is introducing a deal of-the-century game-changing peace plan for the Middle East. Trump's goals for Israel are all counter-intuitive to Satan's goals of world domination but falling right into place with God's eternal purposes for Israel, the Church, and the nations. The last thing Satan wants is peace in the Middle East.

No wonder the Democratic Party, Speaker Pelosi, Senator Schumer, the leftist media, and the entire Washington establishment are in an all-out blitz to get Trump. Knowingly or not, they are being used as political and prophetic pawns in a geopolitical battle as old as man himself. The peace treaty is the kingpin in putting it all together. To get to the woman, to stop Israel, you must kill the great eagle having two wings. That is how the woman escapes the dragon – on two wings of a great eagle (Rev. 12:14). To stop the wings from giving Israel strength to rise above the flood, you must cut off the head of the eagle. You must impeach Trump!

Is President Trump perfect? Absolutely not. Was Rev. Billy Graham perfect? Absolutely not. Are you or I perfect? Absolutely not but God has raised up kings and used imperfect leaders since the beginning of time. Make no mistake, the Lord used Trump in a powerful way with his love and desire to have the best for America but also to have Israel's back to protect the Holy Land. Without jumping too far ahead, President Biden just gave $235 Million dollars to support the Palestinians in Spring 2021. God honors those that blesses Israel and curses those that cause harm to her.

Israel is God's timepiece. If you want to know what time it is on God's prophetic clock, just see what He is doing with Israel. The Lord will further reveal His plans not just in America but worldwide. Already we can see God's judgments in Trump's House, Pelosi's House, Netanyahu's House, and Windsor's Houses - Parliament and the Palace. From the White House to this pastor's house - judgment begins in the "house" - everyone's house." And related to these activities I noted, "God used Trump to secure and prepare Israel's defenses (Golan Heights); then used him to open the gates to the valley of judgment for Gog, Magog, Meshach and Tubal to come against Israel (Ezk. 38-39). God said He would put it in Gog's heart to come against Israel. In fact, He said he would "put a hook in his jaw" and drag him to the mountains of Israel to judge him." And that going forward, "We must from this point forward view every world political event from God's perspective and endgame strategy, not from a political one - but that God is setting the stage for His Son's soon coronation and enthronement in Jerusalem. If so, we can then understand why the Left is fighting so desperately grasping at every political straw."

Months before January 28, Jared Kushner, Trump's son-in-law who is Jewish, had been leading a delegation to the Middle East negotiating the treaty. All of this was in play long before the virus "leaked" from the Wuhan lab or before Speaker Pelosi officially began impeachment articles or Patient Zero arrived in the United States. But on the very day, January 15, that Speaker Pelosi signed the official legislation to begin drafting articles of impeachment, before the ink from her $1,500 a piece commemorative pens could dry, Patient Zero was landing on the West Coast bringing pestilence to the United States. The more pieces we turn over it is becoming increasingly clear; this is not a coincidence. God said, "And if I withhold the rain, if I send locusts and if I send pestilence upon my people, if my people who are called by my name will humble themselves and pray…" (2 Chronicles 7:13-14).

Could it be that our "If my people" prayers were now beginning to be answered? That the painful process of healing had started? Were all these seemingly unrelated calamities transpiring simultaneously upon the world stage setting into motion the providential hand of God to answer our prayers? Are these the sounds of God's clock ticking? The signs of our times? After weeks of writing, it was becoming increasingly clear with each stroke of my keyboard that God is the One managing this world pandemic. What David Wilkerson said years ago is even truer today, "God has everything under control." Had God begun exposing the sins and motives of men's hearts, judging their actions, and bringing a penitent restoration to the earth to fulfill His eternal purposes for man, Israel, and the Church? If so, how is He doing it? I believe God is using economic, societal, and governmental patterns created in the earth by the spiritual principles (laws) operating in the selfish and wicked hearts of unrepentant man, that He may fulfill His eternal plan for His Paradise upon the earth for His people. That is how. Patterns created by principles that reveal God's purposes in the earth. When you can spot them, you can see the bigger picture. They are not random. Before exploring any biblical and possibly prophetic ties this pandemic may have, let us set the stage by reviewing the current events created by this pandemic in the past months.

Jesus said, "I must work the works of him that sent me, while it is day: the night cometh, when no man can work," John 9:4. A fortnight ago who could have seen the calamities gripping the world by some seemingly invisible hand. Like a thief in the night not making a sound the robber has broken into our house while its occupants slumbered and slept (Mt. 25:5). Now that we are "woke" to the deed, does anybody know what time it is? Yesterday, the economy was roaring like a steam locomotive, the Stock Market soaring to historic highs with more Americans punching the clock than ever recorded. Suddenly, in a blink of an eye, it has come to a screeching halt. The trading floor on Wall Street is barren. Stocks have taken a threshing while shareholders helplessly watched their three-year historic yields vanish on a roller coaster ride of record-setting losses. The New York Times reported on March 20, 2020, "With another fall on Friday, the Dow Jones average is now lower than it was when President Trump took office."

Trump's Blue-Collar Bump has become the COVID-19 Dip. Time will reveal if the dip deepens to recession or worse depression. On Broadway there is no business, literally, no business at all. The curtains have come down - no happy feelings, no stolen bows. Just stranded out in the cold, and for now, no sign of "on with the show." On Times Square? Time is finally waiting. Waiting for everyone, anyone: but there is no one. The bars and restaurants, even the sex shops –deserted, empty, desolate. Madison Square Garden – sold out with nothing but vacant seats. The sounds of silence fill her subways and tenement halls. The city that never sleeps is comatose. At least on 9/11, New Yorkers were able to see the hand of the enemy at work: the planes crashing the Towers, the collapse, the clouds of dust enveloping the borough streets infecting every victim's lungs with a powdery grey death while covering their faces with ashes. No test needed. It was evident who the victims were.

On that day, people on the ground, the fortunate ones, could see the wrath approaching and run for safety. Not today, not now. There is no place to run. Everyone it would appear is trapped above the 93rd floor - no way of getting past the flames to the fire escape, no way of knowing where the virus is or how, when, who it will strike next. Gotham has become the global epicenter of this viral earthquake. Governor Andrew Cuomo said Sunday morning that "an estimated 40% to 80% of residents could get the coronavirus over the course of the pandemic." The city already leads the nation with number of confirmed cases and fatalities. Apocalyptic words from Patmos have an ominous ring that runs right through the heart of it. "Alas, alas, that great city Babylon, that mighty city! for in one hour is thy judgment come. And the merchants of the earth shall weep and mourn over her; for no man buys their merchandise anymore," (Rev. 18:10-11).

People have begun fleeing New York in hopes of escaping the virus' wrath. To keep this exodus from becoming a flashpoint of spreading a second wave across the nation, governors like DeSantis of Florida, have asked these refugees to self-quarantine for two-weeks if they enter his state. Soon, in states like Delaware, vehicles with out-of-state tags will be pulled over by law enforcement. The Dragon, the Woman & the Great Eagle - The state of Texas has set up check points on highways leading out of Louisiana. Motorists are required to fill out travel forms asking for driver's license numbers, vehicle license plate numbers, residency while in Texas and required to self-quarantine for fourteen days. Follow up visits by law enforcement is probable to assure that people are being self-quarantined. "And I heard another voice from heaven, saying, come out of her, my people, that ye be not partakers of her sins, and that ye receive not of her plagues,"

Rev. 18:4. But tonight, in Times Square there are no festal crowds gathered to watch a geodesic ball covered in brilliant Waterford Crystals drop down a flagpole ushering in the new year - only desolation and sobering silence are witnesses to this dawn of a new era – the new normal. Another ball of sorts has already dropped. A genome nucleocapsid covered with deadly glycoprotein crown-like spikes has stealthily descended upon Gotham. But the Big Apple is not the only metropolitan city feeling the bite. This scene is being replayed in practically every city on the globe. The NBA, NFL, PGA, NCAA, MLB, MLS, XFL, NASCAR, even the Kentucky Derby have cancelled, postponed, or delayed. No games, no sports, no sports gods, and goddesses for their weekend patrons to worship. Japan and the International Olympic Committee (IOC) have delayed the 2020 summer games for one year. Hollywood is wondering if any of its 2020 movies will be released in theatres.

Sandy Barker-Mitchell is quoted, "In three short months, just like He did with plagues of Egypt, God has taken away everything we worship. God said, 'You want to worship athletes, I will shut down the stadiums. You want to worship musicians; I will shut down the Civic Centers. You want to worship actors; I will shut down theaters. You want to worship money; I will shut down the economy and collapse the stock market. You do not want to go to church and worship Me, I will make it where you cannot go to church.'" What time is it? It is midnight on Times Square.

Yet, partisan political maneuvering persists by some attempting to take advantage of the moment. Democrats in the House and Senate are stalling over partisan policy issues while the funds for the Paycheck Protection Program (PPP) relief for small businesses are now empty. According to the Daily Mail, Mitch McConnell accuses Nancy Pelosi of 'holding American's paychecks hostage' to get cash for hospitals, state and local government as Democrats block $250 billion extra bailout cash for small businesses. If that were not enough, while Americans on ventilators are literally fighting for their next breath, some public "servants" have allegedly taken advantage of classified information to dump millions of dollars in stock holdings before the markets fell.

> The Hill reported on March 20, 2020 "Four senators sold stocks shortly after a January briefing in the Senate on the novel coronavirus outbreak, unloading shares that plummeted in value a month later as the stock market crashed in the face of a global pandemic." One Georgia senator it is reported that she and her husband dumped $18 million in shares before the crash. "According to financial disclosure forms, each sold hundreds of thousands of dollars in stocks within days of the Senate holding a classified briefing on Jan. 24 with Trump administration officials on the threat of the coronavirus outbreak." Members of Congress are among the most vulnerable age group (65+) affected by this global threat. Several members and staff, the count grows with each passing day, have already tested positive and been quarantined. Others have self-quarantined as a precaution.

This is not to bash Democrats or praise the GOP but at this late stage of the game we are on God's time clock. My prayer is that Biden grows in the Bible; that Vice President Harris will fall in love with Him; that Pelosi will realize true power is not as Speaker, but the supremacy of the Savior, and that Trump will see the Trinity and the Republicans need the Redeemer. Every single one of us needs God's grace, forgiveness, and reservation for an afterlife in Heaven. This book is not about black or white and right and wrong but Heaven and Hell and you either stand with God or you will fall with the Devil.

Today is Tuesday, March 30, 2021, as I type this, and this coming Sunday is Easter. Next year on Easter Sunday despite three trips cancelled last year due to COVID-19 we are planning by faith to go with some professional athletes, Grammy winners, and friends from across America and I am helping co-create the trip to Israel. Just like I was not certain if the event with Darryl Strawberry was going to happen in my hometown on May 13, 2020, I am uncertain if the trip Easter 2022 will fly either but either way, we are swinging for the fence. Plus, I must because Darryl and his wife, Tracy are joining us if it happens. I have been feeling the proverbial walls closing for a long time now and the vaccine is the new scheme to divide us by the "have's and have nots." Soon we will be sidelined for traveling and that is part of their plan and the minister with a global vision will be isolated locally like never before.

This morning I am getting reports from a source close to Israel that they are rumors of a false messiah that is soon to be released and he is in his early thirties. One parent is Jewish and the other a Muslim and will perform many interesting accomplishments with an impressive resume. His name Emmanvel not sure what will turn out with him, but the Bible does say that one will eventually appear and mislead many for a couple years of false hope, peace, and optimism but once again Satan is a counterfeit. Satan can only copy but that clown cannot create. He is an impersonator, but no genuine article and the snake is a fraud, not the Almighty embodying faith.

It is prophesied the great reset will come, the New World Order is in the works and Revelation talks about persecutions and beheadings for those that will not take the coming mark. Pastor Sam Thomas in India's dream is to be a martyr for Christ and regardless of if guillotines are in the cards or concentration camps separating the "haves and have nots" either way, to die is Christ and live is gain. On March 24, 2020, I wrote a constant contact email to two thousand friends a week into the lockdown and said we are at war, and this is biological warfare. Without question it is spiritual warfare and I nailed it. What some of you are just seeing I was warned about long ago.

Yes, if you notice every time Satan threw the sink at me God eventually blessed me with a new kitchen. When the Devil tried to knock me out, the Lord promoted me forward as I lifted Him up. Yes, when God is blessing the Devil starts messing but conversely is also true. I now say when the Devil is messing God is ready to bless once more. The beauty of the Sovereignty of God is that the Lord is still on the throne, and He is not afraid of Satan nor is He on the Devil's timeclock. It is the Devil who is worried and knows He is on God's timetable and his minutes are few. Just like Durer's iconic painting, we must armor up and march on because Truth is on our side. God is cleaning house, exposing the frauds, making the cloudy clear, and the old is becoming new. Indeed, God does all things well in His time.

Two men recently posted a video filmed on location at the "COVID" Hotel in McAllen, TX allegedly about our own government possibly hosting human smuggling and illegal aliens. Some predict two million may cross the border illegally within the next year and most likely to be registered to the party of the political left to help ensure they will never lose an election again. While helping fight human trafficking for several years, I know the atrocity is real. While we are still fighting over race issues today as adults, the real issue of slavery today is that innocent children are being captured, tortured, and sexually molested and violated against their will. While most of you are stuck playing checkers the real war is at the chess table. It is a diversion, and you may be, but I am not being played. It is hard to be in the game when you are still sitting on the sidelines or on the couch. #Ouch

We were making such great progress and had some great programs and projects in the works, but most are clueless as to how evil this agenda is. Pause and pray today for those who are imprisoned now. Adrenochrome is a horrible delicacy to those on the Devil's diet and if you are breathing you can still repent and get right with God. Our backyard has a once beautiful solar bird bath and it fell in a violent storm and when the wind knocked it off its pedestal it chipped a hole in the basin. Sadly, today no more birds come to drink because the two-inch hole no longer holds water. I have kept it for two reasons. A reminder of its purpose from the past but that solar light on top of the broken bird basin still shines in the night. Similarly, our nation corporately and many of us personally have taken some hits and some shots, have been knocked down, misquoted, harassed, and followed a time or two. If the enemy had their way, would be left for dead. The good news is God delights in broken things and instead of discarding them He still uses them to radiate His glory. Helen Keller was right, opposed to curse the darkness she would rather light a candle and that night light not only shines in the night but encourages me to shine by day and glow through the evening. Indeed, it is getting dark in America and our world but until He comes or calls me home, you will find this patriot-preacher both standing on post, occupying until He comes and shining a Light in the night.

Back in February 2021, I preached a sermon in my hometown at The Fellowship Church in Maryland and my sermon was Jesus said, "Occupy, Until I Come." The goal then and now was not for me to be seen but that the Gospel could be heard. In my remarks that Sunday I shared, "I believe today He may want some of you to run for public office, some to write a thank you note to someone today. God may want you to do an anonymous act of kindness, but you have only two options you can either be vacant or OCCUPY space. Greater than a President coming to town tomorrow, and you may feel you are standing on post while only guarding a dumpster or does not "feel glamorous" but greater than anything the God of the Universe could come back tonight.

We need to occupy, not violently, but faithfully because not only is the world watching here but God is watching from up There. I submit to you those with the greatest rewards in Glory will not be big ministries. The greatest rewards will be for the folks who felt at times like their assignment was small, overlooked in the corner, or next to the dumpster. I remember at one time thinking, "I signed up to guard the most powerful person on the planet. I signed up to jog next to armored limos with the American and Presidential flags waving in the wind and dying to take a bullet. But leadership never starts with "I" but is in the middle of "Him" and "win" and if you are on post and occupying space you are honoring Christ. When the King comes may we be found on post and faithful.

At one time I wanted to protect presidents but today <u>maybe I am assigned to protect you</u>. The movie "In the Line of Fire" starring Clint Eastwood and "The Bodyguard" starring Kevin Costner are two of my favorite films. Both iconic actors played a current and retired Secret Service agent. Both characters were named Frank. Eastwood took a bullet for a president and Costner took one for Whitney's character a Hollywood star and Grammy singer, but Jesus took the enemy's best shot for you. They both were on post in their respective film, and I love the endorsement of my friend, Tina Marie Griffin who is now on an 84-city tour with some of the doctors quoted in this book warning against the vaccine and governmental overreach said, "Frank is willing to take a bullet for the Truth (cause of Christ)."

Since my parents did not name me Mark, I will shoot it straight and be "frank" with you. In these pages you have read about me being president of student government in middle school, prom king in high school and named an alumnus of the decade in college but the last few years one of the most respected became rejected. I shared "Welcome to the Neighborhood, Welcome to Washington and was considered for a job years ago at the State Department to welcome folks to America. Hands down, my most important assignment has been a preacher of the Gospel and defender of the faith and I have had the honor to literally welcome to Heaven tens of thousands by faith and God's grace. My prayer is that you will make your reservation in Heaven today because tomorrow is not guaranteed for any of us.

In wrapping up this book, I came across a document that says all our restrictions have been lifted, and we are FREE…it is a little old though…. dated 1776." To take it a step further, thousands of years ago the Bible tells us we are free in Christ, but truth be told millions do not respect the Constitution or Christ. They despise the Bill of Rights and the Bible, and they disrespect authority on Earth because they do not love True Authority of Almighty God. It all about self and they are deceived and blinded by the lie of the enemy that you can just do you and get what you want but sin comes with a price. I have said for several years either the bad guys are going down or me and my friends are. Make no mistake, if we go down it was because we lifted Christ and either way glory to His Name. However, if we go down temporarily the born-again Christians will rise and reign with God forever in Heaven. Those who go down unrepented from the grace of God and His glorious Gospel will continue to go down to Hell and never return.

President Abraham Lincoln was not only the right man for his time, but he was constantly cognizant of what time it was. His wife Mary Todd Lincoln gave him a brass pocket watch with his name engraved on it as a reminder to not waste any time while he was able to help.

He had a pocket watch, you may have a Timex or Rolex but all I have in my internal clock is an hourglass and time is ticking and one of the scariest verses in all the Bible is "The summer is ended, the harvest is past, and we are not saved."

In 1863, a young lad was playing the solitary game Hopscotch in front of 1600 Pennsylvania Avenue. His game ceased when he saw a senior citizen crying and with his hands covering his face in frustration. The boy approached the man and said, "Sir, why do you cry?" The man rolled his eyes and said, "Son, you can do nothing for me" and the boy replied, "My heart hurts to see you upset. Please tell me why you are crying?" The man barked, "Well since no one else will listen, I will tell you, my story. My son has a warrant for his arrest for deserting his post during the Civil War and I need to speak to the President."

The young boy's eyes grew wide and said, "Why do you need to speak to him? The man sternly said, "I raised him better than that and I need to speak to President Lincoln for a potential pardon." The boy said two words that echo through history today: "Follow me!" The child immediately grabbed the man's hand and together they walked straight towards the black iron gates. When the officer saw the boy, the gates swung open wide.

After open sesame, the boy was gaining momentum walking across the North Lawn of the Executive Mansion as if he owned the place and had been on the grounds before and he certainly knew the lay of the land. The senior who was discrediting him moments before is now wide eyed in disbelief with this boy's determination. Within two minutes the pair was now entering the foyer of the most powerful home in the world and standing inside the hallowed hallway side by side.

With disbelief but growing faith, the man watched as the boy now called the shots and orchestrated what was to come next. The child told the man to wait while he raced up the red carpet towards the upstairs residence like he owned the place. No less than three minutes the boy is coming back down the stairs but with a six-foot four stately man wearing all black, sporting a full beard and adorning a stove top hat. The man, now in complete shock, is a second away from being toe to toe with the most powerful person in the world.

The little boy that was just out on the street introduced President Abraham Lincoln to the man who just moments before was crying and on the outside looking in. Honest Abe shook his hand and after hearing the sob story of his boy in trouble graciously issued a presidential pardon. How in the world did the older man get in the White House? The boy that he had discounted was Tad Lincoln, Abraham's son. The Bible says, "No man gets to the Father unless you come in with the Son (John 14:6)."

For thousands of years, God's only Son has also been overlooked, bypassed, discounted, and many have used His holy name in vain as a curse word as opposed to using His name with reverence. We mistreated Heaven himself with assaults from Hell and the Book that embodies Love is now in a cancel culture society, as if He, His Word, or His followers promote "Hate Speech." Today you can listen to the lies from Hell or get on board with the Truth and secure your reservation with Christ.

As I finally finish writing this second version of the manuscript assigned by the Lord, in two days we will celebrate Good Friday. It was the day we reflect and honor the supreme sacrifice Jesus paid on our behalf. President Lincoln was shot in the back of the head on Good Friday, and it was reported that the night he headed towards Ford's Theater while exiting the White House paused and tipped his hat to an African American and said, "Goodbye." The butler said the president always said, "Hello" or "see you later" but on that fateful Friday it was goodbye.

I am certain that the "greats" know what time it is, and Lincoln also knew his time was up. With the watch in his pocket, he not only redeemed the time but rarely wasted it. That night it was my ancestor that helped carry the bleeding president across the street and I am sure with blood on his own hands. I believe I also would have blood on mine for not warning you. The Bible says in Ezekiel 3:16-18,

> *"And it came to pass at the end of seven days, that the word of the Lord came unto me, saying, Son of man, I have made thee a watchman unto the house of Israel: therefore, hear the word at my mouth, and give them warning from me. When I say unto the wicked, thou shalt surely die and thou gives him not warning from his wicked way, to save his life; the same wicked man shall die in his iniquity; but his blood will I require at thine hand. Yet if thou warn the wicked and he turn not from his wickedness, nor his wicked way, he shall die in his iniquity; but thou have delivered thy soul."*

Today, respectfully I needed Jesus and He saved me in 1979 at a country church in Brandywine, MD. Thankful my godmother led my mother to the Lord and by His grace and her obedience my entire family is on their way to Heaven. Not because we are "good" but because we have been forgiven by God. You need Jesus, your family needs the Father's forgiveness, the Pelosi's need the Prince of Peace, Cuomo need Christ, Gaetz needs God, Trumps need the Trinity, America needs the Almighty and the world needs The Word. Jesus said, "I am the Way, Truth and Life and no one gets to Heaven but by Him."

The last three out of four years I had flown on my own dime to preach to nearly one third of a million Africans at Mandela Soccer Stadium in Uganda. I miss those dear friends and those times together but praise God for the opportunity and that I seized it when it was presented. The song I sang as a boy is still true, "Red, yellow, black and white, <u>all</u> are precious in God's sight." Do not be fooled by the Deep State and now is the TIME to wake up from your deep sleep. Some saints had been asleep longer than Rip Van Winkle and the game is almost over; and people need the Lord. Jesus asked a few of his followers to stay awake with him three times on the night He was to be betrayed and arrested, In the following days, He would face an unfair trial and sentenced to die. The God who embodied love was killed by hate. Three times instead of being alert, awake and on post, they were all asleep at the wheel. Today, not much has changed. Fear has crippled those in faith, pastors followed the lie and forsook Truth, and some sold out for far less than thirty pieces of silver. Today, I want to be among His disciples who were still alert and awaiting His return.

My ancestor carried President Abraham Lincoln in 1865 and for nearly fifty years now I have been carrying not Lincoln but his ideals. Far greater than carrying the President today in 2021, I am carrying the message of The King of Kings and as a Gospel preacher I have 'Good News' for you! God loves you! Keep in mind it is only good news if you receive it before the clock expires.

Christendom has lost some generals of the faith in the last few years. In evangelist circles we lost Dr. Billy Graham in 2018, Reinhard Bonnke in 2019 and Dr. Luis Palau in March 2021. In April 2021, I was listening to "Elvis Radio" and country artist T.G. Shepherd was the special guest. He was a friend to Elvis and my father, family and I met him while visiting Graceland in 2017. T.G. had a great musical career in his own right and he said, "We lost some of the best country singers this past year. We lost Joe Diffie, Kenny Rogers, Charlie Pride, Mac Davis, Charlie Daniels, just to name a few." Then he paused, reflecting that they were not only famous but more importantly were family and his friends. Not wanting to miss the conclusion of his interview, I sat in my car in my driveway and continued to listen. T.G.'s final statement really hit me when he said, "*But when the singer is gone the song lives on.*"

Yes, we only have a few evangelists left and I love what my eighty-five-year-old friend Dr. Junior Hill said, "*Never has our world needed the evangelist more* but utilized them less." How true and a sad indictment on those that had not seen souls saved in years or failing in these last days to "occupy" in person, until He comes. Shadrach, Meshack and Abednego were in the fire, Daniel was in the lion's den, Paul and Silas went to prison but through it all God was with each of them. We lost Graham, Bonnke, and Palau to name a few and we cannot forget Dr. Fred Price and Bishop Harry Jackson, too; but one thing remains. These faithful servants are <u>gone</u> but the STORY lives *on*. I still believe we make history every time we tell His Story and Charlton Heston was correct when he said, "The Gospel is the greatest story ever told." I love to tell the story and Lord willing, will continue to do so until my time is up.

Regardless of if Pastor Rodney Howard - Browne finds himself again in prison or if Christians end up handcuffed on a train to a concentration camp, or me after sticking my neck out in a guillotine, we are still on post! We have redeemed the time and have preached the Word. Even if we go down in death, we are instantly going up in the afterlife. God wins and so do we! But not only us, but those who get right with the Lord before it is too late.

As a child I vividly recall seeing "Superman" in the theaters, and I loved both George Reeves in black and white but in color no one was better than Christopher Reeve. You may recall when his world was in chaos Superman did his absolute best to circle the globe and despite his cape and superhuman powers, he was unable to turn back time or the tide and was not able to save the day. The theme to the book from the beginning was, "**Ministry Minus Urgency = Catastrophe**!" The subtitle was "**One Minister's Quest to Save the World**." That Minister was not me but the Messiah. Where Superman, Billy Graham, Moody, and thousands of noble and sincere souls have tried, only One could save the world. It is only in Jesus' flawless blood that our dirty souls can be cleansed!

Over the years, on planes, trains, and automobiles I would have never risked my life promoting religion, preaching Mohammed, Buddha, or some false narrative. I went on assignment to proclaim the Name Above All Names and His name is Jesus, The Christ who is the Son of the living God. The Bible says, "Under Heaven there is no other name given among men whereby we must be saved." It is in Christ alone that we find freedom and salvation and it was God's Son that died on that cross and arose from the dead to pay the penalty of the fall of man in the Garden of Eden.

Initially, I picked my dear friend, Alice Marie Johnson for a couple of reasons to write the foreword to this book. First, she is an angel. Second, she is my sister in Christ and third, a cherished friend and of course black lives matter but we both see the big picture that every life matters. Finally, Alice knows firsthand what it means to have served time and she agrees that the Church and too many citizens have wasted time; but the Lord calls us to "redeem the time." As I was in the homestretch of writing this book I spoke to her today on Good Friday, April 2, 2021. I was in a drive through at Chick-Fil-A and called her and she answered on the second ring. It is humbling to have friends in high places! She told me, "Frank, I knew the Lord was granting me freedom not just for me but that I would help liberate others still in bondage, enslaved or incarcerated to sin and who need the Son." More than ever we all need God's endorsement and Him alone.

After just placing my order at my favorite fast-food franchise I said, "Alice, I believe God also granted you freedom before the lockdown to help pastors, churches and countless now who accidentally or inadvertently incarcerated themselves and gladly followed the false narrative and stayed on house arrest. Where the Spirit of the Lord is liberty; and He is going to use you through Christ to help set many captives free before time runs out." Alice forever is one of my favorites and God has BIG plans for her. Thank you, Jesus!

On Good Friday, April 2, 2021, tragedy struck the United States Capitol again when a deranged man who had Muslim ties came at a high rate of speed and barreled through the security checkpoint and struck two U.S. Capitol Police officers. Some had said that Officer William "Billy" Evans pushed his colleague out of harm's way and took the full force and was killed. After striking him, the car slammed against the same barricade that I have driven over many times in the past when I was a driver to a Member of Congress, employed with the U.S. Capitol Police or on official duty with the United States Congress.

On April 5, 2021, I spoke with a friend and U.S. Capitol Police officer on the phone for half an hour. He said, "Frank, I thought after the event on January 6, 2021, I would never see an in the line of duty death again in my career but this one that just happened again really shook me." The brave men and women suit up once again and brave the dark, while shining a light and are "on post" while defending freedom. Keep these brave heroes of "America's Police Department" in your prayers.

I am always looking for symbolism and it is fitting that the officer died on Good Friday. Two thousand years ago, another One paid the full price on that first Good Friday, and He saved the day and died in our place. He did not take a bullet, or full impact of a car used as a weapon but was a recipient of three rusty nails that changed the course of history and snapped the calendar from BC to AD. God bless Officer Evan's family and keep them in your prayers as well as the USCP community.

On April 8, 2021, I had a three in the morning wakeup call and was out the door by a quarter of four for a five thirty boarding on a flight back to Los Angeles. It was an honor to return and preach for the 115th Anniversary of the historic revival that took place at Azusa Street Mission at the invite of my good friend, Apostle Fred Berry. He was bestowing the William Seymour Award to Sean Feucht who has been as bold as a lion the past year taking praise rallies across America. I preached at the event at Azusa that Sean led in music. Despite being one of the main speakers ushering in the New Year celebration in the "City of Angels" we did not officially meet that day. Truth be told, I was disappointed because I was really looking forward to it. He had to race off to another event and I took the picture of Sean and my friend Randy Shepherd together, but it was not meant to be.

God does all things well in His time. When this event came on the calendar and Fred invited us both back for the two-day conference the Lord worked it out. We had a State Senator from California and she presented us all with an award for helping unite Los Angeles and promoting the Gospel and goodwill. My heart is to see unity in the community across America and around the globe. It was an honor to be recognized and honored that night with Sean, Apostle Fred & Wilma Berry and my good friend, Pastor Caleb Cooper from New Mexico.

Apostle Fred asked me to personally pick up Sean at LAX Airport an hour prior to that evening's event and where we did not connect before I was now chaperoning him to the service. It was my honor to carry his guitar to the event and God has used that brother around the world and the greatest are the servants. Sean and I could relate that we both had preached in dangerous regions, and he had ministered in Saudi Arabia, Afghanistan, and Iraq to name a few. His obedience to the call long before the pandemic helped him be the choice candidate to lead the way while during this planned plot the past year.

It was humbling that we would both not only get to be part of such an historic night of unity among races and bringing denominations together but taking a STAND when many churches were still silent and sitting out. Sean had run unsuccessfully for Congress the year before and gave it all he had. If he had won, then this nation-wide tour would have most likely not have happened. What looked like a setback in the eyes of man was a setup by God to not represent Congress but to be an Ambassador of God to a confused, scared, and timid world. That night when the event was over, I was able to finally thank Sean one on one on behalf of tens of thousands of Christians both home and abroad who have been encouraged by his ministry. Sean not only took a stand but understands the importance of occupying territory and being on post until the Lord comes.

In his book <u>BRAZEN – Be A Voice, Not an Echo</u>, Sean talks about during the COVID-19 lockdown in March 2020 that a pastor from New York City emailed him a link to a past sermon he preached while visiting that church months before. The pastor said, "Sean's sermon helped them tremendously to navigate through the pandemic. Sean noted he rarely listens to his past sermons, but he was intrigued, and he wrote, "I referenced a rather obscure passage in the Bible I had never preached on before. The passage contains John's initial reaction to the prophetic vision God unleashed on him in Revelation chapter one. He was alone on the island of Patmos and was overcome with fear and anxiety after just a glimpse of God's vision. John described that moment in Revelation 1:17 (TPT): "When I saw Him, I fell down at his feet as good as dead, but He laid His right hand on me and I heard His reassuring voice saying, "Don't yield to fear, I Am the Beginning, and I Am the End.""

Sean continued, "The Lord spoke directly to John's fear and rebuked it. John had received a glimpse of what lay ahead for the world. There were still twenty chapters ahead of intense and otherworldly Revelation. John had no idea of the events that would pass before his eyes concerning the end of the age – images that could easily bring panic, fear, and discouragement. Before he had a chance to panic, however, God reminded John (and you and me) that He is the Beginning and the End. The vision, John's life, all of eternity are His story and He alone is the One writing it. Because He is the "author and finisher (Hebrews 12L2) of our faith, we can trust that this story will always end up "for the good of those that love Him and are called according to His purposes." (Romans 8:28)."

Sean concluded, "God's gentle yet firm response to John's bewilderment and fear overwhelmed me. Tears ran down my face as I sat listening to my own message. That single scripture cut through my confusion and reminded me that it is not me but God who is writing my story. Hearing myself preach felt like looking over an old journal entry where you shared the testimony of God's goodness. You begin to remember His grace again. The bigger story God was writing with my life came into focus. I have been through plenty of valleys of disappointment, despair, and hopelessness. But not once had He left me hanging in the process. Not one time did God ever fail to come through. He always turned every situation around to bring redemption, hope, and restoration. Lastly, "We are not accountable to the murmurs of the crowd. There is only one voice that matters in the end. There is only One we will ultimately be accountable to for how we steward our lives. His ways are not our ways. He calls us to do crazy things, even when they feel we are at the precipice of our career, or when we feel most comfortable in the lives we have built. There is only One with the pen in hand, writing our story. It is a story so great that "You would not believe, even if you were told (Habakkuk 1:5)."

Filmmaker and podcaster Dinesh D'Souza helped reveal the media's lies about the death of Officer Brian Sicknick and those behind it were caught. The Truth always comes out and Glenn Greenwald wrote on April 19, 2021, "It was crucial for liberal sectors of the media to invent and disseminate a harrowing lie about how U.S. Capitol Police Officer Brian Sicknick died. That is because he is the only one that they could claim was killed by pro-Trump protesters at the January 6, 2021, riot at the Capitol. So, *The New York Times* on January 8 published an emotionally gut-wrenching but complete fiction that never had any evidence – that Officer Sicknick's skull was savagely bashed in with a fire extinguisher by a pro-Trump mob until he died – and, just like the now-discredited Russian bounty story also unveiled by that same paper, cable outlets and other media platforms repeated this lie over and over in the most emotionally manipulative way possible. Nobody on the record claimed it happened.

The autopsy found no blunt trauma to his head. Sicknick's own family kept urging the press to stop spreading this story because he called them the night of January 6 and told them he was fine – obviously inconsistent with the media's claim that he died by having his skull bashed in – and his own mother kept saying that she believed he died of a stroke. But the gruesome story of Sicknick's "murder" was too valuable to allow any questioning. It was too valuable to allow any questions. It was weaponized over and over to depict the pro-Trump mob not as just violent but also barbaric and murderous, because if Sicknick wasn't murdered by them, then nobody was. The others who lost their lives that day were four pro-Trump supporters: two who died of heart attacks, one from an amphetamine overdose, and the other, Ashli Babbitt, who although unarmed, was shot point blank in the neck by the Capitol Police. So crucial was the fairytale of Sicknick's cause of death that it made its way into the official record of President Trump's impeachment trial in the Senate. They had Joe Biden himself recite from the script; even as clear facts mounted proving their narrative was untrue. Because of its centrality to the media narrative and agenda, anyone who tried to point out the serious factual deficiencies in this story – in other words, people trying to be journalists – were smeared by the Democratic Party loyalists who pretend to be journalists as "Sicknick Truthers," white nationalist sympathizers, and supporters of insurrection. Because the truth usually prevails, their lies, yet again, all came crashing down on the heads on Monday. The District of Columbia's chief medical examiner just released his official ruling in the Sicknick case, and it was so definitive that The Washington Post – one of the media outlets that had been pushing the multiple falsehoods – did not even bother to try to mask or mitigate the stark conclusion it revealed:

"Capitol Police officer Brian D. Sicknick suffered two strokes and died of natural causes a day after he confronted rioters at the January 6, insurrection, the district's chief medical examiner has ruled." Using understatement, the paper added: "The ruling likely will make it difficult for prosecutors to pursue homicide chargers in the officer's death." This definitive finding from the medical examiner rids us of the fire extinguisher lie. So, they changed their story to claim pro-Trump protestors still murdered Sicknick, not with a fire extinguisher, but with bear spray. Since bear spray is not known to usually be fatal, that possibility was also ruled out. Francisco Diaz, the medical examiner, said the autopsy found no evidence the 42-year-old officer suffered an allergic reaction to chemical irritants, which Diaz said would have caused Sicknick's throat to quickly seize. Diaz also said there was no evidence or external injuries. Diaz said he had two strokes at the base of the brain stem that caused a clot in an artery that supplies blood to that area of the body but couldn't comment on whether he had a preexisting medical condition, citing privacy laws."

In closing, Greenwald wrote, "What is most depressing about this entire spectacle is that this time, they exploited the tragic death of a young man to achieve their tawdry goals. They never cared in the slightest about Officer Brian Sicknick. They had just spent months glorifying a protest movement whose core view is that police officers are inherently racist and abusive. He had just become their toy, to be played with and exploited in order to depict the January 6 protest as a murderous orgy carried out by savages so primitive and inhumane that they were willing to fatally bash in the skull of a helpless person or spray them with deadly gases until they choked to death on their own lung fluids. None of it was true, but that did not matter – and it still does not to them – because truth, as always, has nothing to do with their actual function. If anything, truth is an impediment to it." Make no mistake, Officer Sicknick fought courageously and valiantly that day and his death was unfortunate and when a society was not on post, he stood his ground and nobly helped defend freedom even at the expense of losing his life. No doubt that mob was wrong to storm the Capitol and our Constitution allows us to peacefully assemble but not fight and enter a building unlaw-fully. My sincere prayers and condolences to the Sicknick family and some may try to abuse a death politically, but God sees all and comfort to the family spiritually. No matter what is said, Officer Sicknick indeed is one of "America's finest" and we owe him and his colleagues in that long, line of a blue a debt of gratitude for their service and sacrifice.

My good friend, Pastor Frank Santora from Faith Church in Danbury, Connecticut, and a campus in New York City wrote a book entitled, <u>Turn It Around</u>. Right when all looks lost, only God can turn things around and what looks like game over is a fresh start when The Master flips the script. Nothing is over when God is in the middle of it!

One of my favorite sermon illustrations is about the Moritz Retzch painting, "CHECKMATE." It was a controversial painting of the Devil playing chess against a born-again Christian. In 1888, the "Columbia Chess Chronicle" featured it to the readers and the backstory was a renowned chess champion looked at the painting and saw something that was overlooked by everyone else. The painter had the audacity to insinuate that Satan not only runs the board but wins in the game of life. This arrogance intrigued but infuriated the chess champion and after further examination he was happy to report that the painting was in error. When asked how, the said with a smile, "Because after further review, The King has one more move!"

The moral of the story is when it looks like game is over or "The End" is when God resurrects dead situations. He got Moses through the Red Sea, little David decapitated a giant named Goliath, and the three Hebrew teens did not burn in the flames. In fact, Jesus was smack in the center of the fire with them, and no one burned! You see, when you are on FIRE for God, the flames cannot hurt you. However, those that die without receiving Christ as Savior will encounter Hell's flames that are never quenched. That is not glamorous but the Gospel Truth. You may be down, discouraged, depressed, been divorced and have some debt, but if you are not dead then God is not done!

Apostle Fred Berry and I were supposed to return last year for the 2020 Olympics in Tokyo and minister during the games and COVID-19 cancelled that. We just learned that we would not be ministering there in 2021, either. You cannot make this up because instead of flying clear around the world to minister in Tokyo, Azusa Street is in "Little Tokyo" and we ministered in the U.S. instead. When you look at the letters in AZUSA it caught my eye that half the word spells USA. The AZ is not for Phoenix or Scottsdale, but AZ represents the Alpha and Omega, Christ is the First and Last and perhaps should He tarry, God may use our stand on the historic anniversary of Azusa that God the Father, Jesus the Son and Holy Spirit could do it again in Los Angeles. The city that was known for stars could be pointed back to The Son.

On a side but powerful note, the famed German Theologian Dietrich Bonhoeffer was killed for his faith on April 9, 1945. On that same date we were honoring the start of the revival that God brought to Los Angeles, and which was the springboard to initiate the entire Pentecostal denomination and movement. The reason that Sean, Apostle Fred, Pastor Caleb, and I could stand that day was because we had been standing nonstop since the pandemic hit. Plus, we all were willing to die for the cause of Christ. Regardless, if we got to be used of the Lord as conduits and catalysts for change, or like Dietrich we had died, either way we were not on an ego trip but on a genuine mission trip. Dietrich was hung for sticking his neck out for the Gospel. John the Baptist was beheaded and one day we could be as well, but the Gospel is worth sharing. You cannot trust those who tanked the economy, enforced unnecessary lockdown, escalated the death rate and those making additional billions of dollars while making it difficult for those of us who lived by faith with no guaranteed salary and who were willing to die delivering the mail. I am sticking with the One who stuck on the cross for mankind's sin and as for me and my house we will serve The Lord.

My buddy, Nikita Koloff recently preached in May 2021 in Newark, DE and it was a door I was able to open for him. He did a Saturday men's breakfast at the church and then preached the paint off the walls on Sunday. He preached a powerful message on Spiritual Warfare and could not have been timelier and the champ in Christ said three things that really hit me like a ton of bricks. First, he noted, "**Who in Hell are you?**" He said most people are not known or harassed by demons in Hell because they hardly know the Lord. Those that are harassed, targeted, mocked, and followed are not always bad but in these last days may be the ones doing it right. Plus, if you are not being bothered by the enemy you may be on his team. #Hello

Secondly, he said he is often asked does he still wrestle since retirement? He is in amazing shape and truth be told he almost fought Stallone in ROCKY IV. Out of 800 to audition to play Ivan Drago he came in second place only to Dolph Lundgren who got the part. Nikita had a screen test with Sly in Hollywood and was in the ring with Rocky! The five-time world wrestling champ is still in great shape but at one time he was 6'4, 289 pounds, seven percent body fat with 34-inch waist. To say he had the "V" shape going on would be an understatement. His answer was profound, "Yes, I wrestle every single day. I either am wrestling Satan or my flesh." He nailed it! Yes, we are in a fight and now is not the time to sit out or run scared.

Lastly, he closed his sermon with this statement. Satan and his demons were having a meeting trying to see how best to trick the world. One demon thought he would score brownie points with his boss and said, "Let's say there is no Heaven." Lucifer replied, "That wouldn't work. Most Christians realize that Heaven is real even though John Lennon in his song "Imagine" wrote in his lyrics that maybe there wasn't one. Another demon said, "Let us say there is no Hell." The Devil said, "That won't work because Jesus preached more on Hell than Heaven." Satan than suggested, "I will tell them that there is no hurry, and we will catch millions off guard and snatch them to hell and they will burn forever in the lake of fire." That statement ladies and gentlemen is the premise of the book! Tell them no <u>urgency</u> is needed, take your time, live your best life now, do it your way, sleep around, enjoy sin, it's all about you and maybe one day you can get right with God but no rush." Jesus said, "Today is the day of salvation!" When Billy Graham was asked what the greatest surprise of his life was, he replied, "The brevity of life. How short it is and we are here one moment and gone the next." I have done my best to sound the alarm, paint a picture that time is short, and we must be ready with our reservations secure, and bags packed.

One of my favorite stories I learned after Meadowlark Lemon died was a picture that perfectly captioned this thought. His hat, shoes and suitcase were next to the door and the next day he was flying out of town for the first time in years to have a reunion with his legendary colleagues - the iconic Harlem Globetrotters. I helped open a door for him to preach in over a dozen states and we did multiple events together but what I am most proud of was the assist I gave to him and another evangelist. When God used me to connect Ronnie Dean, The Preaching Machine with Lark they did 300 events together. That reunion with the Globetrotters never happened on Earth but for those born again will have a big celebration in Heaven. What I love about that picture was when my cherished friend's time was up, his bags were packed, his reservations set in Heaven, and he was ready to go when his number was called. My question to you are your bags packed, reservation secure and ready to stand before a Holy God? Lucifer will let you down, but the Lord will love you and lift you up. You cannot win with the Devil, and you will not lose in the end with the Lord and that is the Gospel Truth.

The first four words of the Bible in Genesis 1:1 say it all, "**In the beginning GOD….** created the Heavens and Earth." Nobody else but King Jesus! Governments, heads of state, Hollywood stars, eastern religions, cults, new age theology or a new world order are NOT your friends or your savior. The Bible says, "Some trust in chariots, and some in horses: but we will remember the name of the LORD our God (Psalms 20:7)." The only One with your best interest in mind is God not globalists and it is high time you put your trust in the Savior not science.

For all my mathematician friends, lovers of education and those infatuated with science; let God "take you to school" to bring you up to speed before the Teacher appears and gives you a "pop quiz" and you are still ill-prepared. Get out a pencil and paper because class is now in session and His bell (trumpet) is about to ring! Gabriel is in Heaven now getting ready to blow the horn, but I picture him now licking his lips before the trumpet is on his lips There are **23,145 verses** in the Old Testament and **7,957 verses** in the New Testament. This gives a total of **31,102 verses**, which is an average of a little more than 26 verses per chapter. John 11:35 ("Jesus wept") is the shortest verse in most English translations.

Before I proceed, that small verse alone in the Gospel with just two words should tell you in the New Testament who Christ is after recalling the first three words in the Bible. GOD not Confucius, Mohammed or Buddha made the world (Genesis 1:1). When you finally grasp that fact then we learn in the first chapters of the Bible about the fall of Adam and Eve bringing the first virus into the world. It was not spelled COVID, or HIV but the virus that infected the world is known as "SIN." Our sin separates us from a Holy God. Know where the media and powers to be fooled you to trust the so-called experts and false narrative to take a vaccine to protect you from a virus that the majority could never die from. In fact, the vaccine will do more harm than good.

The Old Testament teaches that God made Heavens and the Earth. The Devil offered sin and by wanting to become like God and resemble "little gods" like the scientists today pushing transhumanism while desiring to create 'designer babies.' Where Cabbage Patch kids were the craze at Christmas in the early 1980's, multiplied millions are crazy to follow their scam today. The leadership gurus for years who pompously beat their chest like Tarzan espousing they would have 20/20 vision in 2020 are still blind as a bat today sitting in the dark.

In the shortest verse of the Bible found in the New Testament we see that JESUS WEPT. Not because He was weak but heartbroken for YOU! Without a payment for the penalty of sin today mankind would still be duped and damned. However, God saw the gap that was between sinful man and His Holy Heaven, and He sent His only Son on a rescue mission to bridge lost sinners to a loving Savior. God had one Son and He was Ambassador, missionary, and evangelist.

Christmas brought God to man; but Easter brought man to God. His death, burial and resurrection satisfied the payment for our sin since the Garden of Eden. The Bible says, "While we were yet sinners Christ died for us." When you consider that there are 31,102 verses in the bestselling book of all time it is not coincidence that this is what we found. An archeologist would have unearthed the greatest discovery ever and DaVinci Code cannot hang with the One who hung on the cross for the world. Keep in mind Mohammed did not die for you but Jesus, The Christ did and why not live for the One who died in your place?

Nobody took His life, but the Lord of the Universe voluntarily died in our place, and He gave up the Ghost. To quote my dear friend, Ronnie Dean, The Preaching Machine who has preached over 9,000 sermons, "He died the victim of a Roman Cross, 72 hours later God coughed in Greek, He sneezed in Latin, He spit in Chronology, He spoke in Hebrew and thundered like a Lion from His den and said, "Son, you were the victim of a Roman Cross three days ago but today I am making the victor of a Jewish grave. They put you asleep as a Lamb, but I am waking you up the conquering Lion of the Tribe of Judah. He resurrected from the dead, He took the smile of that grinning skull at Golgotha, handcuffed the lightening put thunder in jail and put the machinery of death in reverse. Death, Hell, Satan, or the grave did not have the juice to keep The Big Boy down. God painted a rainbow of victory in the shadow of death to prove He was alive forevermore."

In our Twitter, soundbite world if you want a nugget to nibble on or a fortune cookie to take to the bank this is it. Fellow students, today while school is in session your homework assignment for tonight, "Open up the Bible. In the exact center of the Holy Book (not Quran) but Christ's autobiography, The True Prophet you will find Psalms 118:8. This verse is the exact center of His Word. It summarizes succinctly in a singular sentence not only my book you hold in your hand now but the road map of survival for your life.

"*It is* better to trust in the LORD than to put confidence in man."

The answer is not in a vaccination, but salvation and man will fail but you JESUS is nothing, but the Truth so help us God. Some trust in chariots but we trust in the name of the Lord our God. While many are looking for the return of Trump I am listening for the sound of the Trumpet. Presidents come and go but The King is on His way! Today you have two options to die in your unconfessed sins and go south or repent and believe on the Lord Jesus Christ and enjoy Heaven forever and ever. Hell is too long to be wrong. Tomorrow is not guaranteed and when it is over your soul will go to Heaven or Hell but not both.

Do you know Christ as your Lord and Savior? Time is almost up; the sand is slipping fast and today is the day of Salvation. Presidents come and go but The King is on His Way. #Urgency

"Knight, Death, and the Devil" - 1513

Albrecht Dürer
German, 1471-1528

Albrecht Dürer's masterful engraving encourages the viewer to reflect on the inevitability of
their mortality. Lurking behind the knight on his muscular warhorse, the skeletal, deterio-
rating figure of Death sits astride his aging steed and demonstrates the running hourglass
of Time. The position of the Knight and Death suggests the knight's impending demise.
Despite this Christian soldier's battle-ready appearance, no amount of armor can protect
him (and, by proxy, the rest of humanity) from death, though he shows no outward signs of
fear or of temptation by the devil, who follows closely behind. #OnwardChristianSoldier

ABOUT THE AUTHOR

Child of God. *Saved by Grace*. Almost Home

HOW TO GET TO HEAVEN?

Coming to Christ is as easy as the ABCs.

1) **ADMIT** – that you are a sinner. We all have fallen short of the glory God and our sin separates us from a Holy God (Romans 3:23). Repent, turning away from your sin.

   "There is not a righteous man on earth who does what is right and never sins." Ecclesiastes 7:20

   "For the wages of sin is death, but the gift of God is eternal life in Christ Jesus our Lord." Romans 6:23

2) **BELIEVE** – that Christ is the Son of the Living God and accept God's gift of forgiveness from sin.

   "For God so loved the world that he gave his one and only Son, that whoever believes in him shall not perish but have eternal life." John 3:16

   "Jesus answered, 'I am the way and the truth and the life. No one comes to the Father except through me.' " John 14:6

   "Salvation is found in no one else, for there is no other name under heaven given to men by which we must be saved." Acts 4:12

3) **CONFESS** – with your mouth that Jesus Christ is Lord.

   "That if you confess with your mouth, 'Jesus is Lord,' and believe in your heart that God raised him from the dead, you will be saved. For it is with your heart that you believe and are justified, and it is with your mouth that you confess and are saved . . . for, 'Everyone who calls on the name of the Lord will be saved.'" Romans 10:9-10, 13

ASK CHRIST TO FORGIVE YOU NOW!

PRAYER –

"Dear God, I know I am a sinner and need your forgiveness. I believe that you, Jesus, died for my sins. I choose to turn from my sins. I now receive you, Jesus, as my personal Lord and Savior and invite you to come into my heart and life. I choose to trust and follow you as my Lord. In Jesus' name. Amen"

CONGRATS!

By receiving Jesus Christ, you are born again into God's family. You can be sure of eternal life with God because He has promised it!

WELCOME TO THE FAMILY

"God has given us eternal life, and this life is in his Son. He who has the Son has life; he who does not have the Son of God does not have life." 1 John 5:11-12

Contact our office today to so we can rejoice in your decision to trust Christ as Savior. Please call the office (410) 973-1208 or email Sharon@FrankShelton.com or Frank@FrankShelton.com Feel free to share your prayer requests as well and join our FREE monthly newsletter. Visit www.FrankShelton.com

Check our TV and radio listings when you can catch Frank weekly across America and around the world. Share this book with a friend and may God bless you richly. #HeLives #WeWin #Urgency #TheKingIsComing #FrankShelton

MISSION

Frank Shelton GLOBAL exists to reach the world ONE soul at a time. Regardless, if ministering to homeless, Hollywood or Heads of State our desire is to reach all with the Gospel of Christ before time runs out. After two decades on Capitol Hill, our founder Frank Shelton, Jr. left the pay, perks and prestige of Washington, DC to preach the Gospel across America and around the world. Without a single booking he left his Capitol Hill career on July 27, 2007 "by faith" to be an evangelist.

To date, he has been invited to preach on six continents, he has been a chaplain at three summer Olympics and leads a weekly Bible study to lawmakers assisting in two state capitals. The Church over the years, has been great ministering to the poor but failed to intentionally reach the powerful. Despite getting a "D" in public speaking as a freshman in high school he went on to become one of the most sought-after communicators in America. Previously, where he wrote occasional speeches for a Member of Congress today, he has given his own around the world.

Three years in a row, he spoke to over 120,000 at the iconic Nelson Mandela National Soccer Stadium in Uganda. He was invited to minister to over 700,000 in Nicaragua, received an award by an Ambassador linked to the UN on a faith global initiative and for over four years served as the DC, MD & DE State Coordinator for the Billy Graham Evangelistic Association. His television ministry "BY FAITH with Frank Shelton" airs weekly to over 200M homes coast to coast and four continents. His radio show "BY FAITH" airs in seventeen cities, 80 countries and linked with Wilkins Radio and Salem Radio.

Frank is married to the incredible Ruth Shelton formerly of El Salvador and have two amazing children (Hannah Grace & Andrew Lincoln). They reside in southern Maryland just fifteen from Washington, DC the city of his birth. His parents, Frank and Sharon are his heroes, and his goal is to chase Hell with a water gun shouting in love, "**GOD LOVES YOU!**"

www.FrankShelton.com

Office **(410) 973- 1208** - Facebook, Twitter & Instagram @FrankSheltonJr
Sharon@FrankShelton.com

Invite Frank to your next event Stacy@TheRobinsonAgency.com in ATL (800) 782-2995

Join the conversation **#Urgency @FrankSheltonJr**

FINAL THOUGHT

You may recall in the prelude I mentioned the Hell that I went through writing this book. My car died on top of the bridge the week before Fourth of July weekend (2020) with my Dad and I suspended between Maryland and Virginia. The very next weekend after preaching on world-wide television in Tampa on Fourth of July for my good friend, Dr Rodney Howard-Browne I came home only for my book to be deleted and erased from my computer. I almost died. I lived it once and now wrote it twice. The very next weekend I was bit by a snake while leaving my house and stepped barefoot into the garage. He was on the top step and struck me the second I stepped out. My heart skipped and to be honest I was nervous to come out of the house for a couple days wondering if he or a few "friends" were back waiting for me.

I found it interesting that the snake bit me right after the book was deleted. Talk about snake bitten! Fast forward almost a year and the day I finally wrapped this book up in late May 2021, I had pulled up in my driveway and was talking to my friend in Missouri. Yep, you guessed it Ronnie the Raven (Preaching Machine). With the cell phone up to my ear I walked to the front of my house to turn off the hose that I had been watering my lawn. What I saw next made my heart skip again and it was a five-foot snake stretched against the brick front of my home and was staring at me. He had a meal the size of a tennis ball in his belly, and it was obvious he was still enjoying dinner. As this slimy snake was staring at me and I ran inside to get my son so he could see it firsthand because I have been instructing him what is good and bad and what to keep your eyes open for. The sixty seconds I was gone to fetch our son that snake pregnant with dinner in its belly had already slithered another twenty feet and now was stretched out temporarily parked on the front porch of my home. It was as if he was trying to take ownership and I said not anymore, no way and Devil, your time is up! Andrew grabbed the shovel and handed it to me as he stood a safe distance away, we went to war. After a few forceful chops to his head, neck, and torso we had a fight on our hands. The blade was not as sharp as I would have liked and despite causing great pain to that spineless serpent, I could not decapitate him, and he was still trying to strike.

Andrew grabbed my shrub clippers and as I pinned the snake down with my shovel in the left hand, I methodically began with my right hand clipped that five-foot snake in about a dozen sections, scooped him up and threw him in a trash bag and proceeded to put fifty pounds of trash on top of him in my trash can. He was dead on arrival when the garbage truck came the next morning. A snake bit me after stealing my book but God and I took him out the day my book was done. Glory to God and never forget the King always has the last word and final move. Rambo would have been impressed but I believe my Redeemer was smiling more. #JesusWins

TEN MOST WANTED

The Federal Bureau of Investigation for years had a list for fugitives and felons who were on their radar to be arrested. Now that you realize that time is short, and eternity is around the corner who are some family, friends, and acquaintances that you can point towards Christ? My Dad graduated from the FBI National Academy in 1978 in Quantico, VA. Today, you are now deputized to evangelize.

Over the years, I have officiated one plus hundred funerals. In all my years, I have never once seen a U-Haul behind a hearse. We cannot take our possessions to Heaven, but we can take people with us. We cannot take our fame or fortune, but we can reach friends while time is still on the clock and your stuff will be left behind but let us invest in souls before the sand slides through the hourglass.

Write down the name of TEN friends who need hope and encouragement. Most importantly, who need to hear about God's love for them. God used me in 1982, at age ten to bring 22 friends to church in one week at a Vacation Bible School in Brandywine, Maryland. Who can you share Christ with this week? Friends do not let friends miss Jesus.

Made in the USA
Monee, IL
20 July 2022

10065396R00289